Blackstone's Statutes on

EMPLOYMENT LAW

Blackstone's Statutes on

EMPLOYMENT LAW

1999/2000

Ninth Edition

Edited by

Richard Kidner MA, BCL

Professor of Law, University of Wales, Aberystwyth

BLACKSTONE PRESS LIMITED

First published in Great Britain 1988 by Blackstone Press Limited,
Aldine Place, London W12 8AA. Telephone: (020) 8740 2277
www.blackstonepress.com

ISBN: 1 85431 928 0

First edition, 1988
Second edition, 1991
Third edition, 1993
Fourth edition, 1994
Fifth edition, 1995
Sixth edition, 1996
Seventh edition, 1997
Eighth edition, 1998
Ninth edition, 1999

British Library Cataloguing in Publication Data
A CIP catalogue for this book is available from the British Library

Typeset by Montage Studios Limited, Horsmonden, Kent
Printed by Livesey Ltd, Shrewsbury, Shropshire

CONTENTS

EDITOR'S PREFACE

This collection of statutes is primarily intended for students of Employment Law (whether the subject is called Employment Law or Labour Law or Industrial Law), and it includes all those statutes and parts of statutes which a student may be referred to. The subject is now mainly statutory and it is impossible to study it satisfactorily without constant reference to the statutes, for much of the case law depends to a great extent on interpretation. However, a student does not need to have access to every detail of the vast array of statutory material and accordingly the purpose of this collection is to provide at a low cost those provisions which are central to a study of employment law.

The selection has been made on the basis of what students might be referred to in their courses and the collection is necessarily not comprehensive but I hope that I have not omitted anything of relevance. Generally I have omitted material which relates only to particular employments (such as dock workers or teachers), together with minor, regulatory or empowering provisions. Nevertheless what has been provided covers all the law relevant for students of Employment Law, Trade Union Law and Collective Bargaining and I hope that students will find the collection useful, and a relatively inexpensive aid to the proper understanding of the subject. The statutes are not of course the whole story, but they are an essential prerequisite to appreciating the structure, nature and purpose of Employment Law.

This ninth edition is fully up-to-date and includes materials available to me up to September 1999. There have been a number of major changes to employment legislation over the past year and no doubt there will be further substantial changes in the future. A significant innovation in the Employment Relations Act is that much of it merely provides for the Secretary of State to enact provisions by statutory instrument and we may expect a welter of lengthy orders during the next year, many of which will be extremely detailed. One feature of current practice is that statutes mainly take effect by amending the two principal Consolidation Acts, so that while a statute may not appear in this book under its own title, nevertheless its provisions are fully incorporated into existing legislation. This may make it more difficult to identify the changes, but it has the advantage of presenting the student with the current position as a coherent whole. Additions for this year include the Employment Relations Act (which significantly amends both Consolidation Acts), the Disability Rights Commission Act, the Tax Credits Act, the new COSH regulations, and amendments made by the Sex Discrimination Gender Re-assignment Regulations. Also included are the changes to the Transfer of Undertakings Directive and the amendments to the Transfer of Undertakings Regulations. There are also the new Framework Agreement on Part Time Work and parts of the Code of Practice on disability discrimination. There have been a number of smaller amendments, all of which have duly been incorporated into the text.

The task of selection is becoming ever more difficult and will be even more so in the future when legislation by regulation becomes the norm. As we have already seen with the National Minimum Wage Regulations these are far too detailed to be included here, but nevertheless it is hoped that this book presents within a reasonable compass and at a reasonable price all the major legislation which a student will need to refer to.

Finally, I am most grateful to Blackstone Press for the remarkable efficiency and speed with which this book has been brought to press.

The statutes are arranged in chronological order (and alphabetically within years) and are printed as amended to 5 October 1999.

Richard Kidner

STATUTES OF THE UK PARLIAMENT

EMERGENCY POWERS ACT 1920
(1920, c. 55)

1 Issue of proclamations of emergency

(1) If at any time it appears to His Majesty that there have occurred, or are about to occur, events of such a nature as to be calculated, by interfering with the supply and distribution of food, water, fuel, or light, or with the means of locomotion, to deprive the community, or any substantial portion of the community, of the essentials of life, His Majesty may, by proclamation (hereinafter referred to as a proclamation of emergency), declare that a state of emergency exists.

No such proclamation shall be in force for more than one month, without prejudice to the issue of another proclamation at or before the end of that period.

(2) Where a proclamation of emergency has been made the occasion thereof shall forthwith be communicated to Parliament, and, if Parliament is then separated by such adjournment or prorogation as will not expire within five days, a proclamation shall be issued for the meeting of Parliament within five days, and parliament shall accordingly meet and sit upon the day appointed by that proclamation, and shall continue to sit and act in like manner as if it had stood adjourned or prorogued to the same day.

2 Emergency regulations

(1) Where a proclamation of emergency has been made, and so long as the proclamation is in force, it shall be lawful for His Majesty in Council, by Order, to make regulations for securing the essentials of life to the community, and those regulations may confer or impose on a Secretary of State or other Government department, or any other person in His Majesty's service or acting on His Majesty's behalf, such powers and duties as His Majesty may deem necessary for the preservation of the peace, for securing and regulating the supply and distribution of food, water, fuel, light and other necessities, for maintaining the means of transit or locomotion, and for any other purposes essential to the public safety and the life of the community, and may make such provisions incidental to the powers aforesaid as may appear to His Majesty to be required for making the exercise of those powers effective:

Provided that nothing in this Act shall be construed to authorise the making of any regulations imposing any form of compulsory military service or industrial conscription:

Provided also that no such regulation shall make it an offence for any person or persons to take part in a strike, or peacefully to persuade any other person on persons to take part in a strike.

(2) Any regulations so made shall be laid before Parliament as soon as may be after they are made, and shall not continue in force after the expiration of seven days from the

time when they are so laid unless a resolution is passed by both Houses providing for the continuance thereof.

(3) The regulations may provide for the trial, by courts of summary jurisdiction, of persons guilty of offences against the regulations; so, however, that the maximum penalty which may be inflicted for any offence against any such regulations shall be imprisonment for a term of three months, or a fine not exceeding level 5 on the standard scale, as defined in section 75 of the Criminal Justice Act 1982, or not exceeding a lesser amount, or both such imprisonment and fine, together with the forfeiture of any goods or money in respect of which the offence has been committed: Provided that no such regulations shall alter any existing procedure in criminal cases, or confer any right to punish by fine or imprisonment without trial.

EQUAL PAY ACT 1970
(1970, c. 41)

1 Requirement of equal treatment for men and women in same employment

(1) If the terms of a contract under which a woman is employed at an establishment in Great Britain do not include (directly or by reference to a collective agreement or otherwise) an equality clause they shall be deemed to include one.

(2) An equality clause is a provision which relates to terms (whether concerned with pay or not) of a contract under which a woman is employed (the 'woman's contract'), and has the effect that—

(a) where the woman is employed on like work with a man in the same employment—

(i) if (apart from the equality clause) any term of the woman's contract is or becomes less favourable to the woman than a term of a similar kind in the contract under which that man is employed, that term of the woman's contract shall be treated as so modified as not to be less favourable, and

(ii) if (apart from the equality clause) at any time the woman's contract does not include a term corresponding to a term benefiting that man included in the contract under which he is employed, the woman's contract shall be treated as including such a term;

(b) where the woman is employed on work rated as equivalent with that of a man in the same employment—

(i) if (apart from the equality clause) any term of the woman's contract determined by the rating of the work is or becomes less favourable to the woman than a term of a similar kind in the contract under which that man is employed, that term of the woman's contract shall be treated as so modified as not to be less favourable, and

(ii) if (apart from the equality clause) at any time the woman's contract does not include a term corresponding to a term benefiting that man included in the contract under which he is employed and determined by the rating of the work, the woman's contract shall be treated as including such a term.

(c) where a woman is employed on work which, not being work in relation to which paragraph (a) or (b) above applies, is, in terms of the demands made on her (for instance under such headings as effort, skill and decision), of equal value to that of a man in the same employment—

(i) if (apart from the equality clause) any term of the woman's contract is or becomes less favourable to the woman than a term of a similar kind in the contract under which that man is employed, that term of the woman's contract shall be treated as so modified as not to be less favourable, and

(ii) if (apart from the equality clause) at any time the woman's contract does not include a term corresponding to a term benefiting that man included in the contract under which he is employed, the woman's contract shall be treated as including such a term.

(3) An equality clause shall not operate in relation to a variation between the woman's contract and the man's contract if the employer proves that the variation is genuinely due to a material factor which is not the difference of sex and that factor—

(a) in the case of an equality clause falling within subsection (2)(a) or (b) above, must be a material difference between the woman's case and the man's; and

(b) in the case of an equality clause falling within subsection (2)(c) above, may be such a material difference.

(4) A woman is to be regarded as employed on like work with men if, but only if, her work and theirs is of the same or a broadly similar nature, and the differences (if any) between the things she does and the things they do are not of practical importance in relation to terms and conditions of employment; and accordingly in comparing her work with theirs regard shall be had to the frequency or otherwise with which any such differences occur in practice as well as to the nature and extent of the differences.

(5) A woman is to be regarded as employed on work rated as equivalent with that of any men if, but only if, her job and their job have been given an equal value, in terms of the demand made on a worker under various headings (for instance effort, skill, decision), on a study undertaken with a view to evaluating in those terms the jobs to be done by all or any of the employees in an undertaking or group of undertakings, or would have been given an equal value but for the evaluation being made on a system setting different values for men and women on the same demand under any heading.

(6) Subject to the following subsections, for purposes of this section—

(a) 'employed' means employed under a contract of service or of apprenticeship or a contract personally to execute any work or labour, and related expressions shall be construed accordingly;

(b) [repealed]

(c) Two employers are to be treated as associated if one is a company of which the other (directly or indirectly) has control or if both are companies of which a third person (directly or indirectly) has control,

and men shall be treated as in the same employment with a woman if they are men employed by her employer or any associated employer at the same establishment or at establishments in Great Britain which include that one and at which common terms and conditions of employment are observed either generally or for employees of the relevant classes.

(7) [repealed]

(8) This section shall apply to—

(a) service for purposes of a Minister of the Crown or government department, other than service of a person holding a statutory office, or

(b) service on behalf of the Crown for purposes of a person holding a statutory office or purposes of a statutory body,

as it applies to employment by a private person, and shall so apply as if references to a contract of employment included references to the terms of service.

(9) [repealed]

(10) In this section 'statutory body' means a body set up by or in pursuance of an enactment, and 'statutory office' means an office so set up; and service 'for purposes of' a Minister of the Crown or government department does not include service in any office in Schedule 2 (Ministerial offices) to the House of Commons Disqualification Act 1975 as for the time being in force.

(10A) and (10B) [omitted]

(11) For the purposes of this Act it is immaterial whether the law which (apart from this subsection) in the law applicable to a contract is the law of any part of the United Kingdom or not.

(12) [omitted]

(13) Provisions of this section and sections 2 and 2A below framed with reference to women and their treatment relative to men are to be read as applying equally in a converse case to men and their treatment relative to women.

2 Disputes as to, and enforcement of, requirement of equal treatment

(1) Any claim in respect of the contravention of a term modified or included by virtue of an equality clause, including a claim for arrears of remuneration or damages in respect of the contravention, may be presented by way of a complaint to an employment tribunal.

(1A) Where a dispute arises in relation to the effect of an equality clause the employer may apply to an employment tribunal for an order declaring the rights of the employer and the employee in relation to the matter in question.

(2) Where it appears to the Secretary of State that there may be a question whether the employer of any women is or has been contravening a term modified or included by virtue of their equality clauses, but that it is not reasonable to expect them to take steps to have the question determined, the question may be referred by him as respects all or any of them to an employment tribunal and shall be dealt with as if the reference were of a claim by the women or woman against the employer.

(3) Where it appears to the court in which any proceedings are pending that a claim or counterclaim in respect of the operation of an equality clause could more conveniently be disposed of separately by an employment tribunal, the court may direct that the claim or counterclaim shall be struck out; and (without prejudice to the foregoing) where in proceedings before any court a question arises as to the operation of an equality clause, the court may on the application of any party to the proceedings or otherwise refer that question, or direct it to be referred by a party to the proceedings, to an employment tribunal for determination by the tribunal, and may stay or sist the proceedings in the meantime.

(4) No claim in respect of the operation of an equality clause relating to a woman's employment shall be referred to an employment tribunal otherwise than by virtue of subsection (3) above, if she has not been employed in the employment within the six months preceding the date of the reference.

(5) A woman shall not be entitled, in proceedings brought in respect of a failure to comply with an equality clause (including proceedings before an employment tribunal), to be awarded any payment by way of arrears of remuneration or damages in respect of a time earlier than two years before the date on which the proceedings were instituted.

(6) and (7) [repealed]

2A Procedure before tribunal in certain cases

(1) Where on a complaint or reference made to an employment tribunal under section 2 above, a dispute arises as to whether any work is of equal value as mentioned in section 1(2)(c) above the tribunal may either—

(a) proceed to determine that question; or

(b) unless it is satisfied that there are no reasonable grounds for determining that the work is of equal value as so mentioned, require a member of the panel of independent experts to prepare a report with respect to that question;

and, if it requires the preparation of a report under paragraph (b) of this subsection, it shall not determine that question unless it has received the report.

(2) Without prejudice to the generality of subsection (1) above, there shall be taken, for the purposes of that subsection, to be no reasonable grounds for determining that the work of a woman is of equal value as mentioned in section 1(2)(c) above if—

(a) that work and the work of the man in question have been given different values on a study such as is mentioned in section 1(5) above; and

(b) there are no reasonable grounds for determining that the evaluation contained in the study was (within the meaning of subsection (3) below) made on a system which discriminates on grounds of sex.

(3) An evaluation contained in a study such as is mentioned in section 1(5) above is made on a system which discriminates on grounds of sex where a difference, or coincidence, between values set by that system on different demands under the same or different headings is not justifiable irrespective of the sex of the person on whom those demands are made.

(4) In paragraph (b) of subsection (1) above the reference to a member of the panel of independent experts is a reference to a person who is for the time being designated by the Advisory, Conciliation and Arbitration Service for the purposes of that paragraph as such a member, being neither a member of the Council of that Service nor one of its officers or servants.

3 and **4** [repealed] **5** [omitted]

6 Exclusion from ss. 1 to 5 of pensions etc.

(1) An equality clause shall not operate in relation to terms—

(a) affected by compliance with the laws regulating the employment of women, or

(b) affording special treatment to women in connection with pregnancy or childbirth.

(1A) [repealed]

(1B) An equality clause shall not operate in relation to terms relating to a person's membership of, or rights under, an occupational pension scheme, being terms in relation to which, by reason only of any provision made by or under sections 62 to 64 of the Pensions Act 1995 (equal treatment), an equal treatment rule would not operate if the terms were included in the scheme.

(1C) In subsection (1B), 'occupational pension scheme' has the same meaning as in the Pension Schemes Act 1993 and 'equal treatment rule' has the meaning given by section 62 of the Pensions Act 1995.

(2) [repealed]

7 [repealed]; **7A** [omitted]; **8** [repealed]; **9** [omitted]; **10** [repealed]; **11** [omitted]

HEALTH AND SAFETY AT WORK ETC. ACT 1974
(1974, c. 37)

PART I
HEALTH, SAFETY AND WELFARE IN CONNECTION WITH WORK, AND CONTROL OF DANGEROUS SUBSTANCES AND CERTAIN EMISSIONS INTO THE ATMOSPHERE

Preliminary

1 Preliminary

(1) The provisions of this Part shall have effect with a view to—

(a) securing the health, safety and welfare of persons at work;

(b) protecting persons other than persons at work against risks to health or safety arising out of or in connection with the activities of persons at work;

(c) controlling the keeping and use of explosive or highly flammable or otherwise dangerous substances, and generally preventing the unlawful acquisition, possession and use of such substances;

(2) The provisions of this Part relating to the making of health and safety regulations and the preparation and approval of codes of practice shall in particular have effect with a view to enabling the enactments specified in the third column of Schedule 1 and the regulations, orders and other instruments in force under those enactments to be progressively replaced by a system of regulations and approved codes of practice operating in combination with the other provisions of this Part and designed to maintain or improve the standards of health, safety and welfare established by or under those enactments.

(3) For the purposes of this Part risks arising out of or in connection with the activities of persons at work shall be treated as including risks attributable to the manner of conducting an undertaking, the plant or substances used for the purposes of an undertaking and the condition of premises so used or any part of them.

(4) References in this Part to the general purposes of this Part are references to the purposes mentioned in subsection (1) above.

2 General duties of employers to their employees

(1) It shall be the duty of every employer to ensure, so far as is reasonably practicable, the health, safety and welfare at work of all his employees.

(2) Without prejudice to the generality of an employer's duty under the preceding subsection, the matters to which that duty extends include in particular—

(a) the provision and maintenance of plant and systems of work that are, so far as is reasonably practicable, safe and without risks to health;

(b) arrangements for ensuring, so far as is reasonably practicable, safety and absence of risks to health in connection with the use, handling, storage and transport of articles and substances;

(c) the provision of such information, instruction, training and supervision as is necessary to ensure, so far as is reasonably practicable, the health and safety at work of his employees;

(d) so far as is reasonably practicable as regards any place of work under the employer's control, the maintenance of it in a condition that is safe and without risks to health and the provision and maintenance of means of access to and egress from it that are safe and without such risks;

(e) the provision and maintenance of a working environment for his employees that is, so far as is reasonably practicable, safe, without risks to health, and adequate as regards facilities and arrangements for their welfare at work.

(3) Except in such cases as may be prescribed, it shall be the duty of every employer to prepare and as often as may be appropriate revise a written statement of his general policy with respect to the health and safety at work of his employees and the organisation and arrangements for the time being in force for carrying out that policy, and to bring the statement and any revision of it to the notice of all of his employees.

(4) Regulations made by the Secretary of State may provide for the appointment in prescribed cases by recognised trade unions (within the meaning of the regulations) of safety representatives from amongst the employees, and those representatives shall represent the employees in consultations with the employers under subsection (6) below and shall have such other functions as may be prescribed.

(6) It shall be the duty of every employer to consult any such representatives with a view to the making and maintenance of arrangements which will enable him and his employees to co-operate effectively in promoting and developing measures to ensure the health and safety at work of the employees, and in checking the effectiveness of such measures.

(7) In such cases as may be prescribed it shall be the duty of every employer, if requested to do so by the safety representatives mentioned in subsection (4) above, to establish, in accordance with regulations made by the Secretary of State, a safety committee having the functions of keeping under review the measures taken to ensure the health and safety at work of his employees and such other functions as may be prescribed.

3 General duties of employers and self-employed to persons other than their employees

(1) It shall be the duty of every employer to conduct his undertaking in such a way as to ensure, so far as is reasonably practicable, that persons not in his employment who may be affected thereby are not thereby exposed to risks to their health or safety.

(2) It shall be the duty of every self-employed person to conduct his undertaking in such a way as to ensure, so far as is reasonably practicable, that he and other persons (not being his employees) who may be affected thereby are not thereby exposed to risks to their health or safety.

(3) In such cases as may be prescribed, it shall be the duty of every employer and every self-employed person, in the prescribed circumstances and in the prescribed manner, to give to persons (not being his employees) who may be affected by the way in which he conducts his undertaking the prescribed information about such aspects of the way in which he conducts his undertaking as might affect their health or safety.

4 General duties of persons concerned with premises to persons other than their employees

(1) This section has effect for imposing on persons duties in relation to those who—

(a) are not their employees; but

(b) use non-domestic premises made available to them as a place of work or as a place where they may use plant or substances provided for their use there,

and applies to premises so made available and other non-domestic premises used in connection with them.

(2) It shall be the duty of each person who has, to any extent, control of premises to which this section applies or of the means of access thereto or egress therefrom or of any plant or substance in such premises to take such measures as it is reasonable for a person in his position to take to ensure, so far as is reasonably practicable, that the premises, all means of access thereto or egress therefrom available for use by persons using the premises, and any plant or substance in the premises or, as the case may be, provided for use there, is or are safe and without risks to health.

(3) Where a person has, by virtue of any contract or tenancy, an obligation of any extent in relation to—

(a) the maintenance or repair of any premises to which this section applies or any means of access thereto or egress therefrom; or

(b) the safety of or the absence of risks to health arising from plant or substances in any such premises;

that person shall be treated, for the purposes of subsection (2) above, as being a person who has control of the matters to which his obligation extends.

(4) Any reference in this section to a person having control of any premises or matter is a reference to a person having control of the premises or matter in connection with the carrying on by him of a trade, business or other undertaking (whether for profit or not).

5 [repealed]

6 General duties of manufacturers etc. as regards articles and substances for use at work

(1) It shall be the duty of any person who designs, manufactures, imports or supplies any article for use at work or any article of fairground equipment—

(a) to ensure, so far as is reasonably practicable, that the article is so designed and constructed that it will be safe and without risks to health at all times when it is being set, used, cleaned or maintained by a person at work;

(b) to carry out or arrange for the carrying out of such testing and examination as may be necessary for the performance of the duty imposed on him by the preceding paragraph;

(c) to take such steps as are necessary to secure that persons supplied by that person with the article are provided with adequate information about the use for which the article is designed or has been tested and about any conditions necessary to ensure that it will be safe and without risks to health at all such times as are mentioned in paragraph (a) above and when it is being dismantled or disposed of; and

(d) to take such steps as are necessary to secure, so far as is reasonably practicable, that persons so supplied are provided with all such revisions of information provided to them by virtue of the preceding paragraph as are necessary by reason of its becoming known that anything gives rise to a serious risk to health or safety.

(1A) [omitted]

(2) It shall be the duty of any person who undertakes the design or manufacture of any article for use at work or of any article of fairground equipment to carry out or arrange for the carrying out of any necessary research with a view to the discovery and, so far as is reasonably practicable, the elimination or minimisation of any risks to health or safety to which the design or article may give rise.

(3) It shall be the duty of any person who erects or installs any article for use at work in any premises where that article is to be used by persons at work or who erects or

installs any article of fairground equipment to ensure, so far as is reasonably practicable, that nothing about the way in which the article is erected or installed makes it unsafe or a risk to health at any such time as is mentioned in paragraph (a) of subsection (1) or, as the case may be, in paragraph (a) of subsection (1) or (1A) above.

(4) It shall be the duty of any person who manufactures, imports or supplies any substance—

(a) to ensure, so far as is reasonably practicable, that the substance will be safe and without risks to health at all times when it is being used, handled, processed, stored or transported by a person at work or in premises to which section 4 above applies;

(b) to carry out or arrange for the carrying out of such testing and examination as may be necessary for the performance of the duty imposed on him by the preceding paragraph;

(c) to take such steps as are necessary to secure that persons supplied by that person with the substance are provided with adequate information about any risks to health or safety to which the inherent properties of the substance may give rise, about the results of any relevant tests which have been carried out on or in connection with the substance and about any conditions necessary to ensure that the substance will be safe and without risks to health at all such times as are mentioned in paragraph (a) above and when the substance is being disposed of; and

(d) to take such steps as are necessary to secure, so far as is reasonably practicable, that persons so supplied are provided with all such revisions of information provided to them by virtue of the preceding paragraph as are necessary by reason of its becoming known that anything gives rise to a serious risk to health or safety.

(5) It shall be the duty of any person who undertakes the manufacture of any substance to carry out or arrange for the carrying out of any necessary research with a view to the discovery and, so far as is reasonable practicable, the elimination or minimisation of any risks to health or safety to which the substance may give rise at all such times as are mentioned in paragraph (a) of subsection (4) above.

(6) Nothing in the preceding provisions of this section shall be taken to require a person to repeat any testing, examination or research which has been carried out otherwise than by him or at his instance, in so far as it is reasonable for him to rely on the results thereof for the purposes of those provisions.

(7) Any duty imposed on any person by any of the preceding provisions of this section shall extend only to things done in the course of a trade, business or other undertaking carried on by him (whether for profit or not) and to matters within his control.

(8) Where a person designs, manufactures, imports or supplies an article for use at work or an article of fairground equipment and does so for or to another on the basis of a written undertaking by that other to take specified steps sufficient to ensure, so far as is reasonably practicable, that the article will be safe and without risks to health at all such times as are mentioned in paragraph (a) or, as the case may be, in paragraph (a) of subsection (1) or (1A) above, the undertaking shall have the effect of relieving the first-mentioned person from the duty imposed by virtue of that paragraph to such extent as is reasonable having regard to the terms of the undertaking.

(8A) Nothing in subsection (7) or (8) above shall relieve any person who imports any article or substance from any duty in respect of anything which—

(a) in the case of an article designed outside the United Kingdom, was done by and in the course of any trade, profession or other undertaking carried on by, or was within the control of, the person who designed the article; or

(b) in the case of an article or substance manufactured outside the United Kingdom, was done by and in the course of any trade, profession or other undertaking carried on by, or was within the control of, the person who manufactured the article or substance.

(10) For the purposes of this section an absence of safety or a risk to health shall be disregarded in so far as the case in or in relation to which it would arise is shown to be one the occurrence of which could not reasonably be foreseen; and in determining whether any duty imposed by virtue of paragraph (a) of subsection (1), (1A) or (4) above has been performed regard shall be had to any relevant information or advice which has been provided to any person by the person by whom the article has been designed, manufactured, imported or supplied or, as the case may be, by the person by whom the substance has been manufactured, imported or supplied.

7 General duties of employees at work

It shall be the duty of every employee while at work—

(a) to take reasonable care for the health and safety of himself and of other persons who may be affected by his acts or omissions at work; and

(b) as regards any duty or requirement imposed on his employer or any other person by or under any of the relevant statutory provisions, to co-operate with him so far as is necessary to enable that duty or requirement to be performed or complied with.

8 Duty not to interfere with or misuse things provided pursuant to certain provisions

No person shall intentionally or recklessly interfere with or misuse anything provided in the interests of health, safety or welfare in pursuance of any of the relevant statutory provisions.

9 Duty not to charge employees for things done or provided pursuant to certain specific requirements

No employer shall levy or permit to be levied on any employee of his any charge in respect of anything done or provided in pursuance of any specific requirement of the relevant statutory provisions.

10 to **19** [omitted]

20 Powers of inspectors

(1) Subject to the provisions of section 19 and this section, an inspector may, for the purpose of carrying into effect any of the relevant statutory provisions within the field of responsibility of the enforcing authority which appointed him, exercise the powers set out in subsection (2) below.

(2) The powers of an inspector referred to in the preceding subsection are the following, namely—

(a) at any reasonable time (or, in a situation which in his opinion is or may be dangerous, at any time) to enter any premises which he has reason to believe it is necessary for him to enter for the purpose mentioned in subsection (1) above;

(b) to take with him a constable if he has reasonable cause to apprehend any serious obstruction in the execution of his duty;

(c) without prejudice to the preceding paragraph, on entering any premises by virtue of paragraph (a) above to take with him—

(i) any other person duly authorised by his (the inspector's) enforcing authority; and

(ii) any equipment or materials required for any purpose for which the power of entry is being exercised;

(d) to make such examination and investigation as may in any circumstances be necessary for the purpose mentioned in subsection (1) above;

(e) as regards any premises which he has power to enter, to direct that those premises or any part of them, or anything therein, shall be left undisturbed (whether generally or in particular respects) for so long as is reasonably necessary for the purpose of any examination or investigation under paragraph (d) above;

(f) to take such measurements and photographs and make such recordings as he considers necessary for the purpose of any examination or investigation under paragraph (d) above;

(g) to take samples of any articles or substances found in any premises which he has power to enter, and of the atmosphere in or in the vicinity of any such premises;

(h) in the case of any article or substance found in any premises which he has power to enter, being an article or substance which appears to him to have caused or to be likely to cause danger to health or safety, to cause it to be dismantled or subjected to any process or test (but not so as to damage or destroy it unless this is in the circumstances necessary for the purpose mentioned in subsection (1) above);

(i) in the case of any such article or substance as is mentioned in the preceding paragraph, to take possession of it and detain it for so long as is necessary for all or any of the following purposes, namely—

(i) to examine it and do to it anything which he has power to do under that paragraph;

(ii) to ensure that it is not tampered with before his examinaiton of it is completed;

(iii) to ensure that it is available for use as evidence in any proceedings for an offence under any of the relevant statutory provisions or any proceedings relating to a notice under section 21 or 22;

(j) to require any person whom he has reasonable cause to believe to be able to give any information relevant to any examination or investigation under paragraph (d) above to answer (in the absence of persons other than a person nominated by him to be present and any persons whom the inspector may allow to be present) such questions as the inspector thinks fit to ask and to sign a declaration of the truth of his answers;

(k) to require the production of, inspect, and take copies of or of any entry in—

(i) any books or documents which by virtue of any of the relevant statutory provisions are required to be kept; and

(ii) any other books or documents which it is necessary for him to see for the purposes of any examination or investigation under paragraph (d) above;

(l) to require any person to afford him such facilities and assistance with respect to any matters or things within that person's control or in relation to which that person has responsibilities as are necessary to enable the inspector to exercise any of the powers conferred on him by this section;

(m) any other power which is necessary for the purpose mentioned in subsection (1) above.

(3) The Secretary of State may by regulations make provision as to the procedure to be followed in connection with the taking of samples under subsection (2)(g) above (including provision as to the way in which samples that have been so taken are to be dealt with).

(4) Where an inspector proposes to exercise the power conferred by subsection (2)(h) above in the case of an article or substance found in any premises, he shall, if so requested by a person who at the time is present in and has responsibilities in relation to those premises, cause anything which is to be done by virtue of that power to be done in the presence of that person unless the inspector considers that its being done in that person's presence would be prejudicial to the safety of the State.

(5) Before exercising the power conferred by subsection (2)(h) above in the case of any article or substance, an inspector shall consult such persons as appear to him appropriate for the purpose of ascertaining what dangers, if any, there may be in doing anything which he proposes to do under that power.

(6) Where under the power conferred by subsection (2)(i) above an inspector takes possession of any article or substance found in any premises, he shall leave there, either with a responsible person or, if that is impracticable, fixed in a conspicuous position, a

notice giving particulars of that article or substance sufficient to identify it and stating that he has taken possession of it under that power; and before taking possession of any such substance under that power an inspector shall, if it is practicable for him to do so, take a sample thereof and give to a responsible person at the premises a portion of the sample marked in a manner sufficient to identify it.

(7) No answer given by a person in pursuance of a requirement imposed under subsection (2)(j) above shall be admissible in evidence against that person or the husband or wife of that person in any proceedings.

(8) Nothing in this section shall be taken to compel the production by any person of a document of which he would on grounds of legal professional privilege be entitled to withhold production on an order for discovery in an action in the High Court or, as the case may be, on an order for the production of documents in an action in the Court of Session.

21 Improvement notices

If an inspector is of the opinion that a person—

(a) is contravening one or more of the relevant statutory provisions; or

(b) has contravened one or more of those provisions in circumstances that make it likely that the contravention will continue or be repeated,

he may serve on him a notice (in this Part referred to as 'an improvement notice') stating that he is of that opinion, specifying the provision or provisions as to which he is of that opinion, giving particulars of the reasons why he is of that opinion, and requiring that person to remedy the contravention or, as the case may be, the matters occasioning it within such period (ending not earlier than the period within which an appeal against the notice can be brought under section 24) as may be specified in the notice.

22 Prohibition notices

(1) This section applies to any activities which are being or are likely to be carried on by or under the control of any person, being activities to or in relation to which any of the relevant statutory provisions apply or will, if the activities are so carried on, apply.

(2) If as regards any activities to which this section applies an inspector is of the opinion that, as carried on or likely to be carried on by or under the control of the person in question, the activities involve or, as the case may be, will involve a risk of serious personal injury, the inspector may serve on that person a notice (in this Part referred to as 'a prohibition notice').

(3) A prohibition notice shall—

(a) state that the inspector is of the said opinion;

(b) specify the matters which in his opinion give or, as the case may be, will give rise to the said risk;

(c) where in his opinion any of those matters involves or, as the case may be, will involve a contravention of any of the relevant statutory provisions, state that he is of that opinion, specify the provision or provisions as to which he is of that opinion, and give particulars of the reasons why he is of that opinion; and

(d) direct that the activities to which the notice relates shall not be carried on by or under the control of the person on whom the notice is served unless the matters specified in the notice in pursuance of paragraph (b) above and any associated contraventions of provisions so specified in pursuance of paragraph (c) above have been remedied.

(4) A direction contained in a prohibition notice in pursuance of subsection (3)(d) above shall take effect—

(a) at the end of the period specified in the notice; or

(b) if the notice so declares, immediately.

23 Provisions supplementary to ss 21 and 22

(1) In this section 'a notice' means an improvement notice or a prohibition notice.

(2) A notice may (but need not) include directions as to the measures to be taken to remedy any contravention or matter to which the notice relates; and any such directions—

(a) may be framed to any extent by reference to any approved code of practice; and

(b) may be framed so as to afford the person on whom the notice is served a choice between different ways of remedying the contravention or matter.

(3) Where any of the relevant statutory provisions applies to a building or any matter connected with a building and an inspector proposes to serve an improvement notice relating to a contravention of that provision in connection with that building or matter, the notice shall not direct any measures to be taken to remedy the contravention of that provision which are more onerous than those necessary to secure conformity with the requirements of any building regulations for the time being in force to which that building or matter would be required to conform if the relevant building were being newly erected unless the provision in question imposes specific requirements more onerous than the requirements of any such building regulations to which the building or matter would be required to conform as aforesaid.

In this subsection 'the relevant building', in the case of a building, means that building, and, in the case of a matter connected with a building, means the building with which the matter is connected.

(4) Before an inspector serves in connection with any premises used or about to be used as a place of work a notice requiring or likely to lead to the taking of measures affecting the means of escape in case of fire with which the premises are or ought to be provided, he shall consult the fire authority.

In this subsection 'fire authority' has the meaning assigned by section 43(1) of the Fire Precautions Act 1971.

(5) Where an improvement notice or a prohibition notice which is not to take immediate effect has been served—

(a) the notice may be withdrawn by an inspector at any time before the end of the period specified therein in pursuance of section 21 or section 22(4) as the case may be; and

(b) the period so specified may be extended or further extended by an inspector at any time when an appeal against the notice is not pending.

24 Appeal against improvement or prohibition notice

(1) In this section 'a notice' means an improvement notice or a prohibition notice.

(2) A person on whom a notice is served may within such period from the date of its service as may be prescribed appeal to an employment tribunal; and on such an appeal the tribunal may either cancel or affirm the notice and, if it affirms it, may do so either in its original form or with such modifications as the tribunal may in the circumstances think fit.

(3) Where an appeal under this section is brought against a notice within the period allowed under the preceding subsection, then—

(a) in the case of an improvement notice, the bringing of the appeal shall have the effect of suspending the operation of the notice until the appeal is finally disposed of or, if the appeal is withdrawn, until the withdrawal of the appeal;

(b) in the case of a prohibition notice, the bringing of the appeal shall have the like effect if, but only if, on the application of the appellant the tribunal so directs (and then only from the giving of the direction).

(4) One or more assessors may be appointed for the purposes of any proceedings brought before an employment tribunal under this section.

25 Power to deal with cause of imminent danger

(1) Where, in the case of any article or substance found by him in any premises which he has power to enter, an inspector has reasonable cause to believe that, in the circumstances in which he finds it, the article or substance is a cause of imminent danger of serious personal injury, he may seize it and cause it to be rendered harmless (whether by destruction or otherwise).

(2) Before there is rendered harmless under this section—

(a) any article that forms part of a batch of similar articles; or

(b) any substance,

the inspector shall, if it is practicable for him to do so, take a sample thereof and give to a responsible person at the premises where the article or substance was found by him a portion of the sample marked in a manner sufficient to identify it.

(3) As soon as may be after any article or substance has been seized and rendered harmless under this section, the inspector shall prepare and sign a written report giving particulars of the circumstances in which the article or substance was seized and so dealt with by him, and shall—

(a) give a signed copy of the report to a responsible person at the premises where the article or substance was found by him; and

(b) unless that person is the owner of the article or substance, also serve a signed copy of the report on the owner;

and if, where paragraph (b) above applies, the inspector cannot after reasonable enquiry ascertain the name or address of the owner, the copy may be served on him by giving it to the person to whom a copy was given under the preceding paragraph.

25A to **28** [omitted]; **29** to **32** [repealed]

33 Offences

(1) It is an offence for a person—

(a) to fail to discharge a duty to which he is subject by virtue of sections 2 to 7;

(b) to contravene section 8 or 9;

(c) to contravene any health and safety regulations or any requirement or prohibition imposed under any such regulations (including any requirement or prohibition to which he is subject by virtue of the terms of or any condition or restriction attached to any licence, approval, exemption or other authority issued, given or granted under the regulations);

(d) to contravene any requirement imposed by or under regulations under section 14 or intentionally to obstruct any person in the exercise of his powers under that section;

(e) to contravene any requirement imposed by an inspector under section 20 or 25;

(f) to prevent or attempt to prevent any other person from appearing before an inspector or from answering any question to which an inspector may by virtue of section 20(2) require an answer;

(g) to contravene any requirement or prohibition imposed by an improvement notice or a prohibition notice (including any such notice as modified on appeal);

(h) intentionally to obstruct an inspector in the exercise or performance of his powers or duties or to obstruct a customs officer in the exercise of his powers under section 25A;

(i) to contravene any requirement imposed by a notice under section 27(1);

(j) to use or disclose any information in contravention of section 27(4) or 28;

(k) to make a statement which he knows to be false or recklessly to make a statement which is false where the statement is made—

(i) in purported compliance with a requirement to furnish any information imposed by or under any of the relevant statutory provisions; or

(ii) for the purpose of obtaining the issue of a document under any of the relevant statutory provisions to himself or another person;

(l) intentionally to make a false entry in any register, book, notice or other document required by or under any of the relevant statutory provisions to be kept, served or given or, with intent to deceive, to make use of any such entry which he knows to be false;

(m) with intent to deceive, to use a document issued or authorised to be issued under any of the relevant statutory provisions or required for any purpose thereunder or to make or have in his possession a document so closely resembling any such document as to be calculated to deceive;

(n) falsely to pretend to be an inspector;

(o) to fail to comply with an order made by a court under section 42.

(1A) Subject to any provision made by virtue of section 15(6)(d), a person guilty of an offence under subsection (1)(a) above consisting of a failing to discharge a duty to which he is subject by virtue of sections 2 to 6 shall be liable—

(a) on summary conviction, to a fine not exceeding £20,000;

(b) on conviction on indictment, to a fine.

(2) A person guilty of an offence under paragraph (d), (f), (h) or (n) of subsection (1) above, or of an offence under paragraph (e) of that subsection consisting of contravening a requirement imposed by an inspector under section 20, shall be liable on summary conviction to a fine not exceeding level 5 on the standard scale.

(2A) A person guilty of an offence under subsection (1)(g) or (o) above shall be liable—

(a) on summary conviction, to imprisonment for a term not exceeding six months, or a fine not exceeding £20,000, or both;

(b) on conviction on indictment, to imprisonment for a term not exceeding two years, or a fine, or both.

(3) Subject to any provision made by virtue of section 15(6)(d) or (e) or by virtue of paragraph 2(2) of Schedule 3, a person guilty of an offence under subsection (1) above not falling within subsection (1A), (2) or (2A) above, or of an offence under any of the existing statutory provisions, being an offence for which no other penalty is specified, shall be liable—

(a) on summary conviction, to a fine not exceeding the prescribed sum;

(b) on conviction on indictment—

(i) if the offence is one to which this sub-paragraph applies, to imprisonment for a term not exceeding two years, or a fine, or both;

(ii) if the offence is not one to which the preceding sub-paragraph applies, to a fine.

(4) Subsection (3)(b)(i) above applies to the following offences—

(a) an offence consisting of contravening any of the relevant statutory provisions by doing otherwise than under the authority of a licence issued by the Executive something for the doing of which such a licence is necessary under the relevant statutory provisions;

(b) an offence consisting of contravening a term of or a condition or restriction attached to any such licence as is mentioned in the preceding paragraph;

(c) an offence consisting of acquiring or attempting to acquire, possessing or using an explosive article or substance (within the meaning of any of the relevant statutory provisions) in contravention of any of the relevant statutory provisions;

(d) [repealed];

(e) an offence under subsection (1)(j) above.

(5) and (6) [repealed].

34 and 35 [omitted]

36 Offences due to fault of other person

(1) Where the commission by any person of an offence under any of the relevant statutory provisions is due to the act or default of some other person, that other person shall be guilty of the offence, and a person may be charged with and convicted of the offence by virtue of this subsection whether or not proceedings are taken against the first-mentioned person.

(2) Where there would be or have been the commission of an offence under section 33 by the Crown but for the circumstance that that section does not bind the Crown, and that fact is due to the act or default of a person other than the Crown, that person shall be guilty of the offence which, but for that circumstance, the Crown would be committing or would have committed, and may be charged with and convicted of that offence accordingly.

(3) The preceding provisions of this section are subject to any provision made by virtue of section 15(6).

37 Offences by bodies corporate

(1) Where an offence under any of the relevant statutory provisions committed by a body corporate is proved to have been committed with the consent or connivance of, or to have been attributable to any neglect on the part of, any director, manager, secretary or other similar officer of the body corporate or a person who was purporting to act in any such capacity, he as well as the body corporate shall be guilty of that offence and shall be liable to be proceeded against and punished accordingly.

(2) Where the affairs of a body corporate are managed by its members, the preceding subsection shall apply in relation to the acts and defaults of a member in connection with his functions of management as if he were a director of the body corporate.

38 to **46** [omitted]

47 Civil liability

(1) Nothing in this Part shall be construed—

(a) as conferring a right of action in any civil proceedings in respect of any failure to comply with any duty imposed by sections 2 to 7 or any contravention of section 8; or

(b) as affecting the extent (if any) to which breach of a duty imposed by any of the existing statutory provisions is actionable; or

(c) as affecting the operation of section 12 of the Nuclear Installations Act 1965 (right to compensation by virtue of certain provisions of that Act).

(2) Breach of a duty imposed by health and safety regulations shall, so far as it causes damage, be actionable except in so far as the regulations provide otherwise.

(3) No provision made by virtue of section 15(6)(b) shall afford a defence in any civil proceedings, whether brought by virtue of subsection (2) above or not; but as regards any duty imposed as mentioned in subsection (2) above health and safety regulations may provide for any defence specified in the regulations to be available in any action for breach of that duty.

(4) Subsections (1)(a) and (2) above are without prejudice to any right of action which existed apart from the provisions of this Act, and subsection (3) above is without prejudice to any defence which may be available apart from the provisions of the regulations there mentioned.

(5) Any term of an agreement which purports to exclude or restrict the operation of subsection (2) above, or any liability arising by virtue of that subsection shall be void, except in so far as health and safety regulations provide otherwise.

(6) In this section 'damage' includes the death of, or injury to, any person (including any disease and any impairment of a person's physical or mental condition).

48 to **85** [omitted]

SEX DISCRIMINATION ACT 1975
(1975, c. 65)

PART I
DISCRIMINATION TO WHICH ACT APPLIES

PART II
DISCRIMINATION IN THE EMPLOYMENT FIELD

Discrimination by employers

PART IV
OTHER UNLAWFUL ACTS

PART V
GENERAL EXCEPTIONS FROM PARTS II TO IV

PART VI
EQUAL OPPORTUNITIES COMMISSION

Investigations

PART I
DISCRIMINATION TO WHICH ACT APPLIES

1 Sex discrimination against women

(1) A person discriminates against a woman in any circumstances relevant for the purposes of any provision of this Act if—

(a) on the ground of her sex he treats her less favourably than he treats or would treat a man, or

(b) he applies to her a requirement or condition which he applies or would apply equally to a man but—

(i) which is such that the proportion of women who can comply with it is considerably smaller than the proportion of men who can comply with it, and

(ii) which he cannot show to be justifiable irrespective of the sex of the person to whom it is applied, and

(iii) which is to her detriment because she cannot comply with it.

(2) If a person treats or would treat a man differently according to the man's marital status, his treatment of a woman is for the purposes of subsection (1)(a) to be compared to his treatment of a man having the like marital status.

2 Sex discrimination against men

(1) Section 1, and the provisions of Parts II and III relating to sex discrimination against women, are to be read as applying equally to the treatment of men, and for that purpose shall have effect with such modifications as are requisite.

(2) In the application of subsection (1) no account shall be taken of special treatment afforded to women in connection with pregnancy or childbirth.

2A Discrimination on the grounds of gender reassignment

(1) A person ('A') discriminates against another person ('B') in any circumstances relevant for the purposes of—

(a) any provision of Part II,

(b) section 35A or 35B, or

(c) any other provision of Part III, so far as it applies to vocational training,

if he treats B less favourably than he treats or would treat other persons, and does so on the grounds that B intends to undergo, is undergoing or has undergone gender reassignment.

(2) Subsection (3) applies to arrangements made by any person in relation to another's absence from work or from vocational training.

(3) For the purposes of subsection (1), B is treated less favourably than others under such arrangements if, in the application of the arrangements to any absence due to B undergoing gender reassignment—

(a) he is treated less favourably than he would be if the absence was due to sickness or injury, or

(b) he is treated less favourably than he would be if the absence was due to some other cause and, having regard to the circumstances of the case, it is reasonable for him to be treated no less favourably.

(4) In subsections (2) and (3) 'arrangements' includes terms, conditions or arrangements on which employment, a pupillage or tenancy or vocational training is offered.

(5) For the purposes of subsection (1), a provision mentioned in that subsection framed with reference to discrimination against women shall be treated as applying equally to the treatment of men with such modifications as are requisite.

3 Discrimination against married persons in employment field

(1) A person discriminates against a married person of either sex in any circumstances relevant for the purposes of any provision of Part II if—

(a) on the ground of his or her marital status he treats that person less favourably than he treats or would treat an unmarried person of the same sex, or

(b) he applies to that person a requirement or condition which he applies or would apply equally to an unmarried person but—

(i) which is such that the proportion of married persons who can comply with it is considerably smaller than the proportion of unmarried persons of the same sex who can comply with it, and

(ii) which he cannot show to be justifiable irrespective of the marital status of the person to whom it is applied, and

(iii) which is to that person's detriment because he cannot comply with it.

(2) For the purposes of subsection (1), a provision of Part II framed with reference to discrimination against women shall be treated as applying equally to the treatment of men, and for that purpose shall have effect with such modifications as are requisite.

4 Discrimination by way of victimisation

(1) A person ('the discriminator') discriminates against another person ('the person victimised') in any circumstances relevant for the purposes of any provision of this Act if he treats the person victimised less favourably than in those circumstances he treats or would treat other persons, and does so by reason that the person victimised has—

(a) brought proceedings against the discriminator or any other person under this Act or the Equal Pay Act 1970 or sections 62 to 65 of the Pensions Act 1995, or

(b) given evidence or information in connection with proceedings brought by any person against the discriminator or any other person under this Act or the Equal Pay Act 1970 or sections 62 to 65 of the Pensions Act 1995, or

(c) otherwise done anything under or by reference to this Act or the Equal Pay Act 1970 or sections 62 to 65 of the Pensions Act 1995 in relation to the discriminator or any other person, or

(d) alleged that the discriminator or any other person has committed an act which (whether or not the allegation so states) would amount to a contravention of this Act or give rise to a claim under the Equal Pay Act 1970 or under sections 62 to 65 of the Pensions Act 1995,

or by reason that the discriminator knows the person victimised intends to do any of those things, or suspects the person victimised has done, or intends to do, any of them.

(2) Subsection (1) does not apply to treatment of a person by reason of any allegation made by him if the allegation was false and not made in good faith.

(3) For the purposes of subsection (1), a provision of Part II or III framed with reference to discrimination against women shall be treated as applying equally to the treatment of men and for that purpose shall have effect with such modifications as are requisite.

5 Interpretation

(1) In this Act—

(a) references to discrimination refer to any discrimination falling within sections 1 to 4; and

(b) references to sex discrimination refer to any discrimination falling within section 1 or 2,

and related expressions shall be construed accordingly.

(2) In this Act—

'woman' includes a female of any age, and

'man' includes a male of any age.

(3) A comparison of the cases of persons of different sex or marital status under section 1(1) or 3(1), or a comparison of the cases of persons required for the purposes of section 2A, must be such that the relevant circumstances in the one case are the same, or not materially different, in the other.

PART II
DISCRIMINATION IN THE EMPLOYMENT FIELD

6 Discrimination against applicants and employees

(1) It is unlawful for a person, in relation to employment by him at an establishment in Great Britain, to discriminate against a woman—

(a) in the arrangements he makes for the purpose of determining who should be offered that employment, or

(b) in the terms on which he offers her that employment, or

(c) by refusing or deliberately omitting to offer her that employment.

(2) It is unlawful for a person, in the case of a woman employed by him at an establishment in Great Britain, to discriminate against her—

(a) in the way he affords her access to opportunities for promotion, transfer or training, or to any other benefits, facilities or services, or by refusing or deliberately omitting to afford her access to them, or

(b) by dismissing her, or subjecting her to any other detriment.

(3) [repealed]

(4) Subsections (1)(b) and (2) do not render it unlawful for a person to discriminate against a woman in relation to her membership of, or rights under, an occupational pension scheme in such a way that, were any term of the scheme to provide for discrimination in that way, then, by reason only of any provision made by or under sections 62 to 64 of the Pensions Act 1995 (equal treatment), an equal treatment rule would not operate in relation to that term.

(4A) In subsection (4), 'occupational pension scheme' has the same meaning as in the Pension Schemes Act 1993 and 'equal treatment rule' has the meaning given by section 62 of the Pensions Act 1995.

(5) Subject to section 8(3), subsection (1)(b) does not apply to any provision for the payment of money which, if the woman in question were given the employment, would be included (directly or otherwise) in the contract under which she was employed.

(6) Subsection (2) does not apply to benefits consisting of the payment of money when the provision of those benefits is regulated by the woman's contract of employment.

(7) Subsection (2) does not apply to benefits, facilities or services of any description if the employer is concerned with the provision (for payment or not) of benefits, facilities or services of that description to the public, or to a section of the public comprising the woman in question, unless—

(a) that provision differs in a material respect from the provision of the benefits, facilities or services by the employer to his employees, or

(b) the provision of the benefits, facilities or services to the woman in question is regulated by her contract of employment, or

(c) the benefits, facilities or services relate to training.

(8) In its application to any discrimination falling within section 2A, this section shall have effect with the omission of subsections (4) to (6).

7 Exception where sex is a genuine occupational qualification

(1) In relation to sex discrimination—

(a) section 6(1)(a) or (c) does not apply to any employment where being a man is a genuine occupational qualification for the job, and

(b) section 6(2)(a) does not apply to opportunities for promotion or transfer to, or training for, such employment.

(2) Being a man is a genuine occupational qualification for a job only where—

(a) the essential nature of the job calls for a man for reasons of physiology (excluding physical strength or stamina) or, in dramatic performances or other entertainment, for reasons of authenticity, so that the essential nature or the job would be materially different if carried out by a woman; or

(b) the job needs to be held by a man to preserve decency or privacy because—

(i) it is likely to involve physical contact with men in circumstances where they might reasonably object to its being carried out by a woman, or

(ii) the holder of the job is likely to do his work in circumstances where men might reasonably object to the presence of a woman because they are in a state of undress or are using sanitary facilities; or

(ba) the job is likely to involve the holder of the job doing his work, or living, in a private home and needs to be held by a man because objection might reasonably be taken to allowing to a woman—

(i) the degree of physical or social contact with a person living in the home, or

(ii) the knowledge of intimate details of such a person's life,

which is likely, because of the nature or circumstances of the job or of the home, to be allowed to, or available to, the holder of the job; or

(c) the nature or location of the establishment makes it impracticable for the holder of the job to live elsewhere than in premises provided by the employer, and—

(i) the only such premises which are available for persons holding that kind of job are lived in, or normally lived in, by men and are not equipped with separate sleeping accommodation for women and sanitary facilities which could be used by women in privacy from men, and

(ii) it is not reasonable to expect the employer either to equip those premises with such accommodation and facilities or to provide other premises for women; or

(d) the nature of the establishment, or of the part of it within which the work is done, requires the job to be held by a man because—

(i) it is, or is part of, a hospital, prison or other establishment for persons requiring special care, supervision or attention, and

(ii) those persons are all men (disregarding any woman whose presence is exceptional), and

(iii) it is reasonable, having regard to the essential character of the establishment or that part, that the job should not be held by a woman; or

(e) the holder of the job provides individuals with personal services promoting their welfare or education, or similar personal services, and those services can most effectively be provided by a man, or

(g) the job needs to be held by a man because it is likely to involve the performance of duties outside the United Kingdom in a country whose laws or customs are such that the duties could not, effectively, be performed by a woman, or

(h) the job is one of two to be held by a married couple.

(3) Subsection (2) applies where some only of the duties of the job fall within paragraphs (a) to (g) as well as where all of them do.

(4) Paragraph (a), (b), (c), (d), (e) or (g) of subsection (2) does not apply in relation to the filling of a vacancy at a time when the employer already has male employees—

(a) who are capable of carrying out the duties falling within that paragraph, and

(b) whom it would be reasonable to employ on those duties, and

(c) whose numbers are sufficient to meet the employer's likely requirements in respect of those duties without undue inconvenience.

7A Corresponding exception relating to gender reassignment

(1) In their application to discrimination falling within section 2A, subsections (1) and (2) of section 6 do not make unlawful an employer's treatment of another person if—

(a) in relation to the employment in question—

(i) being a man is a genuine occupational qualification for the job, or

(ii) being a woman is a genuine occupational qualification for the job, and

(b) the employer can show that the treatment is reasonable in view of the circumstances described in the relevant paragraph of section 7(2) and any other relevant circumstances.

(2) In subsection (1) the reference to the employment in question is a reference—

(a) in relation to any paragraph of section 6(1), to the employment mentioned in that paragraph;

(b) in relation to section 6(2)—

(i) in its application to opportunities for promotion or transfer to any employment or for training for any employment, to that employment;

(ii) otherwise, to the employment in which the person discriminated against is employed or from which that person is dismissed.

(3) In determining for the purposes of subsection (1) whether being a man or being a woman is a genuine occupational qualification for a job, section 7(4) applies in relation to dismissal from employment as it applies in relation to the filling of a vacancy.

7B Supplementary exceptions relating to gender reassignment

(1) In relation to discrimination falling within section 2A—

(a) section 6(1)(a) or (c) does not apply to any employment where there is a supplementary genuine occupational qualification for the job,

(b) section 6(2)(a) does not apply to a refusal or deliberate omission to afford access to opportunities for promotion or transfer to or training for such employment, and

(c) section 6(2)(b) does not apply to dismissing an employee from, or otherwise not allowing him to continue in, such employment.

(2) Subject to subsection (3), there is a supplementary genuine occupational qualification for a job only if—

(a) the job involves the holder of the job being liable to be called upon to perform intimate physical searches pursuant to statutory powers;

(b) the job is likely to involve the holder of the job doing his work, or living, in a private home and needs to be held otherwise than by a person who is undergoing or has undergone gender reassignment, because objection might reasonably be taken to allowing to such a person—

(i) the degree of physical or social contact with a person living in the home, or

(ii) the knowledge of intimate details of such a person's life,

which is likely, because of the nature or circumstances of the job or of the home, to be allowed to, or available to, the holder of the job;

(c) the nature of location of the establishment makes it impracticable for the holder of the job to live elsewhere than in premises provided by the employer, and—

(i) the only such premises which are available for persons holding that kind of job are such that reasonable objection could be taken, for the purpose of preserving decency and privacy, to the holder of the job sharing accommodation and facilities with either sex whilst undergoing gender reassignment, and

(ii) it is not reasonable to except the employer either to equip those premises with suitable accommodation or to make alternative arrangements; or

(d) the holder of the job provides vulnerable individuals with personal services promoting their welfare, or similar personal services, and in the reasonable view of the employer those services cannot be effectively provided by a person whilst that person is undergoing gender reassignment.

(3) Paragraphs (c) and (d) of subsection (2) apply only in relation to discrimination against a person who—

(a) intends to undergo gender reassignment, or

(b) is undergoing gender reassignment.

8 Equal Pay Act 1970

(1) [omitted]

(2) Section 1(1) of the Equal Pay Act 1970 does not apply in determining for the purposes of section 6(1)(b) of this Act the terms on which employment is offered.

(3) Where a person offers a woman employment on certain terms, and if she accepted the offer then, by virtue of an equality clause, any of those terms would fall to be modified, or any additional term would fall to be included, the offer shall be taken to contravene section 6(1)(b).

(4) Where a person offers a woman employment on certain terms, and subsection (3) would apply but for the fact that, on her acceptance of the offer, section 1(3) of the Equal Pay Act 1970 (as set out in subsection (1) above) would prevent the equality clause from operating, the offer shall be taken not to contravene section 6(1)(b).

(5) An act does not contravene section 6(2) if—

(a) it contravenes a term modified or included by virtue of an equality clause, or

(b) it would contravene such a term but for the fact that the equality clause is prevented from operating by section 1(3) of the Equal Pay Act 1970.

(6) [omitted]

(7) In its application to any discrimination falling within section 2A, this section shall have effect with the omission of subsections (3), (4) and (5)(b).

9 Discrimination against contract workers

(1) This section applies to any work for a person ('the principal') which is available for doing by individuals ('contract workers') who are employed not by the principal himself but by another person, who supplies them under a contract made with the principal.

(2) It is unlawful for the principal, in relation to work to which this section applies, to discriminate against a woman who is a contract worker—

(a) in the terms on which he allows her to do that work, or

(b) by not allowing her to do it or continue to do it, or

(c) in the way he affords her access to any benefits, facilities or services or by refusing or deliberately omitting to afford her access to them, or

(d) by subjecting her to any other detriment.

(3) Subject to section (3A), the principal does not contravene subsection (2)(b) by doing any act in relation to a woman at a time when if the work were to be done by a person taken into his employment being a man would be a genuine occupational qualification for the job.

(3A) Subsection (3) does not apply in relation to discrimination falling within section 2A.

(3B) In relation to discrimination falling within section 2A, the principal does not contravene subsection (2)(a), (b), (c) or (d) by doing any act in relation to a woman if—

(a) he does it at a time when, if the work were to be done by a person taken into his employment—

(i) being a man would be a genuine occupational qualification for the job, or

(ii) being a woman would be a genuine occupational qualification for the job,

and

(b) he can show that the act is reasonable in view of the circumstances relevant for the purposes of paragraph (a) and any other relevant circumstances.

(3C) In relation to discrimination falling within section 2A, the principal does not contravene subsection (2)(b) by doing any act in relation to a woman at a time when, if the work were to be done by a person taken into his employment, there would be a supplementary genuine occupational qualification for the job.

(4) Subsection (2)(c) does not apply to benefits, facilities or services of any description if the principal is concerned with the provision (for payment or not) of benefits, facilities or services of that description to the public, or to a section of the public to which the woman belongs, unless that provision differs in a material respect from the provision of the benefits, facilities or services by the principal to his contract workers.

10 Meaning of employment at establishment in Great Britain

(1) For the purposes of this Part and section 1 of the Equal Pay Act 1970 ('the relevant purposes'), employment is to be regarded as being at an establishment in Great Britain unless the employee does his work wholly or mainly outside Great Britain.

(2) and (3) [omitted]

(4) Where work is not done at an establishment it shall be treated for the relevant purposes as done at the establishment from which it is done or (where it is not done from any establishment) at the establishment with which it has the closest connection.

(5) to (7) [omitted]

11 [omitted]

12 Trade unions etc.

(1) This section applies to an organisation of workers, an organisation of employers, or any other organisation whose members carry on a particular profession or trade for the purposes of which the organisation exists.

(2) It is unlawful for an organisation to which this section applies, in the case of a woman who is not a member of the organisation, to discriminate against her—

(a) in the terms on which it is prepared to admit her to membership, or

(b) by refusing, or deliberately omitting to accept, her application for membership.

(3) It is unlawful for an organisation to which this section applies, in the case of a woman who is a member of the organisation, to discriminate against her—

(a) in the way it affords her access to any benefits, facilities or services, or by refusing or deliberately omitting to afford her access to them, or

(b) by depriving her of membership, or varying the terms on which she is a member, or

(c) by subjecting her to any other detriment.

(4) This section does not apply to provision made in relation to the death or retirement from work of a member.

13 to **36** [omitted]

PART IV
OTHER UNLAWFUL ACTS

37 Discriminatory practices

(1) In this section 'discriminatory practice' means the application of a requirement or condition which results in an act of discrimination which is unlawful by virtue of any provision of Part II or III taken with section 1(1)(b) or 3(1)(b) or which would be likely to result in such an act of discrimination if the persons to whom it is applied were not all of one sex.

(2) A person acts in contravention of this section if and so long as—

(a) he applies a discriminatory practice, or

(b) he operates practices or other arrangements which in any circumstances would call for the application by him of a discriminatory practice.

(3) Proceedings in respect of a contravention of this section shall be brought only by the Commission in accordance with sections 67 to 71.

38 Discriminatory advertisements

(1) It is unlawful to publish or cause to be published an advertisement which indicates, or might reasonably be understood as indicating, an intention by a person to do any act which is or might be unlawful by virtue of Part II or III.

(2) Subsection (1) does not apply to an advertisement if the intended act would not in fact be unlawful.

(3) For the purposes of subsection (1), use of a job description with a sexual connotation (such as 'waiter', 'salesgirl', 'postman' or 'stewardess') shall be taken to indicate an intention to discriminate, unless the advertisement contains an indication to the contrary.

(4) The publisher of an advertisement made unlawful by subsection (1) shall not be subject to any liability under that subsection in respect of the publication of the advertisement if he proves—

(a) that the advertisement was published in reliance on a statement made to him by the person who caused it to be published to the effect that, by reason of the operation of subsection (2), the publication would not be unlawful, and

(b) that it was reasonable for him to rely on the statement.

(5) A person who knowingly or recklessly makes a statement such as is referred to in subsection (4) which in a material respect is false or misleading commits an offence, and shall be liable on summary conviction to a fine not exceeding level 5 on the standard scale.

39 Instructions to discriminate

It is unlawful for a person—

(a) who has authority over another person, or

(b) in accordance with whose wishes that other person is accustomed to act,

to instruct him to do any act which is unlawful by virtue of Part II or III, or procure or attempt to procure the doing by him of any such act.

40 Pressure to discriminate

(1) It is unlawful to induce, or attempt to induce, a person to do any act which contravenes Part II or III by—

(a) providing or offering to provide him with any benefit, or

(b) subjecting or threatening to subject him to any detriment.

(2) An offer or threat is not prevented from falling within subsection (1) because it is not made directly to the person in question, if it is made in such a way that he is likely to hear of it.

41 Liability of employers and principals

(1) Anything done by a person in the course of his employment shall be treated for the purposes of this Act as done by his employer as well as by him, whether or not it was done with the employer's knowledge or approval.

(2) Anything done by a person as agent for another person with the authority (whether express or implied, and whether precedent or subsequent) of that other person shall be treated for the purposes of this Act as done by that other person as well as by him.

(3) In proceedings brought under this Act against any person in respect of an act alleged to have been done by an employee of his it shall be a defence for that person to prove that he took such steps as were reasonably practicable to prevent the employee from doing that act, or from doing in the course of his employment acts of that description.

42 Aiding unlawful acts

(1) A person who knowingly aids another person to do an act made unlawful by this Act shall be treated for the purposes of this Act as himself doing an unlawful act of the like description.

(2) For the purposes of subsection (1) an employee or agent for whose act the employer or principal is liable under section 41 (or would be so liable but for section 41(3)) shall be deemed to aid the doing of the act by the employer or principal.

(3) A person does not under this section knowingly aid another to do an unlawful act if—

(a) he acts in reliance on a statement made to him by that other person that, by reason of any provision of this Act, the act which he aids would not be unlawful, and

(b) it is reasonable for him to rely on the statement.

(4) A person who knowingly or recklessly makes a statement such as is referred to in subsection (3)(a) which in a material respect is false or misleading commits an offence, and shall be liable on summary conviction to a fine not exceeding level 5 on the standard scale.

43 to **46** [omitted]

PART V
GENERAL EXCEPTIONS FROM PARTS II TO IV

47 Discriminatory training by certain bodies

(1) Nothing in Parts II to IV shall render unlawful any act done in relation to particular work by any person in, or in connection with—

(a) affording women only, or men only, access to facilities for training which would help to fit them for that work, or

(b) encouraging women only, or men only, to take advantage of opportunities for doing that work,

where it reasonably appears to that person that at any time within the 12 months immediately preceding the doing of the act there were no persons of the sex in question doing that work in Great Britain, or the number of persons of that sex doing the work in Great Britain was comparatively small.

(2) Where in relation to particular work it reasonably appears to any person that although the condition for the operation of subsection (1) is not met for the whole of Great Britain it is met for an area within Great Britain, nothing in Parts II to IV shall render unlawful any act done by the training body in, or in connection with—

(a) affording persons who are of the sex in question, and who appear likely to take up that work in that area, access to facilities for training which would help to fit them for that work, or

(b) encouraging persons of that sex to take advantage of opportunities in the area for doing that work.

(3) Nothing in Parts II to IV shall render unlawful any act done by a training body in, or in connection with, affording persons access to facilities for training which would help to fit them for employment, where it reasonably appears to that person that those persons are in special need of training by reason of the period for which they have been discharging domestic or family responsibilities to the exclusion of regular full time employment.

The discrimination in relation to which this subsection applies may result from confining the training to persons who have been discharging domestic or family responsibilities, or from the way persons are selected for training, or both.

(4) The preceding provisions of this section shall not apply in relation to any discrimination which is rendered unlawful by section 6.

48 Other discriminatory training etc.

(1) Nothing in Parts II to IV shall render unlawful any act done by an employer in relation to particular work in his employment, being an act done in, or in connection with,—

(a) affording his female employees only, or his male employees only, access to facilities for training which would help to fit them for that work, or

(b) encouraging women only, or men only, to take advantage of opportunities for doing that work,

where at any time within the twelve months immediately preceding the doing of the act there were no persons of the sex in question among those doing that work or the number of persons of that sex doing the work was comparatively small.

(2) Nothing in section 12 shall render unlawful any act done by an organisation to which that section applies in, or in connection with,—

(a) affording female members of the organisation only, or male members of the organisation only, access to facilities for training which would help to fit them for holding a post of any kind in the organisation, or

(b) encouraging female members only, or male members only, to take advantage of opportunities for holding such posts in the organisation,

where at any time within the twelve months immediately preceding the doing of the act there were no persons of the sex in question among persons holding such posts in the organisation or the number of persons of that sex holding such posts was comparatively small.

(3) Nothing in Parts II to IV shall render unlawful any act done by an organisation to which section 12 applies in, or in connection with, encouraging women only, or men

only, to become members of the organisation where at any time within the twelve months immediately preceding the doing of the act there were no persons of the sex in question among those members or the number of persons of that sex among the members was comparatively small.

49 Trade unions etc.: elective bodies

(1) If an organisation to which section 12 applies comprises a body the membership of which is wholly or mainly elected, nothing in section 12 shall render unlawful provision which ensures that a minimum number of persons of one sex are members of the body—

(a) by reserving seats on the body for persons of that sex, or

(b) by making extra seats on the body available (by election or co-option or otherwise) for persons of that sex on occasions when the number of persons of that sex in the other seats is below the minimum,

where in the opinion of the organisation the provision is in the circumstances needed to secure a reasonable lower limit to the number of members of that sex serving on the body; and nothing in Parts II to IV shall render unlawful any act done in order to give effect to such a provision.

(2) This section shall not be taken as making lawful—

(a) discrimination in the arrangements for determining the persons entitled to vote in an election of members of the body, or otherwise to choose the persons to serve on the body, or

(b) discrimination in any arrangements concerning membership of the organisation itself.

50 Indirect access to benefits etc.

(1) References in this Act to the affording by any person of access to benefits, facilities or services are not limited to benefits, facilities or services provided by that person himself, but include any means by which it is in that person's power to facilitate access to benefits, facilities or services provided by any other person (the 'actual provider').

(2) Where by any provision of this Act the affording by any person of access to benefits, facilities or services in a discriminatory way is in certain circumstances prevented from being unlawful, the effect of the provision shall extend also to the liability under this Act of any actual provider.

51 Acts done for purposes of protection of women

(1) Nothing in the following provisions, namely—

(a) Part II,

(b) Part III so far as it applies to vocational training, or

(c) Part IV so far as it has effect in relation to the provisions mentioned in paragraphs (a) and (b),

shall render unlawful any act done by a person in relation to a woman if—

(i) it was necessary for that person to do it in order to comply with a requirement of an existing statutory provision concerning the protection of women, or

(ii) it was necessary for that person to do it in order to comply with a requirement of a relevant statutory provision (within the meaning of Part I of the Health and Safety at Work etc. Act 1974) and it was done by that person for the purpose of the protection of the woman in question (or of any class of women that included that woman).

(2) In subsection (1)—

(a) the reference in paragraph (i) of that subsection to an existing statutory provision concerning the protection of women is a reference to any such provision having effect for the purpose of protecting women as regards—

(i) pregnancy or maternity, or

(ii) other circumstances giving rise to risks specifically affecting women,

whether the provision relates only to such protection or to the protection of any other class of persons as well; and

(b) the reference in paragraph (ii) of that subsection to the protection of a particular woman or class of women is a reference to the protection of that woman or those women as regards any circumstances falling within paragraph (a)(i) or (ii) above.

(3) In this section 'existing statutory provision' means (subject to subsection (4)) any provision of—

(a) an Act passed before this Act, or

(b) an instrument approved or made by or under such an Act (including one approved or made after the passing of this Act).

(4) Where an Act passed after this Act re-enacts (with or without modification) a provision of an Act passed before this Act, that provision as re-enacted shall be treated for the purposes of subsection (3) as if it continued to be contained in an Act passed before this Act.

51A Acts done under statutory authority to be exempt from certain provisions of Part III

(1) Nothing in—

(a) the relevant provisions of Part III, or

(b) Part IV so far as it has effect in relation to those provisions,

shall render unlawful any act done by a person if it was necessary for that person to do it in order to comply with a requirement of an existing statutory provision within the meaning of section 51.

(2) In subsection (1) 'the relevant provisions of Part III' means the provisions of that Part except so far as they apply to vocational training.

PART VI
EQUAL OPPORTUNITIES COMMISSION

52 to **56A** [omitted]

57 Power to conduct formal investigations

(1) Without prejudice to their general power to do anything requisite for the performance of their duties under section 53(1), the Commission may if they think fit, and shall if required by the Secretary of State, conduct a formal investigation for any purpose connected with the carrying out of those duties.

(2) The Commission may, with the approval of the Secretary of State, appoint, on a full-time or part-time basis, one or more individuals as additional Commissioners for the purposes of a formal investigation.

(3) The Commission may nominate one or more Commissioners, with or without one or more additional Commissioners, to conduct a formal investigation on their behalf, and may delegate any of their functions in relation to the investigation to the persons so nominated.

58 Terms of reference

(1) The Commission shall not embark on a formal investigation unless the requirements of this section have been complied with.

(2) Terms of reference for the investigation shall be drawn up by the Commission or, if the Commission were required by the Secretary of State to conduct the investigation, by the Secretary of State after consulting the Commission.

(3) It shall be the duty of the Commission to give general notice of the holding of the investigation unless the terms of reference confine it to activities of persons named

in them, but in such a case the Commission shall in the prescribed manner give those persons notice of the holding of the investigation.

(3A) Where the terms of reference of the investigation confine it to activities of persons named in them and the Commission in the course of it propose to investigate any act made unlawful by this Act which they believe that a person so named may have done, the Commission shall—

(a) inform that person of their belief and of their proposal to investigate the act in question; and

(b) offer him an opportunity of making oral or written representations with regard to it (or both oral and written representations if he thinks fit);

and a person so named who avails himself of an opportunity under this subsection of making oral representations may be represented—

(i) by counsel or a solicitor; or

(ii) by some other person of his choice, not being a person to whom the Commission object on the ground that he is unsuitable.

(4) The Commission or, if the Commission were required by the Secretary of State to conduct the investigation, the Secretary of State after consulting the Commission may from time to time revise the terms of reference; and subsections (1), (3) and (3A) shall apply to the revised investigation and terms of reference as they applied to the original.

59 Power to obtain information

(1) For the purposes of a formal investigation the Commission, by a notice in the prescribed form served on him in the prescribed manner,—

(a) may require any person to furnish such written information as may be described in the notice, and may specify the time at which, and the manner and form in which, the information is to be furnished;

(b) may require any person to attend at such time and place as is specified in the notice and give oral information about, and produce all documents in his possession or control relating to, any matter specified in the notice.

(2) Except as provided by section 69, a notice shall be served under subsection (1) only where—

(a) service of the notice was authorised by an order made by or on behalf of the Secretary of State, or

(b) the terms of reference of the investigation state that the Commission believe that a person named in them may have done or may be doing acts of all or any of the following descriptions—

(i) unlawful discriminatory acts,

(ii) contraventions of section 37,

(iii) contraventions of sections 38, 39 or 40, and

(iv) acts in breach of a term modified or included by virtue of an equality clause,

and confine the investigation to those acts.

(3) A notice under subsection (1) shall not require a person—

(a) to give information, or produce any documents, which he could not be compelled to give in evidence, or produce, in civil proceedings before the High Court or the Court of Session, or

(b) to attend at any place unless the necessary expenses of his journey to and from that place are paid or tendered to him.

(4) If a person fails to comply with a notice served on him under subsection (1) or the Commission has reasonable cause to believe that he intends not to comply with it, the Commission may apply to a county court for an order requiring him to comply with it or with such directions for the like purpose as may be contained in the order; and section 55 (penalty for neglecting or refusing to give evidence) of the County Courts Act

1984 shall apply to failure without reasonable excuse to comply with any such order as it applies in the cases there provided.

(6) A person commits an offence if he—

(a) wilfully alters, suppresses, conceals or destroys a document which he has been required by a notice or order under this section to produce, or

(b) in complying with such a notice or order, knowingly or recklessly makes any statement which is false in a material particular,

and shall be liable on summary conviction to a fine not exceeding level 5 on the standard scale.

(7) Proceedings for an offence under subsection (6) may (without prejudice to any jurisdiction exercisable apart from this subsection) be instituted—

(a) against any person at any place at which he has an office or other place of business;

(b) against an individual at any place where he resides, or at which he is for the time being.

60 Recommendations and reports on formal investigations

(1) If in the light of any of their findings in a formal investigation it appears to the Commission necessary or expedient, whether during the course of the investigation or after its conclusion,—

(a) to make to any persons, with a view to promoting equality of opportunity between men and women who are affected by any of their activities, recommendations for changes in their policies or procedures, or as to any other matters, or

(b) to make to the Secretary of State any recommendations, whether for changes in the law or otherwise,

the Commission shall make those recommendations accordingly.

(2) The Commission shall prepare a report of their findings in any formal investigation conducted by them.

(3) If the formal investigation is one required by the Secretary of State—

(a) the Commission shall deliver the report to the Secretary of State, and

(b) the Secretary of State shall cause the report to be published,

and unless required by the Secretary of State the Commission shall not publish the report.

(4) If the formal investigation is not one required by the Secretary of State, the Commission shall either publish the report, or make it available for inspection in accordance with subsection (5).

(5) Where under subsection (4) a report is to be made available for inspection, any person shall be entitled, on payment of such fee (if any) as may be determined by the Commission—

(a) to inspect the report during ordinary office hours and take copies of all or any part of the report, or

(b) to obtain from the Commission a copy, certified by the Commission to be correct, of the report.

(6) The Commission may if they think fit determine that the right conferred by subsection (5)(a) shall be exercisable in relation to a copy of the report instead of, or in addition to, the original.

(7) The Commission shall give general notice of the place or places where, and the times when, reports may be inspected under subsection (5).

61 Restriction on disclosure of information

(1) No information given to the Commission by any person ('the informant') in connection with a formal investigation shall be disclosed by the Commission, or by any person who is or has been a Commissioner, additional Commissioner or employee of the Commission, except—

(a) on the order of any court, or

(b) with the informant's consent, or

(c) in the form of a summary or other general statement published by the Commission which does not identify the informant or any other person to whom the information relates, or

(d) in a report of the investigation published by the Commission or made available for inspection under section 60(5), or

(e) to the Commissioners, additional Commissioners or employees of the Commission, or, so far as may be necessary for the proper performance of the functions of the Commission, to other persons, or

(f) for the purpose of any civil proceedings under this Act to which the Commission are a party, or any criminal proceedings.

(2) Any person who discloses information in contravention of subsection (1) commits an offence and shall be liable on summary conviction to a fine not exceeding level 5 on the standard scale.

(3) In preparing any report for publication or for inspection the Commission shall exclude, so far as is consistent with their duties and the object of the report, any matter which relates to the private affairs of any individual or business interests of any person where the publication of that matter might, in the opinion of the Commission, prejudicially affect that individual or person.

PART VII
ENFORCEMENT

62 Restriction of proceedings for breach of Act

(1) Except as provided by this Act no proceedings, whether civil or criminal, shall lie against any person in respect of an act by reason that the act is unlawful by virtue of a provision of this Act.

(2) Subsection (1) does not preclude the making of an order of certiorari, mandamus or prohibition.

(3) [omitted]

63 Jurisdiction of employment tribunals

(1) A complaint by any person ('the complainant') that another person ('the respondent')—

(a) has committed an act of discrimination against the complainant which is unlawful by virtue of Part II, or

(b) is by virtue of section 41 or 42 to be treated as having committed such an act of discrimination against the complainant,

may be presented to an employment tribunal.

(2) Subsection (1) does not apply to a complaint under section 13(1) of an act in respect of which an appeal, or proceedings in the nature of an appeal, may be brought under any enactment.

64 [repealed]

65 Remedies on complaint under section 63

(1) Where an employment tribunal finds that a complaint presented to it under section 63 is well-founded the tribunal shall make such of the following as it considers just and equitable—

(a) an order declaring the rights of the complainant and the respondent in relation to the act to which the complaint relates;

(b) an order requiring the respondent to pay to the complainant compensation of an amount corresponding to any damages he could have been ordered by a county court or by a sheriff court to pay to the complainant if the complaint had fallen to be dealt with under section 66;

(c) a recommendation that the respondent take within a specified period action appearing to the tribunal to be practicable for the purpose of obviating or reducing the adverse effect on the complainant of any act of discrimination to which the complaint relates.

(1A) In applying section 66 for the purposes of subsection (1)(b), no account shall be taken of subsection (3) of that section.

(1B) As respects an unlawful act of discrimination falling within section 1(1)(b) or section 3(1)(b), if the respondent proves that the requirement or condition in question was not applied with the intention of treating the complainant unfavourably on the ground of his sex or marital status as the case may be, an order may be made under subsection (1)(b) only if the employment tribunal—

(a) makes such order under subsection (1)(a) and such recommendation under subsection (1)(c) (if any) as it would have made if it had no power to make an order under subsection (1)(b); and

(b) (where it makes an order under subsection (1)(a) or a recommendation under subsection (1)(c) or both) considers that it is just and equitable to make an order under subsection (1)(b) as well.

(2) [repealed]

(3) If without reasonable justification the respondent to a complaint fails to comply with a recommendation made by an employment tribunal under subsection (1)(c), then, if they think it just and equitable to do so—

(a) the tribunal may increase the amount of compensation required to be paid to the complainant in respect of the complaint by an order made under subsection (1)(b), or

(b) if an order under subsection (1)(b) was not made, the tribunal may make such an order.

66 Claims under Part III

(1) A claim by any person ('the claimant') that another person ('the respondent')—

(a) has committed an act of discrimination against the claimant which is unlawful by virtue of Part III, or

(b) is by virtue of section 41 or 42 to be treated as having committed such an act of discrimination against the claimant,

may be made the subject of civil proceedings in like manner as any other claim in tort or (in Scotland) in reparation for breach of statutory duty.

(2) Proceedings under subsection (1)—

(a) shall be brought in England and Wales only in a county court, and

(b) shall be brought in Scotland only in a sheriff court,

but all such remedies shall be obtainable in such proceedings as, apart from this subsection and section 62(1), would be obtainable in the High Court or the Court of Session, as the case may be.

(3) As respects an unlawful act of discrimination falling within section 1(1)(b) no award of damages shall be made if the respondent proves that the requirement or condition in question was not applied with the intention of treating the claimant unfavourably on the ground of his sex.

(4) For the avoidance of doubt it is hereby declared that damages in respect of an unlawful act of discrimination may include compensation for injury to feelings whether or not they include compensation under any other head.

(5) to (8) [omitted]

67 Issue of non-discrimination notice

(1) This section applies to—

(a) an unlawful discriminatory act, and
(b) a contravention of section 37, and
(c) a contravention of section 38, 39 or 40, and
(d) an act in breach of a term modified or included by virtue of an equality clause,
and so applies whether or not proceedings have been brought in respect of the act.

(2) If in the course of a formal investigation the Commission becomes satisfied that a person is committing, or has committed, any such acts, the Commission may in the prescribed manner serve on him a notice in the prescribed form ('a non-discrimination notice') requiring him—

(a) not to commit any such acts, and
(b) where compliance with paragraph (a) involves changes in any of his practices or other arrangements—
(i) to inform the Commission that he has effected those changes and what those changes are, and
(ii) to take such steps as may be reasonably required by the notice for the purpose of affording that information to other persons concerned.

(3) A non-discrimination notice may also require the person on whom it is served to furnish the Commission with such other information as may be reasonably required by the notice in order to verify that the notice has been complied with.

(4) The notice may specify the time at which, and the manner and form in which, any information is to be furnished to the Commission, but the time at which any information is to be furnished in compliance with the notice shall not be later than five years after the notice has become final.

(5) The Commission shall not serve a non-discrimination notice in respect of any person unless they have first—

(a) given him notice that they are minded to issue a non-discrimination notice in his case, specifying the grounds on which they contemplate doing so, and
(b) offered him an opportunity of making oral or written representations in the matter (or both oral and written representations if he thinks fit) within a period of not less than 28 days specified in the notice, and
(c) taken account of any representations so made by him.

(6) Subsection (2) does not apply to any acts in respect of which the Secretary of State could exercise the powers conferred on him by section 25(2) and (3); but if the Commission become aware of any such acts they shall give notice of them to the Secretary of State.

(7) Section 59(4) shall apply to requirements under subsection (2)(b), (3) and (4) contained in a non-discrimination notice which has become final as it applies to requirements in a notice served under section 59(1).

68 Appeal against non-discrimination notice

(1) Not later than six weeks after a non-discrimination notice is served on any person he may appeal against any requirement of the notice—

(a) to an employment tribunal, so far as the requirement relates to acts which are within the jurisdiction of the tribunal;
(b) to a county court or to a sheriff court so far as the requirement relates to acts which are within the jurisdiction of the court and are not within the jurisdiction of an employment tribunal.

(2) Where the court or tribunal considers a requirement in respect of which an appeal is brought under subsection (1) to be unreasonable because it is based on an incorrect finding of fact or for any other reason, the court or tribunal shall quash the requirement.

(3) On quashing a requirement under subsection (2) the court or tribunal may direct that the non-discrimination notice shall be treated as if, in place of the requirement quashed, it had contained a requirement in terms specified in the direction.

(4) Subsection (1) does not apply to a requirement treated as included in a non-discrimination notice by virtue of a direction under subsection (3).

69 Investigation as to compliance with non-discrimination notice

(1) If—

(a) the terms of reference of a formal investigation state that its purpose is to determine whether any requirements of a non-discrimination notice are being or have been carried out, but section 59(2)(b) does not apply, and

(b) section 58(3) is complied with in relation to the investigation on a date ('the commencement date') not later than the expiration of the period of five years beginning when the non-discrimination notice became final,

the Commission may within the period referred to in subsection (2) serve notices under section 59(1) for the purposes of the investigation without needing to obtain the consent of the Secretary of State.

(2) The said period begins on the commencement date and ends on the later of the following dates—

(a) the date on which the period of five years mentioned in subsection (1)(b) expires;

(b) the date two years after the commencement date.

70 Register of non-discrimination notices

(1) The Commission shall establish and maintain a register ('the register') of non-discrimination notices which have become final.

(2) Any person shall be entitled, on payment of such fee (if any) as may be determined by the Commission,—

(a) to inspect the register during ordinary office hours and take copies of any entry, or

(b) to obtain from the Commission a copy, certified by the Commission to be correct, of any entry in the register.

(3) The Commission may, if they think fit, determine that the right conferred by subsection (2)(a) shall be exercisable in relation to a copy of the register instead of, or in addition to, the original.

(4) The Commission shall give general notice of the place or places where, and the times when, the register or a copy of it may be inspected.

71 Persistent discrimination

(1) If, during the period of five years beginning on the date on which either of the following became final in the case of any person, namely,—

(a) a non-discrimination notice served on him,

(b) a finding by a court or tribunal under section 63 or 66, or section 2 of the Equal Pay Act 1970, that he has done an unlawful discriminatory act or an act in breach of a term modified or included by virtue of an equality clause,

it appears to the Commission that unless restrained he is likely to do one or more acts falling within paragraph (b), or contravening section 37, the Commission may apply to a county court for an injunction, or to the sheriff court for an order, restraining him from doing so; and the court, if satisfied that the application is well-founded, may grant the injunction or order in the terms applied for or in more limited terms.

(2) In proceedings under this section the Commission shall not allege that the person to whom the proceedings relate has done an act which is within the jurisdiction of an employment tribunal unless a finding by an employment tribunal that he did that act has become final.

72 Enforcement of ss 38 to 40

(1) Proceedings in respect of a contravention of section 38, 39 or 40 shall be brought only by the Commission in accordance with the following provisions of this section.

(2) The proceedings shall be—

(a) an application for a decision whether the alleged contravention occurred, or

(b) an application under subsection (4) below,

or both.

(3) An application under subsection (2)(a) shall be made—

(a) in a case based on any provision of Part II, to an employment tribunal, and

(b) in any other case to a county court or sheriff court.

(4) If it appears to the Commission—

(a) that a person has done an act which by virtue of section 38, 39 or 40 was unlawful, and

(b) that unless restrained he is likely to do further acts which by virtue of that section are unlawful,

the Commission may apply to a county court for an injunction, or to a sheriff court for an order, restraining him from doing such act; and the court, if satisfied that the application is well-founded, may grant the injunction or order in the terms applied for or more limited terms.

(5) In proceedings under subsection (4) the Commission shall not allege that the person to whom the proceedings relate has done an act which is unlawful under this Act and within the jurisdiction of an employment tribunal unless a finding by an employment tribunal that he did that act has become final.

73 Preliminary action in employment cases

(1) With a view to making an application under section 71(1) or 72(4) in relation to a person the Commission may present to an employment tribunal a complaint that he has done an act within the jurisdiction of an employment tribunal, and if the tribunal considers that the complaint is well-founded they shall make a finding to that effect and, if they think it just and equitable to do so in the case of an act contravening any provision of Part II may also (as if the complaint had been presented by the person discriminated against) make an order such as is referred to in section 65(1)(a), or a recommendation such as is referred to in section 65(1)(c), or both.

(2) Subsection (1) is without prejudice to the jurisdiction conferred by section 72(2).

(3) Any finding of an employment tribunal under—

(a) this Act, or

(b) the Equal Pay Act 1970,

in respect of any act shall, if it has become final, be treated as conclusive—

(i) by the county court or sheriff court on an application under section 71(1) or 72(4) or in proceedings on an equality clause,

(ii) by an employment tribunal on a complaint made by the person affected by the act under section 63 or in relation to an equality clause.

(4) In section 71 and 72 and this section, the acts 'within the jurisdiction of an employment tribunal' are those in respect of which such jurisdiction is conferred by sections 63 and 72 and by section 2 of the Equal Pay Act 1970.

74 Help for aggrieved persons in obtaining information etc.

(1) With a view to helping a person ('the person aggrieved') who considers he may have been discriminated against in contravention of this Act to decide whether to institute proceedings and, if he does so, to formulate and present his case in the most effective manner, the Secretary of State shall by order prescribe—

(a) forms by which the person aggrieved may question the respondent on his reasons for doing any relevant act, or on any other matter which is or may be relevant;

(b) forms by which the respondent may if he so wishes reply to any questions.

(2) Where the person aggrieved questions the respondent (whether in accordance with an order under subsection (1) or not)—

(a) the question, and any reply by the respondent (whether in accordance with such an order or not) shall, subject to the following provisions of this section, be admissible as evidence in the proceedings;

(b) if it appears to the court or tribunal that the respondent deliberately, and without reasonable excuse, omitted to reply within a reasonable period or that his reply is evasive or equivocal, the court or tribunal may draw any inference from that fact that it considers it just and equitable to draw, including an inference that he committed an unlawful act.

75 Assistance by Commission

(1) Where, in relation to proceedings or prospective proceedings either under this Act or in respect of an equality clause, an individual who is an actual or prospective complainant or claimant applies to the Commission for assistance under this section, the Commission shall consider the application and may grant it if they think fit to do so on the ground that—

(a) the case raises a question of principle, or

(b) it is unreasonable, having regard to the complexity of the case or the applicant's position in relation to the respondent or another person involved or any other matter, to expect the applicant to deal with the case unaided,

or by reason of any other special consideration.

(2) Assistance by the Commission under this section may include—

(a) giving advice;

(b) procuring or attempting to procure the settlement of any matter in dispute;

(c) arranging for the giving of advice or assistance by a solicitor or counsel;

(d) arranging for representation by any person including all such assistance as is usually given by a solicitor or counsel in the steps preliminary or incidental to any proceedings, or in arriving at or giving effect to a compromise to avoid or bring to an end any proceedings,

(e) any other form of assistance which the Commission may consider appropriate,

but paragraph (d) shall not affect the law and practice regulating the descriptions of persons who may appear in, conduct, defend and address the court in, any proceedings.

(3) In so far as expenses are incurred by the Commission in providing the applicant with assistance under this section the recovery of those expenses (as taxed or assessed in such manner as may be prescribed by rules or regulations) shall constitute a first charge for the benefit of the Commission—

(a) on any costs or expenses which (whether by virtue of a judgment or order of a court or tribunal or an agreement or otherwise) are payable to the applicant by any other person in respect of the matter in connection with which the assistance is given, and

(b) so far as relates to any costs or expenses, on his rights under any compromise or settlement arrived at in connection with that matter to avoid or bring to an end any proceedings.

(4) The charge conferred by subsection (3) is subject to any charge under the Legal Aid Act 1988, or any charge or obligation for payment in priority to other debts under the Legal Aid (Scotland) Act 1986, and is subject to any provision in either of those Acts for payment of any sum to the Legal Aid Board or into the Scottish Legal Aid Fund.

(5) In this section 'respondent' includes a prospective respondent and 'rules or regulations'—

(a) in relation to county court proceedings, means county court rules;

(b) in relation to sheriff court proceedings, means sheriff court rules;

(c) in relation to employment tribunal proceedings, means employment tribunal procedure regulations under Part I of the Employment Tribunals Act 1996.

Period within which proceedings to be brought

76 Period within which proceedings to be brought

(1) An employment tribunal shall not consider a complaint under section 63 unless it is presented to the tribunal before the end of

(a) the period of three months beginning when the act complained of was done; or

(b) in a case to which section 85(9A) applies, the period of six months so beginning.

(2) A county court or a sheriff court shall not consider a claim under section 66 unless proceedings in respect of the claim are instituted before the end of

(a) the period of six months beginning when the act complained of was done; or

(b) in a case to which section 66(5) applies, the period of eight months so beginning.

(3) An employment tribunal, county court or sheriff court shall not consider an application under section 72(2)(a) unless it is made before the end of the period of six months beginning when the act to which it relates was done; and a county court or sheriff court shall not consider an application under section 72(4) unless it is made before the end of the period of five years so beginning.

(4) An employment tribunal shall not consider a complaint under section 73(1) unless it is presented to the tribunal before the end of the period of six months beginning when the act complained of was done.

(5) A court or tribunal may nevertheless consider any such complaint, claim or application which is out of time if, in all the circumstances of the case, it considers that it is just and equitable to do so.

(6) For the purposes of this section—

(a) where the inclusion or any term in a contract renders the making of the contract an unlawful act that act shall be treated as extending throughout the duration of the contract, and

(b) any act extending over a period shall be treated as done at the end of that period, and

(c) a deliberate omission shall be treated as done when the person in question decided upon it,

and in the absence of evidence establishing the contrary a person shall be taken for the purposes of this section to decide upon an omission when he does an act inconsistent with doing the omitted act or, if he has done no such inconsistent act, when the period expires within which he might reasonably have been expected to do the omitted act if it was to be done.

PART VIII
SUPPLEMENTAL

77 Validity and revision of contracts

(1) A term of a contract is void where—

(a) its inclusion renders the making of the contract unlawful by virtue of this Act, or

(b) it is included in furtherance of an act rendered unlawful by this Act, or

(c) it provides for the doing of an act which would be rendered unlawful by this Act.

(2) Subsection (1) does not apply to a term the inclusion of which constitutes, or is in furtherance of, or provides for, unlawful discrimination against a party to the contract, but the term shall be unenforceable against that party.

(3) A term in a contract which purports to exclude or limit any provision of this Act or the Equal Pay Act 1970 is unenforceable by any person in whose favour the term would operate apart from this subsection.

(4) Subsection (3) does not apply—

(a) to a contract settling a complaint to which section 63(1) of this Act or section 2 of the Equal Pay Act 1970 applies where the contract is made with the assistance of a conciliation officer;

(aa) to a contract settling a complaint to which section 63(1) of this Act or section 2 of the Equal Pay Act 1970 applies if the conditions regulating compromise contracts under this Act are satisfied in relation to the contract;

(b) to a contract settling a claim to which section 66 applies.

(4A) The conditions regulating compromise contracts under this Act are that—

(a) the contract must be in writing;

(b) the contract must relate to the particular complaint;

(c) the complainant must have received advice from a relevant independent adviser as to the terms and effect of the proposed contract and in particular its effect on his ability to pursue his complaint before an employment tribunal;

(d) there must be in force, when the adviser gives the advice, a contract of insurance, or an indemnity provided for members of a profession or professional body covering the risk of a claim by the complainant in respect of loss arising in consequence of the advice;

(e) the contract must identify the adviser; and

(f) the contract must state that the conditions regulating compromise contracts under this Act are satisfied.

(4B) A person is a relevant independent adviser for the purposes of subsection (4A)(c)—

(a) if he is a qualified lawyer,

(b) if he is an officer, official, employee or member of an independent trade union who has been certified in writing by the trade union as competent to give advice and as authorised to do so on behalf of the trade union,

(c) if he works at an advice centre (whether as an employee or a volunteer) and has been certified in writing by the centre as competent to give advice and as authorised to do so on behalf of the centre, or

(d) if he is a person of a description specified in an order made by the Secretary of State.

(4BA) But a person is not a relevant independent adviser for the purposes of subsection (4A)(c) in relation to the complainant—

(a) if he is, is employed by or is acting in the matter for the other party or a person who is connected with the other party,

(b) in the case of a person within subsection (4B)(b) or (c), if the trade union or advice centre is the other party or a person who is connected with the other party,

(c) in the case of a person within subsection (4B)(c), if the complainant makes a payment for the advice received from him, or

(d) in the case of a person of a description specified in an order under subsection (4B)(d), if any condition specified in the order in relation to the giving of advice by persons of that description is not satisfied.

(4BB) In subsection (4B)(a) 'qualified lawyer' means—

(a) as respects England and Wales, a barrister (whether in practice as such or employed to give legal advice), a solicitor who holds a practising certificate, or a person other than a barrister or solicitor who is an authorised advocate or authorised litigator (within the meaning of the Courts and Legal Services Act 1990), and

(b) as respects Scotland, an advocate (whether in practice as such or employed to give legal advice), or a solicitor who holds a practising certificate.

(4BC) In subsection (4B)(b) 'independent trade union' has the same meaning as in the Trade Union and Labour Relations (Consolidation) Act 1992.

(4C) For the purposes of subsection (4BA) any two persons are to be treated as connected—

(a) if one is a company of which the other (directly or indirectly) has control, or
(b) if both are companies of which a third person (directly or indirectly) has control.

(4D) An agreement under which the parties agree to submit a dispute to arbitration—
(a) shall be regarded for the purposes of subsection (4)(a) and (aa) as being a contract settling a complaint if—
(i) the dispute is covered by a scheme having effect by virtue of an order under section 212A of the Trade Union and Labour Relations (Consolidation) Act 1992, and
(ii) the agreement is to submit it to arbitration in accordance with the scheme, but
(b) shall be regarded for those purposes as neither being nor including such a contract in any other case.

(5) On the application of any person interested in a contract to which subsection (2) applies, a county court or sheriff court may make such order as it thinks just for removing or modifying any term made unenforceable by that subsection; but such an order shall not be made unless all persons affected have been given notice of the application (except where under rules of court notice may be dispensed with) and have been afforded an opportunity to make representations to the court.

(6) An order under subsection (5) may include provision as respects any period before the making of the order.

78 to **81** [omitted]

82 General interpretation provisions

(1) In this Act, unless the context otherwise requires—

'access' shall be construed in accordance with section 50;
'act' includes a deliberate omission;
'advertisement' includes every form of advertisement, whether to the public or not, and whether in a newspaper or other publication, by television or radio, by display of notices, signs, labels, showcards or goods, by distribution of samples, circulars, catalogues, price lists or other material by exhibition of pictures, models or films, or in any other way, and references to the publishing of advertisements shall be construed accordingly;
'associated employer' shall be construed in accordance with subsection (2);
...
'designate' shall be construed in accordance with subsection (3);
'discrimination' and related terms shall be construed in accordance with section 5(1);
'dispose', in relation to premises, includes granting a right to occupy the premises, and any reference to acquiring premises shall be construed accordingly;
'education' includes any form of training or instruction;
...
'employment' means employment under a contract of service or of apprenticeship or a contract personally to execute any work or labour, and related expressions shall be construed accordingly;
'employment agency' means a person who, for profit or not, provides services for the purpose of finding employment for workers or supplying employers with workers;
'equality clause' has the meaning given in section 1(2) of the Equal Pay Act 1970 (as set out in section 8(1) of this Act);
...
'final' shall be construed in accordance with subsection (4);
'firm' has the meaning given by section 4 of the Partnership Act 1890;

'formal investigation' means an investigation under section 57;

. . .

'gender reassignment' means a process which is undertaken under medical supervision for the purpose of reassigning a person's sex by changing physiological or other characteristics of sex, and includes any part of such a process;

'general notice', in relation to any person, means a notice published by him at a time and a manner appearing to him suitable for securing that the notice is seen within a reasonable time by persons likely to be affected by it;

'genuine occupational qualification' shall be construed in accordance with section 7(2), except in the expression 'supplementary genuine occupational qualification', which shall be construed in accordance with section 7B(2);

'Great Britain' includes such of the territorial waters of the United Kingdom as are adjacent to Great Britain;

. . .

'man' includes a male of any age;

. . .

'near relative' shall be construed in accordance with subsection (5);

'non-discrimination notice' means a notice under section 67;

'notice' means a notice in writing;

'prescribed' means prescribed by regulations made by the Secretary of State by statutory instrument;

'profession' includes any vocation or occupation;

. . .

'retirement' includes retirement (whether voluntary or not) on grounds of age, length of service or incapacity;

. . .

'trade' includes any business;

'training' includes any form of education or instruction;

. . .

'woman' includes a female of any age.

(1A) References in this Act to the dismissal of a person from employment or to the expulsion of a person from a position as partner include references—

(a) to the termination of that person's employment or partnership by the expiration of any period (including a period expiring by reference to an event or circumstances), not being a termination immediately after which the employment or partnership is renewed on the same terms; and

(b) to the termination of that person's employment or partnership by any act of his (including the giving of notice) in circumstances such that he is entitled to terminate it without notice by reason of the conduct of the employer or, as the case may be, the conduct of the other partners.

(2) For the purposes of this Act two employers are to be treated as associated if one is a company of which the other (directly or indirectly) has control or if both are companies of which a third person (directly or indirectly) has control.

(3) Any power conferred by this Act to designate establishments or persons may be exercised either by naming them or by identifying them by reference to a class or other description.

(4) For the purposes of this Act a non-discrimination notice or a finding by a court or tribunal becomes final when an appeal against the notice or finding is dismissed, withdrawn or abandoned or when the time for appealing expires without an appeal having been brought; and for this purpose an appeal against a non-discrimination notice shall be taken to be dismissed if, notwithstanding that a requirement of the notice is quashed on appeal, a direction is given in respect of it under section 68(3).

(5) For the purposes of this Act a person is a near relative of another if that person is the wife or husband, or parent or child, a grandparent or grandchild, or a brother or sister of the other (whether of full blood or half-blood or by affinity), and 'child' includes an illegitimate child and the wife or husband of an illegitimate child.

(6) and (7) [omitted]

83 to 87 [omitted]

RACE RELATIONS ACT 1976
(1976, c. 74)

PART I
DISCRIMINATION TO WHICH ACT APPLIES

1 Racial discrimination

(1) A person discriminates against another in any circumstances relevant for the purposes of any provision of this Act if—

(a) on racial grounds he treats that other less favourably than he treats or would treat other persons; or

(b) he applies to that other a requirement or condition which he applies or would apply equally to persons not of the same racial group as that other but—

(i) which is such that the proportion of persons of the same racial group as that other who can comply with it is considerably smaller than the proportion of persons not of that racial group who can comply with it; and

(ii) which he cannot show to be justifiable irrespective of the colour, race, nationality or ethnic or national origins of the person to whom it is applied; and

(iii) which is to the detriment of that other because he cannot comply with it.

(2) It is hereby declared that, for the purposes of this Act, segregating a person from other persons on racial grounds is treating him less favourably than they are treated.

2 Discrimination by way of victimisation

(1) A person ('the discriminator') discriminates against another person ('the person victimised') in any circumstances relevant for the purposes of any provision of this Act if he treats the person victimised less favourably than in those circumstances he treats or would treat other persons, and does so by reason that the person victimised has—

(a) brought proceedings against the discriminator or any other person under this Act; or

(b) given evidence or information in connection with proceedings brought by any person against the discriminator or any other person under this Act; or

(c) otherwise done anything under or by reference to this Act in relation to the discriminator or any other person; or

(d) alleged that the discriminator or any other person has committed an act which (whether or not the allegation so states) would amount to a contravention of this Act,

or by reason that the discriminator knows that the person victimised intends to do any of those things, or suspects that the person victimised has done, or intends to do, any of them.

(2) Subsection (1) does not apply to treatment of a person by reason of any allegation made by him if the allegation was false and not made in good faith.

3 Meaning of 'racial grounds', 'racial group' etc.

(1) In this Act, unless the context otherwise requires—

'racial grounds' means any of the following grounds, namely colour, race, nationality or ethnic or national origins;

'racial group' means a group of persons defined by reference to colour, race, nationality or ethnic or national origins, and references to a person's racial group refer to any racial group into which he falls.

(2) The fact that a racial group comprises two or more distinct racial groups does not prevent it from constituting a particular racial group for the purposes of this Act.

(3) In this Act—

(a) references to discrimination refer to any discrimination falling within section 1 or 2; and

(b) references to racial discrimination refer to any discrimination falling within section 1,

and related expressions shall be construed accordingly.

(4) A comparison of the case of a person of a particular racial group with that of a person not of that group under section 1(1) must be such that the relevant circumstances in the one case are the same, or not materially different, in the other.

PART II
DISCRIMINATION IN THE EMPLOYMENT FIELD

4 Discrimination against applicants and employees

(1) It is unlawful for a person, in relation to employment by him at an establishment in Great Britain, to discriminate against another—

(a) in the arrangements he makes for the purpose of determining who should be offered that employment; or

(b) in the terms on which he offers him that employment; or

(c) by refusing or deliberately omitting to offer him that employment.

(2) It is unlawful for a person, in the case of a person employed by him at an establishment in Great Britain, to discriminate against that employee—

(a) in the terms of employment which he affords him; or

(b) in the way he affords him access to opportunities for promotion, transfer or training, or to any other benefits, facilities or services, or by refusing or deliberately omitting to afford him access to them; or

(c) by dismissing him, or subjecting him to any other detriment.

(3) Except in relation to discrimination falling within section 2, subsections (1) and (2) do not apply to employment for the purposes of a private household.

(4) Subsection (2) does not apply to benefits, facilities or services of any description if the employer is concerned with the provision (for payment or not) of benefits, facilities or services of that description to the public, or to a section of the public comprising the employee in question, unless—

(a) that provision differs in a material respect from the provision of the benefits, facilities or services by the employer to his employees; or

(b) the provision of the benefits, facilities or services to the employee in question is regulated by his contract of employment; or

(c) the benefits, facilities or services relate to training.

5 Exceptions for genuine occupational qualifications

(1) In relation to racial discrimination—

(a) section 4(1)(a) or (c) does not apply to any employment where being of a particular racial group is a genuine occupational qualification for the job; and

(b) section 4(2)(b) does not apply to opportunities for promotion or transfer to, or training for, such employment.

(2) Being of a particular racial group is a genuine occupational qualification for a job only where—

(a) the job involves participation in a dramatic performance or other entertainment in a capacity for which a person of that racial group is required for reasons of authenticity; or

(b) the job involves participation as an artist's or photogaphic model in the production of a work of art, visual image or sequence of visual images for which a person of that racial group is required for reasons of authenticity; or

(c) the job involves working in a place where food or drink is (for payment or not) provided to and consumed by members of the public or a section of the public in a particular setting for which, in that job, a person of that racial group is required for reasons of authenticity; or

(d) the holder of the job provides persons of that racial group with personal services promoting their welfare, and those services can most effectively be provided by a person of that racial group.

(3) Subsection (2) applies where some only of the duties of the job fall within paragraph (a), (b), (c) or (d) as well as where all of them do.

(4) Paragraph (a), (b), (c) or (d) of subsection (2) does not apply in relation to the filling of a vacancy at a time when the employer already has employees of the racial group in question—

(a) who are capable of carrying out the duties falling within that paragraph; and

(b) whom it would be reasonable to employ on those duties; and

(c) whose numbers are sufficient to meet the employer's likely requirements in respect of those duties without undue inconvenience

6 to **80** [omitted]

INSOLVENCY ACT 1986
(1986, c. 45)

PART XII
PREFERENTIAL DEBTS IN COMPANY AND INDIVIDUAL INSOLVENCY

386 Categories of preferential debts

(1) A reference in this Act to the preferential debts of a company or an individual is to the debts listed in Schedule 6 to this Act (money owed to the Inland Revenue for income tax deducted at source; VAT, insurance premium tax, car tax, betting and gaming duties; beer duty; lottery duty; air passenger duty; social security and pension scheme contributions; remuneration etc. of employees; levies on coal and steel production); and references to preferential creditors are to be read accordingly.

(2) In the Schedule 'the debtor' means the company or the individual concerned.

(3) Schedule 6 is to be read with Schedule 4 to the Pension Schemes Act 1993 (occupational pension scheme contributions).

SCHEDULE 6

Category 5: Remuneration, etc., of employees

9. So much of any amount which—

(a) is owed by the debtor to a person who is or has been an employee of the debtor, and

(b) is payable by way of remuneration in respect of the whole or any part of the period of 4 months next before the relevant date,

as does not exceed so much as may be prescribed by order made by the Secretary of State.

10. An amount owed by way of accrued holiday remuneration, in respect of any period of employment before the relevant date, to a person whose employment by the debtor has been terminated, whether before, on or after that date.

11. So much of any sum owed in respect of money advanced for the purpose as has been applied for the payment of a debt which, if it had not been paid, would have been a debt falling within paragraph 9 or 10.

12. [omitted]

Interpretation for Category 5

13.—(1) For the purposes of paragraphs 9 to 12, a sum is payable by the debtor to a person by way of remuneration in respect of any period if—

(a) it is paid as wages or salary (whether payable for time or for piece work or earned wholly or partly by way of commission) in respect of services rendered to the debtor in that period, or

(b) it is an amount falling within the following sub-paragraph and is payable by the debtor in respect of that period.

(2) An amount falls within this sub-paragraph if it is—

(a) a guarantee payment under Part III of the Employment Rights Act 1996 (employee without work to do);

(b) any payment for time off under section 53 (time off to look for work or arrange training) or section 56 (time off for ante-natal care) of that Act or under section 169 of the Trade Union and Labour Relations (Consolidation) Act 1992 (time off for carrying out trade union duties etc.);

(c) remuneration on suspension on medical grounds, or on maternity grounds, under Part VII of the Employment Rights Act 1996; or

(d) remuneration under a protective award under section 189 of the Trade Union and Labour Relations (Consolidation) Act 1992 (redundancy dismissal with compensation).

14.—(1) This paragraph relates to a case in which a person's employment has been terminated by or in consequence of his employer going into liquidation or being adjudged bankrupt or (his employer being a company not in liquidation) by or in consequence of—

(a) a receiver being appointed as mentioned in section 40 of this Act (debenture-holders secured by floating charge), or

(b) the appointment of a receiver under section 53(6) or 54(5) of this Act (Scottish company with property subject to floating charge), or

(c) the taking of possession by debenture-holders (so secured), as mentioned in section 196 of the Companies Act.

(2) For the purposes of paragraphs 9 to 12, holiday remuneration is deemed to have accrued to that person in respect of any period of employment if, by virtue of his contract of employment or of any enactment that remuneration would have accrued in respect of that period if his employment had continued until he became entitled to be allowed the holiday.

(3) The reference in sub-paragraph (2) to any enactment includes an order or direction made under an enactment.

15. Without prejudice to paragraphs 13 and 14—

(a) any remuneration payable by the debtor to a person in respect of a period of holiday or of absence from work through sickness or other good cause is deemed to be wages or (as the case may be) salary in respect of services rendered to the debtor in that period, and

(b) references here and in those paragraphs to remuneration in respect of a period of holiday include any sums which, if they had been paid, would have been treated for the purposes of the enactments relating to social security as earnings in respect of that period.

PUBLIC ORDER ACT 1986
(1986, c. 64)

4 Fear or provocation of violence

(1) A person is guilty of an offence if he—

(a) uses towards another person threatening, abusive or insulting words or behaviour, or

(b) distributes or displays to another person any writing, sign or other visible representation which is threatening, abusive or insulting,

with intent to cause that person to believe that immediate unlawful violence will be used against him or another by any person, or to provoke the immediate use of unlawful violence by that person or another, or whereby that person is likely to believe that such violence will be used or it is likely that such violence will be provoked.

(2) An offence under this section may be committed in a public or a private place, except that no offence is committed where the words or behaviour are used, or the writing, sign or other visible representation is distributed or displayed, by a person inside a dwelling and the other person is also inside that or another dwelling.

(3) A constable may arrest without warrant anyone he reasonably suspects is committing an offence under this section.

(4) A person guilty of an offence under this section is liable on summary conviction to imprisonment for a term not exceeding 6 months or a fine not exceeding level 5 on the standard scale or both.

4A Intentional harassment, alarm or distress

(1) A person is guilty of an offence if, with intent to cause a person harassment, alarm or distress, he—

(a) uses threatening, abusive or insulting words or behaviour, or disorderly behaviour, or

(b) displays any writing, sign or other visible representation which is threatening, abusive or insulting, thereby causing that or another person harassment, alarm or distress.

(2) An offence under this section may be committed in a public or a private place, except that no offence is committed where the words or behaviour are used, or the writing, sign or other visible representation is displayed, by a person inside a dwelling and the person who is harassed, alarmed or distressed is also inside that or another dwelling.

(3) It is a defence for the accused to prove—

(a) that he was inside a dwelling and had no reason to believe that the words or behaviour used, or the writing, sign or other visible representation displayed, would be heard or seen by a person outside that or any other dwelling, or

(b) that his conduct was reasonable.

(4) A constable may arrest without warrant anyone he reasonably suspects is committing an offence under this section.

(5) A person guilty of an offence under this section is liable on summary conviction to imprisonment for a term not exceeding 6 months or a fine not exceeding level 5 on the standard scale or both.

5 Harassment, alarm or distress

(1) A person is guilty of an offence if he—

(a) uses threatening, abusive or insulting words or behaviour, or disorderly behaviour, or

(b) displays any writing, sign or other visible representation which is threatening, abusive or insulting,

within the hearing or sight of a person likely to be caused harassment, alarm or distress thereby.

(2) An offence under this section may be committed in a public or a private place, except that no offence is committed where the words or behaviour are used, or the writing, sign or other visible representation is displayed, by a person inside a dwelling and the other person is also inside that or another dwelling.

(3) It is a defence for the accused to prove—

(a) that he had no reason to believe that there was any person within hearing or sight who was likely to be caused harassment, alarm or distress, or

(b) that he was inside a dwelling and had no reason to believe that the words or behaviour used, or the writing, sign or other visible representation displayed, would be heard or seen by a person outside that or any other dwelling, or

(c) that his conduct was reasonable.

(4) A constable may arrest a person without warrant if—

(a) he engages in offensive conduct which a constable warns him to stop, and

(b) he engages in further offensive conduct immediately or shortly after the warning.

(5) In subsection (4) 'offensive conduct' means conduct the constable reasonably suspects to constitute an offence under this section, and the conduct mentioned in paragraph (a) and the further conduct need not be of the same nature.

(6) A person guilty of an offence under this section is liable on summary conviction to a fine not exceeding level 3 on the standard scale.

6 Mental element: miscellaneous

(3) A person is guilty of an offence under section 4 only if he intends his words or behaviour, or the writing, sign or other visible representation, to be threatening, abusive or insulting, or is aware that it may be threatening, abusive or insulting.

(4) A person is guilty of an offence under section 5 only if he intends his words or behaviour, or the writing, sign or other visible representation, to be threatening, abusive or insulting, or is aware that it may be threatening, abusive or insulting or (as the case may be) he intends his behaviour to be or is aware that it may be disorderly.

14 Imposing conditions on public assemblies

(1) If the senior police officer, having regard to the time or place at which and the circumstances in which any public assembly is being held or is intended to be held, reasonably believes that—

(a) it may result in serious public disorder, serious damage to property or serious disruption to the life of the community, or

(b) the purpose of the persons organising it is the intimidation of others with a view to compelling them not to do an act they have a right to do, or to do an act they have a right not to do,

he may give directions imposing on the persons organising or taking part in the assembly such conditions as to the place at which the assembly may be (or continue to be) held, its maximum duration, or the maximum number of persons who may constitute it, as appear to him necessary to prevent such disorder, damage, disruption or intimidation.

(2) In subsection (1) 'the senior police officer' means—

(a) in relation to an assembly being held, the most senior in rank of the police officers present at the scene, and

(b) in relation to an assembly intended to be held, the chief officer of police.

(3) A direction given by a chief officer of police by virtue of subsection (2)(b) shall be given in writing.

(4) A person who organises a public assembly and knowingly fails to comply with a condition imposed under this section is guilty of an offence, but it is a defence for him to prove that the failure arose from circumstances beyond his control.

(5) A person who takes part in a public assembly and knowingly fails to comply with a condition imposed under this section is guilty of an offence, but it is a defence for him to prove that the failure arose from circumstances beyond his control.

(6) A person who incites another to commit an offence under subsection (5) is guilty of an offence.

(7) A constable in uniform may arrest without warrant anyone he reasonably suspects is committing an offence under subsection (4), (5) or (6).

(8) A person guilty of an offence under subsection (4) is liable on summary conviction to imprisonment for a term not exceeding 3 months or a fine not exceeding level 4 on the standard scale or both.

(9) A person guilty of an offence under subsection (5) is liable on summary conviction to a fine not exceeding level 3 on the standard scale.

(10) A person guilty of an offence under subsection (6) is liable on summary conviction to imprisonment for a term not exceeding 3 months or a fine not exceeding level 4 on the standard scale or both, notwithstanding section 45(3) of the Magistrates' Courts Act 1980.

16 Interpretation

In this Part—

'public assembly' means an assembly of 20 or more persons in a public place which is wholly or partly open to the air;

'public place' means—

(a) any highway, or in Scotland any road within the meaning of the Roads (Scotland) Act 1984, and

(b) any place to which at the material time the public or any section of the public has access, on payment or otherwise, as of right or by virtue of express or implied permission.

SEX DISCRIMINATION ACT 1986
(1986, c. 59)

6 Collective agreements and rules of undertakings

(1) Without prejudice to the generality of section 77 of the 1975 Act (which makes provision with respect to the validity and revision of contracts), that section shall apply, as it applies in relation to the term of a contract, to the following, namely—

(a) any term of a collective agreement, including an agreement which was not intended, or is presumed not to have been intended, to be a legally enforceable contract;

(b) any rule made by an employer for application to all or any of the persons who are employed by him or who apply to be, or are, considered by him for employment;

(c) any rule made by an organisation, authority or body to which subsection (2) below applies for application to all or any of its members or prospective members or to all or any of the persons on whom it has conferred authorisations or qualifications or who are seeking the authorisations or qualifications which it has power to confer;

and that section shall so apply whether the agreement was entered into, or the rule made, before or after the coming into force of this section.

(2) This subsection applies to—

(a) any organisation of workers;

(b) any organisation of employers;

(c) any organisation whose members carry on a particular profession or trade for the purposes of which the organisation exists;

(d) any authority or body which can confer an authorisation or qualification which is needed for, or facilitates, engagement in a particular profession or trade.

(3) For the purposes of the said section 77 a term or rule shall be deemed to provide for the doing of an act which would be rendered unlawful by the 1975 Act if—

(a) it provides for the inclusion in any contract of employment of any term which by virtue of an equality clause would fall either to be modified or to be supplemented by an additional term; and

(b) that clause would not be prevented from operating in relation to the contract by section 1(3) of the Equal Pay Act 1970 (material factors justifying discrimination).

(4) Nothing in the said section 77 shall affect the operation of any term or rule in so far as it provides for the doing of a particular act in circumstances where the doing of that act would not be, or be deemed by virtue of subsection (3) above to be, rendered unlawful by the 1975 Act.

(4A) A person to whom this subsection applies may present a complaint to an employment tribunal that a term or rule is void by virtue of subsection (1) of the said section 77 if he has reason to believe—

(a) that the term or rule may at some future time have effect in relation to him, and

(b) where he alleges that it is void by virtue of paragraph (c) of that subsection, that—

(i) an act for the doing of which it provides may at some such time be done in relation to him, and

(ii) the act would be, or be deemed by virtue of subsection (3) above to be, rendered unlawful by the 1975 Act if done in relation to him in present circumstances.

(4B) In the case of a complaint about—

(a) a term of a collective agreement made by or on behalf of—

(i) an employer,

(ii) an organisation of employers of which an employer is a member, or

(iii) an association of such organisations of one of which an employer is a member, or

(b) a rule made by an employer,

subsection (4A) applies to any person who is, or is genuinely and actively seeking to become, one of his employees.

(4C) In the case of a complaint about a rule made by an organisation, authority or body to which subsection (2) above applies, subsection (4A) applies to any person—

(a) who is, or is genuinely and actively seeking to become, a member of the organisation, authority or body,

(b) on whom the organistion, authority or body has conferred an authorisation or qualification, or

(c) who is genuinely and actively seeking an authorisation or qualification which the organisation, authority or body has power to confer.

(4D) When an employment tribunal finds that a complaint presented to it under subsection (4A) above is well-founded the tribunal shall make an order declaring that the term or rule is void.

(5) The avoidance by virtue of the said section 77 of any term or rule which provides for any person to be discriminated against shall be without prejudice to the following rights except in so far as they enable any person to require another person to be treated less favourably than himself, namely—

(a) such of the rights of the person to be discriminated against; and

(b) such of the rights of any person who will be treated more favourably in direct or indirect consequence of the discrimination,

as are conferred by or in respect of a contract made or modified wholly or partly in pursuance of, or by reference to, that term or rule.

(6) In this section 'collective agreement' means any agreement relating to one or more of the matters mentioned in section 178(2) of the Trade Union and Labour Relations (Consolidation) Act 1992 (meaning of trade dispute), being an agreement made by or on behalf of one or more employers or one or more organisations of employers or associations of such organisations with one or more organisations of workers or associations of such organisations.

(7) Any expression used in this section and in the 1975 Act has the same meaning in this section as in that Act, and this section shall have effect as if the terms of any

service to which Parts II and IV of that Act apply by virtue of subsection (2) of section 85 of that Act (Crown application) were terms of a contract of employment and, in relation to the terms of any such service, as if service for the purposes of any person mentioned in that subsection were employment by that person.

EMPLOYMENT ACT 1989
(1989, c. 38)

1 Overriding of statutory requirements which conflict with certain provisions of 1975 Act

(1) Any provision of—

(a) an Act passed before the Sex Discrimination Act 1975, or

(b) an instrument approved or made by or under such an Act (including one approved or made after the passing of the 1975 Act),

shall be of no effect in so far as it imposes a requirement to do an act which would be rendered unlawful by any of the provisions of that Act referred to in subsection (2).

(2) Those provisions are—

(a) Part II (discrimination as respects employment);

(b) Part III (discrimination as respects education etc.) so far as it applies to vocational training; and

(c) Part IV (other unlawful acts) so far as it has effect in relation to the provisions mentioned in paragraphs (a) and (b) above.

(3) Where in any legal proceedings (of whatever nature) there falls to be determined the question whether subsection (1) operates to negative the effect of any provision in so far as it requires the application by any person of a requirement or condition falling within subsection (1)(b)(i) of section 1 or 3 of the 1975 Act (indirect discrimination on grounds of sex or marital status)—

(a) it shall be for any party to the proceedings who claims that subsection (1) does not so operate in relation to that provision to show the requirement or condition in question to be justifiable as mentioned in subsection (1)(b)(ii) of that section; and

(b) the said subsection (1)(b)(ii) shall accordingly have effect in relation to the requirement or condition as if the reference to the person applying it were a reference to any such party to the proceedings.

(4) Where an Act passed after the 1975 Act, whether before or after the passing of this Act, re-enacts (with or without modification) a provision of an Act passed before the 1975 Act, the provision as re-enacted shall be treated for the purposes of subsection (1) as if it continued to be contained in an Act passed before the 1975 Act.

2 and 3 [omitted]

4 Exemption for discrimination under certain provisions concerned with the protection of women at work

(1) Without prejudice to the operation of section 51 of the 1975 Act nothing in—

(a) Part II of that Act,

(b) Part III of that Act so far as it applies to vocational training, or

(c) Part IV of that Act so far as it has effect in relation to the provisions mentioned in paragraphs (a) and (b) above,

shall render unlawful any act done by a person in relation to a woman if it was necessary for that person to do that act in order to comply with any requirement of any of the provisions specified in Schedule 1 to this Act (which are concerned with the protection of women at work).

(3) In this section 'woman' means a female person of any age.

5 to 30 [omitted]

SOCIAL SECURITY ACT 1989
(1989, c. 24)

SCHEDULE 5
EMPLOYMENT-RELATED SCHEMES FOR PENSIONS OR OTHER BENEFITS: EQUAL TREATMENT FOR MEN AND WOMEN

PART I
COMPLIANCE BY SCHEMES

Schemes to comply with the principle of equal treatment

1. Every employment-related benefit scheme shall comply with the principle of equal treatment.

The principle

2.—(1) The principle of equal treatment is that persons of the one sex shall not, on the basis of sex, be treated less favourably than persons of the other sex in any respect relating to an employment-related benefit scheme.

(2) Sub-paragraphs (3) to (6) below have effect, where applicable, for the purpose of determining whether a scheme complies with the principle of equal treatment.

(3) Where any provision of the scheme imposes on both male and female members a requirement or condition—

(a) which is such that the proportion of persons of the one sex ('the sex affected') who can comply with it is considerably smaller than the proportion of persons of the other sex who can do so, and

(b) which is not justifiable irrespective of the sex of the members,

the imposition of that requirement or condition shall be regarded as less favourable treatment of persons of the sex affected.

(4) No account shall be taken of—

(a) any difference, on the basis of the sex of members, in the levels of contributions—

(i) [lapsed]

(ii) which the employer makes, to the extent that the difference is for the purpose of removing or limiting differences, as between men and women, in the amount or value of money purchase benefits;

(b) any difference, on the basis of sex, in the amount or value of money purchase benefits, to the extent that the difference is justifiable on actuarial grounds;

(c) any special treatment for the benefit of women in connection with pregnancy or childbirth;

(d) any permitted age-related differences;

(e) any difference of treatment in relation to benefits for a deceased member's surviving husband, wife or other dependants;

(f) any difference of treatment in relation to any optional provisions available; or

(g) any provisions of a scheme to the extent that they have been specially arranged for the benefit of one particular member of the scheme;

but where the scheme includes any unfair maternity provisions, it shall to that extent be regarded as according less favourable treatment to women on the basis of sex.

(5) Where the scheme treats persons of the one sex differently according to their marital or family status, that treatment is to be compared with the scheme's treatment of persons of the other sex who have the same status.

(6) The principle of equal treatment applies in relation to members' dependants as it applies in relation to members.

(7) If any question arises whether a condition or requirement falling within sub-paragraphs (3)(a) above is or is not justifiable irrespective of the sex of the members, it shall be for those who assert that it is so justifiable to prove that fact.

(8) In this paragraph—

'money purchase benefits' has the meaning given by section 181(1) of the Pension Schemes Act 1993, but with the substitution for references to a personal or occupational pension scheme of references to an employment-related benefit scheme;

'optional provisions available' means those provisions of a scheme—

(a) which apply only in the case of members who elect for them to do so; and

(b) whose purpose is to secure for those members—

(i) benefits in addition to those otherwise provided under the scheme; or

(ii) a choice with respect to the date on which benefits under the scheme are to commence; or

(iii) a choice between any two or more benefits;

'permitted age-related difference' means any difference, on the basis of sex, in the age—

(a) at which a service-related benefit in respect of old age or retirement commences; or

(b) at which, in consequence of the commencement of such a benefit, any other service-related benefit either ceases to be payable or becomes payable at a reduced rate calcualted by reference to the amount of the benefit so commencing.

(9) For the purposes of this paragraph—

(a) any reference to a person's family status is a reference to his having an unmarried partner or any dependants; and

(b) a person 'has an unmarried partner' if that person and some other person to whom he is not married live together as husband and wife.

Non-compliance: compulsory levelling up

3.—(1) To the extent that any provision of an employment-related benefit scheme does not comply with the principle of equal treatment, it shall be overridden by this Schedule and the more favourable treatment accorded to persons of the one sex shall also be accorded to persons of the other sex.

(2) Where more favourable treatment is accorded to any persons by virtue of sub-paragraph (1) above, that sub-paragraph requires them, in accordance with the principle of equal treatment—

(a) to pay contributions at a level appropriate to the treatment so accorded; and

(b) to bear any other burden which is an incident of that treatment;

but persons of either sex may instead elect to receive the less favourable treatment and, in accordance with the principle of equal treatment, pay contributions at the level appropriate to the treatment and bear the other burdens incidental to it.

(3) Where any provision of a scheme is overridden by sub-paragraph (1) above, nothing in this Schedule shall affect any rights accrued or obligations incurred during the period before the date on which that provision is so overridden.

(4) Sub-paragraph (1) above is without prejudice to the exercise, in compliance with the principle of equal treatment, of any power to amend the scheme.

4. [repealed]

Unfair maternity provisions

5.—(1) In this Schedule 'unfair maternity provisions', in relation to an employment-related benefit scheme, means any provision—

(a) which relates to continuing membership of, or the accrual of rights under, the scheme during any period of paid maternity absence in the case of any woman who is (or who, immediately before the commencement of such a period, was) an employed earner and which treats such a woman otherwise than in accordance with the normal employment requirement; or

(b) which requires the amount of any benefit payable under the scheme to or in respect of any such woman, to the extent that it falls to be determined by reference to her earnings during a period which included a period of paid maternity absence, to be determined otherwise than in accordance with the normal employment requirement.

(2) In the case of any unfair maternity provision—

(a) the more favourable treatment required by paragraph 3(1) above is treatment no less favourable than would be accorded to the women members in accordance with the normal employment requirement;

(b) paragraph 3(2) above does not authorise the making of any such election as is there mentioned; and

(c) paragraph 4(1)(a) above does not authorise the making of any modification which does not satisfy the requirements of paragraph (a) above;

but, in respect of a period of paid maternity absence, a woman shall only be required to pay contributions on the amount of contractual remuneration or statutory maternity pay actually paid to or for her in respect of that period.

(3) In this paragraph—

(a) 'period of paid maternity absence' means any period—

(i) throughout which a woman is absent from work due to pregnancy or confinement; and

(ii) for which her employer (or, if she is no longer in his employment, her former employer) pays her any contractual remuneration or statutory maternity pay;

(b) 'the normal employment requirement' is the requirement that any period of paid maternity absence shall be treated as if it were a period throughout which the woman in question works normally and receives the remuneration likely to be paid for doing so.

Unfair family leave provisions

6.—(1) Where an employment-related benefit scheme includes any unfair family leave provisions (irrespective of any differences on the basis of sex in the treatment accorded to members under those provisions), then—

(a) the scheme shall be regarded to that extent as not complying with the principle of equal treatment; and

(b) subject to sub-paragraph (3) below, this Schedule shall apply accordingly.

(2) In this Schedule 'unfair family leave provisions' means any provision—

(a) which relates to continuing membership of, or the accrual of rights under, the scheme during any period of paid family leave in the case of any member who is an employed earner and which treats such a member otherwise than in accordance with the normal leave requirement; or

(b) which requires the amount of any benefit payable under the scheme to or in respect of any such member to the extent that it falls to be determined by reference to earnings during a period which included a period of paid family leave, to be determined otherwise than in accordance with the normal leave requirement.

(3) In the case of any unfair family leave provision—

(a) the more favourable treatment required by paragraph 3(1) above is treatment no less favourable than would be accorded to the members in accordance with the normal leave requirement;

(b) paragraph 3(2) above does not authorise the making of any such election as is there mentioned; and

(c) paragraph 4(1)(a) above does not authorise the making of any modification which does not satisfy the requirements of paragraph (a) above;

but, in respect of a period of paid family leave, a member shall only be required to pay contributions on the amount of contractual remuneration actually paid to or for him in respect of that period.

(4) In this paragraph—

(a) 'period of paid family leave' means any period—

(i) throughout which a member is absent from work for family reasons; and

(ii) for which the employer pays him any contractual remuneration;

(b) 'the normal leave requirement' is the requirement that any period of paid family leave shall be treated as if it were a period throughout which the member in question works normally but only receives the remuneration in fact paid to him for that period.

Meaning of 'employment-related benefit scheme' etc.

7. In this Schedule—

(a) 'employment-related benefit scheme' means any scheme or arrangement which is comprised in one or more instruments or agreements and which has, or is capable of having, effect in relation to one or more descriptions or categories of employments so as to provide service-related benefits to or in respect of employed or self-employed earners—

(i) who have qualifying service in an employment of any such description or category, or

(ii) who have made arrangements with the trustees or managers of the scheme to enable them to become members of the scheme,

but does not include a limited scheme;

(b) 'limited scheme' means—

(i) any personal scheme for employed earners to which the employer does not contribute;

(ii) any scheme which has only one member, other than a personal scheme for an employed earner to which his employer contributes;

(iii) any contract of insurance which is made for the benefit of employed earners only and to which the employer is not a party;

(c) 'personal scheme' means any scheme or arrangement which falls within paragraph (a) above by virtue of sub-paragraph (ii) of that paragraph (or which would so fall apart from paragraph (b) above);

(d) 'public service scheme' has the same meaning as 'public service pension scheme' in section 1 of the Pension Schemes Act 1993;

(e) 'service-related benefits' means benefits, in the form of pensions or otherwise, payable in money or money's worth in respect of—

(i) termination of service;

(ii) retirement, old age or death;

(iii) interruptions of service by reason of sickness or invalidity;

(iv) accidents, injuries or diseases connected with employment;

(v) unemployment; or

(vi) expenses incurred in connection with children or other dependants;

and includes, in the case of a member who is an employed earner, any other benefit so payable to or in respect of the member in consequence of his employment.

Extension of ban on compulsory membership

8. Section 160(1) of the Pension Schemes Act 1993 (which renders void any provision making membership of a pension scheme compulsory for an employed earner) shall apply in relation to a self-employed earner as it applies in relation to an employed earner, but with the substitution for references to a personal pension scheme of references to an employment-related benefit scheme which would be such a pension scheme if self-employed earners were regarded as employed earners.

Jurisdiction

9.—(1) The court, on the application of any person interested, shall have jurisdiction to determine any question arising as to—

(a) whether any provision of a employment-related benefit scheme does or does not comply with the principle of equal treatment; or

(b) whether, and with what effect, any such provision is overridden by paragraph 3 above.

(2) In sub-paragraph (1) above 'the court' means—

(a) in England and Wales, the High Court or a county court; and

(b) in Scotland, the Court of Session or the sheriff court.

(3) An application under sub-paragraph (1) above may be commenced in a county court notwithstanding—

(a) any financial limit otherwise imposed on the jurisdiction of such a court; or

(b) that the only relief claimed is a declaration or an injunction.

TRADE UNION AND LABOUR RELATIONS (CONSOLIDATION) ACT 1992 (1992, c. 52)

PART I
TRADE UNIONS
CHAPTER I
INTRODUCTORY

Meaning of 'trade union'

Section

1 Meaning of 'trade union'.

The list of trade unions

2 The list of trade unions.
3 Application to have name entered in the list.
4 Removal of name from the list.

Certification as independent trade union

5 Meaning of 'independent trade union'.
6 Application for certificate of independence.
7 Withdrawal or cancellation of certificate.
8 Conclusive effect of Certification Officer's decision.

Supplementary

9 Appeal against decision of Certification Officer.

CHAPTER II
STATUS AND PROPERTY OF TRADE UNIONS

General

10 Quasi-corporate status of trade unions.
11 Exclusion of common law rules as to restraint of trade.

Property of trade union

12 Property to be vested in trustees.
13 Vesting of property in new trustees.
15 Prohibition on use of funds to indemnify unlawful conduct.
16 Remedy against trustees for unlawful use of union property.

Contracts for supply of goods or services

Action short of dismissal

Dismissal

Time off for trade union duties and activities

Right to membership of a trade union

PART IV
INDUSTRIAL RELATIONS
CHAPTER I
COLLECTIVE BARGAINING

Introductory

Enforceability of collective agreements

10	Parties agree
11	Employer rejects request.
12	Negotiations fail.
13–14	Acceptanceof applications.
16	Withdrawal of application.
18–19	Appropriate bargaining unit.
20–29	Union recognition.
30–31	Consequences of recognition.
32	Method not carried out.
35–41	General provisions about admissability.
43–49	General provisions about validity.

PART II
VOLUNTARY RECOGNITION

52	Agreements for recognition.
53–54	Other interpretation.
55	Determination of type of agreement.
56–57	Termination of agreement for recognition.
58–59	Application to CAC to specify method.

PART III
CHANGES AFFECTING BARGAINING UNIT

64–73	Introduction.
74	Employer believes unit has ceased to exist.
82–89	Position where CAC decides new unit.
90–91	Residual workers.
94	Meaning of collective bargaining.
95	Method of collective bargaining.

PART IV
DERECOGNITION: GENERAL

96–98	Introduction.
99–103	Employer employs fewer than 21 workers.
104–110	Employer's request to end arrangements.
112–114	Workers' application to end arrangements.
117–121	Ballot on derecognition.

PART V
DERECOGNITION WHERE RECOGNITION AUTOMATIC

122–126	Introduction.
127–131	Employer's request to end arrangements.
133	Ballot on derecognition.

PART VI
DERECOGNITION WHERE UNION NOT INDEPENDENT

134–136	Introduction.
137–146	Workers' application to end arrangements.
147	Ballot on derecognition.
148	Derecognition: other cases.

PART VII
LOSS OF INDEPENDENCE

PART VIII
DETRIMENT

PART IX
GENERAL

PART I
TRADE UNIONS
CHAPTER I
INTRODUCTORY

Meaning of 'trade union'

1 Meaning of 'trade union'

In this Act a 'trade union' means an organisation (whether temporary or permanent)—

(a) which consists wholly or mainly of workers of one or more descriptions and whose principal purposes include the regulation of relations between workers of that description or those descriptions and employers or employers' associations; or

(b) which consists wholly or mainly of—

(i) constituent or affiliated organisations which fulfil the conditions in paragraph (a) (or themselves consist wholly or mainly of constituent or affiliated organisations which fulfil those conditions), or

(ii) representatives of such constituent or affiliated organisations,

and whose principal purposes include the regulation of relations between workers and employers or between workers and employers' associations, or the regulation of relations between its constituent or affiliated organisations.

The list of trade unions

2 The list of trade unions

(1) The Certification Officer shall keep a list of trade unions containing the names of—

(a) the organisations whose names were, immediately before the commencement of this Act, duly entered in the list of trade unions kept by him under section 8 of the Trade Union and Labour Relations Act 1974, and

(b) the names of the organisations entitled to have their names entered in the list in accordance with this Part.

(2) The Certification Officer shall keep copies of the list of trade unions, as for the time being in force, available for public inspection at all reasonable hours free of charge.

(3) A copy of the list shall be included in his annual report.

(4) The fact that the name of an organisation is included in the list of trade unions is evidence (in Scotland, sufficient evidence) that the organisation is a trade union.

(5) On the application of an organisation whose name is included in the list, the Certification Officer shall issue it with a certificate to that effect.

(6) A document purporting to be such a certificate is evidence (in Scotland, sufficient evidence) that the name of the organisation is entered in the list.

3 Application to have name entered in the list

(1) An organisation of workers, whenever formed, whose name is not entered in the list of trade unions may apply to the Certification Officer to have its name entered in the list.

(2) The application shall be made in such form and manner as the Certification Officer may require and shall be accompanied by—

(a) a copy of the rules of the organisation,
(b) a list of its officers,
(c) the address of its head or main office, and
(d) the name under which it is or is to be known,

and by the prescribed fee.

(3) If the Certification Officer is satisfied—

(a) that the organisation is a trade union,
(b) that subsection (2) has been complied with, and
(c) that entry of the name in the list is not prohibited by subsection (4),

he shall enter the name of the organisation in the list of trade unions.

(4) The Certification Officer shall not enter the name of an organisation in the list of trade unions if the name is the same as that under which another organisation—

(a) was on 30 September 1971 registered as a trade union under the Trade Union Acts 1871 to 1964,

(b) was at any time registered as a trade union or employers' association under the Industrial Relations Act 1971, or

(c) is for the time being entered in the list of trade unions or in the list of employers' associations kept under Part II of this Act,

or if the name is one so nearly resembling any such name as to be likely to deceive the public.

4 Removal of name from the list

(1) If it appears to the Certification Officer, on application made to him or otherwise, that an organisation whose name is entered in the list of trade unions is not a trade union, he may remove its name from the list.

(2) He shall not do so without giving the organisation notice of his intention and considering any representations made to him by the organisation within such period (of not less than 28 days beginning with the date of the notice) as may be specified in the notice.

(3) The Certification Officer shall remove the name of an organisation from the list of trade unions if—

(a) he is requested by the organisation to do so, or
(b) he is satisfied that the organisation has ceased to exist.

Certification as independent trade union

5 Meaning of 'independent trade union'

In this Act an 'independent trade union' means a trade union which—

(a) is not under the domination or control of an employer or group of employers or of one or more employers' associations, and

(b) is not liable to interference by an employer or any such group or association (arising out of the provision of financial or material support or by any other means whatsoever) tending towards such control;

and references to 'independence', in relation to a trade union, shall be construed accordingly.

6 Application for certificate of independence

(1) A trade union whose name is entered on the list of trade unions may apply to the Certification Officer for a certificate that it is independent.
The application shall be made in such form and manner as the Certification Officer may require and shall be accompanied by the prescribed fee.

(2) The Certification Officer shall maintain a record showing details of all applications made to him under this section and shall keep it available for public inspection (free of charge) at all reasonable hours.

(3) If an application is made by a trade union whose name is not entered on the list of trade unions, the Certification Officer shall refuse a certificate of independence and shall enter that refusal on the record.

(4) In any other case, he shall not come to a decision on the application before the end of the period of one month after it has been entered on the record; and before coming to his decision he shall make such enquiries as he thinks fit and shall take into account any relevant information submitted to him by any person.

(5) He shall then decide whether the applicant trade union is independent and shall enter his decision and the date of his decision on the record.

(6) If he decides that the trade union is independent he shall issue a certificate accordingly; and if he decides that it is not, he shall give reasons for his decision.

7 Withdrawal or cancellation of certificate

(1) The Certification Officer may withdraw a trade union's certificate of independence if he is of the opinion that the union is no longer independent.

(2) Where he proposes to do so he shall notify the trade union and enter notice of the proposal in the record.

(3) He shall not come to a decision on the proposal before the end of the period of one month after notice of it was entered on the record; and before coming to his decision he shall make such enquiries as he thinks fit and shall take into account any relevant information submitted to him by any person.

(4) He shall then decide whether the trade union is independent and shall enter his decision and the date of his decision on the record.

(5) He shall confirm or withdraw the certificate accordingly; and if he decides to withdraw it, he shall give reasons for his decision.

(6) Where the name of an organisation is removed from the list of trade unions, the Certification Officer shall cancel any certificate of independence in force in respect of that organisation by entering on the record the fact that the organisation's name has been removed from that list and that the certificate is accordingly cancelled.

8 Conclusive effect of Certification Officer's decision

(1) A certificate of independence which is in force is conclusive evidence for all purposes that a trade union is independent; and a refusal, withdrawal or cancellation of a certificate of independence, entered on the record, is conclusive evidence for all purposes that a trade union is not independent.

(2) A document purporting to be a certificate of independence and to be signed by the Certification Officer, or by a person authorised to act on his behalf, shall be taken to be such a certificate unless the contrary is proved.

(3) A document purporting to be a certified copy of an entry on the record and to be signed by the Certification Officer, or by a person authorised to act on his behalf, shall be taken to be a true copy of such an entry unless the contrary is proved.

(4) If in any proceedings before a court, the Employment Appeal Tribunal, the Central Arbitration Committee, ACAS or an employment tribunal a question arises whether a trade union is independent and there is no certificate of independence in force and no refusal, withdrawal or cancellation of a certificate recorded in relation to that trade union—

(a) that question shall not be decided in those proceedings, and

(b) the proceedings shall instead be stayed or sisted until a certificate of independence has been issued or refused by the Certification Officer.

(5) The body before whom the proceedings are stayed or sisted may refer the question of the independence of the trade union to the Certification Officer who shall proceed in accordance with section 6 as on an application by that trade union.

Supplementary

9 Appeal against decision of Certification Officer

(1) An organisation aggrieved by the refusal of the Certification Officer to enter its name in the list of trade unions, or by a decision of his to remove its name from the list, may appeal to the Employment Appeal Tribunal.

(2) A trade union aggrieved by the refusal of the Certification Officer to issue it with a certificate of independence, or by a decision of his to withdraw its certificate, may appeal to the Employment Appeal Tribunal.

(3) If on appeal the Tribunal is satisfied that the organisation's name should be or remain entered in the list or, as the case may be, that the certificate should be issued or should not be withdrawn, it shall declare that fact and give directions to the Certification Officer accordingly.

(4) The rights of appeal conferred by this section extend to any question of fact or law arising in the proceedings before, or arising from the decision of, the Certification Officer.

CHAPTER II
STATUS AND PROPERTY OF TRADE UNIONS

General

10 Quasi-corporate status of trade unions

(1) A trade union is not a body corporate but—

(a) it is capable of making contracts;

(b) it is capable of suing and being sued in its own name, whether in proceedings relating to property or founded on contract or tort or any other cause of action; and

(c) proceedings for an offence alleged to have been committed by it or on its behalf may be brought against it in its own name.

(2) A trade union shall not be treated as if it were a body corporate except to the extent authorised by the provisions of this Part.

(3) A trade union shall not be registered—

(a) as a company under the Companies Act 1985; or

(b) under the Friendly Societies Act 1974 or the Industrial and Provident Societies Act 1965;

and any such registration of a trade union (whenever effected) is void.

11 Exclusion of common law rules as to restraint of trade

(1) The purposes of a trade union are not, by reason only that they are in restraint of trade, unlawful so as—

(a) to make any member of the trade union liable to criminal proceedings for conspiracy or otherwise, or

(b) to make any agreement or trust void or voidable.

(2) No rule of a trade union is unlawful or unenforceable by reason only that it is in restraint of trade.

Property of trade union

12 Property to be vested in trustees

(1) All property belonging to a trade union shall be vested in trustees in trust for it.

(2) A judgment, order or award made in proceedings of any description brought against a trade union is enforceable, by way of execution, diligence, punishment for contempt or otherwise, against any property held in trust for it to the same extent and in the same manner as if it were a body corporate.

(3) Subsection (2) has effect subject to section 23 (restriction on enforcement of awards against certain property).

13 Vesting of property in new trustees

(1) The provisions of this section apply in relation to the appointment or discharge of trustees in whom any property is vested in trust for a trade union whose name is entered in the list of trade unions.

(2) In the following sections as they apply to such trustees references to a deed shall be construed as references to an instrument in writing—

(a) section 39 of the Trustee Act 1925 and section 38 of the Trustee Act (Northern Ireland) 1958 (retirement of trustee without a new appointment), and

(b) section 40 of the Trustee Act 1925 and section 39 of the Trustee Act (Northern Ireland) 1958 (vesting of trust property in new or continuing trustees).

(3) Where such a trustee is appointed or discharged by a resolution taken by or on behalf of the union, the written record of the resolution shall be treated for the purposes of those sections as an instrument in writing appointing or discharging the trustee.

(4) In section 40 of the Trustee Act 1925 and section 39 of the Trustee Act (Northern Ireland) 1958 as they apply to such trustees, paragraphs (a) and (c) of subsection (4) (which exclude certain property from the section) shall be omitted.

14 [omitted]

15 Prohibition on use of funds to indemnify unlawful conduct

(1) It is unlawful for property of a trade union to be applied in or towards—

(a) the payment for an individual of a penalty which has been or may be imposed on him for an offence or for contempt of court,

(b) the securing of any such payment, or

(c) the provision of anything for indemnifying an individual in respect of such a penalty.

(2) Where any property of a trade union is so applied for the benefit of an individual on whom a penalty has been or may be imposed, then—

(a) in the case of a payment, an amount equal to the payment is recoverable by the union from him, and

(b) in any other case, he is liable to account to the union for the value of the property applied.

(3) If a trade union fails to bring or continue proceedings which it is entitled to bring by virtue of subsection (2), a member of the union who claims that the failure is unreasonable may apply to the court on that ground for an order authorising him to bring or continue the proceedings on the union's behalf and at the union's expense.

(4) In this section 'penalty', in relation to an offence, includes an order to pay compensation and an order for the forfeiture of any property; and references to the imposition of a penalty for an offence shall be construed accordingly.

(5) The Secretary of State may by order designate offences in relation to which the provisions of this section do not apply.

Any such order shall be made by statutory instrument which shall be subject to annulment in pursuance of a resolution of either House of Parliament.

(6) This section does not affect—

(a) any other enactment, any rule of law or any provision of the rules of a trade union which makes it unlawful for the property of a trade union to be applied in a particular way; or

(b) any other remedy available to a trade union, the trustees of its property or any of its members in respect of an unlawful application of the union's property.

(7) In this section 'member', in relation to a trade union consisting wholly or partly of, or of representatives of, constituent or affiliated organisations, includes a member of any of the constituent or affiliated organisations.

16 Remedy against trustees for unlawful use of union property

(1) A member of a trade union who claims that the trustees of the union's property—

(a) have so carried out their functions, or are proposing so to carry out their functions, as to cause or permit an unlawful application of the union's property, or

(b) have complied, or are proposing to comply, with an unlawful direction which has been or may be given, or purportedly given, to them under the rules of the union,

may apply to the court for an order under this section.

(2) In a case relating to property which has already been unlawfully applied, or to an unlawful direction that has already been complied with, an application under this section may be made only by a person who was a member of the union at the time when the property was applied or, as the case may be, the direction complied with.

(3) Where the court is satisfied that the claim is well-founded, it shall make such order as it considers appropriate.

The court may in particular—

(a) require the trustees (if necessary, on behalf of the union) to take all such steps as may be specified in the order for protecting or recovering the property of the union;

(b) appoint a receiver of, or in Scotland a judicial factor on, the property of the union;

(c) remove one or more of the trustees.

(4) Where the court makes an order under this section in a case in which—

(a) property of the union has been applied in contravention of an order of any court, or in compliance with a direction given in contravention of such an order, or

(b) the trustees were proposing to apply property in contravention of such an order or to comply with any such direction,

the court shall by its order remove all the trustees except any trustee who satisfies the court that there is a good reason for allowing him to remain a trustee.

(5) Without prejudice to any other power of the court, the court may on an application for an order under this section grant such interlocutory relief (in Scotland, such interim order) as it considers appropriate.

(6) This section does not affect any other remedy available in respect of a breach of trust by the trustees of a trade union's property.

(7) In this section 'member', in relation to a trade union consisting wholly or partly of, or of representatives of, constituent or affiliated organisations, includes a member of any of the constituent or affiliated organisations.

17-19 [omitted]

Liability of trade unions in proceedings in tort

20 Liability of trade union in certain proceedings in tort

(1) Where proceedings in tort are brought against a trade union—

(a) on the ground that an act—

(i) induces another person to break a contract or interferes or induces another person to interfere with its performance, or

(ii) consists in threatening that a contract (whether one to which the union is a party or not) will be broken or its performance interfered with, or that the union will induce another person to break a contract or interfere with its performance, or

(b) in respect of an agreement or combination by two or more persons to do or to procure the doing of an act which, if it were done without any such agreement or combination, would be actionable in tort on such a ground,
then, for the purpose of determining in those proceedings whether the union is liable in respect of the act in question, that act shall be taken to have been done by the union if, but only if, it is to be taken to have been authorised or endorsed by the trade union in accordance with the following provisions.

(2) An act shall be taken to have been authorised or endorsed by a trade union if it was done, or was authorised or endorsed—

(a) by any person empowered by the rules to do, authorise or endorse acts of the kind in question, or

(b) by the principal executive committee or the president or general secretary, or

(c) by any other committee of the union or any other official of the union (whether employed by it or not).

(3) For the purposes of paragraph (c) of subsection (2)—

(a) any group of persons constituted in accordance with the rules of the union is a committee of the union; and

(b) an act shall be taken to have been done, authorised or endorsed by an official if it was done, authorised or endorsed by, or by any member of, any group of persons of which he was at the material time a member, the purposes of which included organising or co-ordinating industrial action.

(4) The provisions of paragraphs (b) and (c) of subsection (2) apply notwithstanding anything in the rules of the union, or in any contract or rule of law, but subject to the provisions of section 21 (repudiation by union of certain acts).

(5) Where for the purposes of any proceedings an act is by virtue of this section taken to have been done by a trade union, nothing in this section shall affect the liability of any other person, in those or any other proceedings, in respect of that act.

(6) In proceedings arising out of an act which is by virtue of this section taken to have been done by a trade union, the power of the court to grant an injunction or interdict includes power to require the union to take such steps as the court considers appropriate for ensuring—

(a) that there is no, or no further, inducement of persons to take part or to continue to take part in industrial action, and

(b) that no person engages in any conduct after the granting of the injunction or interdict by virtue of having been induced before it was granted to take part or to continue to take part in industrial action.

The provisions of subsections (2) to (4) above apply in relation to proceedings for failure to comply with any such injunction or interdict as they apply in relation to the original proceedings.

(7) In this section 'rules', in relation to a trade union, means the written rules of the union and any other written provision forming part of the contract between a member and the other members.

21 Repudiation by union of certain acts

(1) An act shall not be taken to have been authorised or endorsed by a trade union by virtue only of paragraph (c) of section 20(2) if it was repudiated by the executive, president or general secretary as soon as reasonably practicable after coming to the knowledge of any of them.

(2) Where an act is repudiated—

(a) written notice of the repudiation must be given to the committee or official in question, without delay, and

(b) the union must do its best to give individual written notice of the fact and date of repudiation, without delay—

(i) to every member of the union who the union has reason to believe is taking part, or might otherwise take part, in industrial action as a result of the act, and

(ii) to the employer of every such member.

(3) The notice given to members in accordance with paragraph (b)(i) of subsection (2) must contain the following statement—

'Your union has repudiated the call (or calls) for industrial action to which this notice relates and will give no support to unofficial industrial action taken in response to it (or them). If you are dismissed while taking unofficial industrial action, you will have no right to complain of unfair dismissal.'

(4) If subsection (2) or (3) is not complied with, the repudiation shall be treated as ineffective.

(5) An act shall not be treated as repudiated if at any time after the union concerned purported to repudiate it the executive, president or general secretary has behaved in a manner which is inconsistent with the purported repudiation.

(6) The executive, president or general secretary shall be treated as so behaving if, on a request made to any of them within three months of the purported repudiation by a person who—

(a) is a party to a commercial contract whose performance has been or may be interfered with as a result of the act in question, and

(b) has not been given written notice by the union of the repudiation,

it is not forthwith confirmed in writing that the act has been repudiated.

(7) In this section 'commercial contract' means any contract other than—

(a) a contract of employment, or

(b) any other contract under which a person agrees personally to do work or perform services for another.

22 Limit on damages awarded against trade unions in actions in tort

(1) This section applies to any proceedings in tort brought against a trade union, except—

(a) proceedings for personal injury as a result of negligence, nuisance or breach of duty;

(b) proceedings for breach of duty in connection with the ownership, occupation, possession, control or use of property;

(c) proceedings brought by virtue of Part I of the Consumer Protection Act 1987 (product liability).

(2) In any proceedings in tort to which this section applies the amount which may be awarded against the union by way of damages shall not exceed the following limit—

Number of members of union	*Maximum award of damages*
Less than 5,000	£10,000
5,000 or more but less than 25,000	£50,000
25,000 or more but less than 100,000	£125,000
100,000 or more	£250,000

(3) and (4) [omitted]

(5) In this section—

'breach of duty' means breach of a duty imposed by any rule of law or by or under any enactment;

'personal injury' includes any disease and any impairment of a person's physical or mental condition; and

'property' means any property, whether real or personal (or in Scotland, heritable or moveable).

Restriction on enforcement against certain property

23 Restriction on enforcement of awards against certain property

(1) Where in any proceedings an amount is awarded by way of damages, costs or expenses—

(a) against a trade union,

(b) against trustees in whom property is vested in trust for a trade union, in their capacity as such (and otherwise than in respect of a breach of trust on their part), or

(c) against members or officials of a trade union on behalf of themselves and all of the members of the union,

no part of that amount is recoverable by enforcement against any protected property.

(2) The following is protected property—

(a) property belonging to the trustees otherwise than in their capacity as such;

(b) property belonging to any member of the union otherwise than jointly or in common with the other members;

(c) property belonging to an official of the union who is neither a member nor a trustee;

(d) property comprised in the union's political fund where that fund—

(i) is subject to rules of the union which prevent property which is or has been comprised in the fund from being used for financing strikes or other industrial action, and

(ii) was so subject at the time when the act in respect of which the proceedings are brought was done;

(e) property comprised in a separate fund maintained in accordance with the rules of the union for the purpose only of providing provident benefits.

(3) For this purpose 'provident benefits' includes—

(a) any payment expressly authorised by the rules of the union which is made—

(i) to a member during sickness or incapacity from personal injury or while out of work, or

(ii) to an aged member by way of superannuation, or

(iii) to a member who has met with an accident or has lost his tools by fire or theft;

(b) a payment in discharge or aid of funeral expenses on the death of a member or the wife of a member or as provision for the children of a deceased member.

CHAPTER III
TRADE UNION ADMINISTRATION

Register of members' names and addresses

24 Duty to maintain register of members' names and addresses

(1) A trade union shall compile and maintain a register of the names and addresses of its members, and shall secure, so far as is reasonably practicable, that the entries in the register are accurate and are kept up-to-date.

(2) The register may be kept by means of a computer.

(3) A trade union shall—

(a) allow any member, upon reasonable notice, to ascertain from the register, free of charge and at any reasonable time, whether there is an entry on it relating to him; and

(b) if requested to do so by any member, supply him as soon as reasonably practicable, either free of charge or on payment of a reasonable fee, with a copy of any entry on the register relating to him.

(4) [repealed]

(5) For the purposes of this section a member's address means either his home address or another address which he has requested the union in writing to treat as his postal address.

(6) The remedy for failure to comply with the requirements of this section is by way of application under section 25 (to the Certification Officer) or section 26 (to the court).

24A Securing confidentiality of register during ballots

(1) This section applies in relation to a ballot of the members of a trade union on—

(a) an election under Chapter IV for a position to which that Chapter applies,

(b) a political resolution under Chapter VI, and

(c) a resolution to approve an instrument of amalgamation or transfer under Chapter VII.

(2) Where this section applies in relation to a ballot the trade union shall impose the duty of confidentiality in relation to the register of members' names and addresses on the scrutineer appointed by the union for the purposes of the ballot and on any person appointed by the union as the independent person for the purposes of the ballot.

(3) The duty of confidentiality in relation to the register of members' names and addresses is, when imposed on a scrutineer or on an independent person, a duty—

(a) not to disclose any name or address in the register except in permitted circumstances; and

(b) to take all reasonable steps to secure that there is no disclosure of any such name or address by any other person except in permitted circumstances;

and any reference in this Act to 'the duty of confidentiality' is a reference to the duty prescribed in this subsection.

(4) The circumstances in which disclosure of a member's name and address is permitted are—

(a) where the member consents;

(b) where it is requested by the Certification Officer for the purposes of the discharge of any of his functions or it is required for the purposes of the discharge of any of the functions of an inspector appointed by him;

(c) where it is required for the purposes of the discharge of any of the functions of the scrutineer or independent person, as the case may be, under the terms of his appointment;

(d) where it is required for the purposes of the investigation of crime or of criminal proceedings.

(5) Any provision of this Part which incorporates the duty of confidentiality as respects the register into the appointment of a scrutineer or an independent person has the effect of imposing that duty on the scrutineer or independent person as a duty owed by him to the trade union.

(6) The remedy for failure to comply with the requirements of this section is by way of application under section 25 (to the Certification Officer) or section 26 (to the court).

25 Remedy for failure: application to Certification Officer

(1) A member of a trade union who claims that the union has failed to comply with any of the requirements of section 24 or 24A (duties with respect to register of members' names and addresses) may apply to the Certification Officer for a declaration to that effect.

(2) On an application being made to him, the Certification Officer shall—

(a) make such enquiries as he thinks fit, and

(b) give the applicant and the trade union an opportunity to be heard,

and may make or refuse the declaration asked for.

(3) If he makes a declaration he shall specify in it the provisions with which the trade union has failed to comply.

(4) Where he makes a declaration and is satisfied that steps have been taken by the union with a view to remedying the declared failure, or securing that a failure of the same

or any similar kind does not occur in future, or that the union has agreed to take such steps, he shall specify those steps in the declaration.

(5) Whether he makes or refuses a declaration, he shall give reasons for his decision in writing; and the reasons may be accompanied by written observations on any matter arising from, or connected with, the proceedings.

(5A) Where the Certification Officer makes a declaration he shall also, unless he considers that to do so would be inappropriate, make an enforcement order, that is, an order imposing on the union one or both of the following requirements—

(a) to take such steps to remedy the declared failure, within such period, as may be specified in the order;

(b) to abstain from such acts as may be so specified with a view to securing that a failure of the same or a similar kind does not occur in future.

(5B) Where an enforcement order has been made, any person who is a member of the union and was a member at the time it was made is entitled to enforce obedience to the order as if he had made the application on which the order was made.

(6) In exercising his functions under this section the Certification Officer shall ensure that, so far as is reasonably practicable, an application made to him is determined within six months of being made.

(7) Where he requests a person to furnish information to him in connection with enquiries made by him under this section, he shall specify the date by which that information is to be furnished and, unless he considers that it would be inappropriate to do so, shall proceed with his determination of the application notwithstanding that the information has not been furnished to him by the specified date.

(8) The Certification Officer shall not entertain an application for a declaration as respects an alleged failure to comply with the requirements of section 24A in relation to a ballot to which that section applies unless the application is made before the end of the period of one year beginning with the last day on which votes could be cast in the ballot.

(9) A declaration made by the Certification Officer under this section may be relied on as if it were a declaration made by the court.

(10) An enforcement order made by the Certification Officer under this section may be enforced in the same way as an order of the court.

(11) the following paragraphs have effect in a person applies under section 26 in relation to an alleged failure—

(a) that person may not apply under this section in relation to that failure;

(b) on an application by a different person under this section in relation to that failure, the Certification Officer shall have due regard to any declaration, order, observations or reasons made or given by the court regarding that failure and brought to the Certification Officer's notice.

26 Remedy for failure: application to court

(1) A member of a trade union who claims that the union has failed to comply with any of the requirements of section 24 or 24A (duties with respect to register of members' names and addresses) may apply to the court for a declaration to that effect.

(2) [repealed]

(3) If the court makes a declaration it shall specify in it the provisions with which the trade union has failed to comply.

(4) Where the court makes a declaration it shall also, unless it considers that to do so would be inappropriate, make an enforcement order, that is, an order imposing on the union one or both of the following requirements—

(a) to take such steps to remedy the declared failure, within such period, as may be specified in the order;

(b) to abstain from such acts as may be so specified with a view to securing that a failure of the same or a similar kind does not occur in future.

(5) Where an enforcement order has been made, any person who is a member of the union and was a member at the time it was made, is entitled to enforce obedience to the order as if he had made the application on which the order was made.

(6) Without prejudice to any other power of the court, the court may on an application under this section grant such interlocutory relief (in Scotland, such interim order) as it considers appropriate.

(7) The court shall not entertain an application for a declaration as respects an alleged failure to comply with the requirements of section 24A in relation to a ballot to which that section applies unless the application is made before the end of the period of one year beginning with the last day on which votes could be cast in the ballot.

(8) The following paragraphs have effect if a person applies under section 25 in relation to an alleged failure—

(a) that person may not apply under this section in relation to that failure;

(b) on an application by a different person under this section in relation to that failure, the court shall have due regard to any declaration, order, observations or reasons made or given by the Certification Officer regarding that failure and brought to the court's notice.

Duty to supply copy of rules

27 Duty to supply copy of rules

A trade union shall at the request of any person supply him with a copy of its rules either free of charge or on payment of a reasonable charge.

Accounting records

28 Duty to keep accounting records

(1) A trade union shall—

(a) cause to be kept proper accounting records with respect to its transactions and its assets and liabilities, and

(b) establish and maintain a satisfactory system of control of its accounting records, its cash holdings and all its receipts and remittances.

(2) Proper accounting records shall not be taken to be kept with respect to the matters mentioned in subsection (1)(a) unless there are kept such records as are necessary to give a true and fair view of the state of the affairs of the trade union and to explain its transactions.

29 Duty to keep records available for inspection

(1) A trade union shall keep available for inspection from their creation until the end of the period of six years beginning with the 1 January following the end of the period to which they relate such of the records of the union, or of any branch or section of the union, as are, or purport to be, records required to be kept by the union under section 28.

This does not apply to records relating to periods before 1 January 1988.

(2) In section 30 (right of member to access to accounting records)—

(a) references to a union's accounting records are to any such records as are mentioned in subsection (1) above, and

(b) references to records available for inspection are to records which the union is required by that subsection to keep available for inspection.

(3) The expiry of the period mentioned in subsection (1) above does not affect the duty of a trade union to comply with a request for access made under section 30 before the end of that period.

30 Right of access to accounting records

(1) A member of a trade union has a right to request access to any accounting records of the union which are available for inspection and relate to periods including a time when he was a member of the union.

In the case of records relating to a branch or section of the union, it is immaterial whether he was a member of that branch or section.

(2) Where such access is requested the union shall—

(a) make arrangements with the member for him to be allowed to inspect the records requested before the end of the period of twenty-eight days beginning with the day the request was made,

(b) allow him and any accountant accompanying him for the purpose to inspect the records at the time and place arranged, and

(c) secure that at the time of the inspection he is allowed to take, or is supplied with, any copies of, or of extracts from, records inspected by him which he requires.

(3) The inspection shall be at a reasonable hour and at the place where the records are normally kept, unless the parties to the arrangements agree otherwise.

(4) An 'accountant' means a person who is eligible for appointment as a company auditor under section 25 of the Companies Act 1989.

(5) The union need not allow the member to be accompanied by an accountant if the accountant fails to enter into such agreement as the union may reasonably require for protecting the confidentiality of the records.

(6) Where a member who makes a request for access to a union's accounting records is informed by the union, before any arrangements are made in pursuance of the request—

(a) of the union's intention to charge for allowing him to inspect the records to which the request relates, for allowing him to take copies of, or extracts from, those records or for supplying any such copies, and

(b) of the principles in accordance with which its charges will be determined,

then, where the union complies with the request, he is liable to pay the union on demand such amount, not exceeding the reasonable administrative expenses incurred by the union in complying with the request, as is determined in accordance with those principles.

(7) In this section 'member', in relation to a trade union consisting wholly or partly of, or of representatives of, constituent or affiliated organisations, includes a member of any of the constituent or affiliated organisations.

31 Remedy for failure to comply with request for access

(1) A person who claims that a trade union has failed in any respect to comply with a request made by him under section 30 may apply to the court or to the Certification Officer.

(2) Where on an application to it the court is satisfied that the claim is well-founded, it shall make such order as it considers appropriate for ensuring that the applicant—

(a) is allowed to inspect the records requested,

(b) is allowed to be accompanied by an accountant when making the inspection of those records, and

(c) is allowed to take, or is supplied with, such copies of, or of extracts from, the records as he may require.

(2A) On an application to him the Certification Officer shall—

(a) make such enquiries as he thinks fit, and

(b) give the applicant and the trade union an opportunity to be heard.

(2B) Where the Certification Officer is satisfied that the claim is well-founded he shall make such order as he considers appropriate for ensuring that the applicant—

(a) is allowed to inspect the records requested,

(b) is allowed to be accompanied by an accountant when making the inspection of those records, and

(c) is allowed to take, or is supplied with, such copies of, or of extracts from, the records as he may require.

(2C) In exercising his functions under this section the Certification Officer shall ensure that, so far as is reasonably practicable, an application made to him is determined within six months of being made.

(3) Without prejudice to any other power of the court, the court may on an application to it under this section grant such interlocutory relief (in Scotland, such interim order) as it considers appropriate.

(4) [omitted]

(5) An order made by the Certification Officer under this section may be enforced in the same way as an order of the court.

(6) If a person applies to the court under this section in relation to an alleged failure he may not apply to the Certification Officer under this section in relation to that failure.

(7) If a person applies to the Certification Officer under this section in relation to an alleged failure he may not apply to the court under this section in relation to that failure.

32-45 [omitted]

45D Appeals from Certification Officer

An appeal lies to the Employment Appeal Tribunal on any question of law arising in proceedings before or arising from any decision of the Certification Officer under section 25, 31 or 45C.

CHAPTER IV
ELECTIONS FOR CERTAIN POSITIONS

Duty to hold elections

46 Duty to hold elections for certain positions

(1) A trade union shall secure—

(a) that every person who holds a position in the union to which this Chapter applies does so by virtue of having been elected to it at an election satisfying the requirements of this Chapter, and

(b) that no person continues to hold such a position for more than five years without being re-elected at such an election.

(2) The positions to which this Chapter applies (subject as mentioned below) are—

(a) member of the executive,

(b) any position by virtue of which a person is a member of the executive,

(c) president, and

(d) general secretary;

and the requirements referred to above are those set out in sections 47 to 52 below.

(3) In this Chapter 'member of the executive' includes any person who, under the rules or practice of the union, may attend and speak at some or all of the meetings of the executive, otherwise than for the purpose of providing the committee with factual information or with technical or professional advice with respect to matters taken into account by the executive in carrying out its functions.

(4) This Chapter does not apply to the position of president or general secretary if the holder of that position—

(a) is not, in respect of that position, either a voting member of the executive or an employee of the union,

(b) holds that position for a period which under the rules of the union cannot end more than 13 months after he took it up, and

(c) has not held either position at any time in the period of twelve months ending with the day before he took up that position.

(5) A 'voting member of the executive' means a person entitled in his own right to attend meetings of the executive and to vote on matters on which votes are taken by the

executive (whether or not he is entitled to attend all such meetings or to vote on all such matters or in all circumstances).

(6) The provisions of this Chapter apply notwithstanding anything in the rules or practice of the union; and the terms and conditions on which a person is employed by the union shall be disregarded in so far as they would prevent the union from complying with the provisions of this Chapter.

Requirements to be satisfied with respect to elections

47 Candidates

(1) No member of the trade union shall be unreasonably excluded from standing as a candidate.

(2) No candidate shall be required, directly or indirectly, to be a member of a political party.

(3) A member of a trade union shall not be taken to be unreasonably excluded from standing as a candidate if he is excluded on the ground that he belongs to a class of which all the members are excluded by the rules of the union.

But a rule which provides for such a class to be determined by reference to whom the union chooses to exclude shall be disregarded.

48 Election addresses

(1) The trade union shall—

(a) provide every candidate with an opportunity of preparing an election address in his own words and of submitting it to the union to be distributed to the persons accorded entitlement to vote in the election; and

(b) secure that, so far as reasonably practicable, copies of every election address submitted to it in time are distributed to each of those persons by post along with the voting papers for the election.

(2) The trade union may determine the time by which an election address must be submitted to it for distribution; but the time so determined must not be earlier than the latest time at which a person may become a candidate in the election.

(3) The trade union may provide that election addresses submitted to it for distribution—

(a) must not exceed such length, not being less than one hundred words, as may be determined by the union, and

(b) may, as regards photographs and other matter not in words, incorporate only such matter as the union may determine.

(4) The trade union shall secure that no modification of an election address submitted to it is made by any person in any copy of the address to be distributed except—

(a) at the request or with the consent of the candidate, or

(b) where the modification is necessarily incidental to the method adopted for producing that copy.

(5) The trade union shall secure that the same method of producing copies is applied in the same way to every election address submitted and, so far as reasonably practicable, that no such facility or information as would enable a candidate to gain any benefit from—

(a) the method by which copies of the election addresses are produced, or

(b) the modifications which are necessarily incidental to that method,

is provided to any candidate without being provided equally to all the others.

(6) The trade union shall, so far as reasonably practicable, secure that the same facilities and restrictions with respect to the preparation, submission, length or modification of an election address, and with respect to the incorporation of photographs or other matter not in words, are provided or applied equally to each of the candidates.

(7) The arrangements made by the trade union for the production of the copies to be so distributed must be such as to secure that none of the candidates is required to bear any of the expense of producing the copies.

(8) No-one other than the candidate himself shall incur any civil or criminal liability in respect of the publication of a candidate's election address or of any copy required to be made for the purposes of this section.

49 Appointment of independent scrutineer

(1) The trade union shall, before the election is held, appoint a qualified independent person ('the scrutineer') to carry out—

(a) the functions in relation to the election which are required under this section to be contained in his appointment; and

(b) such additional functions in relation to the election as may be specified in his appointment.

(2) A person is a qualified independent person in relation to an election if—

(a) he satisfies such conditions as may be specified for the purposes of this section by order of the Secretary of State or is himself so specified; and

(b) the trade union has no grounds for believing either that he will carry out any functions conferred on him in relation to the election otherwise than competently or that his independence in relation to the union, or in relation to the election, might reasonably be called into question.

An order under paragraph (a) shall be made by statutory instrument which shall be subject to annulment in pursuance of a resolution of either House of Parliament.

(3) The scrutineer's appointment shall require him—

(a) to be the person who supervises the production of the voting papers and (unless he is appointed under section 51A to undertake the distribution of the voting papers) their distribution and to whom the voting papers are returned by those voting;

(aa) to—

(i) inspect the register of names and addresses of the members of the trade union, or

(ii) examine the copy of the register as at the relevant date which is supplied to him in accordance with subsection (5A)(a),

whenever it appears to him appropriate to do so and, in particular, when the conditions specified in subsection (3A) are satisfied;

(b) to take such steps as appear to him to be appropriate for the purpose of enabling him to make his report (see section 52);

(c) to make his report to the trade union as soon as reasonably practicable after the last date for the return of voting papers; and

(d) to retain custody of all voting papers returned for the purposes of the election and the copy of the register supplied to him in accordance with subsection (5A)(a)—

(i) until the end of the period of one year beginning with the announcement by the union of the result of the election; and

(ii) if within that period an application is made under section 54 (complaint of failure to comply with election requirements), until the Certification Officer or the court authorises him to dispose of the papers or copy.

(3A)-(8) [omitted]

50 Entitlement to vote

(1) Subject to the provisions of this section, entitlement to vote shall be accorded equally to all members of the trade union.

(2) The rules of the union may exclude entitlement to vote in the case of all members belonging to one of the following classes, or to a class falling within one of the following—

(a) members who are not in employment;

(b) members who are in arrears in respect of any subscription or contribution due to the union;

(c) members who are apprentices, trainees or students or new members of the union.

(3) The rules of the union may restrict entitlement to vote to members who fall within—

(a) a class determined by reference to a trade or occupation,

(b) a class determined by reference to a geographical area, or

(c) a class which is by virtue of the rules of the union treated as a separate section within the union,

or to members who fall within a class determined by reference to any combination of the factors mentioned in paragraphs (a), (b) and (c).

The reference in paragraph (c) to a section of a trade union includes a part of the union which is itself a trade union.

(4) Entitlement may not be restricted in accordance with subsection (3) if the effect is that any member of the union is denied entitlement to vote at all elections held for the purposes of this Chapter otherwise than by virtue of belonging to a class excluded in accordance with subsection (2).

51 Voting

(1) The method of voting must be by the marking of a voting paper by the person voting.

(2) Each voting paper must—

(a) state the name of the independent scrutineer and clearly specify the address to which, and the date by which, it is to be returned,

(b) be given one of a series of consecutive whole numbers every one of which is used in giving a different number in that series to each voting paper printed or otherwise produced for the purposes of the election, and

(c) be marked with its number.

(3) Every person who is entitled to vote at the election must—

(a) be allowed to vote without interference from, or constraint imposed by, the union or any of its members, officials or employees, and

(b) so far as is reasonably practicable, be enabled to do so without incurring any direct cost to himself.

(4) So far as is reasonably practicable, every person who is entitled to vote at the election must—

(a) have sent to him by post, at his home address or another address which he has requested the trade union in writing to treat as his postal address, a voting paper which either lists the candidates at the election or is accompanied by a separate list of those candidates; and

(b) be given a convenient opportunity to vote by post.

(5) The ballot shall be conducted so as to secure that—

(a) so far as is reasonably practicable, those voting do so in secret, and

(b) the votes given at the election are fairly and accurately counted.

For the purposes of paragraph (b) an inaccuracy in counting shall be disregarded if it is accidental and on a scale which could not affect the result of the election.

(6) The ballot shall be so conducted as to secure that the result of the election is determined solely by counting the number of votes cast directly for each candidate.

(7) Nothing in subsection (6) shall be taken to prevent the system of voting used for the election being the single transferable vote, that is, a vote capable of being given so as to indicate the voter's order of preference for the candidates and of being transferred to the next choice—

(a) when it is not required to give a prior choice the necessary quota of votes, or

(b) when, owing to the deficiency in the number of votes given for a prior choice, that choice is eliminated from the list of candidates.

51A Counting of votes etc. by independent person

(1) The trade union shall ensure that—

(a) the storage and distribution of the voting papers for the purposes of the election, and

(b) the counting of the votes cast in the election.

are undertaken by one or more independent persons appointed by the union.

(2) A person is an independent person in relation to an election if—

(a) he is the scrutineer, or

(b) he is a person other than the scrutineer and the trade union has no grounds for believing either that he will carry out any functions conferred on him in relation to the election otherwise than competently or that his independence in relation to the union, or in relation to the election, might reasonably be called into question.

(3) An appointment under this section shall require the person appointed to carry out his functions so as to minimise the risk of any contravention of requirements imposed by or under any enactment or the occurrence of any unfairness or malpractice.

(4) The duty of confidentiality as respects the register is incorporated in an appointment under this section.

(5) Where the person appointed to undertake the counting of votes is not the scrutineer, his appointment shall require him to send the voting papers back to the scrutineer as soon as reasonably practicable after the counting has been completed.

(6) The trade union—

(a) shall ensure that nothing in the terms of an appointment under this section is such as to make it reasonable for any person to call into question the independence of the person appointed in relation to the union,

(b) shall ensure that a person appointed under this section duly carries out his functions and that there is no interference with his carrying out of those funtions which would make it reasonable for any person to call into question the independence of the person appointed in relation to the union, and

(c) shall comply with all reasonable requests made by a person appointed under this section for the purposes of, or in connection with, the carrying out of his functions.

52 Scrutineer's report

(1) The scrutineer's report on the election shall state—

(a) the number of voting papers distributed for the purposes of the election,

(b) the number of voting papers returned to the scrutineer,

(c) the number of valid votes cast in the election for each candidate,

(d) the number of spoiled or otherwise invalid voting papers returned, and

(e) the name of the person (or of each of the persons) appointed under section 51A or, if no person was so appointed, that fact.

(2) The report shall also state whether the scrutineer is satisfied—

(a) that there are no reasonable grounds for believing that there was any contravention of a requirement imposed by or under any enactment in relation to the election,

(b) that the arrangements made (whether by him or any other person) with respect to the production, storage, distribution, return or other handling of the voting papers used in the election, and the arrangements for the counting of the votes, included all such security arrangements as were reasonably practicable for the purpose of minimising the risk that any unfairness or malpractice might occur, and

(c) that he has been able to carry out his functions without such interference as would make it reasonable for any person to call his independence in relation to the union into question;

and if he is not satisfied as to any of those matters, the report shall give particulars of his reasons for not being satisfied as to that matter.

(2A)-(6) [omitted]

53 Uncontested elections

Nothing in this Chapter shall be taken to require a ballot to be held at an uncontested election.

Remedy for failure to comply with requirements

54 Remedy for failure to comply with requirements: general

(1) The remedy for a failure on the part of a trade union to comply with the requirements of this Chapter is by way of application under section 55 (to the Certification Officer) or section 56 (to the court).

(2) An application under those sections may be made—

(a) by a person who is a member of the trade union (provided, where the election has been held, he was also a member at the time when it was held), or

(b) by a person who is or was a candidate at the election;

and the references in those sections to a person having a sufficient interest are to such a person.

(3) No such application may be made after the end of the period of one year beginning with the day on which the union announced the result of the election.

55 Application to Certification Officer

(1) A person having a sufficient interest (see section 54(2)) who claims that a trade union has failed to comply with any of the requirements of this Chapter may apply to the Certification Officer for a declaration to that effect.

(2) On an application being made to him, the Certification Officer shall—

(a) make such enquiries as he thinks fit, and

(b) give the applicant and the trade union an opportunity to be heard,

and may make or refuse the declaration asked for.

(3) If he makes a declaration he shall specify in it the provisions with which the trade union has failed to comply.

(4) Where he makes a declaration and is satisfied that steps have been taken by the union with a view to remedying the declared failure, or securing that a failure of the same or any similar kind does not occur in future, or that the union has agreed to take such steps, he shall specify those steps in the declaration.

(5) Whether he makes or refuses a declaration, he shall give reasons for his decision in writing; and the reasons may be accompanied by written observations on any matter arising from, or connected with, the proceedings.

(5A) Where the Certification Officer makes a declaration he shall also, unless he considers that to do so would be inappropriate, make an enforcement order, that is, an order imposing on the union one or more of the following requirements—

(a) to secure the holding of an election in accordance with the order;

(b) to take such other steps to remedy the declared failure as may be specified in the order;

(c) to abstain from such acts as may be so specified with a view to securing that a failure of the same or a similar kind does not occur in future.

The Certification Officer shall in an order imposing any such requirement as is mentioned in paragraph (a) or (b) specify the period within which the union is to comply with the requirements of the order.

(5B) Where the Certification Officer makes an order requiring the union to hold a fresh election, he shall (unless he considers that it would be inappropriate to do so in the particular circumstances of the case) require the election to be conducted in accordance with the requirements of this Chapter and such other provisions as may be made by the order.

(5C) Where an enforcement order has been made—

(a) any person who is a member of the union and was a member at the time the order was made, or

(b) any person who is or was a candidate in the election in question,

is entitled to enforce obedience to the order as if he had made the application on which the order was made.

(6) In exercising his functions under this section the Certification Officer shall ensure that, so far as is reasonably practicable, an application made to him is determined within six months of being made.

(7) Where he requests a person to furnish information to him in connection with enquiries made by him under this section, he shall specify the date by which that information is to be furnished and, unless he considers that it would be inappropriate to do so, shall proceed with his determination of the application notwithstanding that the information has not been furnished to him by the specified date.

(8) A declaration made by the Certification Officer under this section may be relied on as if it were a declaration made by the court.

(9) An enforcement order made by the Certification Officer under this section may be enforced in the same way as an order of the court.

(10) the following paragraphs have effect if a person applies under section 56 in relation to an alleged failure—

(a) that person may not apply under this section in relation to that failure;

(b) on an application by a different person under this section in relation to that failure, the Certification Officer shall have due regard to any declaration, order, observations or reasons made or given by the court regarding that failure and brought to the Certification Officer's notice.

56 Application to court

(1) A person having a sufficient interest (see section 54(2)) who claims that a trade union has failed to comply with any of the requirements of this Chapter may apply to the court for a declaration to that effect.

(2) [repealed]

(3) If the court makes the declaration asked for, it shall specify in the declaration the provisions with which the trade union has failed to comply.

(4) Where the court makes a declaration it shall also, unless it considers that to do so would be inappropriate, make an enforcement order, that is, an order imposing on the union one or more of the following requirements—

(a) to secure the holding of an election in accordance with the order;

(b) to take such other steps to remedy the declared failure as may be specified in the order;

(c) to abstain from such acts as may be so specified with a view to securing that a failure of the same or a similar kind does not occur in future.

The court shall in an order imposing any such requirement as is mentioned in paragraph (a) or (b) specify the period within which the union is to comply with the requirements of the order.

(5) where the court makes an order requiring the union to hold a fresh election, the court shall (unless it considers that it would be inappropriate to do so in the particular circumstances of the case) require the election to be conducted in accordance with the requirements of this Chapter and such other provisions as may be made by the order.

(6) Where an enforcement order has been made—

(a) any person who is a member of the union and was a member at the time the order was made, or

(b) any person who is or was a candidate in the election in question,

is entitled to enforce obedience to the order as if he had made the application on which the order was made.

(7) Without prejudice to any other power of the court, the court may on an application under this section grant such interlocutory relief (in Scotland, such interim order) as it considers appropriate.

(8) The following paragraphs have effect if a person applies under section 55 in relation to an alleged failure—

(a) that person may not apply under this section in relation to that failure;

(b) on an application by a different person under this section in relation to that failure, the court shall have due regard to any declaration, order, observations or reasons made or given by the Certification Officer regarding that failure and brought to the court's notice.

56A Appeals from Certification Officer

An appeal lies to the Employment Appeal Tribunal on any question of law arising in proceedings before or arising from any decision of the Certification Officer under section 55.

57-61 [omitted]

CHAPTER V
RIGHTS OF TRADE UNION MEMBERS

Right to a ballot before industrial action

62 Right to a ballot before industrial action

(1) A member of a trade union who claims that members of the union, including himself, are likely to be or have been induced by the union to take part or to continue to take part in industrial action which does not have the support of a ballot may apply to the court for an order under this section.

In this section 'the relevant time' means the time when the application is made.

(2) For this purpose industrial action shall be regarded as having the support of a ballot only if—

(a) the union has held a ballot in respect of the action—

(i) in relation to which the requirements of section 226B so far as applicable before and during the holding of the ballot were satisfied,

(ii) in relation to which the requirements of sections 227 to 231 were satisfied, and

(iii) in which the majority voting in the ballot answered 'Yes' to the question applicable in accordance with section 229(2) to industrial action of the kind which the applicant has been or is likely to be induced to take part in;

(b) such of the requirements of the following sections as have fallen to be satisfied at the relevant time have been satisfied, namely—

(i) section 226B so far as applicable after the holding of the ballot, and

(ii) section 231B; and

(c) the requirements of section 233 (calling of industrial action with support of ballot) are satisfied.

Any reference in this subsection to a requirement of a provision which is disapplied or modified by section 232 has effect subject to that section.

(3) Where on an application under this section the court is satisfied that the claim is well-founded, it shall make such order as it considers appropriate for requiring the union to take steps for ensuring—

(a) that there is no, or no further, inducement of members of the union to take part or to continue to take part in the industrial action to which the application relates, and

(b) that no member engages in conduct after the making of the order by virtue of having been induced before the making of the order to take part or continue to take part in the action.

(4) Without prejudice to any other power of the court, the court may on an application under this section grant such interlocutory relief (in Scotland, such interim order) as it considers appropriate.

(5) For the purposes of this section an act shall be taken to be done by a trade union if it is authorised or endorsed by the union; and the provisions of section 20(2) to (4) apply for the purpose of determining whether an act is to be taken to be so authorised or endorsed.

Those provisions also apply in relation to proceedings for failure to comply with an order under this section as they apply in relation to the original proceedings.

(6) In this section—

'inducement' includes an inducement which is or would be ineffective, whether because of the member's unwillingness to be influenced by it or for any other reason; and

'industrial action' means a strike or other industrial action by persons employed under contracts of employment.

(7) Where a person holds any office or employment under the Crown on terms which do not constitute a contract of employment between that person and the Crown, those terms shall nevertheless be deemed to constitute such a contract for the purposes of this section.

(8) References in this section to a contract of employment include any contract under which one person personally does work or performs services for another; and related expressions shall be construed accordingly.

(9) Nothing in this section shall be construed as requiring a trade union to hold separate ballots for the purposes of this section and sections 226 to 234 (requirement of ballot before action by trade union).

Right not to be denied access to the courts

63 Right not to be denied access to the courts

(1) This section applies where a matter is under the rules of a trade union required or allowed to be submitted for determination or conciliation in accordance with the rules of the union, but a provision of the rules purporting to provide for that to be a person's only remedy has no effect (or would have no effect if there were one).

(2) Notwithstanding anything in the rules of the union or in the practice of any court, if a member or former member of the union begins proceedings in a court with respect to a matter to which this section applies, then if—

(a) he has previously made a valid application to the union for the matter to be submitted for determination or conciliation in accordance with the union's rules, and

(b) the court proceedings are begun after the end of the period of six months beginning with the day on which the union received the application,

the rules requiring or allowing the matter to be so submitted, and the fact that any relevant steps remain to be taken under the rules, shall be regarded for all purposes as irrelevant to any question whether the court proceedings should be dismissed, stayed or sisted, or adjourned.

(3) An application shall be deemed to be valid for the purposes of subsection (2)(a) unless the union informed the applicant, before the end of the period of 28 days beginning with the date on which the union received the application, of the respects in which the application contravened the requirements of the rules.

(4) If the court is satisfied that any delay in the taking of relevant steps under the rules is attributable to unreasonable conduct of the person who commenced the proceedings, it may treat the period specified in subsection (2)(b) as extended by such further period as it considers appropriate.

(5) In this section—

(a) references to the rules of a trade union include any arbitration or other agreement entered into in pursuance of a requirement imposed by or under the rules; and

(b) references to the relevant steps under the rules, in relation to any matter, include any steps falling to be taken in accordance with the rules for the purposes of or in connection with the determination or conciliation of the matter, or any appeal, review or reconsideration of any determination or award.

(6) This section does not affect any enactment or rule of law by virtue of which a court would apart from this section disregard any such rules of a trade union or any such fact as is mentioned in subsection (2).

Right not to be unjustifiably disciplined

64 Right not to be unjustifiably disciplined

(1) An individual who is or has been a member of a trade union has the right not to be unjustifiably disciplined by the union.

(2) For this purpose an individual is 'disciplined' by a trade union if a determination is made, or purportedly made, under the rules of the union or by an official of the union or a number of persons including an official that—

(a) he should be expelled from the union or a branch or section of the union,

(b) he should pay a sum to the union, to a branch or section of the union or to any other person;

(c) sums tendered by him in respect of an obligation to pay subscriptions or other sums to the union, or to a branch or section of the union, should be treated as unpaid or paid for a different purpose,

(d) he should be deprived to any extent of, or of access to, any benefits, services or facilities which would otherwise be provided or made available to him by virtue of his membership of the union, or a branch or section of the union,

(e) another trade union, or a branch or section of it, should be encouraged or advised not to accept him as a member, or

(f) he should be subjected to some other detriment;

and whether an individual is 'unjustifiably disciplined' shall be determined in accordance with section 65.

(3) Where a determination made in infringement of an individual's right under this section requires the payment of a sum or the performance of an obligation, no person is entitled in any proceedings to rely on that determination for the purpose of recovering the sum or enforcing the obligation.

(4) Subject to that, the remedies for infringement of the right conferred by this section are as provided by sections 66 and 67, and not otherwise.

(5) The right not to be unjustifiably disciplined is in addition to (and not in substitution for) any right which exists apart from this section; and, subject to section 66(4), nothing in this section or sections 65 to 67 affects any remedy for infringement of any such right.

65 Meaning of 'unjustifiably disciplined'

(1) An individual is unjustifiably disciplined by a trade union if the actual or supposed conduct which constitutes the reason, or one of the reasons, for disciplining him is—

(a) conduct to which this section applies, or

(b) something which is believed by the union to amount to such conduct;

but subject to subsection (6) (cases of bad faith in relation to assertion of wrongdoing).

(2) This section applies to conduct which consists in—

(a) failing to participate in or support a strike or other industrial action (whether by members of the union or by others), or indicating opposition to or a lack of support for such action;

(b) failing to contravene, for a purpose connected with such a strike or other industrial action, a requirement imposed on him by or under a contract of employment;

(c) asserting (whether by bringing proceedings or otherwise) that the union, any official or representative of it or a trustee of its property has contravened, or is proposing to contravene, a requirement which is, or is thought to be, imposed by or under the rules of the union or any other agreement or by or under any enactment (whenever passed) or any rule of law;

(d) encouraging or assisting a person—

(i) to perform an obligation imposed on him by a contract of employment, or

(ii) to make or attempt to vindicate any such assertion as is mentioned in paragraph (c);

(e) contravening a requirement imposed by or in consequence of a determination which infringes the individual's or another individual's right not to be unjustifiably disciplined;

(f) failing to agree, or withdrawing agreement, to the making from his wages (in accordance with arrangements between his employer and the union) of deductions representing payments to the union in respect of his membership,

(g) resigning or proposing to resign from the union or from another union, becoming or proposing to become a member of another union, refusing to become a member of another union, or being a member of another union,

(h) working with, or proposing to work with, individuals who are not members of the union or who are or are not members of another union,

(i) working for, or proposing to work for, an employer who employs or who has employed individuals who are not members of the union or who are or are not members of another union, or

(j) requiring the union to do an act which the union is, by any provision of this Act, required to do on the requisition of a member.

(3) This section applies to conduct which involves the Certification Officer being consulted or asked to provide advice or assistance with respect to any matter whatever, or which involves any person being consulted or asked to provide advice or assistance with respect to a matter which forms, or might form, the subject-matter of any such assertion as is mentioned in subsection (2)(c) above.

(4) This section also applies to conduct which consists in proposing to engage in, or doing anything preparatory or incidental to, conduct falling within subsection (2) or (3).

(5) This section does not apply to an act, omission or statement comprised in conduct falling within subsection (2), (3) or (4) above if it is shown that the act, omission or statement is one in respect of which individuals would be disciplined by the union irrespective of whether their acts, omissions or statements were in connection with conduct within subsection (2) or (3) above.

(6) An individual is not unjustifiably disciplined if it is shown—

(a) that the reason for disciplining him, or one of them, is that he made such an assertion as is mentioned in subsection (2)(c), or encouraged or assisted another person to make or attempt to vindicate such an assertion,

(b) that the assertion was false, and

(c) that he made the assertion, or encouraged or assisted another person to make or attempt to vindicate it, in the belief that it was false or otherwise in bad faith, and that there was no other reason for disciplining him or that the only other reasons were reasons in respect of which he does not fall to be treated as unjustifiably disciplined.

(7) In this section—

'conduct' includes statements, acts and omissions;

'contract of employment', in relation to an individual, includes any agreement between that individual and a person for whom he works or normally works,

'employer' includes such a person and related expressions shall be construed accordingly;

'representative', in relation to a union, means a person acting or purporting to act—

(a) in his capacity as a member of the union, or

(b) on the instructions or advice of a person acting or purporting to act in that capacity or in the capacity of an official of the union.

'require' (on the part of an individual) includes request or apply for, and 'requisition' shall be construed accordingly; and

'wages' shall be construed in accordance with the definitions of 'contract of employment', 'employer' and related expressions.

(8) Where a person holds any office or employment under the Crown on terms which do not constitute a contract of employment between him and the Crown, those terms shall nevertheless be deemed to constitute such a contract for the purposes of this section.

66 Complaint of infringement of right

(1) An individual who claims that he has been unjustifiably disciplined by a trade union may present a complaint against the union to an employment tribunal.

(2) The tribunal shall not entertain such a complaint unless it is presented—

(a) before the end of the period of three months beginning with the date of the making of the determination claimed to infringe the right, or

(b) where the tribunal is satisfied—

(i) that it was not reasonably practicable for the complaint to be presented before the end of that period, or

(ii) that any delay in making the complaint is wholly or partly attributable to a reasonable attempt to appeal against the determination or to have it reconsidered or reviewed,

within such further period as the tribunal considers reasonable.

(3) Where the tribunal finds the complaint well-founded, it shall make a declaration to that effect.

(4) Where a complaint relating to an expulsion which is presented under this section is declared to be well-founded, no complaint in respect of the expulsion shall be presented or proceeded with under section 174 (right not to be excluded or expelled from trade union).

67 Further remedies for infringement of right

(1) An individual whose complaint under section 66 has been declared to be well-founded may make an application for one or both of the following—

(a) an award of compensation to be paid to him by the union;

(b) an order that the union pay him an amount equal to any sum which he has paid in pursuance of any such determination as is mentioned in section 64(2)(b).

(2) An application under this section shall be made to the Employment Appeal Tribunal if, when it is made—

(a) the determination infringing the applicant's right not to be unjustifiably disciplined has not been revoked, or

(b) the union has failed to take all the steps necessary for securing the reversal of anything done for the purpose of giving effect to the determination;

and in any other case it shall be made to an employment tribunal.

(3) An application under this section shall not be entertained if made before the end of the period of four weeks beginning with the date of the declaration or after the end of the period of six months beginning with that date.

(4) Where the Employment Appeal Tribunal or employment tribunal is satisfied that it would be required by virtue of subsection (2) to dismiss the application, it may instead transfer it to the tribunal to which it should have been made; and an application so transferred shall be proceeded with as if it had been made in accordance with that subsection when originally made.

(5) The amount of compensation awarded shall, subject to the following provisions, be such as the Employment Appeal Tribunal or employment tribunal considers just and equitable in all the circumstances.

(6) In determining the amount of compensation to be awarded, the same rule shall be applied concerning the duty of a person to mitigate his loss as applies to damages recoverable under the common law in England and Wales or Scotland.

(7) Where the Employment Appeal Tribunal or employment tribunal finds that the infringement complained of was to any extent caused or contributed to by the action of the applicant, it shall reduce the amount of the compensation by such proportion as it considers just and equitable having regard to that finding.

(8) The amount of compensation awarded calculated in accordance with subsections (5) to (7) shall not exceed the aggregate of—

(a) an amount equal to 30 times the limit for the time being imposed by section 227(1)(a) of the Employment Rights Act 1996 (maximum amount of a week's pay for basic award in unfair dismissal cases), and

(b) an amount equal to the limit for the time being imposed by section 124(1) of that Act (maximum compensatory award in such cases);

and, in the case of an award by the Employment Appeal Tribunal, shall not be less than the amount for the time being specified in section 176(6) of this Act (minimum award by Employment Appeal Tribunal in cases of exclusion or expulsion from union).

(9) [repealed]

Right not to suffer deduction of unauthorised union subscriptions

68 Right not to suffer deduction of unauthorised union subscriptions

(1) Where arrangements ('subscription deduction arrangements') exist between the employer of a worker and a trade union relating to the making from workers' wages of deductions representing payments to the union in respect of the workers' membership of the union ('subscription deductions'), the employer shall ensure that no subscription deduction is made from wages payable to the worker on any day unless—

(a) the worker has authorised in writing the making from his wages of subscription deductions; and

(b) the worker has not withdrawn the authorisation.

(2) A worker withdraws an authorisation given for the purposes of subsection (1), in relation to a subscription deduction which falls to be made from wages payable to him on any day, if a written notice withdrawing the authorisation has been received by the employer in time for it to be reasonably practicable for the employer to secure that no such deduction is made.

(3) A worker's authorisation of the making of subscription deductions from his wages shall not give rise to any obligation on the part of the employer to the worker to maintain or continue to maintain subscription deduction arrangements.

(4) In this section and section 68A, 'employer', 'wages' and 'worker' have the same meanings as in the Employment Rights Act 1996.

68A Complaint of infringement of rights

(1) A worker may present a complaint to an employment tribunal that his employer has made a deduction from his wages in contravention of section 68—

(a) within the period of three months beginning with the date of the payment of the wages from which the deduction, or (if the complaint relates to more than one deduction) the last of the deductions, was made, or

(b) where the tribunal is satisfied that it was not reasonably practicable for the complaint to be presented within that period, within such further period as the tribunal considers reasonable.

(2) Where a tribunal finds that a complaint under this section is well-founded, it shall make a declaration to that effect and shall order the employer to pay to the worker the whole amount of the deduction, less any such part of the amount as has already been paid to the worker by the employer.

(3) Where the making of a deduction from the wages of a worker both contravenes section 68(1) and invovles one or more of the contraventions specified in subsection (4) of this section, the aggregate amount which may be ordered by an employment tribunal or court (whether on the same occasion or on different occasions) to be paid in respect of the contraventions shall not exceed the amount, or (where different amounts may be ordered to be paid in respect of different contraventions) the greatest amount, which may be ordered to be paid in respect of any one of them.

(4) The contraventions referred to in subsection (3) are—

(a) a contravention of the requirement not to make a deduction without having given the particulars required by section 8 (itemised pay statements) or 9(1) (standing statements of fixed deductions) of the Employment Rights Act 1996,

(b) a contravention of section 13 of that Act (requirement not to make unauthorised deductions), and

(c) a contravention of section 86(1) or 90(1) of this Act (requirements not to make deductions of political fund contributions in certain circumstances).

Right to terminate membership of union

69 Right to terminate membership of union

In every contract of membership of a trade union, whether made before or after the passing of this Act, a term conferring a right on the member, on giving reasonable notice and complying with any reasonable conditions, to terminate his membership of the union shall be implied.

Supplementary

70 Membership of constituent or affiliated organisation

In this Chapter 'member', in relation to a trade union consisting wholly or partly of, or of representatives of, constituent or affiliated organisations, includes a member of any of the constituent or affiliated organisations.

CHAPTER VA
COLLECTIVE BARGAINING: RECOGNITION

70A Recognition of trade unions

Schedule A1 shall have effect.

70B Training

(1) This section applies where—

(a) a trade union is recognised, in accordance with Schedule A1, as entitled to conduct collective bargaining on behalf of a bargaining unit (within the meaning of Part I of that Schedule), and

(b) a method for the conduct of collective bargaining is specified by the Central Arbitration Committee under paragraph 31(3) of that Schedule (and is not the subject of an agreement under paragraph 31(5)(a) or (b)).

(2) the employer must from time to time invite the trade union to send representatives to a meeting for the purpose of—

(a) consulting about the employer's policy on training for workers within the bargaining unit,

(b) consulting about his plans for training for those workers during the period of six months starting with the day of the meeting, and

(c) reporting about training provided for those workers since the previous meeting.

(3) The date set for a meeting under subsection (2) must not be later than—

(a) in the case of a first meeting, the end of the period of six months starting with the day on which this section first applies in relation to a bargaining unit, and

(b) in the case of each subsequent meeting, the end of the period of six months starting with the day of the previous meeting.

(4) The employer shall, before the period of two weeks ending with the date of a meeting, provide to the trade union any information—

(a) without which the union's representatives would be to a material extent impeded in participating in the meeting, and

(b) which it would be in accordance with good industrial relations practice to disclose for the purposes of the meeting.

(5) Section 182(1) shall apply in relation to the provision of information under subsection (4) as it applies in relation to the disclosure of information under section 181.

(6) The employer shall take account of any written representations about matters raised at a meeting which he receives from the trade union within the period of four weeks starting with the date of the meeting.

(7) Where more than one trade union is recognised as entitled to conduct collective bargaining on behalf of a bargaining unit, a reference in this section to 'the trade union' is a reference to each trade union.

(8) Where at a meeting under this section (Meeting 1) an employer indicates his intention to convene a subsequent meeting (Meeting 2) before the expiry of the period of six months beginning with the date of Meeting 1, for the reference to a period of six months in subsection (2)(b) there shall be substituted a reference to the expected period between Meeting 1 and Meeting 2.

(9)-(10) [omitted]

70C Section 70B: complaint to employment tribunal

(1) A trade union may present a complaint to an employment tribunal that an employer has failed to comply with his obligations under section 70B in relation to a bargaining unit.

(2) An employment tribunal shall not consider a complaint under this section unless it is presented—

(a) before the end of the period of three months beginning with the date of the alleged failure, or

(b) within such further period as the tribunal considers reasonable in a case where it is satisfied that it was not reasonably practicable for the complaint to be presented before the end of that period of three months.

(3) Where an employment tribunal finds a complaint under this section well-founded it—

(a) shall make a declaration to that effect, and

(b) may make an award of compensation to be paid by the employer to each person who was, at the time when the failure occurred, a member of the bargaining unit.

(4) The amount of the award shall not, in relation to each person, exceed two weeks' pay.

(5) For the purpose of subsection (4) a week's pay—

(a) shall be calculated in accordance with Chapter II of Part XIV of the Employment Rights Act 1996 (taking the date of the employer's failure as the calculation date), and

(b) shall be subject to the limit in section 227(1) of that Act.

(6) Proceedings for enforcement of an award of compensation under this section—

(a) may, in relation to each person to whom compensation is payable, be commenced by that person, and

(b) may not be commenced by a trade union.

CHAPTER VI
APPLICATION OF FUNDS FOR POLITICAL OBJECTS

Restriction on use of funds for certain political objects

71 Restriction on use of funds for political objects

(1) The funds of a trade union shall not be applied in the furtherance of the political objects to which this Chapter applies unless—

(a) there is in force in accordance with this Chapter a resolution (a 'political resolution') approving the furtherance of those objects as an object of the union (see section 73 to 81), and

(b) there are in force rules of the union as to—

(i) the making of payments in furtherance of those objects out of a separate fund, and

(ii) the exemption of any member of the union objecting to contribute to that fund,

which comply with this Chapter (see sections 82, 84 and 85) and have been approved by the Certification Officer.

(2) This applies whether the funds are so applied directly, or in conjunction with another trade union, association or body, or otherwise indirectly.

72 Political objects to which restriction applies

(1) The political objects to which this Chapter applies are the expenditure of money—

(a) on any contribution to the funds of, or on the payment of expenses incurred directly or indirectly by, a political party;

(b) on the provision of any service or property for use by or on behalf of any political party;

(c) in connection with the registration of electors, the candidature of any person, the selection of any candidate or the holding of any ballot by the union in connection with any election to a political office;

(d) on the maintenance of any holder of a political office;

(e) on the holding of any conference or meeting by or on behalf of a political party or of any other meeting the main purpose of which is the transaction of business in connection with a political party;

(f) on the production, publication or distribution of any literature, document, film, sound recording or advertisement the main purpose of which is to persuade people to vote for a political party or candidate or to persuade them not to vote for a political party or candidate.

(2) Where a person attends a conference or meeting as a delegate or otherwise as a participator in the proceedings, any expenditure incurred in connection with his attendance as such shall, for the purposes of subsection (1)(e), be taken to be expenditure incurred on the holding of the conference or meeting.

(3) In determining for the purposes of subsection (1) whether a trade union has incurred expenditure of a kind mentioned in that subsection, no account shall be taken of the ordinary administrative expenses of the union.

(4) In this section—

'candidate' means a candidate for election to a political office and includes a prospective candidate;

'contribution', in relation to the funds of a political party, includes any fee payable for affiliation to, or membership of, the party and any loan made to the party;

'electors' means electors at an election to a political office;

'film' includes any record, however made, of a sequence of visual images, which is capable of being used as a means of showing that sequence as a moving picture;

'local authority' means a local authority within the meaning of section 270 of the Local Government Act 1972 or section 235 of the Local Government (Scotland) Act 1973; and

'political office' means the office of member of Parliament, member of the European Parliament or member of a local authority or any position within a political party.

72A Application of funds in breach of section 71

(1) A person who is a member of a trade union and who claims that it has applied its funds in breach of section 71 may apply to the Certification Officer for a declaration that it has done so.

(2) On an application under this section the Certification Officer—

(a) shall make such enquiries as he thinks fit,

(b) shall give the applicant and the union an opportunity to be heard,

(c) shall ensure that, so far as is reasonably practicable, the application is determined within six months of being made,

(d) may make or refuse the declaration asked for,

(e) shall, whether he makes or refuses the declaration, give reasons for his decision in writing, and

(f) may make written observation on any matter arising from, or connected with, the proceedings.

(3) If he makes a declaration he shall specify in it—

(a) the provisions of section 71 breached, and

(b) the amount of the funds applied in breach.

(4) If he makes a declaration and is satisfied that the union has taken or agreed to take steps with a view to—

(a) remedying the declared breach, or

(b) securing that a breach of the same or any similar kind does not occur in future,

he shall specify those steps in making the declaration.

(5) If he makes a declaration he may make such order for remedying the breach as he thinks just under the circumstances.

(6) Where the Certification Officer requests a person to furnish information to him in connection with enquiries made by him under this section, he shall specify the date by which that information is to be furnished and, unless he considers that it would be inappropriate to do so, such proceed with his determination of the application notwithstanding that the information has not been furnished to him by the specified date.

(7) A declaration made by the Certification Officer under this section may be relied on as if it were a declaration made by the court.

(8) Where an order has been made under this section, any person who is a member of the union and was a member at the time it was made is entitled to enforce obedience to the order as if he had made the application on which the order was made.

(9) An order made by the Certification Officer under this section may be enforced in the same way as an order of the court.

(10) If a person applies to the Certification Officer under this section in relation to an alleged breach he may not apply to the court in relation to the breach; but nothing in this subsection shall prevent such a person from exercising any right to appeal against or challenge the Certification Officer's decision on the application to him.

(11) If—

(a) a person applies to the court in relation to an alleged breach, and

(b) the breach is one in relation to which he could have made an application to the Certification Officer under this section,

he may not apply to the Certification Officer under this section in relation to the breach.

Political resolution

73 Passing and effect of political resolution

(1) A political resolution must be passed by a majority of those voting on a ballot of the members of the trade union held in accordance with this Chapter.

(2) A political resolution so passed shall take effect as if it were a rule of the union and may be rescinded in the same manner and subject to the same provisions as such a rule.

(3) If not previously rescinded, a political resolution shall cease to have effect at the end of the period of ten years beginning with the date of the ballot on which it was passed.

(4) Where before the end of that period a ballot is held on a new political resolution, then—

(a) if the new resolution is passed, the old resolution shall be treated as rescinded, and

(b) if it is not passed, the old resolution shall cease to have effect at the end of the period of two weeks beginning with the date of the ballot.

74 Approval of political ballot rules

(1) A ballot on a political resolution must be held in accordance with rules of the trade union (its 'political ballot rules') approved by the Certification Officer.

(2) Fresh approval is required for the purposes of each ballot which it is proposed to hold, notwithstanding that the rules have been approved for the purposes of an earlier ballot.

(3) The Certification Officer shall not approve a union's political ballot rules unless he is satisfied that the requirements set out in—

section 75 (appointment of independent scrutineer),
section 76 (entitlement to vote),
section 77 (voting),
section 77A (counting of votes etc. by independent person), and
section 78 (scrutineer's report),

would be satisfied in relation to a ballot held by the union in accordance with the rules.

75 Appointment of independent scrutineer

(1) The trade union shall, before the ballot is held, appoint a qualified independent person ('the scrutineer') to carry out—

(a) the functions in relation to the ballot which are required under this section to be contained in his appointment; and

(b) such additional functions in relation to the ballot as may be specified in his appointment.

(2) A person is a qualified independent person in relation to a ballot if—

(a) he satisfies such conditions as may be specified for the purposes of this section by order of the Secretary of State or is himself so specified; and

(b) the trade union has no grounds for believing either that he will carry out any functions conferred on him in relation to the ballot otherwise than competently or that his independence in relation to the union, or in relation to the ballot, might reasonably be called into question.

An order under paragraph (a) shall be made by statutory instrument which shall be subject to annulment in pursuance of a resolution of either House of Parliament.

(3) The scrutineer's appointment shall require him—

(a) to be the person who supervises the production of the voting papers and (unless he is appointed under section 77A to undertake the distribution of the voting papers) their distribution and to whom the voting papers are returned by those voting;

(aa) to—

(i) inspect the register of names and addresses of the members of the trade union, or

(ii) examine the copy of the register as at the relevant date which is supplied to him in accordance with subsection (5A)(a),

whenever it appears to him appropriate to do so and, in particular, when the conditions specified in subsection (3A) are satisfied;

(b) to take such steps as appear to him to be appropriate for the purpose of enabling him to make his report (see section 78);

(c) to make his report to the trade union as soon as reasonably practicable after the last date for the return of voting papers; and

(d) to retain custody of all voting papers returned for the purposes of the ballot and the copy of the register supplied to him in accordance with subsection (5A)(a)—

(i) until the end of the period of one year beginning with the announcement by the union of the result of the ballot; and

(ii) if within that period an application is made under section 79 (complaint of failure to comply with ballot rules), until the Certification Officer or the court authorises him to dispose of the papers or copy.

(3A)-(8) [omitted]

76 Entitlement to vote

Entitlement to vote in the ballot shall be accorded equally to all members of the trade union.

77 Voting

(1) The method of voting must be by the marking of a voting paper by the person voting.

(2) Each voting paper must—

(a) state the name of the independent scrutineer and clearly specify the address to which, and the date by which, it is to be returned, and

(b) be given one of a series of consecutive whole numbers every one of which is used in giving a different number in that series to each voting paper printed or otherwise produced for the purposes of the ballot, and

(c) be marked with its number.

(3) Every person who is entitled to vote in the ballot must—

(a) be allowed to vote without interference from, or constraint imposed by, the union or any of its members, officials or employees, and

(b) so far as is reasonably practicable, be enabled to do so without incurring any direct cost to himself.

(4) So far as is reasonably practicable, every person who is entitled to vote in the ballot must—

(a) have a voting paper sent to him by post at his home address or another address which he has requested the trade union in writing to treat as his postal address, and

(b) be given a convenient opportunity to vote by post.

(5) The ballot shall be conducted so as to secure that—

(a) so far as is reasonably practicable, those voting do so in secret, and

(b) the votes given in the ballot are fairly and accurately counted.

For the purposes of paragraph (b) an inaccuracy in counting shall be disregarded if it is accidental and on a scale which could not affect the result of the ballot.

77A Counting of votes etc. by independent person

(1) The trade union shall ensure that—

(a) the storage and distribution of the voting papers for the purposes of the ballot, and

(b) the counting of the votes cast in the ballot,

are undertaken by one or more independent persons appointed by the union.

(2) A person is an independent person in relation to a ballot if—

(a) he is the scrutineer, or

(b) he is a person other than the scrutineer and the trade union has no grounds for believing either that he will carry out any functions conferred on him in relation to the ballot otherwise than competently or that his independence in relation to the union, or in relation to the ballot, might reasonably be called into question.

(3) An appointment under this section shall require the person appointed to carry out his functions so as to minimise the risk of any contravention of requirements imposed by or under any enactment or the occurrence of any unfairness or malpractice.

(4) The duty of confidentiality as respects the register is incorporated in an appointment under this section.

(5) Where the person appointed to undertake the counting of votes is not the scrutineer, his appointment shall require him to send the voting papers back to the scrutineer as soon as reasonably practicable after the counting has been completed.

(6) The trade union—

(a) shall ensure that nothing in the terms of an appointment under this section is such as to make it reasonable for any person to call into question the independence of the person appointed in relation to the union,

(b) shall ensure that a person appointed under this section duly carries out his functions and that there is no interference with his carrying out of those functions which would make it reasonable for any person to call into question the independence of the person appointed in relation to the union, and

(c) shall comply with all reasonable requests made by a person appointed under this section for the purposes of, or in connection with, the carrying out of his functions.

78 Scrutineer's report

(1) The scrutineer's report on the ballot shall state—

(a) the number of voting papers distributed for the purposes of the ballot,

(b) the number of voting papers returned to the scrutineer,

(c) the number of valid votes cast in the ballot for and against the resolution,

(d) the number of spoiled or otherwise invalid voting papers returned, and

(e) the name of the person (or of each of the persons) appointed under section 77A or, if no person was so appointed, that fact.

(2) The report shall also state whether the scrutineer is satisfied—

(a) that there are no reasonable grounds for believing that there was any contravention of a requirement imposed by or under any enactment in relation to the ballot,

(b) that the arrangements made (whether by him or any other person) with respect to the production, storage, distribution, return or other handling of the voting papers used in the ballot, and the arrangements for the counting of the votes, included all such security arrangements as were reasonably practicable for the purpose of minimising the risk that any unfairness or malpractice might occur, and

(c) that he has been able to carry out his functions without such interference as would make it reasonable for any person to call his independence in relation to the union into question;

and if he is not satisfied as to any of those matters, the report shall give particulars of his reasons for not being satisfied as to that matter.

(2A)-(6) [omitted]

79 Remedy for failure to comply with ballot rules: general

(1) The remedy for—

(a) the taking by a trade union of a ballot on a political resolution otherwise than in accordance with political ballot rules approved by the Certification Officer, or

(b) the failure of a trade union, in relation to a proposed ballot on a political resolution, to comply with the political ballot rules so approved,

is by way of application under section 80 (to the Certification Officer) or 81 (to the court).

(2) An application under those sections may be made only by a person who is a member of the trade union and, where the ballot has been held, was a member at the time when it was held.

References in those sections to a person having a sufficient interest are to such a person.

(3) No such application may be made after the end of the period of one year beginning with the day on which the union announced the result of the ballot.

80 Application to Certification Officer

(1) A person having a sufficient interest (see section 79(2)) who claims that a trade union—

(a) has held a ballot on a political resolution otherwise than in accordance with political ballot rules approved by the Certification Officer, or

(b) has failed in relation to a proposed ballot on a political resolution to comply with political ballot rules so approved,

may apply to the Certification Officer for a declaration to that effect.

(2) On an application being made to him, the Certification Officer shall—

(a) make such enquiries as he thinks fit, and

(b) give the applicant and the trade union an opportunity to be heard,

and may make or refuse the declaration asked for.

(3) If he makes a declaration he shall specify in it the provisions with which the trade union has failed to comply.

(4) Where he makes a declaration and is satisfied that steps have been taken by the union with a view to remedying the declared failure, or securing that a failure of the same or any similar kind does not occur in future, or that the union has agreed to take such steps, he shall in making the declaration specify those steps.

(5) Whether he makes or refuses a declaration, he shall give reasons for his decision in writing; and the reasons may be accompanied by written observations on any matter arising from, or connected with, the proceedings.

(5A) Where the Certification Officer makes a declaration he shall also, unless he considers that to do so would be inappropriate, make an enforcement order, that is, an order imposing on the union one or more of the following requirements—

(a) to secure the holding of a ballot in accordance with the order;

(b) to take such other steps to remedy the declared failure as may be specified in the order;

(c) to abstain from such acts as may be so specified with a view to securing that a failure of the same or a similar kind does not occur in future.

The Certification Officer shall in an order imposing any such requirement as is mentioned in paragraph (a) or (b) specify the period within which the union must comply with the requirements of the order.

(5B) Where the Certification Officer makes an order requiring the union to hold a fresh ballot, he shall (unless he considers that it would be inappropriate to do so in the particular circumstances of the case) require the ballot to be conducted in accordance with the union's political ballot rules and such other provisions as may be made by the order.

(5C) Where an enforcement order has been made, any person who is a member of the union and was a member at the time the order was made is entitled to enforce obedience to the order as if he had made the application on which the order was made.

(6) In exercising his functions under this section the Certification Officer shall ensure that, so far as is reasonably practicable, an application made to him is determined within six months of being made.

(7) Where he requests a person to furnish information to him in connection with enquiries made by him under this section, he shall specify the date by which that information is to be furnished and shall, unless he considers that it would be inappropriate to do so, proceed with his determination of the application notwithstanding that the information has not been furnished to him by the specified date.

(8) A declaration made by the Certification Officer under this section may be relied on as if it were a declaration made by the court.

(9) An enforcement order made by the Certification Officer under this section may be enforced in the same way as an order of the court.

(10) The following paragraphs have effect if a person applies under section 81 in relation to a matter—

(a) that person may not apply under this section in relation to that matter;

(b) on an application by a different person under this section in relation to that matter, the Certification Officer shall have due regard to any declaration, order, observations, or reasons made or given by the court regarding that matter and brought to the Certification Officer's notice.

81 Application to court

(1) A person having a sufficient interest (see section 79(2)) who claims that a trade union—

(a) has held a ballot on a political resolution otherwise than in accordance with political ballot rules approved by the Certification Officer, or

(b) has failed in relation to a proposed ballot on a political resolution to comply with political ballot rules so approved,

may apply to the court for a declaration to that effect.

(2) [repealed]

(3) If the court makes the declaration asked for, it shall specify in the declaration the provisions with which the trade union has failed to comply.

(4) Where the court makes a declaration it shall also, unless it considers that to do so would be inappropriate, make an enforcement order, that is, an order imposing on the union one or more of the following requirements—

(a) to secure the holding of a ballot in accordance with the order;

(b) to take such other steps to remedy the declared failure as may be specified in the order;

(c) to abstain from such acts as may be so specified with a view to securing that a failure of the same or a similar kind does not occur in future.

The court shall in an order imposing any such requirement as is mentioned in paragraph (a) or (b) specify the period within which the union must comply with the requirements of the order.

(5) Where the court makes an order requiring the union to hold a fresh ballot, the court shall (unless it considers that it would be inappropriate to do so in the particular circumstances of the case) require the ballot to be conducted in accordance with the union's political ballot rules and such other provisions as may be made by the order.

(6) Where an enforcement order has been made, any person who is a member of the union and was a member at the time the order was made is entitled to enforce obedience to the order as if he had made the application on which the order was made.

(7) Without prejudice to any other power of the court, the court may on an application under this section grant such interlocutory relief (in Scotland, such interim order) as it considers appropriate.

(8) The following paragraphs have effect if a person applies under section 80 in relation to a matter—

(a) that person may not apply under this section in relation to that matter;

(b) on an application by a different person under this section in relation to that matter, the court shall have due regard to any declaration, order, observations or reasons made or given by the Certification Officer regarding that matter and brought to the court's notice.

The political fund

82 Rules as to political fund

(1) The trade union's rules must provide—

(a) that payments in the furtherance of the political objects to which this Chapter applies shall be made out of a separate fund (the 'political fund' of the union);

(b) that a member of the union who gives notice in accordance with section 84 that he objects to contributing to the political fund shall be exempt from any obligation to contribute to it;

(c) that a member shall not by reason of being so exempt—

(i) be excluded from any benefits of the union, or

(ii) be placed in any respect either directly or indirectly under a disability or at a disadvantage as compared with other members of the union (except in relation to the control or management of the political fund); and

(d) that contribution to the political fund shall not be made a condition for admission to the union.

(2) A member of a trade union who claims that he is aggrieved by a breach of any rule made in pursuance of this section may complain to the Certification Officer.

(2A) On a complaint being made to him the Certification Officer shall make such enquiries as he thinks fit.

(3) Where, after giving the member and a representative of the union an opportunity of being heard, the Certification Officer considers that a breach has been committed, he may make such order for remedying the breach as he thinks just under the circumstances.

(3A) Where the Certification Officer requests a person to furnish information to him in connection with enquiries made by him under this section, he shall specify the date by which that information is to be furnished and, unless he considers that it would be inappropriate to do so, shall proceed with his determination of the application notwithstanding that the information has not been furnished to him by the specified date.

(4) Any such order, on being recorded in the county court or, in Scotland, the sheriff court, may be enforced in the same way as an order of that court.

83 Assets and liabilities of political fund

(1) There may be added to a union's political fund only—

(a) sums representing contributions made to the fund by members of the union or by any person other than the union itself, and

(b) property which accrues to the fund in the course of administering the assets of the fund.

(2) The rules of the union shall not be taken to require any member to contribute to the political fund at a time when there is no political resolution in force in relation to the union.

(3) No liability of a union's political fund shall be discharged out of any other fund of the union.

This subsection applies notwithstanding any term or condition on which the liability was incurred or that an asset of the other fund has been charged in connection with the liability.

84 Notice of objection to contributing to political fund.

(1) A member of a trade union may give notice in the following form, or in a form to the like effect, that he objects to contribute to the political fund:—

Name of Trade Union

POLITICAL FUND (EXEMPTION NOTICE)

I give notice that I object to contributing to the Political Fund of the Union, and am in consequence exempt, in manner provided by Chapter VI of Part I of the Trade Union and Labour Relations (Consolidation) Act 1992, from contributing to that fund.

A.B.
Address
day of 19

(2) On the adoption of a political resolution, notice shall be given to members of the union acquainting them—

(a) that each member has a right to be exempted from contributing to the union's political fund, and

(b) that a form of exemption notice can be obtained by or on behalf of a member either by application at or by post from—

(i) the head office or any branch office of the union, or

(ii) the office of the Certification Officer.

(3) The notice to members shall be given in accordance with rules of the union approved for the purpose by the Certification Officer, who shall have regard in each case to the existing practice and character of the union.

(4) On giving an exemption notice in accordance with this section, a member shall be exempt from contributing to the union's political fund—

(a) where the notice is given within one month of the giving of notice to members under subsection (2) following the passing of a political resolution on a ballot held at a time when no such resolution is in force, as from the date on which the exemption notice is given;

(b) in any other case, as from the 1 January next after the exemption notice is given.

(5) An exemption notice continues to have effect until it is withdrawn.

85 Manner of giving effect to exemptions

(1) Effect may be given to the exemption of members from contributing to the political fund of a union either—

(a) by a separate levy of contributions to that fund from the members who are not exempt, or

(b) by relieving members who are exempt from the payment of the whole or part of any periodical contribution required from members towards the expenses of the union.

(2) In the latter case, the rules shall provide—

(a) that relief shall be given as far as possible to all members who are exempt on the occasion of the same periodical payment, and

(b) for enabling each member of the union to know what portion (if any) of any periodical contribution payable by him is a contribution to the political fund.

Duties of employer who deducts union contributions

86 Certificate of exemption or objection to contributing to political fund

(1) If a member of a trade union which has a political fund certifies in writing to his employer that, or to the effect that—

(a) he is exempt from the obligation to contribute to the fund, or

(b) he has, in accordance with section 84, notified the union in writing of his objection to contributing to the fund,

the employer shall ensure that no amount representing a contribution to the political fund is deducted by him from emoluments payable to the member.

(2) The employer's duty under subsection (1) applies from the first day, following the giving of the certificate, on which it is reasonably practicable for him to comply with that subsection, until the certificate is withdrawn.

(3) An employer may not refuse to deduct any union does from emoluments payable to a person who has given a certificate under this section if he continues to deduct union dues from emoluments payable to other members of the union, unless his refusal is not attributable to the giving of the certificate or otherwise connected with the duty imposed by subsection (1).

87 Complaint in respect of employer's failure

(1) A person who claims his employer has failed to comply with section 86 in deducting or refusing to deduct any amount from emoluments payable to him may present a complaint to an employment tribunal.

(2) A tribunal shall not consider a complaint under subsection (1) unless it is presented—

(a) within the period of three months beginning with the date of the payment of the emoluments or (if the complaint relates to more than one payment) the last of the payments, or

(b) where the tribunal is satisfied that it was not reasonably practicable for the complaint to be presented within that period, within such further period as the tribunal considers reasonable.

(3) Where on a complaint under subsection (1) arising out of subsection (3) (refusal to deduct union dues) of section 86 the question arises whether the employer's refusal to deduct an amount was attributable to the giving of the certificate or was otherwise connected with the duty imposed by subsection (1) of that section, it is for the employer to satisfy the tribunal that it was not.

(4) Where a tribunal finds that a complaint under subsection (1) is well-founded—

(a) it shall make a declaration to that effect and, where the complaint arises out of subsection (1) of section 86, order the employer to pay to the complainant the amount deducted in contravention of that subsection less any part of that amount already paid to him by the employer, and

(b) it may, if it considers it appropriate to do so in order to prevent a repetition of the failure, make an order requiring the employer to take, within a specified time, the steps specified in the order in relation to emoluments payable by him to the complainant.

(5) A person who claims his employer has failed to comply with an order made under subsection (4)(b) on a complaint presented by him may present a further complaint to an employment tribunal; but only one complaint may be presented under this subsection in relation to any order.

(6) A tribunal shall not consider a complaint under subsection (5) unless it is presented—

(a) after the end of the period of four weeks beginning with the date of the order, but

(b) before the end of the period of six months beginning with that date.

(7) Where on a complaint under subsection (5) a tribunal finds that an employer has, without reasonable excuse, failed to comply with an order made under subsection (4)(b), it shall order the employer to pay to the complainant an amount equal to two weeks' pay.

(8) Chapter II of Part XIV of the Employment Rights Act 1996 (calculation of a week's pay) applies for the purposes of subsection (7) with the substitution for section 225 of the following—

For the purposes of this Chapter in its application to subsection (7) of section 87 of the Trade Union and Labour Relations (Consolidation) Act 1992, the calculation date is the date of the payment, or (if more than one) the last of the payments, to which the complaint related.

88 [repealed]

Position where political resolution ceases to have effect

89 Administration of political fund where no resolution in force

(1) The following provisions have effect with respect to the political fund of a trade union where there ceases to be any political resolution in force in relation to the union.

(2) If the resolution ceases to have effect by reason of a ballot being held on which a new political resolution is not passed, the union may continue to make payments out of the fund as if the resolution had continued in force for six months beginning with the date of the ballot.

But no payment shall be made which causes the fund to be in deficit or increases a deficit in it.

(3) There may be added to the fund only—

(a) contributions to the fund paid to the union (or to a person on its behalf) before the resolution ceased to have effect, and

(b) property which accrues to the fund in the course of administering the assets of the fund.

(4) The union may, notwithstanding any of its rules or any trusts on which the fund is held, transfer the whole or part of the fund to such other fund of the union as it thinks fit.

(5) If a new political resolution is subsequently passed, no property held immediately before the date of the ballot by or on behalf of the union otherwise than in its political fund, and no sums representing such property, may be added to the fund.

90 Discontinuance of contributions to political fund

(1) Where there ceases to be any political resolution in force in relation to a trade union, the union shall take such steps as are necessary to ensure that the collection of contributions to its political fund is discontinued as soon as is reasonably practicable.

(2) The union may, notwithstanding any of its rules, pay into any of its other funds any such contribution which is received by it after the resolution ceases to have effect.

(3) If the union continues to collect contributions, it shall refund to a member who applies for a refund the contributions made by him collected after the resolution ceased to have effect.

(4) A member of a trade union who claims that the union has failed to comply with subsection (1) may apply to the court for a declaration to that effect.

(5) Where the court is satisfied that the complaint is well-founded, it may, if it considers it appropriate to do so in order to secure that the collection of contributions to the political fund is discontinued, make an order requiring the union to take, within such time as may be specified in the order, such steps as may be so specified.

Such an order may be enforced by a person who is a member of the union and was a member at the time the order was made as if he had made the application.

(6) The remedy for failure to comply with subsection (1) is in accordance with subsections (4) and (5), and not otherwise; but this does not affect any right to recover sums payable to a person under subsection (3).

91 Rules to cease to have effect.

(1) If there ceases to be any political resolution in force in relation to a trade union, the rules of the union made for the purpose of complying with this Chapter also cease to have effect, except so far as they are required to enable the political fund to be administered at a time when there is no such resolution in force.

(2) If the resolution ceases to have effect by reason of a ballot being held on which a new political resolution is not passed, the rules cease to have effect at the end of the period of six months beginning with the date of the ballot.

In any other case the rules cease to have effect when the resolution ceases to have effect.

(3) Nothing in this section affects the operation of section 82(2) (complaint to Certification Officer in respect of breach of rules) in relation to a breach of a rule occurring before the rule in question ceased to have effect.

(4) No member of a trade union who has at any time been exempt from the obligation to contribute to its political fund shall by reason of his having been exempt—

(a) be excluded from any benefits of the union, or

(b) be placed in any respect either directly or indirectly under a disability or at a disadvantage as compared with other members (except in relation to the control or management of the political fund).

Supplementary

92 Manner of making union rules

If the Certification Officer is satisfied, and certifies, that rules of a trade union made for any of the purposes of this Chapter and requiring approval by him have been approved—

(a) by a majority of the members of the union voting for the purpose, or

(b) by a majority of delegates of the union at a meeting called for the purpose,

the rules shall have effect as rules of the union notwithstanding that the rules of the union as to the alteration of rules or the making of new rules have not been complied with.

93 Effect of amalgamation

(1) Where on an amalgamation of two or more trade unions—

(a) there is in force in relation to each of the amalgamating unions a political resolution and such rules as are required by this Chapter, and

(b) the rules of the amalgamated union in force immediately after the amalgamation include such rules as are required by this Chapter,

the amalgamated union shall be treated for the purposes of this Chapter as having passed a political resolution.

(2) That resolution shall be treated as having been passed on the date of the earliest of the ballots on which the resolutions in force immediately before the amalgamation with respect to the amalgamating unions were passed.

(3) Where one of the amalgamating unions is a Northern Ireland union, the references above to the requirements of this Chapter shall be construed as references to the requirements of the corresponding provisions of the law of Northern Ireland.

94 Overseas members of trade union

(1) Where a political resolution is in force in relation to the union—

(a) rules made by the union for the purpose of complying with section 74 (political ballot rules) in relation to a proposed ballot may provide for overseas members of the union not to be accorded entitlement to vote in the ballot, and

(b) rules made by the union for the purpose of complying with section 84 (notice f right to object to contribute to political fund to be given where resolution passed) may provide for notice not to be given by the union to its overseas members.

(2) Accordingly, where provision is made in accordance with subsection (1)(a), the Certification Officer shall not on that ground withhold his approval of the rules; and where provision is made in accordance with subsection (1)(b), section 84(2) (duty to give notice) shall not be taken to require notice to be given to overseas members.

(3) An 'overseas member' means a member of the trade union (other than a merchant seaman or offshore worker) who is outside Great Britain throughout the period during which votes may be cast.

For this purpose—

'merchant seaman' means a person whose employment, or the greater part of it, is carried out on board sea-going ships; and

'offshore worker' means a person in offshore employment, other than one who is in such employment in an area where the law of Northern Ireland applies.

95 Appeals from Certification Officer

An appeal lies to the Employment Appeal Tribunal on any question of law arising in proceedings before or arising from any decision of the Certification Officer under this Chapter.

96 Meaning of 'date of the ballot'

In this Chapter the 'date of the ballot' means, in the case of a ballot in which votes may be cast on more than one day, the last of those days.

97-108 [omitted]

CHAPTER VIIA
BREACH OF RULES

108A Right to apply to Certification Officer

(1) A person who claims that there has been a breach or threatened breach of the rules of a trade union relating to any of the matters mentioned in subsection (2) may apply to the Certification Officer for a declaration to that effect, subject to subsections (3) to (7).

(2) The matters are—

(a) the appointment or election of a person to, or the removal of a person from, any office;

(b) disciplinary proceedings by the union (including expulsion);

(c) the balloting of members on any issue other than industrial action;

(d) the constitution or proceedings of any executive committee or of any decision-making meeting;

(e) such other matters as may be specified in an order made by the Secretary of State.

(3) The applicant must be a member of the union, or have been one at the time of the alleged breach or threatened breach.

(4) A person may not apply under subsection (1) in relation to a claim if he is entitled to apply under section 80 in relation to the claim.

(5) No application may be made regarding—

(a) the dismissal of an employee of the union;

(b) disciplinary proceedings against an employee of the union.

(6) An application must be made—

(a) within the period of six months starting with the day on which the breach or threatened breach is alleged to have taken place, or

(b) if within that period any internal complaints procedure of the union is invoked to resolve the claim, within the period of six months starting with the earlier of the days specified in subsection (7).

(7) Those days are—

(a) the day on which the procedure is concluded, and

(b) the last day of the period of one year beginning with the day on which the procedure is invoked.

(8) The reference in subsection (1) to the rules of a union includes references to the rules of any branch or section of the union.

(9) In subsection (2)(c) 'industrial action' means a strike or other industrial action by persons employed under contracts of employment.

(10) For the purposes of subsection (2)(d) a committee is an executive committee if—

(a) it is a committee of the union concerned and has power to make executive decisions on behalf of the union or on behalf of a constituent body,

(b) it is a committee of a major constituent body and has power to make executive decisions on behalf of that body, or

(c) It is a sub-committee of a committee falling within paragraph (a) or (b).

(11) For the purposes of subsection (2)(d) a decision-making meeting is—

(a) a meeting of members of the union concerned (or the representatives of such members) which has power to make a decision on any matter which, under the rules of the union, is final as regards the union or which, under the rules of the union or a constituent body, is final as regards that body, or

(b) a meeting of members of a major constituent body (or the representatives of such members) which has power to make a decision on any matter which, under the rules of the union or the body, is final as regards that body.

(12) For the purposes of subsections (10) and (11), in relation to the trade union concerned—

(a) a constituent body is any body which forms part of the union, including a branch, group, section or region;

(b) a major constituent body is such a body which has more than 1,000 members.

(13) Any order under subsection (2)(e) shall be made by statutory instrument; and no such order shall be made unless a draft of it has been laid before and approved by resolution of each House of Parliament.

(14) If a person applies to the Certification Officer under this section in relation to an alleged breach or threatened breach he may not apply to the court in relation to the breach or threatened breach; but nothing in this subsection shall prevent such a person from exercising any right to appeal against or challenge the Certification Officer's decision on the application to him.

(15) If—

(a) a person applies to the court in relation to an alleged breach or threatened breach, and

(b) the breach or threatened breach is one in relation to which he could have made an application to the Certification Officer under this section,

he may not apply to the Certification Officer under this section in relation to the breach or threatened breach.

108B Declarations and orders

(1) The Certification Officer may refuse to accept an application under section 108A unless he is satisfied that the applicant has taken all reasonable steps to resolve the claim by the use of any internal complaints procedure of the union.

(2) If he accepts an application under section 108A the Certification Officer—

(a) shall make such enquiries as he thinks fit,

(b) shall give the applicant and the union an opportunity to be heard,

(c) shall ensure that, so far as is reasonably practicable, the application is determined within six months of being made,

(d) may make or refuse the declaration asked for, and

(e) shall, whether he makes or refuses the declaration, give reasons for his decision in writing.

(3) Where the Certification Officer makes a declaration he shall also, unless he considers that to do so would be inappropriate, make an enforcement order, that is, an order imposing on the union one or both of the following requirements—

(a) to take such steps to remedy the breach, or withdraw the threat of a breach, as may be specified in the order;

(b) to abstain from such acts as may be so specified with a view to securing that a breach or threat of the same or a similar kind does not occur in future.

(4) The Certification Officer shall in an order imposing any such requirement as is mentioned in subsection (3)(a) specify the period within which the union is to comply with the requirement.

(5) Where the Certification Officer requests a person to furnish information to him in connection with enquiries made by him under this section, he shall specify the date by which that information is to be furnished and, unless he considers that it would be inappropriate to do so, shall proceed with his determination of the application notwithstanding that the information has not been furnished to him by the specified date.

(6) A declaration made by the Certification Officer under this section may be relied on as if it were a declaration made by the court.

(7) Where an enforcement order has been made, any person who is a member of the union and was a member at the time it was made is entitled to enforce obedience to the order as if he had made the application on which the order was made.

(8) An enforcement order made by the Certification Officer under this section may be enforced in the same way as an order of the court.

(9) An order under section 108A(2)(e) may provide that, in relation to an application under section 108A with regard to a prescribed matter, the preceding provisions of this section shall apply with such omissions or modifications as may be specified in the order; and a prescribed matter is such matter specified under section 108A(2)(e) as is prescribed under this subsection.

108C Appeals from Certification Officer

An appeal lies to the Employment Appeal Tribunal on any question of law arising in proceedings before or arising from any decision of the Certification Officer under this Chapter.

109-114 [repealed]

CHAPTER IX
MISCELLANEOUS AND GENERAL PROVISIONS

115 and **116** [repealed]

Exceptions and adaptations for certain bodies

117 Special register bodies

(1) In this section a 'special register body' means an organisation whose name appeared in the special register maintained under section 84 of the Industrial Relations

Act 1971 immediately before 16 September 1974, and which is a company registered under the Companies Act 1985 or is incorporated by charter or letters patent.

(2) The provisions of this Part apply to special register bodies as to other trade unions, subject to the following exceptions and adaptations.

(3) In Chapter II (status and property of trade unions)—

(a) in section 10 (quasi-corporate status of trade unions)—

(i) subsections (1) and (2) (prohibition on trade union being incorporated) do not apply, and

(ii) subsection (3) (prohibition on registration under certain Acts) does not apply so far as it relates to registration as a company under the Companies Act 1985;

(b) section 11 (exclusion of common law rules as to restraint of trade) applies to the purposes or rules of a special register body only so far as they relate to the regulation of relations between employers or employers' associations and workers;

(c) sections 12 to 14 (vesting of property in trustees; transfer of securities) do not apply; and

(d) in section 20 (liability of trade union in certain proceedings in tort) in subsection (7) the reference to the contract between a member and the other members shall be construed as a reference to the contract between a member and the body.

(4) Sections 33 to 35 (appointment and removal of auditors) do not apply to a special register body which is registered as a company under the Companies Act 1985; and sections 36 and 37 (rights and duties of auditors) apply to the auditors appointed by such a body under Chapter V of Part XI of that Act.

(5) Sections 45B and 45C (disqualification) and Chapter IV (elections) apply only to—

(a) the position of voting member of the executive, and

(b) any position by virtue of which a person is a voting member of the executive.

In this subsection 'voting member of the executive' has the meaning given by section 46(5).

118 Federated trade unions

(1) In this section a 'federated trade union' means a trade union which consists wholly or mainly of constituent or affiliated organisations, or representatives of such organisations, as described in paragraph (b) of the definition of 'trade union' in section 1.

(2) The provisions of this Part apply to federated trade unions subject to the following exceptions and adaptations.

(3) For the purposes of section 22 (limit on amount of damages) as it applies to a federated trade union, the members of such of its constituent or affiliated organisations as have their head or main office in Great Britain shall be treated as members of the union.

(4) The following provisions of Chapter III (trade union administration) do not apply to a federated trade union which consists wholly or mainly of representatives of constituent or affiliated organisations—

(a) section 27 (duty to supply copy of rules),

(b) section 28 (duty to keep accounting records),

(c) sections 32 to 37 (annual return, statement for members, accounts and audit),

(ca) sections 37A to 37E (investigation of financial affairs), and

(d) sections 38 to 42 (members' superannuation schemes).

(5) Sections 29 to 31 (right of member to access to accounting records) do not apply to a federated trade union which has no members other than constituent or affiliated organisations or representatives of such organisations.

(6) Sections 24 to 26 (register of members' names and addresses) and Chapter IV (elections for certain trade union positions) do not apply to a federated trade union—

(a) if it has no individual members other than representatives of constituent or affiliated organisations, or

(b) if its individual members (other than such representatives) are all merchant seamen and a majority of them are ordinarily resident outside the United Kingdom.

For this purpose 'merchant seaman' means a person whose employment, or the greater part of it, is carried out on board sea-going ships.

(7) The provisions of Chapter VI (application of funds for political objects) apply to a trade union which is in whole or part an association or combination of other unions as if the individual members of the component unions were members of that union and not of the component unions.

But nothing in that Chapter prevents a component union from collecting contributions on behalf of the association or combination from such of its members as are not exempt from the obligation to contribute to the political fund of the association or combination.

Interpretation

119 Expressions relating to trade unions

In this Act, in relation to a trade union—

'agent' means a banker or solicitor of, or any person employed as an auditor by, the union or any branch or section of the union;

'branch or section', except where the context otherwise requires, includes a branch or section which is itself a trade union;

'executive' means the principal committee of the union exercising executive functions, by whatever name it is called;

'financial affairs' means affairs of the union relating to any fund which is applicable for the purposes of the union (including any fund of a branch or section of the union which is so applicable);

'general secretary' means the official of the union who holds the office of general secretary or, where there is no such office, holds an office which is equivalent, or (except in section 14(4)) the nearest equivalent, to that of general secretary;

'officer' includes—

(a) any member of the governing body of the union, and

(b) any trustee of any fund applicable for the purposes of the union;

'official' means—

(a) an officer of the union or of a branch or section of the union, or

(b) a person elected or appointed in accordance with the rules of the union to be a representative of its members or of some of them,

and includes a person so elected or appointed who is an employee of the same employer as the members or one or more of the members whom he is to represent;

'president' means the official of the union who holds the office of president or, where there is no such office, who holds an office which is equivalent, or (except in section 14(4) or Chapter IV) the nearest equivalent, to that of president; and

'rules', except where the context otherwise requires, includes the rules of any branch or section of the union.

120 Northern Ireland unions

In this Part a 'Northern Ireland union' means a trade union whose principal office is situated in Northern Ireland.

121 Meaning of 'the court'

In this Part 'the court' (except where the reference is expressed to be to the county court or sheriff court) means the High Court or the Court of Session.

PART II
EMPLOYERS' ASSOCIATIONS

Introductory

122 Meaning of 'employers' association'

(1) In this Act an 'employers' association' means an organisation (whether temporary or permanent)—

(a) which consists wholly or mainly of employers or individual owners of undertakings of one or more descriptions and whose principal purposes include the regulation of relations between employers of that description or those descriptions and workers or trade unions; or

(b) which consists wholly or mainly of—

(i) constituent or affiliated organisations which fulfil the conditions in paragraph (a) (or themselves consist wholly or mainly of constituent or affiliated organisations which fulfil those conditions), or

(ii) representatives of such constituent or affiliated organisations,

and whose principal purposes include the regulation of relations between employers and workers or between employers and trade unions, or the regulation of relations between its constituent or affiliated organisations.

(2) References in this Act to employers' associations include combinations of employers and employers' associations.

123-136 [omitted]

PART III
RIGHTS IN RELATION TO UNION MEMBERSHIP AND ACTIVITIES

Access to employment

137 Refusal of employment on grounds related to union membership

(1) It is unlawful to refuse a person employment—

(a) because he is, or is not, a member of a trade union, or

(b) because he is unwilling to accept a requirement—

(i) to take steps to become or cease to be, or to remain or not to become, a member of a trade union, or

(ii) to make payments or suffer deductions in the event of his not being a member of a trade union.

(2) A person who is thus unlawfully refused employment has a right of complaint to an employment tribunal.

(3) Where an advertisement is published which indicates, or might reasonably be understood as indicating—

(a) that employment to which the advertisement relates is open only to a person who is, or is not, a member of a trade union, or

(b) that any such requirement as is mentioned in subsection (1)(b) will be imposed in relation to employment to which the advertisement relates,

a person who does not satisfy that condition or, as the case may be, is unwilling to accept that requirement, and who seeks and is refused employment to which the advertisement relates, shall be conclusively presumed to have been refused employment for that reason.

(4) Where there is an arrangement or practice under which employment is offered only to persons put forward or approved by a trade union, and the trade union puts forward or approves only persons who are members of the union, a person who is not a member of the union and who is refused employment in pursuance of the arrangement or practice shall be taken to have been refused employment because he is not a member of the trade union.

(5) A person shall be taken to be refused employment if he seeks employment of any description with a person and that person—

(a) refuses or deliberately omits to entertain and process his application or enquiry, or

(b) causes him to withdraw or cease to pursue his application or enquiry, or

(c) refuses or deliberately omits to offer him employment of that description, or

(d) makes him an offer of such employment the terms of which are such as no reasonable employer who wished to fill the post would offer and which is not accepted, or

(e) makes him an offer of such employment but withdraws it or causes him not to accept it.

(6) Where a person is offered employment on terms which include a requirement that he is, or is not, a member of a trade union, or any such requirement as is mentioned in subsection (1)(b), and he does not accept the offer because he does not satisfy or, as the case may be, is unwilling to accept the requirement, he shall be treated as having been refused employment for that reason.

(7) Where a person may not be considered for appointment or election to an office in a trade union unless he is a member of the union, or of a particular branch or section of the union or of one of a number of particular branches or sections of the union, nothing in this section applies to anything done for the purpose of securing compliance with that condition although as holder of the office he would be employed by the union.

For this purpose an 'office' means any position—

(a) by virtue of which the holder is an official of the union, or

(b) to which Chapter IV of Part I applies (duty to hold elections).

(8) The provisions of this section apply in relation to an employment agency acting, or purporting to act, on behalf of an employer as in relation to an employer.

138 Refusal of service of employment agency on grounds related to union membership

(1) It is unlawful for an employment agency to refuse a person any of its services—

(a) because he is, or is not, a member of a trade union, or

(b) because he is unwilling to accept a requirement to take steps to become or cease to be, or to remain or not to become, a member of a trade union.

(2) A person who is thus unlawfully refused any service of an employment agency has a right of complaint to an employment tribunal.

(3) Where an advertisement is published which indicates, or might reasonably be understood as indicating—

(a) that any service of an employment agency is available only to a person who is, or is not, a member of a trade union, or

(b) that any such requirement as is mentioned in subsection (1)(b) will be imposed in relation to a service to which the advertisement relates,

a person who does not satisfy that condition or, as the case may be, is unwilling to accept that requirement, and who seeks to avail himself of and is refused that service, shall be conclusively presumed to have been refused it for that reason.

(4) A person shall be taken to be refused a service if he seeks to avail himself of it and the agency—

(a) refuses or deliberately omits to make the service available to him, or

(b) causes him not to avail himself of the service or to cease to avail himself of it, or

(c) does not provide the same service, on the same terms, as is provided to others.

(5) Where a person is offered a service on terms which include a requirement that he is, or is not, a member of a trade union, or any such requirement as is mentioned in subsection (1)(b), and he does not accept the offer because he does not satisfy or, as the case may be, is unwilling to accept that requirement, he shall be treated as having been refused the service for that reason.

139 Time limit for proceedings

(1) An employment tribunal shall not consider a complaint under section 137 or 138 unless it is presented to the tribunal—

(a) before the end of the period of three months beginning with the date of the conduct to which the complaint relates, or

(b) where the tribunal is satisfied that it was not reasonably practicable for the complaint to be presented before the end of that period, within such further period as the tribunal considers reasonable.

(2) The date of the conduct to which a complaint under section 137 relates shall be taken to be—

(a) in the case of an actual refusal, the date of the refusal;

(b) in the case of a deliberate omission—

(i) to entertain and process the complainant's application or enquiry, or

(ii) to offer employment,

the end of the period within which it was reasonable to except the employer to act;

(c) in the case of conduct causing the complainant to withdraw or cease to pursue his application or enquiry, the date of that conduct;

(d) in a case where an offer was made but withdrawn, the date when it was withdrawn;

(e) in any other case where an offer was made but not accepted, the date on which it was made.

(3) The date of the conduct to which a complaint under section 138 relates shall be taken to be—

(a) in the case of an actual refusal, the date of the refusal;

(b) in the case of a deliberate omission to make a service available, the end of the period within which it was reasonable to expect the employment agency to act;

(c) in the case of conduct causing the complainant not to avail himself of a service or to cease to avail himself of it, the date of that conduct;

(d) in the case of failure to provide the same service, on the same terms, as is provided to others, the date or last date on which the service in fact provided was provided.

140 Remedies

(1) Where the employment tribunal finds that a complaint under section 137 or 138 is well-founded, it shall make a declaration to that effect and may make such of the following as it considers just and equitable—

(a) an order requiring the respondent to pay compensation to the complainant of such amount as the tribunal may determine;

(b) a recommendation that the respondent take within a specified period action appearing to the tribunal to be practicable for the purpose of obviating or reducing the adverse effect on the complainant of any conduct to which the complaint relates.

(2) Compensation shall be assessed on the same basis as damages for breach of statutory duty and may include compensation for injury to feelings.

(3) If the respondent fails without reasonable justification to comply with a recommendation to take action, the tribunal may increase its award of compensation or, if it has not made such an award, make one.

(4) The total amount of compensation shall not exceed the limit for the time being imposed by section 124(1) of the Employment Rights Act 1996 (limit on compensation for unfair dismissal).

141 Complaint against employer and employment agency

(1) Where a person has a right of complaint against a prospective employer and against an employment agency arising out of the same facts, he may present a complaint against either of them or against them jointly.

(2) If a complaint is brought against one only, he or the complainant may request the tribunal to join or sist the other as a party to the proceedings.

The request shall be granted if it is made before the hearing of the complaint begins, but may be refused if it is made after that time; and no such request may be made after the tribunal has made its decision as to whether the complaint is well-founded.

(3) Where a complaint is brought against an employer and an employment agency jointly, or where it is brought against one and the other is joined or sisted as a party to the proceedings, and the tribunal—

(a) finds that the complaint is well-founded as against the employer and the agency, and

(b) makes an award of compensation,

it may order that the compensation shall be paid by the one or the other, or partly by one and partly by the other, as the tribunal may consider just and equitable in the circumstances.

142 Awards against third parties

(1) If in proceedings on a complaint under section 137 or 138 either the complainant or the respondent claims that the respondent was induced to act in the manner complained of by pressure which a trade union or other person exercised on him by calling, organising, procuring or financing a strike or other industrial action, or by threatening to do so, the complainant or the respondent may request the employment tribunal to direct that the person who he claims exercised the pressure be joined or sisted as a party to the proceedings.

(2) The request shall be granted if it is made before the hearing of the complaint begins, but may be refused if it is made after that time; and no such request may be made after the tribunal has made its decision as to whether the complaint is well-founded.

(3) Where a person has been so joined or sisted as a party to the proceedings and the tribunal—

(a) finds that the complaint is well-founded,

(b) makes an award of compensation, and

(c) also finds that the claim in subsection (1) above is well-founded,

it may order that the compensation shall be paid by the person joined instead of by the respondent, or partly by that person and partly by the respondent, as the tribunal may consider just and equitable in the circumstances.

(4) Where by virtue of section 141 (complaint against employer and employment agency) there is more than one respondent, the above provisions apply to either or both of them.

143 Interpretation and other supplementary provisions

(1) In sections 137 to 143—

'advertisement' includes every form of advertisement or notice, whether to the public or not, and references to publishing an advertisement shall be construed accordingly;

'employment' means employment under a contract of employment, and related expressions shall be construed accordingly; and

'employment agency' means a person who, for profit or not, provides services for the purpose of finding employment for workers or supplying employers with workers, but subject to subsection (2) below.

(2) For the purposes of sections 137 to 143 as they apply to employment agencies—

(a) services other than those mentioned in the definition of 'employment agency' above shall be disregarded, and

(b) a trade union shall not be regarded as an employment agency by reason of services provided by it only for, or in relation to, its members.

(3) References in sections 137 to 143 to being or not being a member of a trade union are to being or not being a member of any trade union, of a particular trade union or of one of a number of particular trade unions.

Any such reference includes a reference to being or not being a member of a particular branch or section of a trade union or of one of a number of particular branches or sections of a trade union.

(4) The remedy of a person for conduct which is unlawful by virtue of section 137 or 138 is by way of a complaint to an employment tribunal in accordance with this Part, and not otherwise.

No other legal liability arises by reason that conduct is unlawful by virtue of either of those sections.

Contracts for supply of goods or services

144 Union membership requirement in contract for goods or services void

A term or condition of a contract for the supply of goods or services is void in so far as it purports to require that the whole, or some part, of the work done for the purposes of the contract is done only by persons who are, or are not, members of trade unions or of a particular trade union.

145 Refusal to deal on union membership grounds prohibited

(1) A person shall not refuse to deal with a supplier or prospective supplier of goods or services on union membership grounds.

'Refuse to deal' and 'union membership grounds' shall be construed as follows.

(2) A person refuses to deal with a person if, where he maintains (in whatever form) a list of approved suppliers of goods or services, or of persons from whom tenders for the supply of goods or services may be invited, he fails to include the name of that person in that list.

He does so on union membership grounds if the ground, or one of the grounds, for failing to include his name is that if that person were to enter into a contract with him for the supply of goods or services, work to be done for the purposes of the contract would, or would be likely to, be done by persons who were, or who were not, members of trade unions or of a particular trade union.

(3) A person refuses to deal with a person if, in relation to a proposed contract for the supply of goods or services—

(a) he excludes that person from the group of persons from whom tenders for the supply of the goods or services are invited, or

(b) he fails to permit that person to submit such a tender, or

(c) he otherwise determines not to enter into a contract with that person for the supply of the goods or services.

He does so on union membership grounds if the ground, or one of the grounds, on which he does so is that if the proposed contract were entered into with that person, work to be done for the purposes of the contract would, or would be likely to, be done by persons who were, or who were not, members of trade unions or of a particular trade union.

(4) A person refuses to deal with a person if he terminates a contract with him for the supply of goods or services.

He does so on union membership grounds if the ground, or one of the grounds, on which he does so is that work done, or to be done, for the purposes of the contract has been, or is likely to be, done by persons who are or are not members of trade unions or of a particular trade union.

(5) The obligation to comply with this section is a duty owed to the person with whom there is a refusal to deal and to any other person who may be adversely affected

by its contravention; and a breach of the duty is actionable accordingly (subject to the defences and other incidents applying to actions for breach of statutory duty).

Action short of dismissal

146 Action short of dismissal on grounds related to union membership or activities

(1) An employee has the right not to be subjected to any detriment as an individual by any act, or any deliberate failure to act, by his employer if the act or failure takes place for the purpose of—

(a) preventing or deterring him from being or seeking to become a member of an independent trade union, or penalising him for doing so,

(b) preventing or deterring him from taking part in the activities of an independent trade union at an appropriate time, or penalising him for doing so, or

(c) compelling him to be or become a member of any trade union or of a particular trade union or of one of a number of particular trade unions.

(2) In subsection (1)(b) 'an appropriate time' means—

(a) a time outside the employee's working hours, or

(b) a time within his working hours at which, in accordance with arrangements agreed with or consent given by his employer, it is permissible for him to take part in the activities of a trade union;

and for this purpose 'working hours', in relation to an employee, means any time when, in accordance with his contract of employment, he is required to be at work.

(3) An employee also has the right not to be subjected to any detriment as an individual by any act, or any deliberate failure to act, by his employer if the act or failure takes place for the purpose of enforcing a requirement (whether or not imposed by his contract of employment or in writing) that, in the event of his not being a member of any trade union or of a particular trade union or of one of a number of particular trade unions, he must make one or more payments.

(4) For the purposes of subsection (3) any deduction made by an employer from the remuneration payable to an employee in respect of his employment shall, if it is attributable to his not being a member of any trade union or of a particular trade union or of one of a number of particular trade unions, be treated as a detriment to which he has been subjected as an individual by an act of his employer taking place for the purpose of enforcing a requirement of a kind mentioned in that subsection.

(5) An employee may present a complaint to an employment tribunal on the ground that he has been subjected to a detriment by his employer in contravention of this section.

(6) For the purposes of this section detriment is detriment short of dismissal.

147 Time limit for proceedings

(1) An employment tribunal shall not consider a complaint under section 146 unless it is presented—

(a) before the end of the period of three months beginning with the date of the act or failure to which the complaint relates or, where that act or failure is part of a series of similar acts or failures (or both) the last of them, or

(b) where the tribunal is satisfied that it was not reasonably practicable for the complaint to be presented before the end of that period, within such further period as it considers reasonable.

(2) For the purposes of subsection (1)—

(a) where an act extends over a period, the reference to the date of the act is a reference to the last day of that period;

(b) a failure to act shall be treated as done when it was decided on.

(3) For the purposes of subsection (2), in the absence of evidence establishing the contrary an employer shall be taken to decide on a failure to act—

(a) when he does an act inconsistent with doing the failed act, or

(b) if he has done no such inconsistent act, when the period expires within which he might reasonably have been expected to do the failed act if it was to be done.

148 Consideration of complaint

(1) On a complaint under section 146 it shall be for the employer to show the purpose for which he acted or failed to act.

(2) In determining any question whether the employer acted or failed to act, or the purpose for which he did so, no account shall be taken of any pressure which was exercised on him by calling, organising, procuring or financing a strike or other industrial action, or by threatening to do so; and that question shall be determined as if no such pressure had been exercised.

(3) In determining what was the purpose for which the employer acted or failed to act in a case where—

(a) there is evidence that the employer's purpose was to further a change in his relationship with all or any class of his employees, and

(b) there is also evidence that his purpose was one falling within section 146,

the tribunal shall regard the purpose mentioned in paragraph (a) (and not the purpose mentioned in paragraph (b)) as the purpose for which the employer acted or failed to act, unless it considers that no reasonable employer would act or fail to act in the way concerned having regard to the purpose mentioned in paragraph (a).

(4) Where the tribunal determines that—

(a) the complainant has been subjected to a detriment by an act or deliberate failure to act by his employer, and

(b) the act or failure took place in consequence of a previous act or deliberate failure to act by the employer,

paragraph (a) of subsection (3) is satisfied if the purpose mentioned in that paragraph was the purpose of the previous act or failure.

(5) In subsection (3) 'class', in relation to an employer and his employees, means those employed at a particular place of work, those employees of a particular grade, category or description or those of a particular grade, category or description employed at a particular place of work.

149 Remedies

(1) Where the employment tribunal finds that a complaint under section 146 is well-founded, it shall make a declaration to that effect and may make an award of compensation to be paid by the employer to the complainant in respect of the act or failure complained of.

(2) The amount of the compensation awarded shall be such as the tribunal considers just and equitable in all the circumstances having regard to the infringement complained of and to any loss sustained by the complainant which is attributable to the act or failure which infringed his right.

(3) The loss shall be taken to include—

(a) any expenses reasonably incurred by the complainant in consequence of the act or failure complained of, and

(b) loss of any benefit which he might reasonably be expected to have had but for that act or failure.

(4) In ascertaining the loss, the tribunal shall apply the same rule concerning the duty of a person to mitigate his loss as applies to damages recoverable under the common law of England and Wales or Scotland.

(5) In determining the amount of compensation to be awarded no account shall be taken of any pressure which was exercised on the employer by calling, organising,

procuring or financing a strike or other industrial action, or by threatening to do so; and that question shall be determined as if no such pressure had been exercised.

(6) Where the tribunal finds that the act or failure complained of was to any extent caused or contributed to by action of the complainant, it shall reduce the amount of the compensation by such proportion as it considers just and equitable having regard to that finding.

150 Awards against third parties

(1) If in proceedings on a complaint under section 146—

(a) the complaint is made on the ground that the complainant has been subjected to detriment by an act or failure by his employer taking place for the purpose of compelling him to be or become a member of any trade union or of a particular trade union or of one of a number of particular trade unions, and

(b) either the complainant or the employer claims in proceedings before the tribunal that the employer was induced to act or fail to act in the way complained of by pressure which a trade union or other person exercised on him by calling, organising, procuring or financing a strike or other industrial action, or by threatening to do so,

the complainant or the employer may request the tribunal to direct that the person who he claims exercised the pressure be joined or sisted as a party to the proceedings.

(2) The request shall be granted if it is made before the hearing of the complaint begins, but may be refused if it is made after that time; and no such request may be made after the tribunal has made a declaration that the complaint is well-founded.

(3) Where a person has been so joined or sisted as a party to proceedings and the tribunal—

(a) makes an award of compensation, and

(b) finds that the claim mentioned in subsection (1)(b) is well-founded,

it may order that the compensation shall be paid by the person joined instead of by the employer, or partly by that person and partly by the employer, as the tribunal may consider just and equitable in the circumstances.

151 Interpretation and other supplementary provisions

(1) References in sections 146 to 150 to being, becoming or ceasing to remain a member of a trade union include references to being, becoming or ceasing to remain a member of a particular branch or section of that union and to being, becoming or ceasing to remain a member of one of a number of particular branches or sections of that union; and references to taking part in the activities of a trade union shall be similarly construed.

(2) The remedy of an employee for infringement of the right conferred on him by section 146 is by way of a complaint to an employment tribunal in accordance with this Part, and not otherwise.

Dismissal

152 Dismissal on grounds related to union membership or activities

(1) For purposes of Part X of the Employment Rights Act 1996 (unfair dismissal) the dismissal of an employee shall be regarded as unfair if the reason for it (or, if more than one, the principal reason) was that the employee—

(a) was, or proposed to become, a member of an independent trade union, or

(b) had taken part, or proposed to take part, in the activities of an independent trade union at an appropriate time, or

(c) was not a member of any trade union, or of a particular trade union, or of one of a number of particular trade unions, or had refused, or proposed to refuse, to become or remain a member.

(2) In subsection (1)(b) 'an appropriate time' means—

(a) a time outside the employee's working hours, or

(b) a time within his working hours at which, in accordance with arrangements agreed with or consent given by his employer, it is permissible for him to take part in the activities of a trade union;

and for this purpose 'working hours', in relation to an employee, means any time when, in accordance with his contract of employment, he is required to be at work.

(3) Where the reason, or one of the reasons, for the dismissal was—

(a) the employee's refusal, or proposed refusal, to comply with a requirement (whether or not imposed by his contract of employment or in writing) that, in the event of his not being a member of any trade union, or of a particular trade union, or of one of a number of particular trade unions, he must make one or more payments, or

(b) his objection, or proposed objection, (however expressed) to the operation of a provision (whether or not forming part of his contract of employment or in writing) under which, in the event mentioned in paragraph (a), his employer is entitled to deduct one or more sums from the remuneration payable to him in respect of his employment,

the reason shall be treated as falling within subsection (1)(c).

(4) References in this section to being, becoming or ceasing to remain a member of a trade union include references to being, becoming or ceasing to remain a member of a particular branch or section of that union or of one of a number of particular branches or sections of that trade union; and references to taking part in the activities of a trade union shall be similarly construed.

153 Selection for redundancy on grounds related to union membership or activities

Where the reason or principal reason for the dismissal of an employee was that he was redundant, but it is shown—

(a) that the circumstances constituting the redundancy applied equally to one or more other employees in the same undertaking who held positions similar to that held by him and who have not been dismissed by the employer, and

(b) that the reason (or, if more than one, the principal reason) why he was selected for dismissal was one of those specified in section 152(1),

the dismissal shall be regarded as unfair for the purposes of Part X of the Employment Rights Act 1996 (unfair dismissal).

154 Exclusion of requirement as to qualifying period, &c.

(1) Sections 108 and 109 of the Employment Rights Act 1996 (qualifying period and upper age limit for unfair dismissal protection) do not apply to the dismissal of an employee if it is shown that the reason or principal reason for the dismissal or, in a redundancy case, for selecting the employee for dismissal, was an inadmissible reason.

(2) For the purposes of this section—

'inadmissible', in relation to a reason, means that it is one of those specified in section 152(1); and

'a redundancy case' means a case where the reason or principal reason for the dismissal was that the employee was redundant but the equal application of the circumstances to non-dismissed employees required by section 153(a) is also shown.

155 Matters to be disregarded in assessing contributory fault

(1) Where an employment tribunal makes an award of compensation for unfair dismissal in a case where the dismissal is unfair by virtue of section 152 or 153, the tribunal shall disregard, in considering whether it would be just and equitable to reduce, or further reduce, the amount of any part of the award, any such conduct or action of the complainant as is specified below.

(2) Conduct or action of the complainant shall be disregarded in so far as it constitutes a breach or proposed breach of a requirement—

(a) to be or become a member of any trade union or of a particular trade union or of one of a number of particular trade unions,

(b) to cease to be, or refrain from becoming, a member of any trade union or of a particular trade union or of one of a number of particular trade unions, or

(c) not to take part in the activities of any trade union or of a particular trade union or of one of a number of particular trade unions.

For the purposes of this subsection a requirement means a requirement imposed on the complainant by or under an arrangement or contract of employment or other agreement.

(3) Conduct or action of the complainant shall be disregarded in so far as it constitutes a refusal, or proposed refusal, to comply with a requirement of a kind mentioned in section 152(3)(a) (payments in lieu of membership) or an objection, or proposed objection, (however expressed) to the operation of a provision of a kind mentioned in section 152(3)(b) (deductions in lieu of membership).

156 Minimum basic award

(1) Where a dismissal is unfair by virtue of section 152(1) or 153, the amount of the basic award of compensation, before any reduction is made under section 122 of the Employment Rights Act 1996 shall be not less than £2,900.

(2) But where the dismissal is unfair by virtue of section 153, subsection (2) of that section (reduction for contributory fault) applies in relation to so much of the basic award as is payable because of subsection (1) above.

157-159 [repealed]

160 Awards against third parties

(1) If in proceedings before an employment tribunal on a complaint of unfair dismissal either the employer or the complainant claims—

(a) that the employer was induced to dismiss the complainant by pressure which a trade union or other person exercised on the employer by calling, organising, procuring or financing a strike or other industrial action, or by threatening to do so, and

(b) that the pressure was exercised because the complainant was not a member of any trade union or of a particular trade union or of one of a number of particular trade unions,

the employer or the complainant may request the tribunal to direct that the person who he claims exercised the pressure be joined or sisted as a party to the proceedings.

(2) The request shall be granted if it is made before the hearing of the complaint begins, but may be refused after that time; and no such request may be made after the tribunal has made an award of compensation for unfair dismissal or an order for reinstatement or re-engagement.

(3) Where a person has been so joined or sisted as a party to the proceedings and the tribunal—

(a) makes an award of compensation for unfair dismissal, and

(b) finds that the claim mentioned in subsection (1) is well-founded,

the tribunal may order that the compensation shall be paid by that person instead of the employer, or partly by that person and partly by the employer, as the tribunal may consider just and equitable.

161 Application for interim relief

(1) An employee who presents a complaint of unfair dismissal alleging that the dismissal is unfair by virtue of section 152 may apply to the tribunal for interim relief.

(2) The tribunal shall not entertain an application for interim relief unless it is presented to the tribunal before the end of the period of seven days immediately following the effective date of termination (whether before, on or after that date).

(3) In a case where the employee relies on section 152(1)(a) or (b) the tribunal shall not entertain an application for interim relief unless before the end of that period there is also so presented a certificate in writing signed by an authorised official of the independent trade union of which the employee was or proposed to become a member stating—

(a) that on the date of the dismissal the employee was or proposed to become a member of the union, and

(b) that there appear to be reasonable grounds for supposing that the reason for his dismissal (or, if more than one, the principal reason) was one alleged in the complaint.

(4) An 'authorised official' means an official of the trade union authorised by it to act for the purposes of this section.

(5) A document purporting to be an authorisation of an official by a trade union to act for the purposes of this section and to be signed on behalf of the union shall be taken to be such an authorisation unless the contrary is proved; and a document purporting to be a certificate signed by such an official shall be taken to be signed by him unless the contrary is proved.

(6) For the purposes of subsection (3) the date of dismissal shall be taken to be—

(a) where the employee's contract of employment was terminated by notice (whether given by his employer or by him), the date on which the employer's notice was given, and

(b) in any other case, the effective date of termination.

162 Application to be promptly determined

(1) An employment tribunal shall determine an application for interim relief as soon as practicable after receiving the application and, where appropriate, the requisite certificate.

(2) The tribunal shall give to the employer, not later than seven days before the hearing, a copy of the application and of any certificate, together with notice of the date, time and place of the hearing.

(3) If a request under section 160 (awards against third parties) is made three days or more before the date of the hearing, the tribunal shall also give to the person to whom the request relates, as soon as reasonably practicable, a copy of the application and of any certificate, together with notice of the date, time and place of the hearing.

(4) The tribunal shall not exercise any power it has of postponing the hearing of an application for interim relief except where it is satisfied that special circumstances exist which justify it in doing so.

163 Procedure on hearing of application and making of order

(1) If on hearing an application for interim relief it appears to the tribunal that it is likely that on determining the complaint to which the application relates that it will find that, by virtue of section 152, the complainant has been unfairly dismissed, the following provisions apply.

(2) The tribunal shall announce its findings and explain to both parties (if present) what powers the tribunal may exercise on the application and in what circumstances it will exercise them, and shall ask the employer (if present) whether he is willing, pending the determination or settlement of the complaint—

(a) to reinstate the employee, that is to say, to treat him in all respects as if he had not been dismissed, or

(b) if not, to re-engage him in another job on terms and conditions not less favourable than those which would have been applicable to him if he had not been dismissed.

(3) For this purpose 'terms and conditions not less favourable than those which would have been applicable to him if he had not been dismissed' means as regards

seniority, pension rights and other similar rights that the period prior to the dismissal shall be regarded as continuous with his employment following the dismissal.

(4) If the employer states that he is willing to reinstate the employee, the tribunal shall make an order to that effect.

(5) If the employer states that he is willing to re-engage the employee in another job, and specifies the terms and conditions on which he is willing to do so, the tribunal shall ask the employee whether he is willing to accept the job on those terms and conditions; and—

(a) if the employee is willing to accept the job on those terms and conditions, the tribunal shall make an order to that effect, and

(b) if he is not, then, if the tribunal is of the opinion that the refusal is reasonable, the tribunal shall make an order for the continuation of his contract of employment, and otherwise the tribunal shall make no order.

(6) If on the hearing of an application for interim relief the employer fails to attend before the tribunal, or states that he is unwilling either to reinstate the employee or re-engage him as mentioned in subsection (2), the tribunal shall make an order for the continuation of the employee's contract of employment.

164 Order for continuation of contract of employment

(1) An order under section 163 for the continuation of a contract of employment is an order that the contract of employment continue in force—

(a) for the purposes of pay or any other benefit derived from the employment, seniority, pension rights and other similar matters, and

(b) for the purpose of determining for any purpose the period for which the employee has been continuously employed,

from the date of its termination (whether before or after the making of the order) until the determination or settlement of the complaint.

(2) Where the tribunal makes such an order it shall specify in the order the amount which is to be paid by the employer to the employee by way of pay in respect of each normal pay period, or part of any such period, falling between the date of dismissal and the determination or settlement of the complaint.

(3) Subject as follows, the amount so specified shall be that which the employee could reasonably have been expected to earn during that period, or part, and shall be paid—

(a) in the case of payment for any such period falling wholly or partly after the making of the order, on the normal pay day for that period, and

(b) in the case of a payment for any past period, within such time as may be specified in the order.

(4) If an amount is payable in respect only of part of a normal pay period, the amount shall be calculated by reference to the whole period and reduced proportionately.

(5) Any payment made to an employee by an employer under his contract of employment, or by way of damages for breach of that contract, in respect of a normal pay period or part of any such period shall go towards discharging the employer's liability in respect of that period under subsection (2); and conversely any payment under that subsection in respect of a period shall go towards discharging any liability of the employer under, or in respect of the breach of, the contract of employment in respect of that period.

(6) If an employee, on or after being dismissed by his employer, receives a lump sum which, or part of which, is in lieu of wages but is not referable to any normal pay period, the tribunal shall take the payment into account in determining the amount of pay to be payable in pursuance of any such order.

(7) For the purposes of this section the amount which an employee could reasonably have been expected to earn, his normal pay period and the normal pay day for each such period shall be determined as if he had not been dismissed.

165 Application for variation or revocation of order

(1) At any time between the making of an order under section 163 and the determination or settlement of the complaint, the employer or the employee may apply to an employment tribunal for the revocation or variation of the order on the ground of a relevant change of circumstances since the making of the order.

(2) Sections 161 to 163 apply in relation to such an application as in relation to an original application for interim relief, except that—

(a) no certificate need be presented to the tribunal under section 161(3), and

(b) in the case of an application by the employer, section 162(2) (service of copy of application and notice of hearing) has effect with the substitution of a reference to the employee for the reference to the employer.

166 Consequences of failure to comply with order

(1) If on the application of an employee an employment tribunal is satisfied that the employer has not complied with the terms of an order for the reinstatement or re-engagement of the employee under section 163(4) or (5), the tribunal shall—

(a) make an order for the continuation of the employee's contract of employment, and

(b) order the employer to pay the employee such compensation as the tribunal considers just and equitable in all the circumstances having regard—

(i) to the infringement of the employee's right to be reinstated or re-engaged in pursuance of the order, and

(ii) to any loss suffered by the employee in consequence of the non-compliance.

(2) Section 164 applies to an order under subsection (1)(a) as in relation to an order under section 163.

(3) If on the application of an employee an employment tribunal is satisfied that the employer has not complied with the terms of an order for the continuation of a contract of employment, the following provisions apply.

(4) If the non-compliance consists of a failure to pay an amount by way of pay specified in the order, the tribunal shall determine the amount owed by the employer on the date of the determination.

If on that date the tribunal also determines the employee's complaint that he has been unfairly dismissed, it shall specify that amount separately from any other sum awarded to the employee.

(5) In any other case, the tribunal shall order the employer to pay the employee such compensation as the tribunal considers just and equitable in all the circumstances having regard to any loss suffered by the employee in consequence of the non-compliance.

167 Interpretation and other supplementary provisions

(1) Part X of the Employment Rights Act 1996 (unfair dismissal) has effect subject to the provisions of sections 152 to 166 above.

(2) Those sections shall be construed as one with that Part; and in those sections—

'complaint of unfair dismissal' means a complaint under section 111 of the Employment Rights Act 1996;

'award of compensation for unfair dismissal' means an award of compensation for unfair dismissal under section 112(4) or 117(3)(a) of that Act; and

'order for reinstatement or re-engagement' means an order for reinstatement or re-engagement under section 113 of that Act.

(3) Nothing in those sections shall be construed as conferring a right to complain of unfair dismissal from employment of a description to which that Part does not otherwise apply.

Time off for trade union duties and activities

168 Time off for carrying out trade union duties

(1) An employer shall permit an employee of his who is an official of an independent trade union recognised by the employer to take time off during his working hours for the purpose of carrying out any duties of his, as such an official, concerned with—

(a) negotiations with the employer related to or connected with matters falling within section 178(2) (collective bargaining) in relation to which the trade union is recognised by the employer, or

(b) the performance on behalf of employees of the employer of functions related to or connected with matters falling within that provision which the employer has agreed may be so performed by the trade union, or

(c) receipt of information from the employer and consultation by the employer under section 188 (redundancies) or under the Transfer of Undertakings (Protection of Employment) Regulations 1981.

(2) He shall also permit such an employee to take time off during his working hours for the purpose of undergoing training in aspects of industrial relations—

(a) relevant to the carrying out of such duties as are mentioned in subsection (1), and

(b) approved by the Trades Union Congress or by the independent trade union of which he is an official.

(3) The amount of time off which an employee is to be permitted to take under this section and the purposes for which, the occasions on which and any conditions subject to which time off may be so taken are those that are reasonable in all the circumstances having regard to any relevant provisions of a Code of Practice issued by ACAS.

(4) An employee may present a complaint to an employment tribunal that his employer has failed to permit him to take time off as required by this section.

169 Payment for time off under section 168

(1) An employer who permits an employee to take time off under section 168 shall pay him for the time taken off pursuant to the permission.

(2) Where the employee's remuneration for the work he would ordinarily have been doing during that time does not vary with the amount of work done, he shall be paid as if he had worked at that work for the whole of that time.

(3) Where the employee's remuneration for the work he would ordinarily have been doing during that time varies with the amount of work done, he shall be paid an amount calculated by reference to the average hourly earnings for that work.

The average hourly earnings shall be those of the employee concerned or, if no fair estimate can be made of those earnings, the average hourly earnings for work of that description of persons in comparable employment with the same employer or, if there are no such persons, a figure of average hourly earnings which is reasonable in the circumstances.

(4) A right to be paid an amount under this section does not affect any right of an employee in relation to remuneration under his contract of employment, but—

(a) any contractual remuneration paid to an employee in respect of a period of time off to which this section applies shall go towards discharging any liability of the employer under this section in respect of that period, and

(b) any payment under this section in respect of a period shall go towards discharging any liability of the employer to pay contractual remuneration in respect of that period.

(5) An employee may present a complaint to an employment tribunal that his employer has failed to pay him in accordance with this section.

170 Time off for trade union activities

(1) An employer shall permit an employee of his who is a member of an independent trade union recognised by the employer in respect of that description of employee to take time off during his working hours for the purpose of taking part in—

(a) any activities of the union, and

(b) any activities in relation to which the employee is acting as a representative of the union.

(2) The right conferred by subsection (1) does not extend to activities which themselves consist of industrial action, whether or not in contemplation or furtherance of a trade dispute.

(3) The amount of time off which an employee is to be permitted to take under this section and the purposes for which, the occasions on which and any conditions subject to which time off may be so taken are those that are reasonable in all the circumstances having regard to any relevant provisions of a Code of Practice issued by ACAS.

(4) An employee may present a complaint to an employment tribunal that his employer has failed to permit him to take time off as required by this section.

171 Time limit for proceedings

An employment tribunal shall not consider a complaint under section 168, 169 or 170 unless it is presented to the tribunal—

(a) within three months of the date when the failure occurred, or

(b) where the tribunal is satisfied that it was not reasonably practicable for the complaint to be presented within that period, within such further period as the tribunal considers reasonable.

172 Remedies

(1) Where the tribunal finds a complaint under section 168 or 170 is well-founded, it shall make a declaration to that effect and may make an award of compensation to be paid by the employer to the employee.

(2) The amount of the compensation shall be such as the tribunal considers just and equitable in all the circumstances having regard to the employer's default in failing to permit time off to be taken by the employee and to any loss sustained by the employee which is attributable to the matters complained of.

(3) Where on a complaint under section 169 the tribunal finds that the employer has failed to pay the employee in accordance with that section, it shall order him to pay the amount which it finds to be due.

173 Interpretation and other supplementary provisions

(1) For the purposes of sections 168 and 170 the working hours of an employee shall be taken to be any time when in accordance with his contract of employment he is required to be at work.

(2) The remedy of an employee for infringement of the rights conferred on him by section 168, 169 or 170 is by way of complaint to an employment tribunal in accordance with this Part, and not otherwise.

Right to membership of trade union

174 Right not to be excluded or expelled from union

(1) An individual shall not be excluded or expelled from a trade union unless the exclusion or expulsion is permitted by this section.

(2) The exclusion or expulsion of an individual from a trade union is permitted by this section if (and only if)—

(a) he does not satisfy, or no longer satisfies, an enforceable membership requirement contained in the rules of the union,

(b) he does not qualify, or no longer qualifies, for membership of the union by reason of the union operating only in a particular part or particular parts of Great Britain,

(c) in the case of a union whose purpose is the regulation or relations between its members and one particular employer or a number of particular employers who are associated, he is not, or is no longer, employed by that employer or one of those employers, or

(d) the exclusion or expulsion is entirely attributable to his conduct.

(3) A requirement in relation to membership of a union is 'enforceable' for the purposes of subsection (2)(a) if it restricts membership solely by reference to one or more of the following criteria—

(a) employment in specified trade, industry or profession,

(b) occupational description (including grade, level or category of appointment), and

(c) possession of specified trade, industrial or professional qualifications or work experience.

(4) For the purposes of subsection (2)(d) 'conduct', in relation to an individual, does not include—

(a) his being or ceasing to be, or having been or ceased to be—

(i) a member of another trade union,

(ii) employed by a particular employer or at a particular place, or

(iii) a member of a political party, or

(b) conduct to which section 65 (conduct for which an individual may not be disciplined by a trade union) applies or would apply if the references in that section to the trade union which is relevant for the purposes of that section were references to any trade union.

(5) An individual who claims that he has been excluded or expelled from a trade union in contravention of this section may present a complaint to an employment tribunal.

175 Time limit for proceedings

An employment tribunal shall not entertain a complaint under section 174 unless it is presented—

(a) before the end of the period of six months beginning with the date of the exclusion or expulsion, or

(b) where the tribunal is satisfied that it was not reasonably practicable for the complaint to be presented before the end of that period, within such further period as the tribunal considers reasonable.

176 Remedies

(1) Where the employment tribunal finds a complaint under section 174 is well-founded, it shall make a declaration to that effect.

(2) An individual whose complaint has been declared to be well-founded may make an application for an award of compensation to be paid to him by the union.

The application shall be made to an employment tribunal if when it is made the applicant has been admitted or readmitted to the union, and otherwise to the Employment Appeal Tribunal.

(3) The application shall not be entertained if made—

(a) before the end of the period of four weeks beginning with the date of the declaration, or

(b) after the end of the period of six months beginning with that date.

(4) The amount of compensation awarded shall, subject to the following provisions, be such as the employment tribunal or the Employment Appeal Tribunal considers just and equitable in all the circumstances.

(5) Where the employment tribunal or Employment Appeal Tribunal finds that the exclusion or expulsion complained of was to any extent caused or contributed to by the action of the applicant, it shall reduce the amount of the compensation by such proportion as it considers just and equitable having regard to that finding.

(6) The amount of compensation calculated in accordance with subsections (4) and (5) shall not exceed the aggregate of—

(a) an amount equal to thirty times the limit for the time being imposed by section 227(1)(a) of the Employment Rights Act 1996 (maximum amount of a week's pay for basic award in unfair dismissal cases), and

(b) an amount equal to the limit for the time being imposed by section 124(1) of that Act (maximum compensatory award in such cases);

and, in the case of an award by the Employment Appeal Tribunal, shall not be less than £5,000.

(7) and (8) [repealed]

177 Interpretation and other supplementary provisions

(1) For the purposes of section 174—

(a) 'trade union' does not include an organisation falling within paragraph (b) of section 1,

(b) 'conduct' includes statements, acts and omissions, and

(c) 'employment' includes any relationship whereby an individual personally does work or performs services for another person (related expressions being construed accordingly).

(2) For the purposes of sections 174 to 176—

(a) if an individual's application for membership of a trade union is neither granted nor rejected before the end of the period within which it might reasonably have been expected to be granted if it was to be granted, he shall be treated as having been excluded from the union on the last day of that period, and

(b) an individual who under the rules of a trade union ceases to be a member of the union on the happening of an event specified in the rules shall be treated as having been expelled from the union.

(3) The remedy of an individual for infringement of the rights conferred by section 174 is by way of a complaint to an employment tribunal in accordance with that section, sections 175 and 176 and this section, and not otherwise.

(4) Where a complaint relating to an expulsion which is presented under section 174 is declared to be well-founded, no complaint in respect of the expulsion shall be presented or proceeded with under section 66 (complaint of infringement of right not to be unjustifiably disciplined).

(5) The rights conferred by section 174 are in addition to, and not in substitution for, any right which exists apart from that section; and, subject to subsection (4), nothing in that section, section 175 or 176 or this section affects any remedy for infringement of any such right.

PART IV
INDUSTRIAL RELATIONS

CHAPTER I
COLLECTIVE BARGAINING

Introductory

178 Collective agreements and collective bargaining

(1) In this Act 'collective agreement' means any agreement or arrangement made by or on behalf of one or more trade unions and one or more employers or employers' associations and relating to one or more of the matters specified below; and 'collective

bargaining' means negotiations relating to or connected with one or more of those matters.

(2) The matters referred to above are—

(a) terms and conditions of employment, or the physical conditions in which any workers are required to work;

(b) engagement or non-engagement, or termination or suspension of employment or the duties of employment, of one or more workers;

(c) allocation of work or the duties of employment between workers or groups of workers;

(d) matters of discipline;

(e) a worker's membership or non-membership of a trade union;

(f) facilities for officials of trade unions; and

(g) machinery for negotiation or consultation, and other procedures, relating to any of the above matters, including the recognition by employers or employers' associations of the right of a trade union to represent workers in such negotiation or consultation or in the carrying out of such procedures.

(3) In this Act 'recognition', in relation to a trade union, means the recognition of the union by an employer, or two or more associated employers, to any extent, for the purpose of collective bargaining; and 'recognised' and other related expressions shall be construed accordingly.

Enforceability of collective agreements

179 Whether agreement intended to be a legally enforceable contract

(1) A collective agreement shall be conclusively presumed not to have been intended by the parties to be a legally enforceable contract unless the agreement—

(a) is in writing, and

(b) contains a provision which (however expressed) states that the parties intend that the agreement shall be a legally enforceable contract.

(2) A collective agreement which does satisfy those conditions shall be conclusively presumed to have been intended by the parties to be a legally enforceable contract.

(3) If a collective agreement is in writing and contains a provision which (however expressed) states that the parties intend that one or more parts of the agreement specified in that provision, but not the whole of the agreement, shall be a legally enforceable contract, then—

(a) the specified part or parts shall be conclusively presumed to have been intended by the parties to be a legally enforceable contract, and

(b) the remainder of the agreement shall be conclusively presumed not to have been intended by the parties to be such a contract.

(4) A part of a collective agreement which by virtue of subsection (3)(b) is not a legally enforceable contract may be referred to for the purpose of interpreting a part of the agreement which is such a contract.

180 Effect of provisions restricting right to take industrial action

(1) Any terms of a collective agreement which prohibit or restrict the right of workers to engage in a strike or other industrial action, or have the effect of prohibiting or restricting that right, shall not form part of any contract between a worker and the person for whom he works unless the following conditions are met.

(2) The conditions are that the collective agreement—

(a) is in writing,

(b) contains a provision expressly stating that those terms shall or may be incorporated in such a contract,

(c) is reasonably accessible at his place of work to the worker to whom it applies and is available for him to consult during working hours, and

(d) is one where each trade union which is a party to the agreement is an independent trade union;

and that the contract with the worker expressly or impliedly incorporates those terms in the contract.

(3) The above provisions have effect notwithstanding anything in section 179 and notwithstanding any provision to the contrary in any agreement (including a collective agreement or a contract with any worker).

Disclosure of information for purposes of collective bargaining

181 General duty of employers to disclose information

(1) An employer who recognises an independent trade union shall, for the purposes of all stages of collective bargaining about matters, and in relation to descriptions of workers, in respect of which the union is recognised by him, disclose to representatives of the union, on request, the information required by this section.

In this section and sections 182 to 185 'representative', in relation to a trade union, means an official or other person authorised by the union to carry on such collective bargaining.

(2) The information to be disclosed is all information relating to the employer's undertaking which is in his possession, or that of an associated employer, and is information—

(a) without which the trade union representatives would be to a material extent impeded in carrying on collective bargaining with him, and

(b) which it would be in accordance with good industrial relations practice that he should disclose to them for the purposes of collective bargaining.

(3) A request by trade union representatives for information under this section shall, if the employer so requests, be in writing or be confirmed in writing.

(4) In determining what would be in accordance with good industrial relations practice, regard shall be had to the relevant provisions of any Code of Practice issued by ACAS, but not so as to exclude any other evidence of what that practice is.

(5) Information which an employer is required by virtue of this section to disclose to trade union representatives shall, if they so request, be disclosed or confirmed in writing.

182 Restrictions on general duty

(1) An employer is not required by section 181 to disclose information—

(a) the disclosure of which would be against the interests of national security, or

(b) which he could not disclose without contravening a prohibition imposed by or under an enactment, or

(c) which has been communicated to him in confidence, or which he has otherwise obtained in consequence of the confidence reposed in him by another person, or

(d) which relates specifically to an individual (unless that individual has consented to its being disclosed), or

(e) the disclosure of which would cause substantial injury to his undertaking for reasons other than its effect on collective bargaining, or

(f) obtained by him for the purpose of bringing, prosecuting or defending any legal proceedings.

In formulating the provisions of any Code of Practice relating to the disclosure of information, ACAS shall have regard to the provisions of this subsection.

(2) In the performance of his duty under section 181 an employer is not required—

(a) to produce, or allow inspection of, any document (other than a document prepared for the purpose of conveying or confirming the information) or to make a copy of or extracts from any document, or

(b) to compile or assemble any information where the compilation or assembly would involve an amount of work or expenditure out of reasonable proportion to the value of the information in the conduct of collective bargaining.

183 Complaint of failure to disclose information

(1) A trade union may present a complaint to the Central Arbitration Committee that an employer has failed—

(a) to disclose to representatives of the union information which he was required to disclose to them by section 181, or

(b) to confirm such information in writing in accordance with that section.

The complaint must be in writing and in such form as the Committee may require.

(2) If on receipt of a complaint the Committee is of the opinion that it is reasonably likely to be settled by conciliation, it shall refer the complaint to ACAS and shall notify the trade union and employer accordingly, whereupon ACAS shall seek to promote a settlement of the matter.

If a complaint so referred is not settled or withdrawn and ACAS is of the opinion that further attempts at conciliation are unlikely to result in a settlement, it shall inform the Committee of its opinion.

(3) If the complaint is not referred to ACAS or, if it is so referred, on ACAS informing the Committee of its opinion that further attempts at conciliation are unlikely to result in a settlement, the Committee shall proceed to hear and determine the complaint and shall make a declaration stating whether it finds the complaint well-founded, wholly or in part, and stating the reasons for its findings.

(4) On the hearing of a complaint any person who the Committee considers has a proper interest in the complaint is entitled to be heard by the Committee, but a failure to accord a hearing to a person other than the trade union and employer directly concerned does not affect the validity of any decision of the Committee in those proceedings.

(5) If the Committee finds the complaint wholly or partly well-founded, the declaration shall specify—

(a) the information in respect of which the Committee finds that the complaint is well-founded.

(b) the date (or, if more than one, the earliest date) on which the employer refused or failed to disclose or, as the case may be, to confirm in writing, any of the information in question, and

(c) a period (not being less than one week from the date of the declaration) within which the employer ought to disclose that information, or, as the case may be, to confirm it in writing.

(6) On a hearing of a complaint under this section a certificate signed by or on behalf of a Minister of the Crown and certifying that a particular request for information could not be complied with except by disclosing information the disclosure of which would have been against the interests of national security shall be conclusive evidence of that fact.

A document which purports to be such a certificate shall be taken to be such a certificate unless the contrary is proved.

184 Further complaint of failure to comply with declaration

(1) After the expiration of the period specified in a declaration under section 183(5)(c) the trade union may present a further complaint to the Central Arbitration Committee that the employer has failed to disclose or, as the case may be, to confirm in writing to representatives of the union information specified in the declaration.

The complaint must be in writing and in such form as the Committee may require.

(2) On receipt of a further complaint the Committee shall proceed to hear and determine the complaint and shall make a declaration stating whether they find

the complaint well-founded, wholly or in part, and stating the reasons for their finding.

(3) On the hearing of a further complaint any person who the Committee consider has a proper interest in that complaint shall be entitled to be heard by the Committee, but a failure to accord a hearing to a person other than the trade union and employer directly concerned shall not affect the validity of any decision of the Committee in those proceedings.

(4) If the Committee find the further complaint wholly or partly well-founded the declaration shall specify the information in respect of which the Committee find that that complaint is well-founded.

185 Determination of claim and award

(1) On or after presenting a further complaint under section 184 the trade union may present to the Central Arbitration Committee a claim, in writing, in respect of one or more descriptions of employees (but not workers who are not employees) specified in the claim that their contracts should include the terms and conditions specified in the claim.

(2) The right to present a claim expires if the employer discloses or, as the case may be, confirms in writing, to representatives of the trade union the information specified in the declaration under section 183(5) or 184(4); and a claim presented shall be treated as withdrawn if the employer does so before the Committee make an award on the claim.

(3) If the Committee find, or have found, the further complaint wholly or partly well-founded, they may, after hearing the parties, make an award that in respect of any description of employees specified in the claim the employer shall, from a specified date, observe either—

(a) the terms and conditions specified in the claim; or

(b) other terms and conditions which the Committee consider appropriate.

The date specified may be earlier than that on which the award is made but not earlier than the date specified in accordance with section 183(5)(b) in the declaration made by the Committee on the original complaint.

(4) An award shall be made only in respect of a description of employees, and shall comprise only terms and conditions relating to matters in respect of which the trade union making the claim is recognised by the employer.

(5) Terms and conditions which by an award under this section an employer is required to observe in respect of an employee have effect as part of the employee's contract of employment as from the date specified in the award, except in so far as they are superseded or varied—

(a) by a subsequent award under this section,

(b) by a collective agreement between the employer and the union for the time being representing that employee, or

(c) by express or implied agreement between the employee and the employer so far as that agreement effects an improvement in terms and conditions having effect by virtue of the award.

(6) Where—

(a) by virtue of any enactment, other than one contained in this section, providing for minimum remuneration or terms and conditions, a contract of employment is to have effect as modified by an award, order or other instrument under that enactment, and

(b) by virtue of an award under this section any terms and conditions are to have effect as part of that contract,

that contract shall have effect in accordance with that award, order or other instrument or in accordance with the award under this section, whichever is the more favourable, in respect of any terms and conditions of that contract, to the employee.

(7) No award may be made under this section in respect of terms and conditions of employment which are fixed by virtue of any enactment.

Prohibition of union recognition requirements

186 Recognition requirement in contract for goods or services void

A term or condition of a contract for the supply of goods or services is void in so far as it purports to require a party to the contract—

(a) to recognise one or more trade unions (whether or not named in the contract) for the purpose of negotiating on behalf of workers, or any class of worker, employed by him, or

(b) to negotiate or consult with, or with an official of, one or more trade unions (whether or not so named).

187 Refusal to deal on grounds of union exclusion prohibited

(1) A person shall not refuse to deal with a supplier or prospective supplier of goods or services if the ground or one of the grounds for his action is that the person against whom it is taken does not, or is not likely to—

(a) recognise one or more trade unions for the purpose of negotiating on behalf of workers, or any class of worker, employed by him, or

(b) negotiate or consult with, or with an official of, one or more trade unions.

(2) A person refuses to deal with a person if—

(a) where he maintains (in whatever form) a list of approved suppliers of goods or services, or of persons from whom tenders for the supply of goods or services may be invited, he fails to include the name of that person in that list; or

(b) in relation to a proposed contract for the supply of goods or services—

(i) he excludes that person from the group of persons from whom tenders for the supply of the goods or services are invited, or

(ii) he fails to permit that person to submit such a tender, or

(iii) he otherwise determines not to enter into a contract with that person for the supply of the goods or services; or

(c) he terminates a contract with that person for the supply of goods or services.

(3) The obligation to comply with this section is a duty owed to the person with whom there is a refusal to deal and to any other person who may be adversely affected by its contravention; and a breach of the duty is actionable accordingly (subject to the defences and other incidents applying to actions for breach of statutory duty).

CHAPTER II
PROCEDURE FOR HANDLING REDUNDANCIES

Duty of employer to consult representatives

188 Duty of employer to consult representatives

(1) Where an employer is proposing to dismiss as redundant 20 or more employees at one establishment within a period of 90 days or less, the employer shall consult about the dismissals all the persons who are appropriate representatives of any of the employees who may be affected by the proposed dismissals or may be affected by measures taken in connection with those dismissals.

(1A) The consultation shall begin in good time and in any event—

(a) where the employer is proposing to dismiss 100 or more employees as mentioned in subsection (1), at least 90 days, and

(b) otherwise, at least 30 days,

before the first of the dismissals takes effect.

(1B) For the purposes of this section the appropriate representatives of any affected employees are—

(a) if the employees are of a description in respect of which an independent trade union is recognised by their employer, representatives of the trade union, or

(b) in any other case, whichever of the following employee representatives the employer chooses—

(i) employee representatives appointed or elected by the affected employees otherwise than for the purposes of this section, who (having regard to the purposes for and the method by which they were appointed or elected) have authority from those employees to receive information and to be consulted about the proposed dismissals on their behalf;

(ii) employee representatives elected by the affected employees, for the purposes of this section, in an election satisfying the requirements of section 188A(1).

(2) The consultation shall include consultation about ways of—

(a) avoiding the dismissals,

(b) reducing the numbers of employees to be dismissed, and

(c) mitigating the consequences of the dismissals,

and shall be undertaken by the employer with a view to reaching agreement with the appropriate representatives.

(3) In determining how many employees an employer is proposing to dismiss as redundant no account shall be taken of employees in respect of whose proposed dismissals consultation has already begun.

(4) For the purposes of the consultation the employer shall disclose in writing to the appropriate representatives—

(a) the reasons for his proposals,

(b) the numbers and descriptions of employees whom it is proposed to dismiss as redundant,

(c) the total number of employees of any such description employed by the employer at the establishment in question,

(d) the proposed method of selecting the employees who may be dismissed,

(e) the proposed method of carrying out the dismissals, with due regard to any agreed procedure, including the period over which the dismissals are to take effect.

(f) the proposed method of calculating the amount of any redundancy payments to be made (otherwise than in compliance with an obligation imposed by or by virtue of any enactment) to employees who may be dismissed.

(5) That information shall be given to each of the appropriate representatives by being delivered to them or sent by post to an address notified by them to the employer, or (in the case of representatives of a trade union) sent by post to the union at the address of its head or main office.

(5A) The employer shall allow the appropriate representatives access to the affected employees and shall afford to those representatives such accommodation and other facilities as may be appropriate.

(6) [repealed]

(7) If in any case there are special circumstances which render it not reasonably practicable for the employer to comply with a requirement of subsection (1A), (2) or (4), the employer shall take all such steps towards compliance with that requirement as are reasonably practicable in those circumstances. Where the decision leading to the proposed dismissals is that of a person controlling the employer (directly or indirectly), a failure on the part of that person to provide information to the employer shall not constitute special circumstances rendering it not reasonably practicable for the employer to comply with such a requirement.

(7A) Where—

(a) the employer has invited any of the affected employees to elect employee representatives, and

(b) the invitation was issued long enough before the time when the consultation is required by subsection (1A)(a) or (b) to begin to allow them to elect representatives by that time,

the employer shall be treated as complying with the requirements of this section in relation to those employees if he complies with those requirements as soon as is reasonably practicable after the election of the representatives.

(7B) If, after the employer has invited affected employees to elect representatives, the affected employees fail to do so within a reasonable time, he shall give to each affected employee the information set out in subsection (4).

(8) This section does not confer any rights on a trade union, a representative or an employee except as provided by sections 189 to 192 below.

188A Election of employee representatives

(1) The requirements for the election of employee representatives under section 188(1B)(b)(ii) are that—

(a) the employer shall make such arrangements as are reasonably practical to ensure that the election is fair;

(b) the employer shall determine the number of representatives to be elected so that there are sufficient representatives to represent the interests of all the affected employees having regard to the number and classes of those employees;

(c) the employer shall determine whether the affected employees should be represented either by representatives of all the affected employees or by representatives of particular classes of those employees;

(d) before the election the employer shall determine the term of office as employee representatives so that it is of sufficient length to enable information to be given and consultations under section 188 to be completed;

(e) the candidates for election as employee representatives are affected employees on the date of the election;

(f) no affected employee is unreasonably excluded from standing for election;

(g) all affected employees on the date of the election are entitled to vote for employee representatives;

(h) the employees entitled to vote may vote for as many candidates as there are representatives to be elected to represent them or, if there are to be representatives for particular classes of employees, may vote for as many candidates as there are representatives to be elected to represent their particular class of employee;

(i) the election is conducted so as to secure that—

(i) so far as is reasonably practicable, those voting do so in secret, and

(ii) the votes given at the election are accurately counted.

(2) Where, after an election of employee representatives satisfying the requirements of subsection (1) has been held, one of those elected ceases to act as an employee representative and any of those employees are no longer represented, they shall elect another representative by an election satisfying the requirements of subsection 91)(a), (e), (f) and (i).

189 Complaint and protective award

(1) Where an employer has failed to comply with a requirement of section 188 or section 188A, a complaint may be presented to an employment tribunal on that ground—

(a) in the case of a failure relating to the election of employee representatives, by any of the affected employees or by any of the employees who have been dismissed as redundant;

(b) in the case of any other failure relating to employee representatives, by any of the employee representatives to whom the failure related,

(c) in the case of failure relating to representatives of a trade union, by the trade union, and

(d) in any other case, by any of the affected employees or by any of the employees who have been dismissed as redundant.

(1A) If on a complaint under subsection (1) a question arises as to whether or not any employee representative was an appropriate representative for the purposes of section 188, it shall be for the employer to show that the employee representative had the authority to represent the affected employees.

(1B) On a complaint under subsection (1)(a) it shall be for the employer to show that the requirements in section 188A have been satisfied.

(2) If the tribunal finds the complaint well-founded it shall make a declaration to that effect and may also make a protective award.

(3) A protective award is an award in respect of one or more descriptions of employees—

(a) who has been dismissed as redundant, or whom it is proposed to dismiss as redundant, and

(b) in respect of whose dismissal or proposed dismissal the employer has failed to comply with a requirement of section 188,

ordering the employer to pay remuneration for the protected period.

(4) The protected period—

(a) begins with the date on which the first of the dismissals to which the complaint relates takes effect, or the date of the award, whichever is the earlier, and

(b) is of such length as the tribunal determines to be just and equitable in all the circumstances having regard to the seriousness of the employer's default in complying with any requirement of section 188;

but shall not exceed 90 days.

(5) An employment tribunal shall not consider a complaint under this section unless it is presented to the tribunal—

(a) before the date on which the last of the dismissals to which the complaint relates takes effect, or

(b) during the period of three months beginning with that date, or

(c) where the tribunal is satisfied that it was not reasonably practicable for the complaint to be presented within the period of three months, within such further period as it considers reasonable.

(6) If on a complaint under this section a question arises—

(a) whether there were special circumstances which rendered it not reasonably practicable for the employer to comply with any requirement of section 188, or

(b) whether he took all such steps towards compliance with that requirement as were reasonably practicable in those circumstances,

it is for the employer to show that there were and that he did.

190 Entitlement under protective award

(1) Where an employment tribunal has made a protective award, every employee of a description to which the award relates is entitled, subject to the following provisions and to section 191, to be paid remuneration by his employer for the protected period.

(2) The rate of remuneration payable is a week's pay for each week of the period; and remuneration in respect of a period less than one week shall be calculated by reducing proportionately the amount of a week's pay.

(3) [repealed]

(4) An employee is not entitled to remuneration under a protective award in respect of a period during which he is employed by the employer unless he would be entitled to be paid by the employer in respect of that period—

(a) by virtue of his contract of employment, or

(b) by virtue of sections 87 to 91 of the Employment Rights Act 1996 (rights of employee in period of notice), if that period fell within the period of notice required to be given by section 86(1) of that Act.

(5) Chapter II of Part XIV of the Employment Rights Act 1996 applies with respect to the calculation of a week's pay for the purposes of this section.

The calculation date for the purposes of that Chapter is the date on which the protective award was made or, in the case of an employee who was dismissed before the date on which the protective award was made, the date which by virtue of section 226(5) is the calculation date for the purpose of computing the amount of a redundancy payment in relation to that dismissal (whether or not the employee concerned is entitled to any such payment).

(6) If an employee of a description to which a protective award relates dies during the protected period, the award has effect in his case as if the protected period ended on his death.

191 Termination of employment during protected period

(1) Where the employee is employed by the employer during the protected period and—

(a) he is fairly dismissed by his employer otherwise than as redundant, or

(b) he unreasonably terminates the contract of employment,

then, subject to the following provisions, he is not entitled to remuneration under the protective award in respect of any period during which but for that dismissal or termination he would have been employed.

(2) If an employer makes an employee an offer (whether in writing or not and whether before or after the ending of his employment under the previous contract) to renew his contract of employment, or to re-engage him under a new contract, so that the renewal or re-engagement would take effect before or during the protected period, and either—

(a) the provisions of the contract as renewed, or of the new contract, as to the capacity and place in which he would be employed, and as to the other terms and conditions of his employment, would not differ from the corresponding provisions of the previous contract, or

(b) the offer constitutes an offer of suitable employment in relation to the employee,

the following subsections have effect.

(3) If the employee unreasonably refuses the offer, he is not entitled to remuneration under the protective award in respect of a period during which but for that refusal he would have been employed.

(4) If the employee's contract of employment is renewed, or he is re-engaged under a new contract of employment, in pursuance of such an offer as is referred to in subsection (2)(b), there shall be a trial period in relation to the contract as renewed, or the new contract (whether or not there has been a previous trial period under this section).

(5) The trial period begins with the ending of his employment under the previous contract and ends with the expiration of the period of four weeks beginning with the date on which he starts work under the contract as renewed, or the new contract, or such longer period as may be agreed in accordance with subsection (6) for the purpose of retraining the employee for employment under that contract.

(6) Any such agreement—

(a) shall be made between the employer and the employee or his representative before the employee starts work under the contract as renewed or, as the case may be, the new contract,

(b) shall be in writing,

(c) shall specify the date of the end of the trial period, and

(d) shall specify the terms and conditions of employment which will apply in the employee's case after the end of that period.

(7) If during the trial period—

(a) the employee, for whatever reason, terminates the contract, or gives notice to terminate it and the contract is thereafter, in consequence, terminated, or

(b) the employer, for a reason connected with or arising out of the change to the renewed, or new, employment, terminates the contract, or gives notice to terminate it and the contract is thereafter, in consequence, terminated,

the employee remains entitled under the protective award unless, in a case falling within paragraph (a), he acted unreasonably in terminating or giving notice to terminate the contract.

192 Complaint by employee to employment tribunal

(1) An employee may present a complaint to an employment tribunal on the ground that he is an employee of a description to which a protective award relates and that his employer has failed, wholly or in part, to pay him remuneration under the award.

(2) An employment tribunal shall not entertain a complaint under this section unless it is presented to the tribunal—

(a) before the end of the period of three months beginning with the day (or, if the complaint relates to more than one day, the last of the days) in respect of which the complaint is made of failure to pay remuneration, or

(b) where the tribunal is satisfied that it was not reasonably practicable for the complaint to be presented within the period of three months, within such further period as it may consider reasonable.

(3) Where the tribunal finds a complaint under this section well-founded it shall order the employer to pay the complainant the amount of remuneration which it finds is due to him.

(4) The remedy of an employee for infringement of his right to remuneration under a protective award is by way of complaint under this section, and not otherwise.

Duty of employer to notify Secretary of State

193-194 [omitted]

Supplementary provisions

195 Construction of references to dismissal as redundant etc.

(1) In this Chapter references to dismissal as redundant are references to dismissal for a reason not related to the individual concerned or for a number of reasons all of which are not so related.

(2) For the purposes of any proceedings under this Chapter, where an employee is or is proposed to be dismissed it shall be presumed, unless the contrary is proved, that he is or is proposed to be dismissed as redundant.

196 Construction of references to representatives

(1) For the purposes of this Chapter persons are employee representatives if—

(a) they have been elected by employees for the specific purpose of being consulted by their employer about dismissals proposed by him, or

(b) having been elected or appointed by employees (whether before or after dismissals have been proposed by their employer) otherwise than for that specific purpose, it is appropriate (having regard to the purposes for which they were elected) for the employer to consult them about dismissals proposed by him,

and (in either case) they are employed by the employer at the time when they are elected or appointed.

(2) References in this Chapter to representatives of a trade union, in relation to an employer, are to officials or other persons authorised by the trade union to carry on collective bargaining with the employer.

(3) References in this Chapter to affected employees are to employees who may be affected by the proposed dismissals or who may be affected by measures taken in connection with such dismissals.

197 [omitted]

198 Power to adapt provisions in case of collective agreement

(1) This section applies where there is in force a collective agreement which establishes—

(a) arrangements for providing alternative employment for employees to whom the agreement relates if they are dismissed as redundant by an employer to whom it relates, or

(b) arrangements for handling the dismissal of employees as redundant.

(2) On the application of all the parties to the agreement the Secretary of State may, if he is satisfied having regard to the provisions of the agreement that the arrangements are on the whole at least as favourable to those employees as the foregoing provisions of this Chapter, by order made by statutory instrument adapt, modify or exclude any of those provisions both in their application to all or any of those employees and in their application to any other employees of any such employer.

(3) The Secretary of State shall not make such an order unless the agreement—

(a) provides for procedures to be followed (whether by arbitration or otherwise) in cases where an employee to whom the agreement relates claims that any employer or other person to whom it relates has not complied with the provisions of the agreement, and

(b) provides that those procedures include a right to arbitration or adjudication by an independent referee or body in cases where (by reason of an equality of votes or otherwise) a decision cannot otherwise be reached,

or indicates that any such employee may present a complaint to an employment tribunal that any such employer or other person has not complied with those provisions.

(4) An order under this section may confer on an employment tribunal to whom a complaint is presented as mentioned in subsection (3) such powers and duties as the Secretary of State considers appropriate.

(5) An order under this section may be varied or revoked by a subsequent order thereunder either in pursuance of an application made by all or any of the parties to the agreement in question or without any such application.

CHAPTER III
CODES OF PRACTICE

Codes of Practice issued by ACAS

199 Issue of Codes of Practice by ACAS

(1) ACAS may issue Codes of Practice containing such practical guidance as it thinks fit for the purpose of promoting the improvement of industrial relations.

(2)-(4) [omitted]

200-202 [omitted]

Codes of Practice issued by the Secretary of State

203 Issue of Codes of Practice by the Secretary of State

(1) The Secretary of State may issue Codes of Practice containing such practical guidance as he thinks fit for the purpose—

(a) of promoting the improvement of industrial relations, or

(b) of promoting what appear to him to be desirable practices in relation to the conduct by trade unions of ballots and elections.

(2) [omitted]

204-206 [omitted]

Supplementary provisions

207 Effect of failure to comply with Code

(1) A failure on the part of any person to observe any provision of a Code of Practice issued under this Chapter shall not of itself render him liable to any proceedings.

(2) In any proceedings before an employment tribunal or the Central Arbitration Committee any Code of Practice issued under this Chapter by ACAS shall be admissible in evidence, and any provision of the Code which appears to the tribunal or Committee to be relevant to any question arising in the proceedings shall be taken into account in determining that question.

(3) In any proceedings before a court or employment tribunal or the Central Arbitration Committee any Code of Practice issued under this Chapter by the Secretary of State shall be admissible in evidence, and any provision of the Code which appears to the court, tribunal or Committee to be relevant to any question arising in the proceedings shall be taken into account in determining that question.

208 [omitted]

CHAPTER IV
GENERAL

Functions of ACAS

209 General duty to promote improvement of industrial relations

It is the general duty of ACAS to promote the improvement of industrial relations.

210 Conciliation

(1) Where a trade dispute exists or is apprehended ACAS may, at the request of one or more parties to the dispute or otherwise, offer the parties to the dispute its assistance with a view to bringing about a settlement.

(2) The assistance may be by way of conciliation or by other means, and may include the appointment of a person other than an officer or servant of ACAS to offer assistance to the parties to the dispute with a view to bringing about a settlement.

(3) In exercising its functions under this section ACAS shall have regard to the desirability of encouraging the parties to a dispute to use any appropriate agreed procedures for negotiation or the settlement of disputes.

211 Conciliation officers

(1) ACAS shall designate some of its officers to perform the functions of conciliation officers under any enactment (whenever passed) relating to matters which are or could be the subject to proceedings before an employment tribunal.

(2) References in any such enactment to a conciliation officer are to an officer designated under this section.

212 Arbitration

(1) Where a trade dispute exists or is apprehended ACAS may, at the request of one or more of the parties to the dispute and with the consent of all the parties to the dispute, refer all or any of the matters to which the dispute relates for settlement to the arbitration of—

(a) one or more persons appointed by ACAS for that purpose (not being officers or employees of ACAS), or

(b) the Central Arbitration Committee.

(2) In exercising its functions under this section ACAS shall consider the likelihood of the dispute being settled by conciliation.

(3) Where there exist appropriate agreed procedures for negotiation or the settlement of disputes, ACAS shall not refer a matter for settlement to arbitration under this section unless—

(a) those procedures have been used and have failed to result in a settlement, or

(b) there is, in ACAS's opinion a special reason which justifies arbitration under this section as an alternative to those procedures.

(4) Where a matter is referred to arbitration under subsection (1)(a)—

(a) if more than one arbitrator or arbiter is appointed, ACAS shall appoint one of them to act as chairman; and

(b) the award may be published if ACAS so decides and all the parties consent.

(5) Part I of the Arbitration Act 1996 (general provisions as to arbitration) does not apply to an arbitration under this section.

212A Arbitration scheme for unfair dismissal cases etc.

(1) ACAS may prepare a scheme providing for arbitration in the case of disputes involving proceedings, or claims which could be the subject of proceedings, before an employment tribunal arising out of a contravention or alleged contravention of—

(a) Part X of the Employment Rights Act 1996 (unfair dismissal), or

(b) any enactment specified in an order made by the Secretary of State.

(2) When ACAS has prepared such a scheme it shall submit a draft of the scheme to the Secretary of State who, if he approves it, shall make an order—

(a) setting out the scheme, and

(b) making provision for it to come into effect.

(3) ACAS may from time to time prepare a revised version of such a scheme and, when it has done so, shall submit a draft of the revised scheme to the Secretary of State who, if he approves it, shall make an order—

(a) setting out the revised scheme, and

(b) making provision for it to come into effect.

(4) ACAS may take any steps appropriate for promoting awareness of a scheme prepared under this section.

(5) Where the parties to any dispute within subsection (1) agree in writing to submit the dispute to arbitration in accordance with a scheme having effect by virtue of an order under this section, ACAS shall refer the dispute to the arbitration of a person appointed by ACAS for the purpose (not being an officer or employee of ACAS).

(6) Nothing in the Arbitration Act 1996 shall apply to an arbitration conducted in accordance with a scheme having effect by virtue of an order under this section except to the extent that the order provides for any provision of Part I of that Act so to apply; and the order may provide for any such provision so to apply subject to modifications.

(7) A scheme set out in an order under this section may, in relation to an arbitration conducted in accordance with the law of Scotland, make provision—

(a) that a reference on a preliminary point may be made, or

(b) conferring a right of appeal which shall lie,

to the relevant court on such grounds and in respect of such matters as may be specified in the scheme; and in this subsection 'relevant court' means such court, being the Court of Session or the Employment Appeal Tribunal, as may be specified in the scheme, and a different court may be specified as regards different grounds or matters.

(8) Where a scheme set out in an order under this section includes provision for the making of re-employment orders in arbitrations conducted in accordance with the scheme, the order setting out the scheme may require employment tribunals to enforce such orders—

(a) in accordance with section 117 of the Employment Rights Act 1996 (enforcement by award of compensation), or

(b) in accordance with that section as modified by the order.

For this purpose 're-employment orders' means orders requiring that persons found to have been unfairly dismissed be reinstated, re-engaged or otherwise re-employed.

(9) An order under this section setting out a scheme may provide that, in the case of disputes within subsection (1)(a), such part of an award made in accordance with the scheme as is specified by the order shall be treated as a basic award of compensation for unfair dismissal for the purposes of section 184(1)(d) of the Employment Rights Act 1996 (which specifies such an award as a debt which the Secretary of State must satisfy if the employer has become insolvent).

(10)-(12) [omitted]

212B Dismissal procedures agreements

ACAS may, in accordance with any dismissal procedures agreement (within the meaning of the Employment Rights Act 1996), refer any matter to the arbitration of a person appointed by ACAS for the purpose (not being an officer or employee of ACAS).

213 Advice

(1) ACAS may, on request or otherwise, give employers, employers' associations, workers and trade unions such advice as it thinks appropriate on matters concerned with or affecting or likely to affect industrial relations.

(2) ACAS may also publish general advice on matters concerned with or affecting or likely to affect industrial relations.

214 Inquiry

(1) ACAS may, if it thinks fit, inquire into any question relating to industrial relations generally or to industrial relations in any particular industry or in any particular undertaking or part of an undertaking.

(2) The findings of an inquiry under this section, together with any advice given by ACAS in connection with those findings, may be published by ACAS if—

(a) it appears to ACAS that publication is desirable for the improvement of industrial relations, either generally or in relation to the specific question inquired into, and

(b) after sending a draft of the findings to all parties appearing to be concerned and taking account of their views, it thinks fit.

Courts of inquiry

215 Inquiry and report by court of inquiry

(1) Where a trade dispute exists or is apprehended, the Secretary of State may inquire into the causes and circumstances of the dispute, and, if he thinks fit, appoint a court of inquiry and refer to it any matters appearing to him to be connected with or relevant to the dispute.

(2) The court shall inquire into the matters referred to it and report on them to the Secretary of State; and it may make interim reports if it thinks fit.

(3) Any report of the court, and any minority report, shall be laid before both Houses of Parliament as soon as possible.

(4) The Secretary of State may, before or after the report has been laid before Parliament, publish or cause to be published from time to time, in such manner as he thinks fit, any information obtained or conclusions arrived at by the court as the result or in the course of its inquiry.

(5) No report or publication made or authorised by the court or the Secretary of State shall include any information obtained by the court of inquiry in the course of its inquiry—

(a) as to any trade union, or

(b) as to any individual business (whether carried on by a person, firm, or company),

which is not available otherwise than through evidence given at the inquiry, except with the consent of the secretary of the trade union or of the person, firm, or company in question.

Nor shall any individual member of the court or any person concerned in the inquiry disclose such information without such consent.

(6) The Secretary of State shall from time to time present to Parliament a report of his proceedings under this section.

216 Constitution and proceedings of court of inquiry

(1) A court of inquiry shall consist of—

(a) a chairman and such other persons as the Secretary of State thinks fit to appoint, or

(b) one person appointed by the Secretary of State,

as the Secretary of State thinks fit.

(2) A court may act notwithstanding any vacancy in its number.

(3) A court may conduct its inquiry in public or in private, at its discretion.

(4) The Secretary of State may make rules regulating the procedure of a court of inquiry, including rules as to summoning of witnesses, quorum, and the appointment of committees and enabling the court to call for such documents as the court may determine to be relevant to the subject-matter of the inquiry.

(5) A court of inquiry may, if and to such extent as may be authorised by rules under this section, by order require any person who appears to the court to have knowledge of the subject-matter of the inquiry—

(a) to supply (in writing or otherwise) such particulars in relation thereto as the court may require, and

(b) where necessary, to attend before the court and give evidence on oath;

and the court may administer or authorise any person to administer an oath for that purpose.

(6) Provision shall be made by rules under this section with respect to the cases in which persons may appear by counsel or solicitor in proceedings before a court of inquiry, and except as provided by those rules no person shall be entitled to appear in any such proceedings by counsel or solicitor.

Supplementary provisions

217 [omitted]

218 Meaning of 'trade dispute' in Part IV

(1) In this Part 'trade dispute' means a dispute between employers and workers, or between workers and workers, which is connected with one or more of the following matters—

(a) terms and conditions of employment, or the physical conditions in which any workers are required to work;

(b) engagement or non-engagement, or termination or suspension of employment or the duties of employment, of one or more workers;

(c) allocation of work or the duties of employment as between workers or groups of workers;

(d) matters of discipline;

(e) the membership or non-membership of a trade union on the part of a worker;

(f) facilities for officials of trade unions; and

(g) machinery for negotiation or consultation, and other procedures, relating to any of the foregoing matters, including the recognition by employers or employers' associations of the right of a trade union to represent workers in any such negotiation or consultation or in the carrying out of such procedures.

(2) A dispute between a Minister of the Crown and any workers shall, notwithstanding that he is not the employer of those workers, be treated for the purposes of this Part as a dispute between an employer and those workers if the dispute relates—

(a) to matters which have been referred for consideration by a joint body on which, by virtue of any provision made by or under any enactment, that minister is represented, or

(b) to matters which cannot be settled without that Minister exercising a power conferred on him by or under an enactment.

(3) There is a trade dispute for the purpose of this Part even though it relates to matters occurring outside Great Britain.

(4) A dispute to which a trade union or employer's association is a party shall be treated for the purposes of this Part as a dispute to which workers or, as the case may be, employers are parties.

(5) In this section—

'employment' includes any relationship whereby one person personally does work or performs services for another; and

'worker', in relation to a dispute to which an employer is a party, includes any worker even if not employed by that employer.

PART V
INDUSTRIAL ACTION

Protection of acts in contemplation or furtherance of trade dispute

219 Protection from certain tort liabilities

(1) An act done by a person in contemplation or furtherance of a trade dispute is not actionable in tort on the ground only—

(a) that it induces another person to break a contract or interferes or induces another person to interfere with its performance, or

(b) that it consists in his threatening that a contract (whether one to which he is a party or not) will be broken or its performance interefered with, or that he will induce another person to break a contract or interfere with its performance.

(2) An agreement or combination by two or more persons to do or procure the doing of an act in contemplation or furtherance of a trade dispute is not actionable in tort if the act is one which if done without any such agreement or combination would not be actionable in tort.

(3) Nothing in subsections (1) and (2) prevents an act done in the course of picketing from being actionable in tort unless it is done in the course of attendance declared lawful by section 220 (peaceful picketing).

(4) Subsections (1) and (2) have effect subject to sections 222 to 225 (action excluded from protection) and to sections 226 (requirement of ballot before action by trade union) and 234A (requirement of notice to employer of industrial action); and in those sections 'not protected' means excluded from the protection afforded by this section or, where the expression is used with reference to a particular person, excluded from that protection as respects that person.

220 Peaceful picketing

(1) It is lawful for a person in contemplation or furtherance of a trade dispute to attend—

(a) at or near his own place of work, or

(b) if he is an official of a trade union, at or near the place of work of a member of the union whom he is accompanying and whom he represents,

for the purpose only of peacefully obtaining or communicating information, or peacefully persuading any person to work or abstain from working.

(2) If a person works or normally works—

(a) otherwise than at any one place, or

(b) at a place the location of which is such that attendance there for a purpose mentioned in subsection (1) is impracticable,

his place of work for the purposes of that subsection shall be any premises of his employer from which he works or from which his work is administered.

(3) In the case of a worker not in employment where—

(a) his last employment was terminated in connection with a trade dispute, or

(b) the termination of his employment was one of the circumstances giving rise to a trade dispute,

in relation to that dispute his former place of work shall be treated for the purposes of subsection (1) as being his place of work.

(4) A person who is an official of a trade union by virtue only of having been elected or appointed to be a representative of some of the members of the union shall be regarded for the purposes of subsection (1) as representing only those members; but otherwise an official of a union shall be regarded for those purposes as representing all its members.

221 Restrictions on grant of injunctions and interdicts

(1) Where—

(a) an application for an injunction or interdict is made to a court in the absence of the party against whom it is sought or any representative of his, and

(b) he claims, or in the opinion of the court would be likely to claim, that he acted in contemplation or furtherance of a trade dispute,

the court shall not grant the injunction or interdict unless satisfied that all steps which in the circumstances were reasonable have been taken with a view to securing that notice of the application and an opportunity of being heard with respect to the application have been given to him.

(2) Where—

(a) an application for an interlocutory injunction is made to a court pending the trial of an action, and

(b) the party against whom it is sought claims that he acted in contemplation or furtherance of a trade dispute,

the court shall, in exercising its discretion whether or not to grant the injunction, have regard to the likelihood of that party's succeeding at the trial of the action in establishing any matter which would afford a defence to the action under section 219 (protection from certain tort liabilities) or section 220 (peaceful picketing).

This subsection does not extend to Scotland.

Action excluded from protection

222 Action to enforce trade union membership

(1) An act is not protected if the reason, or one of the reasons, for which it is done is the fact or belief that a particular employer—

(a) is employing, has employed or might employ a person who is not a member of a trade union, or

(b) is failing, has failed or might fail to discriminate against such a person.

(2) For the purposes of subsection (1)(b) an employer discriminates against a person if, but only if, he ensures that his conduct in relation to—

(a) persons, or persons of any description, employed by him, or who apply to be, or are, considered by him for employment, or

(b) the provision of employment for such persons,

is different, in some or all cases, according to whether or not they are members of a trade union, and is more favourable to those who are.

(3) An act is not protected if it constitutes, or is one of a number of acts which together constitute, an inducement or attempted inducement of a person—

(a) to incorporate in a contract to which that person is a party, or a proposed contract to which he intends to be a party, a term or condition which is or would be void by virtue of section 144 (union membership requirement in contract for goods or services), or

(b) to contravene section 145 (refusal to deal with person on grounds relating to union membership).

(4) References in this section to an employer employing a person are to a person acting in the capacity of the person for whom a worker works or normally works.

(5) References in this section to not being a member of a trade union are to not being a member of any trade union, of a particular trade union or of one of a number of particular trade unions.

Any such reference includes a reference to not being a member of a particular branch or section of a trade union or of one of a number of particular branches or sections of a trade union.

223 Action taken because of dismissal for taking unofficial action

An act is not protected if the reason, or one of the reasons, for doing it is the fact or belief that an employer has dismissed one or more employees in circumstances such that by virtue of section 237 (dismissal in connection with unofficial action) they have no right to complain of unfair dismissal.

224 Secondary action

(1) An act is not protected if one of the facts relied on for the purpose of establishing liability is that there has been secondary action which is not lawful picketing.

(2) There is secondary action in relation to a trade dispute when, and only when, a person—

(a) induces another to break a contract of employment or interferes or induces another to interfere with its performance, or

(b) threatens that a contract of employment under which he or another is employed will be broken or its performance interfered with, or that he will induce another to break a contract of employment or to interfere with its performance,

and the employer under the contract of employment is not the employer party to the dispute.

(3) Lawful picketing means acts done in the course of such attendance as is declared lawful by section 220 (peaceful picketing)—

(a) by a worker employed (or, in the case of a worker not in employment, last employed) by the employer party to the dispute, or

(b) by a trade union official whose attendance is lawful by virtue of subsection (1)(b) of that section.

(4) For the purposes of this section an employer shall not be treated as party to a dispute between another employer and workers of that employer; and where more than one employer is in dispute with his workers, the dispute between each employer and his workers shall be treated as a separate dispute.

In this subsection 'worker' has the same meaning as in section 244 (meaning of 'trade dispute').

(5) An act in contemplation or furtherance of a trade dispute which is primary action in relation to that dispute may not be relied on as secondary action in relation to another trade dispute.

Primary action means such action as is mentioned in paragraph (a) or (b) of subsection (2) where the employer under the contract of employment is the employer party to the dispute.

(6) In this section 'contract of employment' includes any contract under which one person personally does work or performs services for another, and related expressions shall be construed accordingly.

225 Pressure to impose union recognition requirement

(1) An act is not protected if it constitutes, or is one of a number of acts which together constitute, an inducement or attempted inducement of a person—

(a) to incorporate in a contract to which that person is a party, or a proposed contract to which he intends to be a party, a term or condition which is or would be void by virtue of section 186 (recognition requirement in contract for goods or services), or

(b) to contravene section 187 (refusal to deal with person on grounds of union exclusion).

(2) An act is not protected if—

(a) it interferes with the supply (whether or not under a contract) of goods or services, or can reasonably be expected to have that effect, and

(b) one of the facts relied upon for the purpose of establishing liability is that a person has—

(i) induced another to break a contract of employment or interfered or induced another to interfere with its performance, or

(ii) threatened that a contract of employment under which he or another is employed will be broken or its performance interfered with, or that he will induce another to break a contract of employment or to interfere with its performance, and

(c) the reason, or one of the reasons, for doing the act is the fact or belief that the supplier (not being the employer under the contract of employment mentioned in paragraph (b)) does not, or might not—

(i) recognise one or more trade unions for the purpose of negotiating on behalf of workers, or any class of worker, employed by him, or

(ii) negotiate or consult with, or with an official of, one or more trade unions.

Requirement of ballot before action by trade union

226 Requirement of ballot before action by trade union

(1) An act done by a trade union to induce a person to take part, or continue to take part, in industrial action

(a) is not protected unless the industrial action has the support of a ballot, and

(b) where section 226A falls to be complied with in relation to the person's employer, is not protected as respects the employer unless the trade union has complied with section 226A in relation to him.

In this section 'the relevant time', in relation to an act by a trade union to induce a person to take part, or continue to take part, in industrial action, means the time at which proceedings are commenced in respect of the act.

(2) Industrial action shall be regarded as having the support of a ballot only if—

(a) the union has held a ballot in respect of the action—

(i) in relation to which the requirements of section 226B so far as applicable before and during the holding of the ballot were satisfied,

(ii) in relation to which the requirements of sections 227 to 231 were satisfied, and

(iii) in which the majority voting in the ballot answered 'Yes' to the question applicable in accordance with section 229(2) to industrial action of the kind to which the act of inducement relates;

(b) such of the requirements of the following sections as have fallen to be satisfied at the relevant time have been satisfied, namely—

(i) section 226B so far as applicable after the holding of the ballot, and

(ii) section 231B;

(bb) section 232A does not prevent the industrial action from being regarded as having the support of the ballot; and

(c) the requirements of section 233 (calling of industrial action with support of ballot) are satisfied.

Any reference in this subsection to a requirement of a provision which is disapplied or modified by section 232 has effect subject to that section.

(3) Where separate workplace ballots are held by virtue of section 228(1)—

(a) industrial action shall be regarded as having the support of a ballot if the conditions specified in subsection (2) are satisfied, and

(b) the trade union shall be taken to have complied with the requirements relating to a ballot imposed by section 226A if those requirements are complied with,

in relation to the ballot for the place of work of the person induced to take part, or continue to take part, in the industrial action.

(3A) If the requirements of section 231A fall to be satisfied in relation to an employer, as respects that employer industrial action shall not be regarded as having the support of a ballot unless those requirements are satisfied in relation to that employer.

(4) For the purposes of this section an inducement, in relation to a person, includes an inducement which is or would be ineffective, whether because of his unwillingness to be influenced by it or for any other reason.

226A Notice of ballot and sample voting paper for employers

(1) The trade union must take such steps as are reasonably necessary to ensure that—

(a) not later than the seventh day before the opening day of the ballot, the notice specified in subsection (2), and

(b) not later than the third day before the opening day of the ballot, the sample voting paper specified in subsection (3),

is received by every person who it is reasonable for the union to believe (at the latest time when steps could be taken to comply with paragraph (a)) will be the employer of persons who will be entitled to vote in the ballot.

(2) The notice referred to in paragraph (a) of subsection (1) is a notice in writing—

(a) stating that the union intends to hold the ballot,

(b) specifying the date which the union reasonably believes will be the opening day of the ballot, and

(c) containing such information in the union's possession as would help the employer to make plans and bring information to the attention of those of his employees who it is reasonable for the union to believe (at the time when the steps to comply with that paragraph are taken) will be entitled to vote in the ballot.

(3) The sample voting paper referred to in paragraph (b) of subsection (1) is—

(a) a sample of the form of voting paper which is to be sent to the employees who it is reasonable for the trade union to believe (at the time when the steps to comply with paragraph (a) of that subsection are taken) will be entitled to vote in the ballot, or

(b) where they are not all to be sent the same form of voting paper, a sample of each form of voting paper which is to be sent to any of them.

(3A) These rules apply for the purposes of paragraph (c) of subsection (2)—

(a) if the union possesses information as to the number, category or work-place of the employees concerned, a notice must contain that information (at least);

(b) if a notice does not name any employees, that fact shall not be a ground for holding that it does not comply with paragraph (c) of subsection (2).

(3B) In subsection (3) references to employees are to employees of the employer concerned.

(4) In this section references to the opening day of the ballot are references to the first day when a voting paper is sent to any person entitled to vote in the ballot.

(5) This section in its application to a ballot in which merchant seamen to whom section 230(2A) applies are entitled to vote, shall have effect with the substitution in subsection (3), for references to the voting paper which is to be sent to the employees, of references to the voting paper which is to be sent or otherwise provided to them.

226B Appointment of scrutineer

(1) The trade union shall, before the ballot in respect of the industrial action is held, appoint a qualified person ('the scrutineer') whose terms of appointment shall require him to carry out in relation to the ballot the functions of—

(a) taking such steps as appear to him to be appropriate for the purpose of enabling him to make a report to the trade union (see section 231B); and

(b) making the report as soon as reasonably practicable after the date of the ballot and, in any event, not later than the end of the period of four weeks beginning with that date.

(2) A person is a qualified person in relation to a ballot if—

(a) he satisfies such conditions as may be specified for the purposes of this section by order of the Secretary of State or is himself so specified; and

(b) the trade union has no grounds for believing either that he will carry out the functions conferred on him under subsection (1) otherwise than competently or that his independence in relation to the union, or in relation to the ballot, might reasonably be called into question.

An order under paragraph (a) shall be made by statutory instrument which shall be subject to annulment in pursuance of a resolution of either House of Parliament.

(3) The trade union shall ensure that the scrutineer duly carries out the functions conferred on him under subsection (1) and that there is no interference with the carrying out of those functions from the union or any of its members, officials or employees.

(4) The trade union shall comply with all reasonable requests made by the scrutineer for the purposes of, or in connection with, the carrying out of those functions.

226C Exclusion for small ballots

Nothing in section 226B, section 229(1A)(a) or section 231B shall impose a requirement on a trade union unless—

(a) the number of members entitled to vote in the ballot, or

(b) where separate workplace ballots are held in accordance with section 228(1), the aggregate of the number of members entitled to vote in each of them,

exceeds 50.

227 Entitlement to vote in ballot

(1) Entitlement to vote in the ballot must be accorded equally to all the members of the trade union who it is reasonable at the time of the ballot for the union to believe will be induced to take part or, as the case may be, to continue to take part in the industrial action in question, and to no others.

(2) [repealed]

228 Separate workplace ballots

(1) Subject to subsection (2), this section applies if the members entitled to vote in a ballot by virtue of section 227 do not all have the same workplace.

(2) This section does not apply if the union reasonably believes that all those members have the same workplace.

(3) Subject to section 228A, a separate ballot shall be held for each workplace; and entitlement to vote in each ballot shall be accorded equally to, and restricted to, members of the union who—

(a) are entitled to vote by virtue of section 227, and

(b) have that workplace.

(4) In this section and section 228A 'workplace' in relation to a person who is employed means—

(a) if the person works at or from a single set of premises, those premises, and

(b) in any other case, the premises with which the person's employment has the closest connection.

228A Separate workplaces: single and aggregate ballots

(1) Where section 228(3) would require separate ballots to be held for each workplace, a ballot may be held in place of some or all of the separate ballots if one of subsections (2) to (4) is satisfied in relation to it.

(2) This subsection is satisfied in relation to a ballot if the workplace of each member entitled to vote in the ballot is the workplace of at least one member of the union who is affected by the dispute.

(3) This subsection is satisfied in relation to a ballot if entitlement to vote is accorded to, and limited to, all the members of the union who—

(a) according to the union's reasonable belief have an occupation of a particular kind or have any of a number of particular kinds of occupation, and

(b) are employed by a particular employer, or by any of a number of particular employers, with whom the union is in dispute.

(4) This subsection is satisfied in relation to a ballot if entitlement to vote is accorded to, and limited to, all the members of the union who are employed by a particular employer, or by any of a number of particular employers, with whom the union is in dispute.

(5) For the purposes of subsection (2) the following are members of the union affected by a dispute—

(a) if the dispute relates (wholly or partly) to a decision which the union reasonably believes the employer has made or will make concerning a matter specified in subsection (1)(a), (b) or (c) of section 244 (meaning of 'trade dispute'), members whom the decision directly affects,

(b) if the dispute relates (wholly or partly) to a matter specified in subsection (1)(d) of that section, members whom the matter directly affects,

(c) if the dispute relates (wholly or partly) to a matter specified in subsection (2)(e) of that section, persons whose membership or non-membership is in dispute,

(d) if the dispute relates (wholly or partly) to a matter specified in subsection (1)(f) of that section, officials of the union who have used or would use the facilities concerned in the dispute.

229 Voting paper

(1) The method of voting in a ballot must be by the marking of a voting paper by the person voting.

(1A) Each voting paper must—

(a) state the name of the independent scrutineer,

(b) clearly specify the address to which, and the date by which, it is to be returned,

(c) be given one of a series of consecutive whole numbers every one of which is used in giving a different number in that series to each voting paper printed or otherwise produced for the purposes of the ballot, and

(d) be marked with its number.

This subsection, in its application to a ballot in which merchant seamen to whom section 230(2A) applies are entitled to vote, shall have effect with the substitution, for the reference to the address to which the voting paper is to be returned, of a reference to the ship to which the seamen belong.

(2) The voting paper must contain at least one of the following questions—

(a) a question (however framed) which requires the person answering it to say, by answering 'Yes' or 'No', whether he is prepared to take part or, as the case may be, to continue to take part in a strike;

(b) a question (however framed) which requires the person answering it to say, by answering 'Yes' or 'No', whether he is prepared to take part or, as the case may be, to continue to take part in industrial action short of a strike.

(2A) For the purposes of subsection (2) an overtime ban and a call-out ban constitute industrial action short of a strike.

(3) The voting paper must specify who, in the event of a vote in favour of industrial action, is authorised for the purposes of section 233 to call upon members to take part or continue to take part in the industrial action.

The person or description of persons so specified need not be authorised under the rules of the union but must be within section 20(2) (persons for whose acts the union is taken to be responsible).

(4) The following statement must (without being qualified or commented upon by anything else on the voting paper) appear on every voting paper—

'If you take part in a strike or other industrial action, you may be in breach of your contract of employment.'.

However, if you are dismissed for taking part in strike or other industrial action which is called officially and is otherwise lawful, the dismissal will be unfair if it takes place fewer than eight weeks after you started taking part in the action, and depending on the circumstances may be unfair if it takes place later.

230 Conduct of ballot

(1) Every person who is entitled to vote in the ballot must—

(a) be allowed to vote without interference from, or constraint imposed by, the union or any of its members, officials or employees, and

(b) so far as is reasonably practicable, be enabled to do so without incurring any direct cost to himself.

(2) Except as regards persons falling within subsection (2A), so far as is reasonably practicable, every person who is entitled to vote in the ballot must—

(a) have a young paper sent to him by post at his home address or any other address which he has requested the trade union in writing to treat as his postal address; and

(b) be given a convenient opportunity to vote by post.

(2A) Subsection (2B) applies to a merchant seaman if the trade union reasonably believes that—

(a) he will be employed in a ship either at sea or at a place outside Great Britain at some time in the period during which votes may be cast, and

(b) it will be convenient for him to receive a voting paper and to vote while on the ship or while at a place where the ship is rather than in accordance with subsection (2).

(2B) Where this subsection applies to a merchant seaman he shall, if it is reasonably practicable—

(a) have a voting paper made available to him while on the ship or while at a place where the ship is, and

(b) be given an opportunity to vote while on the ship or while at a place where the ship is.

(2C) In subsections (2A) and (2B) 'merchant seaman' means a person whose employment, or the greater part of it, is carried out on board sea-going ships.

(3) [repealed]

(4) A ballot shall be conducted so as to secure that—

(a) so far as is reasonably practicable, those voting do so in secret, and

(b) the votes given in the ballot are fairly and accurately counted.

For the purposes of paragraph (b) an inaccuracy in counting shall be disregarded if it is accidental and on a scale which could not affect the result of the ballot.

231 Information as to result of ballot

As soon as is reasonably practicable after the holding of the ballot, the trade union shall take such steps as are reasonably necessary to ensure that all persons entitled to vote in the ballot are informed of the number of—

(a) votes cast in the ballot,

(b) individuals answering 'Yes' to the question, or as the case may be, to each question,

(c) individuals answering 'No' to the question, or, as the case may be, to each question, and

(d) spoiled voting papers.

231A Employers to be informed of ballot result

(1) As soon as reasonably practicable after the holding of the ballot, the trade union shall take such steps as are reasonably necessary to ensure that every relevant employer is informed of the matters mentioned in section 231.

(2) In subsection (1) 'relevant employer' means a person who it is reasonable for the trade union to believe (at the time when the steps are taken) was at the time of the ballot the employer of any persons entitled to vote.

231B Scrutineer's report

(1) The scrutineer's report on the ballot shall state whether the scrutineer is satisfied—

(a) that there are no reasonable grounds for believing that there was any contravention of a requirement imposed by or under any enactment in relation to the ballot,

(b) that the arrangements made with respect to the production, storage, distribution, return or other handling of the voting papers used in the ballot, and the arrangements for the counting of the votes, included all such security arrangements as were reasonably practicable for the purpose of minimising the risk that any unfairness or malpractice might occur, and

(c) that he has been able to carry out the functions conferred on him under section 226B(1) without any interference from the trade union or any of its members, officials or employees;

and if he is not satisfied as to any of those matters, the report shall give particulars of his reason for not being satisfied as to that matter.

(2) If at any time within six months from the date of the ballot—

(a) any person entitled to vote in the ballot, or

(b) the employer of any such person,

requests a copy of the scrutineer's report, the trade union must, as soon as practicable, provide him with one either free of charge or on payment of such reasonable fee as may be specified by the trade union.

232 [omitted]

232A Inducement of member denied entitlement to vote

Industrial action shall not be regarded as having the support of a ballot if the following conditions apply in the case of any person—

(a) he was a member of the trade union at the time when the ballot was held,

(b) it was reasonable at that time for the trade union to believe he would be induced to take part or, as the case may be, to continue to take part in the industrial action,

(c) he was not accorded entitlement to vote in the ballot, and

(d) he was induced by the trade union to take part or, as the case may be, to continue to take part in the industrial action.

232B Small accidental failures to be disregarded

(1) If—

(a) in relation to a ballot there is a failure (or there are failures) to comply with a provision mentioned in subsection (2) or with more than one of those provisions, and

(b) the failure is accidental and on a scale which is unlikely to affect the result of the ballot or, as the case may be, the failures are accidental and taken together are on a scale which is unlikely to affect the result of the ballot,

the failure (or failures) shall be disregarded.

(2) The provisions are section 227(1), section 230(2) and section 230(2A).

233 Calling of industrial action with support of ballot

(1) Industrial action shall not be regarded as having the support of a ballot unless it is called by a specified person and the conditions specified below are satisfied.

(2) A 'specified person' means a person specified or of a description specified in the voting paper for the ballot in accordance with section 229(3).

(3) The conditions are that—

(a) there must have been no call by the trade union to take part or continue to take part in industrial action to which the ballot relates, or any authorisation or endorsement by the union of any such industrial action, before the date of the ballot;

(b) there must be a call for industrial action by a specified person, and industrial action to which it relates must take place, before the ballot ceases to be effective in accordance with section 234.

(4) For the purposes of this section a call shall be taken to have been made by a trade union if it was authorised or endorsed by the union; and the provisions of section 20(2) to (4) apply for the purpose of determining whether a call, or industrial action, is to be taken to have been so authorised or endorsed.

234 Period after which ballot ceases to be effective

(1) Subject to the following provisions, a ballot ceases to be effective for the purposes of section 233(3)(b) in relation to industrial action by members of a trade union at the end of the period, beginning with the date of the ballot—

(a) of four weeks, or

(b) of such longer duration not exceeding eight weeks as is agreed between the union and the members' employer.

(2) Where for the whole or part of that period the calling or organising of industrial action is prohibited—

(a) by virtue of a court order which subsequently lapses or is discharged, recalled or set aside, or

(b) by virtue of an undertaking given to a court by any person from which he is subsequently released or by which he ceases to be bound,

the trade union may apply to the court for an order that the period during which the prohibition had effect shall not count towards the period referred to in subsection (1).

(3) The application must be made forthwith upon the prohibition ceasing to have effect—

(a) to the court by virtue of whose decision it ceases to have effect, or

(b) where an order lapses or an undertaking ceases to bind without any such decision, to the court by which the order was made or to which the undertaking was given;

and no application may be made after the end of the period of eight weeks beginning with the date of the ballot.

(4) The court shall not make an order if it appears to the court—

(a) that the result of the ballot no longer represents the views of the union members concerned, or

(b) that an event is likely to occur as a result of which those members would vote against industrial action if another ballot were to be held.

(5) No appeal lies from the decision of the court to make or refuse an order under this section.

(6) The period between the making of an application under this section and its determination does not count towards the period referred to in subsection (1).

But a ballot shall not by virtue of this subsection (together with any order of the court) be regarded as effective for the purposes of section 233(3)(b) after the end of the period of twelve weeks beginning with the date of the ballot.

Requirement on trade union to give notice of industrial action

234A Notice to employers of industrial action

(1) An act done by a trade union to induce a person to take part, or continue to take part, in industrial action is not protected as respects his employer unless the union has taken or takes such steps as are reasonably necessary to ensure that the employer receives within the appropriate period a relevant notice covering the act.

(2) Subsection (1) imposes a requirement in the case of an employer only if it is reasonable for the union to believe, at the latest time when steps could be taken to ensure that he receives such a notice, that he is the employer of persons who will be or have been induced to take part, or continue to take part, in the industrial action.

(3) For the purposes of this section a relevant notice is a notice in writing which—

(a) contains such information in the union's possession as would help the employer to make plans and bring information to the attention of those of his employees whom the union intends to induce or has induced to take part, or continue to take part, in the industrial action ('the affected employees'),

(b) states whether industrial action is intended to be continuous or discontinuous and specifies—

(i) where it is to be continuous, the intended date for any of the affected employees to begin to take part in the action,

(ii) where it is to be discontinuous, the intended dates for any of the affected employees to take part in the action, and

(c) states that it is given for the purposes of this section.

(4) For the purposes of subsection (1) the appropriate period is the period—

(a) beginning with the day when the union satisfies the requirement of section 231A in relation to the ballot in respect of the industrial action, and

(b) ending with the seventh day before the day, or before the first of the days, specified in the relevant notice.

(5) For the purposes of subsection (1) a relevant notice covers an act done by the union if the person induced is one of the affected employees and—

(a) where he is induced to take part or continue to take part in industrial action which the union intends to be continuous, if—

(i) the notice states that the union intends the industrial action to be continuous, and

(ii) there is no participation by him in the industrial action before the date specified in the notice in consequence of any inducement by the union not covered by a relevant notice; and

(b) where he is induced to take part or continue to take part in industrial action which the union intends to be discontinuous, if there is no participation by him in the industrial action on a day not so specified in consequence of any inducement by the union not covered by a relevant notice.

(5A) These rules apply for the purposes of paragraph (a) of subsection (3)—

(a) if the union possesses information as to the number, category or work-place of the employees concerned, a notice must contain that information (at least);

(b) if a notice does not name any employees, the fact shall not be a ground for holding that it does not comply with paragraph (a) of subsection (3).

(6) For the purposes of this section—

(a) a union intends industrial action to be discontinuous if it intends it to take place only on some days on which there is an opportunity to take the action, and

(b) a union intends industrial action to be continuous if it intends it to be not so restricted.

(7) Subject to subsections (7A) and (7B) where—

(a) continuous industrial action which has been authorised or endorsed by a union ceases to be so authorised or endorsed, and

(b) the industrial action has at a later date again been authorised or endorsed by the union (whether as continuous or discontinuous action),

no relevant notice covering acts done to induce persons to take part in the earlier action shall operate to cover acts done to induce persons to take part in the action authorised or endorsed at the later date and this section shall apply in relation to an act to induce a person to take part, or continue to take part, in the industrial action after that date as if the references in subsection (3)(b)(i) to the industrial action were to the industrial action taking place after that date.

(7A) Subsection (7) shall not apply where industrial action ceases to be authorised or endorsed in order to enable the union to comply with a court order or an undertaking given to a court.

(7B) Subsection (7) shall not apply where—

(a) a union agrees with an employer, before industrial action ceases to be authorised or endorsed, that it will cease to be authorised or endorsed with effect from a date specified in the agreement ('the suspension date') and that it may again be authorised or endorsed with effect from a date not earlier than a date specified in the agreement ('the resumption date'),

(b) the action ceases to be authorised or endorsed with effect from the suspension date, and

(c) the action is again authorised or endorsed with effect from a date which is not earlier than the resumption date or such later date as may be agreed between the union and the employer.

(8) The requirement imposed on a trade union by subsection (1) shall be treated as having been complied with if the steps were taken by other relevant persons or committees whose acts were authorised or endorsed by the union and references to the belief or intention of the union in subsection (2) or as the case may be, subsections (3), (5) and (6) shall be construed as references to the belief or the intention of the person or committee taking the steps.

(9) The provisions of section 20(2) to (4) apply for the purpose of determining for the purposes of subsection (1) who are relevant persons or committees and whether the trade union is to be taken to have authorised or endorsed the steps the person or committee took and for the purposes of subsection (7) whether the trade union is to be taken to have authorised or endorsed the industrial action.

235 Construction of references to contract of employment

In sections 226 to 234A (requirement of ballot before action by trade union) references to a contract of employment include any contract under which one person personally does work or performs services for another; and 'employer' and other related expressions shall be construed accordingly.

Industrial action affecting supply of goods or services to an individual

235A Industrial action affecting supply of goods or services to an individual

(1) Where an individual claims that—

(a) any trade union or other person has done, or is likely to do, an unlawful act to induce any person to take part, or to continue to take part, in industrial action, and

(b) an effect, or a likely effect, of the industrial action is or will be to—

(i) prevent or delay the supply of goods or services, or

(ii) reduce the quality of goods or services supplied,

to the individual making the claim,

he may apply to the High Court or the Court of Session for an order under this section.

(2) For the purposes of this section an act to induce any person to take part, or to continue to take part, in industrial action is unlawful—

(a) if it is actionable in tort by any one or more persons, or

(b) (where it is or would be the act of a trade union) if it could form the basis of an application by a member under section 62.

(3) In determining whether an individual may make an application under this section it is immaterial whether or not the individual is entitled to be supplied with the goods or services in question.

(4) Where on an application under this section the court is satisfied that the claim is well-founded, it shall make such order as it considers appropriate for requiring the person by whom the act of inducement has been, or is likely to be, done to take steps for ensuring—

(a) that no, or no further, act is done by him to induce any persons to take part or to continue to take part in the industrial action, and

(b) that no person engages in conduct after the making of the order by virtue of having been induced by him before the making of the order to take part or continue to take part in the industrial action.

(5) Without prejudice to any other power of the court, the court may on an application under this section grant such interlocutory relief (in Scotland, such interim order) as it considers appropriate.

(6) For the purposes of this section an act of inducement shall be taken to be done by a trade union if it is authorised or endorsed by the union; and the provisions of section 20(2) to (4) apply for the purposes of determining whether such an act is to be taken to be so authorised or endorsed.

Those provisions also apply in relation to proceedings for failure to comply with an order under this section as they apply in relation to the original proceedings.

235B-235C [repealed]

No compulsion to work

236 No compulsion to work

No court shall, whether by way of—

(a) an order for specific performance or specific implement of a contract of employment, or

(b) an injunction or interdict restraining a breach or threatened breach of such a contract,

compel an employee to do any work or attend at any place for the doing of any work.

Loss of unfair dismissal protection

237 Dismissal of those taking part in unofficial industrial action

(1) An employee has no right to complain of unfair dismissal if at the time of dismissal he was taking part in an unofficial strike or other unofficial industrial action.

(1A) Subsection (1) does not apply to the dismissal of the employee if it is shown that the reason (or, if more than one, the principal reason) for the dismissal or, in a redundancy case, for selecting the employee for dismissal was one of those specified in or —

(a) section 99, 100, 101A(d), 103 or 103A of the Employment Rights Act 1996 (dismissal in family, health and safety, working time, employee representative and protected disclosure cases),

(b) section 104 of that Act in its application in relation to time off under section 57A of that Act (dependants);

In this subsection 'redundancy case' has the meaning given in section 105(9) of that Act, and a reference to a specified reason for dismissal includes a reference to specified circumstances of dismissal.

(2) A strike or other industrial action is unofficial in relation to an employee unless—

(a) he is a member of a trade union and the action is authorised or endorsed by that union, or

(b) he is not a member of a trade union but there are among those taking part in the industrial action members of a trade union by which the action has been authorised or endorsed.

Provided that, a strike or other industrial action shall not be regarded as unofficial if none of those taking part in it are members of a trade union.

(3) The provisions of section 20(2) apply for the purpose of determining whether industrial action is to be taken to have been authorised or endorsed by a trade union.

(4) The question whether industrial action is to be so taken in any case shall be determined by reference to the facts as at the time of dismissal.

Provided that, where an act is repudiated as mentioned in section 21, industrial action shall not thereby be treated as unofficial before the end of the next working day after the day on which the repudiation takes place.

(5) In this section the 'time of dismissal' means—

(a) where the employee's contract of employment is terminated by notice, when the notice is given,

(b) where the employee's contract of employment is terminated without notice, when the termination takes effect, and

(c) where the employee is employed under a contract for a fixed term which expires without being renewed under the same contract, when that term expires;

and a 'working day' means any day which is not a Saturday or Sunday, Christmas Day, Good Friday or a bank holiday under the Banking and Financial Dealings Act 1971.

(6) For the purposes of this section membership of a trade union for purposes unconnected with the employment in question shall be disregarded; but an employee who was a member of a trade union when he began to take part in industrial action shall continue to be treated as a member for the purpose of determining whether that action is unofficial in relation to him or another notwithstanding that he may in fact have ceased to be a member.

238 Dismissals in connection with other industrial action

(1) This section applies in relation to an employee who has a right to complain of unfair dismissal (the 'complainant') and who claims to have been unfairly dismissed, where at the date of the dismissal—

(a) the employer was conducting or instituting a lock-out, or

(b) the complainant was taking part in a strike or other industrial action.

(2) In such a case an employment tribunal shall not determine whether the dismissal was fair or unfair unless it is shown—

(a) that one or more relevant employees of the same employer have not been dismissed, or

(b) that a relevant employee has before the expiry of the period of three months beginning with the date of his dismissal been offered re-engagement and that the complainant has not been offered re-engagement.

(2A) Subsection (2) does not apply to the dismissal of the employee if it is shown that the reason (or, if more than one, the principal reason) for the dismissal or, in a redundancy case, for selecting the employee for dismissal was one of those specified in or under—

(a) section 99, 100, 101A(d) or 103 of the Employment Rights Act 1996 (dismissal in family, health and safety, working time and employee representative cases),

(b) section 104 of that Act in its application in relation to time off under section 57A of that Act (dependants).

In this subsection 'redundancy case' has the meaning given in section 105(9) of that Act; and a reference to a specified reason for dismissal includes a reference to specified circumstances of dismissal.

(2B) Subsection (2) does not apply in relation to an employee who is regarded as unfairly dismissed by virtue of section 238A below.

(3) For this purpose 'relevant employees' means—

(a) in relation to a lock-out, employees who were directly interested in the dispute in contemplation or furtherance of which the lock-out occurred, and

(b) in relation to a strike or other industrial action, those employees at the establishment of the employer at or from which the complainant works who at the date of his dismissal were taking part in the action.

Nothing in section 237 (dismissal of those taking part in unofficial industrial action) affects the question who are relevant employees for the purposes of this section.

(4) An offer of re-engagement means an offer (made either by the original employer or by a successor of that employer or an associated employer) to re-engage an employee, either in the job which he held immediately before the date of dismissal or in a different job which would be reasonably suitable in his case.

(5) In this section 'date of dismissal' means—

(a) where the employee's contract of employment was terminated by notice, the date on which the employer's notice was given, and

(b) in any other case, the effective date of termination.

238A Participation in official industrial action

(1) For the purposes of this section an employee takes protected industrial action if he commits an act which, or a series of acts each of which, he is induced to commit by an act which by virtue of section 219 is not actionable in tort.

(2) An employee who is dismissed shall be regarded for the purposes of Part X of the Employment Rights Act 1996 (unfair dismissal) as unfairly dismissed if—

(a) the reason (or, if more than one, the principal reason) for the dismissal is that the employee took protected industrial action, and

(b) subsection (3), (4) or (5) applies to the dismissal.

(3) This subsection applies to a dismissal if it takes place within the period of eight weeks beginning with the day on which the employee started to take protected industrial action.

(4) This subsection applies to a dismissal if—

(a) it takes place after the end of that period, and

(b) the employee had stopped taking protected industrial action before the end of that period.

(5) This subsection applies to a dismissal if—

(a) it takes place after the end of that period,

(b) the employee had not stopped taking protected industrial action before the end of that period, and

(c) the employer had not taken such procedural steps as would have been reasonable for the purposes of resolving the dispute to which the protected industrial action relates.

(6) In determining whether an employer has taken those steps regard shall be had, in particular, to—

(a) whether the employer or a union had complied with procedures established by any applicable collective or other agreement;

(b) Whether the employer or a union offered or agreed to commence or resume negotiations after the start of the protected industrial action;

(c) whether the employer or a union unreasonably refused, after the start of the protected industrial action, a request that conciliation services be used;

(d) whether the employer or a union unreasonably refused, after the start of the protected industrial action, a request that mediation services be used in relation to procedures to be adopted for the purposes of resolving the dispute.

(7) In determining whether an employer has taken those steps no regard shall be had to the merits of the dispute.

(8) For the purposes of this section no account shall be taken of the repudiation of any act by a trade union as mentioned in section 21 in relation to anything which occurs before the end of the next working day (within the meaning of section 237) after the day on which the repudiation takes place.

239 Supplementary provisions relating to unfair dismissal

(1) Sections 237 to 238A (loss of unfair dismissal protection in connection with industrial action) shall be construed as one with Part X of the Employment Rights Act 1996 (unfair dismissal); but sections 108 and 109 of that Act (qualifying period and age limit) shall not apply in relation to section 238A of this Act.

(2) In relation to a complaint to which section 238 or 238A applies, section 111(2) of that Act (time limit for complaint) does not apply, but an employment tribunal shall not consider the complaint unless it is presented to the tribunal—

(a) before the end of the period of six months beginning with the date of the complainant's dismissal (as defined by section 238(5)), or

(b) where the tribunal is satisfied that it was not reasonably practicable for the complaint to be presented before the end of that period, within such further period as the tribunal considers reasonable.

(3) Where it is shown that the condition referred to in section 238(2)(b) is fulfilled (discriminatory re-engagement), the references in—

(a) sections 98 to 106 of the Employment Rights Act 1996, and

(b) sections 152 and 153 of this Act,

to the reason or principal reason for which the complainant was dismissed shall be read as references to the reason or principal reason he has not been offered re-engagement.

(4) In relation to a complaint under section 111 of the 1996 Act (unfair dismissal: complaint to employment tribunal) that a dismissal was unfair by virtue of section 238A of this Act—

(a) no order shall be made under section 113 of the 1996 Act (reinstatement or re-engagement) until after the conclusion of protected industrial action by any employee in relation to the relevant dispute,

(b) regulations under section 7 of the Employment Tribunals Act 1996 may make provision about the adjournment and renewal of applications (including provision requiring adjournment in specified circumstances), and

(c) regulations under section 9 of that Act may require a pre-hearing review to be carried out in specified circumstances.

Criminal offences

240 Breach of contract involving injury to persons or property

(1) A person commits an offence who wilfully and maliciously breaks a contract of service or hiring, knowing or having reasonable cause to believe that the probable consequences of his so doing, either alone or in combination with others, will be—

(a) to endanger human life or cause serious bodily injury, or

(b) to expose valuable property, whether real or personal, to destruction or serious injury.

(2) Subsection (1) applies equally whether the offence is committed from malice conceived against the person endangered or injured or, as the case may be, the owner of the property destroyed or injured, or otherwise.

(3) A person guilty of an offence under this section is liable on summary conviction to imprisonment for a term not exceeding three months or to a fine not exceeding level 2 on the standard scale or both.

(4) This section does not apply to seamen.

241 Intimidation or annoyance by violence or otherwise

(1) A person commits an offence who, with a view to compelling another person to abstain from doing or to do any act which that person has a legal right to do or abstain from doing, wrongfully and without legal authority—

(a) uses violence to or intimidates that person or his wife or children, or injures his property,

(b) persistently follows that person about from place to place,

(c) hides any tools, clothes or other property owned or used by that person, or deprives him of or hinders him in the use thereof,

(d) watches or besets the house or other place where that person resides, works, carries on business or happens to be, or the approach to any such house or place, or

(e) follows that person with two or more other persons in a disorderly manner in or through any street or road.

(2) A person guilty of an offence under this section is liable on summary conviction to imprisonment for a term not exceeding six months or a fine not exceeding level 5 on the standard scale, or both.

(3) A constable may arrest without warrant anyone he reasonably suspects is committing an offence under this section.

242 Restriction of offence of conspiracy: England and Wales

(1) Where in pursuance of any such agreement as is mentioned in section 1(1) of the Criminal Law Act 1977 (which provides for the offence of conspiracy) the acts in question in relation to an offence are to be done in contemplation or furtherance of a trade dispute, the offence shall be disregarded for the purposes of that subsection if it is a summary offence which is not punishable with imprisonment.

(2) This section extends to England and Wales only.

243 Restriction of offence of conspiracy: Scotland

(1) An agreement of combination by two or more persons to do or procure to be done an act in contemplation or furtherance of a trade dispute is not indictable as a conspiracy if that act committed by one person would not be punishable as a crime.

(2) A crime for this purpose means an offence punishable on indictment, or an offence punishable on summary conviction, and for the commission of which the offender is liable under the statute making the offence punishable to be imprisoned either absolutely or at the discretion of the court as an alternative for some other punishment.

(3) Where a person is convicted of any such agreement or combination as is mentioned above to do or procure to be done an act which is punishable only on

summary conviction, and is sentenced to imprisonment, the imprisonment shall not exceed three months or such longer time as may be prescribed by the statute for the punishment of the act when committed by one person.

(4) Nothing in this section—

(a) exempts from punishment a person guilty of a conspiracy for which a punishment is awarded by an Act of Parliament, or

(b) affects the law relating to riot, unlawful assembly, breach of the peace, or sedition or any offence against the State or the Sovereign.

(5) This section extends to Scotland only.

Supplementary

244 Meaning of 'trade dispute' in Part V

(1) In this Part a 'trade dispute' means a dispute between workers and their employer which relates wholly or mainly to one or more of the following—

(a) terms and conditions of employment, or the physical conditions in which any workers are required to work;

(b) engagement or non-engagement, or termination or suspension of employment or the duties of employment, of one or more workers;

(c) allocation of work or the duties of employment between workers or groups of workers;

(d) matters of discipline;

(e) a worker's membership or non-membership of a trade union;

(f) facilities for officials of trade unions; and

(g) machinery for negotiation or consultation, and other procedures, relating to any of the above matters, including the recognition by employers or employers' associations of the right of a trade union to represent workers in such negotiation or consultation or in the carrying out of such procedures.

(2) A dispute between a Minister of the Crown and any workers shall, notwithstanding that he is not the employer of those workers, be treated as a dispute between those workers and their employer if the dispute relates to matters which—

(a) have been referred for consideration by a joint body on which, by virtue of provision made by or under any enactment, he is represented, or

(b) cannot be settled without him exercising a power conferred on him by or under an enactment.

(3) There is a trade dispute even though it relates to matters occurring outside the United Kingdom, so long as the person or persons whose actions in the United Kingdom are said to be in contemplation or furtherance of a trade dispute relating to matters occurring outside the United Kingdom are likely to be affected in respect of one or more of the matters specified in subsection (1) by the outcome of the dispute.

(4) An act, threat or demand done or made by one person or organisation against another which, if restricted, would have led to a trade dispute with that other, shall be treated as being done or made in contemplation of a trade dispute with that other, notwithstanding that because that other submits to the act or threat or accedes to the demand no dispute arises.

(5) In this section—

'employment' includes any relationship whereby one person personally does work or performs services for another; and

'worker', in relation to a dispute with an employer, means—

(a) a worker employed by that employer; or

(b) a person who has ceased to be so employed if his employment was terminated in connection with the dispute or if the termination of his employment was one of the circumstances giving rise to the dispute.

245 Crown employees and contracts

Where a person holds any office or employment under the Crown on terms which do not constitute a contract of employment between that person and the Crown, those terms shall nevertheless be deemed to constitute such a contract for the purposes of—

(a) the law relating to liability in tort of a person who commits an act which—

(i) induces another person to break a contract, interferes with the performance of a contract or induces another person to interfere with its performance, or

(ii) consists in a threat that a contract will be broken or its performance interfered with, or that any person will be induced to break a contract or interfere with its performance, and

(b) the provisions of this or any other Act which refer (whether in relation to contracts generally or only in relation to contracts of employment) to such an act.

246 Minor definitions

In this Part—

'date of the ballot' means, in the case of a ballot in which votes may be cast on more than one day, the last of those days;

'strike' means any concerted stoppage of work;

'working hours', in relation to a person, means any time when under his contract of employment, or other contract personally to do work or perform services, he is required to be at work.

PART VI
ADMINISTRATIVE PROVISIONS

ACAS

247 ACAS

(1) There shall continue to be a body called the Advisory, Conciliation and Arbitration Service (referred to in this Act as 'ACAS').

(2) ACAS is a body corporate of which the corporators are the members of its Council.

(3) Its functions, and those of its officers and servants, shall be performed on behalf of the Crown, but not so as to make it subject to directions of any kind from any Minister of the Crown as to the manner in which it is to exercise its functions under any enactment.

(4) For the purposes of civil proceedings arising out of those functions the Crown Proceedings Act 1947 applies to ACAS as if it were a government department and the Crown Suits (Scotland) Act 1857 applies to it as if it were a public department.

(5)-(6) [omitted]

248 The Council of ACAS

(1) ACAS shall be directed by a Council which, subject to the following provisions, shall consist of a chairman and nine ordinary members appointed by the Secretary of State.

(2) Before appointing those ordinary members of the Council, the Secretary of State shall—

(a) as to three of them, consult such organisations representing employers as he considers appropriate, and

(b) as to three of them, consult such organisations representing workers as he considers appropriate.

(3) The Secretary of State may, if he thinks fit, appoint a further two ordinary members of the Council (who shall be appointed so as to take office at the same time); and before making those appointments he shall—

(a) as to one of them, consult such organisations representing employers as he considers appropriate, and

(b) as to one of them, consult such organisations representing workers as he considers appropriate.

(4) The Secretary of State may appoint up to three deputy chairmen who may be appointed from the ordinary members, or in addition to those members.

(5) The Council shall determine its own procedure, including the quorum necessary for its meetings.

(6) If the Secretary of State has not appointed a deputy charimen, the Council may choose a member to act as chairman in the absence or incapacity of the chairman.

(7) The validity of proceedings of the Council is not affected by any vacancy among the members of the Council or by any defect in the appointment of any of them.

249-253 [omitted]

The Certification Officer

254 The Certification Officer

(1) There shall continue to be an officer called the Certification Officer.

(2) The Certification Officer shall be appointed by the Secretary of State after consultation with ACAS.

(3) The Certification Officer may appoint one or more assistant certification officers and shall appoint an assistant certification officer for Scotland.

(4) The Certification Officer may delegate to an assistant certification officer such functions as he thinks appropriate, and in particular may delegate to the assistant certification officer for Scotland such functions as he thinks appropriate in relation to organisations whose principal office is in Scotland.

References to the Certification Officer in enactments relating to his functions shall be construed accordingly.

(5) ACAS shall provide for the Certification Officer the requisite staff (from among the officers and servants of ACAS) and the requisite accommodation, equipment and other facilities.

(5A) Subject to subsection (6), ACAS shall pay to the Certification Officer such sums as he may require for the performance of any of his functions.

(6) The Secretary of State shall pay to the Certification Officer such sums as he may require for making payments under the scheme under section 115 (payments towards expenditure in connection with secret ballots).

255 [omitted]

256 Procedure before the Certification Officer

(1) Except in relation to matters as to which express provision is made by or under an enactment, the Certification Officer may regulate the procedure to be followed—

(a) on any application or complaint made to him, or

(b) where his approval is sought with respect to any matter.

(2) He shall in particular make provision about the disclosure, and restriction of the disclosure, of the identity of an individual who has made or is proposing to make any such application or complaint.

(2A) Provision under subsection (2) shall be such that if the application or complaint relates to a trade union—

(a) the individual's identity is disclosed to the union unless the Certification Officer thinks the circumstances are such that it should not be so disclosed;

(b) the individual's identity is disclosed to such other persons (if any) as the Certification Officer thinks fit.

(3) [omitted] and (4) [repealed]

256A-258 [omitted]

Central Arbitration Committee

259 The Central Arbitration Committee

(1) There shall continue to be a body called the Central Arbitration Committee.

(2) The functions of the Committee shall be performed on behalf of the Crown, but not so as to make it subject to directions of any kind from any Minister of the Crown as to the manner in which it is to exercise its functions.

(3) ACAS shall provide for the Committee the requisite staff (from among the officers and servants of ACAS) and the requisite accommodation, equipment and other facilities.

260 The members of the Committee

(1) The Central Arbitration Committee shall consist of members appointed by the Secretary of State.

(2) The Secretary of State shall appoint a member as chairman, and may appoint a member as deputy chairman or members as deputy chairmen.

(3) The Secretary of State may appoint as members only persons experienced in industrial relations, and they shall include some persons whose experience is as representatives of employers and some whose experience is as representatives of workers.

(3A) Before making an appointment under subsection (1) or (2) the Secretary of State shall consult ACAS and may consult other persons.

(4) At any time when the chairman of the Committee is absent or otherwise incapable of acting, or there is a vacancy in the office of chairman, and the Committee has a deputy chairman or deputy chairmen—

(a) the deputy chairman, if there is only one, or

(b) if there is more than one, such of the deputy chairmen as they may agree or in default of agreement as the Secretary of State may direct,

may perform any of the functions of chairman of the Committee.

(5) At any time when every person who is chairman or deputy chairman is absent or otherwise incapable of acting, or there is no such person, such member of the Committee as the Secretary of State may direct may perform any of the functions of the chairman of the Committee.

(6) The validity of any proceedings of the Committee shall not be affected by any vacancy among the members of the Committee or by any defect in the appointment of a member of the Committee.

261-265 [omitted]; **266-271** [repealed]; **272** [omitted]

PART VII
MISCELLANEOUS AND GENERAL

Crown employment, etc.

273 Crown employment

(1) The provisions of this Act have effect (except as mentioned below) in relation to Crown employment and persons in Crown employment as in relation to other employment and other workers or employees.

(2) The following provisions are excepted from subsection (1)—

section 87(4)(b) (power of tribunal to make order in respect of employer's failure to comply with duties as to union contributions);

sections 184 and 185 (remedy for failure to comply with declaration as to disclosure of information);

Chapter II of Part IV (procedure for handling redundancies).

(3) In this section 'Crown employment' means employment under or for the purposes of a government department or any officer or body exercising on behalf of the Crown functions conferred by an enactment.

(4) For the purposes of the provisions of this Act as they apply in relation to Crown employment or persons in Crown employment—

(a) 'employee' and 'contract of employment' mean a person in Crown employment and the terms of employment of such a person (but subject to subsection (5) below);

(b) 'dismissal' means the termination of Crown employment;

(c) [repealed]

(d) the reference in 182(1)(e) (disclosure of information for collective bargaining: restrictions on general duty) to the employer's undertaking shall be construed as a reference to the national interest; and

(e) any other reference to an undertaking shall be construed, in relation to a Minister of the Crown, as a reference to his functions or (as the context may require) to the department of which he is in charge, and in relation to a government department, officer or body shall be construed as a reference to the functions of the department, officer or body or (as the context may require) to the department, officer or body.

(5) Sections 137 to 143 (rights in relation to trade union membership: access to employment) apply in relation to Crown employment otherwise than under a contract only where the terms of employment correspond to those of a contract of employment.

(6) This section has effect subject to section 274 (armed forces) and section 275 (exemption on grounds of national security).

274-280 [omitted]

Excluded classes of employment

281 [repealed]

282 Short-term employment

(1) The provisions of Chapter II of Part IV (procedure for handling redundancies) do not apply to employment—

(a) under a contract for a fixed term of three months or less, or

(b) under a contract made in contemplation of the performance of a specific task which is not expected to last for more than three months,

where the employee has not been continuously employed for a period of more than three months.

(2) Chapter I of Part XIV of the Employment Rights Act 1996 (computation of period of continuous employment), and any provision modifying or supplementing that Chapter for the purposes of that Act, apply for the purposes of this section.

283 [repealed]; **284** [omitted]

285 Employment outside Great Britain

(1) The following provisions of this Act do not apply to employment where under his contract of employment an employee works, or in the case of a prospective employee would ordinarily work, outside Great Britain—

In Part III (rights in relation to trade union membership and activities)—

sections 137 to 143 (access to employment),

sections 146 to 151 (action short of dismissal), and

sections 168 to 173 (time off for trade union duties and activities);

In Part IV, sections 193 and 194 (duty to notify Secretary of State of certain redundancies).

(2) For the purposes of subsection (1) employment on board a ship registered in the United Kingdom shall be treated as employment where under his contract a person ordinarily works in Great Britain unless—

(a) the ship is registered at a port outside Great Britain, or

(b) the employment is wholly outside Great Britain, or

(c) the employee or, as the case may be, the person seeking employment or seeking to avail himself of a service of an employment agency, is not ordinarily resident in Great Britain.

286-287 [omitted]

Contracting out, &c.

288 Restriction on contracting out

(1) Any provision in an agreement (whether a contract of employment or not) is void in so far as it purports—

(a) to exclude or limit the operation of any provision of this Act, or

(b) to preclude a person from bringing—

(i) proceedings before an employment tribunal or the Central Arbitration Committee under any provision of this Act, or

(ii) an application to the Employment Appeal Tribunal under section 67 (remedy for infringement of right not to be unjustifiably disciplined) or section 176 (compensation for exclusion or expulsion).

(2) Subsection (1) does not apply to an agreement to refrain from instituting or continuing proceedings where a conciliation officer has taken action under section 18 of the Employment Tribunals Act 1996 (conciliation).

(2A) Subsection (1) does not apply to an agreement to refrain from instituting or continuing any proceedings, other than excepted proceedings, specified in subsection (1)(b) of that section before an employment tribunal if the conditions regulating compromise agreements under this Act are satisfied in relation to the agreement.

(2B) The conditions regulating compromise agreements under this Act are that—

(a) the agreement must be in writing;

(b) the agreement must relate to the particular proceedings;

(c) the complainant must have received advice from a relavant independent adviser as to the terms and effect of the proposed agreement and in particular its effect on his ability to pursue his rights before an employment tribunal;

(d) there must be in force, when the adviser gives the advice, a contract of insurance, or an indemnity provided for members of a profession or professional body covering the risk of a claim by the complainant in respect of loss arising in consequence of the advice;

(e) the agreement must identify the adviser; and

(f) the agreement must state that the conditions regulating compromise agreements under this Act are satisfied.

(2C) The proceedings excepted from subsection (2A) are proceedings on a complaint of non-compliance with section 188.

(3) Subsection (1) does not apply—

(a) to such an agreement as is referred to in section 185(5)(b) or (c) to the extent that it varies or supersedes an award under that section;

(b) to any provision in a collective agreement excluding rights under Chapter II of Part IV (procedure for handling redundancies), if an order under section 198 is in force in respect of it.

(4) A person is a relevant independent adviser for the purposes of subsection (2B)(c)—

(a) if he is a qualified lawyer,

(b) if he is an officer, official, employee or member of an independent trade union who has been certified in writing by the trade union as competent to give advice and as authorised to do so on behalf of the trade union,

(c) if he works at an advice centre (whether as an employee or a volunteer) and has been certified in writing by the centre as competent to give advice and as authorised to do so on behalf of the centre, or

(d) if he is a person of a description specified in an order made by the Secretary of State.

(4A) But a person is not a relevant independent adviser for the purposes of subsection (2B)(c) in relation to the complainant—

(a) if he is, is employed by or is acting in the matter for the other party or a person who is connected with the other party,

(b) in the case of a person within subsection (4)(b) or (c), if the trade union or advice centre is the other party or a person who is connected with the other party,

(c) in the case of a person within subsection (4)(c), if the complainant makes a payment for the advice received from him, or

(d) in the case of a person of a description specified in an order under subsection (4)(d), if any condition specified in the order in relation to the giving of advice by persons of that description is not satisfied.

(4B) In subsection (4)(a) 'qualified lawyer' means—

(a) as respects England and Wales, a barrister (whether in practice as such or employed to give legal advice), a solicitor who holds a practising certificate, or a person other than a barrister or solicitor who is an authorised advocate or authorised litigator (within the meaning of the Courts and Legal Services Act 1990), and

(b) as respects Scotland, an advocate (whether in practice as such or employed to give legal advice), or a solicitor who holds a practising certificate.

(4C) An order under subsection (4)(d) shall be made by statutory instrument which shall be subject to annulment in pursuance of a resolution of either House of Parliament.

(5) For the purposes of subsection (4A) any two persons are to be treated as connected—

(a) if one is a company of which the other (directly or indirectly) has control, or

(b) if both are companies of which a third person (directly or indirectly) has control.

(6) An agreement under which the parties agree to submit a dispute to arbitration—

(a) shall be regarded for the purposes of subsections (2) and (2A) as being an agreement to refrain from instituting or continuing proceedings if—

(i) the dispute is covered by a scheme having effect by virtue of an order under section 212A, and

(ii) the agreement is to submit it to arbitration in accordance with the scheme, but

(b) shall be regarded for those purposes as neither being nor including such an agreement in any other case.

289 Employment governed by foreign law

For the purposes of this Act it is immaterial whether the law which (apart from this Act) governs any person's employment is the law of the United Kingdom, or of a part of the United Kingdom, or not.

290 and **291** [repealed]; **292–294** [omitted]

Interpretation

295 Meaning of 'employee' and related expressions

(1) In this Act—

'contract of employment' means a contract of service or of apprenticeship,

'employee' means an individual who has entered into or works under (or, where the employment has ceased, worked under) a contract of employment, and

'employer', in relation to an employee, means the person by whom the employee is (or, where the employment has ceased, was) employed.

(2) Subsection (1) has effect subject to section 235 and other provisions conferring a wider meaning on 'contract of employment', or related expressions.

296 Meaning of 'worker' and related expressions

(1) In this Act 'worker' means an individual who works, or normally works or seeks to work—

(a) under a contract of employment, or

(b) under any other contract whereby he undertakes to do or perform personally any work or services for another party to the contract who is not a professional client of his, or

(c) in employment under or for the purposes of a government department (otherwise than as a member of the naval, military or air forces of the Crown) in so far as such employment does not fall within paragraph (a) or (b) above.

(2) In this Act 'employer', in relation to a worker, means a person for whom one or more workers work, or have worked or normally work or seek to work.

(3) This section shall have effect subject to section 68(11).

297 Associated employers

For the purposes of this Act any two employers shall be treated as associated if—

(a) one is a company of which the other (directly or indirectly) has control, or

(b) both are companies of which a third person (directly or indirectly) has control;

and 'associated employer' shall be construed accordingly.

298 Minor definitions: general

In this Act, unless the context otherwise requires—

'act' and 'action' each includes omission, and references to doing an act or taking action shall be construed accordingly;

'contravention' includes a failure to comply, and cognate expressions shall be construed accordingly;

'dismiss', 'dismissal' and 'effective date of termination', in relation to an employee, shall be construed in accordance with Part X of the Employment Rights Act 1996;

'post' means a postal service which—

(a) is provided by the Post Office or under a licence granted under section 68 of the British Telecommunications Act 1981, or

(b) does not by virtue of an order made under section 69 of that Act (suspension of postal privilege) infringe the exclusive privilege conferred on the Post Office by section 66(1) of that Act;

'tort', as respects Scotland, means delict, and cognate expressions shall be construed accordingly.

299 Index of defined expressions

In this Act the expressions listed below are defined by or otherwise fall to be construed in accordance with the provisions indicated—

ACAS	section 247(1)
act and action	section 298
advertisement (in sections 137 to 143)	section 143(1)
affected employees (in Part IV, Chapter II)	section 196(3)
agent (of trade union)	section 119
appropriately qualified actuary (in sections 38 to 41)	section 42
associated employer	section 297
branch or section (of trade union)	section 119
collective agreement and collective bargaining	section 178(1)

contract of employment	
—generally	section 295(1)
—in sections 226 to 234	section 235
—in relation to Crown employment	section 273(4)(a)
—in relation to House of Lords or House of Commons staff	sections 277(4) and 278(4)(a)
contravention	section 298
the court (in Part I)	section 121
date of the ballot (in Part V)	section 246
dismiss and dismissal	
—generally	section 298
—in relation to Crown employment	section 273(4)(c)
—in relation to House of Commons staff	section 278(4)(b)
the duty of confidentiality	section 24A(3)
effective date of termination	section 298
employee	
—generally	section 295(1)
—in relation to Crown employment	section 273(4)(a)
—in relation to House of Commons staff	section 278(4)(a)
—excludes police service	section 280
—employee representatives (in Part IV, Chapter II)	section 196(1)
employer	
—in relation to an employee	section 295(1)
—in relation to a worker	section 296(2)
—in relation to health service practitioners	section 279
employment and employment agency (in sections 137 to 143)	section 143(1)
executive (of trade union)	section 119
financial affairs (of trade union)	section 119
financial year (in Part VI)	section 272
general secretary	section 119
independent trade union (and related expressions)	section 5
list	
—of trade unions	section 2
—of employers' associations	section 123
Northern Ireland union (in Part I)	section 120
not protected (in sections 222 to 226)	section 219(4)
officer	
—of trade union	section 119
—of employers' association	section 136
official (of trade union)	section 119
offshore employment	section 287
place of work (in Part V)	section 246
political fund	section 82(1)(a)
political resolution	section 82(1)(a)
post	section 298
prescribed	section 293(1)
president	section 119
recognised, recognition and related expressions	section 178(3)

representatives of trade union (in Part IV, Chapter II)	section 196(2)
rules (of trade union)	section 119
strike (in Part V)	section 246
tort (as respects Scotland)	section 298
trade dispute	
—in Part IV	section 218
—in Part V	section 244
trade union	section 1
undertaking (of employer)	
—in relation to Crown employment	section 273(4)(e) and (f)
—in relation to House of Commons staff	section 278(4)(c) and (d)
worker	
—generally	section 296(1)
—includes health service practitioners	section 279
—excludes police service	section 280
working hours (in Part V)	section 246

300-302 [omitted]

SCHEDULE A1
COLLECTIVE BARGAINING: RECOGNITION

PART I
RECOGNITION

Introduction

1. A trade union (or trade unions) seeking recognition to be entitled to conduct collective bargaining on behalf of a group or groups of workers may make a request in accordance with this Part of this Schedule.

2.—(1) This paragraph applies for the purposes of this Part of this Schedule.

(2) References to the bargaining unit are to the group of workers concerned (or the groups taken together).

(3) References to the proposed bargaining unit are to the bargaining unit proposed in the request for recognition.

(4) References to the employer are to the employer of the workers constituting the bargaining unit concerned.

(5) References to the parties are to the union (or unions) and the employer.

3.—(1) This paragraph applies for the purposes of this part of this Schedule.

(2) The meaning of collective bargaining given by section 178(1) shall not apply.

(3) References to collective bargaining are to negotiations relating to pay, hours and holidays; but this has effect subject to sub-paragraph (4).

(4) If the parties agree matters as the subject of collective bargaining, references to collective bargaining are to negotiations relating to the agreed matters; and this is the case whether the agreement is made before or after the time when the CAC issues a declaration, or the parties agree, that the union is (or unions are) entitled to conduct collective bargaining on behalf of a bargaining unit.

(5) Sub-paragraph (4) does not apply in construing paragraph 31(3).

(6) Sub-paragraphs (2) to (5) do not apply in construing paragraph 35 or 44.

Request for recognition

4.—(1) The union or unions seeking recognition must make a request for recognition to the employer.

(2) Paragraphs 5 to 9 apply to the request.

5. The request is not valid unless it is received by the employer.

6. The request is not valid unless the union (or each of the unions) has a certificate under section 6 that it is independent.

7.—(1) The request is not valid unless the employer, taken with any associated employer or employers, employs—

(a) at least 21 workers on the day the employer receives the request, or

(b) an average of at least 21 workers in the 13 weeks ending with that day.

(2)-(8) [omitted]

8 and 9. [omitted]

Parties agree

10.—(1) If before the end of the first period the parties agree a bargaining unit and that the union is (or unions are) to be recognised as entitled to conduct collective bargaining on behalf of the unit, no further steps are to be taken under this Part of this Schedule.

(2) If before the end of the first period the employer informs the union (or unions) that the employer does not accept the request but is willing to negotiate, sub-paragraph (3) applies.

(3) The parties may conduct negotiations with a view to agreeing a bargaining unit and that the union is (or unions are) to be recognised as entitled to conduct collective bargaining on behalf of the unit.

(4) If such an agreement is made before the end of the second period no further steps are to be taken under this Part of this Schedule.

(5) The employer and the union (or unions) may request ACAS to assist in conducting the negotiations.

(6) The first period is the period of 10 working days starting with the day after that on which the employer receives the request for recognition.

(7) The second period is—

(a) the period of 20 working days starting with the day after that on which the first period ends, or

(b) such longer period (so starting) as the parties may from time to time agree.

Employer rejects request

11.—(1) This paragraph applies if—

(a) before the end of the first period the employer fails to respond to the request, or

(b) before the end of the first period the employer informs the union (or unions) that the employer does not accept the request (without indicating a willingness to negotiate).

(2) The union (or unions) may apply to the CAC to decide both these questions—

(a) whether the proposed bargaining unit is appropriate or some other bargaining unit is appropriate;

(b) whether the union has (or unions have) the support of a majority of the workers constituting the appropriate bargaining unit.

Negotiations fail

12.—(1) Sub-paragraph (2) applies if—

(a) the employer informs the union (or unions) under paragraph 10(2), and

(b) no agreement is made before the end of the second period.

(2) The union (or unions) may apply to the CAC to decide both these questions—

(a) whether the proposed bargaining unit is appropriate or some other bargaining unit is appropriate;

(b) whether the union has (or unions have) the support of a majority of the workers constituting the appropriate bargaining unit.

(3) Sub-paragraph (4) applies if—

(a) the employer informs the union (or unions) under paragraph 10(2), and

(b) before the end of the second period the parties agree a bargaining unit but not that the union is (or unions are) to be recognised as entitled to conduct collective bargaining on behalf of the unit.

(4) The union (or unions) may apply to the CAC to decide the question whether the union has (or unions have) the support of a majority of the workers constituting the bargaining unit.

(5) But no application may be made under this paragraph if within the period of 10 working days starting with the day after that on which the employer informs the union (or unions) under paragraph 10(2) the employer proposes that ACAS be requested to assist in conducting the negotiations and—

(a) the union rejects (or unions reject) the proposals, or

(b) the union fails (or unions fail) to accept the proposal within the period of 10 working days starting with the day after that on which the employer makes the proposal.

Acceptance of applications

13. The CAC must give notice to the parties of receipt of an application under paragraph 11 or 12.

14.—(1) This paragraph applies if—

(a) two or more relevant applications are made,

(b) at least one worker falling within one of the relevant bargaining units also falls within the other relevant bargaining unit (or units), and

(c) the CAC has not accepted any of the applications.

(2) A relevant application is an application under paragraph 11 or 12.

(3) In relation to a relevant application, the relevant bargaining unit is—

(a) the proposed bargaining unit, where the application is under paragraph 11(2) or 12(2);

(b) the agreed bargaining unit, where the application is under paragraph 12(4).

(4) Within the acceptance period the CAC must decide, with regard to each relevant application, whether the 10 per cent test is satisfied.

(5) The 10 per cent test is satisfied if members of the union (or unions) constitute at least 10 per cent of the workers constituting the relevant bargaining unit.

(6) The acceptance period is—

(a) the period of 10 working days starting with the day after that on which the CAC receives the last relevant application, or

(b) such longer period (so starting) as the CAC may specify to the parties by notice containing reasons for the extension.

(7) If the CAC decides that—

(a) the 10 per cent test is satisfied with regard to more than one of the relevant applications, or

(b) the 10 per cent test is satisfied with regard to none of the relevant applications, the CAC must not accept any of the relevant applications.

(8) If the CAC decides that the 10 per cent test is satisfied with regard to one only of the relevant applications the CAC—

(a) must proceed under paragraph 15 with regard to that application, and

(b) must not accept any of the other relevant applications.

(9) The CAC must give notice of its decision to the parties.

(10) If by virtue of this paragraph the CAC does not accept an application, no further steps are to be taken under this Part of this Schedule in relation to that application.

15. [omitted]

Withdrawal of application

16.—(1) If an application under paragraph 11 or 12 is accepted by the CAC, the union (or unions) may not withdraw the application—

(a) after the CAC issues a declaration under paragraph 22(2), or

(b) after the union (or the last of the unions) receives notice under paragraph 22(3) or 23(2).

(2) If an application is withdrawn by the union (or unions)—

(a) the CAC must give notice of the withdrawal to the employer, and

(b) no further steps are to be taken under this Part of this Schedule.

17. [omitted]

Appropriate bargaining unit

18.—(1) If the CAC accepts an application under paragraph 11(2) or 12(2) it must try to help the parties to reach within the appropriate period an agreement as to what the appropriate bargaining unit is.

(2) The appropriate period is—

(a) the period of 20 working days starting with the day after that on which the CAC gives notice of acceptance of the application, or

(b) such longer period (so starting) as the CAC may specify to the parties by notice containing reasons for the extension.

19.—(1) This paragraph applies if—

(a) the CAC accepts an application under paragraph 11(2) or 12(2), and

(b) the parties have not agreed an appropriate bargaining unit at the end of the appropriate period.

(2) The CAC must decide the appropriate bargaining unit within—

(a) the period of 10 working days starting with the day after that on which the appropriate period ends, or

(b) such longer period (so starting) as the CAC may specify to the parties by notice containing reasons for the extension.

(3) In deciding the appropriate bargaining unit the CAC must take these matters into account—

(a) the need for the unit to be compatible with effective management;

(b) the matters listed in sub-paragraph (4), so far as they do not conflict with that need.

(4) The matters are—

(a) the views of the employer and of the union (or unions);

(b) existing national and local bargaining arrangements;

(c) the desirability of avoiding small fragmented bargaining units within an undertaking;

(d) the characteristics of workers falling within the proposed bargaining unit and of any other employees of the employer whom the CAC considers relevant;

(e) the location of workers.

(5) The CAC must give notice of its decision to the parties.

Union recognition

20.—(1) This paragraph applies if—

(a) the CAC accepts an application under paragraph 11(2) or 12(2),

(b) the parties have agreed an appropriate bargaining unit at the end of the appropriate period, or the CAC has decided an appropriate bargaining unit, and

(c) that bargaining unit differs from the proposed bargaining unit.

(2) Within the decision period the CAC must decide whether the application is invalid within the terms of paragraphs 43 to 50.

(3) In deciding whether the application is invalid, the CAC must consider any evidence which it has been given by the employer or the union (or unions).

(4) If the CAC decides that the application is invalid—

(a) the CAC must give notice of its decision to the parties,

(b) the CAC must not proceed with the application, and

(c) no further steps are to be taken under this part of this Schedule.

(5) If the CAC decides that the application is not invalid it must—

(a) proceed with the application, and

(b) give notice to the parties that it is so proceeding.

(6) The decision period is—

(a) the period of 10 working days starting with the day after that on which the parties agree an appropriate bargaining unit or the CAC decides an appropriate bargaining unit, or

(b) such longer period (so starting) as the CAC may specify to the parties by notice containing reasons for the extension.

21.—(1) This paragraph applies if—

(a) the CAC accepts an application under paragraph 11(2) or 12(2),

(b) the parties have agreed an appropriate bargaining unit at the end of the appropriate period, or the CAC has decided an appropriate bargaining unit, and

(c) that bargaining unit is the same as the proposed bargaining unit.

(2) This paragraph also applies if the CAC accepts an application under paragraph 12(4).

(3) The CAC must proceed with the application.

22.—(1) This paragraph applies if—

(a) the CAC proceeds with an application in accordance with paragraph 20 or 21, and

(b) the CAC is satisfied that a majority of the workers constituting the bargaining unit are members of the union (or unions).

(2) The CAC must issue a declaration that the union is (or unions are) recognised as entitled to conduct collective bargaining on behalf of the workers constituting the bargaining unit.

(3) But if any of the three qualifying conditions is fulfilled, instead of issuing a declaration under sub-paragraph (2) the CAC must give notice to the parties that it intends to arrange for the holding of a secret ballot in which the workers constituting the bargaining unit are asked whether they want the union (or unions) to conduct collective bargaining on their behalf.

(4) These are the three qualifying conditions—

(a) the CAC is satisfied that a ballot should be held in the interests of good industrial relations;

(b) a significant number of the union members within the bargaining unit inform the CAC that they do not want the union (or unions) to conduct collective bargaining on their behalf;

(c) membership evidence is produced which leads the CAC to conclude that there are doubts whether a significant number of the union members within the bargaining unit want the union (or unions) to conduct collective bargaining on their behalf.

(5) For the purposes of sub-paragraph (4)(c) membership evidence is—

(a) evidence about the circumstances in which union members became members;

(b) evidence about the length of time for which union members have been members, in a case where the CAC is satisfied that such evidence should be taken into account.

23.—(1) This paragraph applies if—

(a) the CAC proceeds with an application in accordance with paragraph 20 or 21, and

(b) the CAC is not satisfied that a majority of the workers constituting the bargaining unit are members of the union (or unions).

(2) The CAC must give notice to the parties that it intends to arrange for the holding of a secret ballot in which the workers constituting the bargaining unit are asked whether they want the union (or unions) to conduct collective bargaining on their behalf.

24. [omitted]

25.—(1) This paragraph applies if the CAC arranges under paragraph 24 for the holding of a ballot.

(2) The ballot must be conducted by a qualified independent person appointed by the CAC.

(3) The ballot must be conducted within—

(a) the period of 20 working days starting with the day after that on which the qualified independent person is appointed, or

(b) such longer period (so starting) as the CAC may decide.

(4) The ballot must be conducted—

(a) at a workplace or workplaces decided by the CAC,

(b) by post, or

(c) by a combination of the methods described in sub-paragraphs (a) and (b), depending on the CAC's preference.

(5) In deciding how the ballot is to be conducted the CAC must take into account—

(a) the likelihood of the ballot being affected by unfairness or malpractice if it were conducted at a workplace or workplaces;

(b) costs and practicality;

(c) such other matters as the CAC considers appropriate.

(6) The CAC may not decide that the ballot is to be conducted as mentioned in sub-paragraph (4)(c) unless there are special factors making such a decision appropriate; and special factors include—

(a) factors arising from the location of workers or the nature of their employment;

(b) factors put to the CAC by the employer or the union (or unions).

(7) A person is a qualified independent person if—

(a) he satisfies such conditions as may be specified for the purposes of this paragraph by order of the Secretary of State or is himself so specified, and

(b) there are no grounds for believing either that he will carry out any functions conferred on him in relation to the ballot otherwise than competently or that his independence in relation to the ballot might reasonably be called into question.

(8)-(9) [omitted]

26.—(1) An employer who is informed by the CAC under paragraph 25(9) must comply with the following three duties.

(2) The first duty is to co-operate generally, in connection with the ballot, with the union (or unions) and the person appointed to conduct the ballot; and the second and third duties are not to prejudice the generality of this.

(3) The second duty is to give to the union (or unions) such access to the workers constituting the bargaining unit as is reasonable to enable the union (or unions) to inform the workers of the object of the ballot and to seek their support and their opinions on the issues involved.

(4) the third duty is to do the following (so far as it is reasonable to expect the employer to do so)—

(a) to give to the CAC, within the period of 10 working days starting with the day after that on which the employer is informed under paragraph 25(9), the names and home addresses of the workers constituting the bargaining unit;

(b) to give to the CAC, as soon as is reasonably practicable, the name and home address of any worker who joins the unit after the employer has complied with paragraph (a);

(c) to inform the CAC, as soon as is reasonably practicable, of any worker whose name has been given to the CAC under paragraph (a) or (b) but who ceases to be within the unit.

(5) As soon as is reasonably practicable after the CAC receives any information under sub-paragraph (4) it must pass it on to the person appointed to conduct the ballot.

(6) If asked to do so by the union (or unions) the person appointed to conduct the ballot must send to any worker—

(a) whose name and home address have been given under sub-paragraph (5), and

(b) who is still within the unit (so far as the person so appointed is aware),

any information supplied by the union (or unions) to the person so appointed.

(7) The duty under sub-paragraph (6) does not apply unless the union bears (or unions bear) the cost of sending the information.

(8) [omitted]

27.—(1) If the CAC is satisfied that the employer has failed to fulfil any of the three duties imposed by paragraph 26, and the ballot has not been held, the CAC may order the employer—

(a) to take such steps to remedy the failure as the CAC considers reasonable and specifies in the order, and

(b) to do so within such period as the CAC considers reasonable and specifies in the order.

(2) If the CAC is satisfied that the employer has failed to comply with an order under sub-paragraph (1), and the ballot has not been held, the CAC may issue a declaration that the union is (or unions are) recognised as entitled to conduct collective bargaining on behalf of the bargaining unit.

(3) If the CAC issues a declaration under sub-paragraph (2) it shall take steps to cancel the holding of the ballot; and if the ballot is held it shall have no effect.

28. [omitted]

29.—(1) As soon as is reasonably practicable after the CAC is informed of the result of a ballot by the person conducting it, the CAC must act under this paragraph.

(2) The CAC must inform the employer and the union (or unions) of the result of the ballot.

(3) If the result is that the union is (or unions are) supported by—

(a) a majority of the workers voting, and

(b) at least 40 per cent of the workers constituting the bargaining unit,

the CAC must issue a declaration that the union is (or unions are) recognised as entitled to conduct collective bargaining on behalf of the bargaining unit.

(4) If the result is otherwise the CAC must issue a declaration that the union is (or unions are) not entitled to be so recognised.

(5)-(7) [omitted]

Consequences of recognition

30.—(1) This paragraph applies if the CAC issues a declaration under this Part of this Schedule that the union is (or unions are) recognised as entitled to conduct collective bargaining on behalf of a bargaining unit.

(2) The parties may in the negotiation period conduct negotiations with a view to agreeing a method by which they will conduct collective bargaining.

(3) If no agreement is made in the negotiation period the employer or the union (or unions) may apply to the CAC for assistance.

(4) The negotiation period is—

(a) the period of 30 working days starting with the start day, or

(b) such longer period (so starting) as the parties may from time to time agree.

(5) The start day is the day after that on which the parties are notified of the declaration.

31.—(1) This paragraph applies if an application for assistance is made to the CAC under paragraph 30.

(2) The CAC must try to help the parties to reach in the agreement period an agreement on a method by which they will conduct collective bargaining.

(3) If at the end of the agreement period the parties have not made such an agreement the CAC must specify to the parties the method by which they are to conduct collective bargaining.

(4) Any method specified under sub-paragraph (3) is to have effect as if it were contained in a legally enforceable contract made by the parties.

(5) But if the parties agree in writing—

(a) that sub-paragraph (4) shall not apply, or shall not apply to particular parts of the method specified by the CAC, or

(b) to vary or replace the method specified by the CAC,

the written agreement shall have effect as a legally enforceable contract made by the parties.

(6) Specific performance shall be the only remedy available for breach of anything which is a legally enforceable contract by virtue of this paragraph.

(7) If at any time before a specification is made under sub-paragraph (3) the parties jointly apply to the CAC requesting it to stop taking steps under this paragraph, the CAC must company with the request.

(8) The agreement period is—

(a) the period of 20 working days starting with the day after that on which the CAC receives the application under paragraph 30, or

(b) such longer period (so starting) as the CAC may decide with the consent of the parties.

Method not carried out

32.—(1) This paragraph applies if—

(a) the CAC issues a declaration under this Part of this Schedule that the union is (or unions are) recognised as entitled to conduct collective bargaining on behalf of a bargaining unit,

(b) the parties agree a method by which they will conduct collective bargaining, and

(c) one or more of the parties fails to carry out the agreement.

(2) the parties may apply to the CAC for assistance.

(3) Paragraph 31 applies as if 'paragraph 30' (in each place) read 'paragraph 30 or paragraph 32'.

General provisions about admissibility

33-34. [omitted]

35.—(1) An application under paragraph 11 or 12 is not admissible if the CAC is satisfied that there is already in force a collective agreement under which a union is (or unions are) recognised as entitled to conduct collective bargaining on behalf of any workers falling within the relevant bargaining unit.

(2) But sub-paragraph (1) does not apply to an application under paragraph 11 or 12 if—

(a) the union (or unions) recognised under the collective agreement and the union (or unions) making the application under paragraph 11 or 12 are the same, and

(b) the matters in respect of which the union is (or unions are) entitled to conduct collective bargaining do not include pay, hours or holidays.

(3) A declaration of recognition which is the subject of a declaration under paragraph 83(2) must for the purposes of sub-paragraph (1) be treated as ceasing to have effect to the extent specified in paragraph 83(2) on the making of the declaration under paragraph 83(2).

(4) In applying sub-paragraph (1) an agreement for recognition (the agreement in question) must be ignored if—

(a) the union does not have (or none of the unions has) a certificate under section 6 that it is independent,

(b) at some time there was an agreement (the old agreement) between the employer and the union under which the union (whether alone or with other unions) was recognised as entitled to conduct collective bargaining on behalf of a group of workers which was the same or substantially the same as the group covered by the agreement in question, and

(c) the old agreement ceased to have effect in the period of three years ending with the date of the agreement in question.

(5) It is for the CAC to decide whether one group of workers is the same or substantially the same as another, but in deciding the CAC may take account of the views of any person it believes has an interest in the matter.

(6) The relevant bargaining unit is—

(a) the proposed bargaining unit, where the application is under paragraph 11(2) or 12(2);

(b) the agreed bargaining unit, where the application is under paragraph 12(4).

36.—(1) An application under paragraph 11 or 12 is not admissible unless the CAC decides that—

(a) members of the union (or unions) constitute at least 10 per cent of the workers constituting the relevant bargaining unit, and

(b) a majority of the workers constituting the relevant bargaining until would be likely to favour recognition of the union (or unions) as entitled to conduct collective bargaining on behalf of the bargaining unit.

(2) The relevant bargaining unit is—

(a) the proposed bargaining unit, where the application is under paragraph 11(2) or 12(2);

(b) the agreed bargaining unit, where the application is under paragraph 12(4).

(3) The CAC must give reasons for the decision.

37.—(1) This paragraph applies to an application made by more than one union under paragraph 11 or 12.

(2) The application is not admissible unless—

(a) the unions show that they will co-operate with each other in a manner likely to secure and maintain stable and effective collective bargaining arrangements, and

(b) the unions show that, if the employer wishes, they will enter into arrangements under which collective bargaining is conducted by the unions acting together on behalf of the workers constituting the relevant bargaining unit.

(3) The relevant bargaining unit is—

(a) the proposed bargaining unit, where the application is under paragraph 11(2) or 12(2);

(b) the agreed bargaining unit, where the application is under paragraph 11(4).

38. [omitted]

39.—(1) This paragraph applies if the CAC accepts a relevant application relating to a bargaining unit or proceeds under paragraph 20 with an application relating to a bargaining unit.

(2) Another relevant application is not admissible if—

(a) the application is made within the period of 3 years starting with the day after that on which the CAC gave notice of acceptance of the application mentioned in sub-paragraph (1),

(b) the relevant bargaining unit is the same or substantially the same as the bargaining unit mentioned in sub-paragraph (1), and

(c) the application is made by the union (or unions) which made the application mentioned in sub-paragraph (1).

(3) A relevant application is an application under paragraph 11 or 12.

(4) The relevant bargaining unit is—

(a) the proposed bargaining unit, where the application is under paragraph 11(2) or 12(2);

(b) the agreed bargaining unit, where the application is under paragraph 12(4).

(5) This paragraph does not apply if paragraph 40 or 41 applies.

40.—(1) This paragraph applies if the CAC issues a declaration under paragraph 29(4) that a union is (or unions are) not entitled to be recognised as entitled to conduct collective bargaining on behalf of a bargaining unit; and this is so whether the ballot concerned is held under this Part or Part III of this Schedule.

(2) An application under paragraph 11 or 12 is not admissible if—

(a) the application is made within the period of 3 years starting with the day after that on which the declaration was issued,

(b) the relevant bargaining unit is the same or substantially the same as the bargaining unit mentioned in sub-paragraph (1), and

(c) the application is made by the union (or unions) which made the application leading to the declaration.

(3) The relevant bargaining unit is—

(a) the proposed bargaining unit, where the application is under paragraph 11(2) or 12(2);

(b) the agreed bargaining unit, where the application is under paragraph 12(4).

41.—(1) This paragraph applies if the CAC issues a declaration under paragraph 121(3) that bargaining arrangements are to cease to have effect; and that is so whether the ballot concerned is held under Part IV or Part V of this Schedule.

(2) An application under paragraph 11 or 12 is not admissible if—

(a) the application is made within the period of 3 years starting with the day after that on which the declaration was issued,

(b) the relevant bargaining unit is the same or substantially the same as the bargaining unit to which the bargaining arrangements mentioned in sub-paragraph (1) relate, and

(c) the application is made by the union which was a party (or unions which were parties) to the proceedings leading to the declaration.

(3) The relevant bargaining unit is—

(a) the proposed bargaining unit, where the application is under paragraph 11(2) or 12(2);

(b) the agreed bargaining unit, where the application is under paragraph 12(4).

42. [omitted]

General provisions about validity

43.—(1) Paragraphs 44 to 50 apply if the CAC has to decide under paragraph 20 whether an application is valid.

(2) In those paragraphs—

(a) references to the application in question are to that application, and

(b) references to the relevant bargaining unit are to the bargaining unit agreed by the parties or decided by the CAC.

44.—(1) The application in question is invalid if the CAC is satisfied that there is already in force a collective agreement under which a union is (or unions are) recognised as entitled to conduct collective bargaining on behalf of any workers falling within the relevant bargaining unit.

(2) But sub-paragraph (1) does not apply to the application in question if—

(a) the union (or unions) recognised under the collective agreement and the union (or unions) making the application in question are the same, and

(b) the matters in respect of which the union is (or unions are) entitled to conduct collective bargaining do not include pay, hours or holidays.

(3)-(5) [omitted]

45. The application in question is invalid unless the CAC decides that—

(a) members of the union (or unions) constitute at least 10 per cent of the workers constituting the relevant bargaining unit, and

(b) a majority of the workers constituting the relevant bargaining unit would be likely to favour recognition of the union (or unions) as entitled to conduct collective bargaining on behalf of the bargaining unit.

46. [omitted]

47.—(1) This paragraph applies if the CAC accepts an application under paragraph 11 or 12 relating to a bargaining unit or proceeds under paragraph 20 with an application relating to a bargaining unit.

(2) The application in question is invalid if—

(a) the application is made within the period of 3 years starting with the day after that on which the CAC gave notice of acceptance of the application mentioned in sub-paragraph (1),

(b) the relevant bargaining unit is the same or substantially the same as the bargaining unit mentioned in sub-paragraph (1), and

(c) the application is made by the union (or unions) which made the application mentioned in sub-paragraph (1).

(3) This paragraph does not apply if paragraph 48 or 49 applies.

48.—(1) This paragraph applies if the CAC issues a declaration under paragraph 29(4) that a union is (or unions are) not entitled to be recognised as entitled to conduct collective bargaining on behalf of a bargaining unit; and this is so whether the ballot concerned is held under this Part or Part III of this Schedule.

(2) The application in question is invalid if—

(a) the application is made within the period of 3 years starting with the date of the declaration,

(b) the relevant bargaining unit is the same or substantially the same as the bargaining unit mentioned in sub-paragraph (1), and

(c) the application is made by the union (or unions) which made the application leading to the declaration.

49.—(1) This paragraph applies if the CAC issues a declaration under paragraph 121(3) that bargaining arrangements are to cease to have effect; and this is so whether the ballot concerned is held under Part IV or Part V of this Schedule.

(2) The application in question is invalid if—

(a) the application is made within the period of 3 years starting with the day after that on which the declaration was issued,

(b) the relevant bargaining unit is the same or substantially the same as the bargaining unit to which the bargaining arrangements mentioned in sub-paragraph (1) relate, and

(c) the application is made by the union which was a party (or unions which were parties) to the proceedings leading to the declaration.

50-51. [omitted]

PART II
VOLUNTARY RECOGNITION

Agreements for recognition

52.—(1) This paragraph applies for the purposes of this Part of this Schedule.

(2) An agreement is an agreement for recognition if the following conditions are fulfilled in relation to it—

(a) the agreement is made in the permitted period between a union (or unions) and an employer in consequence of a request made under paragraph 4 and valid within the terms of paragraphs 5 to 9;

(b) under the agreement the union is (or unions are) recognised as entitled to conduct collective bargaining on behalf of a group or groups of workers employed by the employer;

(c) if sub-paragraph (5) applies to the agreement, it is satisfied.

(3) The permitted period is the period which begins with the day on which the employer receives the request and ends when the first of the following occurs—

(a) the union withdraws (or unions withdraw) the request;

(b) the union withdraws (or unions withdraw) any application under paragraph 11 or 12 made in consequence of the request;

(c) the CAC gives notice of a decision under paragraph 14(7) which precludes it from accepting such an application under paragraph 11 or 12;

(d) the CAC gives notice under paragraph 15(4)(a) or 20(4)(a) in relation to such an application under paragraph 11 or 12;

(e) the parties give notice to the CAC under paragraph 17(2) in relation to such an application under paragraph 11 or 12;

(f) the CAC issues a declaration under paragraph 22(2) in consequence of such an application under paragraph 11 or 12;

(g) the CAC is notified under paragraph 24(2) in relation to such an application under paragraph 11 or 12;

(h) the last day of the notification period ends (the notification period being that defined by paragraph 24(5) and arising from such an application under paragraph 11 or 12.

(4) Sub-paragraph (5) applies to an agreement if—

(a) at the time it is made the CAC has received an application under paragraph 11 or 12 in consequence of the request mentioned in sub-paragraph (2), and

(b) the CAC has not decided whether the application is admissible or it has decided that it is admissible.

(5) This sub-paragraph is satisfied if, in relation to the application under paragraph 11 or 12, the parties give notice to the CAC under paragraph 17 before the final event (as defined in paragraph 17) occurs.

Other interpretation

53.—(1) This paragraph applies for the purposes of this Part of this Schedule.

(2) In relation to an agreement for recognition, references to the bargaining unit are to the group of workers (or the groups taken together) to which the agreement for recognition relates.

(3) In relation to an agreement for recognition, references to the parties are to the union (or unions) and the employer who are parties to the agreement.

54.—(1) This paragraph applies for the purposes of this Part of this Schedule.

(2) The meaning of collective bargaining given by section 178(1) shall not apply.

(3) Except in paragraph 63(2), in relation to an agreement for recognition references to collective bargaining are to negotiations relating to the matters in respect of which the union is (or unions are) recognised as entitled to conduct negotiations under the agreement for recognition.

(4) In paragraph 63(2) the reference to collective bargaining is to negotiations relating to pay, hours and holidays.

Determination of type of agreement

55.—(1) This paragraph applies if one or more of the parties to an agreement applies to the CAC for a decision whether or not the agreement is an agreement for recognition.

(2) The CAC must give notice of receipt of an application under sub-paragraph (1) to any parties to the agreement who are not parties to the application.

(3) The CAC must within the decision period decide whether the agreement is an agreement for recognition.

(4) If the CAC decides that the agreement is an agreement for recognition it must issue a declaration to that effect.

(5) If the CAC decides that the agreement is not an agreement for recognition it must issue a declaration to that effect.

(6) The decision period is—

(a) the period of 10 working days starting with the day after that on which the CAC receives the application under sub-paragraph (1), or

(b) such longer period (so starting) as the CAC may specify to the parties to the agreement by notice containing reasons for the extension.

Termination of agreement for recognition

56.—(1) The employer may not terminate an agreement for recognition before the relevant period ends.

(2) After that period ends the employer may terminate the agreement, with or without the consent of the union (or unions).

(3) The union (or unions) may terminate an agreement for recognition at any time, with or without the consent of the employer.

(4) Sub-paragraphs (1) to (3) have effect subject to the terms of the agreement or any other agreement of the parties.

(5) The relevant period is the period of three years starting with the day after the date of the agreement.

57.—(1) If an agreement for recognition is terminated, as from the termination the agreement and any provisions relating to the collective bargaining method shall cease to have effect.

(2) For this purpose provisions relating to the collective bargaining method are—

(a) any agreement between the parties as to the method by which collective bargaining is to be conducted with regard to the bargaining unit, or

(b) anything effective as, or as if contained in, a legally enforceable contract and relating to the method by which collective bargaining is to be conducted with regard to the bargaining unit.

Application to CAC to specify method

58.—(1) This paragraph applies if the parties make an agreement for recognition.

(2) The parties may in the negotiation period conduct negotiations with a view to agreeing a method by which they will conduct collective bargaining.

(3) If no agreement is made in the negotiation period the employer or the union (or unions) may apply to the CAC for assistance.

(4) The negotiation period is—

(a) the period of 30 working days starting with the start day, or

(b) such longer period (so starting) as the parties may from time to time agree.

(5) The start day is the day after that on which the agreement is made.

59.—(1) This paragraph applies if—

(a) the parties to an agreement for recognition agree a method by which they will conduct collective bargaining, and

(b) one or more of the parties fails to carry out the agreement as to a method.

(2) The employer or the union (or unions) may apply to the CAC for assistance.

60-63. [omitted]

PART III
CHANGES AFFECTING BARGAINING UNIT

Introduction

64.—(1) This Part of this Schedule applies if—

(a) the CAC has issued a declaration that a union is (or unions are) recognised as entitled to conduct collective bargaining on behalf of a bargaining unit, and

(b) provisions relating to the collective bargaining method apply in relation to the unit.

(2) In such a case, in this Part of this Schedule—

(a) references to the original unit are to the bargaining unit on whose behalf the union is (or unions are) recognised as entitled to conduct collective bargaining, and

(b) references to the bargaining arrangements are to the declaration and to the provisions relating to the collective bargaining method which apply in relation to the original unit.

(3) For this purpose provisions relating to the collective bargaining method are—

(a) the parties' agreement as to the method by which collective bargaining is to be conducted with regard to the original unit,

(b) anything effective as, or as if contained in, a legally enforceable contract and relating to the method by which collective bargaining is to be conducted with regard to the original unit, or

(c) any provision of this Part of this Schedule that a method of collective bargaining is to have effect with regard to the original unit.

65. References in this Part of this Schedule to the parties are to the employer and the union (or unions) concerned.

Either party believes unit no longer appropriate

66.—(1) This paragraph applies if the employer believes or the union believes (or unions believe) that the original unit is no longer an appropriate bargaining unit.

(2) The employer or union (or unions) may apply to the CAC to make a decision as to what is an appropriate bargaining unit.

67.—(1) An application under paragraph 66 is not admissible unless the CAC decides that it is likely that the original unit is no longer appropriate by reason of any of the matters specified in sub-paragraph (2).

(2) The matters are—

(a) a change in the organisation or structure of the business carried on by the employer;

(b) a change in the activities pursued by the employer in the course of the business carried on by him;

(c) a substantial change in the number of workers employed in the original unit.

68-69. [omitted]

70.—(1) This paragraph applies if—

(a) the CAC gives notice of acceptance of the application, and

(b) the parties do not inform the CAC before the end of the first period that they have agreed a bargaining unit or units differing from the original unit.

(2) During the second period—

(a) the CAC must decide whether or not the original unit continues to be an appropriate bargaining unit;

(b) if the CAC decides that the original unit does not so continue, it must decide what other bargaining unit is or units are appropriate;

(c) the CAC must give notice to the parties of its decision or decisions under paragraphs (a) and (b).

(3) In deciding whether or not the original unit continues to be an appropriate bargaining unit the CAC must take into account only these matters—

(a) any change in the organisation or structure of the business carried on by the employer;

(b) any change in the activities pursued by the employer in the course of the business carried on by him;

(c) any substantial change in the number of workers employed in the original unit.

(4) In deciding what other bargaining unit is or units are appropriate the CAC must take these matters into account—

(a) the need for the unit or units to be compatible with effective management;

(b) the matters listed in sub-paragraph (5), so far as they do not conflict with that need.

(5) The matters are—

(a) the views of the employer and of the union (or unions);

(b) existing national and local bargaining arrangements;

(c) the desirability of avoiding small fragmented bargaining units within an undertaking;

(d) the characteristics of workers falling within the original unit and of any other employees of the employer whom the CAC considers relevant;

(e) the location of workers.

(6) If the CAC decides that two or more bargaining units are appropriate its decision must be such that no worker falls within more than one of them.

(7) The second period is—

(a) the period of 10 working days starting with the day after that on which the first period ends, or

(b) such longer period (so starting) as the CAC may specify to the parties by notice containing reasons for the extension.

71. If the CAC gives notice under paragraph 70 of a decision that the original unit continues to be an appropriate bargaining unit no further steps are to be taken under this Part of this Schedule.

72. Paragraph 82 applies if the CAC gives notice under paragraph 70 of—

(a) a decision that the original unit is no longer an appropriate bargaining unit, and

(b) a decision as to the bargaining unit which is (or units which are) appropriate.

73.—(1) This paragraph applies if—

(a) the parties agree under paragraph 69 a bargaining unit or units differing from the original unit,

(b) paragraph 69(2) does not apply, and

(c) at least one worker falling within the original unit does not fall within the new unit (or any of the new units).

(2) In such a case—

(a) the CAC must issue a declaration that the bargaining arrangements, so far as relating to the worker or workers mentioned in sub-paragraph (1)(c), are to cease to have effect on a date specified by the CAC in the declaration, and

(b) the bargaining arrangements shall cease to have effect accordingly.

Employer believes unit has ceased to exist

74.—(1) If the employer—

(a) believes that the original unit has ceased to exist, and

(b) wishes the bargaining arrangements to cease to have effect,

he must give the union (or each of the unions) a notice complying with sub-paragraph (2) and must give a copy of the notice to the CAC.

(2)-(7) [omitted]

75-78. [omitted]

79.—(1) This paragraph applies if—

(a) the CAC gives notice under paragraph 77(4), and

(b) the parties do not inform the CAC before the end of the first period that they have agreed a bargaining unit or units differing from the original unit.

(2) During the second period the CAC—

(a) must decide what other bargaining unit is or units are appropriate;

(b) must give notice of its decision to the parties.

(3) In deciding what other bargaining unit is or units are appropriate, the CAC must take these matters into account—

(a) the need for the unit or units to be compatible with effective management;

(b) the matters listed in sub-paragraph (4), so far as they do not conflict with that need.

(4) The matters are—

(a) the views of the employer and of the union (or unions);

(b) existing national and local bargaining arrangements;

(c) the desirability of avoiding small fragmented bargaining units within an undertaking;

(d) the characteristics of workers falling within the original unit and of any other employees of the employer whom the CAC considers relevant;

(e) the location of workers.

(5) If the CAC decides that two or more bargaining units are appropriate its decision must be such that no worker falls within more than one of them.

(6) The second period is—

(a) the period of 10 working days starting with the day after that on which the first period ends, or

(b) such longer period (so starting) as the CAC may specify to the parties by notice containing reasons for the extension.

80. Paragraph 82 applies if the CAC gives notice under paragraph 79 of a decision as to the bargaining unit which is (or units which are) appropriate.

81.—(1) This paragraph applies if—

(a) the parties agree under paragraph 78 a bargaining unit or units differing from the original unit,

(b) paragraph 78(2) does not apply, and

(c) at least one worker falling within the original unit does not fall within the new unit (or any of the new units).

(2) In such a case—

(a) the CAC must issue a declaration that the bargaining arrangements, so far as relating to the worker or workers mentioned in sub-paragraph (1)(c), are to cease to have effect on a date specified by the CAC in the declaration, and

(b) the bargaining arrangements shall cease to have effect accordingly.

Position where CAC decides new unit

82.—(1) This paragraph applies if the CAC gives notice under paragraph 70 of—

(a) a decision that the original unit is no longer an appropriate bargaining unit, and

(b) a decision as to the bargaining unit which is (or units which are) appropriate.

(2) This paragraph also applies if the CAC gives notice under paragraph 79 of a decision as to the bargaining unit which is (or units which are) appropriate.

(3) The CAC—

(a) must proceed as stated in paragraphs 83 to 89 with regard to the appropriate unit (if there is one only), or

(b) must proceed as stated in paragraphs 83 to 89 with regard to each appropriate unit separately (if there are two or more).

(4) References in those paragraphs to the new unit are to the appropriate unit under consideration.

83.—(1) This paragraph applies if in the CAC's opinion the new unit contains at least one worker falling within a statutory outside bargaining unit.

(2) In such a case—

(a) the CAC must issue a declaration that the relevant bargaining arrangements, so far as relating to workers falling within the new unit, are to cease to have effect on a date specified by the CAC in the declaration, and

(b) the relevant bargaining arrangements shall cease to have effect accordingly.

(3) The relevant bargaining arrangements are—

(a) the bargaining arrangements relating to the original unit, and

(b) the bargaining arrangements relating to each statutory outside bargaining unit containing workers who fall within the new unit.

(4) The bargaining arrangements relating to the original unit are the bargaining arrangements as defined in paragraph 64.

(5) The bargaining arrangements relating to an outside unit are—

(a) the declaration recognising a union (or unions) as entitled to conduct collective bargaining on behalf of the workers constituting the outside unit, and

(b) the provisions relating to the collective bargaining method.

(6) For this purpose the provisions relating to the collective bargaining method are—

(a) any agreement by the employer and the union (or unions) as to the method by which collective bargaining is to be conducted with regard to the outside unit,

(b) anything effective as, or as if contained in, a legally enforceable contract and relating to the method by which collective bargaining is to be conducted with regard to the outside unit, or

(c) any provision of this Part of the Schedule that a method of collective bargaining is to have effect with regard to the outside unit.

(7) A statutory outside bargaining unit is a bargaining unit which fulfils these conditions—

(a) it is not the original unit;

(b) a union is (or unions are) recognised as entitled to conduct collective bargaining on its behalf by virtue of a declaration of the CAC;

(c) the union (or at least one of the unions) is not a party referred to in paragraph 64.

(8) The date specified under sub-paragraph (1)(a) must be—

(a) the date on which the relevant period expires, or

(b) if the CAC believes that to maintain the relevant bargaining arrangements would be impracticable or contrary to the interests of good industrial relations, the date after the date on which the declaration is issued;

and the relevant period is the period of 65 working days starting with the day after that on which the declaration is issued.

84.—(1) This paragraph applies if in the CAC's opinion the new unit contains—

(a) at least one worker falling within a voluntary outside bargaining unit, but

(b) no worker falling within a statutory outside bargaining unit.

(2) In such a case—

(a) the CAC must issue a declaration that the original bargaining arrangements, so far as relating to workers falling within the new unit, are to cease to have effect on a date specified by the CAC in the declaration, and

(b) the original bargaining arrangements shall cease to have effect accordingly.

(3) The original bargaining arrangements are the bargaining arrangements as defined in paragraph 64.

(4) A voluntary outside bargaining unit is a bargaining unit which fulfils these conditions—

(a) it is not the original unit;

(b) a union is (or unions are) recognised as entitled to conduct collective bargaining on its behalf by virtue of an agreement with the employer;

(c) the union (or at least one of the unions) is not a party referred to in paragraph 64.

(5) The date specified under sub-paragraph (2)(a) must be—

(a) the date on which the relevant period expires, or

(b) if the CAC believes that to maintain the original bargaining arrangements would be impracticable or contrary to the interests of good industrial relations, the date after the date on which the declaration is issued;

and the relevant period is the period of 65 working days starting with the day after that on which the declaration is issued.

85.—(1) If the CAC's opinion is not that mentioned in paragraph 83(1) or 84(1) it must—

(a) decide whether the difference between the original unit and the new unit is such that the support of the union (or unions) within the new unit needs to be assessed, and

(b) inform the parties of its decision.

(2) If the CAC's decision is that such support does not need to be assessed—

(a) the CAC must issue a declaration that the union is (or unions are) recognised as entitled to conduct collective bargaining on behalf of the new unit;

(b) so far as it affects workers in the new unit who fall within the original unit, the declaration shall have effect in place of any declaration that the union is (or unions are) recognised as entitled to conduct collective bargaining on behalf of the original unit;

(c) the method of collective bargaining relating to the original unit shall have effect in relation to the new unit, with any modifications which the CAC considers necessary to take account of the change of bargaining unit and specifies in the declaration.

86.—(1) This paragraph applies if the CAC decides under paragraph 85(1) that the support of the union (or unions) within the new unit needs to be assessed.

(2) The CAC must decide these questions—

(a) whether members of the union (or unions) constitute at least 10 per cent of the workers constituting the new unit;

(b) whether a majority of the workers constituting the new unit would be likely to favour recognition of the union (or unions) as entitled to conduct collective bargaining on behalf of the new unit.

(3) If the CAC decides one or both of the questions in the negative—

(a) the CAC must issue a declaration that the bargaining arrangements, so far as relating to workers falling within the new unit, are to cease to have effect on a date specified by the CAC in the declaration, and

(b) the bargaining arrangements shall cease to have effect accordingly.

87.—(1) This paragraph applies if—

(a) the CAC decides both the questions in paragraph 86(2) in the affirmative, and

(b) the CAC is satisfied that a majority of the workers constituting the new unit are members of the union (or unions).

(2) The CAC must issue a declaration that the union is (or unions are) recognised as entitled to conduct collective bargaining on behalf of the workers constituting the new unit.

(3) But if any of the three qualifying conditions is fulfilled, instead of issuing a declaration under sub-paragraph (2) the CAC must give notice to the parties that it intends to arrange for the holding of a secret ballot in which the workers constituting the

new unit are asked whether they want the union (or unions) to conduct collective bargaining on their behalf.

(4) These are the three qualifying conditions—

(a) the CAC is satisfied that a ballot should be held in the interests of good industrial relations;

(b) a significant number of the union members within the new unit inform the CAC that they do not want the union (or unions) to conduct collective bargaining on their behalf;

(c) membership evidence is produced which leads the CAC to conclude that there are doubts whether a significant number of the union members within the new unit want the union (or unions) to conduct collective bargaining on their behalf.

(5) For the purposes of sub-paragraph (4)(c) membership evidence is—

(a) evidence about the circumstances in which union members became members;

(b) evidence about the length of time for which union members have been members, in a case where the CAC is satisfied that such evidence should be taken into account.

(6) If the CAC issues a declaration under sub-paragraph (2)—

(a) so far as it affects workers in the new unit who fall within the original unit, the declaration shall have effect in place of any declaration that the union is (or unions are) recognised as entitled to conduct collective bargaining on behalf of the original unit;

(b) the method of collective bargaining relating to the original unit shall have effect in relation to the new unit, with any modifications which the CAC considers necessary to take account of the change of bargaining unit and specifies in the declaration.

88.—(1) This paragraph, applies if—

(a) the CAC decides both the questions in paragraph 86(2) in the affirmative, and

(b) the CAC is not satisfied that a majority of the workers constituting the new unit are members of the union (or unions).

(2) The CAC must give notice to the parties that it intends to arrange for the holding of a secret ballot in which the workers constituting the new unit are asked whether they want the union (or unions) to conduct collective bargaining on their behalf.

89.—(1)-(3) [omitted]

(4) Paragraph 25 applies if the CAC arranges under this paragraph for the holding of a ballot (as well as if the CAC arranges under paragraph 24 for the holding of a ballot).

(5) Paragraph 26 to 29 apply accordingly, but as if references to the bargaining unit were references to the new unit.

(6) If as a result of the ballot the CAC issues a declaration that the union is (or unions are) recognised as entitled to conduct collective bargaining on behalf of the new unit—

(a) so far as it affects workers in the new unit who fall within the original unit, the declaration shall have effect in place of any declaration that the union is (or unions are) recognised as entitled to conduct collective bargaining on behalf of the original unit;

(b) the method of collective bargaining relating to the original unit shall have effect in relation to the new unit, with any modifications which the CAC considers necessary to take account of the change of bargaining unit and specifies in the declaration.

(7) If as a result of the ballot the CAC issues a declaration that the union is (or unions are) not entitled to be recognised as entitled to conduct collective bargaining on behalf of the new unit—

(a) the CAC must state in the declaration the date on which the bargaining arrangements, so far as relating to workers falling within the new unit, are to cease to have effect, and

(b) the bargaining arrangements shall cease to have effect accordingly.

(8) Paragraph (a) and (b) of sub-paragraph (6) also apply if the CAC issues a declaration under paragraph 272(2).

Residual workers

90.—(1) This paragraph applies if—

(a) the CAC decides an appropriate bargaining unit or units under paragraph 70 or 79, and

(b) at least one worker falling within the original unit does not fall within the new unit (or any of the new units).

(2) In such a case—

(a) the CAC must issue a declaration that the bargaining arrangements, so far as relating to the worker or workers mentioned in sub-paragraph (1)(b), are to cease to have effect on a date specified by the CAC in the declaration, and

(b) the bargaining arrangements shall cease to have effect accordingly.

91.—(1) This paragraph applies if—

(a) the CAC has proceeded as stated in paragraphs 83 to 89 with regard to the new unit (if there is one only) or with regard to each new unit (if there are two or more), and

(b) in so doing the CAC has issued one or more declarations under paragraph 83.

(2) the CAC must—

(a) consider each declaration issued under paragraph 83, and

(b) in relation to each declaration, identify each statutory outside bargaining unit which contains at least one worker who also falls within the new unit to which the declaration relates;

and in this paragraph each statutory outside bargaining unit so identified is referred to as a parent unit.

(3) The CAC must then—

(a) consider each parent unit, and

(b) in relation to each parent unit, identify any workers who fall within the parent unit but who do not fall within the new unit (or any of the new units);

and in this paragraph the workers so identified in relation to a parent unit are referred to as a residual unit.

(4) In relation to each residual unit, the CAC must issue a declaration that the outside union is (or outside unions are) recognised as entitled to conduct collective bargaining on its behalf.

(5) But no such declaration shall be issued in relation to a residual unit if the CAC has received an application under paragraph 66 or 75 in relation to its parent unit.

(6) In this paragraph references to the outside union (or to outside unions) in relation to a residual unit are to the union which is (or unions which are) recognised as entitled to conduct collective bargaining on behalf of its parent unit.

(7) If the CAC issues a declaration under sub-paragraph (4)—

(a) the declaration shall have effect in place of the existing declaration that the outside union is (or outside unions are) recognised as entitled to conduct collective bargaining on behalf of the parent unit, so far as the existing declaration relates to the residual unit;

(b) if there is a method of collective bargaining relating to the parent unit, it shall have effect in relation to the residual unit with any modifications which the CAC considers necessary to take account of the change of bargaining unit and specifies in the declaration.

Applications under this Part

92-93. [omitted]

Meaning of collective bargaining

94.—(1) This paragraph applies for the purposes of this Part of this Schedule.

(2) Except in relation to paragraphs 69(5), 78(5) and 83(6), the meaning of collective bargaining given by section 178(1) shall not apply.

(3) In relation to a new unit references to collective bargaining are to negotiations relating to the matters which were the subject of collective bargaining in relation to the corresponding original unit; and the corresponding original unit is the unit which was the subject of an application under paragraph 66 or 75 in consequence of which the new unit was agreed by the parties or decided by the CAC.

(4) But if the parties agree matters as the subject of collective bargaining in relation to the new unit, references to collective bargaining in relation to that unit are to negotiations relating to the agreed matters; and this is the case whether the agreement is made before or after the time when the CAC issues a declaration that the union is (or unions are) recognised as entitled to conduct collective bargaining on behalf of the new unit.

(5) In relation to a residual unit in relation to which a declaration is issued under paragraph 91, references to collective bargaining are to negotiations relating to the matters which were the subject of collective bargaining in relation to the corresponding parent unit.

(6) In construing paragraphs 69(3)(c), 78(3)(c), 85(2)(c), 87(6)(b) and 89(6)(b)—

(a) sub-paragraphs (3) and (4) do not apply, and

(b) references to collective bargaining are to negotiations relating to pay, hours and holidays.

Method of collective bargaining

95.—(1) This paragraph applies for the purposes of this Part of this Schedule.

(2) Where a method of collective bargaining has effect in relation to a new unit, that method shall have effect as if it were contained in a legally enforceable contract made by the parties.

(3) But if the parties agree in writing—

(a) that sub-paragraph (2) shall not apply, or shall not apply to particular parts of the method, or

(b) to vary or replace the method,

the written agreement shall have effect as a legally enforceable contract made by the parties.

(4) Specific performance shall be the only remedy available for breach of anything which is a legally enforceable contract by virtue of this paragraph.

PART IV
DERECOGNITION: GENERAL

Introduction

96.—(1) This part of this Schedule applies if the CAC has issued a declaration that a union is (or unions are) recognised as entitled to conduct collective bargaining on behalf of a bargaining unit.

(2) In such a case references in this Part of this Schedule to the bargaining arrangements are to the declaration and to the provisions relating to the collective bargaining method.

(3) For this purpose the provisions relating to the collective bargaining method are—

(a) the parties' agreement as to the method by which collective bargaining is to be conducted,

(b) anything effective as, or as if contained in, a legally enforceable contract and relating to the method by which collective bargaining is to be conducted, or

(c) any provision of Part III of this Schedule that a method of collective bargaining is to have effect.

97. For the purposes of this Part of this Schedule the relevant date is the date of the expiry of the period of 3 years starting with the date of the CAC's declaration.

98. References in this Part of this Schedule to the parties are to the employer and the union (or unions) concerned.

Employer employs fewer than 21 workers

99.—(1) This paragraph applies if—

(a) the employer believes that he, taken with any associated employer or employers, employed an average of fewer than 21 workers in any period of 13 weeks, and

(b) that period ends on or after the relevant date.

(2) If the employer wishes the bargaining arrangements to cease to have effect, he must give the union (or each of the unions) a notice complying with sub-paragraph (3) and must give a copy of the notice to the CAC.

(3) A notice complies with this sub-paragraph if it—

(a) identifies the bargaining arrangements,

(b) specifies the period of 13 weeks in question,

(c) states the date on which the notice is given,

(d) is given within the period of 5 working days starting with the day after the last day of the specified period of 13 weeks,

(e) states that the employer, taken with any associated employer or employers, employed an average of fewer than 21 workers in the specified period of 13 weeks, and

(f) states that the bargaining arrangements are to cease to have effect on a date which is specified in the notice and which falls after the end of the period of 35 working days starting with the day after that on which the notice is given.

(4)-(7) [omitted]

100-102. [omitted]

103.—(1) If the CAC accepts an application it—

(a) must give the employer and the union (or unions) an opportunity to put their views on the questions whether the period of 13 weeks specified under paragraph 99(3)(b) ends on or after the relevant date and whether the statement made under paragraph 99(3)(e) is correct;

(b) must decide the questions within the decision period and must give reasons for the decision.

(2) If the CAC decides that the period of 13 weeks specified under paragraph 99(3)(b) ends on or after the relevant date and that the statement made under paragraph 99(3)(e) is correct the bargaining arrangements shall cease to have effect on the termination date.

(3) If the CAC decides that the period of 13 weeks specified under paragraph 99(3)(b) does not end on or after the relevant date or that the statement made under paragraph 99(3)(e) is not correct, the notice under paragraph 99 shall be treated as not having been given.

(4) The decision period is—

(a) the period of 10 working days starting with the day after that on which the CAC gives notice of acceptance of the application, or

(b) such longer period (so starting) as the CAC may specify to the parties by notice containing reasons for the extension.

(5) The termination date is the later of—

(a) the date specified under paragraph 99(3)(f), and

(b) the day after the last day of the decision period.

Employer's request to end arrangements

104.—(1) This paragraph and paragraphs 105 to 111 apply if after the relevant date the employer requests the union (or each of the unions) to agree to end the bargaining arrangements.

(2) The request is not valid unless it—

(a) is in writing,

(b) is received by the union (or each of the unions),

(c) identifies the bargaining arrangements, and

(d) states that it is made under this Schedule.

105. [omitted]

106.—(1) This paragraph applies if—

(a) before the end of the first period the union fails (or unions fail) to respond to the request, or

(b) before the end of the first period the union informs the employer that it does not (or unions inform the employer that they do not) accept the request (without indicating a willingness to negotiate).

(2) The employer may apply to the CAC for the holding of a secret ballot to decide whether the bargaining arrangements should be ended.

107.—(1) This paragraph applies if—

(a) the union informs (or unions inform) the employer under paragraph 105(2), and

(b) no agreement is made before the end of the second period.

(2) The employer may apply to the CAC for the holding of a secret ballot to decide whether the bargaining arrangements should be ended.

(3) But no application may be made if within the period of 10 working days starting with the day after that on which the union informs (or unions inform) the employer under paragraph 105(2) the union proposes (or unions propose) that ACAS be requested to assist in conducting the negotiations and—

(a) the employer rejects the proposals, or

(b) the employer fails to accept the proposal within the period of 10 working days starting with the day after that on which the union makes (or unions make) the proposals.

108-109. [omitted]

110.—(1) An application under paragraph 106 or 107 is not admissible unless the CAC decides that—

(a) at least 10 per cent of the workers constituting the bargaining unit favour an end of the bargaining arrangements, and

(b) a majority of the workers constituting the bargaining unit would be likely to favour an end of the bargaining arrangements.

(2) The CAC must give reasons for the decision.

111. [omitted]

Workers' application to end arrangements

112.—(1) A worker or workers falling within the bargaining unit may after the relevant date apply to the CAC to have the bargaining arrangements ended.

(2) An application is not admissible unless—

(a) it is made in such form as the CAC specifies, and

(b) it is supported by such documents as the CAC specifies.

(3) An application is not admissible unless the worker gives (or workers give) to the employer and to the union (or each of the unions)—

(a) notice of the application, and

(b) a copy of the application and any documents supporting it.

113.—(1) An application under paragraph 112 is not admissible if—

(a) a relevant application was made within the period of 3 years prior to the date of the application under paragraph 112,

(b) the relevant application and the application under paragraph 112 relate to the same bargaining unit, and

(c) the CAC accepted the relevant application.

(2) A relevant application is an application made to the CAC—

(a) by the union (or the unions) under paragraph 101,

(b) by the employer under paragraph 106, 107 or 128, or

(c) by a worker (or workers) under paragraph 112.

114.—(1) An application under paragraph 112 is not admissible unless the CAC decides that—

(a) at least 10 per cent of the workers constituting the bargaining unit favour an end of the bargaining arrangements, and

(b) a majority of the workers constituting the bargaining unit would be likely to favour an end of the bargaining arrangements.

(2) The CAC must give reasons for the decision.

115-116. [omitted]

Ballot on derecognition

117.—(1) This paragraph applies if the CAC accepts an application under paragraph 106 or 107.

(2) This paragraph also applies if—

(a) the CAC accepts an application under paragraph 112, and

(b) in the period mentioned in paragraph 116(1) there is no agreement or withdrawal as there described

(3) the CAC must arrange for the holding of a secret ballot in which the workers constituting the bargaining unit are asked whether the bargaining arrangements should be ended.

(4) The ballot must be conducted by a qualified independent person appointed by the CAC.

(5) The ballot must be conducted within—

(a) the period of 20 working days starting with the day after that on which the qualified independent person is appointed, or

(b) such longer period (so starting) as the CAC may decide.

(6) The ballot must be conducted—

(a) at a workplace or workplaces decided by the CAC,

(b) by post, or

(c) by a combination of the methods described in sub-paragraphs (a) and (b), depending on the CAC's preference.

(7) In deciding how the ballot is to be conducted the CAC must take into account—

(a) the likelihood of the ballot being affected by unfairness or malpractice if it were conducted at a workplace or workplaces;

(b) costs and practicality;

(c) such other matters as the CAC considers appropriate.

(8) The CAC may not decide that the ballot is to be conducted as mentioned in sub-paragraph (6)(c) unless there are special factors making such a decision appropriate; and special factors include—

(a) factors arising from the location of workers or the nature of their employment;

(b) factors put to the CAC by the employer or the union (or unions).

(9) A person is a qualified independent person if—

(a) he satisfies such conditions as may be specified for the purposes of this paragraph by order of the Secretary of State or is himself so specified, and

(b) there are no grounds for believing either that he will carry out any functions conferred on him in relation to the ballot otherwise than competently or that his independence in relation to the ballot might reasonably be called into question.

(10) [omitted]

(11) As soon as is reasonably practicable after the CAC is required under sub-paragraph (3) to arrange for the holding of a ballot it must inform the employer and the union (or unions)—

(a) that it is so required;

(b) of the name of the person appointed to conduct the ballot and the date of his appointment;

(c) of the period within which the ballot must be conducted;

(d) whether the ballot is to be conducted by post or at a workplace or workplaces;

(e) of the workplace or workplaces concerned (if the ballot is to be conducted at a workplace or workplaces).

118.—(1) An employer who is informed by the CAC under paragraph 117(11) must comply with the following three duties.

(2) The first duty is to co-operate generally, in connection with the ballot, with the union (or unions) and the person appointed to conduct the ballot; and the second and third duties are not to prejudice the generality of this.

(3) The second duty is to give to the union (or unions) such access to the workers constituting the bargaining unit as is reasonable to enable the union (or unions) to inform the workers of the object of the ballot and to seek their support and their opinions on the issues involved.

(4) The third duty is to do the following (so far as it is reasonable to expect the employer to do so)—

(a) to give to the CAC, within the period of 10 working days starting with the day after that on which the employer is informed under paragraph 117(11), the names and home addresses of the workers constituting the bargaining unit;

(b) to give to the CAC, as soon as is reasonably practicable, the name and home address of any worker who joins the unit after the employer has complied with paragraph (a);

(c) to inform the CAC, as soon as is reasonably practicable, of any worker whose name has been given to the CAC under paragraph (a) or (b) but who ceases to be within the unit.

(5) As soon as is reasonably practicable after the CAC receives any information under sub-paragraph (4) it must pass it on to the person appointed to conduct the ballot.

(6) If asked to do so by the union (or unions) the person appointed to conduct the ballot must send to any worker—

(a) whose name and home address have been given under sub-paragraph (5), and

(b) who is still within the unit (so far as the person so appointed is aware),

any information supplied by the union (or unions) to the person so appointed.

(7) the duty under sub-paragraph (6) does not apply unless the union bears (or unions bear) the cost of sending the information.

(8) [omitted]

119.—(1) If the CAC is satisfied that the employer has failed to fulfil any of the three duties imposed by paragraph 118, and the ballot has not been held, the CAC may order the employer—

(a) to take such steps to remedy the failure as the CAC considers reasonable and specifies in the order, and

(b) to do so within such period as the CAC considers reasonable and specifies in the order.

(2) If—

(a) the ballot has been arranged in consequence of an application under paragraph 106 or 107,

(b) the CAC is satisfied that the employer has failed to comply with an order under sub-paragraph (1), and

(c) the ballot has not been held,

the CAC may refuse the application.

(3) If—

(a) the ballot has been arranged in consequence of an application under paragraph 112, and

(b) the ballot has not been held,

an order under sub-paragraph (1), on being recorded in the county court, may be enforced in the same way as an order of that court.

(4) If the CAC refuses an application under sub-paragraph (2) it shall take steps to cancel the holding of the ballot; and if the ballot is held it shall have no effect.

120. [omitted]

121.—(1) As soon as is reasonably practicable after the CAC is informed of the result of a ballot by the person conducting it, the CAC must act under this paragraph.

(2) The CAC must inform the employer and the union (or unions) of the result of the ballot.

(3) If the result is that the proposition that the bargaining arrangements should be ended is supported by—

(a) a majority of the workers voting, and

(b) at least 40 per cent of the workers constituting the bargaining unit,

the CAC must issue a declaration that the bargaining arrangements are to cease to have effect on a date specified by the CAC in the declaration.

(4) If the result is otherwise the CAC must refuse the application under paragraph 106, 107 or 112.

(5) If a declaration is issued under sub-paragraph (3) the bargaining arrangements shall cease to have effect accordingly.

(6) The Secretary of State may by order amend sub-paragraph (3) so as to specify a different degree of support; and different provision may be made for different circumstances.

(7) An order under sub-paragraph (6) shall be made by statutory instrument.

(8) No such order shall be made unless a draft of it has been laid before Parliament and approved by a resolution of each House of Parliament.

PART V
DERECOGNITION WHERE RECOGNITION AUTOMATIC

Introduction

122.—(1) This Part of this Schedule applies if—

(a) the CAC has issued a declaration under paragraph 22(2) that a union is (or unions are) recognised as entitled to conduct collective bargaining on behalf of a bargaining unit, and

(b) the parties have agreed under paragraph 30 or 31 a method by which they will conduct collective bargaining.

(2) In such a case references in this Part of this Schedule to the bargaining arrangements are to—

(a) the declaration, and

(b) the parties' agreement.

123.—(1) This Part of this Schedule also applies if—

(a) the CAC has issued a declaration under paragraph 22(2) that a union is (or unions are) recognised as entitled to conduct collective bargaining on behalf of a bargaining unit, and

(b) the CAC has specified to the parties under paragraph 31(3) the method by which they are to conduct collective bargaining.

(2) In such a case references in this Part of this Schedule to the bargaining arrangements are to—

(a) the declaration, and

(b) anything effective as, or as if contained in, a legally enforceable contract by virtue of paragraph 31.

124.—(1) This part of this Schedule also applies if the CAC has issued a declaration under paragraph 87(2) that a union is (or unions are) recognised as entitled to conduct collective bargaining on behalf of a bargaining unit.

(2) In such a case references in this Part of this Schedule to the bargaining arrangements are to—

(a) the declaration, and

(b) paragraph 87(6)(b).

125. For the purposes of this Part of this Schedule the relevant date is the date of the expiry of the period of 3 years starting with the date of the CAC's declaration.

126. References in this Part of this Schedule to the parties are to the employer and the union (or unions) concerned.

Employer's request to end arrangements

127.—(1) The employer may after the relevant date request the union (or each of the unions) to agree to end the bargaining arrangements.

(2) The request is not valid unless it—

(a) is in writing,

(b) is received by the union (or each of the unions),

(c) identifies the bargaining arrangements,

(d) states that it is made under this Schedule, and

(e) states that fewer than half of the workers constituting the bargaining unit are members of the union (or unions).

128.—(1) If before the end of the negotiation period the parties agree to end the bargaining arrangements no further steps are to be taken under this Part of this Schedule.

(2) If no such agreement is made before the end of the negotiation period, the employer may apply to the CAC for the holding of a secret ballot to decide whether the bargaining arrangements should be ended.

(3) The negotiation period is the period of 10 working days starting with the day after—

(a) the day on which the union receives the request, or

(b) the last day on which any of the unions receives the request;

or such longer period (so starting) as the parties may from time to time agree.

129-130. [omitted]

131.—(1) An application under paragraph 128 is not admissible unless the CAC is satisfied that fewer than half of the workers constituting the bargaining unit are members of the union (or unions).

(2) The CAC must give reasons for the decision.

132. [omitted]

Ballot on derecognition

133.—(1) Paragraph 117 applies if the CAC accepts an application under paragraph 128 (as well as in the cases mentioned in paragraph 117(1) and (2)).

(2) Paragraphs 118 to 121 apply accordingly, but as if—

(a) the reference in paragraph 119(2)(a) to paragraph 106 or 107 were to paragraph 106, 107 or 128;

(b) the reference in paragraph 121(4) to paragraph 106, 107 or 112 were to paragraph 106, 107, 112 or 128.

PART VI
DERECOGNITION WHERE UNION NOT INDEPENDENT

Introduction

134.—(1) This Part of this Schedule applies if—

(a) an employer and a union (or unions) have agreed that the union is (or unions are) recognised as entitled to conduct collective bargaining on behalf of a group or groups of workers, and

(b) the union does not have (or none of the unions has) a certificate under section 6 that it is independent.

(2) In such a case references in this part of this Schedule to the bargaining arrangements are to—

(a) the parties' agreement mentioned in sub-paragraph (1)(a), and

(b) any agreement between the parties as to the method by which they will conduct collective bargaining.

135. In this Part of this Schedule—

(a) references to the parties are to the employer and the union (or unions);

(b) references to the bargaining unit are to the group of workers referred to in paragraph 134(1)(a) (or the groups taken together).

136. The meaning of collective bargaining given by section 178(1) shall not apply in relation to this Part of this Schedule.

Workers' application to end arrangements

137.—(1) A worker or workers falling within the bargaining unit may apply to the CAC to have the bargaining arrangements ended.

(2)-(3) [omitted]

138. An application under paragraph 137 is not admissible if the CAC is satisfied that any of the unions has a certificate under section 6 that it is independent.

139.—(1) An application under paragraph 137 is not admissible unless the CAC decides that—

(a) at least 10 per cent of the workers constituting the bargaining unit favour an end of the bargaining arrangements, and

(b) a majority of the workers constituting the bargaining unit would be likely to favour an end of the bargaining arrangements.

(2) The CAC must give reasons for the decision.

140-142. [omitted]

143.—(1) This paragraph applies if—

(a) the CAC accepts an application under paragraph 137,

(b) during the period mentioned in paragraph 142(1) or 145(3) the CAC is satisfied that the union (or each of the unions) has made an application to the Certification Officer under section 6 for a certificate that it is independent, that the application (or each of the applications) to the Certification Officer was made before the application under paragraph 137 and that the Certification Officer has not come to a decision on the application (or each of the applications), and

(c) at the time the CAC is so satisfied there has been no agreement or withdrawal as described in paragraph 142(1) or 145(3).

(2) In such a case paragraph 142(1) or 145(3) shall cease to apply from the time when the CAC is satisfied as mentioned in sub-paragraph (1)(b).

144.—(1) This paragraph applies if the CAC is subsequently satisfied that—

(a) the Certification Officer has come to a decision on the application (or each of the applications) mentioned in paragraph 143(1)(b), and

(b) his decision is that the union (or any of the unions) which made an application under section 6 is independent.

(2) In such a case—

(a) the CAC must give the worker (or workers), the employer and the union (or unions) notice that it is so satisfied, and

(b) the application under paragraph 137 shall be treated as not having been made.

145.—(1) This paragraph applies if the CAC is subsequently satisfied that—

(a) the Certification Officer has come to a decision on the application (or each of the applications) mentioned in paragraph 143(1)(b), and

(b) his decision is that the union (or each of the unions) which made an application under section 6 is not independent.

(2) The CAC must give the worker (or workers), the employer and the union (or unions) notice that it is so satisfied.

(3) In the new negotiation period the CAC must help the employer, the union (or unions) and the worker (or workers) with a view to—

(a) the employer and the union (or unions) agreeing to end the bargaining arrangements, or

(b) the worker (or workers) withdrawing the application.

(4) The new negotiation period is—

(a) the period of 20 working days starting with the day after that on which the CAC gives notice under sub-paragraph (2), or

(b) such longer period (so starting) as the CAC may decide with the consent of the worker (or workers), the employer and the union (or unions).

146.—(1) This paragraph applies if—

(a) the CAC accepts an application under paragraph 137,

(b) paragraph 143 does not apply, and

(c) during the relevant period the CAC is satisfied that a certificate of independence has been issued to the union (or any of the unions) under section 6.

(2) In such a case the relevant period is the period starting with the first day of the negotiation period (as defined in paragraph 142(2)) and ending with the first of the following to occur—

(a) any agreement by the employer and the union (or unions) to end the bargaining arrangements;

(b) any withdrawal of the application by the worker (or workers);

(c) the CAC being informed of the result of a relevant ballot by the person conducting it;

and a relevant ballot is a ballot held by virtue of this Part of this Schedule.

(3) This paragraph also applies if—

(a) the CAC gives notice under paragraph 145(2), and

(b) during the relevant period of CAC is satisfied that a certificate of independence has been issued to the union (or any of the unions) under section 6.

(4) In such a case, the relevant period is the period starting with the first day of the new negotiation period (as defined in paragraph 145(4)) and ending with the first of the following to occur—

(a) any agreement by the employer and the union (or unions) to end the bargaining arrangements;

(b) any withdrawal of the application by the worker (or workers);

(c) the CAC being informed of the result of a relevant ballot by the person conducting it;
and a relevant ballot is a ballot held by virtue of this Part of this Schedule.

(5) If this paragraph applies—

(a) the CAC must give the worker (or workers), the employer and the union (or unions) notice that it is satisfied as mentioned in sub-paragraph (1)(c) or (3)(b), and

(b) the application under paragraph 137 shall be treated as not having been made.

Ballot on derecognition

147.—(1) Paragraph 117 applies if—

(a) the CAC accepts an application under paragraph 137, and

(b) in the period mentioned in paragraph 142(1) or 145(3) there is no agreement or withdrawal as there described,
(as well as in the cases mentioned in paragraph 117(1) and (2)).

(2) Paragraphs 118 to 121 apply accordingly, but as if—

(a) the reference in paragraph 119(3)(a) to paragraph 112 were to paragraph 112 or 137;

(b) the reference in paragraph 121(4) to paragraph 106, 107 or 112 were to paragraph 106, 107, 112 or 137.

(c) the reference in paragraph 119(4) to the CAC refusing an application under paragraph 119(2) included a reference to it being required to give notice under paragraph 146(5).

Derecognition: other cases

148.—(1) This paragraph applies if as a result of a declaration by the CAC another union is (or other unions are) recognised as entitled to conduct collective bargaining on behalf of a group of workers at least one of whom falls within the bargaining unit.

(2) The CAC must issue a declaration that the bargaining arrangements are to cease to have effect on a date specified by the CAC in the declaration.

(3) If a declaration is issued under sub-paragraph (2) the bargaining arrangements shall cease to have effect accordingly.

(4) It is for the CAC to decide whether sub-paragraph (1) if fulfilled, but in deciding the CAC may take account of the views of any person it believes has an interest in the matter.

PART VII
LOSS OF INDEPENDENCE

Introduction

149.—(1) This Part of this Schedule applies if the CAC has issued a declaration that a union is (or unions are) recognised as entitled to conduct collective bargaining on behalf of a bargaining unit.

(2) In such a case references in this Part of this Schedule to the bargaining arrangements are to the declaration and to the provisions relating to the collective bargaining method.

(3) For this purpose the provisions relating to the collective bargaining method are—

(a) the parties' agreement as to the method by which collective bargaining is to be conducted,

(b) anything effective as, or as if contained in, a legally enforceable contract and relating to the method by which collective bargaining is to be conducted, or

(c) any provision of Part III of this Schedule that a method of collective bargaining is to have effect.

150.—(1) This Part of this Schedule also applies if—

(a) the parties have agreed that a union is (or unions are) recognised as entitled to conduct collective bargaining on behalf of a bargaining unit,

(b) the CAC has specified to the parties under paragraph 63(2) the method by which they are to conduct collective bargaining, and

(c) the parties have not agreed in writing to replace the method or that paragraph 63(3) shall not apply.

(2) In such a case references in this Part of this Schedule to the bargaining arrangements are to—

(a) the parties' agreement mentioned in sub-paragraph (1)(a), and

(b) anything effective as, or as if contained in, a legally enforceable contract by virtue of paragraph 63.

151. References in this Part of this Schedule to the parties are to the employer and the union (or unions) concerned.

Loss of certificate

152.—(1) This paragraph applies if—

(a) only one union is a party, and

(b) under section 7 the Certification Officer withdraws the union's certificate of independence.

(2) This paragraph also applies if—

(a) more than one union is a party, and

(b) under section 7 the Certification Officer withdraws the certificate of independence of each union (whether different certificates are withdrawn on the same or on different days).

(3) [omitted]

(4) The bargaining arrangements shall cease to have effect; and the parties shall be taken to agree that the union is (or unions are) recognised as entitled to conduct collective bargaining on behalf of the bargaining unit concerned.

153-155. [omitted]

PART VIII
DETRIMENT

Detriment

156.—(1) A worker has a right not to be subjected to any detriment by any act, or any deliberate failure to act, by his employer if the act or failure takes place on any of the grounds set out in sub-paragraph (2).

(2) The grounds are that—

(a) the worker acted with a view to obtaining or preventing recognition of a union (or unions) by the employer under this Schedule;

(b) the worker indicated that he supported or did not support recognition of a union (or unions) by the employer under this Schedule;

(c) the worker acted with a view to securing or preventing the ending under this Schedule of bargaining arrangements;

(d) the worker indicated that he supported or did not support the ending under this Schedule of bargaining arrangements;

(e) the worker influenced or sought to influence the way in which votes were to be cast by other workers in a ballot arranged under this Schedule;

(f) the worker influenced or sought to influence other workers to vote or to abstain from voting in such a ballot

(g) the worker voted in such a ballot;

(h) the worker proposed to do, failed to do, or proposed to decline to do, any of the things referred to in paragraphs (a) to (g).

(3) A ground does not fall within sub-paragraph (2) if it constitutes an unreasonable act or omission by the worker.

(4) This paragraph does not apply if the worker is an employee and the detriment amounts to dismissal within the meaning of the Employment Rights Act 1996.

(5) A worker may present a complaint to an employment tribunal on the ground that he has been subjected to a detriment in contravention of this paragraph.

(6) Apart from the remedy by way of complaint as mentioned in sub-paragraph (5), a worker has no remedy for infringement of the right conferred on him by this paragraph.

157.—(1) An employment tribunal shall not consider a complaint under paragraph 156 unless it is presented—

(a) before the end of the period of 3 months starting with the date of the act or failure to which the complaint relates or, if that act or failure is part of a series of similar acts or failures (or both), the last of them, or

(b) where the tribunal is satisfied that it was not reasonably practicable for the complaint to be presented before the end of that period, within such further period as it considers reasonable.

(2) For the purposes of sub-paragraph (1)—

(a) where an act extends over a period, the reference to the date of the act is a reference to the last day of that period;

(b) a failure to act shall be treated as done when it was decided on.

(3) For the purposes of sub-paragraph (2), in the absence of evidence establishing the contrary an employer must be taken to decide on a failure to act—

(a) when he does an act inconsistent with doing the failed act, or

(b) if he has done no such inconsistent act, when the period expires within which he might reasonably have been expected to do the failed act if it was to be done.

158. On a complaint under paragraph 156 it shall be for the employer to show the ground on which he acted or failed to act.

159.—(1) If the employment tribunal finds that a complaint under paragraph 156 is well-founded it shall make a declaration to that effect and may make an award of compensation to be paid by the employer to the complainant in respect of the act or failure complained of.

(2) The amount of the compensation awarded shall be such as the tribunal considers just and equitable in all the circumstances having regard to the infringement complained of and to any loss sustained by the complainant which is attributable to the act or failure which infringed his right.

(3) The loss shall be taken to include—

(a) any expenses reasonably incurred by the complainant in consequence of the act or failure complained of, and

(b) loss of any benefit which he might reasonably be expected to have had but for that act or failure.

(4) In ascertaining the loss, the tribunal shall apply the same rule concerning the duty of a person to mitigate his loss as applies to damages recoverable under the common law of England and Wales or Scotland.

(5) If the tribunal finds that the act or failure complained of was to any extent caused or contributed to by action of the complainant, it shall reduce the amount of the compensation by such proportion as it considers just and equitable having regard to the finding.

160.—(1) If the employment tribunal finds that a complaint under paragraph 156 is well-founded and—

(a) the detriment of which the worker has complained is the termination of his worker's contract, but

(b) that contract was not a contract of employment,

any compensation awarded under paragraph 159 must not exceed the limit specified in sub-paragraph (2).

(2) The limit is the total of—

(a) the sum which would be the basic award for unfair dismissal, calculated in accordance with section 119 of the Employment Rights Act 1996, if the worker had been an employee and the contract terminated had been a contract of employment, and

(b) the sum for the time being specified in section 124(1) of that Act which is the limit for a compensatory award to a person calculated in accordance with section 123 of that Act.

Dismissal

161.—(1) For the purposes of Part X of the Employment Rights Act 1996 (unfair dismissal) the dismissal of an employee shall be regarded as unfair if the dismissal was made—

(a) for a reason set out in sub-paragraph (2), or

(b) for reasons the main one of which is one of those set out in sub-paragraph (2).

(2) The reasons are that—

(a) the employee acted with a view to obtaining or preventing recognition of a union (or unions) by the employer under this Schedule;

(b) the employee indicated that he supported or did not support recognition of a union (or unions) by the employer under this Schedule;

(c) the employee acted with a view to securing or preventing the ending under this Schedule of bargaining arrangements;

(d) the employee indicated that he supported or did not support the ending under this Schedule of bargaining arrangements;

(e) the employee influenced or sought to influence the way in which votes were to be cast by other workers in a ballot arranged under this Schedule;

(f) the employee influenced or sought to influence other workers to vote or to abstain from voting in such a ballot;

(g) the employee voted in such a ballot;

(h) the employee proposed to do, failed to do, or proposed to decline to do, any of the things referred to in paragraphs (a) to (g).

(3) A reason does not fall within sub-paragraph (2) if it constitutes an unreasonable act or omission by the employee.

Selection for redundancy

162. For the purposes of Part X of the Employment Rights Act 1996 (unfair dismissal) the dismissal of an employee shall be regarded as unfair if the reason or principal reason for the dismissal was that he was redundant but it is shown—

(a) that the circumstances constituting the redundancy applied equally to one or more other employees in the same undertaking who held positions similar to that held by him and who have not been dismissed by the employer, and

(b) that the reason (or, if more than one, the principal reason) why he was selected for dismissal was one falling within paragraph 161(2).

163. [repealed]

Exclusion of requirement as to qualifying period

164. Sections 108 and 109 of the Employment Rights Act 1996 (qualifying period and upper age limit for unfair dismissal protection) do not apply to a dismissal which by virtue of paragraph 161 or 162 is regarded as unfair for the purposes of Part X of that Act.

Meaning of worker's contract

165. References in this Part of this Schedule to a worker's contract are to the contract mentioned in paragraph (a) or (b) of section 296(1) or the arrangements for the employment mentioned in paragraph (c) of section 296(1).

PART IX
GENERAL

166-170. [omitted]

CAC's general duty

171. In exercising functions under this Schedule in any particular case the CAC must have regard to the object of encouraging and promoting fair and efficient practices and arrangements in the workplace, so far as having regard to that object is consistent with applying other provisions of this Schedule in the case concerned.

172. [omitted]

DISABILITY DISCRIMINATION ACT 1995
(1995, c. 50)

PART I
DISABILITY

Section

PART II
EMPLOYMENT

Discrimination by employers

Enforcement etc.

Discrimination by other persons

Premises occupied under leases

Occupational pension schemes and insurance services

PART I
DISABILITY

1 Meaning of 'disability' and 'disabled person'

(1) Subject to the provisions of Schedule 1, a person has a disability for the purposes of this Act if he has a physical or mental impairment which has a substantial and long-term adverse effect on his ability to carry out normal day-to-day activities.

(2) In this Act 'disabled person' means a person who has a disability.

2 Past disabilities

(1) The provisions of this Part and Parts II and III apply in relation to a person who has had a disability as they apply in relation to a person who has that disability.

(2) Those provisions are subject to the modifications made by Schedule 2.

(3) Any regulations or order made under this Act may include provision with respect to persons who have had a disability.

(4) In any proceedings under Part II or Part III of this Act, the question whether a person had a disability at a particular time ('the relevant time') shall be determined, for the purposes of this section, as if the provisions of, or made under, this Act in force when the act complained of was done had been in force at the relevant time.

(5) The relevant time may be a time before the passing of this Act.

3 [omitted]

PART II
EMPLOYMENT

Discrimination by employers

4 Discrimination against applicants and employees

(1) It is unlawful for an employer to discriminate against a disabled person—

(a) in the arrangements which he makes for the purpose of determining to whom he should offer employment;

(b) in the terms on which he offers that person employment; or

(c) by refusing to offer, or deliberately not offering, him employment.

(2) It is unlawful for an employer to discriminate against a disabled person whom he employs—

(a) in the terms of employment which he affords him;

(b) in the opportunities which he affords him for promotion, a transfer, training or receiving any other benefit;

(c) by refusing to afford him, or deliberately not affording him, any such opportunity; or

(d) by dismissing him, or subjecting him to any other detriment.

(3) Subsection (2) does not apply to benefits of any description if the employer is concerned with the provision (whether or not for payment) of benefits of that description to the public, or to a section of the public which includes the employee in question, unless—

(a) that provision differs in a material respect from the provision of the benefits by the employer to his employees; or

(b) the provision of the benefits to the employee in question is regulated by his contract of employment; or

(c) the benefits relate to training.

(4) In this Part 'benefits' includes facilities and services.

(5) In the case of an act which constitutes discrimination by virtue of section 55, this section also applies to discrimination against a person who is not disabled.

(6) This section applies only in relation to employment at an establishment in Great Britain.

5 Meaning of 'discrimination'

(1) For the purposes of this Part, an employer discriminates against a disabled person if—

(a) for a reason which relates to the disabled person's disability, he treats him less favourably than he treats or would treat others to whom that reason does not or would not apply; and

(b) he cannot show that the treatment in question is justified.

(2) For the purposes of this Part, an employer also discriminates against a disabled person if—

(a) he fails to comply with a section 6 duty imposed on him in relation to the disabled person; and

(b) he cannot show that his failure to comply with that duty is justified.

(3) Subject to subsection (5), for the purposes of subsection (1) treatment is justified if, but only if, the reason for it is both material to the circumstances of the particular case and substantial.

(4) For the purposes of subsection (2), failure to comply with a section 6 duty is justified if, but only if, the reason for the failure is both material to the circumstances of the particular case and substantial.

(5) If, in a case falling within subsection (1), the employer is under a section 6 duty in relation to the disabled person but fails without justification to comply with that duty, his treatment of that person cannot be justified under subsection (3) unless it would have been justified even if he had complied with the section 6 duty.

(6) Regulations may make provision, for purposes of this section, as to circumstances in which—

(a) treatment is to be taken to be justified;

(b) failure to comply with a section 6 duty is to be taken to be justified;

(c) treatment is to be taken not to be justified;

(d) failure to comply with a section 6 duty is to be taken not to be justified.

(7) Regulations under subsection (6) may, in particular—

(a) make provision by reference to the cost of affording any benefit; and

(b) in relation to benefits under occupational pension schemes, make provision with a view to enabling uniform rates of contributions to be maintained.

6 Duty of employer to make adjustments

(1) Where—

(a) any arrangements made by or on behalf of an employer, or

(b) any physical feature of premises occupied by the employer,

place the disabled person concerned at a substantial disadvantage in comparison with persons who are not disabled, it is the duty of the employer to take such steps as it is reasonable, in all the circumstances of the case, for him to have to take in order to prevent the arrangements or feature having that effect.

(2) Subsection (1)(a) applies only in relation to—

(a) arrangements for determining to whom employment should be offered;

(b) any term, condition or arrangements on which employment, promotion, a transfer, training or any other benefit is offered or afforded.

(3) The following are examples of steps which an employer may have to take in relation to a disabled person in order to comply with subsection (1)—

(a) making adjustments to premises;

(b) allocating some of the disabled person's duties to another person;

(c) transferring him to fill an existing vacancy;

(d) altering his working hours;

(e) assigning him to a different place of work;

(f) allowing him to be absent during working hours for rehabilitation, assessment or treatment;

(g) giving him, or arranging for him to be given, training;

(h) acquiring or modifying equipment;

(i) modifying instructions or reference manuals;

(j) modifying procedures for testing or assessment;

(k) providing a reader or interpreter;

(l) providing supervision.

(4) In determining whether it is reasonable for an employer to have to take a particular step in order to comply with subsection (1), regard shall be had, in particular, to—

(a) the extent to which taking the step would prevent the effect in question;

(b) the extent to which it is practicable for the employer to take the step;

(c) the financial and other costs which would be incurred by the employer in taking the step and the extent to which taking it would disrupt any of his activities;

(d) the extent of the employer's financial and other resources;

(e) the availability to the employer of financial or other assistance with respect to taking the step.

This subsection is subject to any provision of regulations made under subsection (8).

(5) In this section, 'the disabled person concerned' means—

(a) in the case of arrangements for determining to whom employment should be offered, any disabled person who is, or has notified the employer that he may be, an applicant for that employment;

(b) in any other case, a disabled person who is—

(i) an applicant for the employment concerned; or

(ii) an employee of the employer concerned.

(6) Nothing in this section imposes any duty on an employer in relation to a disabled person if the employer does not know, and could not reasonably be expected to know—

(a) in the case of an applicant or potential applicant, that the disabled person concerned is, or may be, an applicant for the employment; or

(b) in any case, that that person has a disability and is likely to be affected in the way mentioned in subsection (1).

(7) Subject to the provisions of this section, nothing in this Part is to be taken to require an employer to treat a disabled person more favourably than he treats or would treat others.

(8)-(10) [omitted]

(11) This section does not apply in relation to any benefit under an occupational pension scheme or any other benefit payable in money or money's worth under a scheme or arrangement for the benefit of employees in respect of—

(a) termination of service;

(b) retirement, old age or death;
(c) accident, injury, sickness or invalidity; or
(d) any other prescribed matter.

(12) This section imposes duties only for the purpose of determining whether an employer has discriminated against a disabled person; and accordingly a breach of any such duty is not actionable as such.

7 Exemption for small businesses

(1) Nothing in this Part applies in relation to an employer who has fewer than 15 employees.

(2)-(14) [omitted]

Enforcement etc.

8 Enforcement, remedies and procedure

(1) A complaint by any person that another person—

(a) has discriminated against him in a way which is unlawful under this Part, or

(b) is, by virtue of section 57 or 58, to be treated as having discriminated against him in such a way,

may be presented to an employment tribunal.

(2) Where an employment tribunal finds that a complaint presented to it under this section is well-founded, it shall take such of the following steps as it considers just and equitable—

(a) making a declaration as to the rights of the complainant and the respondent in relation to the matters to which the complaint relates;

(b) ordering the respondent to pay compensation to the complainant;

(c) recommending that the respondent take, within a specified period, action appearing to the tribunal to be reasonable, in all the circumstances of the case, for the purpose of obviating or reducing the adverse effect on the complainant of any matter to which the complaint relates.

(3) Where a tribunal orders compensation under subsection (2)(b), the amount of the compensation shall be calculated by applying the principles applicable to the calculation of damages in claims in tort or (in Scotland) in reparation for breach of statutory duty.

(4) For the avoidance of doubt it is hereby declared that compensation in respect of discrimination in a way which is unlawful under this Part may include compensation for injury to feelings whether or not it includes compensation under any other head.

(5) If the respondent to a complaint fails, without reasonable justification, to comply with a recommendation made by an employment tribunal under subsection (2)(c) the tribunal may, if it thinks it just and equitable to do so—

(a) increase the amount of compensation required to be paid to the complainant in respect of the complaint, where an order was made under subsection (2)(b); or

(b) make an order under subsection (2)(b).

(6)-(8) [omitted]

9 Validity of certain agreements

(1) Any term in a contract of employment or other agreement is void so far as it purports to—

(a) require a person to do anything which would contravene any provision of, or made under, this Part;

(b) exclude or limit the operation of any provision of this Part; or

(c) prevent any person from presenting a complaint to an employment tribunal under this Part.

(2) Paragraphs (b) and (c) of subsection (1) do not apply to an agreement not to institute proceedings under section 8(1), or to an agreement not to continue such proceedings, if—

(a) a conciliation officer has acted under section 18 of the Employment Tribunals Act 1996 in relation to the matter; or

(b) the conditions set out in subsection (3) are satisfied.

(3) The conditions are that—

(a) the complainant must have received advice from a relevant independent adviser as to the terms and effect of the proposed agreement (and in particular its effect on his ability to pursue his complaint before an employment tribunal);

(b) when the adviser gave the advice there must have been in force a contract of insurance, or an indemnity provided for members of a profession or professional body covering the risk of a claim by the complainant in respect of loss arising in consequence of the advice; and

(c) the agreement must be in writing, relate to the particular complaint, identify the adviser and state that the conditions are satisfied.

(4) A person is a relevant independent adviser for the purposes of subsection (3)(a)—

(a) if he is a qualified lawyer,

(b) if he is an officer, official, employee or member of an independent trade union who has been certified in writing by the trade union as competent to give advice and as authorised to do so on behalf of the trade union,

(c) if he works at an advice centre (whether as an employee or a volunteer) and has been certified in writing by the centre as competent to give advice and as authorised to do so on behalf of the centre, or

(d) if he is a person of a description specified in an order made by the Secretary of State.

(4A) But a person is not a relevant independent adviser for the purposes of subsection (3)(a) in relation to the complainant—

(a) if he is, is employed by or is acting in the matter for the other party or a person who is connected with the other party,

(b) in the case of a person within subsection (4)(b) or (c), if the trade union or advice centre is the other party or a person who is connected with the other party,

(c) in the case of a person within subsection (4)(c), if the complainant makes a payment for the advice received from him, or

(d) in the case of a person of a description specified in an order under subsection (4)(d), if any condition specified in the order in relation to the giving of advice by persons of that description is not satisfied.

(4B) In subsection (4)(a) 'qualified lawyer' means—

(a) as respects England and Wales, a barrister (whether in practice as such or employed to give legal advice), a solicitor who holds a practising certificate, or a person other than a barrister or solicitor who is an authorised advocate or authorised litigator (within the meaning of the Courts and Legal Services Act 1990), and

(b) as respects Scotland, an advocate (whether in practice as such or employed to give legal advice), or a solicitor who holds a practising certificate.

(4C) In subsection (4)(b) 'independent trade union' has the same meaning as in the Trade Union and Labour Relations (Consolidation) Act 1992.

(5) For the purposes of subsection (4A) any two persons are to be treated as connected—

(a) if one is a company of which the other (directly or indirectly) has control, or

(b) if both are companies of which a third person (directly or indirectly) has control.

(6) An agreement under which the parties agree to submit a dispute to arbitration—

(a) shall be regarded for the purposes of subsection (2) as being an agreement not to institute, or an agreement not to continue, proceedings if—

(i) the dispute is covered by a scheme having effect by virtue of an order under section 212A of the Trade Union and Labour Relations (Consolidation) Act 1992, and

(ii) the agreement is to submit it to arbitration in accordance with the scheme, but

(b) shall be regarded as neither being nor including such an agreement in any other case.

10 Charities and support for particular groups of persons

(1) Nothing in this Part—

(a) affects any charitable instrument which provides for conferring benefits on one or more categories of person determined by reference to any physical or mental capacity; or

(b) makes unlawful any act done by a charity or recognised body in pursuance of any of its charitable purposes, so far as those purposes are connected with persons so determined.

(2) Nothing in this Part prevents—

(a) a person who provides supported employment from treating members of a particular group of disabled persons more favourably than other persons in providing such employment; or

(b) the Secretary of State from agreeing to arrangements for the provision of supported employment which will, or may, have that effect.

(3) In this section—

'charitable instrument' means an enactment or other instrument (whenever taking effect) so far as it relates to charitable purposes;

'charity' has the same meaning as in the Charities Act 1993;

'recognised body' means a body which is a recognised body for the purposes of Part I of the Law Reform (Miscellaneous Provisions) (Scotland) Act 1990; and

'supported employment' means facilities provided, or in respect of which payments are made, under section 15 of the Disabled Persons (Employment) Act 1944.

(4) In the application of this section to England and Wales, 'charitable purposes' means purposes which are exclusively charitable according to the law of England and Wales.

(5) In the application of this section to Scotland, 'charitable purposes' shall be construed in the same way as if it were contained in the Income Tax Acts.

11 Advertisements suggesting that employers will discriminate against disabled persons

(1) This section applies where—

(a) a disabled person has applied for employment with an employer;

(b) the employer has refused to offer, or has deliberately not offered, him the employment;

(c) the disabled person has presented a complaint under section 8 against the employer;

(d) the employer has advertised the employment (whether before or after the disabled person applied for it); and

(e) the advertisement indicated, or might reasonably be understood to have indicated, that any application for the advertised employment would, or might, be determined to any extent by reference to—

(i) the successful applicant not having any disability or any category of disability which includes the disabled person's disability; or

(ii) the employer's reluctance to take any action of a kind mentioned in section 6.

(2) The tribunal hearing the complaint shall assume, unless the contrary is shown, that the employer's reason for refusing to offer, or deliberately not offering, the employment to the complainant was related to the complainant's disability.

(3) In this section 'advertisement' includes every form of advertisement or notice, whether to the public or not.

Discrimination by other persons

12 Discrimination against contract workers

(1) It is unlawful for a principal, in relation to contract work, to discriminate against a disabled person—

(a) in the terms on which he allows him to do that work;

(b) by not allowing him to do it or continue to do it;

(c) in the way he affords him access to any benefits or by refusing or deliberately omitting to afford him access to them; or

(d) by subjecting him to any other detriment.

(2) Subsection (1) does not apply to benefits of any description if the principal is concerned with the provision (whether or not for payment) of benefits of that description to the public, or to a section of the public which includes the contract worker in question, unless that provision differs in a material respect from the provision of the benefits by the principal to contract workers.

(3) The provisions of this Part (other than subsections (1) to (3) of section 4) apply to any principal, in relation to contract work, as if he were, or would be, the employer of the contract worker and as if any contract worker supplied to do work for him were an employee of his.

(4) In the case of an act which constitutes discrimination by virtue of section 55, this section also applies to discrimination against a person who is not disabled.

(5) This section applies only in relation to contract work done at an establishment in Great Britain (the provisions of section 68 about the meaning of 'employment at an establishment in Great Britain' applying for the purposes of this subsection with the appropriate modifications).

(6) In this section—

'principal' means a person ('A') who makes work available for doing by individuals who are employed by another person who supplies them under a contract made with A;

'contract work' means work so made available; and

'contract worker' means any individual who is supplied to the principal under such a contract.

13 Discrimination by trade organisations

(1) It is unlawful for a trade organisation to discriminate against a disabled person—

(a) in the terms on which it is prepared to admit him to membership of the organisation; or

(b) by refusing to accept, or deliberately not accepting, his application for membership.

(2) It is unlawful for a trade organisation, in the case of a disabled person who is a member of the organisation, to discriminate against him—

(a) in the way it affords him access to any benefits or by refusing or deliberately omitting to afford him access to them;

(b) by depriving him of membership, or varying the terms on which he is a member; or

(c) by subjecting him to any other detriment.

(3) In the case of an act which constitutes discrimination by virtue of section 55, this section also applies to discrimination against a person who is not disabled.

(4) In this section 'trade organisation' means an organisation of workers, an organisation of employers or any other organisation whose members carry on a particular profession or trade for the purposes of which the organisation exists.

14 Meaning of 'discrimination' in relation to trade organisations

(1) For the purposes of this Part, a trade organisation discriminates against a disabled person if—

(a) for a reason which relates to the disabled person's disability, it treats him less favourably than it treats or would treat others to whom that reason does not or would not apply; and

(b) it cannot show that the treatment in question is justified.

(2) For the purposes of this Part, a trade organisation also discriminates against a disabled person if—

(a) it fails to comply with a section 15 duty imposed on it in relation to the disabled person; and

(b) it cannot show that its failure to comply with that duty is justified.

(3) Subject to subsection (5), for the purposes of subsection (1) treatment is justified if, but only if, the reason for it is both material to the circumstances of the particular case and substantial.

(4) For the purposes of subsection (2), failure to comply with a section 15 duty is justified if, but only if, the reason for the failure is both material to the circumstances of the particular case and substantial.

(5) If, in a case falling within subsection (1), the trade organisation is under a section 15 duty in relation to the disabled person concerned but fails without justification to comply with that duty, its treatment of that person cannot be justified under subsection (3) unless the treatment would have been justified even if the organisation had complied with the section 15 duty.

(6) Regulations may make provision, for purposes of this section, as to circumstances in which—

(a) treatment is to be taken to be justified;

(b) failure to comply with a section 15 duty is to be taken to be justified;

(c) treatment is to be taken not to be justified;

(d) failure to comply with a section 15 duty is to be taken not to be justified.

15 Duty of trade organisation to make adjustments

(1) Where—

(a) any arrangements made by or on behalf of a trade organisation, or

(b) any physical feature of premises occupied by the organisation,

place the disabled person concerned at a substantial disadvantage in comparison with persons who are not disabled, it is the duty of the organisation to take such steps as it is reasonable, in all the circumstances of the case, for it to have to take in order to prevent the arrangements or feature having that effect.

(2) Subsection (1)(a) applies only in relation to—

(a) arrangements for determining who should become or remain a member of the organisation;

(b) any term, condition or arrangements on which membership or any benefit is offered or afforded.

(3) In determining whether it is reasonable for a trade organisation to have to take a particular step in order to comply with subsection (1), regard shall be had, in particular, to—

(a) the extent to which taking the step would prevent the effect in question;

(b) the extent to which it is practicable for the organisation to take the step;

(c) the financial and other costs which would be incurred by the organisation in taking the step and the extent to which taking it would disrupt any of its activities;

(d) the extent of the organisation's financial and other resources;

(e) the availability to the organisation of financial or other assistance with respect to taking the step.

This subsection is subject to any provision of regulations made under subsection (7)

(4) In this section 'the disabled person concerned' means—

(a) in the case of arrangements for determining to whom membership should be offered, any disabled person who is, or has notified the organisation that he may be, an applicant for membership;

(b) in any other case, a disabled person who is—

(i) an applicant for membership; or

(ii) a member of the organisation.

(5) Nothing in this section imposes any duty on an organisation in relation to a disabled person if the organisation does not know, and could not reasonably be expected to know that the disabled person concerned—

(a) is, or may be, an applicant for membership; or

(b) has a disability and is likely to be affected in the way mentioned in subsection (1).

(6) Subject to the provisions of this section, nothing in this Part is to be taken to require a trade organisation to treat a disabled person more favourably than it treats or would treat others.

(7) Regulations may make provision for the purposes of subsection (1) as to any of the matters mentioned in paragraphs (a) to (h) of section 6(8) (the references in those paragraphs to an employer being read for these purposes as references to a trade organisation).

(8) Subsection (9) of section 6 applies in relation to such regulations as it applies in relation to regulations made under section 6(8).

(9) Regulations may make provision adding to the duty imposed on trade organisations by this section, including provision of a kind which may be made under subsection (7).

(10) This section imposes duties only for the purpose of determining whether a trade organisation has discriminated against a disabled person; and accordingly a breach of any such duty is not actionable as such.

16 [omitted]

Occupational pension schemes and insurance services

17 Occupational pension schemes

(1) Every occupational pension scheme shall be taken to include a provision ('a non-discrimination rule')—

(a) relating to the terms on which—

(i) persons become members of the scheme; and

(ii) members of the scheme are treated; and

(b) requiring the trustees or managers of the scheme to refrain from any act or omission which, if done in relation to a person by an employer, would amount to unlawful discrimination against that person for the purposes of this Part.

(2) The other provisions of the scheme are to have effect subject to the non-discrimination rule.

(3) Without prejudice to section 67, regulations under this Part may—

(a) with respect to trustees or managers of occupational pension schemes make different provision from that made with respect to employers; or

(b) make provision modifying the application to such trustees or managers of any regulations made under this Part, or of any provisions of this Part so far as they apply to employers.

(4) In determining, for the purposes of this section, whether an act or omission would amount to unlawful discrimination if done by an employer, any provision made under subsection (3) shall be applied as if it applied in relation to the notional employer.

18 Insurance services

(1) This section applies where a provider of insurance services ('the insurer') enters into arrangements with an employer under which the employer's employees, or a class of his employees—

(a) receive insurance services provided by the insurer; or

(b) are given an opportunity to receive such services.

(2) The insurer is to be taken, for the purposes of this Part, to discriminate unlawfully against a disabled person who is a relevant employee if he acts in relation to that employee in a way which would be unlawful discrimination for the purposes of Part III if—

(a) he were providing the service in question to members of the public; and

(b) the employee was provided with, or was trying to secure the provision of, that service as a member of the public.

(3) In this section—

'insurance services' means services of a prescribed description for the provision of benefits in respect of—

(a) termination of service;

(b) retirement, old age or death;

(c) accident, injury, sickness or invalidity; or

(d) any other prescribed matter; and

'relevant employee' means—

(a) in the case of an arrangement which applies to employees of the employer in question, an employee of his;

(b) in the case of an arrangement which applies to a class of employees of the employer, an employee who is in that class.

(4) For the purposes of the definition of 'relevant employee' in subsection (3), 'employee', in relation to an employer, includes a person who has applied for, or is contemplating applying for, employment by that employer or (as the case may be) employment by him in the class in question.

19-49 [omitted]; **50-54** [repealed]

55 Victimisation

(1) For the purposes of Part II or Part III, a person ('A') discriminates against another person ('B') if—

(a) he treats B less favourably than he treats or would treat other persons whose circumstances are the same as B's; and

(b) he does so for a reason mentioned in subsection (2).

(2) The reasons are that—

(a) B has—

(i) brought proceedings against A or any other person under this Act; or

(ii) given evidence or information in connection with such proceedings brought by any person; or

(iii) otherwise done anything under this Act in relation to A or any other person; or

(iv) alleged that A or any other person has (whether or not the allegation so states) contravened this Act; or

(b) A believes or suspects that B has done or intends to do any of those things.

(3) Where B is a disabled person, or a person who has had a disability, the disability in question shall be disregarded in comparing his circumstances with those of any other person for the purposes of subsection (1)(a).

(4) Subsection (1) does not apply to treatment of a person because of an allegation made by him if the allegation was false and not made in good faith.

56 [omitted]

57 Aiding unlawful acts

(1) A person who knowingly aids another person to do an act made unlawful by this Act is to be treated for the purposes of this Act as himself doing the same kind of unlawful act.

(2) For the purposes of subsection (1), an employee or agent for whose act the employer or principal is liable under section 58 (or would be so liable but for section 58(5)) shall be taken to have aided the employer or principal to do the act.

(3) For the purposes of this section, a person does not knowingly aid another to do an unlawful act if—

(a) he acts in reliance on a statement made to him by that other person that, because of any provision of this Act, the act would not be unlawful; and

(b) it is reasonable for him to rely on the statement.

(4) A person who knowingly or recklessly makes such a statement which is false or misleading in a material respect is guilty of an offence.

(5) Any person guilty of an offence under subsection (4) shall be liable on summary conviction to a fine not exceeding level 5 on the standard scale.

58 Liability of employers and principals

(1) Anything done by a person in the course of his employment shall be treated for the purposes of this Act as also done by his employer, whether or not it was done with the employer's knowledge or approval.

(2) Anything done by a person as agent for another person with the authority of that other person shall be treated for the purposes of this Act as also done by that other person.

(3) Subsection (2) applies whether the authority was—

(a) express or implied; or

(b) given before or after the act in question was done.

(4) Subsections (1) and (2) do not apply in relation to an offence under section 57(4).

(5) In proceedings under this Act against any person in respect of an act alleged to have been done by an employee of his, it shall be a defence for that person to prove that he took such steps as were reasonably practicable to prevent the employee from—

(a) doing that act; or

(b) doing, in the course of his employment, acts of that description.

59 Statutory authority and national security etc.

(1) Nothing in this Act makes unlawful any act done—

(a) in pursuance of any enactment; or

(b) in pursuance of any instrument made by a Minister of the Crown under any enactment; or

(c) to comply with any condition or requirement imposed by a Minister of the Crown (whether before or after the passing of this Act) by virtue of any enactment.

(2) In subsection (1) 'enactment' includes one passed or made after the date on which this Act is passed and 'instrument' includes one made after that date.

(3) Nothing in this Act makes unlawful any act done for the purpose of safeguarding national security.

PART VIII
MISCELLANEOUS

60-67 [omitted]

68 Interpretation

(1) In this Act—

. . .

'act' includes a deliberate omission;

. . .

'benefits', in Part II, has the meaning given in section 4(4);

'conciliation officer' means a person designated under section 211 of the Trade Union and Labour Relations (Consolidation) Act 1992;

'employment' means, subject to any prescribed provision, employment under a contract of service or of apprenticeship or a contract personally to do any work, and related expressions are to be construed accordingly;

'employment at an establishment in Great Britain' is to be construed in accordance with subsections (2) to (5);

. . .

'mental impairment' does not have the same meaning as in the Mental Health Act 1983 or the Mental Health (Scotland) Act 1984 but the fact that an impairment would be a mental impairment for the purposes of either of those Acts does not prevent it from being a mental impairment for the purposes of this Act;

'Minister of the Crown' includes the Treasury;

'occupational pension scheme' has the same meaning as in the Pension Schemes Act 1993;

'premises' includes land of any description;

'prescribed' means prescribed by regulations;

'profession' includes any vocation or occupation;

. . .

(2) Where an employee does his work wholly or mainly outside Great Britain, his employment is not to be treated as being work at an establishment in Great Britain even if he does some of his work at such an establishment.

(3) Except in prescribed cases, employment on board a ship, aircraft or hovercraft is to be regarded as not being employment at an establishment in Great Britain.

(4) Employment of a prescribed kind, or in prescribed circumstances, is to be regarded as not being employment at an establishment in Great Britain.

(5) Where work is not done at an establishment it shall be treated as done—

(a) at the establishment from which it is done; or

(b) where it is not done from any establishment, at the establishment with which it has the closest connection.

69-70 [omitted]

SCHEDULE 1
PROVISIONS SUPPLEMENTING SECTION 1

Impairment

1.—(1) 'Mental impairment' includes an impairment resulting from or consisting of a mental illness only if the illness is a clinically well-recognised illness.

(2) Regulations may make provision, for the purposes of this Act—

(a) for conditions of a prescribed description to be treated as amounting to impairments;

(b) for conditions of a prescribed description to be treated as not amounting to impairments.

(3) Regulations made under sub-paragraph (2) may make provision as to the meaning of 'condition' for the purposes of those regulations.

Long-term effects

2.—(1) The effect of an impairment is a long-term effect if—

(a) it has lasted at least 12 months;

(b) the period for which it lasts is likely to be at least 12 months; or

(c) it is likely to last for the rest of the life of the person affected.

(2) Where an impairment ceases to have a substantial adverse effect on a person's ability to carry out normal day-to-day activities, it is to be treated as continuing to have that effect if that effect is likely to recur.

(3) For the purposes of sub-paragraph (2), the likelihood of an effect recurring shall be disregarded in prescribed circumstances.

(4) Regulations may prescribe circumstances in which, for the purposes of this Act—

(a) an effect which would not otherwise be a long-term effect is to be treated as such an effect; or

(b) an effect which would otherwise be a long-term effect is to be treated as not being such an effect.

Severe disfigurement

3.—(1) An impairment which consists of a severe disfigurement is to be treated as having a substantial adverse effect on the ability of the person concerned to carry out normal day-to-day activities.

(2) Regulations may provide that in prescribed circumstances a severe disfigurement is not to be treated as having that effect.

(3) Regulations under sub-paragraph (2) may, in particular, make provision with respect to deliberately acquired disfigurements.

Normal day-to-day activities

4.—(1) An impairment is to be taken to affect the ability of the person concerned to carry out normal day-to-day activities only if it affects one of the following—

(a) mobility;

(b) manual dexterity;

(c) physical co-ordination;

(d) continence;

(e) ability to lift, carry or otherwise move everyday objects;

(f) speech, hearing or eyesight;

(g) memory or ability to concentrate, learn or understand; or

(h) perception of the risk of physical danger.

(2) Regulations may prescribe—

(a) circumstances in which an impairment which does not have an effect falling within sub-paragraph (1) is to be taken to affect the ability of the person concerned to carry out normal day-to-day activities;

(b) circumstances in which an impairment which has an effect falling within sub-paragraph (1) is to be taken not to affect the ability of the person concerned to carry out normal day-to-day activities.

Substantial adverse effects

5. Regulations may make provision for the purposes of this Act—

(a) for an effect of a prescribed kind on the ability of a person to carry out normal day-to-day activities to be treated as a substantial adverse effect;

(b) for an effect of a prescribed kind on the ability of a person to carry out normal day-to-day activities to be treated as not being a substantial adverse effect.

Effect of medical treatment

6.—(1) An impairment which would be likely to have a substantial adverse effect on the ability of the person concerned to carry out normal day-to-day activities, but for the fact that measures are being taken to treat or correct it, is to be treated as having that effect.

(2) In sub-paragraph (1) 'measures' includes, in particular, medical treatment and the use of a prosthesis or other aid.

(3) Sub-paragraph (1) does not apply—

(a) in relation to the impairment of a person's sight, to the extent that the impairment is, in his case, correctable by spectacles or contact lenses or in such other ways as may be prescribed; or

(b) in relation to such other impairments as may be prescribed, in such circumstances as may be prescribed.

Persons deemed to be disabled

7.—(1) Sub-paragraph (2) applies to any person whose name is, both on 12th January 1995 and on the date when this paragraph comes into force, in the register of disabled persons maintained under section 6 of the Disabled Persons (Employment) Act 1944.

(2) That person is to be deemed—

(a) during the initial period, to have a disability, and hence to be a disabled person; and

(b) afterwards, to have had a disability and hence to have been a disabled person during that period.

(3) A certificate of registration shall be conclusive evidence, in relation to the person with respect to whom it was issued, of the matters certified.

(4) Unless the contrary is shown, any document purporting to be a certificate of registration shall be taken to be such a certificate and to have been validly issued.

(5) Regulations may.provide for prescribed descriptions of person to be deemed to have disabilities, and hence to be disabled persons, for the purposes of this Act.

(6) Regulations may prescribe circumstances in which a person who has been deemed to be a disabled person by the provisions of sub-paragraph (1) or regulations made under sub-paragraph (5) is to be treated as no longer being deemed to be such a person.

(7) In this paragraph—

'certificate of registration' means a certificate issued under regulations made under section 6 of the Act of 1944; and

'initial period' means the period of three years beginning with the date on which this paragraph comes into force.

Progressive conditions

8.—(1) Where—

(a) a person has a progressive condition (such as cancer, multiple sclerosis or muscular dystrophy or infection by the human immunodeficiency virus),

(b) as a result of that condition, he has an impairment which has (or had) an effect on his ability to carry out normal day-to-day activities, but

(c) that effect is not (or was not) a substantial adverse effect,

he shall be taken to have an impairment which has such a substantial adverse effect if the condition is likely to result in his having such an impairment.

(2) Regulations may make provision, for the purposes of this paragraph—

(a) for conditions of a prescribed description to be treated as being progressive;

(b) for conditions of a prescribed description to be treated as not being progressive.

SCHEDULE 2
PAST DISABILITIES

1. The modifications referred to in section 2 are as follows.

2. References in Parts II and III to a disabled person are to be read as references to a person who has had a disability.

3. In section 6(1), after 'not disabled' insert 'and who have not had a disability'.
4. In section 6(6), for 'has' substitute 'has had'.
5. For paragraph 2(1) to (3) of Schedule 1, substitute—

'(1) The effect of an impairment is a long-term effect if it has lasted for at least 12 months.

(2) Where an impairment ceases to have a substantial adverse effect on a person's ability to carry out normal day-to-day activities, it is to be treated as continuing to have that effect if that effect recurs.

(3) For the purposes of sub-paragraph (2), the recurrence of an effect shall be disregarded in prescribed circumstances.'

SCHEDULE 3
ENFORCEMENT AND PROCEDURE

PART I
EMPLOYMENT

1. [repealed]

Restriction on proceedings for breach of Part II

2.—(1) Except as provided by section 8, no civil or criminal proceedings may be brought against any person in respect of an act merely because the act is unlawful under Part II.

(2) Sub-paragraph (1) does not prevent the making of an application for judicial review.

Period within which proceedings must be brought

3.—(1) An employment tribunal shall not consider a complaint under section 8 unless it is presented before the end of the period of three months beginning when the act complained of was done.

(2) A tribunal may consider any such complaint which is out of time if, in all the circumstances of the case, it considers that it is just and equitable to do so.

(3) For the purposes of sub-paragraph (1)—

(a) where an unlawful act of discrimination is attributable to a term in a contract, that act is to be treated as extending throughout the duration of the contract;

(b) any act extending over a period shall be treated as done at the end of that period; and

(c) a deliberate omission shall be treated as done when the person in question decided upon it.

(4) In the absence of evidence establishing the contrary, a person shall be taken for the purposes of this paragraph to decide upon an omission—

(a) when he does an act inconsistent with doing the omitted act; or

(b) if he has done no such inconsistent act, when the period expires within which he might reasonably have been expected to do the omitted act if it was to be done.

Evidence

4.—(1) In any proceedings under section 8, a certificate signed by or on behalf of a Minister of the Crown and certifying—

(a) that any conditions or requirements specified in the certificate were imposed by a Minister of the Crown and were in operation at a time or throughout a time so specified, or

(b) [repealed]

shall be conclusive evidence of the matters certified.

(2) A document purporting to be such a certificate shall be received in evidence and, unless the contrary is proved, be deemed to be such a certificate.

JOBSEEKERS ACT 1995
(1995, c. 18)

Trade disputes

14 Trade disputes

(1) Where—

(a) there is a stoppage of work which causes a person not to be employed on any day, and

(b) the stoppage is due to a trade dispute at his place of work,

that person is not entitled to a jobseeker's allowance for the week which includes that day unless he proves that he is not directly interested in the dispute.

(2) A person who withdraws his labour on any day in furtherance of a trade dispute, but to whom subsection (1) does not apply, is not entitled to a jobseeker's allowance for the week which includes that day.

(3) If a person who is prevented by subsection (1) from being entitled to a jobseeker's allowance proves that during the stoppage—

(a) he became bona fide employed elsewhere;

(b) his employment was terminated by reason of redundancy within the meaning of section 139(1) of the Employment Rights Act 1996, or

(c) he bona fide resumed employment with his employer but subsequently left for a reason other than the trade dispute,

subsection (1) shall be taken to have ceased to apply to him on the occurrence of the event referred to in paragraph (a) or (b) or (as the case may be) the first event referred to in paragraph (c).

(4) In this section 'place of work', in relation to any person, means the premises or place at which he was employed.

(5) Where separate branches of work which are commonly carried on as separate businesses in separate premises or at separate places are in any case carried on in separate departments on the same premises or at the same place, each of those departments shall, for the purposes of subsection (4), be deemed to be separate premises or (as the case may be) a separate place.

Denial of jobseeker's allowance

19 Circumstances in which a jobseeker's allowance is not payable

(1) Even though the conditions for entitlement to a jobseeker's allowance are satisfied with respect to a person, the allowance shall not be payable in any of the circumstances mentioned in subsection (5) or (6).

(2) If the circumstances are any of those mentioned in subsection (5), the period for which the allowance is not to be payable shall be such period (of at least one week but not more than 26 weeks) as may be prescribed.

(3) If the circumstances are any of those mentioned in subsection (6), the period for which the allowance is not to be payable shall be such period (of at least one week but not more than 26 weeks) as may be determined by the Secretary of State.

(4) Regulations may prescribe—

(a) circumstances which the Secretary of State is to take into account, and

(b) circumstances which he is not to take into account,

in determining a period under subsection (3).

(5) The circumstances referred to in subsections (1) and (2) are that the claimant—

(a) has, without good cause, refused or failed to carry out any jobseeker's direction which was reasonable, having regard to his circumstances;

(b) has, without good cause

(i) neglected to avail himself of a reasonable opportunity of a place on a training scheme or employment programme;

(ii) after a place on such a scheme or programme has been notified to him by an employment officer as vacant or about to become vacant, refused or failed to apply for it or to accept it when offered to him;

(iii) given up a place on such a scheme or programme; or

(iv) failed to attend such a scheme or programme on which he has been given a place; or

(c) has lost his place on such a scheme or programme through misconduct.

(6) The circumstances referred to in subsections (1) and (3) are that the claimant—

(a) has lost his employment as an employed earner through misconduct;

(b) has voluntarily left such employment without just cause;

(c) has, without good cause, after a situation in any employment has been notified to him by an employment officer as vacant or about to become vacant, refused or failed to apply for it or to accept it when offered to him; or

(d) has, without good cause, neglected to avail himself of a reasonable opportunity of employment.

(7) In such circumstances as may be prescribed, including in particular where he has been dismissed by his employer by reason of redundancy within the meaning of section 139(1) of the Employment Rights Act 1996 after volunteering or agreeing to be so dismissed, a person who might otherwise be regarded as having left his employment voluntarily is to be treated as not having left voluntarily.

(8) to (10) [omitted]

20 Exemptions from section 19

(1) Nothing in section 19, or in regulations under that section, shall be taken to prevent payment of a jobseeker's allowance merely because the claimant refuses to seek or accept employment in a situation which is vacant in consequence of a stoppage of work due to a trade dispute.

(2) to (8) [omitted]

35 Interpretation

(1) In this Act—

...

'trade dispute' means any dispute between employers and employees, or between employees and employees, which is connected with the employment or non-employment or the terms of employment or the conditions of employment of any persons, whether employees in the employment of the employer with whom the dispute arises, or not;

PENSIONS ACT 1995
(1995, c. 26)

Equal treatment

62 The equal treatment rule

(1) An occupational pension scheme which does not contain an equal treatment rule shall be treated as including one.

(2) An equal treatment rule is a rule which relates to the terms on which—

(a) persons become members of the scheme, and

(b) members of the scheme are treated.

(3) Subject to subsection (6), an equal treatment rule has the effect that where—

(a) a woman is employed on like work with a man in the same employment,

(b) a woman is employed on work rated as equivalent with that of a man in the same employment, or

(c) a woman is employed on work which, not being work in relation to which paragraph (a) or (b) applies, is, in terms of the demands made on her (for instance under such headings as effort, skill and decision) of equal value to that of a man in the same employment,

but (apart from the rule) any of the terms referred to in subsection (2) is or becomes less favourable to the woman than it is to the man, the term shall be treated as so modified as not to be less favourable.

(4) An equal treatment rule does not operate in relation to any difference as between a woman and a man in the operation of any of the terms referred to in subsection (2) if the trustees or managers of the scheme prove that the difference is genuinely due to a material factor which—

(a) is not the difference of sex, but

(b) is a material difference between the woman's case and the man's case.

(5) References in subsection (4) and sections 63 to 65 to the terms referred to in subsection (2), or the effect of any of those terms, include—

(a) a term which confers on the trustees or managers of an occupational pension scheme, or any other person, a discretion which, in a case within any of paragraphs (a) to (c) of subsection (3)—

(i) may be exercised so as to affect the way in which persons become members of the scheme, or members of the scheme are treated, and

(ii) may (apart from the equal treatment rule) be so exercised in a way less favourable to the woman than to the man, and

(b) the effect of any exercise of such a discretion;

and references to the terms on which members of the scheme are treated are to be read accordingly.

(6) In the case of a term within subsection (5)(a) the effect of an equal treatment rule is that the term shall be treated as so modified as not to permit the discretion to be exercised in a way less favourable to the woman than to the man.

63 Equal treatment rule: supplementary

(1) The reference in section 62(2) to the terms on which members of a scheme are treated includes those terms as they have effect for the benefit of dependants of members, and the reference in section 62(5) to the way in which members of a scheme are treated includes the way they are treated as it has effect for the benefit of dependants of members.

(2) Where the effect of any of the terms referred to in section 62(2) on persons of the same sex differs according to their family or marital status, the effect of the term is to be compared for the purposes of section 62 with its effect on persons of the other sex who have the same status.

(3) An equal treatment rule has effect subject to paragraphs 5 and 6 of Schedule 5 to the Social Security Act 1989 (employment-related benefit schemes: maternity and family leave provisions).

(4) Section 62 shall be construed as one with section 1 of the Equal Pay Act 1970 (requirement of equal treatment for men and women in the same employment); and sections 2 and 2A of that Act (disputes and enforcement) shall have effect for the purposes of section 62 as if—

(a) references to an equality clause were to an equal treatment rule,

(b) references to employers and employees were to the trustees or managers of the scheme (on the one hand) and the members, or prospective members, of the scheme (on the other),

(c) for section 2(4) there were substituted—

'(4) No claim in respect of the operation of an equal treatment rule in respect of an occupational pension scheme shall be referred to an employment tribunal otherwise than by virtue of subsection (3) above unless the woman concerned has been employed in a description or category of employment to which the scheme relates within the six months preceding the date of the reference', and

(d) references to section 1(2)(c) of the Equal Pay Act 1970 were to section 62(3)(c) of this Act.

(5) Regulations may make provision for the Equal Pay Act 1970 to have effect, in relation to an equal treatment rule, with prescribed modifications; and subsection (4) shall have effect subject to any regulations made by virtue of this subsection.

(6) Section 62, so far as it relates to the terms on which members of a scheme are treated, is to be treated as having had effect in relation to any pensionable service on or after 17th May 1990.

64 Equal treatment rule: exceptions

(1) An equal treatment rule does not operate in relation to any variation as between a woman and a man in the effect of any of the terms referred to in section 62(2) if the variation is permitted by or under any of the provisions of this section.

(2) Where a man and a woman are eligible, in prescribed circumstances, to receive different amounts by way of pension, the variation is permitted by this subsection if, in prescribed circumstances, the differences are attributable only to differences between men and women in the benefits under sections 43 to 55 of the Social Security Contributions and Benefits Act 1992 (State retirement pensions) to which, in prescribed circumstances, they are or would be entitled.

(3) A variation is permitted by this subsection if—

(a) the variation consists of the application of actuarial factors which differ for men and women to the calculation of contributions to a scheme by employers, being factors which fall within a prescribed class or description, or

(b) the variation consists of the application of actuarial factors which differ for men and women to the determination of benefits falling within a prescribed class or description;

and in this subsection 'benefits' include any payment or other benefit made to or in respect of a person as a member of the scheme.

(4) Regulations may—

(a) permit further variations, or

(b) amend or repeal subsection (2) or (3);

and regulations made by virtue of this subsection may have effect in relation to pensionable service on or after 17th May 1990 and before the date on which the regulations are made.

65 Equal treatment rule: consequential alteration of schemes

(1) The trustees or managers of an occupational pension scheme may, if—

(a) they do not (apart from this section) have power to make such alterations to the scheme as may be required to secure conformity with an equal treatment rule, or

(b) they have such power but the procedure for doing so—

(i) is liable to be unduly complex or protracted, or

(ii) involves the obtaining of consents which cannot be obtained, or can only be obtained with undue delay or difficulty,

by resolution make such alterations to the scheme.

(2) The alterations may have effect in relation to a period before the alterations are made.

EMPLOYMENT RIGHTS ACT 1996
(1996, c. 18)

PART I
EMPLOYMENT PARTICULARS

Right to statements of employment particulars

Right to itemised pay statement

Enforcement

PART II
PROTECTION OF WAGES

Deductions by employer

Payments to employer

Cash shortages and stock deficiencies in retail employment

Enforcement

Supplementary

PART III
GUARANTEE PAYMENTS

PART IV
SUNDAY WORKING FOR SHOP AND BETTING WORKERS

Protected shop workers and betting workers

Opting-out of Sunday work

PART IVA
PROTECTED DISCLOSURES

PART V
PROTECTION FROM SUFFERING DETRIMENT IN EMPLOYMENT

Rights not to suffer detriment

PART VIII
MATERNITY LEAVE

71 Ordinary maternity leave.
72 Compulsory maternity leave.
73 Additional maternity leave.
74 Redundancy and dismissal.
75 Sections 71 to 73: Supplemental.

CHAPTER II
PARENTAL LEAVE

76 Entitlement to parental leave.
77 Rights during and after parental leave.
78 Special cases.
79 Supplemental.
80 Complaint to employment tribunal.

PART IX
TERMINATION OF EMPLOYMENT

Minimum period of notice

86 Rights of employer and employee to minimum notice.
87 Rights of employee in period of notice.
88 Employments with normal working hours.
89 Employments without normal working hours.
90 Short-term incapacity benefit and industrial injury benefit.
91 Supplementary.

Written statement of reasons for dismissal

92 Right to written statement of reasons for dismissal.
93 Complaints to employment tribunal.

PART X
UNFAIR DISMISSAL

CHAPTER I
RIGHT NOT TO BE UNFAIRLY DISMISSED

The right

94 The right.

Dismissal

95 Circumstances in which an employee is dismissed.
97 Effective date of termination.

Fairness

98 General.
99 Leave for family reasons.
100 Health and safety cases.
101 Shop workers and betting workers who refuse Sunday work.
101A Working time cases
102 Trustees of occupational pension schemes.
103 Employee representatives.
103A Protected disclosure.
104 Assertion of statutory right.

Exclusion of right

CHAPTER II
REMEDIES FOR UNFAIR DISMISSAL

Introductory

Orders for reinstatement or re-engagement

Compensation

Interim relief

CHAPTER III
SUPPLEMENTARY

PART XI
REDUNDANCY PAYMENTS ETC.

CHAPTER I
RIGHT TO REDUNDANCY PAYMENT

CHAPTER II
RIGHT ON DISMISSAL BY REASON OF REDUNDANCY

Dismissal by reason of redundancy

Exclusions

Supplementary

CHAPTER III
RIGHT BY REASON OF LAY-OFF OR SHORT-TIME

Lay-off and short-time

Exclusions

Supplementary

CHAPTER IV
GENERAL EXCLUSIONS FROM RIGHT

CHAPTER V
OTHER PROVISIONS ABOUT REDUNDANCY PAYMENTS

PART I
EMPLOYMENT PARTICULARS

Right to statements of employment particulars

1 Statement of initial employment particulars

(1) Where an employee begins employment with an employer, the employer shall give to the employee a written statement of particulars of employment.

(2) The statement may (subject to section 2(4)) be given in instalments and (whether or not given in instalments) shall be given not later than two months after the beginning of the employment.

(3) The statement shall contain particulars of—

(a) the names of the employer and employee,

(b) the date when the employment began, and

(c) the date on which the employee's period of continuous employment began (taking into account any employment with a previous employer which counts towards that period).

(4) The statement shall also contain particulars, as at a specified date not more than seven days before the statement (or the instalment containing them) is given, of—

(a) the scale or rate of remuneration or the method of calculating remuneration,

(b) the intervals at which remuneration is paid (that is, weekly, monthly or other specified intervals),

(c) any terms and conditions relating to hours of work (including any terms and conditions relating to normal working hours),

(d) any terms and conditions relating to any of the following—

(i) entitlement to holidays, including public holidays, and holiday pay (the particulars given being sufficient to enable the employee's entitlement, including any entitlement to accrued holiday pay on the termination of employment, to be precisely calculated),

(ii) incapacity for work due to sickness or injury, including any provision for sick pay, and

(iii) pensions and pension schemes,

(e) the length of notice which the employee is obliged to give and entitled to receive to terminate his contract of employment,

(f) the title of the job which the employee is employed to do or a brief description of the work for which he is employed,

(g) where the employment is not intended to be permanent, the period for which it is expected to continue or, if it is for a fixed term, the date when it is to end,

(h) either the place of work or, where the employee is required or permitted to work at various places, an indication of that and of the address of the employer,

(j) any collective agreements which directly affect the terms and conditions of the employment including, where the employer is not a party, the persons by whom they were made, and

(k) where the employee is required to work outside the United Kingdom for a period of more than one month—

(i) the period for which he is to work outside the United Kingdom,

(ii) the currency in which remuneration is to be paid while he is working outside the United Kingdom,

(iii) any additional remuneration payable to him, and any benefits to be provided to or in respect of him, by reason of his being required to work outside the United Kingdom, and

(iv) any terms and conditions relating to his return to the United Kingdom.

(5) Subsection (4)(d)(iii) does not apply to an employee of a body or authority if—

(a) the employee's pension rights depend on the terms of a pension scheme established under any provision contained in or having effect under any Act, and

(b) any such provision requires the body or authority to give to a new employee information concerning the employee's pension rights or the determination of questions affecting those rights.

2 Statement of initial particulars: supplementary

(1) If, in the case of a statement under section 1, there are no particulars to be entered under any of the heads of paragraph (d) or (k) of subsection (4) of that section, or under any of the other paragraphs of subsection (3) or (4) of that section, that fact shall be stated.

(2) A statement under section 1 may refer the employee for particulars of any of the matters specified in subsection (4)(d)(ii) and (iii) of that section to the provisions of some other document which is reasonably accessible to the employee.

(3) A statement under section 1 may refer the employee for particulars of either of the matters specified in subsection (4)(e) of that section to the law or to the provisions of any collective agreement directly affecting the terms and conditions of the employment which is reasonably accessible to the employee.

(4) The particulars required by section 1(3) and (4)(a) to (c), (d)(i), (f) and (h) shall be included in a single document.

(5) Where before the end of the period of two months after the beginning of an employee's employment the employee is to begin to work outside the United Kingdom for a period of more than one month, the statement under section 1 shall be given to him not later than the time when he leaves the United Kingdom in order to begin so to work.

(6) A statement shall be given to a person under section 1 even if his employment ends before the end of the period within which the statement is required to be given.

3 Note about disciplinary procedures and pensions

(1) A statement under section 1 shall include a note—

(a) specifying any disciplinary rules applicable to the employee or referring the employee to the provisions of a document specifying such rules which is reasonably accessible to the employee,

(b) specifying (by description or otherwise)—

(i) a person to whom the employee can apply if dissatisfied with any disciplinary decision relating to him, and

(ii) a person to whom the employee can apply for the purpose of seeking redress of any grievance relating to his employment,

and the manner in which any such application should be made, and

(c) where there are further steps consequent on any such application, explaining those steps or referring to the provisions of a document explaining them which is reasonably accessible to the employee.

(2) Subsection (1) does not apply to rules, disciplinary decisions, grievances or procedures relating to health or safety at work.

(3) The note need not comply with the following provisions of subsection (1)—

(a) paragraph (a),

(b) in paragraph (b), sub-paragraph (i) and the words following sub-paragraph (ii) so far as relating to sub-paragraph (i), and

(c) paragraph (c),

if on the date when the employee's employment began the relevant number of employees was less than twenty.

(4) In subsection (3) 'the relevant number of employees', in relation to an employee, means the number of employees employed by his employer added to the number of employees employed by any associated employer.

(5) The note shall also state whether there is in force a contracting-out certificate (issued in accordance with Chapter I of Part III of the Pension Schemes Act 1993) stating that the employment is contracted-out employment (for the purposes of that Part of that Act).

4 Statement of changes

(1) If, after the material date, there is a change in any of the matters particulars of which are required by sections 1 to 3 to be included or referred to in a statement under section 1, the employer shall give to the employee a written statement containing particulars of the change.

(2) For the purposes of subsection (1)—

(a) in relation to a matter particulars of which are included or referred to in a statement given under section 1 otherwise than in instalments, the material date is the date to which the statement relates,

(b) in relation to a matter particulars of which—

(i) are included or referred to in an instalment of a statement given under section 1, or

(ii) are required by section 2(4) to be included in a single document but are not included in an instalment of a statement given under section 1 which does include other particulars to which that provision applies,

the material date is the date to which the instalment relates, and

(c) in relation to any other matter, the material date is the date by which a statement under section 1 is required to be given.

(3) A statement under subsection (1) shall be given at the earliest opportunity and, in any event, not later than—

(a) one month after the change in question, or

(b) where that change results from the employee being required to work outside the United Kingdom for a period of more than one month, the time when he leaves the United Kingdom in order to begin so to work, if that is earlier.

(4) A statement under subsection (1) may refer the employee to the provisions of some other document which is reasonably accessible to the employee for a change in any of the matters specified in sections 1(4)(d)(ii) and (iii) and 3(1)(a) and (c).

(5) A statement under subsection (1) may refer the employee for a change in either of the matters specifed in section 1(4)(e) to the law or to the provisions of any collective agreement directly affecting the terms and conditions of the employment which is reasonably accessible to the employee.

(6) Where, after an employer has given to an employee a statement under section 1, either—

(a) the name of the employer (whether an individual or a body corporate or partnership) is changed without any change in the identity of the employer, or

(b) the identity of the employer is changed in circumstances in which the continuity of the employee's period of employment is not broken,

and subsection (7) applies in relation to the change, the person who is the employer immediately after the change is not required to give to the employee a statement under section 1; but the change shall be treated as a change falling within subsection (1) of this section.

(7) This subsection applies in relation to a change if it does not involve any change in any of the matters (other than the names of the parties) particulars of which are required by sections 1 to 3 to be included or referred to in the statement under section 1.

(8) A statement under subsection (1) which informs an employee of a change such as is referred to in subsection (6)(b) shall specify the date on which the employee's period of continuous employment began.

5 Exclusion from rights to statements

(1) Sections 1 to 4 apply to an employee who at any time comes or ceases to come within the exceptions from those sections provided by section 199, and under section 209, as if his employment with his employer terminated or began at that time.

(2) The fact that section 1 is directed by subsection (1) to apply to an employee as if his employment began on his ceasing to come within the exceptions referred to in that subsection does not affect the obligation under section 1(3)(b) to specify the date on which his employment actually began.

6 Reasonably accessible document or collective agreement

In sections 2 to 4 references to a document or collective agreement which is reasonably accessible to an employee are references to a document or collective agreement which—

(a) the employee has reasonable opportunities of reading in the course of his employment, or

(b) is made reasonably accessible to the employee in some other way.

7 Power to require particulars of further matters

The Secretary of State may by order provide that section 1 shall have effect as if particulars of such further matters as may be specified in the order were included in the particulars required by that section; and, for that purpose, the order may include such provisions amending that section as appear to the Secretary of State to be expedient.

Right to itemised pay statement

8 Itemised pay statement

(1) An employee has the right to be given by his employer, at or before the time at which any payment of wages or salary is made to him, a written itemised pay statement.

(2) The statement shall contain particulars of—

(a) the gross amount of the wages or salary,

(b) the amounts of any variable, and (subject to section 9) any fixed, deductions from that gross amount and the purposes for which they are made,

(c) the net amount of wages or salary payable, and

(d) where different parts of the net amount are paid in different ways, the amount and method of payment of each part-payment.

9 Standing statement of fixed deductions

(1) A pay statement given in accordance with section 8 need not contain separate particulars of a fixed deduction if—

(a) it contains instead an aggregate amount of fixed deductions, including that deduction, and

(b) the employer has given to the employee, at or before the time at which the pay statement is given, a standing statement of fixed deductions which satisfies subsection (2).

(2) A standing statement of fixed deductions satisfies this subsection if—

(a) it is in writing,

(b) it contains, in relation to each deduction comprised in the aggregate amount of deductions, particulars of—

(i) the amount of the deduction,

(ii) the intervals at which the deduction is to be made, and

(iii) the purpose for which it is made, and

(c) it is (in accordance with subsection (5)) effective at the date on which the pay statement is given.

(3) A standing statement of fixed deductions may be amended, whether by—

(a) addition of a new deduction,

(b) a change in the particulars, or

(c) cancellation of an existing deduction,

by notice in writing, containing particulars of the amendment, given by the employer to the employee.

(4) An employer who has given to an employee a standing statement of fixed deductions shall—

(a) within the period of twelve months beginning with the date on which the first standing statement was given, and

(b) at intervals of not more than twelve months afterwards,

re-issue it in a consolidated form incorporating any amendments notified in accordance with subsection (3).

(5) For the purposes of subsection (2)(c) a standing statement of fixed deductions—

(a) becomes effective on the date on which it is given to the employee, and

(b) ceases to be effective at the end of the period of twelve months beginning with that date or, where it is re-issued in accordance with subsection (4), with the end of the period of twelve months beginning with the date of the last re-issue.

10 [omitted]

Enforcement

11 References to employment tribunals

(1) Where an employer does not give an employee a statement as required by section 1, 4 or 8 (either because he gives him no statement or because the statement he gives does not comply with what is required), the employee may require a reference to be made to an employment tribunal to determine what particulars ought to have been included or referred to in a statement so as to comply with the requirements of the section concerned.

(2) Where—

(a) a statement purporting to be a statement under section 1 or 4, or a pay statement or a standing statement of fixed deductions purporting to comply with section 8 or 9, has been given to an employee, and

(b) a question arises as to the particulars which ought to have been included or referred to in the statement so as to comply with the requirements of this Part,

either the employer or the employee may require the question to be referred to and determined by an employment tribunal.

(3) For the purposes of this section—

(a) a question as to the particulars which ought to have been included in the note required by section 3 to be included in the statement under section 1 does not include any question whether the employment is, has been or will be contracted-out employment (for the purposes of Part III of the Pension Schemes Act 1993), and

(b) a question as to the particulars which ought to have been included in a pay statement or standing statement of fixed deductions does not include a question solely as to the accuracy of an amount stated in any such particulars.

(4) An employment tribunal shall not consider a reference under this section in a case where the employment to which the reference relates has ceased unless an application requiring the reference to be made was made—

(a) before the end of the period of three months beginning with the date on which the employment ceased, or

(b) within such further period as the tribunal considers reasonable in a case where it is satisfied that it was not reasonably practicable for the application to be made before the end of that period of three months.

12 Determination of references

(1) Where, on a reference under section 11(1), an employment tribunal determines particulars as being those which ought to have been included or referred to in a statement given under section 1 or 4, the employer shall be deemed to have given to the employee a statement in which those particulars were included, or referred to, as specified in the decision of the tribunal.

(2) On determining a reference under section 11(2) relating to a statement purporting to be a statement under section 1 or 4, an employment tribunal may—

(a) confirm the particulars as included or referred to in the statement given by the employer,

(b) amend those particulars, or

(c) substitute other particulars for them, as the tribunal may determine to be appropriate; and the statement shall be deemed to have been given by the employer to the employee in accordance with the decision of the tribunal.

(3) Where on a reference under section 11 an employment tribunal finds—

(a) that an employer has failed to give an employee any pay statement in accordance with section 8, or

(b) that a pay statement or standing statement of fixed deductions does not, in relation to a deduction, contain the particulars required to be included in that statement by that section or section 9, the tribunal shall make a declaration to that effect.

(4) Where on a reference in the case of which subsection (3) applies the tribunal further finds that any unnotified deductions have been made from the pay of the employee during the period of thirteen weeks immediately preceding the date of the application for the reference (whether or not the deductions were made in breach of the contract of employment), the tribunal may order the employer to pay the employee a sum not exceeding the aggregate of the unnotified deductions so made.

(5) For the purposes of subsection (4) a deduction is an unnotified deduction if it is made without the employer giving the employee, in any pay statement or standing statement of fixed deductions, the particulars of the deduction required by section 8 or 9.

PART II
PROTECTION OF WAGES

Deductions by employer

13 Right not to suffer unauthorised deductions

(1) An employer shall not make a deduction from wages of a worker employed by him unless—

(a) the deduction is required or authorised to be made by virtue of a statutory provision or a relevant provision of the worker's contract, or

(b) the worker has previously signified in writing his agreement or consent to the making of the deduction.

(2) In this section 'relevant provision', in relation to a worker's contract, means a provision of the contract comprised—

(a) in one or more written terms of the contract of which the employer has given the worker a copy on an occasion prior to the employer making the deduction in question, or

(b) in one or more terms of the contract (whether express or implied and, if express, whether oral or in writing) the existence and effect, or combined effect, of which in relation to the worker the employer has notified to the worker in writing on such an occasion.

(3) Where the total amount of wages paid on any occasion by an employer to a worker employed by him is less than the total amount of the wages properly payable by him to the worker on that occasion (after deductions), the amount of the deficiency shall be treated for the purposes of this Part as a deduction made by the employer from the worker's wages on that occasion.

(4) Subsection (3) does not apply in so far as the deficiency is attributable to an error of any description on the part of the employer affecting the computation by him of the gross amount of the wages properly payable by him to the worker on that occasion.

(5) For the purposes of this section a relevant provision of a worker's contract having effect by virtue of a variation of the contract does not operate to authorise the making of a deduction on account of any conduct of the worker, or any other event occurring, before the variation took effect.

(6) For the purposes of this section an agreement or consent signified by a worker does not operate to authorise the making of a deduction on account of any conduct of the worker, or any other event occurring, before the agreement or consent was signified.

(7) This section does not affect any other statutory provision by virtue of which a sum payable to a worker by his employer but not constituting 'wages' within the meaning of this Part is not to be subject to a deduction at the instance of the employer.

14 Excepted deductions

(1) Section 13 does not apply to a deduction from a worker's wages made by his employer where the purpose of the deduction is the reimbursement of the employer in respect of—

(a) an overpayment of wages, or

(b) an overpayment in respect of expenses incurred by the worker in carrying out his employment,

made (for any reason) by the employer to the worker.

(2) Section 13 does not apply to a deduction from a worker's wages made by his employer in consequence of any disciplinary proceedings if those proceedings were held by virtue of a statutory provision.

(3) Section 13 does not apply to a deduction from a worker's wages made by his employer in pursuance of a requirement imposed on the employer by a statutory provision to deduct and pay over to a public authority amounts determined by that authority as being due to it from the worker if the deduction is made in accordance with the relevant determination of that authority.

(4) Section 13 does not apply to a deduction from a worker's wages made by his employer in pursuance of any arrangements which have been established—

(a) in accordance with a relevant provision of his contract to the inclusion of which in the contract the worker has signified his agreement or consent in writing, or

(b) otherwise with the prior agreement or consent of the worker signified in writing,

and under which the employer is to deduct and pay over to a third person amounts notified to the employer by that person as being due to him from the worker, if the deduction is made in accordance with the relevant notification by that person.

(5) Section 13 does not apply to a deduction from a worker's wages made by his employer where the worker has taken part in a strike or other industrial action and the deduction is made by the employer on account of the worker's having taken part in that strike or other action.

(6) Section 13 does not apply to a deduction from a worker's wages made by his employer with his prior agreement or consent signified in writing where the purpose of the deduction is the satisfaction (whether wholly or in part) of an order of a court or tribunal requiring the payment of an amount by the worker to the employer.

Payments to employer

15 Right not to have to make payments to employer

(1) An employer shall not receive a payment from a worker employed by him unless—

(a) the payment is required or authorised to be made by virtue of a statutory provision or a relevant provision of the worker's contract, or

(b) the worker has previously signified in writing his agreement or consent to the making of the payment.

(2) In this section 'relevant provision', in relation to a worker's contract, means a provision of the contract comprised—

(a) in one or more written terms of the contract of which the employer has given the worker a copy on an occasion prior to the employer receiving the payment in question, or

(b) in one or more terms of the contract (whether express or implied and, if express, whether oral or in writing) the existence and effect, or combined effect, of which in relation to the worker the employer has notified to the worker in writing on such an occasion.

(3) For the purposes of this section a relevant provision of a worker's contract having effect by virtue of a variation of the contract does not operate to authorise the receipt of a payment on account of any conduct of the worker, or any other event occurring, before the variation took effect.

(4) For the purposes of this section an agreement or consent signified by a worker does not operate to authorise the receipt of a payment on account of any conduct of the worker, or any other event occurring, before the agreement or consent was signified.

(5) Any reference in this Part to an employer receiving a payment from a worker employed by him is a reference to his receiving such a payment in his capacity as the worker's employer.

16 Excepted payments

(1) Section 15 does not apply to a payment received from a worker by his employer where the purpose of the payment is the reimbursement of the employer in respect of—

(a) an overpayment of wages, or

(b) an overpayment in respect of expenses incurred by the worker in carrying out his employment,

made (for any reason) by the employer to the worker.

(2) Section 15 does not apply to a payment received from a worker by his employer in consequence of any disciplinary proceedings if those proceedings were held by virtue of a statutory provision.

(3) Section 15 does not apply to a payment received from a worker by his employer where the worker has taken part in a strike or other industrial action and the payment has been required by the employer on account of the worker's having taken part in that strike or other action.

(4) Section 15 does not apply to a payment received from a worker by his employer where the purpose of the payment is the satisfaction (whether wholly or in part) of an order of a court or tribunal requiring the payment of an amount by the worker to the employer.

Cash shortages and stock deficiencies in retail employment

17 Introductory

(1) In the following provisions of this Part—

'cash shortage' means a deficit arising in relation to amounts received in connection with retail transactions, and

'stock deficiency' means a stock deficiency arising in the course of retail transactions.

(2) In the following provisions of this Part 'retail employment', in relation to a worker, means employment involving (whether or not on a regular basis)—

(a) the carrying out by the worker of retail transactions directly with members of the public or with fellow workers or other individuals in their personal capacities, or

(b) the collection by the worker of amounts payable in connection with retail transactions carried out by other persons directly with members of the public or with fellow workers or other individuals in their personal capacities.

(3) References in this section to a 'retail transaction' are to the sale or supply of goods or the supply of services (including financial services).

(4) References in the following provisions of this Part to a deduction made from wages of a worker in retail employment, or to a payment received from such a worker by his employer, on account of a cash shortage or stock deficiency include references to a deduction or payment so made or received on account of—

(a) any dishonesty or other conduct on the part of the worker which resulted in any such shortage or deficiency, or

(b) any other event in respect of which he (whether or not together with any other workers) has any contractual liability and which so resulted,

in each case whether or not the amount of the deduction or payment is designed to reflect the exact amount of the shortage or deficiency.

(5) References in the following provisions of this Part to the recovery from a worker of an amount in respect of a cash shortage or stock deficiency accordingly include references to the recovery from him of an amount in respect of any such conduct or event as is mentioned in subsection (4)(a) or (b).

(6) In the following provisions of this Part 'pay day', in relation to a worker, means a day on which wages are payable to the worker.

18 Limits on amount and time of deductions

(1) Where (in accordance with section 13) the employer of a worker in retail employment makes, on account of one or more cash shortages or stock deficiencies, a deduction or deductions from wages payable to the worker on a pay day, the amount or aggregate amount of the deduction or deductions shall not exceed one-tenth of the gross amount of the wages payable to the worker on that day.

(2) Where the employer of a worker in retail employment makes a deduction from the worker's wages on account of a cash shortage or stock deficiency, the employer shall not be treated as making the deduction in accordance with section 13 unless (in addition to the requirements of that section being satisfied with respect to the deduction)—

(a) the deduction is made, or

(b) in the case of a deduction which is one of a series of deductions relating to the shortage or deficiency, the first deduction in the series was made, not later than the end of the relevant period.

(3) In subsection (2) 'the relevant period' means the period of twelve months beginning with the date when the employer established the existence of the shortage or deficiency or (if earlier) the date when he ought reasonably to have done so.

19 Wages determined by reference to shortages etc.

(1) This section applies where—

(a) by virtue of an agreement between a worker in retail employment and his employer, the amount of the worker's wages or any part of them is or may be determined by reference to the incidence of cash shortages or stock deficiencies, and

(b) the gross amount of the wages payable to the worker on any pay day is, on account of any such shortages or deficiencies, less than the gross amount of the wages that would have been payable to him on that day if there had been no such shortages or deficiencies.

(2) The amount representing the difference between the two amounts referred to in subsection (1)(b) shall be treated for the purposes of this Part as a deduction from the wages payable to the worker on that day made by the employer on account of the cash shortages or stock deficiencies in question.

(3) The second of the amounts referred to in subsection (1)(b) shall be treated for the purposes of this Part (except subsection (1)) as the gross amount of the wages payable to him on that day.

(4) Accordingly—

(a) section 13, and

(b) if the requirements of section 13 and subsection (2) of section 18 are satisfied, subsection (1) of section 18,

have effect in relation to the amount referred to in subsection (2) of this section.

20 Limits on method and timing of payments

(1) Where the employer of a worker in retail employment receives from the worker a payment on account of a cash shortage or stock deficiency, the employer shall not be treated as receiving the payment in accordance with section 15 unless (in addition to the requirements of that section being satisfied with respect to the payment) he has previously—

(a) notified the worker in writing of the worker's total liability to him in respect of that shortage or deficiency, and

(b) required the worker to make the payment by means of a demand for payment made in accordance with the following provisions of this section.

(2) A demand for payment made by the employer of a worker in retail employment in respect of a cash shortage or stock deficiency—

(a) shall be made in writing, and

(b) shall be made on one of the worker's pay days.

(3) A demand for payment in respect of a particular cash shortage or stock deficiency, or (in the case of a series of such demands) the first such demand, shall not be made—

(a) earlier than the first pay day of the worker following the date when he is notified of his total liability in respect of the shortage or deficiency in pursuance of subsection (1)(a) or, where he is so notified on a pay day, earlier than that day, or

(b) later than the end of the period of twelve months beginning with the date when the employer established the existence of the shortage or deficiency or (if earlier) the date when he ought reasonably to have done so.

(4) For the purposes of this Part a demand for payment shall be treated as made by the employer on one of a worker's pay days if it is given to the worker or posted to, or left at, his last known address—

(a) on that pay day, or

(b) in the case of a pay day which is not a working day of the employer's business, on the first such working day following that pay day.

(5) Legal proceedings by the employer of a worker in retail employment for the recovery from the worker of an amount in respect of a cash shortage or stock deficiency shall not be instituted by the employer after the end of the period referred to in subsection (3)(b) unless the employer has within that period made a demand for payment in respect of that amount in accordance with this section.

21 Limit on amount of payments

(1) Where the employer of a worker in retail employment makes on any pay day one or more demands for payment in accordance with section 20, the amount or aggregate amount required to be paid by the worker in pursuance of the demand or demands shall not exceed—

(a) one-tenth of the gross amount of the wages payable to the worker on that day, or

(b) where one or more deductions falling within section 18(1) are made by the employer from those wages, such amount as represents the balance of that one-tenth after subtracting the amount or aggregate amount of the deduction or deductions.

(2) Once an amount has been required to be paid by means of a demand for payment made in accordance with section 20 on any pay day, that amount shall not be taken into account under subsection (1) as it applies to any subsequent pay day, even though the employer is obliged to make further requests for it to be paid.

(3) Where in any legal proceedings the court finds that the employer of a worker in retail employment is (in accordance with section 15 as it applies apart from section 20(1)) entitled to recover an amount from the worker in respect of a cash shortage or stock deficiency, the court shall, in ordering the payment by the worker to the employer of that amount, make such provision as appears to the court to be necessary to ensure that it is paid by the worker at a rate not exceeding that at which it could be recovered from him by the employer in accordance with this section.

22 Final instalments of wages

(1) In this section 'final instalment of wages', in relation to a worker, means—

(a) the amount of wages payable to the worker which consists of or includes an amount payable by way of contractual remuneration in respect of the last of the periods for which he is employed under his contract prior to its termination for any reason (but excluding any wages referable to any earlier such period), or

(b) where an amount in lieu of notice is paid to the worker later than the amount referred to in paragraph (a), the amount so paid,

in each case whether the amount in question is paid before or after the termination of the worker's contract.

(2) Section 18(1) does not operate to restrict the amount of any deductions which may (in accordance with section 13(1)) be made by the employer of a worker in retail employment from the worker's final instalment of wages.

(3) Nothing in section 20 or 21 applies to a payment falling within section 20(1) which is made on or after the day on which any such worker's final instalment of wages is paid; but (even if the requirements of section 15 would otherwise be satisfied with respect to it) his employer shall not be treated as receiving any such payment in accordance with that section if the payment was first required to be made after the end of the period referred to in section 20(3)(b).

(4) Section 21(3) does not apply to an amount which is to be paid by a worker on or after the day on which his final instalment of wages is paid.

Enforcement

23 Complaints to employment tribunals

(1) A worker may present a complaint to an employment tribunal—

(a) that his employer has made a deduction from his wages in contravention of section 13 (including a deduction made in contravention of that section as it applies by virtue of section 18(2)),

(b) that his employer has received from him a payment in contravention of section 15 (including a payment received in contravention of that section as it applies by virtue of section 20(1)),

(c) that his employer has recovered from his wages by means of one or more deductions falling within section 18(1) an amount or aggregate amount exceeding the limit applying to the deduction or deductions under that provision, or

(d) that his employer has received from him in pursuance of one or more demands for payment made (in accordance with section 20) on a particular pay day, a payment or payments of an amount or aggregate amount exceeding the limit applying to the demand or demands under section 21(1).

(2) Subject to subsection (4), an employment tribunal shall not consider a complaint under this section unless it is presented before the end of the period of three months beginning with—

(a) in the case of a complaint relating to a deduction by the employer, the date of payment of the wages from which the deduction was made, or

(b) in the case of a complaint relating to a payment received bv the employer, the date when the payment was received.

(3) Where a complaint is brought under this section in respect of—

(a) a series of deductions or payments, or

(b) a number of payments falling within subsection (1)(d) and made in pursuance of demands for payment subject to the same limit under section 21(1) but received by the employer on different dates,

the references in subsection (2) to the deduction or payment are to the last deduction or payment in the series or to the last of the payments so received.

(4) Where the employment tribunal is satisfied that it was not reasonably practicable for a complaint under this section to be presented before the end of the relevant period of three months, the tribunal may consider the complaint if it is presented within such further period as the tribunal considers reasonable.

(5) No complaint shall be presented under this section in respect of any deduction made in contravention of section 86 of the Trade Union and Labour Relations (Consolidation) Act 1992 (deduction of political fund contribution where certificate of exemption or objection has been given).

24 Determination of complaints

Where a tribunal finds a complaint under section 23 well-founded, it shall make a declaration to that effect and shall order the employer—

(a) in the case of a complaint under section 23(1)(a), to pay to the worker the amount of any deduction made in contravention of section 13,

(b) in the case of a complaint under section 23(1)(b), to repay to the worker the amount of any payment received in contravention of section 15,

(c) in the case of a complaint under section 23(1)(c), to pay to the worker any amount recovered from him in excess of the limit mentioned in that provision, and

(d) in the case of a complaint under section 23(1)(d), to repay to the worker any amount received from him in excess of the limit mentioned in that provision.

25 Determinations: supplementary

(1) Where, in the case of any complaint under section 23(1)(a), a tribunal finds that, although neither of the conditions set out in section 13(1)(a) and (b) was satisfied with respect to the whole amount of the deduction, one of those conditions was satisfied with respect to any lesser amount, the amount of the deduction shall for the purposes of section 24(a) be treated as reduced by the amount with respect to which that condition was satisfied.

(2) Where, in the case of any complaint under section 23(1)(b), a tribunal finds that, although neither of the conditions set out in section 15(1)(a) and (b) was satisfied with respect to the whole amount of the payment, one of those conditions was satisfied with respect to any lesser amount, the amount of the payment shall for the purposes of section 24(b) be treated as reduced by the amount with respect to which that condition was satisfied.

(3) An employer shall not under section 24 be ordered by a tribunal to pay or repay to a worker any amount in respect of a deduction or payment, or in respect of any combination of deductions or payments, in so far as it appears to the tribunal that he has already paid or repaid any such amount to the worker.

(4) Where a tribunal has under section 24 ordered an employer to pay or repay to a worker any amount in respect of a particular deduction or payment falling within section

23(1)(a) to (d), the amount which the employer is entitled to recover (by whatever means) in respect of the matter in relation to which the deduction or payment was originally made or received shall be treated as reduced by that amount.

(5) Where a tribunal has under section 24 ordered an employer to pay or repay to a worker any amount in respect of any combination of deductions or payments falling within section 23(1)(c) or (d), the aggregate amount which the employer is entitled to recover (by whatever means) in respect of the cash shortages or stock deficiencies in relation to which the deductions or payments were originally made or required to be made shall be treated as reduced by that amount.

26 Complaints and other remedies

Section 23 does not affect the jurisdiction of an employment tribunal to consider a reference under section 11 in relation to any deduction from the wages of a worker; but the aggregate of any amounts ordered by an employment tribunal to be paid under section 12(4) and under section 24 (whether on the same or different occasions) in respect of a particular deduction shall not exceed the amount of the deduction.

Supplementary

27 Meaning of 'wages' etc.

(1) In this Part 'wages', in relation to a worker, means any sums payable to the worker in connection with his employment, including—

(a) any fee, bonus, commission, holiday pay or other emolument referable to his employment, whether payable under his contract or otherwise,

(b) statutory sick pay under Part XI of the Social Security Contributions and Benefits Act 1992,

(c) statutory maternity pay under Part XII of that Act,

(d) a guarantee payment (under section 28 of this Act),

(e) any payment for time off under Part VI of this Act or section 169 of the Trade Union and Labour Relations (Consolidation) Act 1992 (payment for time off for carrying out trade union duties etc.),

(f) remuneration on suspension on medical grounds under section 64 of this Act and remuneration on suspension on maternity grounds under section 68 of this Act,

(g) any sum payable in pursuance of an order for reinstatement or re-engagement under section 113 of this Act,

(h) any sum payable in pursuance of an order for the continuation of a contract of employment under section 130 of this Act or section 164 of the Trade Union and Labour Relations (Consolidation) Act 1992, and

(j) remuneration under a protective award under section 189 of that Act,

but excluding any payments within subsection (2).

(2) Those payments are—

(a) any payment by way of an advance under an agreement for a loan or by way of an advance of wages (but without prejudice to the application of section 13 to any deduction made from the worker's wages in respect of any such advance),

(b) any payment in respect of expenses incurred by the worker in carrying out his employment,

(c) any payment by way of a pension, allowance or gratuity in connection with the worker's retirement or as compensation for loss of office,

(d) any payment referable to the worker's redundancy, and

(e) any payment to the worker otherwise than in his capacity as a worker.

(3) Where any payment in the nature of a non-contractual bonus is (for any reason) made to a worker by his employer, the amount of the payment shall for the purposes of this Part—

(a) be treated as wages of the worker, and

(b) be treated as payable to him as such on the day on which the payment is made.

(4) In this Part 'gross amount', in relation to any wages payable to a worker, means the total amount of those wages before deductions of whatever nature.

(5) For the purposes of this Part any monetary value attaching to any payment or benefit in kind furnished to a worker by his employer shall not be treated as wages of the worker except in the case of any voucher, stamp or similar document which is—

(a) of a fixed value expressed in monetary terms, and

(b) capable of being exchanged (whether on its own or together with other vouchers, stamps or documents, and whether immediately or only after a time) for money, goods or services (or for any combination of two or more of those things).

PART III
GUARANTEE PAYMENTS

28 Right to guarantee payment

(1) Where throughout a day during any part of which an employee would normally be required to work in accordance with his contract of employment the employee is not provided with work by his employer by reason of—

(a) a diminution in the requirements of the employer's business for work of the kind which the employee is employed to do, or

(b) any other occurrence affecting the normal working of the employer's business in relation to work of the kind which the employee is employed to do,

the employee is entitled to be paid by his employer an amount in respect of that day.

(2) In this Act a payment to which an employee is entitled under subsection (1) is referred to as a guarantee payment.

(3) In this Part—

(a) a day falling within subsection (1) is referred to as a 'workless day', and

(b) 'workless period' has a corresponding meaning.

(4) In this Part 'day' means the period of twenty-four hours from midnight to midnight.

(5) Where a period of employment begun on any day extends, or would normally extend, over midnight into the following day—

(a) if the employment before midnight is, or would normally be, of longer duration than that after midnight, the period of employment shall be treated as falling wholly on the first day, and

(b) in any other case, the period of employment shall be treated as falling wholly on the second day.

29 Exclusions from right to guarantee payment

(1) An employee is not entitled to a guarantee payment unless he has been continuously employed for a period of not less than one month ending with the day before that in respect of which the guarantee payment is claimed.

(2) An employee who is employed—

(a) under a contract for a fixed term of three months or less, or

(b) under a contract made in contemplation of the performance of a specific task which is not expected to last for more than three months,

is not entitled to a guarantee payment unless he has been continuously employed for a period of more than three months ending with the day before that in respect of which the guarantee payment is claimed.

(3) An employee is not entitled to a guarantee payment in respect of a workless day if the failure to provide him with work for that day occurs in consequence of a strike, lock-out or other industrial action involving any employee of his employer or of an associated employer.

(4) An employee is not entitled to a guarantee payment in respect of a workless day if—

(a) his employer has offered to provide alternative work for that day which is suitable in all the circumstances (whether or not it is work which the employee is under his contract employed to perform), and

(b) the employee has unreasonably refused that offer.

(5) An employee is not entitled to a guarantee payment if he does not comply with reasonable requirements imposed by his employer with a view to ensuring that his services are available.

30 Calculation of guarantee payment

(1) Subject to section 31, the amount of a guarantee payment payable to an employee in respect of any day is the sum produced by multiplying the number of normal working hours on the day by the guaranteed hourly rate; and, accordingly, no guarantee payment is payable to an employee in whose case there are no normal working hours on the day in question.

(2) The guaranteed hourly rate, in relation to an employee, is the amount of one week's pay divided by the number of normal working hours in a week for that employee when employed under the contract of employment in force on the day in respect of which the guarantee payment is payable.

(3) But where the number of normal working hours differs from week to week or over a longer period, the amount of one week's pay shall be divided instead by—

(a) the average number of normal working hours calculated by dividing by twelve the total number of the employee's normal working hours during the period of twelve weeks ending with the last complete week before the day in respect of which the guarantee payment is payable, or

(b) where the employee has not been employed for a sufficient period to enable the calculation to be made under paragraph (a), a number which fairly represents the number of normal working hours in a week having regard to such of the considerations specified in subsection (4) as are appropriate in the circumstances.

(4) The considerations referred to in subsection (3)(b) are—

(a) the average number of normal working hours in a week which the employee could expect in accordance with the terms of his contract, and

(b) the average number of normal working hours of other employees engaged in relevant comparable employment with the same employer.

(5) If in any case an employee's contract has been varied, or a new contract has been entered into, in connection with a period of short-time working, subsections (2) and (3) have effect as if for the references to the day in respect of which the guarantee payment is payable there were substituted references to the last day on which the original contract was in force.

31 Limits on amount of and entitlement to guarantee payment

(1) The amount of a guarantee payment payable to an employee in respect of any day shall not exceed £15.35.

(2) An employee is not entitled to guarantee payments in respect of more than the specified number of days in any period of three months.

(3) The specified number of days for the purposes of subsection (2) is the number of days, not exceeding five, on which the employee normally works in a week under the contract of employment in force on the day in respect of which the guarantee payment is claimed.

(4) But where that number of days varies from week to week or over a longer period, the specified number of days is instead—

(a) the average number of such days, not exceeding five, calculated by dividing by twelve the total number of such days during the period of twelve weeks ending with the last complete week before the day in respect of which the guarantee payment is claimed, and rounding up the resulting figure to the next whole number, or

(b) where the employee has not been employed for a sufficient period to enable the calculation to be made under paragraph (a), a number which fairly represents the number of the employee's normal working days in a week, not exceeding five, having regard to such of the considerations specified in subsection (5) as are appropriate in the circumstances.

(5) The considerations referred to in subsection (4)(b) are—

(a) the average number of normal working days in a week which the employee could expect in accordance with the terms of his contract, and

(b) the average number of such days of other employees engaged in relevant comparable employment with the same employer.

(6) If in any case an employee's contract has been varied, or a new contract has been entered into, in connection with a period of short-time working, subsections (3) and (4) have effect as if for the references to the day in respect of which the guarantee payment is claimed there were substituted references to the last day on which the original contract was in force.

(7) The Secretary of State may by order vary—

(a) the length of the period specified in subsection (2);

(b) a limit specified in subsection (3) or (4).

32 Contractual remuneration

(1) A right to a guarantee payment does not affect any right of an employee in relation to remuneration under his contract of employment ('contractual remuneration').

(2) Any contractual remuneration paid to an employee in respect of a workless day goes towards discharging any liability of the employer to pay a guarantee payment in respect of that day; and, conversely, any guarantee payment paid in respect of a day goes towards discharging any liability of the employer to pay contractual remuneration in respect of that day.

(3) For the purposes of subsection (2), contractual remuneration shall be treated as paid in respect of a workless day—

(a) where it is expressed to be calculated or payable by reference to that day or any part of that day, to the extent that it is so expressed, and

(b) in any other case, to the extent that it represents guaranteed remuneration, rather than remuneration for work actually done, and is referable to that day when apportioned rateably between that day and any other workless period falling within the period in respect of which the remuneration is paid.

33 [omitted]

34 Complaints to employment tribunals

(1) An employee may present a complaint to an employment tribunal that his employer has failed to pay the whole or any part of a guarantee payment to which the employee is entitled.

(2) An employment tribunal shall not consider a complaint relating to a guarantee payment in respect of any day unless the complaint is presented to the tribunal—

(a) before the end of the period of three months beginning with that day, or

(b) within such further period as the tribunal considers reasonable in a case where it is satisfied that it was not reasonably practicable for the complaint to be presented before the end of that period of three months.

(3) Where an employment tribunal finds a complaint under this section well-founded, the tribunal shall order the employer to pay to the employee the amount of guarantee payment which it finds is due to him.

35 [omitted]

PART IV
SUNDAY WORKING FOR SHOP AND BETTING WORKERS

Protected shop workers and betting workers

36 Protected shop workers and betting workers

(1) Subject to subsection (5), a shop worker or betting worker is to be regarded as 'protected' for the purposes of any provision of this Act if (and only if) subsection (2) or (3) applies to him.

(2) This subsection applies to a shop worker or betting worker if—

(a) on the day before the relevant commencement date he was employed as a shop worker or a betting worker but not to work only on Sunday,

(b) he has been continuously employed during the period beginning with that day and ending with the day which, in relation to the provision concerned, is the appropriate date, and

(c) throughout that period, or throughout every part of it during which his relations with his employer were governed by a contract of employment, he was a shop worker or a betting worker.

(3) This subsection applies to any shop worker or betting worker whose contract of employment is such that under it he—

(a) is not, and may not be, required to work on Sunday, and

(b) could not be so required even if the provisions of this Part were disregarded.

(4) Where on the day before the relevant commencement date an employee's relations with his employer had ceased to be governed by a contract of employment, he shall be regarded as satisfying subsection (2)(a) if—

(a) that day fell in a week which counts as a period of employment with that employer under section 212(2) or (3) or under regulations under section 219, and

(b) on the last day before the relevant commencement date on which his relations with his employer were governed by a contract of employment, the employee was employed as a shop worker or a betting worker but not to work only on Sunday.

(5) A shop worker is not a protected shop worker, and a betting worker is not a protected betting worker, if—

(a) he has given his employer an opting-in notice on or after the relevant commencement date, and

(b) after giving the notice, he has expressly agreed with his employer to do shop work, or betting work, on Sunday or on a particular Sunday.

(6) In this Act 'opting-in notice', in relation to a shop worker or a betting worker, means written notice, signed and dated by the shop worker or betting worker, in which the shop worker or betting worker expressly states that he wishes to work on Sunday or that he does not object to Sunday working.

(7) In this Act 'the relevant commencement date' means—

(a) in relation to a shop worker, 26th August 1994, and

(b) in relation to a betting worker, 3rd January 1995.

37 Contractual requirements relating to Sunday work

(1) Any contract of employment under which a shop worker or betting worker who satisfies section 36(2)(a) was employed on the day before the relevant commencement date is unenforceable to the extent that it—

(a) requires the shop worker to do shop work, or the betting worker to do betting work, on Sunday on or after that date, or

(b) requires the employer to provide the shop worker with shop work, or the betting worker with betting work, on Sunday on or after that date.

(2) Subject to subsection (3), any agreement entered into after the relevant commencement date between a protected shop worker, or a protected betting worker, and his employer is unenforceable to the extent that it—

(a) requires the shop worker to do shop work, or the betting worker to do betting work, on Sunday, or

(b) requires the employer to provide the shop worker with shop work, or the betting worker with betting work, on Sunday.

(3) Where, after giving an opting-in notice, a protected shop worker or a protected betting worker expressly agrees with his employer to do shop work or betting work on Sunday or on a particular Sunday (and so ceases to be protected), his contract of employment shall be taken to be varied to the extent necessary to give effect to the terms of the agreement.

(4) [repealed]

(5) For the purposes of section 36(2)(b), the appropriate date—

(a) in relation to subsections (2) and (3) of this section, is the day on which the agreement is entered into, and

(b) [repealed]

38 Contracts with guaranteed hours

(1) This section applies where—

(a) under the contract of employment under which a shop worker or betting worker who satisfies section 36(2)(a) was employed on the day before the relevant commencement date, the employer is, or may be, required to provide him with shop work, or betting work, for a specified number of hours each week,

(b) under the contract the shop worker or betting worker was, or might have been, required to work on Sunday before that date, and

(c) the shop worker has done shop work, or the betting worker betting work, on Sunday in that employment (whether or not before that day) but has, on or after that date, ceased to do so.

(2) So long as the shop worker remains a protected shop worker, or the betting worker remains a protected betting worker, the contract shall not be regarded as requiring the employer to provide him with shop work, or betting work, on weekdays in excess of the hours normally worked by the shop worker or betting worker on weekdays before he ceased to do shop work, or betting work, on Sunday.

(3) For the purposes of section 36(2)(b), the appropriate date in relation to this section is any time in relation to which the contract is to be enforced.

39 Reduction of pay etc.

(1) This section applies where—

(a) under the contract of employment under which a shop worker or betting worker who satisfies section 36(2)(a) was employed on the day before the relevant commencement date, the shop worker or betting worker was, or might have been, required to work on Sunday before the relevant commencement date,

(b) the shop worker has done shop work, or the betting worker has done betting work, on Sunday in that employment (whether or not before that date) but has, on or after that date, ceased to do so, and

(c) it is not apparent from the contract what part of the remuneration payable, or of any other benefit accruing, to the shop worker or betting worker was intended to be attributable to shop work, or betting work, on Sunday.

(2) So long as the shop worker remains a protected shop worker, or the betting worker remains a protected betting worker, the contract shall be regarded as enabling the employer to reduce the amount of remuneration paid, or the extent of the other benefit provided, to the shop worker or betting worker in respect of any period by the relevant proportion.

(3) In subsection (2) 'the relevant proportion' means the proportion which the hours of shop work, or betting work, which (apart from this Part) the shop worker, or betting worker, could have been required to do on Sunday in the period ('the contractual Sunday hours') bears to the aggregate of those hours and the hours of work actually done by the shop worker, or betting worker, in the period.

(4) Where, under the contract of employment, the hours of work actually done on weekdays in any period would be taken into account in determining the contractual Sunday hours, they shall be taken into account in determining the contractual Sunday hours for the purposes of subsection (3).

(5) For the purposes of section 36(2)(b), the appropriate date in relation to this section is the end of the period in respect of which the remuneration is paid or the benefit accrues.

Opting-out of Sunday work

40 Notice of objection to Sunday working

(1) A shop worker or betting worker to whom this section applies may at any time give his employer written notice, signed and dated by the shop worker or betting worker, to the effect that he objects to Sunday working.

(2) In this Act 'opting-out notice' means a notice given under subsection (1) by a shop worker or betting worker to whom this section applies.

(3) This section applies to any shop worker or betting worker who under his contract of employment—

(a) is or may be required to work on Sunday (whether or not as a result of previously giving an opting-in notice), but

(b) is not employed to work only on Sunday.

41 Opted-out shop workers and betting workers

(1) Subject to subsection (2), a shop worker or betting worker is to be regarded as 'opted-out' for the purposes of any provision of this Act if (and only if)—

(a) he has given his employer an opting-out notice,

(b) he has been continuously employed during the period beginning with the day on which the notice was given and ending with the day which, in relation to the provision concerned, is the appropriate date, and

(c) throughout that period, or throughout every part of it during which his relations with his employer were governed by a contract of employment, he was a shop worker or a betting worker.

(2) A shop worker is not an opted-out shop worker, and a betting worker is not an opted-out betting worker, if—

(a) after giving the opting-out notice concerned, he has given his employer an opting-in notice, and

(b) after giving the opting-in notice, he has expressly agreed with his employer to do shop work, or betting work, on Sunday or on a particular Sunday.

(3) In this Act 'notice period', in relation to an opted-out shop worker or an opted-out betting worker, means, subject to section 42(2), the period of three months beginning with the day on which the opting-out notice concerned was given.

42 Explanatory statement

(1) Where a person becomes a shop worker or betting worker to whom section 40 applies, his employer shall, before the end of the period of two months beginning with the day on which that person becomes such a worker, give him a written statement in the prescribed form.

(2) If—

(a) an employer fails to comply with subsection (1) in relation to any shop worker or betting worker, and

(b) the shop worker or betting worker, on giving the employer an opting-out notice, becomes an opted-out shop worker or an opted-out betting worker,

section 41(3) has effect in relation to the shop worker or betting worker with the substitution for 'three months' of 'one month'.

(3) An employer shall not be regarded as failing to comply with subsection (1) in any case where, before the end of the period referred to in that subsection, the shop worker or betting worker has given him an opting-out notice.

(4) Subject to subsection (6), the prescribed form in the case of a shop worker is as follows—

'STATUTORY RIGHTS IN RELATION TO SUNDAY SHOP WORK

You have become employed as a shop worker and are or can be required under your contract of employment to do the Sunday work your contract provides for.

However, if you wish, you can give a notice, as described in the next paragraph, to your employer and you will then have the right not to work in or about a shop on any Sunday on which the shop is open once three months have passed from the date on which you gave the notice.

Your notice must—

be in writing;

be signed and dated by you;

say that you object to Sunday working.

For three months after you give the notice, your employer can still require you to do all the Sunday work your contract provides for. After the three month period has ended, you have the right to complain to an employment tribunal if, because of your refusal to work on Sundays on which the shop is open, your employer—

dismisses you, or

does something else detrimental to you, for example, failing to promote you.

Once you have the rights described, you can surrender them only by giving your employer a further notice, signed and dated by you, saying that you wish to work on Sunday or that you do not object to Sunday working and then agreeing with your employer to work on Sundays or on a particular Sunday.'

(5) Subject to subsection (6), the prescribed form in the case of a betting worker is as follows—

'STATUTORY RIGHTS IN RELATION TO SUNDAY BETTING WORK

You have become employed under a contract of employment under which you are or can be required to do Sunday betting work, that is to say, work—

at a track on a Sunday on which your employer is taking bets at the track, or

in a licensed betting office on a Sunday on which it is open for business.

However, if you wish, you can give a notice, as described in the next paragraph, to your employer and you will then have the right not to do Sunday betting work once three months have passed from the date on which you gave the notice.

Your notice must—

be in writing;

be signed and dated by you;

say that you object to doing Sunday betting work.

For three months after you give the notice, your employer can still require you to do all the Sunday betting work your contract provides for. After the three month period has ended, you have the right to complain to an employment tribunal if, because of your refusal to do Sunday betting work, your employer—

dismisses you, or

does something else detrimental to you, for example, failing to promote you.

Once you have the rights described, you can surrender them only by giving your employer a further notice, signed and dated by you, saying that you wish to do Sunday betting work or that you do not object to doing Sunday betting work and then agreeing with your employer to do such work on Sundays or on a particular Sunday.'

(6) The Secretary of State may by order amend the prescribed forms set out in subsections (4) and (5).

43 Contractual requirements relating to Sunday work

(1) Where a shop worker or betting worker gives his employer an opting-out notice, the contract of employment under which he was employed immediately before he gave that notice becomes unenforceable to the extent that it—

(a) requires the shop worker to do shop work, or the betting worker to do betting work, on Sunday after the end of the notice period, or

(b) requires the employer to provide the shop worker with shop work, or the betting worker with betting work, on Sunday after the end of that period.

(2) Subject to subsection (3), any agreement entered into between an opted-out shop worker, or an opted-out betting worker, and his employer is unenforceable to the extent that it—

(a) requires the shop worker to do shop work, or the betting worker to do betting work, on Sunday after the end of the notice period, or

(b) requires the employer to provide the shop worker with shop work, or the betting worker with betting work, on Sunday after the end of that period.

(3) Where, after giving an opting-in notice, an opted-out shop worker or an opted-out betting worker expressly agrees with his employer to do shop work or betting work on Sunday or on a particular Sunday (and so ceases to be opted-out), his contract of employment shall be taken to be varied to the extent necessary to give effect to the terms of the agreement.

(4) [repealed]

(5) For the purposes of section 41(1)(b), the appropriate date—

(a) in relation to subsections (2) and (3) of this section, is the day on which the agreement is entered into,

(b) [repealed]

PART IVA
PROTECTED DISCLOSURES

43A Meaning of 'protected disclosure'

In this Act a 'protected disclosure' means a qualifying disclosure (as defined by section 43B) which is made by a worker in accordance with any of sections 43C to 43H.

43B Disclosures qualifying for protection

(1) In this Part a 'qualifying disclosure' means any disclosure of information which, in the reasonable belief of the worker making the disclosure, tends to show one or more of the following—

(a) that a criminal offence has been committed, is being committeed or is likely to be committed,

(b) that a person has failed, is failing or is likely to fail to comply with any legal obligation to which he is subject,

(c) that a miscarriage of justice has occurred, is occurring or is likely to occur,

(d) that the health or safety of any individual has been, is being or is likely to be endangered,

(e) that the environment has been, is being or is likely to be damaged, or

(f) that information tending to show any matter falling within any one of the preceding paragraphs has been, is being or is likely to be deliberately concealed.

(2) For the purposes of subsection (1), it is immaterial whether the relevant failure occurred, occurs or would occur in the United Kingdom or elsewhere, and whether the law applying to it is that of the United Kingdom or of any other country or territory.

(3) A disclosure of information is not a qualifying disclosure if the person making the disclosure commits an offence by making it.

(4) A disclosure of information in respect of which a claim to legal professional privilege (or, in Scotland, to confidentiality as between client and professional legal adviser) could be maintained in legal proceedings is not a qualifying disclosure if it is made by a person to whom the information had been disclosed in the course of obtaining legal advice.

(5) In this Part 'the relevant failure', in relation to a qualifying disclosure, means the matter falling within paragraphs (a) to (f) of subsection (1).

43C Disclosure to employer or other responsible person

(1) A qualifying disclosure is made in accordance with this section if the worker makes the disclosure in good faith—

(a) to his employer, or

(b) where the worker reasonably believes that the relevant failure relates solely or mainly to—

(i) the conduct of a person other than his employer, or

(ii) any other matter for which a person other than his employer has legal responsiblity,

to that other person.

(2) A worker who, in accordance with a procedure whose use by him is authorised by his employer, makes a qualifying disclosure to a person other than his employer, is to be treated for the purposes of this Part as making the qualifying disclosure to his employer.

43D Disclosure to legal adviser

A qualifying disclosure is made in accordance with this section if it is made in the course of obtaining legal advice.

43E Disclosure to Minister of the Crown

A qualifying disclosure is made in accordance with this section if—

(a) the worker's employer is—

(i) an individual appointed under any enactment by a Minister of the Crown, or

(ii) a body any of whose members are so appointed, and

(b) the disclosure is made in good faith to a Minister of the Crown.

43F Disclosure to prescribed person

(1) A qualifying disclosure is made in accordance with this section if the worker—

(a) makes the disclosure in good faith to a person prescribed by an order made by the Secretary of State for the purposes of this section, and

(b) reasonably believes—

(i) that the relevant failure falls within any description of matters in respect of which that person is so prescribed, and

(i) that the information disclosed, and any allegation contained in it, are substantially true.

(2) An order prescribing persons for the purposes of this section may specify persons or descriptions of persons and shall specify the descriptions of matters in respect of which each person, or persons of each description, is or are prescribed.

43G Disclosure in other cases

(1) A qualifying disclosure is made in accordance with this section if—

(a) the worker makes the disclosure in good faith,
(b) he reasonably believes that the information disclosed, and any allegation contained in it, are substantially true,
(c) he does not make the disclosure for purposes of personal gain,
(d) any of the conditions in subsection (2) is met, and
(e) in all the circumstances of the case, it is reasonable for him to make the disclosure.

(2) The conditions referred to in subsection (1)(d) are—
(a) that, at the time he makes the disclosure, the worker reasonably believes that he will be subjected to a detriment by his employer if he makes a disclosure to his employer or in accordance with section 43F,
(b) that, in a case where no person is prescribed for the purposes of section 43F in relation to the relevant failure, the worker reasonably believes that it is likely that evidence relating to the relevant failure will be concealed or destroyed if he makes a disclosure to his employer, or
(c) that the worker has previously made a disclosure of substantially the same information—
(i) to his employer, or
(ii) in accordance with section 43F.

(3) In determining for the purposes of subsection (1)(e) whether it is reasonable for the worker to make the disclosure, regard shall be had, in particular, to—
(a) the identity of the person to whom the disclosure is made,
(b) the seriousness of the relevant failure,
(c) whether the relevant failure is continuing or is likely to occur in the future,
(d) whether the disclosure is made in breach of a duty of confidentiality owed by the employer to any other person,
(e) in a case falling within subsection (2)(c)(i) or (ii), any action which the employer or the person to whom the previous disclosure in accordance with section 43F was made has taken or might reasonably be expected to have taken as a result of the previous disclosure, and
(f) in a case falling within subsection (2)(c)(i), whether in making the disclosure to the employer the worker complied with any procedure whose use by him was authorised by the employer.

(4) For the purposes of this section a subsequent disclosure may be regarded as a disclosure of substantially the same information as that disclosed by a previous disclosure as mentioned in subsection (2)(c) even though the subsequent disclosure extends to information about action taken or not taken by any person as a result of the previous disclosure.

43H Disclosure of exceptionally serious failure

(1) A qualifying disclosure is made in accordance with this section if—
(a) the worker makes the disclosure in good faith,
(b) he reasonably believes that the information disclosed, and any allegation contained in it, are substantially true,
(c) he does not make the disclosure for purposes of personal gain,
(d) the relevant failure is of an exceptionally serious nature, and
(e) in all the circumstances of the case, it is reasonable for him to make the disclosure.

(2) In determining for the purposes of subsection (1)(e) whether it is reasonable for the worker to make the disclosure, regard shall be had, in particular, to the identity of the person to whom the disclosure is made.

43J Contractual duties of confidentiality

(1) Any provision in an agreement to which this section applies is void in so far as it purports to preclude the worker from making a protected disclosure.

(2) This section applies to any agreement between a worker and his employer (whether a worker's contract or not), including an agreement to refrain from instituting or continuing any proceedings under this Act or any proceedings for breach of contract.

43K Extension of meaning of 'worker' etc. for Part IVA

(1) For the purposes of this Part 'worker' includes an individual who is not a worker as defined by section 230(3) but who—

(a) works or worked for a person in circumstances in which—

(i) he is or was introduced or supplied to do that work by a third person, and

(ii) the terms on which he is or was engaged to do the work are or were in practice substantially determined not by him but by the person for whom he works or worked, by the third person or by both of them,

(b) contracts or contracted with a person, for the purposes of that person's business, for the execution of work to be done in a place not under the control or management of that person and would fall within section 230(3)(b) if for 'personally' in that provision there were substituted '(whether personally or otherwise)',

(c) works or worked as a person providing general medical services, general dental services, general ophthalmic services or pharmaceutical services in accordance with arrangements made—

(i) by a Health Authority under section 29, 35, 38 or 41 of the National Health Service Act 1997, or

(ii) by a Health Board under section 19, 25, 26 or 27 of the National Health Service (Scotland) Act 1978, or

(d) is or was provided with work experience provided pursuant to a training course or programme or with training for employment (or with both) otherwise than—

(i) under a contract of employment, or

(ii) by an educational establishment on a course run by that establishment;

and any reference to a worker's contract, to employment or to a worker being 'employed' shall be construed accordingly.

(2) For the purposes of this Part 'employer' includes—

(a) in relation to a worker falling within paragraph (a) of subsection (1), the person who substantially determines or determined the terms on which he is or was engaged,

(b) in relation to a worker falling within paragraph (c) of that subsection, the authority or board referred to in that paragraph, and

(c) in relation to a worker falling within paragraph (d) of that subsection, the person providing the work experience or training.

(3) In this section 'educational establishment' includes any university, college, school or other educational establishment.

43L Other interpretative provisions

(1) In this Part—

'qualifying disclosure' has the meaning given by section 43B;

'the relevant failure', in relation to a qualifying disclosure, has the meaning given by section 43B(5).

(2) In determining for the purposes of this Part whether a person makes a disclosure for purposes of personal gain, there shall be disregarded any reward payable by or under any enactment.

(3) Any reference in this Part to the disclosure of information shall have effect, in relation to any case where the person receiving the information is already aware of it, as a reference to bringing the information to his attention.

PART V
PROTECTION FROM SUFFERING DETRIMENT IN EMPLOYMENT

Rights not to suffer detriment

44 Health and safety cases

(1) An employee has the right not to be subjected to any detriment by any act, or any deliberate failure to act, by his employer done on the ground that—

(a) having been designated by the employer to carry out activities in connection with preventing or reducing risks to health and safety at work, the employee carried out (or proposed to carry out) any such activities,

(b) being a representative of workers on matters of health and safety at work or member of a safety committee—

(i) in accordance with arrangements established under or by virtue of any enactment, or

(ii) by reason of being acknowledged as such by the employer,

the employee performed (or proposed to perform) any functions as such a representative or a member of such a committee,

(ba) the employee took part (or proposed to take part) in consultation with the employer pursuant to the Health and Safety (Consultation with Employees) Regulations 1996 or in an election of representatives of employee safety within the meaning of those Regulations (whether as a candidate or otherwise),

(c) being an employee at a place where—

(i) there was no such representative or safety committee, or

(ii) there was such a representative or safety committee but it was not reasonably practicable for the employee to raise the matter by those means,

he brought to his employer's attention, by reasonable means, circumstances connected with his work which he reasonably believed were harmful or potentially harmful to health or safety,

(d) in circumstances of danger which the employee reasonably believed to be serious and imminent and which he could not reasonably have been expected to avert, he left (or proposed to leave) or (while the danger persisted) refused to return to his place of work or any dangerous part of his place of work, or

(e) in circumstances of danger which the employee reasonably believed to be serious and imminent, he took (or proposed to take) appropriate steps to protect himself or other persons from the danger.

(2) For the purposes of subsection (1)(e) whether steps which an employee took (or proposed to take) were appropriate is to be judged by reference to all the circumstances including, in particular, his knowledge and the facilities and advice available to him at the time.

(3) An employee is not to be regarded as having been subjected to any detriment on the ground specified in subsection (1)(e) if the employer shows that it was (or would have been) so negligent for the employee to take the steps which he took (or proposed to take) that a reasonable employer might have treated him as the employer did.

(4) This section does not apply where the detriment in question amounts to dismissal (within the meaning of Part X).

45 Sunday working for shop and betting workers

(1) An employee who is—

(a) a protected shop worker or an opted-out shop worker, or

(b) a protected betting worker or an opted-out betting worker,

has the right not to be subjected to any detriment by any act, or any deliberate failure to act, by his employer done on the ground that the employee refused (or proposed to refuse) to do shop work, or betting work, on Sunday or on a particular Sunday.

(2) Subsection (1) does not apply to anything done in relation to an opted-out shop worker or an opted-out betting worker on the ground that he refused (or proposed to refuse) to do shop work, or betting work, on any Sunday or Sundays falling before the end of the notice period.

(3) An employee who is a shop worker or a betting worker has the right not to be subjected to any detriment by any act, or any deliberate failure to act, by his employer done on the ground that the employee gave (or proposed to give) an opting-out notice to his employer.

(4) Subsections (1) and (3) do not apply where the detriment in question amounts to dismissal (within the meaning of Part X).

(5) For the purposes of this section a shop worker or betting worker who does not work on Sunday or on a particular Sunday is not to be regarded as having been subjected to any detriment by—

(a) a failure to pay remuneration in respect of shop work, or betting work, on a Sunday which he has not done,

(b) a failure to provide him with any other benefit, where that failure results from the application (in relation to a Sunday on which the employee has not done shop work, or betting work) of a contractual term under which the extent of that benefit varies according to the number of hours worked by the employee or the remuneration of the employee, or

(c) a failure to provide him with any work, remuneration or other benefit which by virtue of section 38 or 39 the employer is not obliged to provide.

(6) Where an employer offers to pay a sum specified in the offer to any one or more employees—

(a) who are protected shop workers or opted-out shop workers or protected betting workers or opted-out betting workers, or

(b) who under their contracts of employment are not obliged to do shop work, or betting work, on Sunday,

if they agree to do shop work, or betting work, on Sunday or on a particular Sunday subsections (7) and (8) apply.

(7) An employee to whom the offer is not made is not to be regarded for the purposes of this section as having been subjected to any detriment by any failure to make the offer to him or to pay him the sum specified in the offer.

(8) An employee who does not accept the offer is not to be regarded for the purposes of this section as having been subjected to any detriment by any failure to pay him the sum specified in the offer.

(9) For the purposes of section 36(2)(b) or 41(1)(b), the appropriate date in relation to this section is the date of the act or failure to act.

(10) For the purposes of subsection (9)—

(a) where an act extends over a period, the 'date of the act' means the first day of that period, and

(b) a deliberate failure to act shall be treated as done when it was decided on;

and, in the absence of evidence establishing the contrary, an employer shall be taken to decide on a failure to act when he does an act inconsistent with doing the failed act or, if he has done no such inconsistent act, when the period expires within which he might reasonably have been expected to do the failed act if it was to be done.

45A Working time cases

(1) A worker has the right not to be subjected to any detriment by any act, or any deliberate failure to act, by his employer done on the ground that the worker—

(a) refused (or proposed to refuse) to comply with a requirement which the employer imposed (or proposed to impose) in contravention of the Working Time Regulations 1998,

(b) refused (or proposed to refuse) to forgo a right conferred on him by those Regulations,

(c) failed to sign a workforce agreement for the purposes of those Regulations, or to enter into, or agree to vary or extend, any other agreement with his employer which is provided for in those Regulations,

(d) being—

(i) a representative of members of the workforce for the purposes of Schedule 1 to those Regulations, or

(ii) a candidate in an election in which any person elected will, on being elected, be such a representative,

performed (or proposed to perform) any functions or activities as such a representative or candidate,

(e) brought proceedings against the employer to enforce a right conferred on him by those Regulations, or

(f) alleged that the employer had infringed such a right.

(2) It is immaterial for the purposes of subsection (1)(e) or (f)—

(a) whether or not the worker has the right, or

(b) whether or not the right has been infringed,

but, for those provisions to apply, the claim to the right and that it has been infringed must be made in good faith.

(3) It is sufficient for subsection (1)(f) to apply that the worker, without specifying the right, made it reasonably clear to the employer what the right claimed to have been infringed was.

(4) This section does not apply where a worker is an employee and the detriment in question amounts to dismissal within the meaning of Part X.

46 Trustees of occupational pension schemes

(1) An employee has the right not to be subjected to any detriment by any act, or any deliberate failure to act, by his employer done on the ground that, being a trustee of a relevant occupational pension scheme which relates to his employment, the employee performed (or proposed to perform) any functions as such a trustee.

(2) This section does not apply where the detriment in question amounts to dismissal (within the meaning of Part X).

(3) In this section 'relevant occupational pension scheme' means an occupational pension scheme (as defined in section 1 of the Pension Schemes Act 1993) established under a trust.

47 Employee representatives

(1) An employee has the right not to be subjected to any detriment by any act, or any deliberate failure to act, by his employer done on the ground that, being—

(a) an employee representative for the purposes of Chapter II of Part IV of the Trade Union and Labour Relations (Consolidation) Act 1992 (redundancies) or Regulations 10 and 11 of the Transfer of Undertakings (Protection of Employment) Regulations 1981, or

(b) a candidate in an election in which any person elected will, on being elected, be such an employee representative,

he performed (or proposed to perform) any functions or activities as such an employee representative or candidate.

(1A) An employee has the right not to be subjected to any detriment by any act, or by any deliberate failure to act, by his employer done on the ground of his participation in an election of employee representatives for the purposes of Chapter II of Part IV of the Trade Union and Labour Relations (Consolidation) Act 1992 (redundancies) or Regulations 10 and 11 of the Transfer of Undertakings (Protection of Employment) Regulations 1981.

(2) This section does not apply where the detriment in question amounts to a dismissal (within the meaning of Part X).

47A Employees exercising right to time off work for study or training

(1) An employee has the right not to be subjected to any detriment by any act, or any deliberate failure to act, by his employer or the principal (within the meaning of section 63A(3)) done on the ground that, being a person entitled to—

(a) time off under section 63A(1) or (3), and

(b) remuneration under section 63B(1) in respect of that time taken off,

the employee exercised (or proposed to exercise) that right or received (or sought to receive) such remuneration.

(2) This section does not apply where the detriment in question amounts to dismissal (within the meaning of Part X).

47B Protected disclosures

(1) A worker has the right not to be subjected to any detriment by any act, or any deliberate failure to act, by his employer done on the ground that the worker has made a protected disclosure.

(2) This section does not apply where—

(a) the worker is an employee, and

(b) the detriment in question amounts to dismissal (within the meaning of Part X).

(3) For the purposes of this section, and of sections 48 and 49 so far as relating to this section, 'worker', 'worker's contract', 'employment' and 'employer' have the extended meaning given by section 43K.

47C Leave for family and domestic reasons

(1) An employee has the right not to be subjected to any detriment by any act, or any deliberate failure to act, by his employer done for a prescribed reason.

(2) A prescribed reason is one which is prescribed by regulations made by the Secretary of State and which relates to—

(a) pregnancy, childbirth or maternity,

(b) ordinary, compulsory or additional maternity leave,

(c) parental leave, or

(d) time off under section 57A.

(3) A reason prescribed under this section in relation to parental leave may relate to action which an employee takes, agrees to take or refuses to take under or in respect of a collective or workforce agreement.

(4) Regulations under this section may make different provision for different cases or circumstances.

Enforcement

48 Complaints to employment tribunals

(1) An employee may present a complaint to an employment tribunal that he has been subjected to a detriment in contravention of section 44, 45, 46, 47, 47A or 47C.

(1ZA) A worker may present a complaint to an employment tribunal that he has been subjected to a detriment in contravention of section 45A.

(1A) A worker may present a complaint to an employment tribunal that he has been subjected to a detriment in contravention of section 47B.

(2) On such a complaint it is for the employer to show the ground on which any act, or deliberate failure to act, was done.

(3) An employment tribunal shall not consider a complaint under this section unless it is presented—

(a) before the end of the period of three months beginning with the date of the act or failure to act to which the complaint relates or, where that act or failure is part of a series of similar acts or failures, the last of them, or

(b) within such further period as the tribunal considers reasonable in a case where it is satisfied that it was not reasonably practicable for the complaint to be presented before the end of that period of three months.

(4) For the purposes of subsection (3)—

(a) where an act extends over a period, the 'date of the act' means the last day of hat period, and

(b) a deliberate failure to act shall be treated as done when it was decided on;

and, in the absence of evidence establishing the contrary, an employer shall be taken to decide on a failure to act when he does an act inconsistent with doing the failed act or, if he has done no such inconsistent act, when the period expires within which he might reasonably have been expected to do the failed act if it was to be done.

(5) In this section and section 49 any reference to the employer includes, where a person complains that he has been subjected to a detriment in contravention of section 47A, the principal (within the meaning of section 63A(3)).

49 Remedies

(1) Where an employment tribunal finds a complaint under section 48 well-founded, the tribunal—

(a) shall make a declaration to that effect, and

(b) may make an award of compensation to be paid by the employer to the complainant in respect of the act or failure to act to which the complaint relates.

(2) Subject to subsections (5A) and (6) the amount of the compensation awarded shall be such as the tribunal considers just and equitable in all the circumstances having regard to—

(a) the infringement to which the complaint relates, and

(b) any loss which is attributable to the act, or failure to act, which infringed the complainant's right.

(3) The loss shall be taken to include—

(a) any expenses reasonably incurred by the complainant in consequence of the act, or failure to act, to which the complaint relates, and

(b) loss of any benefit which he might reasonably be expected to have had but for that act or failure to act.

(4) In ascertaining the loss the tribunal shall apply the same rule concerning the duty of a person to mitigate his loss as applies to damages recoverable under the common law of England and Wales or (as the case may be) Scotland.

(5) Where the tribunal finds that the act, or failure to act, to which the complaint relates was to any extent caused or contributed to by action of the complainant, it shall reduce the amount of the compensation by such proportion as it considers just and equitable having regard to that finding.

(5A) Where—

(a) the complaint is made under section 48(1ZA),

(b) the detriment to which the worker is subjected is the termination of his worker's contract, and

(c) that contract is not a contract of employment,

any compensation must not exceed the compensation that would be payable under Chapter II of Part X if the worker had been an employee and had been dismissed for the reason specified in section 101A.

(6) Where—

(a) the complaint is made under section 48(1A),

(b) the detriment to which the worker is subjected is the termination of his worker's contract, and

(c) that contract is not a contract of employment,

any compensation must not exceed the compensation that would be payable under Chapter II of Part X if the worker had been an employee and had been dismissed for the reason specified in section 103A.

49A [omitted]

PART VI
TIME OFF WORK

Public duties

50 Rights to time off for public duties

(1) An employer shall permit an employee of his who is a justice of the peace to take time off during the employee's working hours for the purpose of performing any of the duties of his office.

(2) An employer shall permit an employee of his who is a member of—

(a) a local authority,

(b) a statutory tribunal,

(c) a police authority,

(ca) the Service Authority for the National Criminal Intelligence Service or the Service Authority for the National Crime Squad,

(d) a board of prison visitors or a prison visiting committee,

(e) a relevant health body,

(f) a relevant education body, or

(g) the Environment Agency or the Scottish Environment Protection Agency,

to take time off during the employee's working hours for the purposes specified in subsection (3).

(3) The purposes referred to in subsection (2) are—

(a) attendance at a meeting of the body or any of its committees or sub-committees, and

(b) the doing of any other thing approved by the body, or anything of a class so approved, for the purpose of the discharge of the functions of the body or of any of its committees or sub-committees.

(4) The amount of time off which an employee is to be permitted to take under this section, and the occasions on which and any conditions subject to which time off may be so taken, are those that are reasonable in all the circumstances having regard, in particular, to—

(a) how much time off is required for the performance of the duties of the office or as a member of the body in question, and how much time off is required for the performance of the particular duty,

(b) how much time off the employee has already been permitted under this section or sections 168 and 170 of the Trade Union and Labour Relations (Consolidation) Act 1992 (time off for trade union duties and activities), and

(c) the circumstances of the employer's business and the effect of the employee's absence on the running of that business.

(5) In subsection (2)(a) 'a local authority' means—

(a) a local authority within the meaning of the Local Government Act 1972,

(b) a council constituted under section 2 of the Local Government etc. (Scotland) Act 1994,

(c) the Common Council of the City of London,

(d) a National Park authority, or

(e) the Broads Authority.

(6) The reference in subsection (2) to a member of a police authority is to a person appointed as such a member under Schedule 2 to the Police Act 1996.

(7) In subsection (2)(d)—

(a) 'a board of prison visitors' means a board of visitors appointed under section 6(2) of the Prison Act 1952, and

(b) 'a prison visiting committee' means a visiting committee appointed under section 19(3) of the Prisons (Scotland) Act 1989 or constituted by virtue of rules made under section 39 (as read with section 8(1)) of that Act.

(8) In subsection (2)(e) 'a relevant health body' means—

(a) a National Health Service trust established under Part I of the National Health Service and Community Care Act 1990 or the National Health Service (Scotland) Act 1978,

(b) a Health Authority established under section 8 of the National Health Service Act 1977 or a Special Health Authority established under section 11 of that Act, or

(c) a Health Board constituted under section 2 of the National Health Service (Scotland) Act 1978.

(9) In subsection (2)(f) 'a relevant education body' means—

(a) a managing or governing body of an educational establishment maintained by a local education authority,

(b) a governing body of a further education corporation or higher education corporation,

(c) a school council appointed under section 125(1) of the Local Government (Scotland) Act 1973,

(d) a school board within the meaning of section 1(1) of the School Boards (Scotland) Act 1988,

(e) a board of management of a self-governing school within the meaning of section 135(1) of the Education (Scotland) Act 1980,

(f) a board of management of a college of further education within the meaning of section 36(1) of the Further and Higher Education (Scotland) Act 1992,

(g) a governing body of a central institution within the meaning of section 135(1) of the Education (Scotland) Act 1980, or

(h) a governing body of a designated institution within the meaning of Part II of the Further and Higher Education (Scotland) Act 1992.

(10) The Secretary of State may by order—

(a) modify the provisions of subsections (1) and (2) and (5) to (9) by adding any office or body, removing any office or body or altering the description of any office or body, or

(b) modify the provisions of subsection (3).

(11) For the purposes of this section the working hours of an employee shall be taken to be any time when, in accordance with his contract of employment, the employee is required to be at work.

51 Complaints to employment tribunals

(1) An employee may present a complaint to an employment tribunal that his employer has failed to permit him to take time off as required by section 50.

(2) An employment tribunal shall not consider a complaint under this section that an employer has failed to permit an employee to take time off unless it is presented—

(a) before the end of the period of three months beginning with the date on which the failure occurred, or

(b) within such further period as the tribunal considers reasonable in a case where it is satisfied that it was not reasonably practicable for the complaint to be presented before the end of that period of three months.

(3) Where an employment tribunal finds a complaint under this section well-founded, the tribunal—

(a) shall make a declaration to that effect, and

(b) may make an award of compensation to be paid by the employer to the employee.

(4) The amount of the compensation shall be such as the tribunal considers just and equitable in all the circumstances having regard to—

(a) the employer's default in failing to permit time off to be taken by the employee, and

(b) any loss sustained by the employee which is attributable to the matters to which the complaint relates.

Looking for work and making arrangements for training

52 Right to time off to look for work or arrange training

(1) An employee who is given notice of dismissal by reason of redundancy is entitled to be permitted by his employer to take reasonable time off during the employee's working hours before the end of his notice in order to—

(a) look for new employment, or

(b) make arrangements for training for future employment.

(2) An employee is not entitled to take time off under this section unless, on whichever is the later of—

(a) the date on which the notice is due to expire, and

(b) the date on which it would expire were it the notice required to be given by section 86(1),

he will have been (or would have been) continuously employed for a period of two years or more.

(3) For the purposes of this section the working hours of an employee shall be taken to be any time when, in accordance with his contract of employment, the employee is required to be at work.

53 Right to remuneration for time off under section 52

(1) An employee who is permitted to take time off under section 52 is entitled to be paid remuneration by his employer for the period of absence at the appropriate hourly rate.

(2) The appropriate hourly rate, in relation to an employee, is the amount of one week's pay divided by the number of normal working hours in a week for that employee when employed under the contract of employment in force on the day when the notice of dismissal was given.

(3) But where the number of normal working hours differs from week to week or over a longer period, the amount of one week's pay shall be divided instead by the average number of normal working hours calculated by dividing by twelve the total number of the employee's normal working hours during the period of twelve weeks ending with the last complete week before the day on which the notice was given.

(4) If an employer unreasonably refuses to permit an employee to take time off from work as required by section 52, the employee is entitled to be paid an amount equal to the remuneration to which he would have been entitled under subsection (1) if he had been permitted to take the time off.

(5) The amount of an employer's liability to pay remuneration under subsection (1) shall not exceed, in respect of the notice period of any employee, forty per cent. of a week's pay of that employee.

(6) A right to any amount under subsection (1) or (4) does not affect any right of an employee in relation to remuneration under his contract of employment ('contractual remuneration').

(7) Any contractual remuneration paid to an employee in respect of a period of time off under section 52 goes towards discharging any liability of the employer to pay

remuneration under subsection (1) in respect of that period; and, conversely, any payment of remuneration under subsection (1) in respect of a period goes towards discharging any liability of the employer to pay contractual remuneration in respect of that period.

54 Complaints to employment tribunals

(1) An employee may present a complaint to an employment tribunal that his employer—

(a) has unreasonably refused to permit him to take time off as required by section 52, or

(b) has failed to pay the whole or any part of any amount to which the employee is entitled under section 53(1) or (4).

(2) An employment tribunal shall not consider a complaint under this section unless it is presented—

(a) before the end of the period of three months beginning with the date on which it is alleged that the time off should have been permitted, or

(b) within such further period as the tribunal considers reasonable in a case where it is satisfied that it was not reasonably practicable for the complaint to be presented before the end of that period of three months.

(3) Where an employment tribunal finds a complaint under this section well-founded, the tribunal shall—

(a) make a declaration to that effect, and

(b) order the employer to pay to the employee the amount which it finds due to him.

(4) The amount which may be ordered by a tribunal to be paid by an employer under subsection (3) (or, where the employer is liable to pay remuneration under section 53, the aggregate of that amount and the amount of that liability) shall not exceed, in respect of the notice period of any employee, forty per cent. of a week's pay of that employee.

Ante-natal care

55 Right to time off for ante-natal care

(1) An employee who—

(a) is pregnant, and

(b) has, on the advice of a registered medical practitioner, registered midwife or registered health visitor, made an appointment to attend at any place for the purpose of receiving ante-natal care,

is entitled to be permitted by her employer to take time off during the employee's working hours in order to enable her to keep the appointment.

(2) An employee is not entitled to take time off under this section to keep an appointment unless, if her employer requests her to do so, she produces for his inspection—

(a) a certificate from a registered medical practitioner, registered midwife or registered health visitor stating that the employee is pregnant, and

(b) an appointment card or some other document showing that the appointment has been made.

(3) Subsection (2) does not apply where the employee's appointment is the first appointment during her pregnancy for which she seeks permission to take time off in accordance with subsection (1).

(4) For the purposes of this section the working hours of an employee shall be taken to be any time when, in accordance with her contract of employment, the employee is required to be at work.

56 Right to remuneration for time off under section 55

(1) An employee who is permitted to take time off under section 55 is entitled to be paid remuneration by her employer for the period of absence at the appropriate hourly rate.

(2) The appropriate hourly rate, in relation to an employee, is the amount of one week's pay divided by the number of normal working hours in a week for that employee when employed under the contract of employment in force on the day when the time off is taken.

(3) But where the number of normal working hours differs from week to week or over a longer period, the amount of one week's pay shall be divided instead by—

(a) the average number of normal working hours calculated by dividing by twelve the total number of the employee's normal working hours during the period of twelve weeks ending with the last complete week before the day on which the time off is taken, or

(b) where the employee has not been employed for a sufficient period to enable the calculation to be made under paragraph (a), a number which fairly represents the number of normal working hours in a week having regard to such of the considerations specified in subsection (4) as are appropriate in the circumstances.

(4) The considerations referred to in subsection (3)(b) are—

(a) the average number of normal working hours in a week which the employee could expect in accordance with the terms of her contract, and

(b) the average number of normal working hours of other employees engaged in relevant comparable employment with the same employer.

(5) A right to any amount under subsection (1) does not affect any right of an employee in relation to remuneration under her contract of employment ('contractual remuneration').

(6) Any contractual remuneration paid to an employee in respect of a period of time off under section 55 goes towards discharging any liability of the employer to pay remuneration under subsection (1) in respect of that period; and, conversely, any payment of remuneration under subsection (1) in respect of a period goes towards discharging any liability of the employer to pay contractual remuneration in respect of that period.

57 Complaints to employment tribunals

(1) An employee may present a complaint to an employment tribunal that her employer—

(a) has unreasonably refused to permit her to take time off as required by section 55, or

(b) has failed to pay the whole or any part of any amount to which the employee is entitled under section 56.

(2) An employment tribunal shall not consider a complaint under this section unless it is presented—

(a) before the end of the period of three months beginning with the date of the appointment concerned, or

(b) within such further period as the tribunal considers reasonable in a case where it is satisfied that it was not reasonably practicable for the complaint to be presented before the end of that period of three months.

(3) Where an employment tribunal finds a complaint under this section well-founded, the tribunal shall make a declaration to that effect.

(4) If the complaint is that the employer has unreasonably refused to permit the employee to take time off, the tribunal shall also order the employer to pay to the employee an amount equal to the remuneration to which she would have been entitled under section 56 if the employer had not refused.

(5) If the complaint is that the employer has failed to pay the employee the whole or part of any amount to which she is entitled under section 56, the tribunal shall also order the employer to pay to the employee the amount which it finds due to her.

Dependants

57A Time off for dependants

(1) An employee is entitled to be permitted by his employer to take a reasonable amount of time off during the employee's working hours in order to take action which is necessary—

(a) to provide assistance on an occasion when a dependant falls ill, gives birth or is injured or assaulted,

(b) to make arrangements for the provision of care for a dependant who is ill or injured,

(c) in consequence of the death of a dependant,

(d) because of the unexpected disruption or termination of arrangements for the care of a dependant, or

(e) to deal with an incident which involves a child of the employee and which occurs unexpectedly in a period during which an educational establishment which the child attends is responsible for him.

(2) Subsection (1) does not apply unless the employee—

(a) tells his employer the reason for his absence as soon as reasonably practicable, and

(b) expect where paragraph (a) cannot be complied with until after the employee has returned to work, tells his employer for how long he expects to be absent.

(3) Subject to subsections (4) and (5), for the purposes of this section 'dependant' means, in relation to an employee—

(a) a spouse,

(b) a child,

(c) a parent,

(d) a person who lives in the same household as the employee, otherwise than by reason of being his employee, tenant, lodger or boarder.

(4) For the purposes of subsection (1)(a) or (b) 'dependant' includes, in addition to the persons mentioned in subsection (3), any person who reasonably relies on the employee—

(a) for assistance on an occasion when the person falls ill or is injured or assaulted, or

(b) to make arrangements for the provision of care in the event of illness or injury.

(5) For the purposes of subsection (1)(d) 'dependant' includes, in addition to the persons mentioned in subsection (3), any person who reasonably relies on the employee to make arrangements for the provision of care.

(6) A reference in this section to illness or injury includes a reference to mental illness or injury.

57B Complaint to employment tribunal

(1) An employee may present a complaint to an employment tribunal that his employer has unreasonably refused to permit him to take time off as required by section 57A.

(2) An employment tribunal shall not consider a complaint under this section unless it is presented—

(a) before the end of the period of three months beginning with the date when the refusal occurred, or

(b) within such further period as the tribunal considers reasonable in a case where it is satisfied that it was not reasonably practicable for the complaint to be presented before the end of that period of three months.

(3) Where an employment tribunal finds a complaint under subsection (1) well-founded, it—

(a) shall make a declaration to that effect, and

(b) may make an award of compensation to be paid by the employer to the employee.

(4) the amount of compensation shall be such as the tribunal considers just and equitable in all the circumstances having regard to—

(a) the employer's default in refusing to permit time off to be taken by the employee, and

(b) any loss sustained by the employee which is attributable to the matters complained of.

Occupational pension scheme trustees

58 Right to time off for pension scheme trustees

(1) The employer in relation to a relevant occupational pension scheme shall permit an employee of his who is a trustee of the scheme to take time off during the employee's working hours for the purpose of—

(a) performing any of his duties as such a trustee, or

(b) undergoing training relevant to the performance of those duties.

(2) The amount of time off which an employee is to be permitted to take under this section and the purposes for which, the occasions on which and any conditions subject to which time off may be so taken are those that are reasonable in all the circumstances having regard, in particular, to—

(a) how much time off is required for the performance of the duties of a trustee of the scheme and the undergoing of relevant training, and how much time off is required for performing the particular duty or for undergoing the particular training, and

(b) the circumstances of the employer's business and the effect of the employee's absence on the running of that business.

(3) In this section—

(a) 'relevant occupational pension scheme' means an occupational pension scheme (as defined in section 1 of the Pension Schemes Act 1993) established under a trust, and

(b) references to the employer, in relation to such a scheme, are to an employer of persons in the description or category of employment to which the scheme relates, and

(c) reference to training are to training on the employer's premises or elsewhere.

(4) For the purposes of this section the working hours of an employee shall be taken to be any time when, in accordance with his contract of employment, the employee is required to be at work.

59 Right to payment for time off under section 58

(1) An employer who permits an employee to take time off under section 58 shall pay him for the time taken off pursuant to the permission.

(2) Where the employee's remuneration for the work he would ordinarily have been doing during that time does not vary with the amount of work done, he must be paid as if he had worked at that work for the whole of that time.

(3) Where the employee's remuneration for the work he would ordinarily have been doing during that time varies with the amount of work done, he must be paid an amount calculated by reference to the average hourly earnings for that work.

(4) The average hourly earnings mentioned in subsection (3) are—

(a) those of the employee concerned, or

(b) if no fair estimate can be made of those earnings, the average hourly earnings for work of that description of persons in comparable employment with the same employer or, if there are no such persons, a figure of average hourly earnings which is reasonable in the circumstances.

(5) A right to be paid an amount under subsection (1) does not affect any right of an employee in relation to remuneration under his contract of employment ('contractual remuneration').

(6) Any contractual remuneration paid to an employee in respect of a period of time off under section 58 goes towards discharging any liability of the employer under subsection (1) in respect of that period; and, conversely, any payment under subsection (1) in respect of a period goes towards discharging any liability of the employer to pay contractual remuneration in respect of that period.

60 Complaints to employment tribunals

(1) An employee may present a complaint to an employment tribunal that his employer—

(a) has failed to permit him to take time off as required by section 58, or

(b) has failed to pay him in accordance with section 59.

(2) An employment tribunal shall not consider a complaint under this section unless it is presented—

(a) before the end of the period of three months beginning with the date when the failure occurred, or

(b) within such further period as the tribunal considers reasonable in a case where it is satisfied that it was not reasonably practicable for the complaint to be presented before the end of that period of three months.

(3) Where an employment tribunal finds a complaint under subsection (1)(a) well-founded, the tribunal—

(a) shall make a declaration to that effect, and

(b) may make an award of compensation to be paid by the employer to the employee.

(4) The amount of the compensation shall be such as the tribunal considers just and equitable in all the circumstances having regard to—

(a) the employer's default in failing to permit time off to be taken by the employee, and

(b) any loss sustained by the employee which is attributable to the matters complained of.

(5) Where on a complaint under subsection (1)(b) an employment tribunal finds that an employer has failed to pay an employee in accordance with section 59, it shall order the employer to pay the amount which it finds to be due.

Employee representatives

61 Right to time off for employee representatives

(1) An employee who is—

(a) an employee representative for the purposes of Chapter II of Part IV of the Trade Union and Labour Relations (Consolidation) Act 1992 (redundancies) or Regulations 10 and 11 of the Transfer of Undertakings (Protection of Employment) Regulations 1981, or

(b) a candidate in an election in which any person elected will, on being elected, be such an employee representative,

is entitled to be permitted by his employer to take reasonable time off during the employee's working hours in order to perform his functions as such an employee representative or candidate or in order to undergo training to perform such functions.

(2) For the purposes of this section the working hours of an employee shall be taken to be any time when, in accordance with his contract of employment, the employee is required to be at work.

62 Right to remuneration for time off under section 61

(1) An employee who is permitted to take time off under section 61 is entitled to be paid remuneration by his employer for the time taken off at the appropriate hourly rate.

(2) The appropriate hourly rate, in relation to an employee, is the amount of one week's pay divided by the number of normal working hours in a week for that employee when employed under the contract of employment in force on the day when the time off is taken.

(3) But where the number of normal working hours differs from week to week or over a longer period, the amount of one week's pay shall be divided instead by—

(a) the average number of normal working hours calculated by dividing by twelve the total number of the employee's normal working hours during the period of twelve weeks ending with the last complete week before the day on which the time off is taken, or

(b) where the employee has not been employed for a sufficient period to enable the calculation to be made under paragraph (a), a number which fairly represents the number of normal working hours in a week having regard to such of the considerations specified in subsection (4) as are appropriate in the circumstances.

(4) The considerations referred to in subsection (3)(b) are—

(a) the average number of normal working hours in a week which the employee could expect in accordance with the terms of his contract, and

(b) the average number of normal working hours of other employees engaged in relevant comparable employment with the same employer.

(5) A right to any amount under subsection (1) does not affect any right of an employee in relation to remuneration under his contract of employment ('contractual remuneration').

(6) Any contractual remuneration paid to an employee in respect of a period of time off under section 61 goes towards discharging any liability of the employer to pay remuneration under subsection (1) in respect of that period; and, conversely, any payment of remuneration under subsection (1) in respect of a period goes towards discharging any liability of the employer to pay contractual remuneration in respect of that period.

63 Complaints to employment tribunals

(1) An employee may present a complaint to an employment tribunal that his employer—

(a) has unreasonably refused to permit him to take time off as required by section 61, or

(b) has failed to pay the whole or any part of any amount to which the employee is entitled under section 62.

(2) An employment tribunal shall not consider a complaint under this section unless it is presented—

(a) before the end of the period of three months beginning with the day on which the time off was taken or on which it is alleged the time off should have been permitted, or

(b) within such further period as the tribunal considers reasonable in a case where it is satisfied that it was not reasonably practicable for the complaint to be presented before the end of that period of three months.

(3) Where an employment tribunal finds a complaint under this section well-founded, the tribunal shall make a declaration to that effect.

(4) If the complaint is that the employer has unreasonably refused to permit the employee to take time off, the tribunal shall also order the employer to pay to the employee an amount equal to the remuneration to which he would have been entitled under section 62 if the employer had not refused.

(5) If the complaint is that the employer has failed to pay the employee the whole or part of any amount to which he is entitled under section 62, the tribunal shall also order the employer to pay to the employee the amount which it finds due to him.

63A Right to time off for young person for study or training

(1) An employee who—

(a) is aged 16 or 17,

(b) is not receiving full-time secondary or further education, and

(c) has not attained such standard of achievement as is prescribed by regulations made by the Secretary of State,

is entitled to be permitted by his employer to take time off during the employee's working hours in order to undertake study or training leading to a relevant qualification.

(2) [omitted]

(3) An employee who—

(a) satisfies the requirements of paragraphs (a) to (c) of subsection (1), and

(b) is for the time being supplied by his employer to another person ('the principal') to perform work in accordance with a contract made between the employer and the principal,

is entitled to be permitted by the principal to take time off during the employee's working hours in order to undertake study or training leading to a relevant qualification.

(4) Where an employee—

(a) is aged 18,

(b) is undertaking study or training leading to a relevant qualification, and

(c) began such study or training before attaining that age,

subsections (1) and (3) shall apply to the employee, in relation to that study or training, as if 'or 18' were inserted at the end of subsection (1)(a).

(5) The amount of time off which an employee is to be permitted to take under this section, and the occasions on which and any conditions subject to which time off may be so taken, are those that are reasonable in all the circumstances having regard, in particular, to—

(a) the requirements of the employee's study or training, and

(b) the circumstances of the business of the employer or the principal and the effect of the employee's time off on the running of that business.

(6) [omitted]

(7) References in this section to study or training are references to study or training on the premises of the employer or (as the case may be) principal or elsewhere.

(8) For the purposes of this section the working hours of an employee shall be taken to be any time when, in accordance with his contract of employment, the employee is required to be at work.

63B Right to remuneration for time off under section 63A

(1) An employee who is permitted to take time off under section 63A is entitled to be paid remuneration by his employer for the time taken off at the appropriate hourly rate.

(2) The appropriate hourly rate, in relation to an employee, is the amount of one week's pay divided by the number of normal working hours in a week for that employee when employed under the contract of employment in force on the day when the time off is taken.

(3) But where the number of normal working hours differs from week to week or over a longer period, the amount of one week's pay shall be divided instead by—

(a) the average number of normal working hours calculated by dividing by twelve the total number of the employee's working hours during the period of twelve weeks ending with the last complete week before the day on which the time off is taken, or

(b) where the employee has not been employed for a sufficient period to enable the calculation to be made under paragraph (a), a number which fairly represents the number of normal working hours in a week having regard to such of the considerations specified in subsection (4) as are appropriate in the circumstances.

(4) The considerations referred to in subsection (3)(b) are—

(a) the average number of normal working hours in a week which the employee could expect in accordance with the terms of his contract, and

(b) the average number of normal working hours of other employees engaged in relevant comparable employment with the same employer.

(5) A right to any amount under subsection (1) does not affect any right of an employee in relation to remuneration under his contract of employment ('contractual remuneration').

(6) Any contractual remuneration paid to an employee in respect of a period of time off under section 63A goes towards discharging any liability of the employer to pay remuneration under subsection (1) in respect of that period; and, conversely, any payment of remuneration under subsection (1) in respect of a period goes towards discharging any liability of the employer to pay contractual remuneration in respect of that period.

63C Complaints to employment tribunals

(1) An employee may present a complaint to an employment tribunal that—

(a) his employer, or the principal referred to in subsection (3) of section 63A, has unreasonably refused to permit him to take time off as required by that section, or

(b) his employer has failed to pay the whole or any part of any amount to which the employee is entitled under section 63B.

(2) An employment tribunal shall not consider a complaint under this section unless it is presented—

(a) before the end of the period of three months beginning with the day on which the time off was taken or on which it is alleged the time off should have been permitted, or

(b) within such further period as the tribunal considers reasonable in a case where it is satisfied that it was not reasonably practicable for the complaint to be presented before the end of that period of three months.

(3) Where an employment tribunal finds a complaint under this section well-founded, the tribunal shall make a declaration to that effect.

(4) If the complaint is that the employer or the principal has unreasonably refused to permit the employee to take time off, the tribunal shall also order the employer or the principal, as the case may be, to pay to the employee an amount equal to the remuneration to which he would have been entitled under section 63B if the employer or the principal had not refused.

(5) If the complaint is that the employer has failed to pay the employee the whole or part of any amount to which he is entitled under section 63B, the tribunal shall also order the employer to pay to the employee the amount which it finds due to him.

PART VII
SUSPENSION FROM WORK

Suspension on medical grounds

64 Right to remuneration on suspension on medical grounds

(1) An employee who is suspended from work by his employer on medical grounds is entitled to be paid by his employer remuneration while he is so suspended for a period not exceeding twenty-six weeks.

(2) For the purposes of this Part an employee is suspended from work on medical grounds if he is suspended from work in consequence of—

(a) a requirement imposed by or under a provision of an enactment or of an instrument made under an enactment, or

(b) a recommendation in a provision of a code of practice issued or approved under section 16 of the Health and Safety at Work etc. Act 1974,

and the provision is for the time being specified in subsection (3).

(3) The provisions referred to in subsection (2) are—

Regulation 16 of the Control of Lead at Work Regulations 1980,

Regulation 16 of the Ionising Radiations Regulations 1985, and

Regulation 11 of the Control of Substances Hazardous to Health Regulations 1988.

(4) The Secretary of State may by order add provisions to or remove provisions from the list of provisions specified in subsection (3).

(5) For the purposes of this Part an employee shall be regarded as suspended from work on medical grounds only if and for so long as he—

(a) continues to be employed by his employer, but

(b) is not provided with work or does not perform the work he normally performed before the suspension.

65 Exclusions from right to remuneration

(1) An employee is not entitled to remuneration under section 64 unless he has been continuously employed for a period of not less than one month ending with the day before that on which the suspension begins.

(2) An employee who is employed—

(a) under a contract for a fixed term of three months or less, or

(b) under a contract made in contemplation of the performance of a specific task which is not expected to last for more than three months,

is not entitled to remuneration under section 64 unless he has been continuously employed for a period of more than three months ending with the day before that on which the suspension begins.

(3) An employee is not entitled to remuneration under section 64 in respect of any period during which he is incapable of work by reason of disease or bodily or mental disablement.

(4) An employee is not entitled to remuneration under section 64 in respect of any period if—

(a) his employer has offered to provide him with suitable alternative work during the period (whether or not it is work which the employee is under his contract, or was under the contract in force before the suspension, employed to perform) and the employee has unreasonably refused to perform that work, or

(b) he does not comply with reasonable requirements imposed by his employer with a view to ensuring that his services are available.

Suspension on maternity grounds

66 Meaning of suspension on maternity grounds

(1) For the purposes of this Part an employee is suspended from work on maternity grounds if, in consequence of any relevant requirement or relevant recommendation, she is suspended from work by her employer on the ground that she is pregnant, has recently given birth or is breastfeeding a child.

(2) In subsection (1)—

'relevant requirement' means a requirement imposed by or under a specified provision of an enactment or of an instrument made under an enactment, and

'relevant recommendation' means a recommendation in a specified provision of a code of practice issued or approved under section 16 of the Health and Safety at Work etc. Act 1974;

and in this subsection 'specified provision' means a provision for the time being specified in an order made by the Secretary of State under this subsection.

(3) For the purposes of this Part an employee shall be regarded as suspended from work on maternity grounds only if and for so long as she—

(a) continues to be employed by her employer, but

(b) is not provided with work or (disregarding alternative work for the purposes of section 67) does not perform the work she normally performed before the suspension.

67 Right to offer of alternative work

(1) Where an employer has available suitable alternative work for an employee, the employee has a right to be offered to be provided with the alternative work before being suspended from work on maternity grounds.

(2) For alternative work to be suitable for an employee for the purposes of this section—

(a) the work must be of a kind which is both suitable in relation to her and appropriate for her to do in the circumstances, and

(b) the terms and conditions applicable to her for performing the work, if they differ from the corresponding terms and conditions applicable to her for performing the work she normally performs under her contract of employment, must not be substantially less favourable to her than those corresponding terms and conditions.

68 Right to remuneration

(1) An employee who is suspended from work on maternity grounds is entitled to be paid remuneration by her employer while she is so suspended.

(2) An employee is not entitled to remuneration under this section in respect of any period if—

(a) her employer has offered to provide her during the period with work which is suitable alternative work for her for the purposes of section 67, and

(b) the employee has unreasonably refused to perform that work.

General

69 Calculation of remuneration

(1) The amount of remuneration payable by an employer to an employee under section 64 or 68 is a week's pay in respect of each week of the period of suspension; and if in any week remuneration is payable in respect of only part of that week the amount of a week's pay shall be reduced proportionately.

(2) A right to remuneration under section 64 or 68 does not affect any right of an employee in relation to remuneration under the employee's contract of employment ('contractual remuneration').

(3) Any contractual remuneration paid by an employer to an employee in respect of any period goes towards discharging the employer's liability under section 64 or 68 in respect of that period; and, conversely, any payment of remuneration in discharge of an employer's liability under section 64 or 68 in respect of any period goes towards discharging any obligation of the employer to pay contractual remuneration in respect of that period.

70 Complaints to employment tribunals

(1) An employee may present a complaint to an employment tribunal that his or her employer has failed to pay the whole or any part of remuneration to which the employee is entitled under section 64 or 68.

(2) An employment tribunal shall not consider a complaint under subsection (1) relating to remuneration in respect of any day unless it is presented—

(a) before the end of the period of three months beginning with that day, or

(b) within such further period as the tribunal considers reasonable in a case where it is satisfied that it was not reasonably practicable for the complaint to be presented within that period of three months.

(3) Where an employment tribunal finds a complaint under subsection (1) well-founded, the tribunal shall order the employer to pay the employee the amount of remuneration which it finds is due to him or her.

(4) An employee may present a complaint to an employment tribunal that in contravention of section 67 her employer has failed to offer to provide her with work.

(5) An employment tribunal shall not consider a complaint under subsection (4) unless it is presented—

(a) before the end of the period of three months beginning with the first day of the suspension, or

(b) within such further period as the tribunal considers reasonable in a case where it is satisfied that it was not reasonably practicable for the complaint to be presented within that period of three months.

(6) Where an employment tribunal finds a complaint under subsection (4) well-founded, the tribunal may make an award of compensation to be paid by the employer to the employee.

(7) The amount of the compensation shall be such as the tribunal considers just and equitable in all the circumstances having regard to—

(a) the infringement of the employee's right under section 67 by the failure on the part of the employer to which the complaint relates, and

(b) any loss sustained by the employee which is attributable to that failure.

PART VIII

CHAPTER I
MATERNITY LEAVE

71 Ordinary maternity leave

(1) An employee may, provided that she satisfies any conditions which may be prescribed, be absent from work at any time during an ordinary maternity leave period.

(2) An ordinary maternity leave period is a period calculated in accordance with regulations made by the Secretary of State.

(3) Regulations under subsection (2)—

(a) shall secure that no ordinary maternity leave period is less than 18 weeks;

(b) may allow an employee to choose, subject to any prescribed restrictions, the date on which an ordinary maternity leave period starts.

(4) Subject to section 74, an employee who exercises her right under subsection (1)—

(a) is entitled to the benefit of the terms and conditions of employment which would have applied if she had not been absent,

(b) is bound by any obligations arising under those terms and conditions (except in so far as they are inconsistent with subsection (1)), and

(c) is entitled to return from leave to the job in which she was employed before her absence.

(5) In subsection (4)(a) 'terms and conditions of employment'—

(a) includes matters connected with an employee's employment whether or not they arise under her contract of employment, but

(b) does not include terms and conditions about remuneration.

(6) The Secretary of State may make regulations specifying matters which are, or are not, to be treated as remuneration for the purposes of this section.

(7) An employee's right to return under subsection (4)(c) is a right to return—

(a) with her seniority, pension rights and similar rights as they would have been if she had not been absent (subject to paragraph 5 of Schedule 5 to the Social Security Act 1989 (equal treatment under pension schemes: maternity)), and

(b) on terms and conditions not less favourable than those which would have applied if she had not been absent.

72 Compulsory maternity leave

(1) An employer shall not permit an employee who satisfies prescribed conditions to work during a compulsory maternity leave period.

(2) A compulsory maternity leave period is a period calculated in accordance with regulations made by the Secretary of State.

(3) Regulations under subsection (2) shall secure—

(a) that no compulsory leave period is less than two weeks, and

(b) that every compulsory maternity leave period falls within an ordinary maternity leave period.

(4) Subject to subsection (5), any provision of or made under the Health and Safety at Work etc. Act 1974 shall apply in relation to the prohibition under subsection (1) as if it were imposed by regulations under section 15 of that Act.

(5) Section 33(1)(c) of the 1974 Act shall not apply in relation to the prohibition under subsection (1); and an employer who contravenes that subsection shall be—

(a) guilty of an offence, and

(b) liable on summary conviction to a fine not exceeding level 2 on the standard scale.

73 Additional maternity leave

(1) An employee who satisfies prescribed conditions may be absent from work at any time during an additional maternity leave period.

(2) An additional maternity leave period is a period calculated in accordance with regulations made by the Secretary of State.

(3) Regulations under subsection (2) may allow an employee to choose, subject to prescribed restrictions, the date on which an additional maternity leave period ends.

(4) Subject to section 74, an employee who exercises her right under subsection (1)—

(a) is entitled, for such purposes and to such extent as may be prescribed, to the benefit of the terms and conditions of employment which would have applied if she had not been absent,

(b) is bound, for such purposes and to such extent as may be prescribed, by obligations arising under those terms and conditions (except in so far as they are inconsistent with subsection (1), and

(c) is entitled to return from leave to a job of a prescribed kind.

(5) In subsection (4)(a) 'terms and conditions of employment'—

(a) includes matters connected with an employee's employment whether or not they arise under her contract of employment, but

(b) does not include terms and conditions about remuneration.

(6) The Secretary of State may make regulations specifying matters which are, or are not, to be treated as remuneration for the purposes of this section.

(7) The Secretary of State may make regulations making provision, in relation to the right to return under subsection (4)(c), about—

(a) seniority, pension rights and similar rights;

(b) terms and conditions of employment on return.

74 Redundancy and dismissal

(1) Regulations under section 71 or 73 may make provision about redundancy during an ordinary or additional maternity leave period.

(2) Regulations under section 71 or 73 may make provision about dismissal (other than by reason of redundancy) during an ordinary or additional maternity leave period.

(3) Regulations made by virtue of subsection (1) or (2) may include—

(a) provision requiring an employer to offer alternative employment;

(b) provision for the consequences of failure to comply with the regulations (which may include provision for a dismissal to be treated as unfair for the purposes of Part X).

(4) Regulations under section 73 may make provision—

(a) for section 73(4)(c) not to apply in specified cases, and

(b) about dismissal at the conclusion of an additional maternity leave period.

75 Section 71 to 73: supplemental.

(1) Regulations under section 71, 72 or 73 may—

(a) make provision about notices to be given, evidence to be produced and other procedures to be followed by employees and employers;

(b) make provision for the consequences of failure to give notices, to produce evidence or to comply with other procedural requirements;

(c) make provision for the consequences of failure to act in accordance with a notice given by virtue of paragraph (a);

(d) make special provision for cases where an employee has a right which corresponds to a right under this Chapter and which arises under her contract of employment or otherwise;

(e) make provision modifying the effect of Chapter II of Part XIV (calculation of a week's pay) in relation to an employee who is or has been absent from work on ordinary or additional maternity leave;

(f) make provision applying, modifying or excluding an enactment, in such circumstances as may be specified and subject to any conditions specified, in relation to a person entitled to ordinary, compulsory or additional maternity leave;

(g) make different provision for different cases or circumstances.

(2) In sections 71 to 73 'prescribed' means prescribed by regulations made by the Secretary of State.

CHAPTER II
PARENTAL LEAVE

76 Entitlement to parental leave

(1) The Secretary of State shall make regulations entitling an employee who satisfies specified conditions—

(a) as to duration of employment, and

(b) as to having, or expecting to have, responsibility for a child,

to be absent from work on parental leave for the purpose of caring for a child.

(2) The regulations shall include provision for determining—

(a) the extent of an employee's entitlement to parental leave in respect of a child;

(b) when parental leave may be taken.

(3) Provision under subsection (2)(a) shall secure that where an employee is entitled to parental leave in respect of a child he is entitled to a period or total period of leave of at least three months; but this subsection is without prejudice to any provision which may be made by the regulations for cases in which—

(a) a person ceases to satisfy conditions under subsection (1);

(b) an entitlement to parental leave is transferred.

(4) Provision under subsection (2)(b) may, in particular, refer to—

(a) a child's age, or

(b) a specified period of time starting from a specified event.

(5) Regulations under subsection (1) may—

(a) specify things which are, or are not, to be taken as done for the purpose of caring for a child;

(b) require parental leave to be taken as a single period of absence in all cases or in specified cases;

(c) require parental leave to be taken as a series of periods of absence in all cases or in specified cases;

(d) require all or specified parts of a period of parental leave to be taken at or by specified times;

(e) make provision about the postponement by an employer or a period of parental leave which an employee wishes to take;

(f) specify a minimum or maximum period of absence which may be taken as part of a period of parental leave.

(g) specify a maximum aggregate of periods of parental leave which may be taken during a specified period of time.

77 Rights during and after parental leave

(1) Regulations under section 76 shall provide—

(a) that an employee who is absent on parental leave is entitled, for such purposes and to such extent as may be prescribed, to the benefit of the terms and conditions of employment which would have applied if he had not been absent,

(b) that an employee who is absent on parental leave is bound, for such purposes and to such extent as may be prescribed, by any obligations arising under those terms and conditions (except in so far as they are inconsistent with section 76(1)), and

(c) that an employee who is absent on parental leave is entitled, subject to section 78(1), to return from leave to a job of such kind as the regulations may specify.

(2) In subsection (1)(a) 'terms and conditions of employment'—

(a) includes matters connected with an employee's employment whether or not they arise under a contract of employment, but

(b) does not include terms and conditions about remuneration.

(3) Regulations under section 76 may specify matters which are, or are not, to be treated as remuneration for the purposes of subsection (2)(b) above.

(4) The regulations may make provision, in relation to the right to return mentioned in subsection (1)(c), about—

(a) seniority, pension rights and similar rights;

(b) terms and conditions of employment on return.

78 Special cases

(1) Regulations under section 76 may make provision—

(a) about redundancy during a period of parental leave;

(b) about dismissal (other than by reason of redundancy) during a period of parental leave.

(2) Provision by virtue of subsection (1) may include—

(a) provision requiring an employer to offer alternative employment;

(b) provision for the consequences of failure to comply with the regulations (which may include provision for a dismissal to be treated as unfair for the purposes of Part X).

(3) Regulations under section 76 may provide for an employee to be entitled to choose to exercise all or part of his entitlement to parental leave—

(a) by varying the terms of his contract of employment as to hours of work, or

(b) by varying his normal working practice as to hours of work,

in a way specified in or permitted by the regulations for a period specified in the regulations.

(4) Provision by virtue of subsection (3)—

(a) may restrict an entitlement to specified circumstances;

(b) may make an entitlement subject to specified conditions (which may include conditions relating to obtaining the employer's consent);

(c) may include consequential and incidental provision.

(5) Regulations under section 76 may make provision permitting all or part of an employee's entitlement to parental leave in respect of a child to be transferred to another employee in specified circumstances.

(6) The reference in section 77(1)(c) to absence on parental leave includes, where appropriate, a reference to a continuous period of absence attributable partly to maternity leave and partly to parental leave.

(7) Regulations under section 76 may provide for specified provisions of the regulations not to apply in relation to an employee if any provision of his contract of employment—

(a) confers an entitlement to absence from work for the purpose of caring for a child, and

(b) incorporates or operates by reference to all or part of a collective agreement, or workforce agreement, of a kind specified in the regulations.

79 Supplemental

(1) Regulations under section 76 may, in particular—

(a) make provision about notices to be given and evidence to be produced by employees to employers, by employers to employees, and by employers to other employers;

(b) make provision requiring employers or employees to keep records;

(c) make provision about other procedures to be followed by employees and employers;

(d) make provision (including provision creating criminal offences) specifying the consequences of failure to give notices, to produce evidence, to keep records or to comply with other procedural requirements;

(e) make provision specifying the consequences of failure to act in accordance with a notice given by virtue of paragraph (a);

(f) make special provision for cases where an employee has a right which corresponds to a right conferred by the regulations and which arises under his contract of employment or otherwise;

(g) make provision applying, modifying or excluding an enactment, in such circumstances as may be specified and subject to any conditions specified, in relation to a person entitled to paternal leave;

(h) make different provision for different cases or circumstances.

(2) The regulations may make provision modifying the effect of Chapter II of Part XIV (calculation of a week's pay) in relation to an employee who is or has been absent from work on parental leave.

(3) Without prejudice to the generality of section 76, the regulations may make any provision which appears to the Secretary of State to be necessary or expedient—

(a) for the purpose of implementing Council Directive 96/34/EC on the framework agreement on parental leave, or

(b) for the purpose of dealing with any matter arising out of or related to the United Kingdom's obligations under that Directive.

80 Complaint to employment tribunal

(1) An employee may present a complaint to an employment tribunal that his employer—

(a) has unreasonably postponed a period of parental leave requested by the employee, or

(b) has prevented or attempted to prevent the employee from taking parental leave.

(2) An employment tribunal shall not consider a complaint under this … it is presented—

(a) before the end of the period of three months beginning with the … date) of the matters complained of, or

(b) within such further period as the tribunal considers reasonable in … it is satisfied that it was not reasonably practicable for the complaint to be presented before the end of that period of three months.

(3) Where an employment tribunal finds a complaint under this section well-founded it—

(a) shall make a declaration to that effect, and

(b) may make an award of compensation to be paid by the employer to the employee.

(4) The amount of compensation shall be such as the tribunal considers just and equitable in all the circumstances having regard to—

(a) the employer's behaviour, and

(b) any loss sustained by the employee which is attributable to the matters complained of.

81 to **85** [repealed]

PART IX
TERMINATION OF EMPLOYMENT

Minimum period of notice

86 Rights of employer and employee to minimum notice

(1) The notice required to be given by an employer to terminate the contract of employment of a person who has been continuously employed for one month or more—

(a) is not less than one week's notice if his period of continuous employment is less than two years,

(b) is not less than one week's notice for each year of continuous employment if his period of continuous employment is two years or more but less than twelve years, and

(c) is not less than twelve weeks' notice if his period of continuous employment is twelve years or more.

(2) The notice required to be given by an employee who has been continuously employed for one month or more to terminate his contract of employment is not less than one week.

(3) Any provision for shorter notice in any contract of employment with a person who has been continuously employed for one month or more has effect subject to subsections (1) and (2); but this section does not prevent either party from waiving his right to notice on any occasion or from accepting a payment in lieu of notice.

(4) Any contract of employment of a person who has been continuously employed for three months or more which is a contract for a term certain of one month or less shall have effect as if it were for an indefinite period; and, accordingly, subsections (1) and (2) apply to the contract.

(5) Subsections (1) and (2) do not apply to a contract made in contemplation of the performance of a specific task which is not expected to last for more than three months unless the employee has been continuously employed for a period of more than three months.

(6) This section does not affect any right of either party to a contract of employment to treat the contract as terminable without notice by reason of the conduct of the other party.

87 Rights of employee in period of notice

(1) If an employer gives notice to terminate the contract of employment of a person who has been continuously employed for one month or more, the provisions of sections 88 to 91 have effect as respects the liability of the employer for the period of notice required by section 86(1).

(2) If an employee who has been continuously employed for one month or more gives notice to terminate his contract of employment, the provisions of sections 88 to 91 have effect as respects the liability of the employer for the period of notice required by section 86(2).

(3) In sections 88 to 91 'period of notice' means—

(a) where notice is given by an employer, the period of notice required by section 86(1), and

(b) where notice is given by an employee, the period of notice required by section 86(2).

(4) This section does not apply in relation to a notice given by the employer or the employee if the notice to be given by the employer to terminate the contract must be at least one week more than the notice required by section 86(1).

88 Employments with normal working hours

(1) If an employee has normal working hours under the contract of employment in force during the period of notice and during any part of those normal working hours—

(a) the employee is ready and willing to work but no work is provided for him by his employer,

(b) the employee is incapable of work because of sickness or injury,

(c) the employee is absent from work wholly or partly because of pregnancy or childbirth or on parental leave, or

(d) the employee is absent from work in accordance with the terms of his employment relating to holidays,

the employer is liable to pay the employee for the part of normal working hours covered by any of paragraphs (a), (b), (c) and (d) a sum not less than the amount of remuneration for that part of normal working hours calculated at the average hourly rate of remuneration produced by dividing a week's pay by the number of normal working hours.

(2) Any payments made to the employee by his employer in respect of the relevant part of the period of notice (whether by way of sick pay, statutory sick pay, maternity pay, statutory maternity pay, holiday pay or otherwise) go towards meeting the employer's liability under this section.

(3) Where notice was given by the employee, the employer's liability under this section does not arise unless and until the employee leaves the service of the employer in pursuance of the notice.

89 Employments without normal working hours

(1) If an employee does not have normal working hours under the contract of employment in force in the period of notice, the employer is liable to pay the employee for each week of the period of notice a sum not less than a week's pay.

(2) The employer's liability under this section is conditional on the employee being ready and willing to do work of a reasonable nature and amount to earn a week's pay.

(3) Subsection (2) does not apply—

(a) in respect of any period during which the employee is incapable of work because of sickness or injury,

(b) in respect of any period during which the employee is absent from work wholly or partly because of pregnancy or childbirth or on parental leave, or

(c) in respect of any period during which the employee is absent from work in accordance with the terms of his employment relating to holidays.

(4) Any payment made to an employee by his employer in respect of a period within subsection (3) (whether by way of sick pay, statutory sick pay, maternity pay, statutory maternity pay, holiday pay or otherwise) shall be taken into account for the purposes of this section as if it were remuneration paid by the employer in respect of that period.

(5) Where notice was given by the employee, the employer's liability under this section does not arise unless and until the employee leaves the service of the employer in pursuance of the notice.

90 Short-term incapacity benefit and industrial injury benefit

(1) This section has effect where the arrangements in force relating to the employment are such that—

(a) payments by way of sick pay are made by the employer to employees to whom the arrangements apply, in cases where any such employees are incapable of work because of sickness or injury, and

(b) in calculating any payment so made to any such employee an amount representing, or treated as representing, short-term incapacity benefit or industrial injury benefit is taken into account, whether by way of deduction or by way of calculating the payment as a supplement to that amount.

(2) If—

(a) during any part of the period of notice the employee is incapable of work because of sickness or injury,

(b) one or more payments by way of sick pay are made to him by the employer in respect of that part of the period of notice, and

(c) in calculating any such payment such an amount as is referred to in paragraph (b) of subsection (1) is taken into account as mentioned in that paragraph,

for the purposes of section 88 or 89 the amount so taken into account shall be treated as having been paid by the employer to the employee by way of sick pay in respect of that part of that period, and shall go towards meeting the liability of the employer under that section accordingly.

91 Supplementary

(1) An employer is not liable under section 88 or 89 to make any payment in respect of a period during which an employee is absent from work with the leave of the employer granted at the request of the employee, including any period of time off taken in accordance with—

(a) Part VI of this Act, or

(b) section 168 or 170 of the Trade Union and Labour Relations (Consolidation) Act 1992 (trade union duties and activities).

(2) No payment is due under section 88 or 89 in consequence of a notice to terminate a contract given by an employee if, after the notice is given and on or before the termination of the contract, the employee takes part in a strike of employees of the employer.

(3) If, during the period of notice, the employer breaks the contract of employment, payments received under section 88 or 89 in respect of the part of the period after the breach go towards mitigating the damages recoverable by the employee for loss of earnings in that part of the period of notice.

(4) If, during the period of notice, the employee breaks the contract and the employer rightfully treats the breach as terminating the contract, no payment is due to the employee under section 88 or 89 in respect of the part of the period falling after the termination of the contract.

(5) If an employer fails to give the notice required by section 86, the rights conferred by sections 87 to 90 and this section shall be taken into account in assessing his liability for breach of the contract.

(6) Sections 86 to 90 and this section apply in relation to a contract all or any of the terms of which are terms which take effect by virtue of any provision contained in or having effect under an Act (whether public or local) as in relation to any other contract; and the reference in this subsection to an Act includes, subject to any express provision to the contrary, an Act passed after this Act.

Written statement of reasons for dismissal

92 Right to written statement of reasons for dismissal

(1) An employee is entitled to be provided by his employer with a written statement giving particulars of the reasons for the employee's dismissal—

(a) if the employee is given by the employer notice of termination of his contract of employment,

(b) if the employee's contract of employment is terminated by the employer without notice, or

(c) if the employee is employed under a contract for a fixed term and that term expires without being renewed under the same contract.

(2) Subject to subsection (4), an employee is entitled to a written statement under this section only if he makes a request for one; and a statement shall be provided within fourteen days of such a request.

(3) Subject to subsection (4), an employee is not entitled to a written statement under this section unless on the effective date of termination he has been, or will have been, continuously employed for a period of not less than one year ending with that date.

(4) An employee is entitled to a written statement under this section without having to request it and irrespective of whether she has been continuously employed for any period if she is dismissed—

(a) at any time while she is pregnant, or

(b) after childbirth in circumstances in which her ordinary or additional maternity leave period ends by reason of the dismissal.

(5) A written statement under this section is admissible in evidence in any proceedings.

(6) Subject to subsection (7), in this section 'the effective date of termination'—

(a) in relation to an employee whose contract of employment is terminated by notice, means the date on which the notice expires,

(b) in relation to an employee whose contract of employment is terminated without notice, means the date on which the termination takes effect, and

(c) in relation to an employee who is employed under a contract for a fixed term which expires without being renewed under the same contract, means the date on which the term expires.

(7) Where—

(a) the contract of employment is terminated by the employer, and

(b) the notice required by section 86 to be given by an employer would, if duly given on the material date, expire on a date later than the effective date of termination (as defined by subsection (6)),

the later date is the effective date of termination.

(8) In subsection (7)(b) 'the material date' means—

(a) the date when notice of termination was given by the employer, or

(b) where no notice was given, the date when the contract of employment was terminated by the employer.

93 Complaints to employment tribunal

(1) A complaint may be presented to an employment tribunal by an employee on the ground that—

(a) the employer unreasonably failed to provide a written statement under section 92, or

(b) the particulars of reasons given in purported compliance with that section are inadequate or untrue.

(2) Where an employment tribunal finds a complaint under this section well-founded, the tribunal—

(a) may make a declaration as to what it finds the employer's reasons were for dismissing the employee, and

(b) shall make an award that the employer pay to the employee a sum equal to the amount of two weeks' pay.

(3) An employment tribunal shall not consider a complaint under this section relating to the reasons for a dismissal unless it is presented to the tribunal at such a time that the tribunal would, in accordance with section 111, consider a complaint of unfair dismissal in respect of that dismissal presented at the same time.

PART X
UNFAIR DISMISSAL

CHAPTER I
RIGHT NOT TO BE UNFAIRLY DISMISSED

The right

94 The right

(1) An employee has the right not to be unfairly dismissed by his employer.

(2) Subsection (1) has effect subject to the following provisions of this Part (in particular sections 108 to 110) and to the provisions of the Trade Union and Labour Relations (Consolidation) Act 1992 (in particular sections 237 to 239).

Dismissal

95 Circumstances in which an employee is dismissed

(1) For the purposes of this Part an employee is dismissed by his employer if (and, subject to subsection (2) and section 96, only if)—

(a) the contract under which he is employed is terminated by the employer (whether with or without notice),

(b) he is employed under a contract for a fixed term and that term expires without being renewed under the same contract, or

(c) the employee terminates the contract under which he is employed (with or without notice) in circumstances in which he is entitled to terminate it without notice by reason of the employer's conduct.

(2) An employee shall be taken to be dismissed by his employer for the purposes of this Part if—

(a) the employer gives notice to the employee to terminate his contract of employment, and

(b) at a time within the period of that notice the employee gives notice to the employer to terminate the contract of employment on a date earlier than the date on which the employer's notice is due to expire;

and the reason for the dismissal is to be taken to be the reason for which the employer's notice is given.

96 [repealed]

97 Effective date of termination

(1) Subject to the following provisions of this section, in this Part 'the effective date of termination'—

(a) in relation to an employee whose contract of employment is terminated by notice, whether given by his employer or by the employee, means the date on which the notice expires,

(b) in relation to an employee whose contract of employment is terminated without notice, means the date on which the termination takes effect, and

(c) in relation to an employee who is employed under a contract for a fixed term which expires without being renewed under the same contract, means the date on which the term expires.

(2) Where—

(a) the contract of employment is terminated by the employer, and

(b) the notice required by section 86 to be given by an employer would, if duly given on the material date, expire on a date later than the effective date of termination (as defined by subsection (1)),

for the purposes of sections 108(1), 119(1) and 227(3) the later date is the effective date of termination.

(3) In subsection (2)(b) 'the material date' means—

(a) the date when notice of termination was given by the employer, or

(b) where no notice was given, the date when the contract of employment was terminated by the employer.

(4) Where—

(a) the contract of employment is terminated by the employee,

(b) the material date does not fall during a period of notice given by the employer to terminate that contract, and

(c) had the contract been terminated not by the employee but by notice given on the material date by the employer, that notice would have been required by section 86 to expire on a date later than the effective date of termination (as defined by subsection (1)),

for the purposes of sections 108(1), 119(1) and 227(3) the later date is the effective date of termination.

(5) In subsection (4) 'the material date' means—

(a) the date when notice of termination was given by the employee, or

(b) where no notice was given, the date when the contract of employment was terminated by the employee.

(6) [repealed]

Fairness

98 General

(1) In determining for the purposes of this Part whether the dismissal of an employee is fair or unfair, it is for the employer to show—

(a) the reason (or, if more than one, the principal reason) for the dismissal, and

(b) that it is either a reason falling within subsection (2) or some other substantial reason of a kind such as to justify the dismissal of an employee holding the position which the employee held.

(2) A reason falls within this subsection if it—

(a) relates to the capability or qualifications of the employee for performing work of the kind which he was employed by the employer to do,

(b) relates to the conduct of the employee,

(c) is that the employee was redundant, or

(d) is that the employee could not continue to work in the position which he held without contravention (either on his part or on that of his employer) of a duty or restriction imposed by or under an enactment.

(3) In subsection (2)(a)—

(a) 'capability', in relation to an employee, means his capability assessed by reference to skill, aptitude, health or any other physical or mental quality, and

(b) 'qualifications', in relation to an employee, means any degree, diploma or other academic, technical or professional qualification relevant to the position which he held.

(4) Where the employer has fulfilled the requirements of subsection (1), the determination of the question whether the dismissal is fair or unfair (having regard to the reason shown by the employer)—

(a) depends on whether in the circumstances (including the size and administrative resources of the employer's undertaking) the employer acted reasonably or unreasonably in treating it as a sufficient reason for dismissing the employee, and

(b) shall be determined in accordance with equity and the substantial merits of the case.

(5) [repealed]

(6) Subsection (4) is subject to—

(a) sections 99 to 107 of this Act, and

(b) sections 152, 153 and 238 of the Trade Union and Labour Relations (Consolidation) Act 1992 (dismissal on ground of trade union membership or activities or in connection with industrial action).

99 Leave for family reasons

(1) An employee who is dismissed shall be regarded for the purposes of this Part as unfairly dismissed if—

(a) the reason or principal reason for the dismissal is of a prescribed kind, or

(b) the dismissal takes place in prescribed circumstances.

(2) In this section 'prescribed' means prescribed by regulations made by the Secretary of State.

(3) A reason or set of circumstances prescribed under this section must relate to—

(a) pregnancy, childbirth or maternity,

(b) ordinary, compulsory or additional maternity leave,

(c) parental leave, or

(d) time off under section 57A;

and it may also relate to redundancy or other factors.

(4) A reason or set of circumstances prescribed under subsection (1) satisfies subsection (3)(c) or (d) if it relates to action which an employee—

(a) takes,

(b) agrees to take, or

(c) refuses to take,

under or in respect of a collective or workforce agreement which deals with parental leave.

(5) Regulations under this section may—

(a) make different provision for different cases or circumstances;

(b) apply any enactment, in such circumstances as may be specified, in relation to persons regarded as unfairly dismissed by reason of this section.

100 Health and safety cases

(1) An employee who is dismissed shall be regarded for the purposes of this Part as unfairly dismissed if the reason (or, if more than one, the principal reason) for the dismissal is that—

(a) having been designated by the employer to carry out activities in connection with preventing or reducing risks to health and safety at work, the employee carried out (or proposed to carry out) any such activities,

(b) being a representative of workers on matters of health and safety at work or member of a safety committee—

(i) in accordance with arrangements established under or by virtue of any enactment, or

(ii) by reason of being acknowledged as such by the employer, the employee performed (or proposed to perform) any functions as such a representative or a member of such a committee,

(ba) the employee took part (or proposed to take part) in consultation with the employer pursuant to the Health and Safety (Consultation with Employees) Regulations 1996 or in an election of representatives of employee safety within the meaning of those Regulations (whether as a candidate or otherwise),

(c) being an employee at a place where—

(i) there was no such representative or safety committee, or

(ii) there was such a representative or safety committee but it was not reasonably practicable for the employee to raise the matter by those means,

he brought to his employer's attention, by reasonable means, circumstances connected with his work which he reasonably believed were harmful or potentially harmful to health or safety,

(d) in circumstances of danger which the employee reasonably believed to be serious and imminent and which he could not reasonably have been expected to avert, he left (or proposed to leave) or (while the danger persisted) refused to return to his place of work or any dangerous part of his place of work, or

(e) in circumstances of danger which the employee reasonably believed to be serious and imminent, he took (or proposed to take) appropriate steps to protect himself or other persons from the danger.

(2) For the purposes of subsection (1)(e) whether steps which an employee took (or proposed to take) were appropriate is to be judged by reference to all the circumstances including, in particular, his knowledge and the facilities and advice available to him at the time.

(3) Where the reason (or, if more than one, the principal reason) for the dismissal of an employee is that specified in subsection (1)(e), he shall not be regarded as unfairly dismissed if the employer shows that it was (or would have been) so negligent for the employee to take the steps which he took (or proposed to take) that a reasonable employer might have dismissed him for taking (or proposing to take) them.

101 Shop workers and betting workers who refuse Sunday work

(1) Where an employee who is—

(a) a protected shop worker or an opted-out shop worker, or

(b) a protected betting worker or an opted-out betting worker,

is dismissed, he shall be regarded for the purposes of this Part as unfairly dismissed if the reason (or, if more than one, the principal reason) for the dismissal is that he refused (or proposed to refuse) to do shop work, or betting work, on Sunday or on a particular Sunday.

(2) Subsection (1) does not apply in relation to an opted-out shop worker or an opted-out betting worker where the reason (or principal reason) for the dismissal is that he refused (or proposed to refuse) to do shop work, or betting work, on any Sunday or Sundays falling before the end of the notice period.

(3) A shop worker or betting worker who is dismissed shall be regarded for the purposes of this Part as unfairly dismissed if the reason (or, if more than one, the principal reason) for the dismissal is that the shop worker or betting worker gave (or proposed to give) an opting-out notice to the employer.

(4) For the purposes of section 36(2)(b) or 41(1)(b), the appropriate date in relation to this section is the effective date of termination.

101A Working time cases

An employee who is dismissed shall be regarded for the purposes of this Part as unfairly dismissed if the reason (or, if more than one, the principal reason) for the dismissal is that the employee—

(a) refused (or proposed to refuse) to comply with a requirement which the employer imposed (or proposed to impose) in contravention of the Working Time Regulations 1998,

(b) refused (or proposed to refuse) to forgo a right conferred on him by those Regulations,

(c) failed to sign a workforce agreement for the purposes of those Regulations, or to enter into, or agree to vary or extend, any other agreement with his employer which is provided for in those Regulations, or

(d) being—

(i) a representative of members of the workforce for the purposes of Schedule 1 to those Regulations, or

(ii) a candidate in an election in which any person elected will, on being elected, be such a representative,

performed (or proposed to perform) any functions or activities as such a representative or candidate.

102 Trustees of occupational pension schemes

(1) An employee who is dismissed shall be regarded for the purposes of this Part as unfairly dismissed if the reason (or, if more than one, the principal reason) for the dismissal is that, being a trustee of a relevant occupational pension scheme which relates to his employment, the employee performed (or proposed to perform) any functions as such a trustee.

(2) In this section 'relevant occupational pension scheme' means an occupational pension scheme (as defined in section 1 of the Pension Schemes Act 1993) established under a trust.

103 Employee representatives

(1) An employee who is dismissed shall be regarded for the purposes of this Part as unfairly dismissed if the reason (or, if more than one, the principal reason) for the dismissal is that the employee, being—

(a) an employee representative for the purposes of Chapter II of Part IV of the Trade Union and Labour Relations (Consolidation) Act 1992 (redundancies) or Regulations 10 and 11 of the Transfer of Undertakings (Protection of Employment) Regulations 1981, or

(b) a candidate in an election in which any person elected will, on being elected, be such an employee representative,

performed (or proposed to perform) any functions or activities as such an employee representative or candidate.

(2) An employee who is dismissed shall be regarded for the purposes of this Part as unfairly dismissed if the reason (or, if more than one, the principal reason) for the dismissal is that the employee took part in an election of employee representatives for the purposes of Chapter II of Part IV of the Trade Union and Labour Relations (Consolidation) Act 1992 (redundancies) or Regulations 10 and 11 of the Transfer of Undertakings (Protection of Employment) Regulations 1981.

103A Protected disclosure

An employee who is dismissed shall be regarded for the purposes of this Part as unfairly dismissed if the reason (or, if more than one, the principal reason) for the dismissal is that the employee made a protected disclosure.

104 Assertion of statutory right

(1) An employee who is dismissed shall be regarded for the purposes of this Part as unfairly dismissed if the reason (or, if more than one, the principal reason) for the dismissal is that the employee—

(a) brought proceedings against the employer to enforce a right of his which is a relevant statutory right, or

(b) alleged that the employer had infringed a right of his which is a relevant statutory right.

(2) It is immaterial for the purposes of subsection (1)—

(a) whether or not the employee has the right, or

(b) whether or not the right has been infringed;

but, for that subsection to apply, the claim to the right and that it has been infringed must be made in good faith.

(3) It is sufficient for subsection (1) to apply that the employee, without specifying the right, made it reasonably clear to the employer what the right claimed to have been infringed was.

(4) The following are relevant statutory rights for the purposes of this section—

(a) any right conferred by this Act for which the remedy for its infringement is by way of a complaint or reference to an employment tribunal,

(b) the right conferred by section 86 of this Act,

(c) the rights conferred by sections 68, 86, 146, 168, 169 and 170 of the Trade Union and Labour Relations (Consolidation) Act 1992 (deductions from pay, union activities and time off), and

(d) the rights conferred by the Working Time Regulations 1998.

(5) In this section any reference to an employer includes, where the right in question is conferred by section 63A, the principal (within the meaning of section 63A(3)).

104A The national minimum wage

(1) An employee who is dismissed shall be regarded for the purposes of this Part as unfairly dismissed if the reason (or, if more than one, the principal reason) for the dismissal is that—

(a) any action was taken, or was proposed to be taken, by or on behalf of the employee with a view to enforcing, or otherwise securing the benefit of, a right of the employee's to which this section applies; or

(b) the employer was prosecuted for an offence under section 31 of the National Minimum Wage Act 1998 as a result of action taken by or on behalf of the employee for the purpose of enforcing, or otherwise securing the benefit of, a right of the employee's to which this section applies; or

(c) the employee qualifies, or will or might qualify, for the national minimum wage or for a particular rate of national minimum wage.

(2) It is immaterial for the purposes of paragraph (a) or (b) of subsection (1) above—

(a) whether or not the employee has the right, or

(b) whether or not the right has been infringed,

but, for that subsection to apply, the claim to the right and, if applicable, the claim that it has been infringed must be made in good faith.

(3) The following are the rights to which this section applies—

(a) any right conferred by, or by virtue of, any provision of the National Minimum Wage Act 1998 for which the remedy for its infringement is by way of a complaint to an employment tribunal; and

(b) any right conferred by section 17 of the National Minimum Wage Act 1998 (worker receiving less than national minimum wage entitled to additional remuneration).

104B Tax credit

(1) An employee who is dismissed shall be regarded for the purposes of this Part as unfairly dismissed if the reason (or, if more than one, the principal reason) for the dismissal is that—

(a) any action was taken, or was proposed to be taken, by or on behalf of the employee with a view to enforcing, or otherwise securing the benefit of, a right conferred on the employee by regulations under section 6(2)(a) or (c) of the Tax Credits Act 1999;

(b) a penalty was imposed on the employer, or proceedings for a penalty were brought against him, under section 9 of that Act, as a result of action taken by or on behalf of the employee for the purpose of enforcing, or otherwise securing the benefit of, such a right; or

(c) the employee is entitled, or will or may be entitled, to working families' tax credit or disabled person's tax credit.

(2) It is immaterial for the purposes of paragraph (a) or (b) of subsection (1) above—

(a) whether or not the employee has the right, or

(b) whether or not the right has been infringed,

but, for that subsection to apply, the claim to the right and, if applicable, the claim that it has been infringed must be made in good faith.

105 Redundancy

(1) An employee who is dismissed shall be regarded for the purposes of this Part as unfairly dismissed if—

(a) the reason (or, if more than-one, the principal reason) for the dismissal is that the employee was redundant,

(b) it is shown that the circumstances constituting the redundancy applied equally to one or more other employees in the same undertaking who held positions similar to that held by the employee and who have not been dismissed by the employer, and

(c) it is shown that any of subsections (2) to (7C) applies.

(2) [repealed]

(3) This subsection applies if the reason (or, if more than one, the principal reason) for which the employee was selected for dismissal was one of those specified in subsection (1) of section 100 (read with subsections (2) and (3) of that section).

(4) This subsection applies if either—

(a) the employee was a protected shop worker or an opted-out shop worker, or a protected betting worker or an opted-out betting worker, and the reason (or, if more than one, the principal reason) for which the employee was selected for dismissal was that specified in subsection (1) of section 101 (read with subsection (2) of that section), or

(b) the employee was a shop worker or a betting worker and the reason (or, if more than one, the principal reason) for which the employee was selected for dismissal was that specified in subsection (3) of that section.

(4A) This subsection applies if the reason (or, if more than one, the principal reason) for which the employee was selected for dismissal was one of those specified in section 101A.

(5) This subsection applies if the reason (or, if more than one, the principal reason) for which the employee was selected for dismissal was that specified in section 102(1).

(6) This subsection applies if the reason (or, if more than one, the principal reason) for which the employee was selected for dismissal was that specified in section 103.

(6A) This subsection applies if the reason (or, if more than one, the principal reason) for which the employee was selected for dismissal was that specified in section 103A.

(7) This subsection applies if the reason (or, if more than one, the principal reason) for which the employee was selected for dismissal was one of those specified in subsection (1) of section 104 (read with subsections (2) and (3) of that section).

(7A) This subsection applies if the reason (or, if more than one, the principal reason) for which the employee was selected for dismissal was one of those specified in subsection (1) of section 104A (read with subsection (2) of that section).

(7B) This subsection applies if the reason (or, if more than one, the principal reason) for which the employee has selected for dismissal was one of those specified in subsection (1) of section 104B (read with subsection (2) of that section).

(7C) This subsection applies if—

(a) the reason (or, if more than one, the principal reason) for which the employee was selected for dismissal was the reason mentioned in section 238A(2) of the Trade Union and Labour Relations (Consolidation) Act 1992 (participation in official industrial action), and

(b) subsection (3), (4) or (5) of that section applies to the dismissal.

(8) For the purposes of section 36(2)(b) or 41(1)(b), the appropriate date in relation to this section is the effective date of terrnination.

(9) In this Part 'redundancy case' means a case where paragraphs (a) and (b) of subsection (1) of this section are satisfied.

106 Replacements

(1) Where this section applies to an employee he shall be regarded for the purposes of section 98(1)(b) as having been dismissed for a substantial reason of a kind such as to justify the dismissal of an employee holding the position which the employee held.

(2) This section applies to an employee where—

(a) on engaging him the employer informs him in writing that his employment will be terminated on the resumption of work by another employee who is, or will be, absent wholly or partly because of pregnancy or childbirth, and

(b) the employer dismisses him in order to make it possible to give work to the other employee.

(3) This section also applies to an employee where—

(a) on engaging him the employer informs him in writing that his employment will be terminated on the end of a suspension of another employee from work on medical grounds or maternity grounds (within the meaning of Part VII), and

(b) the employer dismisses him in order to make it possible to allow the resumption of work by the other employee.

(4) Subsection (1) does not affect the operation of section 98(4) in a case to which this section applies.

107 Pressure on employer to dismiss unfairly

(1) This section applies where there falls to be determined for the purposes of this Part a question—

(a) as to the reason, or principal reason, for which an employee was dismissed,

(b) whether the reason or principal reason for which an employee was dismissed was a reason fulfilling the requirement of section 98(1)(b), or

(c) whether an employer acted reasonably in treating the reason or principal reason for which an employee was dismissed as a sufficient reason for dismissing him.

(2) In determining the question no account shall be taken of any pressure which by calling, organising, procuring or financing a strike or other industrial action, or threatening to do so, was exercised on the employer to dismiss the employee; and the question shall be determined as if no such pressure had been exercised.

Exclusion of right

108 Qualifying period of employment

(1) Section 94 does not apply to the dismissal of an employee unless he has been continuously employed for a period of not less than one year ending with the effective date of termination.

(2) If an employee is dismissed by reason of any such requirement or recommendation as is referred to in section 64(2), subsection (1) has effect in relation to that dismissal as if for the words 'one year' there were substituted the words 'one month'.

(3) Subsection (1) does not apply if—

(a) [repealed]

(b) subsection (1) of section 99 (read with subsection (2) of that section) or subsection (3) of that section applies,

(c) subsection (1) of section 100 (read with subsections (2) and (3) of that section) applies,

(d) subsection (1) of section 101 (read with subsection (2) of that section) or subsection (3) of that section applies,

(dd) section 101A applies,

(e) section 102 applies,

(f) section 103 applies,

(ff) section 103A applies,

(g) subsection (1) of section 104 (read with subsections (2) and (3) of that section) applies,

(gg) subsection (1) of section 104A (read with subsection (2) of that section) applies,

(gh) subsection (1) of section 104B (read with subsection (2) of that section) applies, or

(h) section 105 applies.

109 Upper age limit

(1) Section 94 does not apply to the dismissal of an employee if on or before the effective date of termination he has attained—

(a) in a case where—

(i) in the undertaking in which the employee was employed there was a normal retiring age for an employee holding the position held by the employee, and

(ii) the age was the same whether the employee holding that position was a man or a woman,

that normal retiring age, and

(b) in any other case, the age of sixty-five.

(2) Subsection (1) does not apply if—

(a) [repealed]

(b) subsection (1) of section 99 (read with subsection (2) of that section) or subsection (3) of that section applies,

(c) subsection (1) of section 100 (read with subsections (2) and (3) of that section) applies,

(d) subsection (1) of section 101 (read with subsection (2) of that section) or subsection (3) of that section applies,

(dd) section 101A applies,

(e) section 102 applies,

(f) section 103 applies,

(ff) section 103A applies,

(g) subsection (1) of section 104 (read with subsections (2) and (3) of that section) applies,

(gg) subsection (1) of section 104A (read with subsection (2) of that section) applies,

(gh) subsection (1) of section 104B (read with subsection (2) of that section) applies, or

(h) section 105 applies.

110 [omitted]

CHAPTER II
REMEDIES FOR UNFAIR DISMISSAL

Introductory

111 Complaints to employment tribunal

(1) A complaint may be presented to an employment tribunal against an employer by any person that he was unfairly dismissed by the employer.

(2) Subject to subsection (3), an employment tribunal shall not consider a complaint under this section unless it is presented to the tribunal—

(a) before the end of the period of three months beginning with the effective date of termination, or

(b) within such further period as the tribunal considers reasonable in a case where it is satisfied that it was not reasonably practicable for the complaint to be presented before the end of that period of three months.

(3) Where a dismissal is with notice, an employment tribunal shall consider a complaint under this section if it is presented after the notice is given but before the effective date of termination.

(4) In relation to a complaint which is presented as mentioned in subsection (3), the provisions of this Act, so far as they relate to unfair dismissal, have effect as if—

(a) references to a complaint by a person that he was unfairly dismissed by his employer included references to a complaint by a person that his employer has given him notice in such circumstances that he will be unfairly dismissed when the notice expires,

(b) references to reinstatement included references to the withdrawal of the notice by the employer,

(c) references to the effective date of termination included references to the date which would be the effective date of termination on the expiry of the notice, and

(d) references to an employee ceasing to be employed included references to an employee having been given notice of dismissal.

112 The remedies: orders and compensation

(1) This section applies where, on a complaint under section 111, an employment tribunal finds that the grounds of the complaint are well-founded.

(2) The tribunal shall—

(a) explain to the complainant what orders may be made under section 113 and in what circumstances they may be made, and

(b) ask him whether he wishes the tribunal to make such an order.

(3) If the complainant expresses such a wish, the tribunal may make an order under section 113.

(4) If no order is made under section 113, the tribunal shall make an award of compensation for unfair dismissal (calculated in accordance with sections 118 to 127A) to be paid by the employer to the employee.

Orders for reinstatement or re-engagement

113 The orders

An order under this section may be—

(a) an order for reinstatement (in accordance with section 114), or

(b) an order for re-engagement (in accordance with section 115),

as the tribunal may decide.

114 Order for reinstatement

(1) An order for reinstatement is an order that the employer shall treat the complainant in all respects as if he had not been dismissed.

(2) On making an order for reinstatement the tribunal shall specify—

(a) any amount payable by the employer in respect of any benefit which the complainant might reasonably be expected to have had but for the dismissal (including arrears of pay) for the period between the date of termination of employment and the date of reinstatement,

(b) any rights and privileges (including seniority and pension rights) which must be restored to the employee, and

(c) the date by which the order must be complied with.

(3) If the complainant would have benefited from an improvement in his terms and conditions of employment had he not been dismissed, an order for reinstatement shall require him to be treated as if he had benefited from that improvement from the date on which he would have done so but for being dismissed.

(4) In calculating for the purposes of subsection (2)(a) any amount payable by the employer, the tribunal shall take into account, so as to reduce the employer's liability, any sums received by the complainant in respect of the period between the date of termination of employment and the date of reinstatement by way of—

(a) wages in lieu of notice or ex gratia payments paid by the employer, or

(b) remuneration paid in respect of employment with another employer,

and such other benefits as the tribunal thinks appropriate in the circumstances.

(5) [repealed]

115 Order for re-engagement

(1) An order for re-engagement is an order, on such terms as the tribunal may decide, that the complainant be engaged by the employer, or by a successor of the employer or by an associated employer, in employment comparable to that from which he was dismissed or other suitable employment.

(2) On making an order for re-engagement the tribunal shall specify the terms on which re-engagement is to take place, including—

(a) the identity of the employer,

(b) the nature of the employment,

(c) the remuneration for the employment,

(d) any amount payable by the employer in respect of any benefit which the complainant might reasonably be expected to have had but for the dismissal (including arrears of pay) for the period between the date of termination of employment and the date of re-engagement,

(e) any rights and privileges (including seniority and pension rights) which must be restored to the employee, and

(f) the date by which the order must be complied with.

(3) In calculating for the purposes of subsection (2)(d) any amount payable by the employer, the tribunal shall take into account, so as to reduce the employer's liability, any sums received by the complainant in respect of the period between the date of termination of employment and the date of re-engagement by way of—

(a) wages in lieu of notice or ex gratia payments paid by the employer, or

(b) remuneration paid in respect of employment with another employer,

and such other benefits as the tribunal thinks appropriate in the circumstances.

(4) [repealed]

116 Choice of order and its terms

(1) In exercising its discretion under section 113 the tribunal shall first consider whether to make an order for reinstatement and in so doing shall take into account—

(a) whether the complainant wishes to be reinstated,

(b) whether it is practicable for the employer to comply with an order for reinstatement, and

(c) where the complainant caused or contributed to some extent to the dismissal, whether it would be just to order his reinstatement.

(2) If the tribunal decides not to make an order for reinstatement it shall then consider whether to make an order for re-engagement and, if so, on what terms.

(3) In so doing the tribunal shall take into account—

(a) any wish expressed by the complainant as to the nature of the order to be made,

(b) whether it is practicable for the employer (or a successor or an associated employer) to comply with an order for re-engagement, and

(c) where the complainant caused or contributed to some extent to the dismissal, whether it would be just to order his re-engagement and (if so) on what terms.

(4) Except in a case where the tribunal takes into account contributory fault under subsection (3)(c) it shall, if it orders re-engagement, do so on terms which are, so far as is reasonably practicable, as favourable as an order for reinstatement.

(5) Where in any case an employer has engaged a permanent replacement for a dismissed employee, the tribunal shall not take that fact into account in determining, for the purposes of subsection (1)(b) or (3)(b), whether it is practicable to comply with an order for reinstatement or re-engagement.

(6) Subsection (5) does not apply where the employer shows—

(a) that it was not practicable for him to arrange for the dismissed employee's work to be done without engaging a permanent replacement, or

(b) that—

(i) he engaged the replacement after the lapse of a reasonable period, without having heard from the dismissed employee that he wished to be reinstated or re-engaged, and

(ii) when the employer engaged the replacement it was no longer reasonable for him to arrange for the dismissed employee's work to be done except by a permanent replacement.

117 Enforcement of order and compensation

(1) An employment tribunal shall make an award of compensation, to be paid by the employer to the employee, if—

(a) an order under section 113 is made and the complainant is reinstated or re-engaged, but

(b) the terms of the order are not fully complied with.

(2) Subject to section 124, the amount of the compensation shall be such as the tribunal thinks fit having regard to the loss sustained by the complainant in consequence of the failure to comply fully with the terms of the order.

(3) Subject to subsections (1) and (2), if an order under section 113 is made but the complainant is not reinstated or re-engaged in accordance with the order, the tribunal shall make—

(a) an award of compensation for unfair dismissal (calculated in accordance with sections 118 to 127A), and

(b) except where this paragraph does not apply, an additional award of compensation of an amount not less than twenty-six nor more than fifty-two weeks' pay,

to be paid by the employer to the employee.

(4) Subsection (3)(b) does not apply where—

(a) the employer satisfies the tribunal that it was not practicable to comply with the order,

(b) [repealed]

(5) and (6) [repealed]

(7) Where in any case an employer has engaged a permanent replacement for a dismissed employee, the tribunal shall not take that fact into account in determining for the purposes of subsection (4)(a) whether it was practicable to comply with the order for reinstatement or re-engagement unless the employer shows that it was not

practicable for him to arrange for the dismissed employee's work to be done without engaging a permanent replacement.

(8) Where in any case an employment tribunal finds that the complainant has unreasonably prevented an order under section 113 from being complied with, in making an award of compensation for unfair dismissal it shall take that conduct into account as a failure on the part of the complainant to mitigate his loss.

Compensation

118 General

(1) Where a tribunal makes an award of compensation for unfair dismissal under section 112(4) or 117(3)(a) the award shall consist of—

(a) a basic award (calculated in accordance with sections 119 to 122 and 126), and

(b) a compensatory award (calculated in accordance with sections 123, 124, 126 and 127A(1), (3) and (4)).

(2) and (3) [repealed]

(4) Where section 127A(2) applies, the award shall also include a supplementary award.

119 Basic award

(1) Subject to the provisions of this section, sections 120 to 122 and section 126, the amount of the basic award shall be calculated by—

(a) determining the period, ending with the effective date of termination, during which the employee has been continuously employed,

(b) reckoning backwards from the end of that period the number of years of employment falling within that period, and

(c) allowing the appropriate amount for each of those years of employment.

(2) In subsection (1)(c) 'the appropriate amount' means—

(a) one and a half weeks' pay for a year of employment in which the employee was not below the age of forty-one,

(b) one week's pay for a year of employment (not within paragraph (a)) in which he was not below the age of twenty-two, and

(c) half a week's pay for a year of employment not within paragraph (a) or (b).

(3) Where twenty years of employment have been reckoned under subsection (1), no account shall be taken under that subsection of any year of employment earlier than those twenty years.

(4) Where the effective date of termination is after the sixty-fourth anniversary of the day of the employee's birth, the amount arrived at under subsections (1) to (3) shall be reduced by the appropriate fraction.

(5) In subsection (4) 'the appropriate fraction' means the fraction of which—

(a) the numerator is the number of whole months reckoned from the sixty-fourth anniversary of the day of the employee's birth in the period beginning with that anniversary and ending with the effective date of termination, and

(b) the denominator is twelve.

(6) [repealed]

120 Basic award: minimum in certain cases

(1) The amount of the basic award (before any reduction under section 122) shall not be less than £2,900 where the reason (or, if more than one, the principal reason)—

(a) in a redundancy case, for selecting the employee for dismissal, or

(b) otherwise, for the dismissal,

is one of those specified in section 100(1)(a) and (b), 101A(d), 102(1) or 103.

(2) [repealed]

121 Basic award of two weeks' pay in certain cases

The amount of the basic award shall be two weeks' pay where the tribunal finds that the reason (or, where there is more than one, the principal reason) for the dismissal of the employee is that he was redundant and the employee—

(a) by virtue of section 138 is not regarded as dismissed for the purposes of Part XI, or

(b) by virtue of section 141 is not, or (if he were otherwise entitled) would not be, entitled to a redundancy payment.

122 Basic award: reductions

(1) Where the tribunal finds that the complainant has unreasonably refused an offer by the employer which (if accepted) would have the effect of reinstating the complainant in his employment in all respects as if he had not been dismissed, the tribunal shall reduce or further reduce the amount of the basic award to such extent as it considers just and equitable having regard to that finding.

(2) Where the tribunal considers that any conduct of the complainant before the dismissal (or, where the dismissal was with notice, before the notice was given) was such that it would be just and equitable to reduce or further reduce the amount of the basic award to any extent, the tribunal shall reduce or further reduce that amount accordingly.

(3) Subsection (2) does not apply in a redundancy case unless the reason for selecting the employee for dismissal was one of those specified in section 100(1)(a) and (b), 101A(d), 102(1) or 103; and in such a case subsection (2) applies only to so much of the basic award as is payable because of section 120.

(3A) Where the complainant has been awarded any amount in respect of the dismissal under a designated dismissal procedures agreement, the tribunal shall reduce or further reduce the amount of the basic award to such extent as it considers just and equitable having regard to that award.

(4) The amount of the basic award shall be reduced or further reduced by the amount of—

(a) any redundancy payment awarded by the tribunal under Part XI in respect of the same dismissal, or

(b) any payment made by the employer to the employee on the ground that the dismissal was by reason of redundancy (whether in pursuance of Part XI or otherwise).

123 Compensatory award

(1) Subject to the provisions of this section and sections 124, 126, 127 and 127A(1), (3) and (4), the amount of the compensatory award shall be such amount as the tribunal considers just and equitable in all the circumstances having regard to the loss sustained by the complainant in consequence of the dismissal in so far as that loss is attributable to action taken by the employer.

(2) The loss referred to in subsection (1) shall be taken to include—

(a) any expenses reasonably incurred by the complainant in consequence of the dismissal, and

(b) subject to subsection (3), loss of any benefit which he might reasonably be expected to have had but for the dismissal.

(3) The loss referred to in subsection (1) shall be taken to include in respect of any loss of—

(a) any entitlement or potential entitlement to a payment on account of dismissal by reason of redundancy (whether in pursuance of Part XI or otherwise), or

(b) any expectation of such a payment,

only the loss referable to the amount (if any) by which the amount of that payment would have exceeded the amount of a basic award (apart from any reduction under section 122) in respect of the same dismissal.

(4) In ascertaining the loss referred to in subsection (1) the tribunal shall apply the same rule concerning the duty of a person to mitigate his loss as applies to damages recoverable under the common law of England and Wales or (as the case may be) Scotland.

(5) In determining, for the purposes of subsection (1), how far any loss sustained by the complainant was attributable to action taken by the employer, no account shall be taken of any pressure which by—

(a) calling, organising, procuring or financing a strike or other industrial action, or

(b) threatening to do so,

was exercised on the employer to dismiss the employee; and that question shall be determined as if no such pressure had been exercised.

(6) Where the tribunal finds that the dismissal was to any extent caused or contributed to by any action of the complainant, it shall reduce the amount of the compensatory award by such proportion as it considers just and equitable having regard to that finding.

(7) If the amount of any payment made by the employer to the employee on the ground that the dismissal was by reason of redundancy (whether in pursuance of Part XI or otherwise) exceeds the amount of the basic award which would be payable but for section 122(4), that excess goes to reduce the amount of the compensatory award.

124 Limit of compensatory award etc.

(1) The amount of—

(a) any compensation awarded to a person under section 117(1) and (2), or

(b) a compensatory award to a person calculated in accordance with section 123,

shall not exceed £50,000.

(1A) Subsection (1) shall not apply to compensation awarded, or a compensatory award made, to a person in a case where he is regarded as unfairly dismissed by virtue of section 100, 103A, 105(3) or 105(6A).

(2) [repealed]

(3) In the case of compensation awarded to a person under section 117(1) and (2), the limit imposed by this section may be exceeded to the extent necessary to enable the award fully to reflect the amount specified as payable under section 114(2)(a) or section 115(2)(d).

(4) Where—

(a) a compensatory award is an award under paragraph (a) of subsection (3) of section 117, and

(b) an additional award falls to be made under paragraph (b) of that subsection,

the limit imposed by this section on the compensatory award may be exceeded to the extent necessary to enable the aggregate of the compensatory and additional awards fully to reflect the amount specified as payable under section 114(2)(a) or section 115(2)(d).

(5) The limit imposed by this section applies to the amount which the employment tribunal would, apart from this section, award in respect of the subject matter of the complaint after taking into account—

(a) any payment made by the respondent to the complainant in respect of that matter, and

(b) any reduction in the amount of the award required by any enactment or rule of law.

125 [repealed]

126 Acts which are both unfair dismissal and discrimination

(1) This section applies where compensation falls to be awarded in respect of any act both under—

(a) the provisions of this Act relating to unfair dismissal, and

(b) any one or more of the Sex Discrimination Act 1975, the Race Relations Act 1976 and the Disability Discrimination Act 1995.

(2) An employment tribunal shall not award compensation under any one of those Acts in respect of any loss or other matter which is or has been taken into account under any other of them, by the tribunal (or another employment tribunal) in awarding compensation on the same or another complaint in respect of that act.

127 [repealed]

127A Internal appeal procedures

(1) Where in a case in which an award of compensation for unfair dismissal falls to be made under section 112(4) or 117(3)(a) the tribunal finds that—

(a) the employer provided a procedure for appealing against dismissal, and

(b) the complainant was, at the time of the dismissal or within a reasonable period afterwards, given written notice stating that the employer provided the procedure and including details of it, but

(c) the complainant did not appeal against the dismissal under the procedure (otherwise than because the employer prevented him from doing so),

the tribunal shall reduce the compensatory award included in the award of compensation for unfair dismissal by such amount (if any) as it considers just and equitable.

(2) Where in a case in which an award of compensation for unfair dismissal falls to be made under section 112(4) or 117(3)(a) the tribunal finds that—

(a) the employer provided a procedure for appealing against dismissal, but

(b) the employer prevented the complainant from appealing against the dismissal under the procedure,

the award of compensation for unfair dismissal shall include a supplementary award of such amount (if any) as the tribunal considers just and equitable.

(3) In determining the amount of a reduction under subsection (1) or a supplementary award under subsection (2) the tribunal shall have regard to all the circumstances of the case, including in particular the chances that an appeal under the procedure provided by the employer would have been successful.

(4) The amount of such a reduction or supplementary award shall not exceed the amount of two weeks' pay.

127B [repealed]

Interim relief

128 Interim relief pending determination of complaint

(1) An employee who presents a complaint to an employment tribunal—

(a) that he has been unfairly dismissed by his employer, and

(b) that the reason (or, if more than one, the principal reason) for the dismissal is one of those specified in section 100(1)(a) and (b), 101A(d), 102(1), 103 or 103A, or in paragraph 161(2) Schedule A1 to the Trade Union and Labour Relations Consolidation Act 1992,

may apply to the tribunal for interim relief.

(2) The tribunal shall not entertain an application for interim relief unless it is presented to the tribunal before the end of the period of seven days immediately following the effective date of termination (whether before, on or after that date).

(3) The tribunal shall determine the application for interim relief as soon as practicable after receiving the application.

(4) The tribunal shall give to the employer not later than seven days before the date of the hearing a copy of the application together with notice of the date, time and place of the hearing.

(5) The tribunal shall not exercise any power it has of postponing the hearing of an application for interim relief except where it is satisfied that special circumstances exist which justify it in doing so.

129 Procedure on hearing of application and making of order

(1) This section applies where, on hearing an employee's application for interim relief, it appears to the tribunal that it is likely that on determining the complaint to which the application relates the tribunal will find that the reason (or, if more than one, the principal reason) for his dismissal is one of those specified in section 100(1)(a) and (b), 101A(d), 102(1), 103 or 103A or in paragraph 161(2) Schedule A1 to the Trade Union and Labour Relations Consolidation Act 1992.

(2) The tribunal shall announce its findings and explain to both parties (if present)—

(a) what powers the tribunal may exercise on the application, and

(b) in what circumstances it will exercise them.

(3) The tribunal shall ask the employer (if present) whether he is willing, pending the determination or settlement of the complaint—

(a) to reinstate the employee (that is, to treat him in all respects as if he had not been dismissed), or

(b) if not, to re-engage him in another job on terms and conditions not less favourable than those which would have been applicable to him if he had not been dismissed.

(4) For the purposes of subsection (3)(b) 'terms and conditions not less favourable than those which would have been applicable to him if he had not been dismissed' means, as regards seniority, pension rights and other similar rights, that the period prior to the dismissal should be regarded as continuous with his employment following the dismissal.

(5) If the employer states that he is willing to reinstate the employee, the tribunal shall make an order to that effect.

(6) If the employer—

(a) states that he is willing to re-engage the employee in another job, and

(b) specifies the terms and conditions on which he is willing to do so,

the tribunal shall ask the employee whether he is willing to accept the job on those terms and conditions.

(7) If the employee is willing to accept the job on those terms and conditions, the tribunal shall make an order to that effect.

(8) If the employee is not willing to accept the job on those terms and conditions—

(a) where the tribunal is of the opinion that the refusal is reasonable, the tribunal shall make an order for the continuation of his contract of employment, and

(b) otherwise, the tribunal shall make no order.

(9) If on the hearing of an application for interim relief the employer—

(a) fails to attend before the tribunal, or

(b) states that he is unwilling either to reinstate or re-engage the employee as mentioned in subsection (3),

the tribunal shall make an order for the continuation of the employee's contract of employment.

130 Order for continuation of contract of employment

(1) An order under section 129 for the continuation of a contract of employment is an order that the contract of employment continue in force—

(a) for the purposes of pay or any other benefit derived from the employment, seniority, pension rights and other similar matters, and

(b) for the purposes of determining for any purpose the period for which the employee has been continuously employed, from the date of its termination (whether before or after the making of the order) until the determination or settlement of the complaint.

(2) Where the tribunal makes such an order it shall specify in the order the amount which is to be paid by the employer to the employee by way of pay in respect of each normal pay period, or part of any such period, falling between the date of dismissal and the determination or settlement of the complaint.

(3) Subject to the following provisions, the amount so specified shall be that which the employee could reasonably have been expected to earn during that period, or part, and shall be paid—

(a) in the case of a payment for any such period falling wholly or partly after the making of the order, on the normal pay day for that period, and

(b) in the case of a payment for any past period, within such time as may be specified in the order.

(4) If an amount is payable in respect only of part of a normal pay period, the amount shall be calculated by reference to the whole period and reduced proportionately.

(5) Any payment made to an employee by an employer under his contract of employment, or by way of damages for breach of that contract, in respect of a normal pay period, or part of any such period, goes towards discharging the employer's liability in respect of that period under subsection (2); and, conversely, any payment under that subsection in respect of a period goes towards discharging any liability of the employer under, or in respect of breach of, the contract of employment in respect of that period.

(6) If an employee, on or after being dismissed by his employer, receives a lump sum which, or part of which, is in lieu of wages but is not referable to any normal pay period, the tribunal shall take the payment into account in determining the amount of pay to be payable in pursuance of any such order.

(7) For the purposes of this section, the amount which an employee could reasonably have been expected to earn, his normal pay period and the normal pay day for each such period shall be determined as if he had not been dismissed.

131 Application for variation or revocation of order

(1) At any time between—

(a) the making of an order under section 129, and

(b) the determination or settlement of the complaint,

the employer or the employee may apply to an employment tribunal for the revocation or variation of the order on the ground of a relevant change of circumstances since the making of the order.

(2) Sections 128 and 129 apply in relation to such an application as in relation to an original application for interim relief except that, in the case of an application by the employer, section 128(4) has effect with the substitution of a reference to the employee for the reference to the employer.

132 Consequence of failure to comply with order

(1) If, on the application of an employee, an employment tribunal is satisfied that the employer has not complied with the terms of an order for the reinstatement or re-engagement of the employee under section 129(5) or (7), the tribunal shall—

(a) make an order for the continuation of the employee's contract of employment, and

(b) order the employer to pay compensation to the employee.

(2) Compensation under subsection (1)(b) shall be of such amount as the tribunal considers just and equitable in all the circumstances having regard—

(a) to the infringement of the employee's right to be reinstated or re-engaged in pursuance of the order, and

(b) to any loss suffered by the employee in consequence of the non-compliance.

(3) Section 130 applies to an order under subsection (1)(a) as in relation to an order under section 129.

(4) If on the application of an employee an employment tribunal is satisfied that the employer has not complied with the terms of an order for the continuation of a contract of employment subsection (5) or (6) applies.

(5) Where the non-compliance consists of a failure to pay an amount by way of pay specified in the order—

(a) the tribunal shall determine the amount owed by the employer on the date of the determination, and

(b) if on that date the tribunal also determines the employee's complaint that he has been unfairly dismissed, it shall specify that amount separately from any other sum awarded to the employee.

(6) In any other case, the tribunal shall order the employer to pay the employee such compensation as the tribunal considers just and equitable in all the circumstances having regard to any loss suffered by the employee in consequence of the non-compliance.

CHAPTER III
SUPPLEMENTARY

133 Death of employer or employee

(1) Where—

(a) an employer has given notice to an employee to terminate his contract of employment, and

(b) before that termination the employee or the employer dies,

this Part applies as if the contract had been duly terminated by the employer by notice expiring on the date of the death.

(2) Where—

(a) an employee's contract of employment has been terminated,

(b) by virtue of subsection (2) or (4) of section 97 a date later than the effective date of termination as defined in subsection (1) of that section is to be treated for certain purposes as the effective date of termination, and

(c) the employer or the employee dies before that date,

subsection (2) or (4) of section 97 applies as if the notice referred to in that subsection as required by section 86 expired on the date of the death.

(3) Where an employee has died, sections 113 to 116 do not apply; and, accordingly, if the employment tribunal finds that the grounds of the complaint are well-founded, the case shall be treated as falling within section 112(4) as a case in which no order is made under section 113.

(4) Subsection (3) does not prejudice an order for reinstatement or re-engagement made before the employee's death.

(5) Where an order for reinstatement or re-engagement has been made and the employee dies before the order is complied with—

(a) if the employer has before the death refused to reinstate or re-engage the employee in accordance with the order, subsections (3) to (6) of section 117 apply, and an award shall be made under subsection (3)(b) of that section, unless the employer satisfies the tribunal that it was not practicable at the time of the refusal to comply with the order, and

(b) if there has been no such refusal, subsections (1) and (2) of that section apply if the employer fails to comply with any ancillary terms of the order which remain capable of fulfilment after the employee's death as they would apply to such a failure to comply fully with the terms of an order where the employee had been reinstated or re-engaged.

134 and **134A** [omitted]

PART XI
REDUNDANCY PAYMENTS ETC.

CHAPTER I
RIGHT TO REDUNDANCY PAYMENT

135 The right

(1) An employer shall pay a redundancy payment to any employee of his if the employee—

(a) is dismissed by the employer by reason of redundancy, or

(b) is eligible for a redundancy payment by reason of being laid off or kept on short-time.

(2) Subsection (1) has effect subject to the following provisions of this Part (including, in particular, sections 140 to 144, 149 to 152, 155 to 161 and 164).

CHAPTER II
RIGHT ON DISMISSAL BY REASON OF REDUNDANCY

Dismissal by reason of redundancy

136 Circumstances in which an employee is dismissed

(1) Subject to the provisions of this section and sections 137 and 138, for the purposes of this Part an employee is dismissed by his employer if (and only if)—

(a) the contract under which he is employed by the employer is terminated by the employer (whether with or without notice),

(b) he is employed under a contract for a fixed term and that term expires without being renewed under the same contract, or

(c) the employee terminates the contract under which he is employed (with or without notice) in circumstances in which he is entitled to terminate it without notice by reason of the employer's conduct.

(2) Subsection (1)(c) does not apply if the employee terminates the contract without notice in circumstances in which he is entitled to do so by reason of a lock-out by the employer.

(3) An employee shall be taken to be dismissed by his employer for the purposes of this Part if—

(a) the employer gives notice to the employee to terminate his contract of employment, and

(b) at a time within the obligatory period of notice the employee gives notice in writing to the employer to terminate the contract of employment on a date earlier than the date on which the employer's notice is due to expire.

(4) In this Part the 'obligatory period of notice', in relation to notice given by an employer to terminate an employee's contract of employment, means—

(a) the actual period of the notice in a case where the period beginning at the time when the notice is given and ending at the time when it expires is equal to the minimum period which (by virtue of any enactment or otherwise) is required to be given by the employer to terminate the contract of employment, and

(b) the period which—

(i) is equal to the minimum period referred to in paragraph (a), and

(ii) ends at the time when the notice expires,

in any other case.

(5) Where in accordance with any enactment or rule of law—

(a) an act on the part of an employer, or

(b) an event affecting an employer (including, in the case of an individual, his death), operates to terminate a contract under which an employee is employed by him, the act or event shall be taken for the purposes of this Part to be a termination of the contract by the employer.

137 [repealed]

138 No dismissal in cases of renewal of contract or re-engagement

(1) Where—

(a) an employee's contract of employment is renewed, or he is re-engaged under a new contract of employment in pursuance of an offer (whether in writing or not) made before the end of his employment under the previous contract, and

(b) the renewal or re-engagement takes effect either immediately on, or after an interval of not more than four weeks after, the end of that employment, the employee shall not be regarded for the purposes of this Part as dismissed by his employer by reason of the ending of his employment under the previous contract.

(2) Subsection (1) does not apply if—

(a) the provisions of the contract as renewed, or of the new contract, as to—

(i) the capacity and place in which the employee is employed, and

(ii) the other terms and conditions of his employment, differ (wholly or in part) from the corresponding provisions of the previous contract, and

(b) during the period specified in subsection (3)—

(i) the employee (for whatever reason) terminates the renewed or new contract, or gives notice to terminate it and it is in consequence terminated, or

(ii) the employer, for a reason connected with or arising out of any difference between the renewed or new contract and the previous contract, terminates the renewed or new contract, or gives notice to terminate it and it is in consequence terminated.

(3) The period referred to in subsection (2)(b) is the period—

(a) beginning at the end of the employee's employment under the previous contract, and

(b) ending with—

(i) the period of four weeks beginning with the date on which the employee starts work under the renewed or new contract, or

(ii) such longer period as may be agreed in accordance with subsection (6) for the purpose of retraining the employee for employment under that contract;

and is in this Part referred to as the 'trial period'.

(4) Where subsection (2) applies, for the purposes of this Part—

(a) the employee shall be regarded as dismissed on the date on which his employment under the previous contract (or, if there has been more than one trial period, the original contract) ended, and

(b) the reason for the dismissal shall be taken to be the reason for which the employee was then dismissed, or would have been dismissed had the offer (or original offer) of renewed or new employment not been made, or the reason which resulted in that offer being made.

(5) Subsection (2) does not apply if the employee's contract of employment is again renewed, or he is again re-engaged under a new contract of employment, in circumstances such that subsection (1) again applies.

(6) For the purposes of subsection (3)(b)(ii) a period of retraining is agreed in accordance with this subsection only if the agreement—

(a) is made between the employer and the employee or his representative before the employee starts work under the contract as renewed, or the new contract,

(b) is in writing,

(c) specifies the date on which the period of retraining ends, and

(d) specifies the terms and conditions of employment which will apply in the employee's case after the end of that period.

139 Redundancy

(1) For the purposes of this Act an employee who is dismissed shall be taken to be dismissed by reason of redundancy if the dismissal is wholly or mainly attributable to—

(a) the fact that his employer has ceased or intends to cease—

(i) to carry on the business for the purposes of which the employee was employed by him, or

(ii) to carry on that business in the place where the employee was so employed, or

(b) the fact that the requirements of that business—

(i) for employees to carry out work of a particular kind, or

(ii) for employees to carry out work of a particular kind in the place where the employee was employed by the employer,

have ceased or diminished or are expected to cease or diminish.

(2) For the purposes of subsection (1) the business of the employer together with the business or businesses of his associated employers shall be treated as one (unless either of the conditions specified in paragraphs (a) and (b) of that subsection would be satisfied without so treating them).

(3) For the purposes of subsection (1) the activities carried on by a local education authority with respect to the schools maintained by it, and the activities carried on by the governors of those schools, shall be treated as one business (unless either of the conditions specified in paragraphs (a) and (b) of that subsection would be satisfied without so treating them).

(4) Where—

(a) the contract under which a person is employed is treated by section 136(5) as terminated by his employer by reason of an act or event, and

(b) the employee's contract is not renewed and he is not re-engaged under a new contract of employment,

he shall be taken for the purposes of this Act to be dismissed by reason of redundancy if the circumstances in which his contract is not renewed, and he is not re-engaged, are wholly or mainly attributable to either of the facts stated in paragraphs (a) and (b) of subsection (1).

(5) In its application to a case within subsection (4), paragraph (a)(i) of subsection (1) has effect as if the reference in that subsection to the employer included a reference to any person to whom, in consequence of the act or event, power to dispose of the business has passed.

(6) In subsection (1) 'cease' and 'diminish' mean cease and diminish either permanently or temporarily and for whatever reason.

Exclusions

140 Summary dismissal

(1) Subject to subsections (2) and (3), an employee is not entitled to a redundancy payment by reason of dismissal where his employer, being entitled to terminate his contract of employment without notice by reason of the employee's conduct, terminates it either—

(a) without notice,

(b) by giving shorter notice than that which, in the absence of conduct entitling the employer to terminate the contract without notice, the employer would be required to give to terminate the contract, or

(c) by giving notice which includes, or is accompanied by, a statement in writing that the employer would, by reason of the employee's conduct, be entitled to terminate the contract without notice.

(2) Where an employee who—

(a) has been given notice by his employer to terminate his contract of employment, or

(b) has given notice to his employer under section 148(1) indicating his intention to claim a redundancy payment in respect of lay-off or short-time,

takes part in a strike at any relevant time in circumstances which entitle the employer to treat the contract of employment as terminable without notice, subsection (1) does not apply if the employer terminates the contract by reason of his taking part in the strike.

(3) Where the contract of employment of an employee who—

(a) has been given notice by his employer to terminate his contract of employment, or

(b) has given notice to his employer under section 148(1) indicating his intention to claim a redundancy payment in respect of lay-off or short-time,

is terminated as mentioned in subsection (1) at any relevant time otherwise than by reason of his taking part in a strike, an employment tribunal may determine that the employer is liable to make an appropriate payment to the employee if on a reference to the tribunal it appears to the tribunal, in the circumstances of the case, to be just and equitable that the employee should receive it.

(4) In subsection (3) 'appropriate payment' means—

(a) the whole of the redundancy payment to which the employee would have been entitled apart from subsection (1), or

(b) such part of that redundancy payment as the tribunal thinks fit.

(5) In this section 'relevant time'—

(a) in the case of an employee who has been given notice by his employer to terminate his contract of employment, means any time within the obligatory period of notice, and

(b) in the case of an employee who has given notice to his employer under section 148(1), means any time after the service of the notice.

141 Renewal of contract or re-engagement

(1) This section applies where an offer (whether in writing or not) is made to an employee before the end of his employment—

(a) to renew his contract of employment, or

(b) to re-engage him under a new contract of employment,

with renewal or re-engagement to take effect either immediately on, or after an interval of not more than four weeks after, the end of his employment.

(2) Where subsection (3) is satisfied, the employee is not entitled to a redundancy payment if he unreasonably refuses the offer.

(3) This subsection is satisfied where—

(a) the provisions of the contract as renewed, or of the new contract, as to—

(i) the capacity and place in which the employee would be employed, and

(ii) the other terms and conditions of his employment,

would not differ from the corresponding provisions of the previous contract, or

(b) those provisions of the contract as renewed, or of the new contract, would differ from the corresponding provisions of the previous contract but the offer constitutes an offer of suitable employment in relation to the employee.

(4) The employee is not entitled to a redundancy payment if—

(a) his contract of employment is renewed, or he is re-engaged under a new contract of employment, in pursuance of the offer,

(b) the provisions of the contract as renewed or new contract as to the capacity or place in which he is employed or the other terms and conditions of his employment differ (wholly or in part) from the corresponding provisions of the previous contract,

(c) the employment is suitable in relation to him, and

(d) during the trial period he unreasonably terminates the contract, or unreasonably gives notice to terminate it and it is in consequence terminated.

142 Employee anticipating expiry of employer's notice

(1) Subject to subsection (3), an employee is not entitled to a redundancy payment where—

(a) he is taken to be dismissed by virtue of section 136(3) by reason of giving to his employer notice terminating his contract of employment on a date earlier than the date on which notice by the employer terminating the contract is due to expire,

(b) before the employee's notice is due to expire, the employer gives him a notice such as is specified in subsection (2), and

(c) the employee does not comply with the requirements of that notice.

(2) The employer's notice referred to in subsection (1)(b) is a notice in writing—

(a) requiring the employee to withdraw his notice terminating the contract of employment and to continue in employment until the date on which the employer's notice terminating the contract expires, and

(b) stating that, unless he does so, the employer will contest any liability to pay to him a redundancy payment in respect of the termination of his contract of employment.

(3) An employment tribunal may determine that the employer is liable to make an appropriate payment to the employee if on a reference to the tribunal it appears to the tribunal, having regard to—

(a) the reasons for which the employee seeks to leave the employment, and

(b) the reasons for which the employer requires him to continue in it,

to be just and equitable that the employee should receive the payment.

(4) In subsection (3) 'appropriate payment' means—

(a) the whole of the redundancy payment to which the employee would have been entitled apart from subsection (1), or

(b) such part of that redundancy payment as the tribunal thinks fit.

143 Strike during currency of employer's notice

(1) This section applies where—

(a) an employer has given notice to an employee to terminate his contract of employment ('notice of termination'),

(b) after the notice is given the employee begins to take part in a strike of employees of the employer, and

(c) the employer serves on the employee a notice of extension.

(2) A notice of extension is a notice in writing which—

(a) requests the employee to agree to extend the contract of employment beyond the time of expiry by a period comprising as many available days as the number of working days lost by striking ('the proposed period of extension'),

(b) indicates the reasons for which the employer makes that request, and

(c) states that the employer will contest any liability to pay the employee a redundancy payment in respect of the dismissal effected by the notice of termination unless either—

(i) the employee complies with the request, or

(ii) the employer is satisfied that, in consequence of sickness or injury or otherwise, the employee is unable to comply with it or that (even though he is able to comply with it) it is reasonable in the circumstances for him not to do so.

(3) Subject to subsections (4) and (5), if the employee does not comply with the request contained in the notice of extension, he is not entitled to a redundancy payment by reason of the dismissal effected by the notice of termination.

(4) Subsection (3) does not apply if the employer agrees to pay a redundancy payment to the employee in respect of the dismissal effected by the notice of termination even though he has not complied with the request contained in the notice of extension.

(5) An employment tribunal may determine that the employer is liable to make an appropriate payment to the employee if on a reference to the tribunal it appears to the tribunal that—

(a) the employee has not complied with the request contained in the notice of extension and the employer has not agreed to pay a redundancy payment in respect of the dismissal effected by the notice of termination, but

(b) either the employee was unable to comply with the request or it was reasonable in the circumstances for him not to comply with it.

(6) In subsection (5) 'appropriate payment' means—

(a) the whole of the redundancy payment to which the employee would have been entitled apart from subsection (3), or

(b) such part of that redundancy payment as the tribunal thinks fit.

(7) If the employee—

(a) complies with the request contained in the notice of extension, or

(b) does not comply with it but attends at his proper or usual place of work and is ready and willing to work on one or more (but not all) of the available days within the proposed period of extension,

the notice of termination has effect, and shall be deemed at all material times to have had effect, as if the period specified in it had been appropriately extended; and sections 87 to 91 accordingly apply as if the period of notice required by section 86 were extended to a corresponding extent.

(8) In subsection (7) 'appropriately extended' means—

(a) in a case within paragraph (a) of that subsection, extended beyond the time of expiry by an additional period equal to the proposed period of extension, and

(b) in a case within paragraph (b) of that subsection, extended beyond the time of expiry up to the end of the day (or last of the days) on which he attends at his proper or usual place of work and is ready and willing to work.

144 Provisions supplementary to section 143

(1) For the purposes of section 143 an employee complies with the request contained in a notice of extension if, but only if, on each available day within the proposed period of extension, he—

(a) attends at his proper or usual place of work, and

(b) is ready and willing to work,

whether or not he has signified his agreement to the request in any other way.

(2) The reference in section 143(2) to the number of working days lost by striking is a reference to the number of working days in the period—

(a) beginning with the date of service of the notice of termination, and

(b) ending with the time of expiry,

which are days on which the employee in question takes part in a strike of employees of his employer.

(3) In section 143 and this section—

'available day', in relation to an employee, means a working day beginning at or after the time of expiry which is a day on which he is not taking part in a strike of employees of the employer,

'available day within the proposed period of extension' means an available day which begins before the end of the proposed period of extension,

'time of expiry', in relation to a notice of termination, means the time at which the notice would expire apart from section 143, and

'working day', in relation to an employee, means a day on which, in accordance with his contract of employment, he is normally required to work.

(4) Neither the service of a notice of extension nor any extension by virtue of section 143(7) of the period specified in a notice of termination affects—

(a) any right either of the employer or of the employee to terminate the contract of employment (whether before, at or after the time of expiry) by a further notice or without notice, or

(b) the operation of this Part in relation to any such termination of the contract of employment.

Supplementary

145 The relevant date

(1) For the purposes of the provisions of this Act relating to redundancy payments 'the relevant date' in relation to the dismissal of an employee has the meaning given by this section.

(2) Subject to the following provisions of this section, 'the relevant date'—

(a) in relation to an employee whose contract of employment is terminated by notice, whether given by his employer or by the employee, means the date on which the notice expires,

(b) in relation to an employee whose contract of employment is terminated without notice, means the date on which the termination takes effect, and

(c) in relation to an employee who is employed under a contract for a fixed term which expires without being renewed under the same contract, means the date on which the term expires.

(3) Where the employee is taken to be dismissed by virtue of section 136(3) the 'relevant date' means the date on which the employee's notice to terminate his contract of employment expires.

(4) Where the employee is regarded by virtue of section 138(4) as having been dismissed on the date on which his employment under an earlier contract ended, 'the relevant date' means—

(a) for the purposes of section 164(1), the date which is the relevant date as defined by subsection (2) in relation to the renewed or new contract or, where there has been more than one trial period, the last such contract, and

(b) for the purposes of any other provision, the date which is the relevant date as defined by subsection (2) in relation to the previous contract or, where there has been more than one such trial period, the original contract.

(5) Where—

(a) the contract of employment is terminated by the employer, and

(b) the notice required by section 86 to be given by an employer would, if duly given on the material date, expire on a date later than the relevant date (as defined by the previous provisions of this section),

for the purposes of sections 155, 162(1) and 227(3) the later date is the relevant date.

(6) In subsection (5)(b) 'the material date' means—

(a) the date when notice of termination was given by the employer, or

(b) where no notice was given, the date when the contract of employment was terminated by the employer.

(7) [repealed]

146 Provisions supplementing sections 138 and 141

(1) In sections 138 and 141—

(a) references to re-engagement are to re-engagement by the employer or an associated employer, and

(b) references to an offer are to an offer made by the employer or an associated employer.

(2) For the purposes of the application of section 138(1) or 141(1) to a contract under which the employment ends on a Friday, Saturday or Sunday—

(a) the renewal or re-engagement shall be treated as taking effect immediately on the ending of the employment under the previous contract if it takes effect on or before the next Monday after that Friday, Saturday or Sunday, and

(b) the interval of four weeks to which those provisions refer shall be calculated as if the employment had ended on that next Monday.

(3) [repealed]

CHAPTER III
RIGHT BY REASON OF LAY-OFF OR SHORT-TIME

Lay-off and short-time

147 Meaning of 'lay-off' and 'short-time'

(1) For the purposes of this Part an employee shall be taken to be laid off for a week if—

(a) he is employed under a contract on terms and conditions such that his remuneration under the contract depends on his being provided by the employer with work of the kind which he is employed to do, but

(b) he is not entitled to any remuneration under the contract in respect of the week because the employer does not provide such work for him.

(2) For the purposes of this Part an employee shall be taken to be kept on short-time for a week if by reason of a diminution in the work provided for the employee by his employer (being work of a kind which under his contract the employee is employed to do) the employee's remuneration for the week is less than half a week's pay.

148 Eligibility by reason of lay-off or short-time

(1) Subject to the following provisions of this Part, for the purposes of this Part an employee is eligible for a redundancy payment by reason of being laid off or kept on short-time if—

(a) he gives notice in writing to his employer indicating (in whatever terms) his intention to claim a redundancy payment in respect of lay-off or short-time (referred to in this Part as 'notice of intention to claim'), and

(b) before the service of the notice he has been laid off or kept on short-time in circumstances in which subsection (2) applies.

(2) This subsection applies if the employee has been laid off or kept on short-time—

(a) for four or more consecutive weeks of which the last before the service of the notice ended on, or not more than four weeks before, the date of service of the notice, or

(b) for a series of six or more weeks (of which not more than three were consecutive) within a period of thirteen weeks, where the last week of the series before the service of the notice ended on, or not more than four weeks before, the date of service of the notice.

Exclusions

149 Counter-notices

Where an employee gives to his employer notice of intention to claim but—

(a) the employer gives to the employee, within seven days after the service of that notice, notice in writing (referred to in this Part as a 'counter-notice') that he will contest any liability to pay to the employee a redundancy payment in pursuance of the employee's notice, and

(b) the employer does not withdraw the counter-notice by a subsequent notice in writing,

the employee is not entitled to a redundancy payment in pursuance of his notice of intention to claim except in accordance with a decision of an employment tribunal.

150 Resignation

(1) An employee is not entitled to a redundancy payment by reason of being laid off or kept on short-time unless he terminates his contract of employment by giving such period of notice as is required for the purposes of this section before the end of the relevant period.

(2) The period of notice required for the purposes of this section—

(a) where the employee is required by his contract of employment to give more than one week's notice to terminate the contract, is the minimum period which he is required to give, and

(b) otherwise, is one week.

(3) In subsection (1) 'the relevant period'—

(a) if the employer does not give a counter-notice within seven days after the service of the notice of intention to claim, is three weeks after the end of those seven days,

(b) if the employer gives a counter-notice within that period of seven days but withdraws it by a subsequent notice in writing, is three weeks after the service of the notice of withdrawal, and

(c) if—

(i) the employer gives a counter-notice within that period of seven days, and does not so withdraw it, and

(ii) a question as to the right of the employee to a redundancy payment in pursuance of the notice of intention to claim is referred to an employment tribunal,

is three weeks after the tribunal has notified to the employee its decision on that reference.

(4) For the purposes of subsection (3)(c) no account shall be taken of—

(a) any appeal against the decision of the tribunal, or

(b) any proceedings or decision in consequence of any such appeal.

151 Dismissal

(1) An employee is not entitled to a redundancy payment by reason of being laid off or kept on short-time if he is dismissed by his employer.

(2) Subsection (1) does not prejudice any right of the employee to a redundancy payment in respect of the dismissal.

152 Likelihood of full employment

(1) An employee is not entitled to a redundancy payment in pursuance of a notice of intention to claim if—

(a) on the date of service of the notice it was reasonably to be expected that the employee (if he continued to be employed by the same employer) would, not later than four weeks after that date, enter on a period of employment of not less than thirteen weeks during which he would not be laid off or kept on short-time for any week, and

(b) the employer gives a counter-notice to the employee within seven days after the service of the notice of intention to claim.

(2) Subsection (1) does not apply where the employee—

(a) continues or has continued, during the next four weeks after the date of service of the notice of intention to claim, to be employed by the same employer, and

(b) is or has been laid off or kept on short-time for each of those weeks.

Supplementary

153 The relevant date

For the purposes of the provisions of this Act relating to redundancy payments 'the relevant date' in relation to a notice of intention to claim or a right to a redundancy payment in pursuance of such a notice—

(a) in a case falling within paragraph (a) of subsection (2) of section 148, means the date on which the last of the four or more consecutive weeks before the service of the notice came to an end, and

(b) in a case falling within paragraph (b) of that subsection, means the date on which the last of the series of six or more weeks before the service of the notice came to an end.

154 Provisions supplementing sections 148 and 152

For the purposes of sections 148(2) and 152(2)—

(a) it is immaterial whether a series of weeks consists wholly of weeks for which the employee is laid off or wholly of weeks for which he is kept on short-time or partly of the one and partly of the other, and

(b) no account shall be taken of any week for which an employee is laid off or kept on short-time where the lay-off or short-time is wholly or mainly attributable to a strike or a lock-out (whether or not in the trade or industry in which the employee is employed and whether in Great Britain or elsewhere).

CHAPTER IV
GENERAL EXCLUSIONS FROM RIGHT

155 Qualifying period of employment

An employee does not have any right to a redundancy payment unless he has been continuously employed for a period of not less than two years ending with the relevant date.

156 Upper age limit

(1) An employee does not have any right to a redundancy payment if before the relevant date he has attained—

(a) in a case where—

(i) in the business for the purposes of which the employee was employed there was a normal retiring age of less than sixty-five for an employee holding the position held by the employee, and

(ii) the age was the same whether the employee holding that position was a man or woman,

that normal retiring age, and

(b) in any other case, the age of sixty-five.

(2) [repealed]

157 [omitted]

158 Pension rights

(1) The Secretary of State shall by regulations make provision for excluding the right to a redundancy payment, or reducing the amount of any redundancy payment, in such cases to which subsection (2) applies as are prescribed by the regulations.

(2) This subsection applies to cases in which an employee has (whether by virtue of any statutory provision or otherwise) a right or claim (whether or not legally enforceable) to a periodical payment or lump sum by way of pension, gratuity or superannuation allowance which—

(a) is to be paid by reference to his employment by a particular employer, and

(b) is to be paid, or to begin to be paid, at the time when he leaves the employment or within such period after he leaves the employment as may be prescribed by the regulations.

(3) The regulations shall secure that the right to a redundancy payment shall not be excluded, and that the amount of a redundancy payment shall not be reduced, by reason of any right or claim to a periodical payment or lump sum, in so far as the payment or lump sum—

(a) represents compensation for loss of employment or for loss or diminution of emoluments or of pension rights, and

(b) is payable under a statutory provision (whether passed or made before or after the passing of this Act).

(4) In relation to any case where (in accordance with any provision of this Part) an employment tribunal determines that an employer is liable to pay part (but not the whole) of a redundancy payment the references in this section to a redundancy payment, or to the amount of a redundancy payment, are to the part of the redundancy payment, or to the amount of the part.

159 Public offices etc.

A person does not have any right to a redundancy payment in respect of any employment which—

(a) is employment in a public office within the meaning of section 39 of the Superannuation Act 1965, or

(b) is for the purposes of pensions and other superannuation benefits treated (whether by virtue of that Act or otherwise) as service in the civil service of the State.

160 Overseas government employment

(1) A person does not have any right to a redundancy payment in respect of employment in any capacity under the Government of an overseas territory.

(2) The reference in subsection (1) to the Government of an overseas territory includes a reference to—

(a) a Government constituted for two or more overseas territories, and

(b) any authority established for the purpose of providing or administering services which are common to, or relate to matters of common interest to, two or more overseas territories.

(3) In this section references to an overseas territory are to any territory or country outside the United Kingdom.

161 Domestic servants

(1) A person does not have any right to a redundancy payment in respect of employment as a domestic servant in a private household where the employer is the parent (or step-parent), grandparent, child (or step-child), grandchild or brother or sister (or half-brother or half-sister) of the employee.

(2) Subject to that, the provisions of this Part apply to an employee who is employed as a domestic servant in a private household as if—

(a) the household were a business, and

(b) the maintenance of the household were the carrying on of that business by the employer.

CHAPTER V
OTHER PROVISIONS ABOUT REDUNDANCY PAYMENTS

162 Amount of a redundancy payment

(1) The amount of a redundancy payment shall be calculated by—

(a) determining the period, ending with the relevant date, during which the employee has been continuously employed,

(b) reckoning backwards from the end of that period the number of years of employment falling within that period, and

(c) allowing the appropriate amount for each of those years of employment.

(2) In subsection (1)(c) 'the appropriate amount' means—

(a) one and a half weeks' pay for a year of employment in which the employee was not below the age of forty-one,

(b) one week's pay for a year of employment (not within paragraph (a)) in which he was not below the age of twenty-two, and

(c) half a week's pay for each year of employment not within paragraph (a) or (b).

(3) Where twenty years of employment have been reckoned under subsection (1), no account shall be taken under that subsection of any year of employment earlier than those twenty years.

(4) Where the relevant date is after the sixty-fourth anniversary of the day of the employee's birth, the amount arrived at under subsections (1) to (3) shall be reduced by the appropriate fraction.

(5) In subsection (4) 'the appropriate fraction' means the fraction of which—

(a) the numerator is the number of whole months reckoned from the sixty-fourth anniversary of the day of the employee's birth in the period beginning with that anniversary and ending with the relevant date, and

(b) the denominator is twelve.

(6) Subsections (1) to (5) apply for the purposes of any provision of this Part by virtue of which an employment tribunal may determine that an employer is liable to pay to an employee—

(a) the whole of the redundancy payment to which the employee would have had a right apart from some other provision, or

(b) such part of the redundancy payment to which the employee would have had a right apart from some other provision as the tribunal thinks fit,

as if any reference to the amount of a redundancy payment were to the amount of the redundancy payment to which the employee would have been entitled apart from that other provision.

(7) [repealed]

(8) This section has effect subject to any regulations under section 158 by virtue of which the amount of a redundancy payment, or part of a redundancy payment, may be reduced.

163 References to employment tribunals

(1) Any question arising under this Part as to—

(a) the right of an employee to a redundancy payment, or

(b) the amount of a redundancy payment,

shall be referred to and determined by an employment tribunal.

(2) For the purposes of any such reference, an employee who has been dismissed by his employer shall, unless the contrary is proved, be presumed to have been so dismissed by reason of redundancy.

(3) Any question whether an employee will become entitled to a redundancy payment if he is not dismissed by his employer and he terminates his contract of employment as mentioned in section 150(1) shall for the purposes of this Part be taken to be a question as to the right of the employee to a redundancy payment.

(4) Where an order under section 157 is in force in respect of an agreement, this section has effect in relation to any question arising under the agreement as to the right of an employee to a payment on the termination of his employment, or as to the amount of such a payment, as if the payment were a redundancy payment and the question arose under this Part.

164 Claims for redundancy payment

(1) An employee does not have any right to a redundancy payment unless, before the end of the period of six months beginning with the relevant date—

(a) the payment has been agreed and paid,

(b) the employee has made a claim for the payment by notice in writing given to the employer,

(c) a question as to the employee's right to, or the amount of, the payment has been referred to an employment tribunal, or

(d) a complaint relating to his dismissal has been presented by the employee under section 111.

(2) An employee is not deprived of his right to a redundancy payment by subsection (1) if, during the period of six months immediately following the period mentioned in that subsection, the employee—

(a) makes a claim for the payment by notice in writing given to the employer,

(b) refers to an employment tribunal a question as to his right to, or the amount of, the payment, or

(c) presents a complaint relating to his dismissal under section 111,

and it appears to the tribunal to be just and equitable that the employee should receive a redundancy payment.

(3) In determining under subsection (2) whether it is just and equitable that an employee should receive a redundancy payment an employment tribunal shall have regard to—

(a) the reason shown by the employee for his failure to take any such step as is referred to in subsection (2) within the period mentioned in subsection (1), and

(b) all the other relevant circumstances.

165 Written particulars of redundancy payment

(1) On making any redundancy payment, otherwise than in pursuance of a decision of a tribunal which specifies the amount of the payment to be made, the employer shall give to the employee a written statement indicating how the amount of the payment has been calculated.

(2) An employer who without reasonable excuse fails to comply with subsection (1) is guilty of an offence and liable on summary conviction to a fine not exceeding level 1 on the standard scale.

(3) If an employer fails to comply with the requirements of subsection (1), the employee may by notice in writing to the employer require him to give to the employee a written statement complying with those requirements within such period (not being less than one week beginning with the day on which the notice is given) as may be specified in the notice.

(4) An employer who without reasonable excuse fails to comply with a notice under subsection (3) is guilty of an offence and liable on summary conviction to a fine not exceeding level 3 on the standard scale.

CHAPTER VI
PAYMENTS BY SECRETARY OF STATE

166 Applications for payments

(1) Where an employee claims that his employer is liable to pay to him an employer's payment and either—

(a) that the employee has taken all reasonable steps, other than legal proceedings, to recover the payment from the employer and the employer has refused or failed to pay it, or has paid part of it and has refused or failed to pay the balance, or

(b) that the employer is insolvent and the whole or part of the payment remains unpaid,

the employee may apply to the Secretary of State for a payment under this section.

(2) In this Part 'employer's payment', in relation to an employee, means—

(a) a redundancy payment which his employer is liable to pay to him under this Part,

(aa) a payment which his employer is liable to make to him under an agreement to refrain from instituting or continuing proceedings for a contravention or alleged contravention of section 135 which has effect by virtue of section 203(2)(e) or (f), or

(b) a payment which his employer is, under an agreement in respect of which an order is in force under section 157, liable to make to him on the termination of his contract of employment.

(3) In relation to any case where (in accordance with any provision of this Part) an employment tribunal determines that an employer is liable to pay part (but not the whole) of a redundancy payment the reference in subsection (2)(a) to a redundancy payment is to the part of the redundancy payment.

(4) In subsection (1)(a) 'legal proceedings'—

(a) does not include any proceedings before an employment tribunal, but

(b) includes any proceedings to enforce a decision or award of an employment tribunal.

(5) An employer is insolvent for the purposes of subsection (1)(b)—

(a) where the employer is an individual, if (but only if) subsection (6) is satisfied, and

(b) where the employer is a company, if (but only if) subsection (7) is satisfied.

(6) This subsection is satisfied in the case of an employer who is an individual—

(a) in England and Wales if—

(i) he has been adjudged bankrupt or has made a composition or arrangement with his creditors, or

(ii) he has died and his estate falls to be administered in accordance with an order under section 421 of the Insolvency Act 1986, and

(b) in Scotland if—

(i) sequestration of his estate has been awarded or he has executed a trust deed for his creditors or has entered into a composition contract, or

(ii) he has died and a judicial factor appointed under section 11A of the Judicial Factors (Scotland) Act 1889 is required by that section to divide his insolvent estate among his creditors.

(7) This subsection is satisfied in the case of an employer which is a company—

(a) if a winding up order or an administration order has been made, or a resolution for voluntary winding up has been passed, with respect to the company,

(b) if a receiver or (in England and Wales only) a manager of the company's undertaking has been duly appointed, or (in England and Wales only) possession has been taken, by or on behalf of the holders of any debentures secured by a floating charge, of any property of the company comprised in or subject to the charge, or

(c) if a voluntary arrangement proposed in the case of the company for the purposes of Part I of the Insolvency Act 1986 has been approved under that Part of that Act.

167 Making of payments

(1) Where, on an application under section 166 by an employee in relation to an employer's payment, the Secretary of State is satisfied that the requirements specified in subsection (2) are met, he shall pay to the employee out of the National Insurance Fund a sum calculated in accordance with section 168 but reduced by so much (if any) of the employer's payment as has already been paid.

(2) The requirements referred to in subsection (1) are—

(a) that the employee is entitled to the employer's payment, and

(b) that one of the conditions specified in paragraphs (a) and (b) of subsection (1) of section 166 is fulfilled,

and, in a case where the employer's payment is a payment such as is mentioned in subsection (2)(b) of that section, that the employee's right to the payment arises by virtue of a period of continuous employment (computed in accordance with the provisions of the agreement in question) which is not less than two years.

(3) Where under this section the Secretary of State pays a sum to an employee in respect of an employer's payment—

(a) all rights and remedies of the employee with respect to the employer's payment, or (if the Secretary of State has paid only part of it) all the rights and remedies of the employee with respect to that part of the employer's payment, are transferred to and vest in the Secretary of State, and

(b) any decision of an employment tribunal requiring the employer's payment to be paid to the employee has effect as if it required that payment, or that part of it which the Secretary of State has paid, to be paid to the Secretary of State.

(4) Any money recovered by the Secretary of State by virtue of subsection (3) shall be paid into the National Insurance Fund.

168 Amount of payments

(1) The sum payable to an employee by the Secretary of State under section 167—

(a) where the employer's payment to which the employee's application under section 166 relates is a redundancy payment or a part of a redundancy payment, is a sum equal to the amount of the redundancy payment or part,

(aa) where the employer's payment to which the employee's application under section 166 relates is a payment which his employer is liable to make to him under an agreement having effect by virtue of section 203(2)(e) or (f), is a sum equal to the amount of the employer's payment or of any redundancy payment which the employer would have been liable to pay to the employee but for the agreement, whichever is less, and

(b) where the employer's payment to which the employee's application under section 166 relates is a payment which the employer is liable to make under an agreement in respect of which an order is in force under section 157, is a sum equal to the amount of the employer's payment or of the relevant redundancy payment, whichever is less.

(2) The reference in subsection (1)(b) to the amount of the relevant redundancy payment is to the amount of the redundancy payment which the employer would have been liable to pay to the employee on the assumptions specified in subsection (3).

(3) The assumptions referred to in subsection (2) are that—

(a) the order in force in respect of the agreement had not been made,

(b) the circumstances in which the employer's payment is payable had been such that the employer was liable to pay a redundancy payment to the employee in those circumstances,

(c) the relevant date, in relation to any such redundancy payment, had been the date on which the termination of the employee's contract of employment is treated as having taken effect for the purposes of the agreement, and

(d) in so far as the provisions of the agreement relating to the circumstances in which the continuity of an employee's period of employment is to be treated as broken, and the weeks which are to count in computing a period of employment, are inconsistent with the provisions of Chapter I of Part XIV, the provisions of the agreement were substituted for those provisions.

169 Information relating to applications for payments

(1) Where an employee makes an application to the Secretary of State under section 166, the Secretary of State may, by notice in writing given to the employer, require the employer—

(a) to provide the Secretary of State with such information, and

(b) to produce for examination on behalf of the Secretary of State documents in his custody or under his control of such description,

as the Secretary of State may reasonably require for the purpose of determining whether the application is well-founded.

(2) Where a person on whom a notice is served under subsection (1) fails without reasonable excuse to comply with a requirement imposed by the notice, he is guilty of

an offence and liable on summary conviction to a fine not exceeding level 3 on the standard scale.

(3) A person is guilty of an offence if—

(a) in providing any information required by a notice under subsection (1), he makes a statement which he knows to be false in a material particular or recklessly makes a statement which is false in a material particular, or

(b) he produces for examination in accordance with a notice under subsection (1) a document which to his knowledge has been wilfully falsified.

(4) A person guilty of an offence under subsection (3) is liable—

(a) on summary conviction, to a fine not exceeding the statutory maximum or to imprisonment for a term not exceeding three months, or to both, or

(b) on conviction on indictment, to a fine or to imprisonment for a term not exceeding two years, or to both.

170 References to employment tribunals

(1) Where on an application made to the Secretary of State for a payment under section 166 it is claimed that an employer is liable to pay an employer's payment, there shall be referred to an employment tribunal—

(a) any question as to the liability of the employer to pay the employer's payment, and

(b) any question as to the amount of the sum payable in accordance with section 168.

(2) For the purposes of any reference under this section an employee who has been dismissed by his employer shall, unless the contrary is proved, be presumed to have been so dismissed by reason of redundancy.

CHAPTER VII
SUPPLEMENTARY

Application of Part to particular cases

171 and **172** [omitted]

173 Employees paid by person other than employer

(1) For the purposes of the operation of the provisions of this Part (and Chapter I of Part XIV) in relation to any employee whose remuneration is, by virtue of any statutory provision, payable to him by a person other than his employer, each of the references to the employer specified in subsection (2) shall be construed as a reference to the person by whom the remuneration is payable.

(2) The references referred to in subsection (1) are the first reference in section 135(1), the third reference in section 140(3), the first reference in section 142(3) and the first reference in section 143(2)(c) and the references in sections 142(2)(b), 143(4) and (5), 149(a) and (b), 150(3), 152(1)(b), 158(4), 162(6), 164 to 169, 170(1) and 214(5).

Death of employer or employee

174 Death of employer: dismissal

(1) Where the contract of employment of an employee is taken for the purposes of this Part to be terminated by his employer by reason of the employer's death, this Part has effect in accordance with the following provisions of this section.

(2) Section 138 applies as if—

(a) in subsection (1)(a), for the words 'in pursuance' onwards there were substituted 'by a personal representative of the deceased employer',

(b) in subsection (1)(b), for the words 'either immediately' onwards there were substituted 'not later than eight weeks after the death of the deceased employer', and

(c) in subsections (2)(b) and (6)(a), for the word 'employer' there were substituted 'personal representative of the deceased employer'.

(3) Section 141(1) applies as if—

(a) for the words 'before the end of his employment' there were substituted 'by a personal representative of the deceased employer', and

(b) for the words 'either immediately' onwards there were substituted 'not later than eight weeks after the death of the deceased employer.'

(4) For the purposes of section 141—

(a) provisions of the contract as renewed, or of the new contract, do not differ from the corresponding provisions of the contract in force immediately before the death of the deceased employer by reason only that the personal representative would be substituted for the deceased employer as the employer, and

(b) no account shall be taken of that substitution in determining whether refusal of the offer was unreasonable or whether the employee acted reasonably in terminating or giving notice to terminate the new or renewed employment.

(5) Section 146 has effect as if—

(a) subsection (1) were omitted, and

(b) in subsection (2), paragraph (a) were omitted and, in paragraph (b), for the word 'four' there were substituted 'eight'.

(6) For the purposes of the application of this Part (in accordance with section 161(2)) in relation to an employee who was employed as a domestic servant in a private household, references in this section and sections 175 and 218(4) and (5) to a personal representative include a person to whom the management of the household has passed, otherwise than in pursuance of a sale or other disposition for valuable consideration, in consequence of the death of the employer.

175 Death of employer: lay-off and short-time

(1) Where an employee is laid off or kept on short-time and his employer dies, this Part has effect in accordance with the following provisions of this section.

(2) Where the employee—

(a) has been laid off or kept on short-time for one or more weeks before the death of the employer,

(b) has not given the deceased employer notice of intention to claim before the employer's death,

(c) after the employer's death has his contract of employment renewed, or is re-engaged under a new contract, by a personal representative of the deceased employer, and

(d) after renewal or re-engagement is laid off or kept on short-time for one or more weeks by the personal representative,

the week in which the employer died and the first week of the employee's employment by the personal representative shall be treated for the purposes of Chapter III as consecutive weeks (and references to four weeks or thirteen weeks shall be construed accordingly).

(3) The following provisions of this section apply where—

(a) the employee has given the deceased employer notice of intention to claim before the employer's death,

(b) the employer's death occurred before the end of the period of four weeks after the service of the notice, and

(c) the employee has not terminated his contract of employment by notice expiring before the employer's death.

(4) If the contract of employment is not renewed, and the employee is not re-engaged under a new contract, by a personal representative of the deceased employer before the end of the period of four weeks after the service of the notice of intention to claim—

(a) sections 149 and 152 do not apply, but
(b) (subject to that) Chapter III applies as if the employer had not died and the employee had terminated the contract of employment by a week's notice, or by the minimum notice which he is required to give to terminate the contract (if longer than a week), expiring at the end of that period.

(5) If—
(a) the contract of employment is renewed, or the employee is re-engaged under a new contract, by a personal representative of the deceased employer before the end of the period of four weeks after the service of the notice of intention to claim, and
(b) the employee was laid off or kept on short-time by the deceased employer for one or more of those weeks and is laid off or kept on short-time by the personal representative for the week, or for the next two or more weeks, following the renewal or re-engagement,
subsection (6) has effect.

(6) Where this subsection has effect Chapter III applies as if—
(a) all the weeks mentioned in subsection (5) were consecutive weeks during which the employee was employed (but laid off or kept on short-time) by the same employer, and
(b) the periods specified by section 150(3)(a) and (b) as the relevant period were extended by any week or weeks any part of which was after the death of the employer and before the date on which the renewal or re-engagement took effect.

176 Death of employee

(1) Where an employee whose employer has given him notice to terminate his contract of employment dies before the notice expires, this Part applies as if the contract had been duly terminated by the employer by notice expiring on the date of the employee's death.

(2) Where—
(a) an employee's contract of employment has been terminated by the employer,
(b) (by virtue of subsection (5) of section 145) a date later than the relevant date as defined by the previous provisions of that section is the relevant date for the purposes of certain provisions of this Act, and
(c) the employee dies before that date,
that subsection applies as if the notice to which it refers would have expired on the employee's death.

(3) Where—
(a) an employer has given notice to an employee to terminate his contract of employment and has offered to renew his contract of employment or to re-engage him under a new contract, and
(b) the employee dies without having accepted or refused the offer and without the offer having been withdrawn,
section 141(2) applies as if for the words 'he unreasonably refuses' there were substituted 'it would have been unreasonable on his part to refuse'.

(4) Where an employee's contract of employment has been renewed or he has been re-engaged under a new contract—
(a) if he dies during the trial period without having terminated, or given notice to terminate, the contract, section 141(4) applies as if for paragraph (d) there were substituted—

'(d) it would have been unreasonable for the employee during the trial period to terminate or give notice to terminate the contract.', and

(b) if during that trial period he gives notice to terminate the contract but dies before the notice expires, sections 138(2) and 141(4) apply as if the notice had expired (and the contract had been terminated by its expiry) on the date of the employee's death.

(5) Where in the circumstances specified in paragraphs (a) and (b) of subsection (3) of section 136 the employee dies before the notice given by him under paragraph (b) of that subsection expires—

(a) if he dies before his employer has given him a notice such as is specified in subsection (2) of section 142, subsections (3) and (4) of that section apply as if the employer had given him such a notice and he had not complied with it, and

(b) if he dies after his employer has given him such a notice, that section applies as if the employee had not died but did not comply with the notice.

(6) Where an employee has given notice of intention to claim—

(a) if he dies before he has given notice to terminate his contract of employment and before the relevant period (as defined in subsection (3) of section 150) has expired, that section does not apply, and

(b) if he dies within the period of seven days after the service of the notice of intention to claim, and before the employer has given a counter-notice, Chapter III applies as if the employer had given a counter-notice within that period of seven days.

(7) Where a claim for a redundancy payment is made by a personal representative of a deceased employee—

(a) if the employee died before the end of the period of six months beginning with the relevant date, subsection (1) of section 164, and

(b) if the employee died after the end of the period of six months beginning with the relevant date but before the end of the following period of six months, subsection (2) of that section,

applies as if for the words 'six months' there were substituted 'one year'.

177 [omitted]

Other supplementary provisions

178 and 179 [omitted]

180 Offences

(1) Where an offence under this Part committed by a body corporate is proved—

(a) to have been committed with the consent or connivance of, or

(b) to be attributable to any neglect on the part of,

any director, manager, secretary or other similar officer of the body corporate, or any person who was purporting to act in any such capacity, he (as well as the body corporate) is guilty of the offence and liable to be proceeded against and punished accordingly.

(2) In this section 'director', in relation to a body corporate established by or under any enactment for the purpose of carrying on under national ownership any industry or part of an industry or undertaking, being a body corporate whose affairs are managed by its members, means a member of that body corporate.

181 Interpretation

(1) In this Part—

'counter-notice' shall be construed in accordance with section 149(a),

'dismissal' and 'dismissed' shall be construed in accordance with sections 136 to 138,

'employer's payment' has the meaning given by section 166,

'notice of intention to claim' shall be construed in accordance with section 148(1),

'obligatory period of notice' has the meaning given by section 136(4), and

'trial period' shall be construed in accordance with section 138(3).

(2) In this Part—

(a) references to an employee being laid off or being eligible for a redundancy payment by reason of being laid off, and

(b) references to an employee being kept on short-time or being eligible for a redundancy payment by reason of being kept on short-time,

shall be construed in accordance with sections 147 and 148.

PART XII
INSOLVENCY OF EMPLOYERS

182 Employee's rights on insolvency of employer

If, on an application made to him in writing by an employee, the Secretary of State is satisfied that—

(a) the employee's employer has become insolvent,

(b) the employee's employment has been terminated, and

(c) on the appropriate date the employee was entitled to be paid the whole or part of any debt to which this Part applies,

the Secretary of State shall, subject to section 186, pay the employee out of the National Insurance Fund the amount to which, in the opinion of the Secretary of State, the employee is entitled in respect of the debt.

183 Insolvency

(1) An employer has become insolvent for the purposes of this Part—

(a) where the employer is an individual, if (but only if) subsection (2) is satisfied, and

(b) where the employer is a company, if (but only if) subsection (3) is satisfied.

(2) This subsection is satisfied in the case of an employer who is an individual—

(a) in England and Wales if—

(i) he has been adjudged bankrupt or has made a composition or arrangement with his creditors, or

(ii) he has died and his estate falls to be administered in accordance with an order under section 421 of the Insolvency Act 1986, and

(b) in Scotland if—

(i) sequestration of his estate has been awarded or he has executed a trust deed for his creditors or has entered into a composition contract, or

(ii) he has died and a judicial factor appointed under section 11A of the Judicial Factors (Scotland) Act 1889 is required by that section to divide his insolvent estate among his creditors.

(3) This subsection is satisfied in the case of an employer which is a company—

(a) if a winding up order or an administration order has been made, or a resolution for voluntary winding up has been passed, with respect to the company,

(b) if a receiver or (in England and Wales only) a manager of the company's undertaking has been duly appointed, or (in England and Wales only) possession has been taken, by or on behalf of the holders of any debentures secured by a floating charge, of any property of the company comprised in or subject to the charge, or

(c) if a voluntary arrangement proposed in the case of the company for the purposes of Part I of the Insolvency Act 1986 has been approved under that Part of that Act.

184 Debts to which Part applies

(1) This Part applies to the following debts—

(a) any arrears of pay in respect of one or more (but not more than eight) weeks,

(b) any amount which the employer is liable to pay the employee for the period of notice required by section 86(1) or (2) or for any failure of the employer to give the period of notice required by section 86(1),

(c) any holiday pay—

(i) in respect of a period or periods of holiday not exceeding six weeks in all, and

(ii) to which the employee became entitled during the twelve months ending with the appropriate date,

(d) any basic award of compensation for unfair dismissal or so much of an award under a designated dismissal procedures agreement as does not exceed any basic award of compensation for unfair dismissal to which the employee would be entitled but for the agreement, and

(e) any reasonable sum by way of reimbursement of the whole or part of any fee or premium paid by an apprentice or articled clerk.

(2) For the purposes of subsection (1)(a) the following amounts shall be treated as arrears of pay—

(a) a guarantee payment,

(b) any payment for time off under Part VI of this Act or section 169 of the Trade Union and Labour Relations (Consolidation) Act 1992 (payment for time off for carrying out trade union duties etc.),

(c) remuneration on suspension on medical grounds under section 64 of this Act and remuneration on suspension on maternity grounds under section 68 of this Act, and

(d) remuneration under a protective award under section 189 of the Trade Union and Labour Relations (Consolidation) Act 1992.

(3) In subsection (1)(c) 'holiday pay', in relation to an employee, means—

(a) pay in respect of a holiday actually taken by the employee, or

(b) any accrued holiday pay which, under the employee's contract of employment, would in the ordinary course have become payable to him in respect of the period of a holiday if his employment with the employer had continued until he became entitled to a holiday.

(4) A sum shall be taken to be reasonable for the purposes of subsection (1)(e) in a case where a trustee in bankruptcy, or (in Scotland) a permanent or interim trustee (within the meaning of the Bankruptcy (Scotland) Act 1985), or liquidator has been or is required to be appointed—

(a) as respects England and Wales, if it is admitted to be reasonable by the trustee in bankruptcy or liquidator under section 348 of the Insolvency Act 1986 (effect of bankruptcy on apprenticeships etc.), whether as originally enacted or as applied to the winding up of a company by rules under section 411 of that Act, and

(b) as respects Scotland, if it is accepted by the permanent or interim trustee or liquidator for the purposes of the sequestration or winding up.

185 The appropriate date

In this Part 'the appropriate date'—

(a) in relation to arrears of pay (not being remuneration under a protective award made under section 189 of the Trade Union and Labour Relations (Consolidation) Act 1992 and to holiday pay, means the date on which the employer became insolvent,

(b) in relation to a basic award of compensation for unfair dismissal and to remuneration under a protective award so made, means whichever is the latest of—

(i) the date on which the employer became insolvent,

(ii) the date of the termination of the employee's employment, and

(iii) the date on which the award was made, and

(c) in relation to any other debt to which this Part applies, means whichever is the latter of—

(i) the date on which the employer became insolvent, and

(ii) the date of the termination of the employee's employment.

186 Limit on amount payable under section 182

(1) The total amount payable to an employee in respect of any debt to which this Part applies, where the amount of the debt is referable to a period of time, shall not exceed—

(a) £220 in respect of any one week, or

(b) in respect of a shorter period, an amount bearing the same proportion to £220 as that shorter period bears to a week.

(2) [repealed]

187 [omitted]

188 Complaints to employment tribunals

(1) A person who has applied for a payment under section 182 may present a complaint to an employment tribunal—

(a) that the Secretary of State has failed to make any such payment, or

(b) that any such payment made by him is less than the amount which should have been paid.

(2) An employment tribunal shall not consider a complaint under subsection (1) unless it is presented—

(a) before the end of the period of three months beginning with the date on which the decision of the Secretary of State on the application was communicated to the applicant, or

(b) within such further period as the tribunal considers reasonable in a case where it is not reasonably practicable for the complaint to be presented before the end of that period of three months.

(3) Where an employment tribunal finds that the Secretary of State ought to make a payment under section 182, the tribunal shall—

(a) make a declaration to that effect, and

(b) declare the amount of any such payment which it finds the Secretary of State ought to make.

189 Transfer to Secretary of State of rights and remedies

(1) Where, in pursuance of section 182, the Secretary of State makes a payment to an employee in respect of a debt to which this Part applies—

(a) on the making of the payment any rights and remedies of the employee in respect of the debt (or, if the Secretary of State has paid only part of it, in respect of that part) become rights and remedies of the Secretary of State, and

(b) any decision of an employment tribunal requiring an employer to pay that debt to the employee has the effect that the debt (or the part of it which the Secretary of State has paid) is to be paid to the Secretary of State.

(2) Where a debt (or any part of a debt) in respect of which the Secretary of State has made a payment in pursuance of section 182 constitutes—

(a) a preferential debt within the meaning of the Insolvency Act 1986 for the purposes of any provision of that Act (including any such provision as applied by any order made under that Act) or any provision of the Companies Act 1985, or

(b) a preferred debt within the meaning of the Bankruptcy (Scotland) Act 1985 for the purposes of any provision of that Act (including any such provision as applied by section 11A of the Judicial Factors (Scotland) Act 1889),

the rights which become rights of the Secretary of State in accordance with subsection (1) include any right arising under any such provision by reason of the status of the debt (or that part of it) as a preferential or preferred debt.

(3) In computing for the purposes of any provision mentioned in subsection (2)(a) or (b) the aggregate amount payable in priority to other creditors of the employer in respect of—

(a) any claim of the Secretary of State to be paid in priority to other creditors of the employer by virtue of subsection (2), and

(b) any claim by the employee to be so paid made in his own right,
any claim of the Secretary of State to be so paid by virtue of subsection (2) shall be treated as if it were a claim of the employee.

(4) But the Secretary of State shall be entitled, as against the employee, to be so paid in respect of any such claim of his (up to the full amount of the claim) before any payment is made to the employee in respect of any claim by the employee to be so paid made in his own right.

(5) Any sum recovered by the Secretary of State in exercising any right, or pursuing any remedy, which is his by virtue of this section shall be paid into the National Insurance Fund.

190 [omitted]

PART XIII
MISCELLANEOUS

CHAPTER I
PARTICULAR TYPES OF EMPLOYMENT

Crown employment etc.

191 Crown employment

(1) Subject to sections 192 and 193, the provisions of this Act to which this section applies have effect in relation to Crown employment and persons in Crown employment as they have effect in relation to other employment and other employees or workers.

(2) This section applies to—

(a) Parts I to III,

(aa) Part IVA,

(b) Part V, apart from section 45,

(c) Parts VI to VIII,

(d) in Part IX, sections 92 and 93,

(e) Part X, apart from section 101, and

(f) this Part and Parts XIV and XV.

(3) In this Act 'Crown employment' means employment under or for the purposes of a government department or any officer or body exercising on behalf of the Crown functions conferred by a statutory provision.

(4) For the purposes of the application of provisions of this Act in relation to Crown employment in accordance with subsection (1)—

(a) references to an employee or a worker shall be construed as references to a person in Crown employment,

(b) references to a contract of employment, or a workers contract, shall be construed as references to the terms of employment of a person in Crown employment,

(c) references to dismissal, or to the termination of a worker's contract, shall be construed as references to the termination of Crown employment,

(d) references to redundancy shall be construed as references to the existence of such circumstances as are treated, in accordance with any arrangements falling within section 177(3) for the time being in force, as equivalent to redundancy in relation to Crown employment, and

(e) references to an undertaking shall be construed—

(i) in relation to a Minister of the Crown, as references to his functions or (as the context may require) to the department of which he is in charge, and

(ii) in relation to a government department, officer or body, as references to the functions of the department, officer or body or (as the context may require) to the department, officer or body.

(5) Where the terms of employment of a person in Crown employment restrict his right to take part in—

(a) certain political activities, or

(b) activities which may conflict with his official functions,

nothing in section 50 requires him to be allowed time off work for public duties connected with any such activities.

(6) Sections 159 and 160 are without prejudice to any exemption or immunity of the Crown.

192 Armed forces

(1) Section 191—

(a) applies to service as a member of the naval, military or air forces of the Crown but subject to the following provisions of this section, and

(b) applies to employment by an association established for the purposes of Part XI of the Reserve Forces Act 1996.

(2) The provisions of this Act which have effect by virtue of section 191 in relation to service as a member of the naval, military or air forces of the Crown are—

(a) Part I,

(aa) in Part V, section 45A, and sections 48 and 49 so far as relating to that section,

(ab) section 47C

(b) in Part VI, sections 55 to 57B,

(c) Parts VII and VIII,

(d) in Part IX, sections 92 and 93,

(e) Part X, apart from sections 100 to 103 and 134, and

(f) this Part and Parts XIV and XV.

(3)-(8) [omitted]

193 National security

(1) Part IVA and section 47B of this Act do not apply in relation to employment for the purposes of—

(a) the Security Service,

(b) the Secret Intelligence Service, or

(c) the Government Communications Headquarters.

194 and **195** [omitted]

Excluded classes of employment

196 [repealed]

197 Fixed-term contracts

(1) and (2) [repealed]

(3) An employee employed under a contract of employment for a fixed term of two years or more is not entitled to a redundancy payment in respect of the expiry of that term without its being renewed (whether by the employer or by an associated employer of his) if, before the term expires, the employee has agreed in writing to exclude any right to a redundancy payment in that event.

(4) An agreement such as is mentioned in subsection (3) may be contained—

(a) in the contract itself, or

(b) in a separate agreement.

(5) Where—

(a) an agreement such as is mentioned in subsection (3) is made during the currency of a fixed term, and

(b) the term is renewed,

the agreement shall not be construed as applying to the term as renewed; but this subsection is without prejudice to the making of a further agreement in relation to the renewed term.

198 Short-term employment

Sections 1 to 7 do not apply to an employee if his employment continues for less than one month.

199 Mariners

(1) Sections 1 to 7, Part II and sections 86 to 91 do not apply to a person employed as a seaman in a ship registered in the United Kingdom under a crew agreement the provisions and form of which are of a kind approved by the Secretary of State.

(2) Sections 8 to 10, Part III, sections 44, 45, 47, 47C, 50 to 57B and 61 to 63, Parts VII and VIII, sections 92 and 93 and Parts X to XII do not apply to employment as master, or as a member of the crew, of a fishing vessel where the employee is remunerated only by a share in the profits or gross earnings of the vessel.

(3) [repealed]

(4) Sections 8 to 10 and 50 to 54 and Part XII do not apply to employment as a merchant seaman.

(5) In subsection (4) 'employment as a merchant seaman'—

(a) does not include employment in the fishing industry or employment on board a ship otherwise than by the owner, manager or charterer of that ship except employment as a radio officer, but

(b) subject to that, includes—

(i) employment as a master or a member of the crew of any ship,

(ii) employment as a trainee undergoing training for the sea service, and

(iii) employment in or about a ship in port by the owner, manager or charterer of the ship to do work of the kind ordinarily done by a merchant seaman on a ship while it is in port.

(6) Section 197(3) does not apply to a contract of employment, if the employee is—

(a) employed as a master or seaman in a British ship, and

(b) ordinarily resident in Great Britain.

(7) The provisions mentioned in subsection (8) apply to employment on board a ship registered in the register maintained under section 8 of the Merchant Shipping Act 1995 in and only if—

(a) the ship's entry in the register specifies a port in Great Britain as the port to which the vessel is to be treated as belonging,

(b) under his contract of employment the person employed does not work wholly outside Great Britain, and

(c) the person employed is ordinarily resident in Great Britain.

(8) The provisions are—

(a) sections 8 to 10,

(b) Parts II, III and V,

(c) Part VI, apart from sections 58 to 60,

(d) Parts VII and VIII,

(e) sections 92 and 93, and

(f) Part X.

200 Police officers

(1) Sections 8 to 10, Part III, Part IVA, sections 45, 45A, 47, 47B, 47C, 50 to 57B and 61 to 63, Parts VII and VIII, sections 92 and 93, and Part X (except sections 100

and 134A and the other provisions of that Part so far as relating to the right not to be unfairly dismissed in a case where the dismissal is unfair by virtue of section 100) do not apply to employment under a contract of employment in police service or to persons engaged in such employment.

(2) In subsection (1) 'police service' means—

(a) service as a member of a constabulary maintained by virtue of an enactment; or

(b) subject to section 126 of the Criminal Justice and Public Order Act 1994 (prison staff not to be regarded as in police service), service in any other capacity by virtue of which a person has the powers or privileges of a constable.

201 [omitted]

CHAPTER II
OTHER MISCELLANEOUS MATTERS

Restrictions on disclosure of information

202 National security

(1) Where in the opinion of any Minister of the Crown the disclosure of any information would be contrary to the interests of national security—

(a) nothing in any of the provisions to which this section applies requires any person to disclose the information, and

(b) no person shall disclose the information in any proceedings in any court or tribunal relating to any of those provisions.

(2) This section applies to—

(a) Part I, so far as it relates to employment particulars,

(b) in Part V, sections 44, 45A, 47 and 47C, and sections 48 and 49 so far as relating to those sections,

(c) in Part VI, sections 55 to 57B and 61 to 63,

(d) in Part VII, sections 66 to 68, and sections 69 and 70 so far as relating to those sections,

(e) Part VIII,

(f) in Part IX, sections 92 and 93 where they apply by virtue of section 92(4),

(g) Part X so far as relating to a dismissal which is treated as unfair—

(i) by section 99, 100, 101A(d) or 103, or by section 104 in its application in relation to time off under section 57A,

(ii) by subsection (1) of section 105 by reason of the application of subsection (2), (3) or (6) of that section or by reason of the application of subsection (4A) in so far as it applies where the reason (or, if more than one, the principal reason) for which an employee was selected for dismissal was that specified in section 101A(d), and

(h) this Part and Parts XIV and XV (so far as relating to any of the provisions in paragraphs (a) to (g)).

Contracting out etc. and remedies

203 Restrictions on contracting out

(1) Any provision in an agreement (whether a contract of employment or not) is void in so far as it purports—

(a) to exclude or limit the operation of any provision of this Act, or

(b) to preclude a person from bringing any proceedings under this Act before an employment tribunal.

(2) Subsection (1)—

(a) does not apply to any provision in a collective agreement excluding rights under section 28 if an order under section 35 is for the time being in force in respect of it,

(b) does not apply to any provision in a dismissal procedures agreement excluding the right under section 94 if that provision is not to have effect unless an order under section 110 is for the time being in force in respect of it,

(c) does not apply to any provision in an agreement if an order under section 157 is for the time being in force in respect of it,

(d) does not apply to any provision of an agreement relating to dismissal from employment such as is mentioned in section 197(3),

(e) does not apply to any agreement to refrain from instituting or continuing proceedings where a conciliation officer has taken action under section 18 of the Employment Tribunals Act 1996, and

(f) does not apply to any agreement to refrain from instituting or continuing any proceedings within section 18(1)(d) (proceedings under this Act where conciliation available) of the Employment Tribunals Act 1996 if the conditions regulating compromise agreements under this Act are satisfied in relation to the agreement.

(3) For the purposes of subsection (2)(f) the conditions regulating compromise agreements under this Act are that—

(a) the agreement must be in writing,

(b) the agreement must relate to the particular proceedings,

(c) the employee or worker must have received advice from a relevant independent adviser as to the terms and effect of the proposed agreement and, in particular, its effect on his ability to pursue his rights before an employment tribunal,

(d) there must be in force, when the adviser gives the advice, a contract of insurance, or an indemnity provided for members of a profession or professional body covering the risk of a claim by the employee or worker in respect of loss arising in consequence of the advice,

(e) the agreement must identify the adviser, and

(f) the agreement must state that the conditions regulating compromise agreements under this Act are satisfied.

(3A) A person is a relevant independent adviser for the purposes of subsection (3)(c)—

(a) if he is a qualified lawyer,

(b) if he is an officer, official, employee or member of an independent trade union who has been certified in writing by the trade union as competent to give advice and as authorised to do so on behalf of the trade union,

(c) if he works at an advice centre (whether as an employee or a volunteer) and has been certified in writing by the centre as competent to give advice and as authorised to do so on behalf of the centre, or

(d) if he is a person of a description specified in an order made by the Secretary of State.

(3B) But a person is not a relevant independent adviser for the purposes of subsection (3)(c) in relation to the employee or worker—

(a) if he is, is employed by or is acting in the matter for the employer or an associated employer,

(b) in the case of a person within subsection (3A)(b) or (c), if the trade union or advice centre is the employer or an associated employer,

(c) in the case of a person within subsection (3A)(c), if the employee or worker makes a payment for the advice received from him, or

(d) in the case of a person of a description specified in an order under subsection (3A)(d), if any condition specified in the order in relation to the giving of advice by persons of that description is not satisfied.

(4) In subsection (3A)(a) 'qualified lawyer' means—

(a) as respects England and Wales, a barrister (whether in practice as such or employed to give legal advice), a solicitor who holds a practising certificate, or a person other than a barrister or solicitor who is an authorised advocate or authorised litigator (within the meaning of the Courts and Legal Services Act 1990), and

(b) as respects Scotland, an advocate (whether in practice as such or employed to give legal advice), or a solicitor who holds a practising certificate.

(5) An agreement under which the parties agree to submit a dispute to arbitration—

(a) shall be regarded for the purposes of subsection (2)(e) and (f) as being an agreement to refrain from instituting or continuing proceedings if—

(i) the dispute is covered by a scheme having effect by virtue of an order under section 212A of the Trade Union and Labour Relations (Consolidation) Act 1992, and

(ii) the agreement is to submit it to arbitration in accordance with the scheme,

but

(b) shall be regarded as neither being nor including such an agreement in any other case.

204 Law governing employment

(1) For the purposes of this Act it is immaterial whether the law which (apart from this Act) governs any person's employment is the law of the United Kingdom, or of a part of the United Kingdom, or not.

(2) [repealed]

205 Remedy for infringement of certain rights

(1) The remedy of an employee for infringement of any of the rights conferred by section 8, Part III, Parts V to VIII, section 92, Part X and Part XII is, where provision is made for a complaint or the reference of a question to an employment tribunal, by way of such a complaint or reference and not otherwise.

(1ZA) In relation to the right conferred by section 45A, the reference in subsection (1) to an employee has effect as a reference to a worker.

(1A) In relation to the right conferred by section 47B, the reference in subsection (1) to an employee has effect as a reference to a worker.

(2) The remedy of a worker in respect of any contravention of section 13, 15, 18(1) or 21(1) is by way of a complaint under section 23 and not otherwise.

General provisions about death of employer or employee

206 Institution or continuance of tribunal proceedings

(1) Where an employer has died, any tribunal proceedings arising under any of the provisions of this Act to which this section applies may be defended by a personal representative of the deceased employer.

(2) This section and section 207 apply to—

(a) Part I, so far as it relates to itemised pay statements,
(b) Part III,
(c) Part V,
(d) Part VI, apart from sections 58 to 60,
(e) Parts VII and VIII,
(f) in Part IX, sections 92 and 93, and
(g) Parts X to XII.

(3) Where an employee has died, any tribunal proceedings arising under any of the provisions of this Act to which this section applies may be instituted or continued by a personal representative of the deceased employee.

(4) If there is no personal representative of a deceased employee, any tribunal proceedings arising under any of the provisions of this Act to which this section applies may be instituted or continued on behalf of the estate of the deceased employee by any appropriate person appointed by the employment tribunal.

(5) In subsection (4) 'appropriate person' means a person who is—

(a) authorised by the employee before his death to act in connection with the proceedings, or

(b) the widow or widower, child, parent or brother or sister of the deceased employee;

and in Part XI and the following provisions of this section and section 207 references to a personal representative include a person appointed under subsection (4).

(6) In a case where proceedings are instituted or continued by virtue of subsection (4), any award made by the employment tribunal shall be—

(a) made in such terms, and

(b) enforceable in such manner,

as the Secretary of State may by regulations provide.

(7) Any reference in the provisions of this Act to which this section applies to the doing of anything by or in relation to an employer or employee includes a reference to the doing of the thing by or in relation to a personal representative of the deceased employer or employee.

(8) Any reference in the provisions of this Act to which this section applies to a thing required or authorised to be done by or in relation to an employer or employee includes a reference to a thing required or authorised to be done by or in relation to a personal representative of the deceased employer or employee.

(9) Subsections (7) and (8) do not prevent a reference to a successor of an employer including a personal representative of a deceased employer.

207 Rights and liabilities accruing after death

(1) Any right arising under any of the provisions of this Act to which this section applies which accrues after the death of an employee devolves as if it had accrued before his death.

(2) Where an employment tribunal determines under any provision of Part XI that an employer is liable to pay to a personal representative of a deceased employee—

(a) the whole of a redundancy payment to which he would have been entitled but for some provision of Part XI or section 206, or

(b) such part of such a redundancy payment as the tribunal thinks fit,

the reference in subsection (1) to a right includes any right to receive it.

(3) Where—

(a) by virtue of any of the provisions to which this section applies a personal representative is liable to pay any amount, and

(b) the liability has not accrued before the death of the employer,

it shall be treated as a liability of the deceased employer which had accrued immediately before his death.

208 [repealed]; **209** [omitted]

PART XIV
INTERPRETATION

CHAPTER I
CONTINUOUS EMPLOYMENT

210 Introductory

(1) References in any provision of this Act to a period of continuous employment are (unless provision is expressly made to the contrary) to a period computed in accordance with this Chapter.

(2) In any provision of this Act which refers to a period of continuous employment expressed in months or years—

(a) a month means a calendar month, and

(b) a year means a year of twelve calendar months.

(3) In computing an employee's period of continuous employment for the purposes of any provision of this Act, any question—

(a) whether the employee's employment is of a kind counting towards a period of continuous employment, or

(b) whether periods (consecutive or otherwise) are to be treated as forming a single period of continuous employment,

shall be determined week by week; but where it is necessary to compute the length of an employee's period of employment it shall be computed in months and years of twelve months in accordance with section 211.

(4) Subject to sections 215 to 217, a week which does not count in computing the length of a period of continuous employment breaks continuity of employment.

(5) A person's employment during any period shall, unless the contrary is shown, be presumed to have been continuous.

211 Period of continuous employment

(1) An employee's period of continuous employment for the purposes of any provision of this Act—

(a) (subject to subsections (2) and (3)) begins with the day on which the employee starts work, and

(b) ends with the day by reference to which the length of the employee's period of continuous employment is to be ascertained for the purposes of the provision.

(2) For the purposes of sections 155 and 162(1), an employee's period of continuous employment shall be treated as beginning on the employee's eighteenth birthday if that is later than the day on which the employee starts work.

(3) If an employee's period of continuous employment includes one or more periods which (by virtue of section 215, 216 or 217) while not counting in computing the length of the period do not break continuity of employment, the beginning of the period shall be treated as postponed by the number of days falling within that intervening period, or the aggregate number of days falling within those periods, calculated in accordance with the section in question.

212 Weeks counting in computing period

(1) Any week during the whole or part of which an employee's relations with his employer are governed by a contract of employment counts in computing the employee's period of employment.

(2) [repealed]

(3) Subject to subsection (4), any week (not within subsection (1)) during the whole or part of which an employee is—

(a) incapable of work in consequence of sickness or injury,

(b) absent from work on account of a temporary cessation of work, or

(c) absent from work in circumstances such that, by arrangement or custom, he is regarded as continuing in the employment of his employer for any purpose,

(d) [repealed]

(4) Not more than twenty-six weeks count under subsection (3)(a) between any periods falling under subsection (1).

213 Intervals in employment

(1) Where in the case of an employee a date later than the date which would be the effective date of termination by virtue of subsection (1) of section 97 is treated for certain purposes as the effective date of termination by virtue of subsection (2) or (4) of that section, the period of the interval between the two dates counts as a period of employment in ascertaining for the purposes of section 108(1) or 119(1) the period for which the employee has been continuously employed.

(2) Where an employee is by virtue of section 138(1) regarded for the purposes of Part XI as not having been dismissed by reason of a renewal or re-engagement taking effect after an interval, the period of the interval counts as a period of employment in ascertaining for the purposes of section 155 or 162(1) the period for which the employee has been continuously employed (except so far as it is to be disregarded under section 214 or 215).

(3) Where in the case of an employee a date later than the date which would be the relevant date by virtue of subsections (2) to (4) of section 145 is treated for certain purposes as the relevant date by virtue of subsection (5) of that section, the period of the interval between the two dates counts as a period of employment in ascertaining for the purposes of section 155 or 162(1) the period for which the employee has been continuously employed (except so far as it is to be disregarded under section 214 or 215).

214 Special provisions for redundancy payments

(1) This section applies where a period of continuous employment has to be determined in relation to an employee for the purposes of the application of section 155 or 162(1).

(2) The continuity of a period of employment is broken where—

(a) a redundancy payment has previously been paid to the employee (whether in respect of dismissal or in respect of lay-off or short-time), and

(b) the contract of employment under which the employee was employed was renewed (whether by the same or another employer) or the employee was re-engaged under a new contract of employment (whether by the same or another employer).

(3) The continuity of a period of employment is also broken where—

(a) a payment has been made to the employee (whether in respect of the termination of his employment or lay-off or short-time) in accordance with a scheme under section 1 of the Superannuation Act 1972 or arrangements falling within section 177(3), and

(b) he commenced new, or renewed, employment.

(4) The date on which the person's continuity of employment is broken by virtue of this section—

(a) if the employment was under a contract of employment, is the date which was the relevant date in relation to the payment mentioned in subsection (2)(a) or (3)(a), and

(b) if the employment was otherwise than under a contract of employment, is the date which would have been the relevant date in relation to the payment mentioned in subsection (2)(a) or (3)(a) had the employment been under a contract of employment.

(5) For the purposes of this section a redundancy payment shall be treated as having been paid if—

(a) the whole of the payment has been paid to the employee by the employer,

(b) a tribunal has determined liability and found that the employer must pay part (but not all) of the redundancy payment and the employer has paid that part, or

(c) the Secretary of State has paid a sum to the employee in respect of the redundancy payment under section 167.

215 Employment abroad etc.

(1) This Chapter applies to a period of employment—

(a) (subject to the following provisions of this section) even where during the period the employee was engaged in work wholly or mainly outside Great Britain, and

(b) even where the employee was excluded by or under this Act from any right conferred by this Act.

(2) For the purposes of sections 155 and 162(1) a week of employment does not count in computing a period of employment if the employee—

(a) was employed outside Great Britain during the whole or part of the week, and

(b) was not during that week an employed earner for the purposes of the Social Security Contributions and Benefits Act 1992 in respect of whom a secondary Class 1 contribution was payable under that Act (whether or not the contribution was in fact paid).

(3) Where by virtue of subsection (2) a week of employment does not count in computing a period of employment, the continuity of the period is not broken by reason only that the week does not count in computing the period; and the number of days which, for the purposes of section 211(3), fall within the intervening period is seven for each week within this subsection.

(4) Any question arising under subsection (2) whether—

(a) a person was an employed earner for the purposes of the Social Security Contributions and Benefits Act 1992, or

(b) if so, whether a secondary Class 1 contribution was payable in respect of him under that Act,

shall be determined by an officer of the Commissioners of the Inland Revenue.

(5) Part II of the Social Security Contributions (Transfer of Functions, etc.) Act 1999 (decisions and appeals) shall apply in relation to the determination of any issue by the Inland Revenue under subsection (4) as if it were a decision falling within section 8(1) of that Act.

(6) Subsection (2) does not apply in relation to a person who is—

(a) employed as a master or seaman in a British ship, and

(b) ordinarily resident in Great Britain.

216 Industrial disputes

(1) A week does not count under section 212 if during the week, or any part of the week, the employee takes part in a strike.

(2) The continuity of an employee's period of employment is not broken by a week which does not count under this Chapter (whether or not by virtue only of subsection (1)) if during the week, or any part of the week, the employee takes part in a strike; and the number of days which, for the purposes of section 211(3), fall within the intervening period is the number of days between the last working day before the strike and the day on which work was resumed.

(3) The continuity of an employee's period of employment is not broken by a week if during the week, or any part of the week, the employee is absent from work because of a lock-out by the employer; and the number of days which, for the purposes of section 211(3), fall within the intervening period is the number of days between the last working day before the lock-out and the day on which work was resumed.

217 [omitted]

218 Change of employer

(1) Subject to the provisions of this section, this Chapter relates only to employment by the one employer.

(2) If a trade or business, or an undertaking (whether or not established by or under an Act), is transferred from one person to another—

(a) the period of employment of an employee in the trade or business or undertaking at the time of the transfer counts as a period of employment with the transferee, and

(b) the transfer does not break the continuity of the period of employment.

(3) If by or under an Act (whether public or local and whether passed before or after this Act) a contract of employment between any body corporate and an employee is modified and some other body corporate is substituted as the employer—

(a) the employee's period of employment at the time when the modification takes effect counts as a period of employment with the second body corporate, and

(b) the change of employer does not break the continuity of the period of employment.

(4) If on the death of an employer the employee is taken into the employment of the personal representatives or trustees of the deceased—

(a) the employee's period of employment at the time of the death counts as a period of employment with the employer's personal representatives or trustees, and

(b) the death does not break the continuity of the period of employment.

(5) If there is a change in the partners, personal representatives or trustees who employ any person—

(a) the employee's period of employment at the time of the change counts as a period of employment with the partners, personal representatives or trustees after the change, and

(b) the change does not break the continuity of the period of employment.

(6) If an employee of an employer is taken into the employment of another employer who, at the time when the employee enters the second employer's employment, is an associated employer of the first employer—

(a) the employee's period of employment at that time counts as a period of employment with the second employer, and

(b) the change of employer does not break the continuity of the period of employment.

(7) to (10) [omitted]

219 [omitted]

CHAPTER II
A WEEK'S PAY

Introductory

220 Introductory

The amount of a week's pay of an employee shall be calculated for the purposes of this Act in accordance with this Chapter.

Employments with normal working hours

221 General

(1) This section and sections 222 and 223 apply where there are normal working hours for the employee when employed under the contract of employment in force on the calculation date.

(2) Subject to section 222, if the employee's remuneration for employment in normal working hours (whether by the hour or week or other period) does not vary with the amount of work done in the period, the amount of a week's pay is the amount which is payable by the employer under the contract of employment in force on the calculation date if the employee works throughout his normal working hours in a week.

(3) Subject to section 222, if the employee's remuneration for employment in normal working hours (whether by the hour or week or other period) does vary with the amount of work done in the period, the amount of a week's pay is the amount of remuneration for the number of normal working hours in a week calculated at the average hourly rate of remuneration payable by the employer to the employee in respect of the period of twelve weeks ending—

(a) where the calculation date is the last day of a week, with that week, and

(b) otherwise, with the last complete week before the calculation date.

(4) In this section references to remuneration varying with the amount of work done includes remuneration which may include any commission or similar payment which varies in amount.

(5) This section is subject to sections 227 and 228.

222 Remuneration varying according to time of work

(1) This section applies if the employee is required under the contract of employment in force on the calculation date to work during normal working hours on days of the week, or at times of the day, which differ from week to week or over a longer period so that the remuneration payable for, or apportionable to, any week varies according to the incidence of those days or times.

(2) The amount of a week's pay is the amount of remuneration for the average number of weekly normal working hours at the average hourly rate of remuneration.

(3) For the purposes of subsection (2)—

(a) the average number of weekly hours is calculated by dividing by twelve the total number of the employee's normal working hours during the relevant period of twelve weeks, and

(b) the average hourly rate of remuneration is the average hourly rate of remuneration payable by the employer to the employee in respect of the relevant period of twelve weeks.

(4) In subsection (3) 'the relevant period of twelve weeks' means the period of twelve weeks ending—

(a) where the calculation date is the last day of a week, with that week, and

(b) otherwise, with the last complete week before the calculation date.

(5) This section is subject to sections 227 and 228.

223 Supplementary

(1) For the purposes of sections 221 and 222, in arriving at the average hourly rate of remuneration, only—

(a) the hours when the employee was working, and

(b) the remuneration payable for, or apportionable to, those hours,

shall be brought in.

(2) If for any of the twelve weeks mentioned in sections 221 and 222 no remuneration within subsection (1)(b) was payable by the employer to the employee, account shall be taken of remuneration in earlier weeks so as to bring up to twelve the number of weeks of which account is taken.

(3) Where—

(a) in arriving at the average hourly rate of remuneration, account has to be taken of remuneration payable for, or apportionable to, work done in hours other than normal working hours, and

(b) the amount of that remuneration was greater than it would have been if the work had been done in normal working hours (or, in a case within section 234(3), in normal working hours falling within the number of hours without overtime),

account shall be taken of that remuneration as if the work had been done in such hours and the amount of that remuneration had been reduced accordingly.

Employments with no normal working hours

224 Employment with no normal working hours

(1) This section applies where there are no normal working hours for the employee when employed under the contract of employment in force on the calculation date.

(2) The amount of a week's pay is the amount of the employee's average weekly remuneration in the period of twelve weeks ending—

(a) where the calculation date is the last day of a week, with that week, and

(b) otherwise, with the last complete week before the calculation date.

(3) In arriving at the average weekly remuneration no account shall be taken of a week in which no remuneration was payable by the employer to the employee and

remuneration in earlier weeks shall be brought in so as to bring up to twelve the number of weeks of which account is taken.

(4) This section is subject to sections 227 and 228.

The calculation date

225 Rights during employment

(1) Where the calculation is for the purposes of section 30, the calculation date is—

(a) where the employee's contract has been varied, or a new contract entered into, in connection with a period of short-time working, the last day on which the original contract was in force, and

(b) otherwise, the day in respect of which the guarantee payment is payable.

(2) Where the calculation is for the purposes of section 53 or 54, the calculation date is the day on which the employer's notice was given.

(3) Where the calculation is for the purposes of section 56, the calculation date is the day of the appointment.

(4) Where the calculation is for the purposes of section 62, the calculation date is the day on which the time off was taken or on which it is alleged the time off should have been permitted.

(4A) Where the calculation is for the purposes of section 63B, the calculation date is the day on which the time off was taken or on which it is alleged the time off should have been permitted.

(5) Where the calculation is for the purposes of section 69—

(a) in the case of an employee suspended on medical grounds, the calculation date is the day before that on which the suspension begins, and

(b) in the case of an employee suspended on maternity grounds, the calculation date is—

(i) where the day before that on which the suspension begins falls during a period of ordinary or additional maternity leave, the day before the beginning of that period,

(ii) otherwise, the day before that on which the suspension begins.

226 Rights on termination

(1) Where the calculation is for the purposes of section 88 or 89, the calculation date is the day immediately preceding the first day of the period of notice required by section 86(1) or (2).

(2) Where the calculation is for the purposes of section 93, 117 or 125, the calculation date is—

(a) if the dismissal was with notice, the date on which the employer's notice was given, and

(b) otherwise, the effective date of termination.

(3) Where the calculation is for the purposes of section 119, 121 or 127A, the calculation date is—

(a) [repealed]

(b) if by virtue of subsection (2) or (4) of section 97 a date later than the effective date of termination as defined in subsection (1) of that section is to be treated for certain purposes as the effective date of termination, the effective date of termination as so defined, and

(c) otherwise, the date specified in subsection (6).

(4) Where the calculation is for the purposes of section 147(2), the calculation date is the day immediately preceding the first of the four, or six, weeks referred to in section 148(2).

(5) Where the calculation is for the purposes of section 162, the calculation date is—

(a) [repealed]

(b) if by virtue of subsection (5) of section 145 a date is to be treated for certain purposes as the relevant date which is later than the relevant date as defined by the previous provisions of that section, the relevant date as so defined, and

(c) otherwise, the date specified in subsection (6).

(6) The date referred to in subsections (3)(c) and (5)(c) is the date on which notice would have been given had—

(a) the contract been terminable by notice and been terminated by the employer giving such notice as is required by section 86 to terminate the contract, and

(b) the notice expired on the effective date of termination, or the relevant date,

(whether or not those conditions were in fact fulfilled).

Maximum amount of week's pay

227 Maximum amount

(1) For the purpose of calculating—

(a) a basic award of compensation for unfair dismissal,

(b) an additional award of compensation for unfair dismissal, or

(c) a redundancy payment, the amount of a week's pay shall not exceed £220.

(2)-(4) [repealed]

Miscellaneous

228 New employments and other special cases

(1) In any case in which the employee has not been employed for a sufficient period to enable a calculation to be made under the preceding provisions of this Chapter, the amount of a week's pay is the amount which fairly represents a week's pay.

(2) In determining that amount the employment tribunal—

(a) shall apply as nearly as may be such of the preceding provisions of this Chapter as it considers appropriate, and

(b) may have regard to such of the considerations specified in subsection (3) as it thinks fit.

(3) The considerations referred to in subsection (2)(b) are—

(a) any remuneration received by the employee in respect of the employment in question,

(b) the amount offered to the employee as remuneration in respect of the employment in question,

(c) the remuneration received by other persons engaged in relevant comparable employment with the same employer, and

(d) the remuneration received by other persons engaged in relevant comparable employment with other employers.

(4) The Secretary of State may by regulations provide that in cases prescribed by the regulations the amount of a week's pay shall be calculated in such manner as may be so prescribed.

229 Supplementary

(1) In arriving at—

(a) an average hourly rate of remuneration, or

(b) average weekly remuneration,

under this Chapter, account shall be taken of work for a former employer within the period for which the average is to be taken if, by virtue of Chapter I of this Part, a period of employment with the former employer counts as part of the employee's continuous period of employment.

(2) Where under this Chapter account is to be taken of remuneration or other payments for a period which does not coincide with the periods for which the remuneration or other payments are calculated, the remuneration or other payments shall be apportioned in such manner as may be just.

CHAPTER III
OTHER INTERPRETATION PROVISIONS

230 Employees, workers etc.

(1) In this Act 'employee' means an individual who has entered into or works under (or, where the employment has ceased, worked under) a contract of employment.

(2) In this Act 'contract of employment' means a contract of service or apprenticeship, whether express or implied, and (if it is express) whether oral or in writing.

(3) In this Act 'worker' (except in the phrases 'shop worker' and 'betting worker') means an individual who has entered into or works under (or, where the employment has ceased, worked under)—

(a) a contract of employment, or

(b) any other contract, whether express or implied and (if it is express) whether oral or in writing, whereby the individual undertakes to do or perform personally any work or services for another party to the contract whose status is not by virtue of the contract that of a client or customer of any profession or business undertaking carried on by the individual;

and any reference to a worker's contract shall be construed accordingly.

(4) In this Act 'employer', in relation to an employee or a worker, means the person by whom the employee or worker is (or, where the employment has ceased, was) employed.

(5) In this Act 'employment'—

(a) in relation to an employee, means (except for the purposes of section 171) employment under a contract of employment, and

(b) in relation to a worker, means employment under his contract; and 'employed' shall be construed accordingly.

(6) This section has effect subject to sections 43K and 47B(3); and for the purposes of Part XIII so far as relating to Part IVA or section 47B, 'worker', 'worker's contract' and, in relation to a worker, 'employer', 'employment' and 'employed' have the extended meaning given by section 43K.

231 Associated employer

For the purposes of this Act any two employers shall be treated as associated if—

(a) one is a company of which the other (directly or indirectly) has control, or

(b) both are companies of which a third person (directly or indirectly) has control;

and 'associated employer' shall be construed accordingly.

232 Shop workers

(1) In this Act 'shop worker' means an employee who, under his contract of employment, is or may be required to do shop work.

(2) In this Act 'shop work' means work in or about a shop in England or Wales on a day on which the shop is open for the serving of customers.

(3) Subject to subsection (4), in this Act 'shop' includes any premises where any retail trade or business is carried on.

(4) Where premises are used mainly for purposes other than those of retail trade or business and would not (apart from subsection (3)) be regarded as a shop, only such part of the premises as—

(a) is used wholly or mainly for the purposes of retail trade or business, or

(b) is used both for the purposes of retail trade or business and for the purposes of wholesale trade and is used wholly or mainly for those two purposes considered together, is to be regarded as a shop for the purposes of this Act.

(5) In subsection (4)(b) 'wholesale trade' means the sale of goods for use or resale in the course of a business or the hire of goods for use in the course of a business.

(6) In this section 'retail trade or business' includes—

(a) the business of a barber or hairdresser,

(b) the business of hiring goods otherwise than for use in the course of a trade or business, and

(c) retail sales by auction,

but does not include catering business or the sale at theatres and places of amusement of programmes, catalogues and similar items.

(7) In subsection (6) 'catering business' means—

(a) the sale of meals, refreshments or intoxicating liquor for consumption on the premises on which they are sold, or

(b) the sale of meals or refreshments prepared to order for immediate consumption off the premises;

and in paragraph (a) 'intoxicating liquor' has the same meaning as in the Licensing Act 1964.

(8) In this Act—

'notice period', in relation to an opted-out shop worker, has the meaning given by section 41(3),

'opted-out', in relation to a shop worker, shall be construed in accordance with section 41(1) and (2),

'opting-in notice', in relation to a shop worker, has the meaning given by section 36(6),

'opting-out notice', in relation to a shop worker, has the meaning given by section 40(2), and

'protected', in relation to a shop worker, shall be construed in accordance with section 36(1) to (5).

233 Betting workers

(1) In this Act 'betting worker' means an employee who, under his contract of employment, is or may be required to do betting work.

(2) In this Act 'betting work' means—

(a) work at a track in England or Wales for a bookmaker on a day on which the bookmaker acts as such at the track, being work which consists of or includes dealing with betting transactions, and

(b) work in a licensed betting office in England or Wales on a day on which the office is open for use for the effecting of betting transactions.

(3) In subsection (2) 'betting transactions' includes the collection or payment of winnings on a bet and any transaction in which one or more of the parties is acting as a bookmaker.

(4) In this section 'bookmaker' means any person who—

(a) whether on his own account or as servant or agent to any other person, carries on (whether occasionally or regularly) the business of receiving or negotiating bets or conducting pool betting operations, or

(b) by way of business in any manner holds himself out, or permits himself to be held out, as a person who receives or negotiates bets or conducts such operations.

(5) Expressions used in this section and in the Betting, Gaming and Lotteries Act 1963 have the same meaning in this section as in that Act.

(6) In this Act—

'notice period', in relation to an opted-out betting worker, has the meaning given by section 41(3),

'opted-out', in relation to a betting worker, shall be construed in accordance with section 41(1) and (2),
'opting-in notice', in relation to a betting worker, has the meaning given by section 36(6),
'opting-out notice', in relation to a betting worker, has the meaning given by section 40(2), and
'protected', in relation to a betting worker, shall be construed in accordance with section 36(1) to (5).

234 Normal working hours

(1) Where an employee is entitled to overtime pay when employed for more than a fixed number of hours in a week or other period, there are for the purposes of this Act normal working hours in his case.

(2) Subject to subsection (3), the normal working hours in such a case are the fixed number of hours.

(3) Where in such a case—

(a) the contract of employment fixes the number, or minimum number, of hours of employment in a week or other period (whether or not it also provides for the reduction of that number or minimum in certain circumstances), and

(b) that number or minimum number of hours exceeds the number of hours without overtime,

the normal working hours are that number or minimum number of hours (and not the number of hours without overtime).

235 Other definitions

(1) In this Act, except in so far as the context otherwise requires—
'act' and 'action' each includes omission and references to doing an act or taking action shall be construed accordingly,
'basic award of compensation for unfair dismissal' shall be construed in accordance with section 118,
'business' includes a trade or profession and includes any activity carried on by a body of persons (whether corporate or unincorporated),
'childbirth' means the birth of a living child or the birth of a child whether living or dead after twenty-four weeks of pregnancy,
'collective agreement' has the meaning given by section 178(1) and (2) of the Trade Union and Labour Relations (Consolidation) Act 1992,
'conciliation officer' means an officer designated by the Advisory, Conciliation and Arbitration Service under section 211 of that Act,
'dismissal procedures agreement' means an agreement in writing with respect to procedures relating to dismissal made by or on behalf of one or more independent trade unions and one or more employers or employers' associations,
'employers' association' has the same meaning as in the Trade Union and Labour Relations (Consolidation) Act 1992,
'expected week of childbirth' means the week, beginning with midnight between Saturday and Sunday, in which it is expected that childbirth will occur,
'guarantee payment' has the meaning given by section 28,
'independent trade union' means a trade union which—

(a) is not under the domination or control of an employer or a group of employers or of one or more employers' associations, and

(b) is not liable to interference by an employer or any such group or association (arising out of the provision of financial or material support or by any other means whatever) tending towards such control, 'job', in relation to an employee, means the nature of the work which he is employed to do in accordance with his contract and the capacity and place in which he is so employed,

'position', in relation to an employee, means the following matters taken as a whole—

(a) his status as an employee,

(b) the nature of his work, and

(c) his terms and conditions of employment,

'protected disclosure' has the meaning given by section 43A,

'redundancy payment' has the meaning given by Part XI,

'relevant date' has the meaning given by sections 145 and 153,

'renewal' includes extension, and any reference to renewing a contract or a fixed term shall be construed accordingly,

'statutory provision' means a provision, whether of a general or a special nature, contained in, or in any document made or issued under, any Act, whether of a general or special nature,

'successor', in relation to the employer of an employee, means (subject to subsection (2)) a person who in consequence of a change occurring (whether by virtue of a sale or other disposition or by operation of law) in the ownership of the undertaking, or of the part of the undertaking, for the purposes of which the employee was employed, has become the owner of the undertaking or part,

'trade union' has the meaning given by section 1 of the Trade Union and Labour Relations (Consolidation) Act 1992,

'week'—

(a) in Chapter I of this Part means a week ending with Saturday, and

(b) otherwise, except in section 86, means, in relation to an employee whose remuneration is calculated weekly by a week ending with a day other than Saturday, a week ending with that other day and, in relation to any other employee, a week ending with Saturday.

(2) The definition of 'successor' in subsection (1) has effect (subject to the necessary modifications) in relation to a case where—

(a) the person by whom an undertaking or part of an undertaking is owned immediately before a change is one of the persons by whom (whether as partners, trustees or otherwise) it is owned immediately after the change, or

(b) the persons by whom an undertaking or part of an undertaking is owned immediately before a change (whether as partners, trustees or otherwise) include the persons by whom, or include one or more of the persons by whom, it is owned immediately after the change,

as it has effect where the previous owner and the new owner are wholly different persons.

(3) References in this Act to redundancy, dismissal by reason of redundancy and similar expressions shall be construed in accordance with section 139.

(4) In sections 136(2), 154 and 216(3) and paragraph 14 of Schedule 2 'lock-out' means—

(a) the closing of a place of employment,

(b) the suspension of work, or

(c) the refusal by an employer to continue to employ any number of persons employed by him in consequence of a dispute,

done with a view to compelling persons employed by the employer, or to aid another employer in compelling persons employed by him, to accept terms or conditions of or affecting employment.

(5) In sections 91(2), 140(2) and (3), 143(1), 144(2) and (3), 154 and 216(1) and (2) and paragraph 14 of Schedule 2 'strike' means—

(a) the cessation of work by a body of employed persons acting in combination, or
(b) a concerted refusal, or a refusal under a common understanding, of any number of employed persons to continue to work for an employer in consequence of a dispute,

done as a means of compelling their employer or any employed person or body of employed persons, or to aid other employees in compelling their employer or any employed person or body of employed persons, to accept or not to accept terms or conditions of or affecting employment.

236-245 [omitted]

EMPLOYMENT TRIBUNALS ACT 1996
(1996, c. 17)

PART I
EMPLOYMENT TRIBUNALS

Jurisdiction

PART III
SUPPLEMENTARY

General

PART I
EMPLOYMENT TRIBUNALS

1 [omitted]

Jurisdiction

2 Enactments conferring jurisdiction on employment tribunals

Employment tribunals shall exercise the jurisdiction conferred on them by or by virtue of this Act or any other Act, whether passed before or after this Act.

3 Power to confer further jurisdiction on employment tribunals

(1) The appropriate Minister may by order provide that proceedings in respect of—

(a) any claim to which this section applies, or

(b) any claim to which this section applies and which is of a description specified in the order,

may, subject to such exceptions (if any) as may be so specified, be brought before an employment tribunal.

(2) Subject to subsection (3), this section applies to—

(a) a claim for damages for breach of a contract of employment or other contract connected with employment,

(b) a claim for a sum due under such a contract, and

(c) a claim for the recovery of a sum in pursuance of any enactment relating to the terms or performance of such a contract,

if the claim is such that a court in England and Wales or Scotland would under the law for the time being in force have jurisdiction to hear and determine an action in respect of the claim.

(3) This section does not apply to a claim for damages, or for a sum due, in respect of personal injuries.

(4) Any jurisdiction conferred on an employment tribunal by virtue of this section in respect of any claim is exercisable concurrently with any court in England and Wales or in Scotland which has jurisdiction to hear and determine an action in respect of the claim.

(5) In this section—

'appropriate Minister', as respects a claim in respect of which an action could be heard and determined by a court in England and Wales, means the Lord Chancellor and, as respects a claim in respect of which an action could be heard and determined by a court in Scotland, means the Lord Advocate, and

'personal injuries' includes any disease and any impairment of a person's physical or mental condition.

(6) In this section a reference to breach of a contract includes a reference to breach of—

(a) a term implied in a contract by or under any enactment or otherwise,

(b) a term of a contract as modified by or under any enactment or otherwise, and

(c) a term which, although not contained in a contract, is incorporated in the contract by another term of the contract.

Membership etc.

4 Composition of a tribunal

(1) Subject to the following provisions of this section and to section 7(3)(A), proceedings before an employment tribunal shall be heard by—

(a) the person who, in accordance with regulations made under section 1(1), is the chairman, and

(b) two other members selected as the other members in accordance with regulations so made or, with appropriate consent, one other member selected as the other member in accordance with regulations so made,

and in paragraph (b) 'appropriate consent' means either consent given at the beginning of the hearing by such of the parties as are then present in person or represented, or consent given by each of the parties.

(2) Subject to subsection (5), the proceedings specified in subsection (3) shall be heard by the person mentioned in subsection (1)(a) alone.

(3) The proceedings referred to in subsection (2) are—

(a) proceedings on a complaint under section 68A, 87 or 192 of the Trade Union and Labour Relations (Consolidation) Act 1992 or on an application under section 161, 165 or 166 of that Act,

(b) proceedings on a complaint under section 126 of the Pension Schemes Act 1993,

(c) proceedings on a reference under section 11, 163 or 170 of the Employment Rights Act 1996, on a complaint under section 23, 34 or 188 of that Act, on a complaint under section 70(1) of that Act relating to section 64 of that Act, on an application under section 128, 131 or 132 of that Act or for an appointment under section 206(4) of that Act,

(ca) proceedings on a complaint under regulation 11(5) of the Transfer of Undertakings (Protection of Employment) Regulations 1981,

(cc) proceedings on a complaint under section 11 of the National Minimum Wage Act 1998,

(cd) proceedings on an appeal under section 19 or 22 of the National Minimum Wage Act 1998,

(d) proceedings in respect of which an employment tribunal has jurisdiction by virtue of section 3 of this Act,

(e) proceedings in which the parties have given their written consent to the proceedings being heard in accordance with subsection (2) (whether or not they have subsequently withdrawn it),

(f) . . .

(g) proceedings in which the person (or, where more than one, each of the persons) against whom the proceedings are brought does not, or has ceased to, contest the case.

(4) The Secretary of State may by order amend the provisions of subsection (3).

(5) Proceedings specified in subsection (3) shall be heard in accordance with subsection (1) if a person who, in accordance with regulations made under section 1(1), may be the chairman of an employment tribunal, having regard to—

(a) whether there is a likelihood of a dispute arising on the facts which makes it desirable for the proceedings to be heard in accordance with subsection (1),

(b) whether there is a likelihood of an issue of law arising which would make it desirable for the proceedings to be heard in accordance with subsection (2),

(c) any views of any of the parties as to whether or not the proceedings ought to be heard in accordance with either of those subsections, and

(d) whether there are other proceedings which might be heard concurrently but which are not proceedings specified in subsection (3), decides at any stage of the proceedings that the proceedings are to be heard in accordance with subsection (1).

(6)-(6C) [omitted]; (7) [repealed]

5 [omitted]

Procedure

6 Conduct of hearings

(1) A person may appear before an employment tribunal in person or be represented by—

(a) counsel or a solicitor,

(b) a representative of a trade union or an employers' association, or

(c) any other person whom he desires to represent him.

(2) Part I of the Arbitration Act 1996 does not apply to any proceedings before an employment tribunal.

7 [omitted]

8 Procedure in contract cases

(1) Where in proceedings brought by virtue of section 3 an employment tribunal finds that the whole or part of a sum claimed in the proceedings is due, the tribunal shall order the respondent to the proceedings to pay the amount which it finds due.

(2) An order under section 3 may provide that an employment tribunal shall not in proceedings in respect of a claim, or a number of claims relating to the same contract, order the payment of an amount exceeding such sum as may be specified in the order as the maximum amount which an employment tribunal may order to be paid in relation to a claim or in relation to a contract.

(3) An order under section 3 may include provisions—

(a) as to the manner in which and time within which proceedings are to be brought by virtue of that section, and

(b) modifying any other enactment.

(4) An order under that section may make different provision in relation to proceedings in respect of different descriptions of claims.

9-14 [omitted]

15 Enforcement

(1) Any sum payable in pursuance of a decision of an employment tribunal in England and Wales which has been registered in accordance with employment tribunal procedure regulations shall, if a county court so orders, be recoverable by execution issued from the county court or otherwise as if it were payable under an order of that court.

(2) Any order for the payment of any sum made by an employment tribunal in Scotland (or any copy of such an order certified by the Secretary of the Tribunals) may be enforced as if it were an extract registered decree arbitral bearing a warrant for execution issued by the sheriff court of any sheriffdom in Scotland.

(3) In this section a reference to a decision or order of an employment tribunal—

(a) does not include a decision or order which, on being reviewed, has been revoked by the tribunal, and

(b) in relation to a decision or order which on being reviewed, has been varied by the tribunal shall be construed as a reference to the decision or order as so varied.

16 and **17** [omitted]

Conciliation

18 Conciliation

(1) This section applies in the case of employment tribunal proceedings and claims which could be the subject of employment tribunal proceedings—

(a) under—

(i) section 2(1) of the Equal Pay Act 1970,

(ii) section 63 of the Sex Discrimination Act 1975, or

(iii) section 54 of the Race Relations Act 1976,

(b) arising out of a contravention, or alleged contravention, of section 64, 68, 86, 137, 138, 146, 168, 169, 170, 174, 188 or 190 of the Trade Union and Labour Relations (Consolidation) Act 1992,

(c) under section 8 of the Disability Discrimination Act 1995,

(d) arising out of a contravention, or alleged contravention, of section 8, 13, 15, 18(1), 21(1), 28, 92 or 135, or of Part V, VI, VII or X, of the Employment Rights Act 1996,

(dd) under or by virtue of section 11, 18, 20(1)(a) or 24 of the National Minimum Wage Act 1998,

(e) which are proceedings in respect of which an employment tribunal has jurisdiction by virtue of section 3 of this Act, or

(f) arising out of a contravention, or alleged contravention, of a provision specified by an order under subsection (8)(b) as a provision to which this paragraph applies.

(2) Where an application has been presented to an employment tribunal and a copy of it has been sent to a conciliation officer, it is the duty of the conciliation officer—

(a) if he is requested to do so by the person by whom and the person against whom the proceedings are brought, or

(b) if, in the absence of any such request, the conciliation officer considers that he could act under this subsection with a reasonable prospect of success,

to endeavour to promote a settlement of the proceedings without their being determined by an employment tribunal.

(3) Where at any time—

(a) a person claims that action has been taken in respect of which proceedings could be brought by him before an employment tribunal, but

(b) before any application relating to that action has been presented by him a request is made to a conciliation officer (whether by that person or by the person against whom the proceedings could be instituted) to make his services available to them,

the conciliation officer shall act in accordance with subsection (2) as if an application had been presented to an employment tribunal.

(4) Where a person who has presented a complaint to an employment tribunal under section 111 of the Employment Rights Act 1996 has ceased to be employed by the employer against whom the complaint was made, the conciliation officer shall (for the purpose of promoting a settlement of the complaint in accordance with subsection (2)) in particular—

(a) seek to promote the reinstatement or re-engagement of the complainant by the employer, or by a successor of the employer or by an associated employer, on terms appearing to the conciliation officer to be equitable, or

(b) where the complainant does not wish to be reinstated or re-engaged, or where reinstatement or re-engagement is not practicable, and the parties desire the conciliation officer to act, seek to promote agreement between them as to a sum by way of compensation to be paid by the employer to the complainant.

(5) Where at any time—

(a) a person claims that action has been taken in respect of which a complaint could be presented by him to an employment tribunal under section 111 of the Employment Rights Act 1996, but

(b) before any complaint relating to that action has been presented by him a request is made to a conciliation officer (whether by that person or by the employer) to make his services available to them,

the conciliation officer shall act in accordance with subsection (4) as if a complaint had been presented to an employment tribunal under section 111.

(6) In proceeding under this section a conciliation officer shall, where appropriate, have regard to the desirability of encouraging the use of other procedures available for the settlement of grievances.

(7) Anything communicated to a conciliation officer in connection with the performance of his functions under this section shall not be admissible in evidence in any proceedings before an employment tribunal, except with the consent of the person who communicated it to that officer.

(8) The Secretary of State may by order—

(a) direct that further provisions of the Employment Rights Act 1996 be added to the list in subsection (1)(d), or

(b) specify a provision of any other Act as a provision to which subsection (1)(f) applies.

19 [omitted]

PART II
THE EMPLOYMENT APPEAL TRIBUNAL

Introductory

20 The Appeal Tribunal

(1) The Employment Appeal Tribunal ('the Appeal Tribunal') shall continue in existence.

(2) The Appeal Tribunal shall have a central office in London but may sit at any time and in any place in Great Britain.

(3) The Appeal Tribunal shall be a superior court of record and shall have an official seal which shall be judicially noticed.

Jurisdiction

21 Jurisdiction of Appeal Tribunal

(1) An appeal lies to the Appeal Tribunal on any question of law arising from any decision of, or arising in any proceedings before, an employment tribunal under or by virtue of—

(a) the Equal Pay Act 1970,
(b) the Sex Discrimination Act 1975,
(c) the Race Relations Act 1976,
(d) the Trade Union and Labour Relations (Consolidation) Act 1992,
(e) the Disability Discrimination Act 1995,
(f) the Employment Rights Act 1996,
(ff) the National Minimum Wage Act 1998,
(fg) the Tax Credits Act 1999, or
(g) this Act,

or under the Working Time Regulations 1998.

(2) No appeal shall lie except to the Appeal Tribunal from any decision of an employment tribunal under or by virtue of the Acts listed or the Regulations referred to in subsection (1).

(3) Subsection (1) does not affect any provision contained in, or made under, any Act which provides for an appeal to lie to the Appeal Tribunal (whether from an employment tribunal, the Certification Officer or any other person or body) otherwise than on a question to which that subsection applies.

(4) The Appeal Tribunal also has any jurisdiction in respect of matters other than appeals which is conferred on it by or under—

(a) the Trade Union and Labour Relations (Consolidation) Act 1992,

(b) this Act, or

(c) any other Act.

Membership etc.

22 Membership of Appeal Tribunal

(1) The Appeal Tribunal shall consist of—

(a) such number of judges as may be nominated from time to time by the Lord Chancellor from the judges (other than the Lord Chancellor) of the High Court and the Court of Appeal,

(b) at least one judge of the Court of Session nominated from time to time by the Lord President of the Court of Session, and

(c) such number of other members as may be appointed from time to time by Her Majesty on the joint recommendation of the Lord Chancellor and the Secretary of State ('appointed members').

(2) The appointed members shall be persons who appear to the Lord Chancellor and the Secretary of State to have special knowledge or experience of industrial relations either—

(a) as representatives of employers, or

(b) as representatives of workers (within the meaning of the Trade Union and Labour Relations (Consolidation) Act 1992).

(3) The Lord Chancellor shall, after consultation with the Lord President of the Court of Session, appoint one of the judges nominated under subsection (1) to be the President of the Appeal Tribunal.

(4) No judge shall be nominated a member of the Appeal Tribunal except with his consent.

23 to **27** [omitted]

28 Composition of Appeal Tribunal

(1) The Appeal Tribunal may sit, in accordance with directions given by the President of the Appeal Tribunal, either as a single tribunal or in two or more divisions concurrently.

(2) Subject to subsections (3) to (5), proceedings before the Appeal Tribunal shall be heard by a judge and either two or four appointed members, so that in either case there is an equal number—

(a) of persons whose knowledge or experience of industrial relations is as representatives of employers, and

(b) of persons whose knowledge or experience of industrial relations is as representatives of workers.

(3) With the consent of the parties, proceedings before the Appeal Tribunal may be heard by a judge and one appointed member or by a judge and three appointed members.

(4) Proceedings on an appeal on a question arising from any decision of, or arising in any proceedings before, an employment tribunal consisting of the person mentioned in section 4(1)(a) alone shall be heard by a judge alone unless a judge directs that the proceedings shall be heard in accordance with subsections (2) and (3).

(5) [repealed]

Procedure

29 Conduct of hearings

(1) A person may appear before the Appeal Tribunal in person or be represented by—

(a) counsel or a solicitor,

(b) a representative of a trade union or an employers' association, or

(c) any other person whom he desires to represent him.

(2) The Appeal Tribunal has in relation to—

(a) the attendance and examination of witnesses,

(b) the production and inspection of documents, and

(c) all other matters incidental to its jurisdiction,

the same powers, rights, privileges and authority (in England and Wales) as the High Court and (in Scotland) as the Court of Session.

30 to **32** [omitted]

33 Restriction of vexatious proceedings

(1) If, on an application made by the Attorney General or the Lord Advocate under this section, the Appeal Tribunal is satisfied that a person has habitually and persistently and without any reasonable ground—

(a) instituted vexatious proceedings, whether in an employment tribunal or before the Appeal Tribunal, and whether against the same person or against different persons, or

(b) made vexatious applications in any proceedings, whether in an employment tribunal or before the Appeal Tribunal,

the Appeal Tribunal may, after hearing the person or giving him an opportunity of being heard, make a restriction of proceedings order.

(2) A 'restriction of proceedings order' is an order that—

(a) no proceedings shall without the leave of the Appeal Tribunal be instituted in any employment tribunal or before the Appeal Tribunal by the person against whom the order is made,

(b) any proceedings instituted by him in any employment tribunal or before the Appeal Tribunal before the making of the order shall not be continued by him without the leave of the Appeal Tribunal, and

(c) no application (other than one for leave under this section) is to be made by him in any proceedings in any employment tribunal or before the Appeal Tribunal without the leave of the Appeal Tribunal.

(3) A restriction of proceedings order may provide that it is to cease to have effect at the end of a specified period, but otherwise it remains in force indefinitely.

(4) Leave for the institution or continuance of, or for the making of an application in, any proceedings in an employment tribunal or before the Appeal Tribunal by a person who is the subject of a restriction of proceedings order shall not be given unless the Appeal Tribunal is satisfied—

(a) that the proceedings or application are not an abuse of the process of the tribunal in question, and

(b) that there are reasonable grounds for the proceedings or application.

(5) A copy of a restriction of proceedings order shall be published in the London Gazette and the Edinburgh Gazette.

34 [omitted]

Decisions and further appeals

35 Powers of Appeal Tribunal

(1) For the purpose of disposing of an appeal, the Appeal Tribunal may—

(a) exercise any of the powers of the body or officer from whom the appeal was brought, or

(b) remit the case to that body or officer.

(2) Any decision or award of the Appeal Tribunal on an appeal has the same effect, and may be enforced in the same manner, as a decision or award of the body or officer from whom the appeal was brought.

36 Enforcement of decisions etc.

(1) Any sum payable in England and Wales in pursuance of an award of the Appeal Tribunal—

(a) made under section 67 or 176 of the Trade Union and Labour Relations (Consolidation) Act 1992, and

(b) registered in accordance with Appeal Tribunal procedure rules,

is, if a county court so orders, recoverable by execution issued from the county court or otherwise as if it were payable under an order of that court.

(2) Any order by the Appeal Tribunal for the payment in Scotland of any sum in pursuance of such an award (or any copy of such an order certified by the Secretary of the Tribunals) may be enforced as if it were an extract registered decree arbitral bearing a warrant for execution issued by the sheriff court of any sheriffdom in Scotland.

(3) Any sum payable in pursuance of an award of the Appeal Tribunal under section 67 or 176 of the Trade Union and Labour Relations (Consolidation) Act 1992 shall be treated as if it were a sum payable in pursuance of a decision of an employment tribunal for the purposes of section 14 of this Act.

(4) No person shall be punished for contempt of the Appeal Tribunal except by, or with the consent of, a judge.

(5) A magistrates' court shall not remit the whole or part of a fine imposed by the Appeal Tribunal unless it has the consent of a judge who is a member of the Appeal Tribunal.

37 Appeals from Appeal Tribunal

(1) Subject to subsection (3), an appeal on any question of law lies from any decision or order of the Appeal Tribunal to the relevant appeal court with the leave of the Appeal Tribunal or of the relevant appeal court.

(2) In subsection (1) the 'relevant appeal court' means—

(a) in the case of proceedings in England and Wales, the Court of Appeal, and

(b) in the case of proceedings in Scotland, the Court of Session;.

(3) No appeal lies from a decision of the Appeal Tribunal refusing leave for the institution or continuance of, or for the making of an application in, proceedings by a person who is the subject of a restriction of proceedings order made under section 33.

(4) This section is without prejudice to section 13 of the Administration of Justice Act 1960 (appeal in case of contempt of court).

PART III
SUPPLEMENTARY

38 to **41** [omitted]

42 Interpretation

(1) In this Act—

'the Appeal Tribunal' means the Employment Appeal Tribunal,

'Appeal Tribunal procedure rules' shall be construed in accordance with section 30(1),

'appointed member' shall be construed in accordance with section 22(1)(c),

'conciliation officer' means an officer designated by the Advisory, Conciliation and Arbitration Service under section 211 of the Trade Union and Labour Relations (Consolidation) Act 1992, 'contract of employment' means a contract of service or apprenticeship, whether express or implied, and (if it is express) whether oral or in writing,

'employee' means an individual who has entered into or works under (or, where the employment has ceased, worked under) a contract of employment,

'employer', in relation to an employee, means the person by whom the employee is (or, where the employment has ceased, was) employed,

'employers' association' has the same meaning as in the Trade Union and Labour Relations (Consolidation) Act 1992,

'employment' means employment under a contract of employment and 'employed' shall be construed accordingly,

'employment tribunal procedure regulations' shall be construed in accordance with section 7(1),

'statutory provision' means a provision, whether of a general or a special nature, contained in, or in any document made or issued under, any Act, whether of a general or special nature,

'successor', in relation to the employer of an employee, means (subject to subsection (2)) a person who in consequence of a change occurring (whether by virtue of a sale or other disposition or by operation of law) in the ownership of the undertaking, or of the part of the undertaking, for the purposes of which the employee was employed, has become the owner of the undertaking or part, and

'trade union' has the meaning given by section 1 of the Trade Union and Labour Relations (Consolidation) Act 1992.

(2) The definition of 'successor' in subsection (1) has effect (subject to the necessary modifications) in relation to a case where—

(a) the person by whom an undertaking or part of an undertaking is owned immediately before a change is one of the persons by whom (whether as partners, trustees or otherwise) it is owned immediately after the change, or

(b) the persons by whom an undertaking or part of an undertaking is owned immediately before a change (whether as partners, trustees or otherwise) include the persons by whom, or include one or more of the persons by whom, it is owned immediately after the change,

as it has effect where the previous owner and the new owner are wholly different persons.

(3) For the purposes of this Act any two employers shall be treated as associated if—

(a) one is a company of which the other (directly or indirectly) has control, or

(b) both are companies of which a third person (directly or indirectly) has control;

and 'associated employer' shall be construed accordingly.

43 to **48** [omitted]

NATIONAL MINIMUM WAGE ACT 1998
(1998, c. 39)

Entitlement to the national minimum wage

The Low Pay Commission

6 Referrals of matters to the Low Pay Commission at any time.

Records

9 Duty of employers to keep records.
10 Worker's right of access to records.
11 Failure of employer to allow access to records.
12 Employer to provide worker with national minimum wage statement.

Officers

14 Powers of officers.

Information

15 Information obtained by officers.

Enforcement

17 Non-compliance: worker entitled to additional remuneration.
18 Enforcement in the case of special classes of worker.
19 Power of officer to issue enforcement notice.
20 Non-compliance: power of officer to sue on behalf of worker.
21 Financial penalty for non-compliance.
22 Appeals against penalty notices.

Rights not to suffer unfair dismissal or other detriment

23 The right not to suffer detriment.
24 Enforcement of the right.

Civil procedure, evidence and appeals

28 Reversal of burden of proof.

Offences

31 Offences.
32 Offences by bodies corporate etc.
33 Proceedings for offences.

Special classes of person

34 Agency workers who are not otherwise 'workers'.
35 Home workers who are not otherwise 'workers'.
36 Crown employment.
37 Armed forces.

Extensions

41 Power to apply Act to individuals who are not otherwise 'workers'.

Exclusions

44 Voluntary workers.
44A Religious and other communities: resident workers.
45 Prisoners.

Miscellaneous

48 Application of Act to superior employers.
49 Restrictions on contracting out.

Supplementary

Entitlement to the national minimum wage

1 Workers to be paid at least the national minimum wage

(1) A person who qualifies for the national minimum wage shall be remunerated by his employer in respect of his work in any pay reference period at a rate which is not less than the national minimum wage.

(2) A person qualifies for the national minimum wage if he is an individual who—

(a) is a worker;

(b) is working, or ordinarily works, in the United Kingdom under his contract; and

(c) has ceased to be of compulsory school age.

(3) The national minimum wage shall be such single hourly rate as the Secretary of State may from time to time prescribe.

(4) For the purposes of this Act a 'pay reference period' is such period as the Secretary of State may prescribe for the purpose.

(5) Subsections (1) to (4) above are subject to the following provisions of this Act.

Regulations relating to the national minimum wage

2 Determination of hourly rate of remuneration

(1) The Secretary of State may by regulations make provision for determining what is the hourly rate at which a person is to be regarded for the purposes of this Act as remunerated by his employer in respect of his work in any pay reference period.

(2) The regulations may make provision for determining the hourly rate in cases where—

(a) the remuneration, to the extent that it is at a periodic rate, is at a single rate;

(b) the remuneration is, in whole or in part, at different rates applicable at different times or in different circumstances;

(c) the remuneration is, in whole or in part, otherwise than at a periodic rate or rates;

(d) the remuneration consists, in whole or in part, of benefits in kind.

(3) The regulations may make provision with respect to—

(a) circumstances in which, times at which, or the time for which, a person is to be treated as, or as not, working, and the extent to which a person is to be so treated;

(b) the treatment of periods of paid or unpaid absence from, or lack of, work and of remuneration in respect of such periods.

(4) The provision that may be made by virtue of paragraph (a) of subsection (3) above includes provision for or in connection with—

(a) treating a person as, or as not, working for a maximum or minimum time, or for a proportion of the time, in any period;

(b) determining any matter to which that paragraph relates by reference to the terms of an agreement.

(5) The regulations may make provision with respect to—

(a) what is to be treated as, or as not, forming part of a person's remuneration, and the extent to which it is to be so treated;

(b) the valuation of benefits in kind;

(c) the treatment of deductions from earnings;

(d) the treatment of any charges or expenses which a person is required to bear.

(6) The regulations may make provision with respect to—

(a) the attribution to a period, or the apportionment between two or more periods, of the whole or any part of any remuneration or work, whether or not the remuneration is received or the work is done within the period or periods in question;

(b) the aggregation of the whole or any part of the remuneration for different periods;

(c) the time at which remuneration is to be treated as received or accruing.

(7) Subsections (2) to (6) above are without prejudice to the generality of subsection (1) above.

(8) No provision shall be made under this section which treats the same circumstances differently in relation to—

(a) different areas;
(b) different sectors of employment;
(c) undertakings of different sizes;
(d) persons of different ages; or
(e) persons of different occupations.

3 Exclusion of, and modifications for, certain classes of person

(1) This section applies to persons who have not attained the age of 26.

(1A) This section also applies to persons who have attained the age of 26 who are—

(a) within the first six months after the commencement of their employment with an employer by whom they have not previously been employed;

(b) participating in a scheme under which shelter is provided in return for work;

(c) participating in a scheme designed to provide training, work experience or temporary work;

(d) participating in a scheme to assist in the seeking or obtaining of work; or

(e) attending a course of higher education requiring attendance for a period of work experience.

(2) The Secretary of State may by regulations make provision in relation to any of the persons to whom this section applies—

(a) preventing them being persons who qualify for the national minimum wage; or

(b) prescribing an hourly rate for the national minimum wage other than the single hourly rate for the time being prescribed under section 1(3) above.

(3) No provision shall be made under subsection (2) above which treats persons differently in relation to—

(a) different areas;
(b) different sectors of employment;
(c) undertakings of different sizes; or
(d) different occupations.

(4) If any description of persons who have attained the age of 26 is added by regulations under section 4 below to the descriptions of person to whom this section applies, no provision shall be made under subsection (2) above which treats persons of that description differently in relation to different ages over 26.

4 Power to add to the persons to whom section 3 applies

(1) The Secretary of State may by regulations amend section 3 above by adding descriptions of persons who have attained the age of 26 to the descriptions of person to whom that section applies.

(2) No amendment shall be made under subsection (1) above which treats persons differently in relation to—

(a) different areas;
(b) different sectors of employment;
(c) undertakings of different sizes;
(d) different ages over 26; or

(f) different occupations.

The Low Pay Commission

5 [omitted]

6 Referral of matters to the Low Pay Commission at any time

(1) The Secretary of State may at any time refer to the Low Pay Commission such matters relating to this Act as the Secretary of State thinks fit.

(2)–(4) [omitted]

7–8 [omitted]

Records

9 Duty of employers to keep records

For the purposes of this Act, the Secretary of State may by regulations make provision requiring employers—

(a) to keep, in such form and manner as may be prescribed, such records as may be prescribed; and

(b) to preserve those records for such period as may be prescribed.

10 Worker's right of access to records

(1) A worker may, in accordance with the following provisions of this section,—

(a) require his employer to produce any relevant records; and

(b) inspect and examine those records and copy any part of them.

(2) The rights conferred by subsection (1) above are exercisable only if the worker believes on reasonable grounds that he is or may be being, or has or may have been, remunerated for any pay reference period by his employer at a rate which is less than the national minimum wage.

(3) The rights conferred by subsection (1) above are exercisable only for the purpose of establishing whether or not the worker is being, or has been, remunerated for any pay reference period by his employer at a rate which is less than the national minimum wage.

(4) The rights conferred by subsection (1) above are exercisable—

(a) by the worker alone; or

(b) by the worker accompanied by such other person as the worker may think fit.

(5) The rights conferred by subsection (1) above are exercisable only if the worker gives notice (a 'production notice') to his employer requesting the production of any relevant records relating to such period as may be described in the notice.

(6) If the worker intends to exercise the right conferred by subsection (4)(b) above, the production notice must contain a statement of that intention.

(7) Where a production notice is given, the employer shall give the worker reasonable notice of the place and time at which the relevant records will be produced.

(8) The place at which the relevant records are produced must be—

(a) the worker's place of work; or

(b) any other place at which it is reasonable, in all the circumstances, for the worker to attend to inspect the relevant records; or

(c) such other place as may be agreed between the worker and the employer.

(9) The relevant records must be produced—

(a) before the end of the period of fourteen days following the date of receipt of the production notice; or

(b) at such later time as may be agreed during that period between the worker and the employer.

(10) In this section—

'records' means records which the worker's employer is required to keep and, at the time of receipt of the production notice, preserve in accordance with section 9 above;

'relevant records' means such parts of, or such extracts from, any records as are relevant to establishing whether or not the worker has, for any pay reference period to which the records relate, been remunerated by the employer at a rate which is at least equal to the national minimum wage.

11 Failure of employer to allow access to records

(1) A complaint may be presented to an employment tribunal by a worker on the ground that the employer—

(a) failed to produce some or all of the relevant records in accordance with subsections (8) and (9) of section 10 above; or

(b) failed to allow the worker to exercise some or all of the rights conferred by subsection (1)(b) or (4)(b) of that section.

(2) Where an employment tribunal finds a complaint under this section well-founded, the tribunal shall—

(a) make a declaration to that effect; and

(b) make an award that the employer pay to the worker a sum equal to 80 times the hourly amount of the national minimum wage (as in force when the award is made).

(3) An employment tribunal shall not consider a complaint under this section unless it is presented to the tribunal before the expiry of the period of three months following—

(a) the end of the period of fourteen days mentioned in paragraph (a) of subsection (9) of section 10 above; or

(b) in a case where a later day was agreed under paragraph (b) of that subsection, that later day.

(4) Where the employment tribunal is satisfied that it was not reasonably practicable for a complaint under this section to be presented before the expiry of the period of three months mentioned in subsection (3) above, the tribunal may consider the complaint if it is presented within such further period as the tribunal considers reasonable.

(5) Expressions used in this section and in section 10 above have the same meaning in this section as they have in that section.

12 Employer to provide worker with national minimum wage statement

(1) Regulations may make provision for the purpose of conferring on a worker the right to be given by his employer, at or before the time at which any payment of remuneration is made to the worker, a written statement.

(2) The regulations may make provision with respect to the contents of any such statement and may, in particular, require it to contain—

(a) prescribed information relating to this Act or any regulations under it; or

(b) prescribed information for the purpose of assisting the worker to determine whether he has been remunerated at a rate at least equal to the national minimum wage during the period to which the payment of remuneration relates.

(3) Any statement required to be given under this section to a worker by his employer may, if the worker is an employee, be included in the written itemised pay statement required to be given to him by his employer under section 8 of the Employment Rights Act 1996 or Article 40 of the Employment Rights (Northern Ireland) Order 1996, as the case may be.

(4) The regulations may make provision for the purpose of applying—

(a) sections 11 and 12 of the Employment Rights Act 1996 (references to employment tribunals and determination of references), or

(b) in relation to Northern Ireland, Articles 43 and 44 of the Employment Rights (Northern Ireland) Order 1996 (references to industrial tribunals and determination of references), in relation to a worker and any such statement as is mentioned in subsection (1) above as they apply in relation to an employee and a statement required to be given to him by his employer under section 8 of that Act or Article 40 of that Order, as the case may be.

Officers

13 [omitted]

14 Powers of officers

(1) An officer acting for the purposes of this Act shall have power for the performance of his duties—

(a) to require the production by a relevant person of any records required to be kept and preserved in accordance with regulations under section 9 above and to inspect and examine those records and to copy any material part of them;

(b) to require a relevant person to furnish to him (either alone or in the presence of any other person, as the officer thinks fit) an explanation of any such records;

(c) to require a relevant person to furnish to him (either alone or in the presence of any other person, as the officer thinks fit) any additional information known to the relevant person which might reasonably be needed in order to establish whether this Act, or any enforcement notice under section 19 below, is being or has been complied with;

(d) at all reasonable times to enter any relevant premises in order to exercise any power conferred on the officer by paragraphs (a) to (c) above.

(2) No person shall be required under paragraph (b) or (c) of subsection (1) above to answer any question or furnish any information which might incriminate the person or, if married, the person's spouse.

(3) The powers conferred by subsection (1) above include power, on reasonable written notice, to require a relevant person—

(a) to produce any such records as are mentioned in paragraph (a) of that subsection to an officer at such time and place as may be specified in the notice; or

(b) to attend before an officer at such time and place as may be specified in the notice to furnish any such explanation or additional information as is mentioned in paragraph (b) or (c) of that subsection.

(4) In this section 'relevant person' means any person whom an officer acting for the purposes of this Act has reasonble cause to believe to be—

(a) the employer of a worker;

(b) a person who for the purposes of section 34 below is the agent or the principal;

(c) a person who supplies work to an individual who qualifies for the national minimum wage;

(d) a worker, servant or agent of a person falling within paragraph (a), (b) or (c) above; or

(e) a person who qualifies for the national minimum wage.

(5) In this section 'relevant premises' means any premises which an officer acting for the purposes of this Act has reasonable cause to believe to be—

(a) premises at which an employer carries on business;

(b) premises which an employer uses in connection with his business (including any place used, in connection with that business, for giving out work to home workers, within the meaning of section 35 below); or

(c) premises of a person who for the purposes of section 34 below is the agent or the principal.

Information

15 Information obtained by officers

(1) This section applies to any information obtained by an officer acting for the purposes of this Act, whether by virtue of paragraph (a) or paragraph (b) of section 13(1) above.

(2) Information to which this section applies vests in the Secretary of State.

(3) Information to which this section applies may be used for any purpose relating to this Act by—

(a) the Secretary of State; or

(b) any relevant authority whose officer obtained the information.

(4) Information to which this section applies—

(a) may be supplied by, or with the authorisation of, the Secretary of State to any relevant authority for any purpose relating to this Act; and

(b) may be used by the recipient for any purpose relating to this Act.

(5) Information supplied under subsection (4) above—

(a) shall not be supplied by the recipient to any other person or body unless it is supplied for the purposes of any civil or criminal proceedings relating to this Act; and

(b) shall not be supplied in those circumstances without the authorisation of the Secretary of State.

(6) This section does not limit the circumstances in which information may be supplied or used apart from this section.

(7) Subsection (2) above does not affect the title or rights of—

(a) any person whose property the information was immediately before it was obtained as mentioned in subsection (1) above; or

(b) any person claiming title or rights through or under such a person otherwise than by virtue of any power conferred by or under this Act.

(8) In this section 'relevant authority' means any Minister of the Crown who, or government department or other body which, is party to arrangements made with the Secretary of State which are in force under section 13(1)(b) above.

16 [omitted]

Enforcement

17 Non-compliance: worker entitled to additional remuneration

(1) If a worker who qualifies for the national minimum wage is remunerated for any pay reference period by his employer at a rate which is less than the national minimum wage, the worker shall be taken to be entitled under his contract to be paid, as additional remuneration in respect of that period, the amount described in subsection (2) below.

(2) That amount is the difference between—

(a) the relevant remuneration received by the worker for the pay reference period; and

(b) the relevant remuneration which the worker would have received for that period had he been remunerated by the employer at a rate equal to the national minimum wage.

(3) In subsection (2) above, 'relevant remuneration' means remuneration which falls to be brought into account for the purposes of regulations under section 2 above.

18 Enforcement in the case of special classes of worker

(1) If the persons who are the worker and the employer for the purposes of section 17 above would not (apart from this section) fall to be regarded as the worker and the employer for the purposes of—

(a) Part II of the Employment Rights Act 1996 (protection of wages), or

(b) in relation to Northern Ireland, Part IV of the Employment Rights (Northern Ireland) Order 1996,

they shall be so regarded for the purposes of the application of that Part in relation to the entitlement conferred by that section.

(2) In the application by virtue of subsection (1) above of—

(a) Part II of the Employment Rights Act 1996, or

(b) Part IV of the Employment Rights (Northern Ireland) Order 1996, in a case where there is or was, for the purposes of that Part, no worker's contract between the persons who are the worker and the employer for the purposes of section 17 above, it shall be assumed that there is or, as the case may be, was such a contract.

(3) For the purpose of enabling the amount described as additional remuneration in subsection (1) of section 17 above to be recovered in civil proceedings on a claim in contract in a case where in fact there is or was no worker's contract between the persons who are the worker and the employer for the purposes of that section, it shall be assumed for the purpose of any civil proceedings, so far as relating to that amount, that there is or, as the case may be, was such a contract.

19 Power of officer to issue enforcement notice

(1) If an officer acting for the purposes of this Act is of the opinion that a worker who qualifies for the national minimum wage has not been remunerated for any pay reference period by his employer at a rate at least equal to the national minimum wage, the officer may serve a notice (an 'enforcement notice') on the employer requiring the employer to remunerate the worker for pay reference periods ending on or after the date of the notice at a rate equal to the national minimum wage.

(2) An enforcement notice may also require the employer to pay to the worker within such time as may be specified in the notice the sum due to the worker under section 17 above in respect of the employer's previous failure to remunerate the worker at a rate at least equal to the national minimum wage.

(3) The same enforcement notice may relate to more than one worker (and, where it does so, may be so framed as to relate to workers specified in the notice or to workers of a description so specified).

(4) A person on whom an enforcement notice is served may appeal against the notice before the end of the period of four weeks following the date of service of the notice.

(5) An appeal under subsection (4) above lies to an employment tribunal.

(6) On an appeal under subsection (4) above, the employment tribunal shall dismiss the appeal unless it is established—

(a) that, in the case of the worker or workers to whom the enforcement notice relates, the facts are such that an officer who was aware of them would have had no reason to serve any enforcement notice on the appellant; or

(b) where the enforcement notice relates to two or more workers, that the facts are such that an officer who was aware of them would have had no reason to include some of the workers in any enforcement notice served on the appellant; or

(c) where the enforcement notice imposes a requirement under subsection (2) above in relation to a worker,—

(i) that no sum was due to the worker under section 17 above; or

(ii) that the amount specified in the notice as the sum due to the worker under that section is incorrect;

and in this subsection any reference to a worker includes a reference to a person whom the enforcement notice purports to treat as a worker.

(7) Where an appeal is allowed by virtue of paragraph (a) of subsection (6) above, the employment tribunal shall rescind the enforcement notice.

(8) If, in a case where subsection (7) above does not apply, an appeal is allowed by virtue of paragraph (b) or (c) of subsection (6) above—

(a) the employment tribunal shall rectify the enforcement notice; and

(b) the enforcement notice shall have effect as if it had originally been served as so rectified.

(9) The powers of an employment tribunal in allowing an appeal in a case where subsection (8) above applies shall include power to rectify, as the tribunal may consider appropriate in consequence of its decision on the appeal, any penalty notice which has been served under section 21 below in respect of the enforcement notice.

(10) Where a penalty notice is rectified under subsection (9) above, it shall have effect as if it had originally been served as so rectified.

20 Non-compliance: power of officer to sue on behalf of worker

(1) If an enforcement notice is not complied with in whole or in part, an officer acting for the purposes of this Act may, on behalf of any worker to whom the notice relates,—

(a) present a complaint under section 23(1)(a) of the Employment Rights Act 1996 (deductions from worker's wages in contravention of section 13 of that Act) to an employment tribunal in respect of any sums due to the worker by virtue of section 17 above; or

(b) in relation to Northern Ireland, present a complaint under Article 55(1)(a) of the Employment Rights (Northern Ireland) Order 1996 (deductions from worker's wages in contravention of Article 45 of that Order) to an industrial tribunal in respect of any sums due to the worker by virtue of section 17 above; or

(c) commence other civil proceedings for the recovery, on a claim in contract, of any sums due to the worker by virtue of section 17 above.

(2) The powers conferred by subsection (1) above for the recovery of sums due from an employer to a worker shall not be in derogation of any right which the worker may have to recover such sums by civil proceedings.

21 Financial penalty for non-compliance

(1) If an officer acting for the purposes of this Act is satisfied that a person on whom an enforcement notice has been served has failed, in whole or in part, to comply with the notice, the officer may serve on that person a notice (a 'penalty notice') requiring the person to pay a financial penalty to the Secretary of State.

(2) A penalty notice must state—

(a) the amount of the financial penalty;

(b) the time within which the financial penalty is to be paid (which must not be less than four weeks from the date of service of the notice);

(c) the period to which the financial penalty relates;

(d) the respects in which the officer is of the opinion that the enforcement notice has not been complied with; and

(e) the calculation of the amount of the financial penalty.

(3) The amount of the financial penalty shall be calculated at a rate equal to twice the hourly amount of the national minimum wage (as in force at the date of the penalty notice) in respect of each worker to whom the failure to comply relates for each day during which the failure to comply has continued in respect of the worker.

(4) The Secretary of State may by regulations from time to time amend the multiplier for the time being specified in subsection (3) above in relation to the hourly amount of the national minimum wage.

(5) A financial penalty under this section—

(a) in England and Wales, shall be recoverable, if a county court so orders, by execution issued from the county court or otherwise as if it were payable under an order of that court;

(b) in Scotland, may be enforced in the same manner as an extract registered decree arbitral bearing a warrant for execution issued by the sheriff court of any sheriffdom in Scotland;

(c) in Northern Ireland, shall be recoverable, if the county court so orders, as if it were payable under an order of that court.

(6) Where a person has appealed under subsection (4) of section 19 above against an enforcement notice and the appeal has not been withdrawn or finally determined, then, notwithstanding the appeal,—

(a) the enforcement notice shall have effect; and

(b) an officer may serve a penalty notice in respect of the enforcement notice.

(7) If, in a case falling within subsection (6) above, an officer serves a penalty notice in respect of the enforcement notice, the penalty notice—

(a) shall not be enforceable until the appeal has been withdrawn or finally determined; and

(b) shall be of no effect if the enforcement notice is rescinded as a result of the appeal; but

(c) subject to paragraph (b) above and section 22(4) and (6)(a) below, as from the withdrawal or final determination of the appeal shall be enforceable as if paragraph (a) above had not had effect.

(8) Any sums received by the Secretary of State by virtue of this section shall be paid into the Consolidated Fund.

22 Appeals against penalty notices

(1) A person on whom a penalty notice is served may appeal against the notice before the end of the period of four weeks following the date of service of the notice.

(2) An appeal under subsection (1) above lies to an employment tribunal.

(3) On an appeal under subsection (1) above, the employment tribunal shall dismiss the appeal unless it is shown—

(a) that, in the case of each of the allegations of failure to comply with the enforcement notice, the facts are such that an officer who was aware of them would have had no reason to serve any penalty notice on the appellant; or

(b) that the penalty notice is incorrect in some of the particulars which affect the amount of the financial penalty; or

(c) that the calculation of the amount of the financial penalty is incorrect;

and for the purposes of any appeal realting to a penalty notice, the enforcement notice in question shall (subject to rescission or rectification on any appeal brought under section 19 above) be taken to be correct.

(4) Where an appeal is allowed by virtue of paragraph (a) of subsection (3) above, the employment tribunal shall rescind the penalty notice.

(5) If, in a case where subsection (4) above does not apply, an appeal is allowed by virtue of paragraph (b) or (c) of subsection (3) above—

(a) the employment tribunal shall rectify the penalty notice; and

(b) the penalty notice shall have effect as if it had originally been served as so rectified.

(6) Where a person has appealed under subsection (1) above against a penalty notice and the appeal has not been withdrawn or finally determined, the penalty notice—

(a) shall not be enforceable until the appeal has been withdrawn or finally determined; but

(b) subject to subsection (4) above and section 21(7)(a) and (b) above, as from the withdrawal or final determination of the appeal shall be enforceable as if paragraph (a) above had not had effect.

Rights not to suffer unfair dismissal or other detriment

23 The right not to suffer detriment

(1) A worker has the right not to be subjected to any detriment by any act, or any deliberate failure to act, by his employer, done on the ground that—

(a) any action was taken, or was proposed to be taken, by or on behalf of the worker with a view to enforcing, or otherwise securing the benefit of, a right of the worker's to which this section applies; or

(b) the employer was prosecuted for an offence under section 31 below as a result of action taken by or on behalf of the worker for the purpose of enforcing, or otherwise securing the benefit of, a right of the worker's to which this section applies; or

(c) the worker qualifies, or will or might qualify, for the national minimum wage or for a particular rate of national minimum wage.

(2) It is immaterial for the purposes of paragraph (a) or (b) of subsection (1) above—

(a) whether or not the worker has the right, or

(b) whether or not the right has been infringed,

but, for that subsection to apply, the claim to the right and, if applicable, the claim that it has been infringed must be made in good faith.

(3) The following are the rights to which this section applies—

(a) any right conferred by, or by virtue of, any provision of this Act for which the remedy for its infringement is by way of a complaint to an employment tribunal; and

(b) any right conferred by section 17 above.

(4) This section does not apply where the detriment in question amounts to dismissal within the meaning of—

(a) Part X of the Employment Rights Act 1996 (unfair dismissal), or

(b) Part XI, of the Employment Rights (Northern Ireland) Order 1996 (corresponding provision for Northern Ireland),

except wherein relation to Northern Ireland the person in question is dismissed in circumstances in which by virtue of Article 240 of that Order (fixed term contracts), Part XI does not apply to the dismissal.

24 Enforcement of the right

(1) A worker may present a complaint to an employment tribunal that he has been subjected to a detriment in contravention of section 23 above.

(2) Subject to the following provisions of this section, the provisions of—

(a) sections 48(2) to (4) and 49 of the Employment Rights Act 1996 (complaints to employment tribunals and remedies), or

(b) in relation to Northern Ireland, Articles 71(2) to (4) and 72 of the Employment Rights (Northern Ireland) Order 1996 (complaints to industrial tribunals and remedies),

shall apply in relation to a complaint under this section as they apply in relation to a complaint under section 48 of that Act or Article 71 of that Order (as the case may be), but taking references in those provisions to the employer as references to the employer within the meaning of section 23(1) above.

(3) Where—

(a) the detriment to which the worker is subjected is the termination of his worker's contract, but

(b) that contract is not a contract of employment,

any compensation awarded under section 49 of the Employment Rights Act 1996 or Article 72 of the Employment Rights (Northern Ireland) Order 1996 by virtue of subsection (2) above must not exceed the limit specified in subsection (4) below.

(4) The limit mentioned in subsection (3) above is the total of—

(a) the sum which would be the basic award for unfair dismissal, calculated in accordance with section 119 of the Employment Rights Act 1996 or Article 153 of the Employment Rights (Northern Ireland) Order 1996 (as the case may be), if the worker had been an employee and the contract terminated had been a contract of employment; and

(b) the sum for the time being specified in section 124(1) of that Act or Article 158(1) of that Order (as the case may be) which is the limit for a compensatory award to a person calculated in accordance with section 123 of that Act or Article 157 of that Order (as the case may be).

(5) Where the worker has been working under arrangements which do not fall to be regarded as a worker's contract for the purposes of—

(a) the Employment Rights Act 1996, or

(b) in relation to Northern Ireland, the Employment Rights (Northern Ireland) Order 1996,

he shall be treated for the purposes of subsections (3) and (4) above as if any arrangements under which he has been working constituted a worker's contract falling within section 230(3)(b) of that Act or Article 3(3)(b) of that Order (as the case may be).

25-27 [omitted]

28 Reversal of burden of proof

(1) Where in any civil proceedings any question arises as to whether an individual qualifies or qualified at any time for the national minimum wage, it shall be presumed that the individual qualifies or, as the case may be, qualified at that time for the national minimum wage unless the contrary is established.

(2) Where—

(a) a complaint is made—

(i) to an employment tribunal under section 23(1)(a) of the Employment Rights Act 1996 (unauthorised deductions from wages), or

(ii) to an industrial tribunal under Article 55(1)(a) of the Employment Rights (Northern Ireland) Order 1996, and

(b) the complaint relates in whole or in part to the deduction of the amount described as additional remuneration in section 17(1) above,

it shall be presumed for the purposes of the complaint, so far as relating to the deduction of that amount, that the worker in question was remunerated at a rate less than the national minimum wage unless the contrary is established.

(3) Where in any civil proceedings a person seeks to recover on a claim in contract the amount described as additional remuneration in section 17(1) above, it shall be presumed for the purposes of the proceedings, so far as relating to that amount, that the worker in question was remunerated at a rate less than the national minimum wage unless the contrary is established.

29–30 [omitted]

Offences

31 Offences

(1) If the employer of a worker who qualifies for the national minimum wage refuses or wilfully neglects to remunerate the worker for any pay reference period at a rate which is at least equal to the national minimum wage, that employer is guilty of an offence.

(2) If a person who is required to keep or preserve any record in accordance with regulations under section 9 above fails to do so, that person is guilty of an offence.

(3) If a person makes, or knowingly causes or allows to be made, in a record required to be kept in accordance with regulations under section 9 above any entry which he knows to be false in a material particular, that person is guilty of an offence.

(4) If a person, for purposes connected with the provisions of this Act, produces or furnishes, or knowingly causes or allows to be produced or furnished, any record or information which he knows to be false in a material particular, that person is guilty of an offence.

(5) If a person—

(a) intentionally delays or obstructs an officer acting for the purposes of this Act in the exercise of any power conferred by this Act, or

(b) refuses or neglects to answer any question, furnish any information or produce any document when required to do so under section 14(1) above,

that person is guilty of an offence.

(6) Where the commission by any person of an offence under subsection (1) or (2) above is due to the act or default of some other person, that other person is also guilty of the offence.

(7) A person may be charged with and convicted of an offence by virtue of subsection (6) above whether or not proceedings are taken against any other person.

(8) In any proceedings for an offence under subsection (1) or (2) above it shall be a defence for the person charged to prove that he exercised all due diligence and took all reasonable precautions to secure that the provisions of this Act, and of any relevant regulations made under it, were complied with by himself and by any person under his control.

(9) A person guilty of an offence under this section shall be liable on summary conviction to a fine not exceeding level 5 on the standard scale.

32 Offences by bodies corporate etc.

(1) This section applies to any offence under this Act.

(2) If an offence committed by a body corporate is proved—

(a) to have been committed with the consent or connivance of an officer of the body, or

(b) to be attributable to any neglect on the part of such an officer,

the officer as well as the body corporate is guilty of the offence and liable to be proceeded against and punished accordingly.

(3) In subsection (2) above 'officer', in relation to a body corporate, means a director, manager, secretary or other similar officer of the body, or a person purporting to act in any such capacity.

(4) If the affairs of a body corporate are managed by its members, subsection (2) above applies in relation to the acts and defaults of a member in connection with his functions of management as if he were a director of the body corporate.

(5) If an offence committed by a partnership in Scotland is proved—

(a) to have been committed with the consent or connivance of a partner, or

(b) to be attributable to any neglect on the part of a partner,

the partner as well as the partnership is guilty of the offence and liable to be proceeded against and punished accordingly.

(6) In subsection (5) above, 'partner' includes a person purporting to act as a partner.

33 Proceedings for offences

(1) The persons who may conduct proceedings for an offence under this Act—

(a) in England and Wales, before a magistrates' court, or

(b) in Northern Ireland, before a court of summary jurisdiction,

shall include any person authorised for the purpose by the Secretary of State even if that person is not a barrister or solicitor.

(2) In England and Wales or Northern Ireland, proceedings for an offence under this Act may be begun at any time within whichever of the following periods expires the later, that is to say—

(a) the period of 6 months from the date on which evidence, sufficient in the opinion of the Secretary of State to justify a prosecution for the offence, comes to the knowledge of the Secretary of State, or

(b) the period of 12 months from the commission of the offence,

notwithstanding anything in any other enactment (including an enactment comprised in Northern Ireland legislation) or in any instrument made under an enactment.

(3) For the purposes of subsection (2) above, a certificate purporting to be signed by or on behalf of the Secretary of State as to the date on which such evidence as is mentioned in paragraph (a) of that subsection came to the knowledge of the Secretary of State shall be conclusive evidence of that date.

(4) In Scotland, proceedings for an offence under this Act may, notwithstanding anything in section 136 of the Criminal Procedure (Scotland) Act 1995, be commenced at any time within—

(a) the period of 6 months from the date on which evidence, sufficient in the opinion of the procurator fiscal to justify proceedings, comes to the knowledge of the procurator fiscal, or

(b) the period of 12 months from the commission of the offence,

whichever period expires the later.

(5) For the purposes of subsection (4) above—

(a) a certificate purporting to be signed by or on behalf of the procurator fiscal as to the date on which such evidence as is mentioned above came to the knowledge of the procurator fiscal shall be conclusive evidence of that date; and

(b) subsection (3) of section 136 of the said Act of 1995 (date of commencement of proceedings) shall have effect as it has effect for the purposes of that section.

Special classes of person

34 Agency workers who are not otherwise 'workers'

(1) This section applies in any case where an individual ('the agency worker')—

(a) is supplied by a person ('the agent') to do work for another ('the principal') under a contract or other arrangements made between the agent and the principal; but

(b) is not, as respects that work, a worker, beause of the absence of a worker's contract between the individual and the agent or the principal; and

(c) is not a party to a contract under which he undertakes to do the work for another party to the contract whose status is, by virtue of the contract, that of a client or customer of any profession or business undertaking carried on by the individual.

(2) In a case where this section applies, the other provisions of this Act shall have effect as if there were a worker's contract for the doing of the work by the agency worker made between the agency worker and—

(a) whichever of the agent and the principal is responsible for paying the agency worker in respect of the work; or

(b) if neither the agent nor the principal is so responsible, whichever of them pays the agency worker in respect of the work.

35 Home workers who are not otherwise 'workers'

(1) In determining for the purposes of this Act whether a home worker is or is not a worker, section 54(3)(b) below shall have effect as if for the word 'personally' there were substituted '(whether personally or otherwise)'.

(2) In this section 'home worker' means an individual who contracts with a person, for the purposes of that person's business, for the execution of work to be done in a place not under the control or management of that person.

36 Crown employment

(1) Subject to section 37 below, the provisions of this Act have effect in relation to Crown employment and persons in Crown employment as they have effect in relation to other employment and other workers.

(2) In this Act, subject to section 37 below, 'Crown employment' means employment under or for the purposes of a government department or any officer or body exercising on behalf of the Crown functions conferred by statutory provision.

(3) For the purposes of the application of the other provisions of this Act in relation to Crown employment in accordance with subsection (1) above—

(a) references to an employee or a worker shall be construed as references to a person in Crown employment;

(b) references to a contract of employment or a worker's contract shall be construed as references to the terms of employment of a person in Crown employment; and

(c) references to dismissal, or to the termination of a worker's contract, shall be construed as references to the termination of Crown employment.

37 Armed forces

(1) A person serving as a member of the naval, military or air forces of the Crown does not qualify for the national minimum wage in respect of that service.

(2) Section 36 above applies to employment by an association established for the purposes of Part XI of the Reserve Forces Act 1996, notwithstanding anything in subsection (1) above.

38–43 [omitted]

Exclusions

44 Voluntary workers

(1) A worker employed by a charity, a voluntary organisation, an associated fund-raising body or a statutory body does not qualify for the national minimum wage in respect of that employment if he receives, and under the terms of his employment (apart from this Act) is entitled to,—

(a) no monetary payments of any description, or no monetary payments except in respect of expenses—

(i) actually incurred in the performance of his duties; or

(ii) reasonably estimated as likely to be or to have been so incurred; and

(b) no benefits in kind of any description, or no benefits in kind other than the provision of some or all of his subsistence or of such accommodation as is reasonable in the circumstances of the employment.

(2) A person who would satisfy the conditions in subsection (1) above but for receiving monetary payments made solely for the purpose of providing him with means of subsistence shall be taken to satisfy those conditions if—

(a) he is employed to do the work in question as a result of arrangements made between a charity acting in pursuance of its charitable purposes and the body for which the work is done; and

(b) the work is done for a charity, a voluntary organisation, an associated fund-raising body or a statutory body.

(3) For the purposes of subsection (1)(b) above—

(a) any training (other than that which a person necessarily acquires in the course of doing his work) shall be taken to be a benefit in kind; but

(b) there shall be left out of account any training provided for the sole or main purpose of improving the worker's ability to perform the work which he has agreed to do.

(4) In this section—

'associated fund-raising body' means a body of persons the profits of which are applied wholly for the purposes of a charity or voluntary organisation;

'charity' means a body of persons, or the trustees of a trust, established for charitable purposes only;

'receive', in relation to a monetary payment or a benefit in kind, means receive in respect of, or otherwise in connection with, the employment in question (whether or not under the terms of the employment);

'statutory body' means a body established by or under an enactment (including an enactment comprised in Northern Ireland legislation);

'subsistence' means such subsistence as is reasonable in the circumstances of the employment in question, and does not include accommodation;

'voluntary organisation' means a body of persons, or the trustees of a trust, which is established only for charitable purposes (whether or not those purposes are charitable within the meaning of any rule of law), benevolent purposes or philanthropic purposes, but which is not a charity.

44A Religious and other communities: resident workers

(1) A residential member of a community to which this section applies does not qualify for the national minimum wage in respect of employment by the community.

(2) Subject to subsection (3), this section applies to a community if—

(a) it is a charity or is established by a charity,

(b) a purpose of the community is to practise or advance a belief of a religious or similar nature, and

(c) all or some of its members live together for that purpose.

(3) This section does not apply to a community which—

(a) is an independent school, or

(b) provides a course of further or higher education.

(4) The residential members of a community are those who live together as mentioned in subsection (2)(c).

(5) and (6) [omitted]

45 Prisoners

(1) A prisoner does not qualify for the national minimum wage in respect of any work which he does in pursuance of prison rules.

(2) In this section—

'prisoner' means a person detained in, or on temporary release from, a prison;

'prison' includes any other institution to which prison rules apply;

'prison rules' means—

(a) in relation to England and Wales, rules made under section 47 of the Prison Act 1952;

(b) in relation to Scotland, rules made under section 39 of the Prisons (Scotland) Act 1989; and

(c) in relation to Northern Ireland, rules made under section 13 of the Prison Act (Northern Ireland) 1953.

46–47 [omitted]

Miscellaneous

48 Application of Act to superior employers

Where—

(a) the immediate employer of a worker is himself in the employment of some other person, and

(b) the worker is employed on the premises of that other person,

that other person shall be deemed for the purposes of this Act to be the employer of the worker jointly with the immediate employer.

49 Restrictions on contracting out

(1) Any provision in any agreement (whether a worker's contract or not) is void in so far as it purports—

(a) to exclude or limit the operation of any provision of this Act; or

(b) to preclude a person from bringing proceedings under this Act before an employment tribunal.

(2) Subsection (1) above does not apply to any agreement to refrain from instituting or continuing proceedings where a conciliation officer has taken action under—

(a) section 18 of the Employment Tribunals Act 1996 (conciliation), or

(b) in relation to Northern Ireland, Article 20 of the Industrial Tribunals (Northern Ireland) Order 1996.

(3) Subsection (1) above does not apply to any agreement to refrain from instituting or continuing before an employment tribunal any proceedings within—

(a) section 18(1)(dd) of the Employment Tribunals Act 1996 (proceedings under or by virtue of this Act where conciliation is available), or

(b) in relation to Northern Ireland, Article 20(1)(cc) of the Industrial Tribunals (Northern Ireland) Order 1996,

if the conditions regulating compromise agreements under this Act are satisfied in relation to the agreement.

(4) For the purposes of subsection (3) above the conditions regulating compromise agreements under this Act are that—

(a) the agreement must be in writing,

(b) the agreement must relate to the particular proceedings,

(c) the employee or worker must have received advice from a relevant independent adviser as to the terms and effect of the proposed agreement and, in particular, its effect on his ability to pursue his rights before an employment tribunal,

(d) there must be in force, when the adviser gives the advice, a contract of insurance, or an indemnity provided for members of a profession or a professional body, covering the risk of a claim by the employee or worker in respect of loss arising in consequence of the advice,

(e) the agreement must identify the adviser, and

(f) the agreement must state that the conditions regulating compromise agreements under this Act are satisfied.

(5) A person is a relevant independent adviser for the purposes of subsection (4)(c) above—

(a) if he is a qualified lawyer,

(b) if he is an officer, official, employee or member of an independent trade union who has been certified in writing by the trade union as competent to give advice and as authorised to do so on behalf of the trade union,

(c) if he works at an advice centre (whether as an employee or a volunteer) and has been certified in writing by the centre as competent to give advice and as authorised to do so on behalf of the centre, or

(d) if he is a person of a description specified in an order made by the Secretary of State.

(6) But a person is not a relevant independent adviser for the purposes of subsection (4)(c) above in relation to the employee or worker—

(a) if he is employed by, or is acting in the matter for, the employer or an associated employer,

(b) in the case of a person within subsection (5)(b) or (c) above, if the trade union or advice centre is the employer or an associated employer,

(c) in the case of a person within subsection (5)(c) above, if the employee or worker makes a payment for the advice received from him, or

(d) in the case of a person of a description specified in an order under subsection (5)(d) above, if any condition specified in the order in relation to the giving of advice by persons of that description is not satisfied.

(7) In this section 'qualified lawyer' means—

(a) as respects England and Wales—

(i) a barrister (whether in practice as such or employed to give legal advice);

(ii) a solicitor who holds a practising certificate; or

(iii) a person other than a barrister or solicitor who is an authorised advocate or authorised litigator (within the meaning of the Courts and Legal Services Act 1990);

(b) as respects Scotland—

(i) an advocate (whether in practice as such or employed to give legal advice); or

(ii) a solicitor who holds a practising certificate; and

(c) as respects Northern Ireland—

(i) a barrister (whether in practice as such or employed to give legal advice); or
(ii) a solicitor who holds a practising certificate.

(8) For the purposes of this section any two employers shall be treated as associated if—

(a) one is a company of which the other (directly or indirectly) has control; or

(b) both are companies of which a third person (directly or indirectly) has control;

and 'associated employer' shall be construed accordingly.

(9) In the application of this section in relation to Northern Ireland—

(a) subsection (4)(c) above shall have effect as if for 'advice from a relevant independent adviser' there were substituted 'independent legal advice from a qualified lawyer'; and

(b) subsection (4)(d) above shall have effect as if for 'contract of insurance, or an indemnity provided for members of a profession or a professional body,' there were substituted 'policy of insurance'.

(10) In subsection (4) above, as it has effect by virtue of subsection (9) above, 'independent', in relation to legal advice received by an employee or worker, means that the advice is given by a lawyer who is not acting in the matter for the employer or an associated employer.

(11) The Secretary of State may by order repeal subsections (9) and (10) above and this subsection.

50–53 [omitted]

Supplementary

54 Meaning of 'worker', 'employee' etc.

(1) In this Act 'employee' means an individual who has entered into or works under (or, where the employment has ceased, worked under) a contract of employment.

(2) In this Act 'contract of employment' means a contract of service or apprenticeship, whether express or implied, and (if it is express) whether oral or in writing.

(3) In this Act 'worker' (except in the phrases 'agency worker' and 'home worker') means an individual who has entered into or works under (or, where the employment has ceased, worked under)—

(a) a contract of employment; or

(b) any other contract, whether express or implied and (if it is express) whether oral or in writing, whereby the individual undertakes to do or perform personally any work or services for another party to the contract whose status is not by virtue of the contract that of a client or customer of any profession or business undertaking carried on by the individual;

and any reference to a worker's contract shall be construed accordingly.

(4) In this Act 'employer', in relation to an employee or a worker, means the person by whom the employee or worker is (or, where the employment has ceased, was) employed.

(5) In this Act 'employment'—

(a) in relation to an employee, means employment under a contract of employment; and

(b) in relation to a worker, means employment under his contract;

and 'employed' shall be construed accordingly.

55 Interpretation

(1) In this Act, unless the context otherwise requires,—

'civil proceedings' means proceedings before an employment tribunal or civil proceedings before any other court;

'enforcement notice' shall be construed in accordance with section 19 above;

'government department' includes a Northern Ireland department, except in section 52(a) above;

'industrial tribunal' means a tribunal established under Article 3 of the Industrial Tribunals (Northern Ireland) Order 1996;

'notice' means notice in writing;

'pay reference period' shall be construed in accordance with section 1(4) above;

'penalty notice' shall be construed in accordance with section 21 above;

'person who qualifies for the national minimum wage' shall be construed in accordance with section 1(2) above; and related expressions shall be construed accordingly;

'prescribe' means prescribe by regulations;

'regulations' means regulations made by the Secretary of State, except in the case of regulations under section 47(2) or (4) above made by the Secretary of State and the Minister of Agriculture, Fisheries and Food acting jointly or by the Department of Agriculture for Northern Ireland.

(2) Any reference in this Act to a person being remunerated for a pay reference period is a reference to the person being remunerated by his employer in respect of his work in that pay reference period.

(3) Any reference in this Act to doing work includes a reference to performing services; and 'work' and other related expressions shall be construed accordingly.

(4) For the purposes of this Act, a person ceases to be of compulsory school age in Scotland when he ceases to be of school age in accordance with sections 31 and 33 of the Education (Scotland) Act 1980.

(5) Any reference in this Act to a person ceasing to be of compulsory school age shall, in relation to Northern Ireland, be construed in accordance with Article 46 of the Education and Libraries (Northern Ireland) Order 1986.

(6) Any reference in this Act to an employment tribunal shall, in relation to Northern Ireland, be construed as a reference to an industrial tribunal.

56 [omitted]

DISABILITY RIGHTS COMMISSION ACT 1999
(1999, c. 17)

1 The Disability Rights Commission

(1) There shall be a body known as the Disability Rights Commission (referred to in this Act as 'the Commission')

(2)-(4) [omitted]

2 General functions

(1) The Commission shall have the following duties—

(a) to work towards the elimination of discrimination against disabled persons;

(b) to promote the equalisation of opportunities for disabled persons;

(c) to take such steps as it considers appropriate with a view to encouraging good practice in the treatment of disabled persons; and

(d) to keep under review the working of the Disability Discrimination Act 1995 (referred to in this Act as 'the 1995 Act') and this Act.

(2) The Commission may, for any purpose connected with the performance of its functions—

(a) make proposals or give other advice to any Minister of the Crown as to any aspect of the law or a proposed change to the law;

(b) make proposals or give other advice to any Government agency or other public authority as to the practical application of any law;

(c) undertake, or arrange for or support (whether financially or otherwise), the carrying out of research or the provision of advice or information.

Nothing in this subsection is to be regarded as limiting the Commission's powers.

(3) The commission shall make proposals or give other advice under subsection (2)(a) on any matter specified in a request from a Minister of the Crown.

(4) The Commission may make charges for facilities or services made available by it for any purpose.

(5) In this section—

'disabled persons' includes persons who have had a disability;

'discrimination' means anything which is discrimination for the purpose of any provision of Part II or Part III of the 1995 Act; and

'the law' includes Community law and the international obligations of the United Kingdom.

3 Formal investigations

(1) The commission may decide to conduct a formal investigation for any purpose connected with the performance of its duties under section 2(1).

(2) The Commission shall conduct a formal investigation if directed to do so by the Secretary of State for any such purpose.

(3) The commission may at any time decide to stop or to suspend the conduct of a formal investigation; but any such decision requires the approval of the Secretary of State if the investigation is being conducted in pursuance of a direction under subsection (2).

(4) The Commission may, as respects any formal investigation which it has decided or been directed to conduct—

(a) nominate one or more commissioners, with or without one or more additional commissioners appointed for the purposes of the investigation, to conduct the investigation on its behalf; and

(b) authorise those persons to exercise such of its functions in relation to the investigation (which may include drawing up or revising terms of reference) as it may determine.

(5) [omitted]

4 Non-discrimination notices

(1) If in the course of a formal investigation the Commission is satisfied that a person has committed or is committing an unlawful act, it may serve on him a notice (referred to in this Act as a non-discrimination notice) which—

(a) gives details of the unlawful act which the Commission has found that he has committed or is committing; and

(b) requires him not to commit any further unlawful acts of the same kind (and, if the finding is that he is committing an unlawful act, to cease doing so).

(2) The notice may include recommendations to the person concerned as to action which the Commission considers he could reasonably be expected to take with a view to complying with the requirement mentioned in subsection (1)(b).

(3) the notice may require the person concerned—

(a) to propose an adequate action plan (subject to and in accordance with Part III of Schedule 3) with a view to securing compliance with the requirement mentioned in subsection (1)(b); and

(b) once an action plan proposed by him has become final, to take any action which—

(i) is specified in the plan; and

(ii) he has not already taken,

at the time or times specified in the plan.

(4) For the purposes of subsection (3)—

(a) an action plan is a document drawn up by the person concerned specifying action (including action he has already taken) intended to change anything in his practices, policies, procedures or other arrangements which—

(i) caused or contributed to the commission of the unlawful act concerned; or

(ii) is liable to cause or contribute to a failure to comply with the requirement mentioned in subsection (1)(b); and

(b) an action plan is adequate if the action specified in it would be sufficient to ensure, within a reasonable time, that he is not prevented from complying with that requirement by anything in his practices, policies, procedures or other arrangements;

and the action specified in an action plan may include ceasing an activity or taking continuing action over a period.

(5) In this section 'unlawful act' means an act which is unlawful discrimination for the purposes of any provision of Part II or Part III of the 1995 Act or any other unlawful act of a description prescribed for the purposes of this section.

(6) [omitted]

5 Agreements in lieu of enforcement action

(1) If the Commission has reason to believe that a person has committed or is committing an unlawful act, it may (subject to section 3(3)) enter into an agreement in writing under this section with that person on the assumption that that belief is well founded (whether or not that person admits that he committed or is committing the act in question).

(2) An agreement under this section is one by which—

(a) the Commission undertakes not to take any relevant enforcement action in relation to the unlawful act in question; and

(b) the person concerned undertakes—

(i) not to commit any further unlawful acts of the same kind (and, where appropriate, to cease committing the unlawful act in question); and

(ii) to take such action (which may include ceasing an activity or taking continuing action over any period) as may be specified in the agreement.

(3) Those undertakings are binding on the parties to the agreement; but undertakings under subsection (2)(b) are enforceable by the Commission only as provided by subsection (8).

(4) For the purposes of subsection (2)(a), 'relevant enforcement action' means—

(a) beginning a formal investigation into the commission by the person concerned of the unlawful act in question;

(b) if such an investigation has begun (whether or not the investigation is confined to that matter), taking any further steps in the investigation of that matter; and

(c) taking any steps, or further steps, with a view to the issue of a non-discrimination notice based on the commission of the unlawful act in question.

(5) The action specified in an undertaking under subsection (2)(b)(ii) must be action intended to change anything in the practices, policies, procedures or other arrangements of the person concerned which—

(a) caused or contributed to the commission of the unlawful act in question; or

(b) is liable to cause or contribute to a failure to comply with his undertaking under subsection (2)(b)(i).

(6) An agreement under this section—

(a) may include terms providing for incidental or supplementary matters (including the termination of the agreement, or the right of either party to terminate it, in certain circumstances); and

(b) may be varied or revoked by agreement of the parties.

(7) An agreement under this section may not include any provisions other than terms mentioned in subsections (2) and (6)(a) unless their inclusion is authorised by

regulations made by the Secretary of State for the purposes of this section; but any provisions so authorised are not enforceable by the commission under subsection (8).

(8) The commission may apply to a county court or by summary application to the sheriff for an order under this subsection if—

(a) the other party to an agreement under this section has failed to comply with any undertaking under subsection (2)(b); or

(b) the Commission has reasonable cause to believe that he intends not to comply with any such undertaking.

(9) An order under subsection (8) is an order requiring the other party to comply with the undertaking or with such directions for the same purpose as are contained in the order.

(10) Nothing in the section affects the Commission's powers to settle or compromise legal proceedings of any description.

(11) In this section 'unlawful act' means an act which is unlawful discrimination for the purposes of any provision of Part II or Part III of the 1995 Act or any other unlawful act of a description prescribed for the purposes of this section.

(12) [omitted]

6 Persistent discrimination

(1) This section applies during the period of five years beginning on the date on which—

(a) a non-discrimination notice served on a person,

(b) a finding by a court or tribunal in proceedings under section 8 or 25 of the 1995 Act that a person has committed an act which is unlawful discrimination for the purposes of any provision of Part II or Part III of that Act, or

(c) a finding by a court or tribunal in any other proceedings that a person has committed an act of a description prescribed under subsection (4)(b),

has become final.

(2) If during that period it appears to the Commission that unless restrained the person concerned is likely to do one or more unlawful acts, the Commission may apply to a county court for an injunction, or to the sheriff for interdict, restraining him from doing so.

(3) The court, if satisfied that the application is well-founded, may grant the injunction or interdict in the terms applied for or in more limited terms.

(4) In this section 'unlawful act' means an act which is unlawful discrimination for the purposes of any provision of Part II or Part III of the 1995 Act or any other unlawful act of a description prescribed for the purposes of this section.

(5) A finding of a court or tribunal becomes final for the purposes of this section when an appeal against it is dismissed, withdrawn or abandoned or when the time for appealing expires without an appeal having been brought.

7 to **16** and Schedules [omitted]

EMPLOYMENT RELATIONS ACT 1999
(1999, c. 26)

ARRANGEMENT OF SECTIONS

Trade unions

Disciplinary and grievance hearings

1-2 [omitted]

3 Detriment related to trade union membership. Blacklists

(1) The Secretary of State may make regulations prohibiting the compilation of lists which—

(a) contain details of members of trade unions or persons who have taken part in the activities of trade unions, and

(b) are compiled with a view to being used by employers or employment agencies for the purposes of discrimination in relation to recruitment or in relation to the treatment of workers.

(2) The Secretary of State may make regulations prohibiting—

(a) the use of lists to which subsection (1) applies;

(b) the sale or supply of lists to which subsection (1) applies.

(3) Regulations under this section may, in particular—

(a) confer jurisdiction (including exclusive jurisdiction) on employment tribunals and on the Employment Appeal Tribunal;

(b) include provision for or about the grant and enforcement of specified remedies by courts and tribunals;

(c) include provision for the making of awards of compensation calculated in accordance with the regulations;

(d) include provision permitting proceedings to be brought by trade unions on behalf of members in specified circumstances;

(e) include provision about cases where an employee is dismissed by his employer and the reason or principal reason for the dismissal, or why the employee was selected for dismissal, relates to a list to which subsection (1) applies;

(f) create criminal offences;

(g) in specified cases or circumstances, extend liability for a criminal offence created under paragraph (f) to a person who aids the commission of the offence or to a person who is an agent, principal, employee, employer or officer of a person who commits the offence;

(h) provide for specified obligations or offences not to apply in specified circumstances;

(i) include supplemental, incidental, consequential and transitional provision, including provision amending an enactment;

(j) make different provision for different cases or circumstances.

(4) Regulations under this section creating an offence may not provide for it to be punishable—

(a) by imprisonment,

(b) by a fine in excess of level 5 on the standard scale in the case of an offence triable only summarily, or

(c) by a fine in excess of the statutory maximum in the case of summary conviction for an offence triable either way.

(5) In this section—

'list' includes any index or other set of items whether recorded electronically or by any other means, and

'worker' has the meaning given by section 13.

(6) Subject to subsection (5), expressions used in this section and in the Trade Union and Labour Relations (Consolidation) Act 1992 have the same meaning in this section as in that Act.

4-9 [omitted]

Disciplinary and grievance hearings

10 Right to be accompanied

(1) This section applies where a worker—

(a) is required or invited by his employer to attend a disciplinary or grievance hearing, and

(b) reasonably requests to be accompanied at the hearing.

(2) Where this section applies the employer must permit the worker to be accompanied at the hearing by a single companion who—

(a) is chosen by the worker and is within subsection (3),

(b) is to be permitted to address the hearing (but not to answer questions on behalf of the worker), and

(c) is to be permitted to confer with the worker during the hearing.

(3) A person is within this subsection if he is—

(a) employed by a trade union of which he is an official within the meaning of section 1 and 119 of the Trade Union and Labour Relations (Consolidation) Act 1992,

(b) an official of a trade union (within that meaning) whom the union has reasonably certified in writing as having experience of, or as having received training in, acting as a worker's companion at disciplinary or grievance hearings, or

(c) another of the employer's workers.

(4) If—

(a) a worker has a right under this section to be accompanied at a hearing,

(b) his chosen companion will not be available at the time proposed for the hearing by the employer, and

(c) the worker proposes an alternative time which satisfies subsection (5),

the employer must postpone the hearing to the time proposed by the worker.

(5) An alternative time must—

(a) be reasonable, and

(b) fall before the end of the period of five working days beginning with the first working day after the day proposed by the employer.

(6) An employer shall permit a worker to take time off during working hours for the purpose of accompanying another of the employer's workers in accordance with a request under subsection (1)(b).

(7) Sections 168(3) and (4), 169 and 171 to 173 of the Trade Union and Labour Relations (Consolidation) Act 1992 (time off for carrying out trade union duties) shall apply in relation to subsection (6) above as they apply in relation to section 168(1) of that Act.

11 Complaint to employment tribunal

(1) A worker may present a complaint to an employment tribunal that his employer has failed, or threatened to fail, to comply with section 10(2) or (4).

(2) A tribunal shall not consider a complaint under this section in relation to a failure or threat unless the complaint is presented—

(a) before the end of the period of three months beginning with the date of the failure or threat, or

(b) within such further period as the tribunal considers reasonable in a case where it is satisfied that it was not reasonably practicable for the complaint to be presented before the end of that period of three months.

(3) Where a tribunal finds that a complaint under this section is well-founded it shall order the employer to pay compensation to the worker of an amount not exceeding two weeks' pay.

(4) Chapter II of Part XIV of the Employment Rights Act 1996 (calculation of a week's pay) shall apply for the purposes of subsection (3); and in applying that Chapter the calculation date shall be taken to be—

(a) in the case of a claim which is made in the course of a claim for unfair dismissal, the date on which the employer's notice of dismissal was given or, if there was no notice, the effective date of termination, and

(b) in any other case, the date on which the relevant hearing took place (or was to have taken place).

(5) The limit in section 227(1) of the Employment Rights Act 1996 (maximum amount of week's pay) shall apply for the purposes of subsection (3) above.

(6) No award shall be made under subsection (3) in respect of a claim which is made in the course of a claim for unfair dismissal if the tribunal makes a supplementary award under section 127A(2) of the Employment Rights Act 1996 (internal appeal procedures).

12 Detriment and dismissal

(1) A worker has the right not to be subjected to any detriment by any act, or any deliberate failure to act, by his employer done on the ground that he—

(a) exercised or sought to exercise the right under section 10(2) or (4), or

(b) accompanied or sought to accompany another worker (whether of the same employer or not) pursuant to a request under that section.

(2) Section 48 of the Employment Rights Act 1996 shall apply in relation to contraventions of subsection (1) above as it applies in relation to contraventions of certain sections of that Act.

(3) A worker who is dismissed shall be regarded for the purposes of Part X of the Employment Rights Act 1996 as unfairly dismissed if the reason (or, if more than one, the principal reason) for the dismissal is that he—

(a) exercised or sought to exercise the right under section 10(2) or (4), or

(b) accompanied or sought to accompany another worker (whether of the same employer or not) pursuant to a request under that section.

(4) Sections 108 and 109 of that Act (qualifying period of employment and upper age limit) shall not apply in relation to subsection (3) above.

(5) Sections 128 to 132 of that Act (interim relief) shall apply in relation to dismissal for the reason specified in subsection (3)(a) or (b) above as they apply in relation to dismissal for a reason specified in section 128(1)(b) of that Act.

(6) In the application of Chapter II of Part X of that Act in relation to subsection (3) above, a reference to an employee shall be taken as a reference to a worker.

13 Interpretation

(1) In sections 10 to 12 and this section 'worker' means an individual who is—

(a) a worker within the meaning of section 230(3) of the Employment Rights Act 1996,

(b) an agency worker,

(c) a home worker,

(d) a person in Crown employment within the meaning of section 191 of that Act, other than a member of the naval, military, air or reserve forces of the Crown, or

(e) employed as a relevant member of the House of Lords staff or the House of Commons staff within the meaning of section 194(6) or 195(5) of that Act.

(2) In subsection (1) 'agency worker' means an individual who—

(a) is supplied by a person ('the agent') to do work for another ('the principal') by arrangement between the agent and the principal,

(b) is not a party to a worker's contract, within the meaning of section 230(3) of that Act, relating to that work, and

(c) is not a party to a contract relating to that work under which he undertakes to do the work for another party to the contract whose status is, by virtue of the contract, that of a client or customer of any professional or business undertaking carried on by the individual;

and, for the purposes of sections 10 to 12, both the agent and the principal are employers of an agency worker.

(3) In subsection (1) 'home worker' means an individual who—

(a) contracts with a person, for the purposes of the person's business, for the execution of work to be done in a place not under the person's control or management, and

(b) is not a party to a contract relating to that work under which the work is to be executed for another party to the contract whose status is, by virtue of the contract, that of a client or customer of any professional or business undertaking carried on by the individual;

and, for the purposes of sections 10 to 12, the person mentioned in paragraph (a) is the home worker's employer.

(4) For the purposes of section 10 a disciplinary hearing is a hearing which could result in—

(a) the administration of a formal warning to a worker by his employer,

(b) the taking of some other action in respect of a worker by his employer, or

(c) the confirmation of a warning issued or some other action taken.

(5) For the purposes of section 10 a grievance hearing is a hearing which concerns the performance of a duty by an employer in relation to a worker.

(6) For the purposes of section 10(5)(b) in its application to a part of Great Britain a working day is a day other than—

(a) a Saturday or a Sunday,

(b) Christmas Day or Good Friday, or

(c) a day which is a bank holiday under the Banking and Financial Dealings act 1971 in that part of Great Britain.

14 Contracting out and conciliation

Sections 10 to 13 of this Act shall be treated as provisions of Part V of the Employment Rights act 1996 for the purposes of—

(a) section 203(1), (2)(e) and (f), (3) and (4) of that Act (restrictions on contracting out), and

(b) section 18(1)(d) of the Employment Tribunals Act 1996 (conciliation).

15 National security employees

Sections 10 to 13 of this Act shall not apply in relation to a person employed for the purposes of—

(a) the Security Service,

(b) the Secret Intelligence Service, or

(c) the Government Communications Headquarters.

16 [omitted]

17 Collective agreements: detriment and dismissal.

(1) The Secretary of State may make regulations about cases where a worker—

(a) is subjected to detriment by his employer, or

(b) is dismissed,

on the grounds that he refuses to enter into a contract which includes terms which differ from the terms of a collective agreement which applies to him.

(2) The regulations may—

(a) make provision which applies only in specified classes of case;

(b) make different provision for different circumstances;

(c) include supplementary, incidental and transitional provision.

(3) In this section—

'collective agreement' has the meaning given by section 178(1) of the Trade Union and Labour Relations (Consolidation) Act 1992; and

'employer' and 'worker' have the same meaning as in section 296 of that Act.

(4) The payment of higher wages or higher rates of pay or overtime or the payment of any signing on or other bonuses or the provision of other benefits having a monetary value to other workers employed by the same employer shall not constitute a detriment to any worker not receiving the same or similar payments or benefits within the meaning of subsection (1)(a) of this section so long as—

(a) there is no inhibition in the contract of employment of the worker receiving the same from being the member of any trade union, and

(b) the said payments of higher wages or rates of pay or overtime or bonuses or the provision of other benefits are in accordance with the terms of a contract of employment and reasonably relate to services provided by the worker under that contract.

18 [omitted]

19 Part-time work: discrimination

(1) The Secretary of State shall make regulations for the purpose of securing that persons in part-time employment are treated, for such purposes and to such extent as the regulations may specify, no less favourably than persons in full-time employment.

(2) The regulations may—

(a) specify classes of person who are to be taken to be, or not to be, in part-time employment;

(b) specify classes of person who are to be taken to be, or not to be, in full-time employment;

(c) specify circumstances in which persons in part-time employment are to be taken to be, or not to be, treated less favourably than persons in full-time employment;

(d) make provision which has effect in relation to persons in part-time employment generally or provision which has effect only in relation to specified classes of persons in part-time employment.

(3) The regulations may—

(a) confer jurisdiction (including exclusive jurisdiction) on employment tribunals and on the Employment Appeal Tribunal;

(b) create criminal offences in relation to specified acts or omissions by an employer, by an organisation or employers, by an organisation of workers or by an organisation existing for the purposes of a profession or trade carried on by the organisation's members;

(c) In specified cases or circumstances, extend liability for a criminal offence created under paragraph (b) to a person who aids the commission of the offence or to a person who is an agent, principal, employee, employer or officer of a person who commits the offence;

(d) provide for specified obligations or offences not to apply in specified circumstances;

(e) make provision about notices or information to be given, evidence to be produced and other procedures to be followed;

(f) amend, apply with or without modifications, or make provision similar to any provision of the Employment Rights Act 1996 (including, in particular, Parts V, X and XIII) or the Trade Union and Labour Relations (Consolidation) Act 1992;

(g) provide for the provisions of specified agreements to have effect in place of provisions of the regulations to such extent and in such circumstances as may be specified;

(h) include supplemental, incidental, consequential and transitional provision, including provision amending an enactment;

(i) make different provision for different cases or circumstances.

(4) Without prejudice to the generality of this section the regulations may make any provision which appears to the Secretary of State to be necessary or expedient—

(a) for the purpose of implementing Council Directive 97/81/EC on the framework agreement on part-time work in its application to terms and conditions of employment;

(b) for the purpose of dealing with any matter arising out of or related to the United Kingdom's obligations under that Directive;

(c) for the purpose of any matter dealt with by the framework agreement or for the purpose of applying the provisions of the framework agreement to any matter relating to part-time workers.

(5) Regulations under this section which create an offence—

(a) shall provide for it to be triable summarily only, and

(b) may not provide for it to be punishable by imprisonment or by a fine in excess of level 5 on the standard scale.

20-22 [omitted]

23 Power to confer rights on individuals

(1) This section applies to any right conferred on an individual against an employer (however defined) under or by virtue of any of the following—

(a) the Trade Union and Labour Relations (Consolidation) Act 1992;

(b) the Employment Rights Act 1996;

(c) this Act;

(d) any instrument made under section 2(2) of the European Communities Act 1972.

(2) The Secretary of State may by order make provision which has the effect of conferring any such right on individuals who are of a specified description.

(3) the reference in subsection (2) to individuals includes a reference to individuals expressly excluded from exercising the right.

(4) An order under this section may—

(a) provide that individuals are to be treated as parties to workers' contracts or contracts of employment;

(b) make provision as to who are to be regarded as the employers of individuals;

(c) make provision which has the effect of modifying the operation of any right as conferred on individuals by the order;

(d) include such consequential, incidental or supplementary provisions as the Secretary of State thinks fit.

(5)-(7) [omitted]

24-29 [omitted]

Miscellaneous

30 Partnerships at work

(1) The Secretary of State may spend money or provide money to other persons for the purpose of encouraging and helping employers (or their representatives) and employees (or their representatives) to improve the way they work together.

(2) Money may be provided in such way as the Secretary of State thinks fit (whether as grants or otherwise) and on such terms as he thinks fit (whether as to repayment or otherwise).

31-33 [omitted]

34 Indexation of amounts, etc.

(1) This section applies to the sums specified in the following provisions—

(a) section 31(1) of the Employment Rights Act 1996 (guarantee payments: limits);

(b) section 120(1) of that Act (unfair dismissal: minimum amount of basic award);

(c) section 124(1) of that Act (unfair dismissal: limit of compensatory award);

(d) section 186(1)(a) and (b) of that Act (employee's rights on insolvency of employer: maximum amount payable);

(e) section 227(1) of that Act (maximum amount of a week's pay for purposes of certain calculations);

(f) section 156(1) of the Trade Union and Labour Relations (Consolidation) Act 1992 (unfair dismissal: minimum basic award);

(g) section 176(6) of that Act (right to membership of trade union: remedies).

(2) If the retail prices index for September of a year is higher or lower than the index for the previous September, the Secretary of State shall as soon as practicable make an order in relation to each sum mentioned in subsection (1)—

(a) increasing each sum, if the new index is higher, or

(b) decreasing each sum, if the new index is lower,

by the same percentage as the amount of the increase or decrease of the index.

(3) In making the calculation required by subsection (2) the Secretary of State shall—

(a) in the case of the sum mentioned in subsection (1)(a), round the result up to the nearest 10 pence,

(b) in the case of the sums mentioned in subsection (1)(b), (c), (f) and (g), round the result up to the nearest £100, and

(c) in the case of the sums mentioned in subsection (1)(d) and (e), round the result up to the nearest £10.

(4) [omitted]

(5) In this section 'retail prices index' means—

(a) the general index of retail prices (for all items) published by the Office for National Statistics, or

(b) where that index is not published for a month, any substituted index or figures published by that Office.

(6) [omitted]

35-37 [omitted]

38 Transfer of undertakings

(1) This section applies where regulations under section 2(2) of the European Communities Act 1972 (general implementation of Treaties) make provision for the purpose of implementing, or for a purpose concerning, a Community obligation of the

United Kingdom which relates to the treatment of employees on the transfer of an undertaking or business or part of an undertaking or business.

(2) The Secretary of State may by regulations make the same or similar provision in relation to the treatment of employees in circumstances other than those to which the Community obligation applies (including circumstances in which there is no transfer, or no transfer to which the Community obligation applies).

(3) [omitted]

39-47 [omitted]

TAX CREDITS ACT 1999
(1999, c. 10)

6 Payment of tax credit by employers, etc.

(1) On the making to any person ('the employee') of any payment of, or on account of, any income assessable to income tax under Schedule E, any tax credit to which he is entitled shall, subject to and in accordance with regulations made by the Board under this section, be paid by the person making the payment ('the employer').

(2) the Board shall make regulations with respect to the payment of tax credit by employers, and those regulations may, in particular, include provision—

(a) for requiring employers to make payments of tax credit by reference to notifications of entitlement furnished to them by the Board;

(b) [omitted]

(c) for requiring employers to provide information to employees (in their itemised pay statements or otherwise);

SCHEDULE 3
RIGHTS OF EMPLOYEES NOT TO SUFFER UNFAIR DISMISSAL OR OTHER DETRIMENT

The right not to suffer detriment

1.—(1) An employee has the right not to be subjected to any detriment by any act, or any deliberate failure to act, by his employer, done on the ground that—

(a) any action was taken, or was proposed to be taken, by or on behalf of the employee with a view to enforcing, or otherwise securing the benefit of, a right conferred on the employee by regulations under section 6(2)(a) or (c) above;

(b) a penalty was imposed on the employer, or proceedings for a penalty were brought against him, under section 9 above, as a result of action taken by or on behalf of the employee for the purpose of enforcing, or otherwise securing the benefit of, such a right; or

(c) the employee is entitled, or will or may be entitled, to tax credit.

(2) It is immaterial for the purposes of paragraph (a) or (b) of sub-paragraph (1) above—

(a) whether or not the employee has the right; or

(b) whether or not the right has been infringed;

but, for that sub-paragraph to apply, the claim to the right and, if applicable, the claim that it has been infringed, must be made in good faith.

(3) This paragraph does not apply where the detriment in question amounts to dismissal within the meaning of—

(a) Part X of the Employment Rights Act 1996 (unfair dismissal), or

(b) Part XI of the Employment Rights (Northern Ireland) Order 1996 (corresponding provision for Northern Ireland),

except where in relation to Northern Ireland the employee is dismissed in circumstances in which, by virtue of Article 240 of that Order (fixed term contracts), Part XI does not apply to the dismissal.

Enforcement of right not to suffer detriment

2.—(1) An employee may present a complaint to an employment tribunal or, in Northern Ireland, an industrial tribunal that he has been subjected to a detriment in contravention of paragraph 1 above.

(2) The provisions of—

(a) sections 48(2) to (4) and 49 of the Employment Rights Act 1996 (complaints to employment tribunals and remedies); or

(b) in relation to Northern Ireland, Articles 71(2) to (4) and 72 of the Employment Rights (Northern Ireland) Order 1996 (complaints to industrial tribunals and remedies),

shall apply in relation to a complaint under this paragraph as they apply in relation to a complaint under section 48 of that Act or Article 71 of that Order (as the case may be), but so that references in those provisions to the employer are construed in accordance with section 6 above.

STATUTORY INSTRUMENTS

THE TRANSFER OF UNDERTAKINGS (PROTECTION OF EMPLOYMENT) REGULATIONS 1981 (SI 1981 No. 1794)

Interpretation

2.—(1) In these Regulations—

'collective agreement', 'employers' association', and 'trade union' have the same meanings respectively as in the 1974 Act or, in Northern Ireland, the 1976 order;

'collective bargaining' has the same meaning as it has in the 1975 Act or, in Northern Ireland, the 1976 order;

'contract of employment' means any agreement between an employee and his employer determining the terms and conditions of his employment;

'employee' means any individual who works for another person whether under a contract of service or apprenticeship or otherwise but does not include anyone who provides services under a contract for services and references to a person's employer shall be construed accordingly;

'the 1974 Act', 'the 1975 Act', 'the 1978 Act' and 'the 1976 order' mean, respectively, the Trade Union and Labour Relations Act 1974, the Employment Protection Act 1975, the Employment Protection (Consolidation) Act 1978 and the Industrial Relations (Northern Ireland) Order 1976;

'recognised', in relation to a trade union, means recognised to any extent by an employer, or two or more associated employers, (within the meaning of the 1978 Act), for the purpose of collective bargaining;

'relevant transfer' means a transfer to which these Regulations apply and 'transferor' and 'transferee' shall be construed accordingly; and

'undertaking' includes any trade or business

(2) References in these Regulations to the transfer of part of an undertaking are references to a transfer of a part which is being transferred as a business and, accordingly, do not include references to a transfer of a ship without more.

(3) For the purposes of these Regulations the representative of a trade union recognised by an employer is an official or other person authorised to carry on collective bargaining with the employer by that union.

A relevant transfer

3.—(1) Subject to the provisions of these Regulations, these Regulations apply to a transfer from one person to another of an undertaking situated immediately before the transfer in the United Kingdom or a part of one which is so situated.

(2) Subject as aforesaid, these Regulations so apply whether the transfer is effected by sale or by some other disposition or by operation of law.

(3) Subject as aforesaid, these Regulations so apply notwithstanding—

(a) that the transfer is governed or effected by the law of a country or territory outside the United Kingdom;

(b) that persons employed in the undertaking or part transferred ordinarily work outside the United Kingdom;

(c) that the employment of any of those persons is governed by any such law.

(4) It is hereby declared that a transfer of an undertaking or part of one—

(a) may be effected by a series of two or more transactions; and

(b) may take place whether or not any property is transferred to the transferee by the transferor.

(5) [omitted]

Transfers by receivers and liquidators

4.—(1) Where the receiver of the property or part of the property of a company or the administrator of a company appointed under Part II of the Insolvency Act 1986 or, in the case of a creditors' voluntary winding up, the liquidator of a company transfers the company's undertaking, or part of the company's undertaking (the 'relevant undertaking') to a wholly owned subsidiary of the company, the transfer shall for the purposes of these Regulations be deemed not to have been effected until immediately before—

(a) the transferee company ceases (otherwise than by reason of its being wound up) to be a wholly owned subsidiary of the transferor company; or

(b) the relevant undertaking is transferred by the transferee company to another person;

whichever first occurs, and, for the purposes of these Regulations, the transfer of the relevant undertaking shall be taken to have been effected immediately before that date by one transaction only.

In this Regulation—

'creditors' voluntary winding up' has the same meaning as in the Companies Act 1948 or, in Northern Ireland, the Companies Act (Northern Ireland) 1960; and

'wholly owned subsidiary' has the same meaning as it has for the purposes of section 150 of the Companies Act 1948 and section 144 of the Companies Act (Northern Ireland) 1960.

Effect of relevant transfer on contracts of employment, etc.

5.—(1) Except where objection is made under paragraph (4A) below a relevant transfer shall not operate so as to terminate the contract of employment of any person employed by the transferor in the undertaking or part transferred but any such contract which would otherwise have been terminated by the transfer shall have effect after the transfer as if originally made between the person so employed and the transferee.

(2) Without prejudice to paragraph (1) above but subject to paragraph (4A) below, on the completion of a relevant transfer—

(a) all the transferor's rights, powers, duties and liabilities under or in connection with any such contract, shall be transferred by virtue of this Regulation to the transferee; and

(b) anything done before the transfer is completed by or in relation to the transferor in respect of that contract or a person employed in that undertaking or part shall be deemed to have been done by or in relation to the transferee.

(3) Any reference in paragraph (1) or (2) above to a person employed in an undertaking or part of one transferred by a relevant transfer is a reference to a person so employed immediately before the transfer, including, where the transfer is effected by a series of two or more transactions, a person so employed immediately before any of those transactions.

(4) Paragraph (2) above shall not transfer or otherwise affect the liability of any person to be prosecuted for, convicted of and sentenced for any offence.

(4A) Paragraphs (1) and (2) above shall not operate to transfer his contract of employment and the rights, powers, duties and liabilities under or in connection with it if the employee informs the transferor or the transferee that he objects to becoming employed by the transferee.

(4B) Where an employee so objects the transfer of the undertaking or part in which he is employed shall operate so as to terminate his contract of employment with the transferor but he shall not be treated, for any purpose, as having been dismissed by the transferor.

(5) Paragraphs (1) and (4A) above are without prejudice to any right of an employee arising apart from these Regulations to terminate his contract of employment without notice if a substantial change is made in his working conditions to his detriment; but no such right shall arise by reason only that, under that paragraph, the identity of his employer changes unless the employee shows that, in all the circumstances, the change is a significant change and is to his detriment.

Effect of relevant transfer on collective agreements

6. Where at the time of a relevant transfer there exists a collective agreement made by or on behalf of the transferor with a trade union recognised by the transferor in respect of any employee whose contract of employment is preserved by Regulation 5(1) above, then,—

(a) without prejudice to section 18 of the 1974 Act or Article 63 of the 1976 Order (collective agreements presumed to be unenforceable in specified circumstances) that agreement, in its application in relation to the employee, shall, after the transfer, have effect as if made by or on behalf of the transferee with that trade union, and accordingly anything done under or in connection with it, in its application as aforesaid, by or in relation to the transferor before the transfer, shall, after the transfer, be deemed to have been done by or in relation to the transferee; and

(b) any order made in respect of that agreement, in its application in relation to the employee, shall, after the transfer, have effect as if the transferee were a party to the agreement.

Exclusion of occupational pensions schemes

7.—(1) Regulations 5 and 6 above shall not apply—

(a) to so much of a contract of employment or collective agreement as relates to an occupational pension scheme within the meaning of the Social Security Pensions Act 1975 or the Social Security Pensions (Northern Ireland) Order 1975; or

(b) to any rights, powers, duties or liabilities under or in connection with any such contract or subsisting by virtue of any such agreement and relating to such a scheme or otherwise arising in connection with that person's employment and relating to such a scheme.

(2) For the purposes of paragraph (1) above any provisions of the occupational pension scheme which do not relate to benefits for old age, invalidity or survivors shall be treated as not being part of the scheme.

Dismissal of employee because of relevant transfer

8.—(1) Where either before or after a relevant transfer, any employee of the transferor or transferee is dismissed, that employee shall be treated for the purposes of Part V of the 1978 Act and Articles 20 to 41 of the 1976 Order (unfair dismissal) as unfairly dismissed if the transfer or a reason connected with it is the reason or principal reason for his dismissal.

(2) Where an economic, technical or organisational reason entailing changes in the workforce of either the transferor or the transferee before or after a relevant transfer is the reason or principal reason for dismissing an employee—

(a) paragraph (1) above shall not apply to his dismissal; but

(b) without prejudice to the application of section 57(3) of the 1978 Act or Article 22(10) of the 1976 Order (test of fair dismissal), the dismissal shall for the purposes of section 57(1)(b) of that Act and Article 22(1)(b) of that Order (substantial reason for dismissal) be regarded as having been for a substantial reason of a kind such as to justify the dismissal of an employee holding the position which that employee held.

(3) The provisions of this Regulation apply whether or not the employee in question is employed in the undertaking or part of the undertaking transferred or to be transferred.

(4) Paragraph (1) above shall not apply in relation to the dismissal of any employee which was required by reason of the application of section 5 of the Aliens Restriction (Amendment) Act 1919 to his employment.

(5) Paragraph (1) above shall not apply in relation to a dismissal of an employee if—

(a) the application of section 54 of the 1978 Act to the dismissal of the employee is excluded by or under any provision of Part V or sections 141 to 149 of the 1978 Act or of section 237 or 238 of the Trade Union and Labour Relations (Consolidation) Act 1992; or

(b) the application of Article 20 of the 1976 Order to the dismissal of the employee is excluded by or under any provision of Part III or Article 76 of that Order.

Effect of relevant transfer on trade union recognition

9.—(1) This Regulation applies where after a relevant transfer the undertaking or part of the undertaking transferred maintains an identity distinct from the remainder of the transferee's undertaking.

(2) Where before such a transfer an independent trade union is recognised to any extent by the transferor in respect of employees of any description who in consequence of the transfer become employees of the transferee, then, after the transfer—

(a) the union shall be deemed to have been recognised by the transferee to the same extent in respect of employees of that description so employed; and

(b) any agreement for recognition may be varied or rescinded accordingly.

Duty to inform and consult representatives

10.—(1) In this Regulation and Regulation 11 below references to affected employees, in relation to a relevant transfer, are to any employees of the transferor or the transferee (whether or not employed in the undertaking or the part of the undertaking to be transferred) who may be affected by the transfer or may be affected by measures taken in connection with it; and references to the employer shall be construed accordingly.

(2) Long enough before a relevant transfer to enable the employer of any affected employees to consult all the persons who are appropriate representatives of any of those affected employees, the employer shall inform those representatives of—

(a) the fact that the relevant transfer is to take place, when, approximately, it is to take place and the reasons for it; and

(b) the legal, economic and social implications of the transfer for the affected employees; and

(c) the measures which he envisages he will, in connection with the transfer, take in relation to those employees or, if he envisages that no measures will be so taken, that fact; and

(d) if the employer is the transferor, the measures which the transferee envisages he will, in connection with the transfer, take in relation to such of those employees as, by virtue of Regulation 5 above, become employees of the transferee after the transfer or, if he envisages that no measures will be so taken, that fact.

(2A) For the purposes of this Regulation the appropriate representatives of any employees are—

(a) if the employees are of a description in respect of which an independent trade union is recognised by their employer, representatives of the trade union, or

(b) in any other case, whichever of the following employee representatives the employer chooses—

(i) employee representatives appointed or elected by the affected employees otherwise than for the purposes of this Regulation, who (having regard to the purposes for and the method by which they were appointed or elected) have authority from those employees to receive information and to be consulted about the transfer on their behalf;

(ii) employee representatives elected by them, for the purposes of this Regulation, in an election satisfying the requirements of Regulation 10A(1).

(3) The transferee shall give the transferor such information at such a time as will enable the transferor to perform the duty imposed on him by virtue of paragraph (2)(d) above.

(4) The information which is to be given to the appropriate representatives shall be given to each of them by being delivered to them, or sent by post to an address notified by them to the employer, or (in the case of representatives of a trade union) sent by post to the union at the address of its head or main office.

(5) Where an employer of any affected employees envisages that he will, in connection with the transfer, be taking measures in relation to any such employees he shall consult all the persons who are appropriate representatives of any of the affected employees in relation to whom he envisages taking measures with a view to seeking their agreement to measures to be taken.

(6) In the course of those consultations the employer shall—

(a) consider any representations made by the appropriate representatives; and

(b) reply to those representations and, if he rejects any of those representations, state his reasons.

(6A) The employer shall allow the appropriate representatives access to the affected employees and shall afford to those representatives such accommodation and other facilities as may be appropriate.

(7) If in any case there are special circumstances which render it not reasonably practicable for an employer to perform a duty imposed on him by any of paragraphs (2) to (6), he shall take all such steps towards performing that duty as are reasonably practicable in the circumstances.

(8) Where—

(a) the employer has invited any of the affected employees to elect employee representatives, and

(b) the invitation was issued long enough before the time when the employer is required to give information under paragraph (2) above to allow them to elect representatives by that time,

the employer shall be treated as complying with the requirements of this Regulation in relation to those employees if he complies with those requirements as soon as is reasonably practicable after the election of the representatives.

(8A) If, after the employer has invited affected employees to elect representatives, they fail to do so within a reasonable time, he shall give to each affected employee the information set out in paragraph (2).

Election of employee representatives

10A.—(1) The requirements for the election of employee representatives under Regulation 10(2A) are that—

(a) the employer shall make such arrangements as are reasonably practical to ensure that the election is fair;

(b) the employer shall determine the number of representatives to be elected so that there are sufficient representatives to represent the interests of all the affected employees having regard to the number and classes of those employees;

(c) the employer shall determine whether the affected employees should be represented either by representatives of all the affected employees or by representatives of particular classes of those employees;

(d) before the election the employer shall determine the term of office as employee representatives so that it is of sufficient length to enable information to be given and consultations under Regulation 10 to be completed;

(e) the candidates for election as employee representatives are affected employees on the date of the election;

(f) no affected employee is unreasonably excluded from standing for election;

(g) all affected employees on the date of the election are entitled to vote for employee representatives;

(h) the employees entitled to vote may vote for as many candidates as there are representatives to be elected to represent them or, if there are to be representatives for particular classes of employees, may vote for as many candidates as there are representatives to be elected to represent their particular class of employee;

(i) the election is conducted so as to secure that—

(i) so far as is reasonably practicable, those voting do so in secret, and

(ii) the votes given at the election are accurately counted.

(2) Where, after an election of employee representatives satisfying the requirements of paragraph (1) has been held, one of those elected ceases to act as an employee representative and any of those employees are no longer represented, those employees shall elect another representative by an election satisfying the requirements of paragraph (1)(a), (e), (f) and (i).

Failure to inform or consult

11.—(1) Where an employer has failed to comply with a requirement of Regulation 10 or Regulation 10A, a complaint may be presented to an employment tribunal on that ground—

(a) in the case of a failure relating to the election of employee representatives, by any of his employees who are affected employees;

(b) in the case of any other failure relating to employee representatives, by any of the employee representatives to whom the failure related,

(c) in the case of failure relating to representatives of a trade union, by the trade union, and

(d) in any other case, by any of his employees who are affected employees.

(2) If on a complaint under paragraph (1) above a question arises whether or not it was reasonably practicable for an employer to perform a particular duty or what steps he took towards performing it, it shall be for him to show—

(a) that there were special circumstances which rendered it not reasonably practicable for him to perform the duty; and

(b) that he took all such steps towards its performance as were reasonably practicable in those circumstances.

(2A) If on a complaint under paragraph (1) a question arises as to whether or not any employee representative was an appropriate representative for the purposes of Regulation 10, it shall be for the employer to show that the employee representative had the necessary authority to represent the affected employees.

(2B) On a complaint under sub-paragraph (1)(a) it shall be for the employer to show that the requirements in Regulation 10A have been satisfied.

(3) On any such complaint against a transferor that he had failed to perform the duty imposed upon him by virtue of paragraph (2)(d) or, so far as relating thereto, paragraph (7) of Regulation 10 above, he may not show that it was not reasonably practicable for him to perform the duty in question for the reason that the transferee had failed to give him the requisite information at the requisite time in accordance with

Regulation 10(3) above unless he gives the transferee notice of his intention to show that fact; and the giving of the notice shall make the transferee a party to the proceedings.

(4) Where the tribunal finds a complaint under paragraph (3) above well-founded it shall make a declaration to that effect and may—

(a) order the employer to pay appropriate compensation to such descriptions of affected employees as may be specified in the award; or

(b) if the complaint is that the transferor did not perform the duty mentioned in sub-paragraph (3) above and the transferor (after giving due notice) shows the facts so mentioned, order the transferee to pay appropriate compensation to such descriptions of affected employees as may be specified in the award.

(5) An employee may present a complaint to an employment tribunal on the ground that he is an employee of a description to which an order under paragraph (4) above relates and that the transferor or the transferee has failed, wholly or in part, to pay him compensation in pursuance of the order.

(6) Where the tribunal finds a complaint under paragraph (5) above well-founded it shall order the employer to pay the complainant the amount of compensation which it finds is due to him.

(7) [revoked]

(8) An employment tribunal shall not consider a complaint under paragraph (1) or (5) above unless it is presented to the tribunal before the end of the period of three months beginning with—

(a) the date on which the relevant transfer is completed, in the case of a complaint under paragraph (1);

(b) the date of the tribunal's order under paragraph (4) above, in the case of a complaint under paragraph (5);

or within such further period as the tribunal considers reasonable in a case where it is satisfied that it was not reasonably practicable for the complaint to be presented before the end of the period of three months.

(9) Section 129 of the 1978 Act (complaint to be sole remedy for breach of relevant rights) and section 133 of that Act (functions of conciliation officer) and Articles 58(2) and 62 of the 1976 Order (which make corresponding provision for Northern Ireland) shall apply to the rights conferred by this Regulation and to proceedings under this Regulation as they apply to the rights conferred by that Act or that Order and the employment tribunal proceedings mentioned therein.

(10) An appeal shall lie and shall lie only to the Employment Appeal Tribunal on a question of law arising from any decision of, or arising in any proceedings before, an employment tribunal under or by virtue of these Regulations; and section 13(1) of the Tribunals and Inquiries Act 1971 (appeal from certain tribunals to the High Court) shall not apply in relation to any such proceedings.

(11) In this Regulation 'appropriate compensation' means such sum not exceeding thirteen weeks' pay for the employee in question as the tribunal considers just and equitable having regard to the seriousness of the failure of the employer to comply with his duty.

(12) Schedule 14 to the 1978 Act or, in Northern Ireland, Schedule 2 to the 1976 Order shall apply for calculating the amount of a week's pay for an employee for the purposes of paragraph (11) above; and, for the purposes of that calculation, the calculation date shall be—

(a) in the case of an employee who is dismissed by reason of redundancy (within the meaning of section 81 of the 1978 Act or, in Northern Ireland, section 11 of the Contracts of Employment and Redundancy Payments Act (Northern Ireland) 1965) the date which is the calculation date for the purposes of any entitlement of his to a redundancy payment (within the meaning of that section) or which would be that calculation date if he were so entitled;

(b) in the case of an employee who is dismissed for any other reason, the effective date of termination (within the meaning of section 55 of the 1978 Act or, in Northern Ireland, Article 21 of the 1976 Order) of his contract of employment;

(c) in any other case, the date of the transfer in question.

Construction of references to employee representatives

11A. For the purposes of Regulations 10 and 11 above persons are employee representatives if—

(a) they have been elected by employees for the specific purpose of being given information and consulted by their employer under Regulation 10 above; or

(b) having been elected or appointed by employees otherwise than for that specific purpose, it is appropriate (having regard to the purposes for which they were elected) for their employer to inform and consult them under that Regulation,

and (in either case) they are employed by the employer at the time when they are elected or appointed.

Restriction on contracting out

12. Any provision of any agreement (whether a contract of employment or not) shall be void in so far as it purports to exclude or limit the operation of Regulation 5, 8 or 10 above or to preclude any person from presenting a complaint to an employment tribunal under Regulation 11 above.

Exclusion of employment abroad or as a dock worker

13.—(1) Regulation 8, 10 and 11 of these Regulations do not apply to employment where under his contract of employment the employee ordinarily works outside the United Kingdom.

(2) For the purposes of this Regulation a person employed to work on board a ship registered in the United Kingdom shall, unless—

(a) the employment is wholly outside the United Kingdom, or

(b) he is not ordinarily resident in the United Kingdom

be regarded as a person who under his contract ordinarily works in the United Kingdom

(3) [revoked]

THE MANAGEMENT OF HEALTH AND SAFETY AT WORK REGULATIONS 1992 (SI 1992 No. 2051)

1 Citation, commencement and interpretation.
3 Risk assessment.
4 Health and safety arrangements.
5 Health surveillance.
6 Health and safety assistance.
7 Procedures for serious and imminent danger and for danger areas.
8 Information for employees.
9 Co-operation and Co-ordination.
10 Persons working in host employers' or self-employed persons' undertakings.
11 Capabilities and training.
12 Employees' duties.
13 Temporary workers.
15 Exclusion of civil liability.
16 Extension outside Great Britain.

Citation, commencement and interpretation

1.—(1) [omitted]

(2) In these Regulations—

'the 1978 Act' means the Employment Protection (Consolidation) Act 1978;

'the assessment' means, in the case of an employer or self-employed person, the assessment made or changed by him in accordance with regulation 3;

'child'—

(a) as respects England and Wales, means a person who is not over compulsory school age, construed—

(i) before the coming into force of section 8 of the Education Act 1996 in accordance with paragraph 1 of Schedule 40 to that Act; and

(ii) in accordance with section 8 from its coming into force;

(b) as respects Scotland, means a person who is not over school age, construed in accordance with section 31 of the Education (Scotland) Act 1980;

'employment business' means a business (whether or not carried on with a view to profit and whether or not carried on in conjunction with any other business) which supplies persons (other than seafarers) who are employed in it to work for and under the control of other persons in any capacity;

'fixed-term contract of employment' means a contract of employment for a specific term which is fixed in advance or which can be ascertained in advance by reference to some relevant circumstance;

'given birth' means 'delivered a living child or, after twenty-four weeks of pregnancy, a stillborn child';

'new or expectant mother' means an employee who is pregnant; who has given birth within the previous six months; or who is breastfeeding;

'the preventive and protective measures' means the measures which have been identified by the employer or by the self-employed person in consequence of the assessment as the measures he needs to take to comply with the requirements and prohibitions imposed upon him by or under the relevant statutory provisions and by Part II of the Fire Precautions (Workplace) Regulations 1997;

'young person' means any person who has not attained the age of eighteen.

(3) Any reference in these Regulations to—

(a) a numbered regulation is a reference to the regulation in these Regulations so numbered; or

(b) a numbered paragraph is a reference to the paragraph so numbered in the regulation in which the reference appears.

Disapplication of these Regulations

2. [omitted]

Risk assessment

3.—(1) Every employer shall make a suitable and sufficient assessment of—

(a) the risks to health and safety of his employees to which they are exposed whilst they are at work; and

(b) the risks to the health and safety of persons not in his employment arising out of or in connection with the conduct by him of his undertaking,

for the purpose of identifying the measures he needs to take to comply with the requirements and prohibitions imposed upon him by or under the relevant statutory provisions and by Part II of the Fire Precautions (Workplace) Regulations 1997.

(2) Every self-employed person shall make a suitable and sufficient assessment of—

(a) the risks to his own health and safety to which he is exposed whilst he is at work; and

(b) the risks to the health and safety of persons not in his employment arising out of or in connection with the conduct by him of his undertaking,

for the purpose of identifying the measures he needs to take to comply with the requirements and prohibitions imposed upon him by or under the relevant statutory provisions.

(3) Any assessment such as is referred to in paragraph (1) or (2) shall be reviewed by the employer or self-employed person who made it if—

(a) there is reason to suspect that it is no longer valid; or

(b) there has been a significant change in the matters to which it relates;

and where as a result of any such review changes to an assessment are required, the employer or self-employed person concerned shall make them.

(3A) Subject to paragraph (3B), an employer shall not employ a young person unless he has, in relation to risks to the health and safety of young persons, made or reviewed an assessment in accordance with paragraphs (1) and (3C).

(3B) Where an employer is employing a young person when this paragraph comes into force he shall, in relation to risks to the health and safety of young persons, review the assessment forthwith.

(3C) In making or reviewing the assessment, an employer who employs or is to employ a young person shall take particular account of—

(a) the inexperience, lack of awareness of risks and immaturity of young persons;

(b) the fitting-out and layout of the workplace and the workstation;

(c) the nature, degree and duration of exposure to physical, biological and chemical agents;

(d) the form, range and use of work equipment and the way in which it is handled;

(e) the organisation of processes and activities;

(f) the extent of the health and safety training provided or to be provided to young persons; and

(g) risks from agents, processes and work listed in the Annex to Council Directive 94/33/EC on the protection of young people at work.

(4) Where the employer employs five or more employees, he shall record—

(a) the significant findings of the assessment; and

(b) any group of his employees identified by it as being especially at risk.

Health and safety arrangements

4.—(1) Every employer shall make and give effect to such arrangements as are appropriate, having regard to the nature of his activities and the size of his undertaking, for the effective planning, organisation, control, monitoring and review of the preventive and protective measures.

(2) Where the employer employs five or more employees, he shall record the arrangements referred to in paragraph (1).

Health surveillance

5. Every employer shall ensure that his employees are provided with such health surveillance as is appropriate having regard to the risks to their health and safety which are identified by the assessment.

Health and safety assistance

6.—(1) Every employer shall, subject to paragraphs (6) and (7), appoint one or more competent persons to assist him in undertaking the measures he needs to take to comply with the requirements and prohibitions imposed upon him by or under the relevant statutory provisions and by Part II of the Fire Precautions (Workplace) Regulations 1997.

(2) Where an employer appoints persons in accordance with paragraph (1), he shall make arrangements for ensuring adequate co-operation between them.

(3) The employer shall ensure that the number of persons appointed under paragraph (1), the time available for them to fulfil their functions and the means at their disposal are adequate having regard to the size of his undertaking, the risks to which his employees are exposed and the distribution of those risks throughout the undertaking.

(4) The employer shall ensure that—

(a) any person appointed by him in accordance with paragraph (1) who is not in his employment—

(i) is informed of the factors known by him to affect, or suspected by him of affecting, the health and safety of any other person who may be affected by the conduct of his undertaking, and

(ii) has access to the information referred to in regulation 8; and

(b) any person appointed by him in accordance with paragraph (1) is given such information about any person working in his undertaking who is—

(i) employed by him under a fixed-term contract of employment, or

(ii) employed in an employment business,

as is necessary to enable that person properly to carry out the function specified in that paragraph.

(5) A person shall be regarded as competent for the purposes of paragraph (1) where he has sufficient training and experience or knowledge and other qualities to enable him properly to assist in undertaking the measures referred to in that paragraph.

(6) Paragraph (1) shall not apply to a self-employed employer who is not in partnership with any other person where he has sufficient training and experience or knowledge and other qualities properly to undertake the measures referred to in that paragraph himself.

(7) Paragraph (1) shall not apply to individuals who are employers and who are together carrying on business in partnership where at least one of the individuals concerned has sufficient training and experience or knowledge and other qualities—

(a) properly to undertake the measures he needs to take to comply with the requirements and prohibitions imposed upon him by or under the relevant statutory provisions; and

(b) properly to assist his fellow partners in undertaking the measures they need to take to comply with the requirements and prohibitions imposed upon them by or under the relevant statutory provisions.

Procedures for serious and imminent danger and for danger areas

7.—(1) Every employer shall—

(a) establish and where necessary give effect to appropriate procedures to be followed in the event of serious and imminent danger to persons at work in his undertaking;

(b) nominate a sufficient number of competent persons to implement those procedures insofar as they relate to the evacuation from premises of persons at work in his undertaking; and

(c) ensure that none of his employees has access to any area occupied by him to which it is necessary to restrict access on grounds of health and safety unless the employee concerned has received adequate health and safety instruction.

(2) Without prejudice to the generality of paragraph (1)(a), the procedures referred to in that sub-paragraph shall—

(a) so far as is practicable, require any persons at work who are exposed to serious and imminent danger to be informed of the nature of the hazard and of the steps taken or to be taken to protect them from it;

(b) enable the persons concerned (if necessary by taking appropriate steps in the absence of guidance or instruction and in the light of their knowledge and the technical means at their disposal) to stop work and immediately proceed to a place of safety in the event of their being exposed to serious, imminent and unavoidable danger; and

(c) save in exceptional cases for reasons duly substantiated (which cases and reasons shall be specified in those procedures), require the persons concerned to be prevented from resuming work in any situation where there is still a serious and imminent danger.

(3) A person shall be regarded as competent for the purposes of paragraph (1)(b) where he has sufficient training and experience or knowledge and other qualities to enable him properly to implement the evacuation procedures referred to in that sub-paragraph.

Information for employees

8.—(1) Every employer shall provide his employees with comprehensible and relevant information on—

(a) the risks to their health and safety identified by the assessment;

(b) the preventive and protective measures;

(c) the procedures referred to in regulation 7(1)(a) and the measures referred to in regulation 4(2)(a) of the Fire Precautions (Workplace) Regulations 1997;

(d) the identity of those persons nominated by him in accordance with regulation 7(1)(b) and regulation 4(2)(b) of the Fire Precautions (Workplace) Regulations 1997; and

(e) the risks notified to him in accordance with regulation 9(1)(c).

(2) Every employer shall, before employing a child, provide a parent of the child with comprehensible and relevant information on—

(a) the risks to his health and safety identified by the assessment;

(b) the preventive and protective measures; and

(c) the risks notified to him in accordance with regulation 9(1)(c).

(3) The reference in paragraph (2) to a parent of the child includes—

(a) in England and Wales, a person who has parental responsibility, within the meaning of section 3 of the Children Act 1989, for him; and

(b) in Scotland, a person who has parental rights, within the meaning of section 8 of the Law Reform (Parent and Child (Scotland)) Act 1986, for him.

Co-operation and co-ordination

9.—(1) Where two or more employers share a workplace (whether on a temporary or a permanent basis) each such employer shall—

(a) co-operate with the other employers concerned so far as is necessary to enable them to comply with the requirements and prohibitions imposed upon them by or under the relevant statutory provisions and by Part II of the Fire Precautions (Workplace) Regulations 1997;

(b) (taking into account the nature of his activities) take all reasonable steps to co-ordinate the measures he takes to comply with the requirements and prohibitions imposed upon him by or under the relevant statutory provisions and by Part II of the Fire Precautions (Workplace) Regulations 1997 with the measures the other employers concerned are taking to comply with the requirements and prohibitions imposed upon them by that legislation; and

(c) take all reasonable steps to inform the other employers concerned of the risks to their employees' health and safety arising out of or in connection with the conduct by him of his undertaking.

(2) Paragraph (1) shall apply to employers sharing a workplace with self-employed persons and to self-employed persons sharing a workplace with other self-employed persons as it applies to employers sharing a workplace with other employers; and the references in that paragraph to employers and the reference in the said paragraph to their employees shall be construed accordingly.

Persons working in host employers' or self-employed persons' undertakings

10.—(1) Every employer and every self-employed person shall ensure that the employer of any employees from an outside undertaking who are working in his undertaking is provided with comprehensible information on—

(a) the risks to those employees' health and safety arising out of or in connection with the conduct by that first-mentioned employer or by that self-employed person of his undertaking; and

(b) the measures taken by that first-mentioned employer or by that self-employed person in compliance with the requirements and prohibitions imposed upon him by or under the relevant statutory provisions and by Part II of the Fire Precautions (Workplace) Regulations 1997 insofar as the said requirements and prohibitions relate to those employees.

(2) Paragraph (1) shall apply to a self-employed person who is working in the undertaking of an employer or a self-employed person as it applies to employees from an outside undertaking who are working therein; and the reference in that paragraph to the employer of any employees from an outside undertaking who are working in the undertaking of an employer or a self-employed person and the references in the said paragraph to employees from an outside undertaking who are working in the undertaking of an employer or a self-employed person shall be construed accordingly.

(3) Every employer shall ensure that any person working in his undertaking who is not his employee and every self-employed person (not being an employer) shall ensure that any person working in his undertaking is provided with appropriate instructions and comprehensible information regarding any risks to that person's health and safety which arise out of the conduct by that employer or self-employed person of his undertaking.

(4) Every employer shall—

(a) ensure that the employer of any employees from an outside undertaking who are working in his undertaking is provided with sufficient information to enable that second-mentioned employer to identify any person nominated by that first-mentioned employer in accordance with regulation 7(1)(b) to implement evacuation procedures as far as those employees are concerned; and

(b) take all reasonable steps to ensure that any employees from an outside undertaking who are working in his undertaking receive sufficient information to enable them to identify any person nominated by him in accordance with regulation 7(1)(b) to implement evacuation procedures as far as they are concerned.

(5) Paragraph (4) shall apply to a self-employed person who is working in an employer's undertaking as it applies to employees from an outside undertaking who are working therein; and the reference in that paragraph to the employer of any employees from an outside undertaking who are working in an employer's undertaking and the references in the said paragraph to employees from an outside undertaking who are working in an employer's undertaking shall be construed accordingly.

Capabilities and training

11.—(1) Every employer shall, in entrusting tasks to his employees, take into account their capabilities as regards health and safety.

(2) Every employer shall ensure that his employees are provided with adequate health and safety training—

(a) on their being recruited into the employer's undertaking; and

(b) on their being exposed to new or increased risks because of—

(i) their being transferred or given a change of responsibilities within the employer's undertaking,

(ii) the introduction of new work equipment into or a change respecting work equipment already in use within the employer's undertaking,

(iii) the introduction of new technology into the employer's undertaking, or

(iv) the introduction of a new system of work into or a change respecting a system of work already in use within the employer's undertaking.

(3) The training referred to in paragraph (2) shall—

(a) be repeated periodically where appropriate;

(b) be adapted to take account of any new or changed risks to the health and safety of the employees concerned; and

(c) take place during working hours.

Employees' duties

12.—(1) Every employee shall use any machinery, equipment, dangerous substance, transport equipment, means of production or safety device provided to him by his employer in accordance both with any training in the use of the equipment concerned which has been received by him and the instructions respecting that use which have been provided to him by the said employer in compliance with the requirements and prohibitions imposed upon that employer by or under the relevant statutory provisions.

(2) Every employee shall inform his employer or any other employee of that employer with specific responsibility for the health and safety of his fellow employees—

(a) of any work situation which a person with the first-mentioned employee's training and instruction would reasonably consider represented a serious and immediate danger to health and safety; and

(b) of any matter which a person with the first-mentioned employee's training and instruction would reasonably consider represented a shortcoming in the employer's protection arrangements for health and safety,

insofar as that situation or matter either affects the health and safety of that first-mentioned employee or arises out of or in connection with his own activities at work, and has not previously been reported to his employer or to any other employee of that employer in accordance with this paragraph.

Temporary workers

13.—(1) Every employer shall provide any person whom he has employed under a fixed-term contract of employment with comprehensible information on—

(a) any special occupational qualifications or skills required to be held by that employee if he is to carry out his work safely; and

(b) any health surveillance required to be provided to that employee by or under any of the relevant statutory provisions,

and shall provide the said information before the employee concerned commences his duties.

(2) Every employer and every self-employed person shall provide any person employed in an employment business who is to carry out work in his undertaking with comprehensible information on—

(a) any special occupational qualifications or skills required to be held by that employee if he is to carry out his work safely; and

(b) any health surveillance required to be provided to that employee by or under any of the relevant statutory provisions.

(3) Every employer and every self-employed person shall ensure that every person carrying on an employment business whose employees are to carry out work in his undertaking is provided with comprehensible information on—

(a) any special occupational qualifications or skills required to be held by those employees if they are to carry out their work safely; and

(b) the specific features of the jobs to be filled by those employees (insofar as those features are likely to affect their health and safety);

and the person carrying on the employment business concerned shall ensure that the information so provided is given to the said employees.

13A.—(1) Where—

(a) the persons working in an undertaking include women of child-bearing age; and

(b) the work is of a kind which could involve risk, by reason of her condition, to the health and safety of a new or expectant mother, or to that of her baby, from any processes or working conditions, or physical, biological or chemical agents, including those specified in Annexes I and II of Council Directive 92/85/EEC on the introduction of measures to encourage improvements in the safety and health at work of pregnant workers and workers who have recently given birth or are breastfeeding,

the assessment required by regulation 3(1) shall also include an assessment of such risk.

(2) Where, in the case of an individual employee, the taking of any other action the employer is required to take under the relevant statutory provisions would not avoid the risk referred to in paragraph (1) the employer shall, if it is reasonable to do so, and would avoid such risks, alter her working conditions or hours of work.

(3) If it is not reasonable to alter the working conditions or hours of work, or if it would not avoid such risk, the employer shall, subject to section 46 of the 1978 Act, suspend the employee from work for so long as is necessary to avoid such risk.

(4) In paragraphs (1) to (3) references to risk, in relation to risk from any infectious or contagious disease, are references to a level of risk at work which is in addition to the level to which a new or expectant mother may be expected to be exposed outside the workplace.

13B. Where—

(a) a new or expectant mother works at night; and

(b) a certificate from a registered medical practitioner or a registered midwife shows that it is necessary for her health or safety that she should not be at work for any period of such work identified in the certificate

the employer shall, subject to section 46 of the 1978 Act, suspend her from work for so long as is necessary for her health or safety.

13C.—(1) Nothing in paragraph (2) or (3) of regulation 13A shall require the employer to take any action in relation to an employee until she has notified the employer in writing that she is pregnant, has given birth within the previous six months, or is breastfeeding.

(2) Nothing in paragraph (2) or (3) of regulation 13A or in regulation 13B shall require the employer to maintain action taken in relation to an employee—

(a) in a case—

(i) to which regulation 13A(2) or (3) relates; and

(ii) where the employee has notified her employer that she is pregnant,

where she has failed, within a reasonable time of being requested to do so in writing by her employer, to produce for the employer's inspection a certificate from a registered medical practitioner or a registered midwife showing that she is pregnant;

(b) once the employer knows that she is no longer a new or expectant mother; or

(c) if the employer cannot establish whether she remains a new or expectant mother.

Protection of young persons

13D.—(1) Every employer shall ensure that young persons employed by him are protected at work from any risks to their health or safety which are a consequence of their lack of experience, of absence of awareness of existing or potential risks or the fact that young persons have not yet fully matured.

(2) Subject to paragraph (3), no employer shall employ a young person for work—

(a) which is beyond his physical or psychological capacity;

(b) involving harmful exposure to agents which are toxic or carcinogenic, cause heritable genetic damage or harm to the unborn child or which in any other way chronically affect human health;

(c) involving harmful exposure to radiation;

(d) involving the risk of accidents which it may reasonably be assumed cannot be recognised or avoided by young persons owing to their insufficient attention to safety or lack of experience or training; or

(e) in which there is a risk to health from—

(i) extreme cold or heat;

(ii) noise; or

(iii) vibration,

and in determining whether work will involve harm or risk for the purposes of this paragraph, regard shall be had to the results of the assessment.

(3) Nothing in paragraph (2) shall prevent the employment of a young person who is no longer a child for work—

(a) where it is necessary for his training;

(b) where the young person will be supervised by a competent person; and

(c) where any risk will be reduced to the lowest level that is reasonably practicable.

(4) The provisions contained in this regulation are without prejudice to—

(a) the provisions contained elsewhere in these Regulations; and

(b) any prohibition or restriction, arising otherwise than by this regulation, on the employment of any person.

Exemption certificates

14. [omitted]

Exclusion of civil liability

15.—(1) Breach of a duty imposed by these Regulations shall not confer a right of action in any civil proceedings.

(2) Paragraph (1) shall not apply to any duty imposed by these Regulations on an employer:

(a) to the extent that it relates to risk referred to in regulation 13A(1) to an employee; or

(b) which is contained in regulation 13D.

Extension outside Great Britain

16.—(1) These Regulations shall, subject to regulation 2, apply to and in relation to the premises and activities outside Great Britain to which sections 1 to 59 and 80 to 82 of the Health and Safety at Work etc. Act 1974 apply by virtue of the Health and Safety at Work etc. Act 1974 (Application Outside Great Britain) Order 1989 as they apply within Great Britain.

(2) For the purposes of Part I of the 1974 Act, the meaning of 'at work' shall be extended so that an employee or a self-employed person shall be treated as being at work throughout the time that he is present at the premises to and in relation to which these Regulations apply by virtue of paragraph (1); and, in that connection, these Regulations shall have effect subject to the extension effected by this paragraph.

THE EMPLOYMENT TRIBUNALS EXTENSION OF JURISDICTION (ENGLAND AND WALES) ORDER 1994 (SI 1994 No. 1623)

Citation, commencement and interpretation

1.—(1) This Order may be cited as the Employment Tribunals Extension of Jurisdiction (England and Wales) Order 1994 and comes into force on the first day after it is made.

(2) In this Order—

'contract claim' means a claim in respect of which proceedings may be brought before an employment tribunal by virtue of article 3 or 4; and

'the 1978 Act' means the Employment Protection (Consolidation) Act 1978.

2. [omitted]

Extension of jurisdiction

3. Proceedings may be brought before an employment tribunal in respect of a claim of an employee for the recovery of damages or any other sum (other than a claim for damages, or for a sum due, in respect of personal injuries) if—

(a) the claim is one to which section 131(2) of the 1978 Act applies and which a court in England and Wales would under the law for the time being in force have jurisdiction to hear and determine;

(b) the claim is not one to which article 5 applies; and

(c) the claim arises or is outstanding on the termination of the employee's employment.

4. Proceedings may be brought before an employment tribunal in respect of a claim of an employer for the recovery of damages or any other sum (other than a claim for damages, or for a sum due, in respect of personal injuries) if—

(a) the claim is one to which section 131(2) of the 1978 Act applies and which a court in England and Wales would under the law for the time being in force have jurisdiction to hear and determine;

(b) the claim is not one to which article 5 applies;

(c) the claim arises or is outstanding on the termination of the employment of the employee against whom it is made; and

(d) proceedings in respect of a claim of that employee have been brought before an employment tribunal by virtue of this Order.

5. This article applies to a claim for breach of a contractual term of any of the following descriptions—

(a) a term requiring the employer to provide living accommodation for the employee;

(b) a term imposing an obligation on the employer or the employee in connection with the provision of living accommodation;

(c) a term relating to intellectual property;

(d) a term imposing an obligation of confidence;

(e) a term which is a covenant in restraint of trade.

In this article, 'intellectual property' includes copyright, rights in performances, moral rights, design right, registered designs, patents and trade marks.

Manner in which proceedings may be brought

6. Proceedings on a contract claim may be brought before an employment tribunal by presenting a complaint to an employment tribunal.

Time within which proceedings may be brought

7. An employment tribunal shall not entertain a complaint in respect of an employee's contract claim unless it is presented—

(a) within the period of three months beginning with the effective date of termination of the contract giving rise to the claim, or

(b) where there is no effective date of termination, within the period of three months beginning with the last day upon which the employee worked in the employment which has terminated, or

(c) where the tribunal is satisfied that it was not reasonably practicable for the complaint to be presented within whichever of those periods is applicable, within such further period as the tribunal considers reasonable.

8. An employment tribunal shall not entertain a complaint in respect of an employer's contract claim unless—

(a) it is presented at a time when there is before the tribunal a complaint in respect of a contract claim of a particular employee which has not been settled or withdrawn;

(b) it arises out of a contract with that employee; and

(c) it is presented—

(i) within the period of six weeks beginning with the day, or if more than one the last of the days, on which the employer (or other person who is the respondent party to the employee's contract claim) received from the tribunal a copy of an originating application in respect of a contract claim of that employee; or

(ii) where the tribunal is satisfied that it was not reasonably practicable for the complaint to be presented within that period, within such further period as the tribunal considers reasonable.

Death and bankruptcy

9.—(1) Where proceedings in respect of a contract claim have been brought before an employment tribunal and an employee or employer party to them dies before their conclusion, the proceedings shall not abate by reason of the death and the tribunal may, if it thinks it necessary in order to ensure that all matters in dispute may be effectually and completely determined and adjudicated upon, order the personal representatives of the deceased party, or other persons whom the tribunal considers appropriate, to be made parties and the proceedings to be carried on as if they had been substituted for the deceased party.

(2) Where proceedings in respect of a contract claim have been brought before an employment tribunal and the employee or employer who is the applicant party to them becomes bankrupt before their conclusion, the proceedings shall not abate by reason of the bankruptcy and the tribunal may, if it thinks it necessary in order to ensure that all matters in dispute may be effectually and completely adjudicated upon, order the person in whom the interest of the bankrupt party has vested to be made a party and the proceedings to be carried on as if he had been substituted for the bankrupt party.

Limit on payment to be ordered

10. An employment tribunal shall not in proceedings in respect of a contract claim, or in respect of a number of contract claims relating to the same contract, order the payment of an amount exceeding £25,000.

THE EMPLOYMENT PROTECTION (CONTINUITY OF EMPLOYMENT) REGULATIONS 1996
(SI 1996 No. 3147)

Application

2. These Regulations apply to any action taken in relation to the dismissal of an employee which consists of—

(a) his making a claim in accordance with a dismissal procedures agreement designated by an order under section 110 of the Employment Rights Act 1996,

(b) the presentation by him of a relevant complaint of dismissal,

(c) any action taken by a conciliation officer under section 18 of the Employment Tribunals Act 1996, or

(d) the making of a relevant compromise contract.

Continuity of employment where employee re-engaged

3.—(1) The provisions of this regulation shall have effect to preserve the continuity of a person's period of employment for the purposes of—

(a) Chapter I of Part XIV of the Employment Rights Act 1996 (continuous employment), and

(b) that Chapter as applied by subsection (2) of section 282 of the Trade Union and Labour Relations (Consolidation) Act 1992 for the purposes of that section.

(2) If in consequence of any action to which these Regulations apply a dismissed employee is reinstated or re-employed by his employer or by a successor or associated employer of the employer—

(a) the continuity of that employee's period of employment shall be preserved, and

(b) the period beginning with the date on which the dismissal takes effect and ending with the date of reinstatement or re-engagement shall count in the computation of the employee's period of continuous employment.

Exclusion of operation of section 214 of the Employment Rights Act 1996 where redundancy or equivalent payment repaid

4.—(1) Section 214 of the Employment Rights Act 1996 (continuity broken where employee re-employed after the making of a redundancy payment or equivalent payment) shall not apply where—

(a) in consequence of any action to which these Regulations apply a dismissed employee is reinstated or re-employed by his employer or by a successor or associated employer of the employer,

(b) the terms upon which he is so reinstated or re-engaged include provision for him to repay the amount of a redundancy payment or an equivalent payment paid in respect of the relevant dismissal, and

(c) that provision is complied with.

(2) For the purposes of this regulation the cases in which a redundancy payment shall be treated as having been paid are the cases mentioned in section 214(5) of the Employment Rights Act 1996.

THE WORKING TIME REGULATIONS 1998
(SI 1998 No. 1833)

ARRANGEMENT OF REGULATIONS

PART I
GENERAL

PART II
RIGHTS AND OBLIGATIONS CONCERNING WORKING TIME

PART I
GENERAL

1 [omitted]

2 Interpretation

(1) In these Regulations—

'the 1996 Act' means the Employment Rights Act 1996;

'adult worker' means a worker who has attained the age of 18;

'the armed forces' means any of the naval, military and air forces of the Crown;

'calendar year' means the period of twelve months beginning with 1 January in any year;

'the civil protection services' includes the police, fire brigades and ambulance services, the security and intelligence services, customs and immigration officers, the prison service, the coastguard, and lifeboat crew and other voluntary rescue services;

'collective agreement' means a collective agreement within the meaning of section 178 of the Trade Union and Labour Relations (Consolidation) Act 1992, the trade union parties to which are independent trade unions within the meaning of section 5 of that Act;

'day' means a period of 24 hours beginning at midnight;

'employer', in relation to a worker, means the person by whom the worker is (or, where the employment has ceased, was) employed;

'employment', in relation to a worker, means employment under his contract, and 'employed' shall be construed accordingly;

'night time', in relation to a worker, means a period—

(a) the duration of which is not less than seven hours, and

(b) which includes the period between midnight and 5 a.m.,

which is determined for the purposes of these Regulations by a relevant agreement, or, in default of such a determination, the period between 11 p.m. and 6 a.m.,

'night work' means work during night time;

'night worker' means a worker—

(a) who, as a normal course, works at least three hours of his daily working time during night time, or

(b) who is likely, during night time, to work at least such proportion of his annual working time as may be specified for the purposes of these Regulations in a collective agreement or a workforce agreement;

and, for the purpose of paragraph (a) of this definition, a person works hours as a normal course (without prejudice to the generality of that expression) if he works such hours on the majority of days on which he works;

'relevant agreement', in relation to a worker, means a workforce agreement which applies to him, any provision of a collective agreement which forms part of a contract between him and his employer, or any other agreement in writing which is legally enforceable as between the worker and his employer;

'relevant training' means work experience provided pursuant to a training course or programme, training for employment, or both, other than work experience or training—

(a) the immediate provider of which is an educational institution or a person whose main business is the provision of training, and

(b) which is provided on a course run by that institution or person;

'rest period', in relation to a worker, means a period which is not working time, other than a rest break or leave to which the worker is entitled under these Regulations;

'worker' means an individual who has entered into or works under (or, where the employment has ceased, worked under)—

(a) a contract of employment; or

(b) any other contract, whether express or implied and (if it is express) whether oral or in writing, whereby the individual undertakes to do or perform personally any work or services for another party to the contract whose status is not by virtue of the contract that of a client or customer of any profession or business undertaking carried on by the individual;

and any reference to a worker's contract shall be construed accordingly;

'worker employed in agriculture' has the same meaning as in the Agricultural Wages Act 1948 or the Agricultural Wages (Scotland) Act 1949, and a reference to a worker partly employed in agriculture is to a worker employed in agriculture whose employer also employs him for non-agricultural purposes;

'workforce agreement' means an agreement between an employer and worker employed by him or their representatives in respect of which the conditions set out in Schedule 1 to these Regulations are satisfied;

'working time', in relation to a worker, means—

(a) any period during which he is working, at his employer's disposal and carrying out his activity or duties,

(b) any period during which he is receiving relevant training, and

(c) any additional period which is to be treated as working time for the purpose of these Regulations under a relevant agreement;

and 'work' shall be construed accordingly;

'Working Time Directive' means Council Directive 93/104/EC of 23 November 1993 concerning certain aspects of the organisation of working time;

'young worker' means a worker who has attained the age of 15 but not the age of 18 and who, as respects England and Wales, is over compulsory school age (construed in accordance with section 8 of the Education Act 1996) and, as respects Scotland, is over school age (construed in accordance with section 31 of the Education (Scotland) Act 1980), and

'Young Workers Directive' means Council Directive 94/33/EC of 22 June 1994 on the protection of young people at work.

(2) In the absence of a definition in these Regulations, words and expressions used in particular provisions which are also used in corresponding provisions of the Working Time Directive or the Young Workers Directive have the same meaning as they have in those corresponding provisions.

(3) [omitted]

PART II
RIGHTS AND OBLIGATIONS CONCERNING WORKING TIME

3 General

The provisions of this Part have effect subject to the exceptions provided for in Part III of these Regulations.

4 Maximum weekly working time

(1) Subject to regulation 5, a worker's working time, including overtime, in any reference period which is applicable in his case shall not exceed an average of 48 hours for each seven days.

(2) An employer shall take all reasonable steps, in keeping with the need to protect the health and safety of workers, to ensure that the limit specified in paragraph (1) is complied with in the case of each worker employed by him in relation to whom it applies.

(3) Subject to paragraphs (4) and (5) and any agreement under regulation 23(b), the reference periods which apply in the case of a worker are—

(a) where a relevant agreement provides for the application of this regulation in relation to successive periods of 17 weeks, each such period, or

(b) in any other case, any period of 17 weeks in the course of his employment.

(4) Where a worker has worked for his employer for less than 17 weeks, the reference period applicable in his case is the period that has elapsed since he started work for his employer.

(5) Paragraphs (3) and (4) shall apply to a worker who is excluded from the scope of certain provisions of these Regulations by regulation 21 as if for each reference to 17 weeks there were substituted a reference to 26 weeks.

(6) For the purposes of this regulation, a worker's average working time for each seven days during a reference period shall be determined according to the formula—

$$\frac{\mathbf{A} + \mathbf{B}}{\mathbf{C}}$$

where—

A is the aggregate number of hours comprised in the worker's working time during the course of the reference period;

B is the aggregate number of hours comprised in his working time during the course of the period beginning immediately after the end of the reference period and ending when the number of days in that subsequent period on which he has worked equals the number of excluded days during the reference period; and

C is the number of weeks in the reference period.

(7) In paragraph (6), 'excluded days' means days comprised in—

(a) any period of annual leave taken by the worker in exercise of his entitlement under regulation 13;

(b) any period of sick leave taken by the worker;

(c) any period of maternity leave taken by the worker; and

(d) any period in respect of which the limit specified in paragraph (1) did not apply in relation to the worker by virtue of regulation 5.

5 Agreement to exclude the maximum

(1) The limit specified in regulation 4(1) shall not apply in relation to a worker who has agreed with his employer in writing that it should not apply in his case, provided that the employer complies with the requirements of paragraph (4).

(2) An agreement for the purposes of paragraph (1)—

(a) may either relate to a specified period or apply indefinitely; and

(b) subject to any provision in the agreement for a different period of notice, shall be terminable by the worker by giving not less than seven days' notice to his employer in writing.

(3) Where an agreement for the purposes of paragraph (1) makes provision for the termination of the agreement after a period of notice, the notice period provided for shall not exceed three months.

(4) The requirements referred to in paragraph (1) are that the employer—

(a) maintains up-to-date records which—

(i) identify each of the workers whom he employs who has agreed that the limit specified in regulation 4(1) should not apply in his case;

(ii) set out any terms on which the worker agreed that the limit should not apply; and

(iii) specify the number of hours worked by him for the employer during each reference period since the agreement came into effect (excluding any period which ended more than two years before the most recent entry in the records);

(b) permits any inspector appointed by the Health and Safety Executive or any other authority which is responsible under regulation 28 for the enforcement of these Regulations to inspect those records on request; and

(c) provides any such inspector with such information as he may request regarding any case in which a worker has agreed that the limit specified in regulation 4(1) should not apply in his case.

6 Length of night work

(1) A night worker's normal hours of work in any reference period which is applicable in his case shall not exceed an average of eight hours for each 24 hours.

(2) An employer shall take all reasonable steps, in keeping with the need to protect the health and safety of workers, to ensure that the limit specified in paragraph (1) is complied with in the case of each night worker employed by him.

(3) The reference periods which apply in the case of a night worker are—

(a) where a relevant agreement provides for the application of this regulation in relation to successive periods of 17 weeks, each such period, or

(b) in any other case, any period of 17 weeks in the course of his employment.

(4) Where a worker has worked for his employer for less than 17 weeks, the reference period applicable in his case is the period that has elapsed since he started work for his employer.

(5) For the purposes of this regulation, a night worker's average normal hours of work for each 24 hours during a reference period shall be determined according to the formula—

$$\frac{A}{B - C}$$

where—

A is the number of hours during the reference period which are normal working hours for that worker;

B is the number of days during the reference period; and

C is the total number of hours during the reference period comprised in rest periods spent by the worker in pursuance of his entitlement under regulation 11, divided by 24.

(6) A night worker's normal hours of work for the purposes of this regulation are his normal working hours for the purposes of the 1996 Act in a case where section 234 of that Act (which provides for the interpretation of normal working hours in the case of certain employees) applies to him.

(7) An employer shall ensure that no night worker employed by him whose work involves special hazards or heavy physical or mental strain works for more than eight hours in any 24-hour period during which the night worker performs night work.

(8) For the purposes of paragraph (7), the work of a night worker shall be regarded as involving special hazards or heavy physical or mental strain if—

(a) it is identified as such in—

(i) a collective agreement, or

(ii) a workforce agreement,

which takes account of the specific effects and hazards of night work, or

(b) it is recognised in a risk assessment made by the employer under regulation 3 of the Management of Health and Safety at Work Regulations 1992 as involving a significant risk to the health or safety of workers employed by him.

7 Health assessment and transfer of night workers to day work

(1) An employer—

(a) shall not assign an adult worker to work which is to be undertaken during periods such that the worker will become a night worker unless—

(i) the employer has ensured that the worker will have the opportunity of a free health assessment before he takes up the assignment; or

(ii) the worker had a health assessment before being assigned to work to be undertaken during such periods on an earlier occasion, and the employer has no reason to believe that that assessment is no longer valid, and

(b) shall ensure that each night worker employed by him has the opportunity of a free health assessment at regular intervals of whatever duration may be appropriate in his case.

(2) Subject to paragraph (4), an employer—

(a) shall not assign a young worker to work during the period between 10 p.m. and 6 a.m. ('the restricted period') unless—

(i) the employer has ensured that the young worker will have the opportunity of a free assessment of his health and capacities before he takes up the assignment; or

(ii) the young worker had an assessment of his health and capacities before being assigned to work during the restricted period on an earlier occasion, and the employer has no reason to believe that that assessment is no longer valid; and

(b) shall ensure that each young worker employed by him and assigned to work during the restricted period has the opportunity of a free assessment of his health and capacities at regular intervals of whatever duration may be appropriate in his case.

(3) For the purposes of paragraphs (1) and (2), an assessment is free if it is at no cost to the worker to whom it relates.

(4) The requirements in paragraph (2) do not apply in a case where the work a young worker is assigned to do is of an exceptional nature.

(5) No person shall disclose an assessment made for the purposes of this regulation to any person other than the worker to whom it relates, unless—

(a) the worker has given his consent in writing to the disclosure, or

(b) the disclosure is confined to a statement that the assessment shows the worker to be fit—

(i) in a case where paragraph (1)(a)(i) or (2)(a)(i) applies, to take up an assignment, or

(ii) in a case where paragraph (1)(b) or (2)(b) applies, to continue to undertake an assignment.

(6) Where—

(a) a registered medical practitioner has advised an employer that a worker employed by the employer is suffering from health problems which the practitioner considers to be connected with the fact that the worker performs night work, and

(b) it is possible for the employer to transfer the worker to work—

(i) to which the worker is suited, and

(ii) which is to be undertaken during periods such that the worker will cease to be a night worker,

the employer shall transfer the worker accordingly.

8 Pattern of work

Where the pattern according to which an employer organises work is such as to put the health and safety of a worker employed by him at risk, in particular because the work is monotonous or the work-rate is predetermined, the employer shall ensure that the worker is given adequate rest breaks.

9 Records

An employer shall—

(a) keep records which are adequate to show whether the limits specified in regulations 4(1) and 6(1) and (7) and the requirements in regulations 7(1) and (2) are being complied with in the case of each worker employed by him in relation to whom they apply; and

(b) retain such records for two years from the date on which they were made.

10 Daily rest

(1) An adult worker is entitled to a rest period of not less than eleven consecutive hours in each 24-hour period during which he works for his employer.

(2) Subject to paragraph (3), a young worker is entitled to a rest period of not less than twelve consecutive hours in each 24-hour period during which he works for his employer.

(3) The minimum rest period provided for in paragraph (2) may be interrupted in the case of activities involving periods of work that are split up over the day or of short duration.

11 Weekly rest period

(1) Subject to paragraph (2), an adult worker is entitled to an uninterrupted rest period of not less than 24 hours in each seven-day period during which he works for his employer.

(2) If his employer so determines, an adult worker shall be entitled to either—

(a) two uninterrupted rest periods each of not less than 24 hours in each 14-day period during which he works for his employer; or

(b) one uninterrupted rest period of not less than 48 hours in each such 14-day period,

in place of the entitlement provided for in paragraph (1).

(3) Subject to paragraph (8), a young worker is entitled to a rest period of not less than 48 hours in each seven-day period during which he works for his employer.

(4) For the purpose of paragraphs (1) to (3), a seven-day period or (as the case may be) 14-day period shall be taken to begin—

(a) at such times on such days as may be provided for for the purposes of this regulation in a relevant agreement; or

(b) where there are no provisions of a relevant agreement which apply, at the start of each week or (as the case may be) every other week.

(5) In a case where, in accordance with paragraph (4), 14-day periods are to be taken to begin at the start of every other week, the first such period applicable in the case of a particular worker shall be taken to begin—

(a) if the worker's employment began on or before the date on which these Regulations come into force, on 5 October 1998; or

(b) if the worker's employment begins after the date on which these Regulations come into force, at the start of the week in which that employment begins.

(6) For the purposes of paragraphs (4) and (5), a week starts at midnight between Sunday and Monday.

(7) The minimum rest period to which an adult worker is entitled under paragraph (1) or (2) shall not include any part of a rest period to which the worker is entitled under regulation 10(1), except where this is justified by objective or technical reasons or reasons concerning the organisation of work.

(8) The minimum rest period to which a young worker is entitled under paragraph (3)—

(a) may be interrupted in the case of activities involving periods of work that are split up over the day or are of short duration; and

(b) may be reduced where this is justified by technical or organisation reasons, but not to less than 36 consecutive hours.

12 Rest breaks

(1) Where an adult worker's daily working time is more than six hours, he is entitled to a rest break.

(2) The details of the rest break to which an adult worker is entitled under paragraph (1), including its duration and the terms on which it is granted, shall be in accordance with any provisions for the purposes of this regulation which are contained in a collective agreement or a workforce agreement.

(3) Subject to the provisions of any applicable collective agreement or workforce agreement, the rest break provided for in paragraph (1) is an uninterrupted period of not less than 20 minutes, and the worker is entitled to spend it away from his workstation if he has one.

(4) Where a young worker's daily working time is more than four and a half hours, he is entitled to a rest break of at least 30 minutes, which shall be consecutive if possible, and he is entitled to spend it away from his workstation if he has one.

(5) If, on any day, a young worker is employed by more than one employer, his daily working time shall be determined for the purpose of paragraph (4) by aggregating the number of hours worked by him for each employer.

13 Entitlement to annual leave

(1) Subject to paragraphs (5) and (7), a worker is entitled in each leave year to a period of leave determined in accordance with paragraph (2).

(2) The period of leave to which a worker is entitled under paragraph (1) is—

(a) in any leave year beginning on or before 23 November 1998, three weeks;

(b) in any leave year beginning after 23 November 1998 but before 23 November 1999, three weeks and a proportion of a fourth week equivalent to the proportion of the year beginning on 23 November 1998 which has elapsed at the start of that leave year; and

(c) in any leave year beginning after 23 November 1999, four weeks.

(3) A worker's leave year, for the purposes of this regulation, begins—

(a) on such date during the calendar year as may be provided for in a relevant agreement; or

(b) where there are no provisions of a relevant agreement which apply—

(i) if the worker's employment began on or before 1 October 1998, on that date and each subsequent anniversary of that date; or

(ii) if the worker's employment begins after 1 October 1998, on the date on which that employment begins and each subsequent anniversary of that date.

(4) Paragraph (3) does not apply to a worker to whom Schedule 2 applies (workers employed in agriculture) except where, in the case of a worker partly employed in agriculture, a relevant agreement so provides.

(5) Where the date on which a worker's employment begins is later than the date on which (by virtue of a relevant agreement) his first leave year begins, the leave to which he is entitled in that leave year is a proportion of the period applicable under paragraph (2) equal to the proportion of that leave year remaining on the date on which his employment begins.

(6) Where by virtue of paragraph (2)(b) or (5) the period of leave to which a worker is entitled is or includes a proportion of a week, the proportion shall be determined in days and any fraction of a day shall be treated as a whole day.

(7) The entitlement conferred by paragraph (1) does not arise until a worker has been continuously employed for thirteen weeks.

(8) For the purposes of paragraph (7), a worker has been continuously employed for thirteen weeks if his relations with his employer have been governed by a contract during the whole or part of each of those weeks.

(9) Leave to which a worker is entitled under this regulation may be taken in instalments, but—

(a) it may only be taken in the leave year in respect of which it is due, and

(b) it may not be replaced by a payment in lieu except where the worker's employment is terminated.

14 Compensation related to entitlement to leave

(1) This regulation applies where—

(a) a worker's employment is terminated during the course of his leave year, and

(b) on the date on which the termination takes effect ('the termination date'), the proportion he has taken of the leave to which he is entitled in the leave year under regulation 13(1) differs from the proportion of the leave year which has expired.

(2) Where the proportion of leave taken by the worker is less than the proportion of the leave year which has expired, his employer shall make him a payment in lieu of leave in accordance with paragraph (3).

(3) The payment due under paragraph (2) shall be—

(a) such sum as may be provided for for the purposes of this regulation in a relevant agreement, or

(b) where there are no provisions of a relevant agreement which apply, a sum equal to the amount that would be due to the worker under regulation 16 in respect of a period of leave determined according to the formula—

$$(\mathbf{A} \times \mathbf{B}) - \mathbf{C}$$

where—

A is the period of leave to which the worker is entitled under regulation 13(1);

B is the proportion of the worker's leave year which expired before the termination date, and

C is the period of leave taken by the worker between the start of the leave year and the termination date.

(4) A relevant agreement may provide that, where the proportion of leave taken by the worker exceeds the proportion of the leave year which has expired, he shall compensate his employer, whether by a payment, by undertaking additional work or otherwise.

15 Dates on which leave is taken

(1) A worker may take leave to which he is entitled under regulation 13(1) on such days as he may elect by giving notice to his employer in accordance with paragraph (3), subject to any requirement imposed on him by his employer under paragraph (2).

(2) A worker's employer may require the worker—

(a) to take leave to which the worker is entitled under regulation 13(1); or

(b) not to take such leave,

on particular days, by giving notice to the worker in accordance with paragraph (3).

(3) A notice under paragraph (1) or (2)—

(a) may relate to all or part of the leave to which a worker is entitled in a leave year;

(b) shall specify the days on which leave is or (as the case may be) is not to be taken and, where the leave on a particular day is to be in respect of only part of the day, its duration; and

(c) shall be given to the employer or, as the case may be, the worker before the relevant date.

(4) The relevant date, for the purposes of paragraph (3), is the date—

(a) in the case of a notice under paragraph (1) or (2)(a), twice as many days in advance of the earliest day specified in the notice as the number of days or part-days to which the notice relates, and

(b) in the case of a notice under paragraph (2)(b), as many days in advance of the earliest day so specified as the number of days or part-days to which the notice relates.

(5) Any right or obligation under paragraphs (1) to (4) may be varied or excluded by a relevant agreement.

(6) This regulation does not apply to a worker to whom Schedule 2 applies (workers employed in agriculture) except where, in the case of a worker partly employed in agriculture, a relevant agreement so provides.

16 Payment in respect of periods of leave

(1) A worker is entitled to be paid in respect of any period of annual leave to which he is entitled under regulation 13, at the rate of a week's pay in respect of each week of leave.

(2) Sections 221 to 224 of the 1996 Act shall apply for the purpose of determining the amount of a week's pay for the purposes of this regulation, subject to the modifications set out in paragraph (3).

(3) The provisions referred to in paragraph (2) shall apply—

(a) as if references to the employee were references to the worker;

(b) as if references to the employee's contract of employment were references to the worker's contract;

(c) as if the calculation date were the first day of the period of leave in question; and

(d) as if the references to sections 227 and 228 did not apply.

(4) A right to payment under paragraph (1) does not affect any right of a worker to remuneration under his contract ('contractual remuneration').

(5) Any contractual remuneration paid to a worker in respect of a period of leave goes towards discharging any liability of the employer to make payments under this regulation in respect of that period; and, conversely, any payment of remuneration under this regulation in respect of a period goes towards discharging any liability of the employer to pay contractual remuneration in respect of that period.

17 Entitlements under other provisions

Where during any period a worker is entitled to a rest period, rest break or annual leave both under a provision of these Regulations and under a separate provision (including a provision of his contract), he may not exercise the two rights separately, but may, in taking a rest period, break or leave during that period, take advantage of whichever right is, in any particular respect, the more favourable.

PART III
EXCEPTIONS

18 Excluded sectors

Regulations 4(1) and (2), 6(1), (2) and (7), 7(1) and (6), 8, 10(1), 11(1) and (2), 12(1), 13 and 16 do not apply—

(a) to the following sectors of activity—

(i) air, rail, road, sea, inland waterway and lake transport;

(ii) sea fishing;

(iii) other work at sea; or

(b) to the activities of doctors in training, or

(c) where characteristics peculiar to certain specified services such as the armed forces or the police, or to certain specific activities in the civil protection services, inevitably conflict with the provisions of these Regulations.

19 Domestic service

Regulations 4(1) and (2), 6(1), (2) and (7), 7(1), (2) and (6) and 8 do not apply in relation to a worker employed as a domestic servant in a private household.

20 Unmeasured working time

Regulations 4(1) and (2), 6(1), (2) and (7), 10(1), 11(1) and (2) and 12(1) do not apply in relation to a worker where, on account of the specific characteristics of the activity in which he is engaged, the duration of his working time is not measured or predetermined or can be determined by the worker himself, as may be the case for—

(a) managing executives or other persons with autonomous decision-taking powers;

(b) family workers; or

(c) workers officiating at religious ceremonies in churches and religious communities.

21 Other special cases

Subject to regulation 24, regulations 6(1), (2) and (7), 10(1), 11(1) and (2) and 12(1) do not apply in relation to a worker—

(a) where the worker's activities are such that his place of work and place of residence are distant from one another or his different places of work are distant from one another;

(b) where the worker is engaged in security and surveillance activities requiring a permanent presence in order to protect property and persons, as may be the case for security guards and caretakers or security firms;

(c) where the worker's activities involve the need for continuity of service or production, as may be the case in relation to—

(i) services relating to the reception, treatment or care provided by hospitals or similar establishments, residential institutions and prisons;

(ii) work at docks or airports;

(iii) press, radio, television, cinematographic production, postal and telecommunications services and civil protection services;

(iv) gas, water and electricity production, transmission and distribution, household refuse collection and incineration;

(v) industries in which work cannot be interrupted on technical grounds;
(vi) research and development activities;
(vii) agriculture;

(d) where there is a foreseeable surge of activity, as may be the case in relation to—

(i) agriculture;
(ii) tourism; and
(iii) postal services;

(e) where the worker's activities are affected by—

(i) an occurrence due to unusual and unforeseeable circumstances, beyond the control of the worker's employer;

(ii) exceptional events, the consequences of which could not have been avoided despite the exercise of all due care by the employer; or

(iii) an accident or the imminent risk of an accident.

22 Shift workers

(1) Subject to regulation 24—

(a) regulation 10(1) does not apply in relation to a shift worker when he changes shift and cannot take a daily rest period between the end of one shift and the start of the next one;

(b) paragraphs (1) and (2) of regulation 11 do not apply in relation to a shift worker when he changes shift and cannot take a weekly rest period between the end of one shift and the start of the next one; and

(c) neither regulation 10(1) nor paragraphs (1) and (2) of regulation 11 apply to workers engaged in activities involving periods of work split up over the day, as may be the case for cleaning staff.

(2) For the purposes of this regulation—

'shift worker' means any worker whose work schedule is part of shift work; and

'shift work' means any method of organising work in shifts whereby workers succeed each other at the same workstations according to a certain pattern, including a rotating pattern, and which may be continuous or discontinuous, entailing the need for workers to work at different times over a given period of days or weeks.

23 Collective and workforce agreements

A collective agreement or a workforce agreement may—

(a) modify or exclude the application of regulations 6(1) to (3) and (7), 10(1), 11(1) and (2) and 12(1), and

(b) for objective or technical reasons or reasons concerning the organisation of work, modify the application of regulation 4(3) and (4) by the substitution, for each reference to 17 weeks, of a different period, being a period not exceeding 52 weeks, in relation to particular workers or groups of workers.

24 Compensatory rest

Where the application of any provision of these Regulations is excluded by regulation 21 or 22, or is modified or excluded by means of a collective agreement or a workforce agreement under regulation 23(a), and a worker is accordingly required by his employer to work during a period which would otherwise be a rest period or rest break—

(a) his employer shall wherever possible allow him to take an equivalent period of compensatory rest, and

(b) in exceptional cases in which it is not possible, for objective reasons, to grant such a period of rest, his employer shall afford him such protection as may be appropriate in order to safeguard the worker's health and safety.

25 Workers in the armed forces

(1) Regulation 9 does not apply in relation to a worker serving as a member of the armed forces.

(2) Regulations 10(2) and 11(3) do not apply in relation to a young worker serving as a member of the armed forces.

(3) In a case where a young worker is accordingly required to work during a period which would otherwise be a rest period, he shall be allowed an appropriate period of compensatory rest.

26 Young workers employed on ships

Regulations 7(2), 10(2), 11(3) and 12(4) do not apply in relation to a young worker whose employment is subject to regulation under section 55(2)(b) of the Merchant Shipping Act 1995.

27 Young workers: *force majeure*

(1) Regulations 10(2) and 12(4) do not apply in relation to a young worker where his employer requires him to undertake work which no adult worker is available to perform and which—

(a) is occasioned by either—

(i) an occurrence due to unusual and unforeseeable circumstances, beyond the employer's control, or

(ii) exceptional events, the consequences of which could not have been avoided despite the exercise of all due care by the employer;

(b) is of a temporary nature; and

(c) must be performed immediately.

(2) Where the application of regulation 10(2) or 12(4) is excluded by paragraph (1), and a young worker is accordingly requried to work during a period which would otherwise be a rest period or rest break, his employer shall allow him to take an equivalent period of compensatory rest within the following three weeks.

PART IV
MISCELLANEOUS

28 Enforcement

(1) In this regulation and regulation 29—

'the 1974 Act' means the Health and Safety at Work etc. Act 1974;

'the relevant requirements' means the following provisions—

(a) regulations 4(2), 6(2) and (7), 7(1), (2) and (6), 8 and 9; and

(b) regulation 24, in so far as it applies where regulation 6(1), (2) or (7) is modified or excluded, and

'the relevant statutory provisions' has the same meaning as in the 1974 Act.

(2) It shall be the duty of the Health and Safety Executive to make adequate arrangements for the enforcement of the relevant requirements except to the extent that a local authority is made responsible for their enforcement by paragraph (3).

(3) Where the relevant requirements apply in relation to workers employed in premises in respect of which a local authority is responsible, under the Health and Safety (Enforcing Authority) Regulations 1998, for enforcing any of the relevant statutory provisions, it shall be the duty of that authority to enforce those requirements.

(4) The duty imposed on local authorities by paragraph (3) shall be performed in accordance with such guidance as may be given to them by the Health and Safety Commission.

(5) The following provisions of the 1974 Act shall apply in relation to the enforcement of the relevant requirements as they apply in relation to the enforcement of the relevant statutory provisions, and as if any reference in those provisions to an

enforcing authority were a reference to the Health and Safety Executive and any local authority made responsible for the enforcement of the relevant requirements—

(a) section 19;

(b) section 20(1), (2)(a) to (d) and (j) to (m), (7) and (8); and

(c) sections 21, 22, 23(1), (2) and (5), 24 and 26; and

(d) section 28, in so far as it relates to information obtained by an inspector in pursuance of a requirement imposed under section 20(2)(j) or (k).

(6) Any function of the Health and Safety Commission under the 1974 Act which is exercisable in relation to the enforcement by the Health and Safety Executive of the relevant statutory provisions shall be exercisable in relation to the enforcement by the Executive of the relevant requirements.

29 Offences

(1) An employer who fails to comply with any of the relevant requirements shall be guilty of an offence.

(2) The following provisions of section 33(1) of the 1974 Act shall apply where an inspector is exercising or has exercised any power conferred by a provision specified in regulation 28(5)—

(a) paragraph (e), in so far as it refers to section 20;

(b) paragraphs (f) and (g);

(c) paragraph (h), in so far as it refers to an inspector;

(d) paragraph (j) in so far as it refers to section 28; and

(e) paragraph (k).

(3) An employer guilty of an offence under paragraph (1) shall be liable—

(a) on summary conviction, to a fine not exceeding the statutory maximum;

(b) on conviction on indictment, to a fine.

(4) A person gulity of an offence under a provision of section 33(1) of the 1974 Act as applied by paragraph (2) shall be liable to the penalty prescribed in relation to that provision by subsection (2), (2A) or (3) of section 33, as the case may be.

(5) Sections 36(1), 37 to 39 and 42(1) to (3) of the 1974 Act shall apply in relation to the offences provided for in paragraphs (1) and (2) as they apply in relation to offences under the relevant statutory provisions.

30 Remedies

(1) A worker may present a complaint to an employment tribunal that his employer—

(a) has refused to permit him to exercise any right he has under—

(i) regulation 10(1) or (2), 11(1), (2) or (3), 12(1) or (4) or 13(1);

(ii) regulation 24, in so far as it applies where regulation 10(1), 11(1) or (2) or 12(1) is modified or excluded; or

(iii) regulation 25(3) or 27(2); or

(b) has failed to pay him the whole or any part of any amount due to him under regulation 14(2) or 16(1).

(2) An employment tribunal shall not consider a complaint under this regulation unless it is presented—

(a) before the end of the period of three months (or, in a case to which regulation 38(2) applies, six months) beginning with the date on which it is alleged that the exercise of the right should have been permitted (or in the case of a rest period or leave extending over more than one day, the date on which it should have been permitted to begin) or, as the case may be, the payment should have been made;

(b) within such further period as the tribunal considers reasonable in a case where it is satisfied that it was not reasonably practicable for the complaint to be presented before the end of that period of three or, as the case may be, six months.

(3) Where an employment tribunal finds a complaint under paragraph (1)(a) well-founded, the tribunal—

(a) shall make a declaration to that effect, and

(b) may make an award of compensation to be paid by the employer to the worker.

(4) The amount of the compensation shall be such as the tribunal considers just and equitable in all the circumstances having regard to—

(a) the employer's default in refusing to permit the worker to exercise his right, and

(b) any loss sustained by the worker which is attributable to the matters complained of.

(5) Where on a complaint under paragraph (1)(b) an employment tribunal finds that an employer has failed to pay a worker in accordance with regulation 14(2) or 16(1), it shall order the employer to pay to the worker the amount which it finds to be due to him.

31 to 34 [amend other statutes]

35 Restrictions on contracting out

(1) Any provision in an agreement (whether a contract of employment or not) is void in so far as it purports—

(a) to exclude or limit the operation of any provision of these Regulations, save in so far as these Regulations provide for an agreement to have that effect, or

(b) to preclude a person from bringing proceedings under these Regulations before an employment tribunal.

(2) Paragraph (1) does not apply to—

(a) any agreement to refrain from instituting or continuing proceedings where a conciliation officer has taken action under section 18 of the Employment Tribunals Act 1996 (conciliation); or

(b) any agreement to refrain from instituting or continuing proceedings within section 18(1)(ff) of the Employment Tribunals Act 1996 (proceedings under these Regulations where conciliation is available), if the conditions regulating compromise agreements under these Regulations are satisfied in relation to the agreement.

(3) For the purposes of paragraph (2)(b) the conditions regulating compromise agreements under these Regulations are that—

(a) the agreement must be in writing,

(b) the agreement must relate to the particular complaint,

(c) the worker must have received advice from a relevant independent adviser as to the terms and effect of the proposed agreement and, in particular, its effect on his ability to pursue his rights before an employment tribunal,

(d) there must be in force, when the adviser gives the advice, a contract of insurance, or an indemnity provided for members of a profession or professional body, covering the risk of a claim by the worker in respect of loss arising in consequence of the advice,

(e) the agreement must identify the adviser, and

(f) the agreement must state that the conditions regulating compromise agreements under these Regulations are satisfied.

(4) A person is a relevant independent adviser for the purposes of paragraph (3)(c)—

(a) if he is a qualified lawyer,

(b) if he is an officer, official, employee or member of an independent trade union who has been certified in writing by the trade union as competent to give advice and as authorised to do so on behalf of the trade union, or

(c) if he works at an advice centre (whether as an employee or as a volunteer) and has been certified in writing by the centre as competent to give advice and as authorised to do so on behalf of the centre.

(5) But a person is not a relevant independent adviser for the purposes of paragraph (3)(c) in relation to the worker—

(a) if he is, is employed by or is acting in the matter for the employer or an associated employer,

(b) in the case of a person within paragraph (4)(b) or (c), if the trade union or advice centre is the employer or an associated employer, or

(c) in the case of a person within paragraph (4)(c), if the worker makes a payment for the advice received from him.

(6) In paragraph (4)(a), 'qualified lawyer' means—

(a) as respects England and Wales, a barrister (whether in practice as such or employed to give legal advice), a solicitor who holds a practising certificate, or a person other than a barrister or solicitor who is an authorised advocate or authorised litigator (within the meaning of the Courts and Legal Services Act 1990); and

(b) as respects Scotland, an advocate (whether in practice as such or employed to give legal advice), or a solicitor who holds a practising certificate.

(7) For the puproses of paragraph (5) any two employers shall be treated as associated if—

(a) one is a company of which the other (directly or indirectly) has control; or

(b) both are companies of which a third person (directly or indirectly) has control; and 'associated employer' shall be construed accordingly.

PART V
SPECIAL CLASSES OF PERSON

36 Agency workers not otherwise 'workers'

(1) This regulation applies in any case where an individual ('the agency worker')—

(a) is supplied by a person ('the agent') to do work for another ('the principal') under a contract or other arrangements made between the agent and the principal; but

(b) is not, as respects that work, a worker, because of the absence of a worker's contract between the individual and the agent or the principal; and

(c) is not a party to a contract under which he undertakes to do the work for another party to the contract whose status is, by virtue of the contract, that of a client or customer of any profession or business undertaking carried on by the individual.

(2) In a case where this regulation applies, the other provisions of these Regulations shall have effect as if there were a worker's contract for the doing of the work by the agency worker made between the agency worker and—

(a) whichever of the agent and the principal is responsible for paying the agency worker in respect of the work; or

(b) if neither the agent nor the principal is so responsible, whichever of them pays the agency worker in respect of the work,

and as if that person were the agency worker's employer.

37 Crown employment

(1) Subject to paragraph (4) and regulation 38, these Regulations have effect in relation to Crown employment and persons in Crown employment as they have effect in relation to other employment and other workers.

(2) In paragraph (1) 'Crown employment' means employment under or for the purposes of a government department or any officer or body exercising on behalf of the Crown functions conferred by a statutory provision.

(3) For the purposes of the application of the provisions of these Regulations in relation to Crown employment in accordance with paragraph (1)—

(a) references to a worker shall be construed as references to a person in Crown employment; and

(b) references to a worker's contract shall be construed as references to the terms of employment of a person in Crown employment.

(4) No act or omission by the Crown which is an offence under regulation 29 shall make the Crown criminally liable, but the High Court or, in Scotland, the Court of Session may, on the application of a person appearing to the Court to have an interest, declare any such act or omission unlawful.

38 to **41** [omitted]

42 Non-employed trainees

For the purposes of these Regulations, a person receiving relevant training, otherwise than under a contract of employment, shall be regarded as a worker, and the person whose undertaking is providing the training shall be regarded as his employer.

43 [omitted]

SCHEDULE 1
WORKFORCE AGREEMENTS

1. An agreement is a workforce agreement for the purposes of these Regulations if the following conditions are satisfied—

(a) the agreement is in writing;

(b) it has effect for a specified period not exceeding five years;

(c) it applies either—

(i) to all of the relevant members of the workforce, or

(ii) to all of the relevant members of the workforce who belong to a particular group;

(d) the agreement is signed—

(i) in the case of an agreement of the kind referred to in sub-paragraph (c)(i), by the representatives of the workforce, and in the case of an agreement of the kind referred to in sub-paragraph (c)(ii) by the representatives of the group to which the agreement applies (excluding, in either case, any representative not a relevant member of the workforce on the date on which the agreement was first made available for signature), or

(ii) if the employer employed 20 or fewer workers on the date referred to in sub-paragraph (d)(i), either by the appropriate representatives in accordance with that sub-paragraph or by the majority of the workers employed by him;

(e) before the agreement was made available for signature, the employer provided all the workers to whom it was intended to apply on the date on which it came into effect with copies of the text of the agreement and such guidance as those workers might reasonably require in order to understand it fully.

2. For the purposes of this Schedule—

'a particular group' is a group of the relevant members of a workforce who undertake a particular function, work at a particular workplace or belong to a particular department or unit within their employer's business;

'relevant members of the workforce' are all of the workers employed by a particular employer, excluding any worker whose terms and conditions of employment are provided for, wholly or in part, in a collective agreement;

'representatives of the workforce' are workers duly elected to represent the relevant members of the workforce, 'representatives of the group' are workers duly elected to represent the members of a particular group, and representatives are 'duly elected' if the election at which they were elected satisfied the requirements of paragraph 3 of this Schedule.

3. The requirements concerning elections referred to in paragraph 2 are that—

(a) the number of representatives to be elected is determined by the employer;

(b) the candidates for election as representatives of the workforce are relevant members of the workforce, and the candidates for election as representataives of a group are members of the group;

(c) no worker who is eligible to be a candidate is unreasonably excluded from standing for election;

(d) all the relevant members of the workforce are entitled to vote for representatives of the workforce, and all the members of a particular group are entitled to vote for representatives of the group;

(e) the workers entitled to vote may vote for as many candidates as there are representatives to be elected;

(f) the election is conducted so as to secure that—

(i) so far as is reasonably practicable, those voting do so in secret, and

(ii) the votes given at the election are fairly and accurately counted.

THE CONTROL OF SUBSTANCES HAZARDOUS TO HEALTH REGULATIONS 1999
(SI 1999 No. 437)

1. [omitted]

Interpretation

2.—(1) In these Regulations, unless the context otherwise requires—

'the 1974 Act' means the Health and Safety at Work etc. Act 1974;

'the Agreement' means the Agreement on the European Economic Area signed at Oporto on 2nd May 1992 as adjusted by the Protocol signed at Brussels on 17th March 1993 and adopted as respects Great Britain by the European Economic Area Act 1993;

'approved' means approved for the time being in writing;

'approved supply list' has the meaning assigned to it in regulation 4 of the Chemicals (Hazard Information and Packaging for Supply) Regulations 1994;

'biological agent' means any micro-organism, cell culture, or human endoparasite, including any which have been genetically modified, which may cause any infection, allergy, toxicity or otherwise create a hazard to human health;

'carcinogen' means—

(a) any substance or preparation which if classified in accordance with the classification provided for by regulation 5 of the Chemicals (Hazard Information and Packaging for Supply) Regulations 1994 would be in the category of danger, carcinogenic (category 1) or carcinogenic (category 2) whether or not the substance or preparation would be required to be classified under those Regulations; or

(b) any substance or preparation—

(i) listed in Schedule 1, or

(ii) arising from a process specified in Schedule 1 which is a substance hazardous to health;

'the Executive' means the Health and Safety Executive;

'fumigation' means an operation in which a substance is released into the atmosphere so as to form a gas to control or kill pests or other undesirable organisms and 'fumigate' and 'fumigant' shall be construed accordingly;

'maximum exposure limit' for a substance hazardous to health means the maximum exposure limit approved by the Health and Safety Commission for that substance in relation to the reference period specified therein when calculated by a method approved by the Health and Safety Commission;

'member State' means a State which is a Contracting Party to the Agreement;

'micro-organism' means a microbiological entity, cellular or non-celular, which is capable of replication or of transferring genetic material;

'mine' has the meaning assigned to it by section 180 of the Mines and Quarries Act 1954;

'occupational exposure standard' for a substance hazardous to health means the standard approved by the Health and Safety Commission for that substance in relation to the specified reference period when calculated by a method approved by the Health and Safety Commission;

'preparation' means a mixture or solution of two or more substances;

'registered dentist' has the meaning assigned to it in section 53(1) of the Dentists Act 1984;

'respirate dust' means airborne material which is capable of penetrating to the gas exchange region of the lung;

'substance' means any natural or artificial substance whether in solid or liquid form or in the form of a gas or vapour (including micro-organisms);

'substance hazardous to health' means any substance (including any preparation) which is—

(a) a substance which is listed in Part 1 of the approved supply list as dangerous for supply within the meaning of the Chemicals (Hazard Information and Packaging for Supply) Regulations 1994 and for which an indication of danger specified for the substance in Part V of that list is very toxic, toxic, harmful, corrosive or irritant;

(b) a substance for which the Health and Safety Commission has approved an occupational exposure standard;

(c) a biological agent;

(d) dust of any kind, which is a substance within paragraph (a) or (b) above, when present at a concentration in air equal to or greater than—

(i) $10mg/m^3$, as a time weighted average over an 8-hour period, of total inhalable dust, or

(ii) $4mg/m^3$, as a time weighted average over an 8-hour period, of respirable dust;

(e) a substance, not being a substance mentioned in sub-paragraphs (a) to (d) above, which creates a hazard to the health of any person which is comparable with the hazards created by substances mentioned in those sub-paragraphs.

'total inhalable dust' means airborne material which is capable of entering the nose and mouth during breathing and is thereby available for deposition in the respiratory tract.

(2) In these Regulations, any reference to an employee being exposed to a substance hazardous to health is a reference to the exposure of that employee to a substance hazardous to health arising out of or in connection with work which is under the control of his employer.

(3) In these Regulations, unless the context otherwise requires—

(a) a reference to a numbered regulation or Schedule is a reference to the regulation or Schedule in these Regulations so numbered; and

(b) a reference to a numbered paragraph is a reference to the paragraph so numbered in the regulation or Schedule in which that reference appears.

Duties under these Regulations

3.—(1) Where any duty is placed by these Regulations on an employer in respect of his employees, he shall, so far as is reasonably practicable, be under a like duty in respect of any other person, whether at work or not, who may be affected by the work carried on by the employer except that the duties of the employer—

(a) under regulation 11 (health surveillance) shall not extend to persons who are not his employees; and

(b) under regulations 10 and 12(1) and (2) (which relate respectively to monitoring and information, training etc.) shall not extend to persons who are not his employees, unless those persons are on the premises where the work is being carried on.

(2) These Regulations shall apply to a self-employed person as they apply to an employer and an employee and as if that self-employed person were both an employer and employee, except that regulations 10 and 11 shall not apply to a self-employed person.

(3) The duties imposed by these Regulations shall not extend to the master or crew of a sea-going ship or to the employer of such persons in relation to the normal shipboard activities of a ship's crew under the direction of the master.

Prohibitions relating to certain substances

4.—(1) Those substances described in column 1 of Schedule 2 are prohibited to the extent set out in the corresponding entry in column 2 of that Schedule.

(2) The importation into the United Kingdom, other than from another member State, of the following substances and articles is prohibited, namely—

(a) 2-naphthylamine, benzidine, 4-aminodiphenyl, 4-nitrodiphenyl, their salts and any substance containing any of those compounds in a total concentration equal to or greater than 0.1 per cent. by mass;

(b) matches made with white phosphorus,

and any contravention of this paragraph shall be punishable under the Customs and Excise Management Act 1979 and not as a contravention of a health and safety regulation.

(3) A person shall not supply during the course of or for use at work any substance or article specified in paragraph (2).

(4) A person shall not supply during the course of or for use at work, benzene or any substance containing benzene unless its intended use is not prohibited by item 11 of Schedule 2.

Application of regulations 6 to 12

5.—(1) Regulations 6 to 12 shall have effect with a view to protecting persons against risks to their health, whether immediate or delayed, arising from exposure to substances hazardous to health except—

(a) where and to the extent that the following Regulations apply, namely—

(i) the Control of Lead at Work Regulations 1998,

(ii) the Control of Asbestos at Work Regulations 1987;

(b) where the substance is hazardous to health solely by virtue of its radioactive, explosive or flammable properties, or solely because it is at a high or low temperature or a high pressure;

(c) where the risk to health is a risk to the health of a person to whom the substance is administered in the course of his medical treatment;

(d) where the substance hazardous to health is total inhalable dust which is below ground in any mine of coal.

(2) In paragraph 1(c) 'medical treatment' means medical or dental examination or treatment which is conducted by, or under the direction of, a registered medical practitioner or registered dentist and includes any such examination, treatment or administration of any substance conducted for the purpose of research.

(3) Nothing in these Regulations shall prejudice any requirement imposed by or under any enactment relating to public health or the protection of the environment.

Assessment of health risks created by work involving substances hazardous to health

6.—(1) An employer shall not carry on any work which is liable to expose any employees to any substance hazardous to health unless he has made a suitable and sufficient assessment of the risks created by that work to the health of those employees and of the steps that need to be taken to meet the requirements of these Regulations.

(2) The assessment required by paragraph (1) shall be reviewed regularly and forthwith if—

(a) there is reason to suspect that the assessment is no longer valid; or

(b) there has been a significant change in the work to which the assessment relates,

and, where as a result of the review, changes in the assessment are required, those changes shall be made.

Prevention or control of exposure to substances hazardous to health

7.—(1) Every employer shall ensure that the exposure of his employees to substances hazardous to health is either prevented or, where this is not reasonably practicable, adequately controlled.

(2) So far as is reasonably practicable, the prevention or adequate control of exposure of employees to a substance hazardous to health, except to a carcinogen or a biological agent, shall be secured by measures other than the provision of personal protective equipment.

(3) Without prejudice to the generality of paragraph (1), where the assessment made under regulation 6 shows that it is not reasonably practicable to prevent exposure to a carcinogen by using an alternative substance or process, the employer shall apply all the following measures, namely—

(a) the total enclosure of the process and handling systems unless this is not reasonably practicable;

(b) the use of plant, processes and systems of work which minimise the generation of, or suppress and contain, spills, leaks, dust, fumes and vapours of carcinogens;

(c) the limitation of the quantities of a carcinogen at the place of work;

(d) the keeping of the number of persons who might be exposed to a carcinogen to a minimum;

(e) the prohibition of eating, drinking and smoking in areas that may be contaminated by carcinogens;

(f) the provision of hygiene measures including adequate washing facilities and regular cleaning of walls and surfaces;

(g) the designation of those areas and installations which may be contaminated by carcinogens, and the use of suitable and sufficient warning signs; and

(h) the safe storage, handling and disposal of carcinogens and use of closed and clearly labelled containers.

(4) Where the measures taken in accordance with paragraph (2) or (3), as the case may be, do not prevent, or provide adequate control of, exposure to substances hazardous to health to which those paragraphs apply, then, in addition to taking those measures, the employer shall provide those employees with such suitable personal protective equipment as will adequately control their exposure to those substances.

(5) Any personal protective equipment provided by an employer in pursuance of this regulation shall comply with any provision in the Personal Protective Equipment (EC Directive) Regulations 1992 which is applicable to that item of personal protective equipment.

(6) Where there is exposure to a substance for which a maximum exposure limit has been approved, the control of exposure shall, so far as the inhalation of that substance is concerned, only be treated as being adequate if the level of exposure is reduced so far as is reasonably practicable and in any case below the maximum exposure limit.

(7) Without prejudice to the generality of paragraph (1), where there is exposure to a substance for which an occupational exposure standard has been approved, the control of exposure shall, so far as the inhalation of that substance is concerned, be treated as being adequate if—

(a) that occupational exposure standard is not exceeded; or

(b) where that occupational exposure standard is exceeded, the employer identifies the reasons for the standard being exceeded and takes appropriate action to remedy the situation as soon as is reasonably practicable.

(8) Where respiratory protective equipment is provided in pursuance of this regulation, then it shall—

(a) be suitable for the purpose; and

(b) comply with paragraph (5) or, where no requirement is imposed by virtue of that paragraph, be of a type approved or shall conform to a standard approved, in either case, by the Executive.

(9) In the event of the failure of a control measure which might result in the escape of carcinogens into the workplace, the employer shall ensure that—

(a) only those persons who are responsible for the carrying out of repairs and other necessary work are permitted in the affected area and they are provided with suitable respiratory protective equipment and protective clothing; and

(b) employees and other persons who may be affected are informed of the failure forthwith.

(10) Schedule 3 of these Regulations shall have effect in relation to biological agents.

(11) In this regulation, 'adequate' means adequate having regard only to the nature of the substance and the nature and degree of exposure to substances hazardous to health and 'adequately' shall be construed accordingly.

Use of control measures etc.

8.—(1) Every employer who provides any control measure, personal protective equipment or other thing or facility pursuant to these Regulations shall take all reasonable steps to ensure that it is properly used or applied as the case may be.

(2) Every employee shall make full and proper use of any control measure, personal protective equipment or other thing or facility provided pursuant to these Regulations and shall take all reasonable steps to ensure it is returned after use to any accommoda-

tion provided for it and, if he discovers any defect therein, shall report it forthwith to his employer.

Maintenance, examination and test of control measures etc.

9.—(1) Every employer who provides any control measure to meet the requirements of regulation 7 shall ensure that it is maintained in an efficient state, in efficient working order and in good repair and, in the case of personal protective equipment, in a clean condition.

(2) Where engineering controls are provided to meet the requirements of regulation 7, the employer shall ensure that thorough examinations and tests of those engineering controls are carried out—

(a) in the case of local exhaust ventilation plant, at least once every 14 months, or for local exhaust ventilation plant used in conjunction with a process specified in column 1 of Schedule 4, at not more than the interval specified in the corresponding entry in column 2 of that Schedule;

(b) in any other case, at suitable intervals.

(3) Where respiratory protective equipment (other than disposable respiratory protective equipment) is provided to meet the requirements of regulation 7, the employer shall ensure that at suitable intervals thorough examinations and, where appropriate, tests of that equipment are carried out.

(4) Every employer shall keep a suitable record of the examinations and tests carried out in pursuance of paragraphs (2) and (3) and of any repairs carried out as a result of those examinations and tests, and that record or a suitable summary thereof shall be kept available for at least 5 years from the date on which it was made.

Monitoring exposure at the workplace

10.—(1) In any case in which—

(a) it is requisite for ensuring the maintenance of adequate control of the exposure of employees to substances hazardous to health; or

(b) it is otherwise requisite for protecting the health of employees,

the employer shall ensure that the exposure of employees to substances hazardous to health is monitored in accordance with a suitable procedure.

(2) Where a substance or process is specified in column 1 of Schedule 5, monitoring shall be carried out at least at the frequency specified in the corresponding entry in column 2 of that Schedule.

(3) The employer shall keep a suitable record of any monitoring carried out for the purpose of this regulation and that record or a suitable summary thereof shall be kept available—

(a) where the record is representative of the personal exposures of identifiable employees, for at least 40 years;

(b) in any other case, for at least 5 years.

Health surveillance

11.—(1) Where it is appropriate for the protection of the health of his employees who are, or are liable to be, exposed to a substance hazardous to health, the employer shall ensure that such employees are under suitable health surveillance.

(2) Health surveillance shall be treated as being appropriate where—

(a) the employee is exposed to one of the substances specified in Column 1 of Schedule 6 and is engaged in a process specified in Column 2 of that Schedule, unless that exposure is not significant; or

(b) the exposure of the employee to a substance hazardous to health is such that an identifiable disease or adverse health effect may be related to the exposure, there is a reasonable likelihood that the disease or effect may occur under the particular conditions of his work and there are valid techniques for detecting indications of the disease or the effect.

(3) The employer shall ensure that a health record, containing particulars approved by the Executive, in respect of each of his employees to whom paragraph (1) relates is made and maintained and that that record or a copy thereof is kept in a suitable form for at least 40 years from the date of the last entry made in it.

(4) Where an employer who holds records in accordance with paragraph (3) ceases to trade, he shall forthwith notify the Executive thereof in writing and offer those records to the Executive.

(5) If an employee is exposed to a substance specified in Schedule 6 and is engaged in a process specified therein, the health surveillance required under paragraph (1) shall include medical surveillance under the supervision of an employment medical adviser or appointed doctor at intervals of not more than 12 months or at such shorter intervals as the employment medical adviser or appointed doctor may require.

(6) Where an employee is subject to medical surveillance in accordance with paragraph (5) and an employment medical adviser or appointed doctor has certified by an entry in the health record of that employee that in his professional opinion that employee should not be engaged in work which exposes him to that substance or that he should only be so engaged under conditions specified in the record, the employer shall not permit the employee to be engaged in such work except in accordance with the conditions, if any, specified in the health record, unless that entry has been cancelled by an employment medical adviser or appointed doctor.

(7) Where an employee is subject to medical surveillance in accordance with paragraph (5) and an employment medical adviser or appointed doctor has certified by an entry in his health record that medical surveillance should be continued after his exposure to that substance has ceased, the employer shall ensure that the medical surveillance of that employee is continued in accordance with that entry while he is employed by the employer, unless that entry has been cancelled by an employment medical adviser or appointed doctor.

(8) On reasonable notice being given, the employer shall allow any of his employees access to the health record which relates to him.

(9) An employee to whom this regulation applies shall, when required by his employer and at the cost of the employer, present himself during his working hours for such health surveillance procedures as may be required for the purposes of paragraph (1) and, in the case of an employee who is subject to medical surveillance in accordance with paragraph (5), shall furnish the employment medical adviser or appointed doctor with such information concerning his health as the employment medical adviser or appointed doctor may reasonably require.

(10) Where, for the purpose of carrying out his functions under these Regulations, an employment medical adviser or appointed doctor requires to inspect any workplace or any record kept for the purposes of these Regulations, the employer shall permit him to do so.

(11) Where an employee or an employer is aggrieved by a decision recorded in the health record by an employment medical adviser or appointed doctor to suspend an employee from work which exposes him to a substance hazardous to health (or to impose conditions on such work), he may, by an application in writing to the Executive within 28 days of the date on which he was notified of the decision, apply for that decision to be reviewed in accordance with a procedure approved for the purposes of this paragraph by the Health and Safety Commission, and the result of that review shall be notified to the employee and employer and entered in the health record in accordance with the approved procedure.

(12) In this regulation—

'appointed doctor' means a registered medical practitioner who is appointed for the time being in writing by the Executive for the purposes of this regulation;

'employment medical adviser' means an employment medical adviser appointed under section 56 of the 1974 Act;

'health surveillance' includes biological monitoring.

Information, instruction and training for persons who may be exposed to substances hazardous to health

12.—(1) An employer who undertakes work which may expose any of his employees to substances hazardous to health shall provide that employee with such information, instruction and training as is suitable and sufficient for him to know—

(a) the risks to health created by such exposure; and

(b) the precautions which should be taken.

(2) Without prejudice to the generality of paragraph (1), the information provided under that paragraph shall include—

(a) information on the results of any monitoring of exposure at the workplace in accordance with regulation 10 and, in particular, in the case of any substance hazardous to health for which a maximum exposure has been approved, the employee or his representatives shall be informed forthwith, if the results of such monitoring show that the maximum exposure limit has been exceeded; and

(b) information on the collective results of any health surveillance undertaken in accordance with regulation 11 in a form calculated to prevent it from being identified as relating to any particular person.

(3) Every employer shall ensure that any person (whether or not his employee) who carries out any work in connection with the employer's duties under these Regulations has the necessary information, instruction and training.

Provisions relating to certain fumigations

13.—(1) This regulation shall apply to fumigations in which the fumigant used or intended to be used is hydrogen cyanide, phosphine or methyl bromide, except that paragraph (2) shall not apply to fumigations using the fumigant specified in column 1 of Schedule 7 when the nature of the fumigation is that specified in the corresponding entry in column 2 of that Schedule.

(2) An employer shall not undertake any fumigation to which this regulation applies unless he has—

(a) notified the persons specified in Part I of Schedule 8 of his intention to undertake the fumigation; and

(b) provided to those persons the information specified in Part II of that Schedule,

at least 24 hours in advance, or such shorter time in advance, as the persons required to be notified may agree.

(3) An employer who undertakes a fumigation to which this regulation applies shall ensure that, before the fumigant is released, suitable warning notices have been affixed at all points of reasonable access to the premises or to those parts of the premises in which the fumigation is to be carried out and that after the fumigation has been completed, and the premises are safe to enter, those warning notices are removed.

Exemption certificates

14.—(1) Subject to paragraph (2) the Executive may, by a certificate in writing, exempt any person or class of persons or any substance or class of substances from all or any of the requirements or prohibitions imposed by these Regulations and any such exemption may be granted subject to conditions and to a limit of time and may be revoked by a certificate in writing at any time.

(2) The Executive shall not grant any such exemption unless having regard to the circumstances of the case and, in particular, to—

(a) the conditions, if any, which it proposes to attach to the exemption; and

(b) any other requirements imposed by or under any enactments which apply to the case, it is satisfied that the health and safety of persons who are likely to be affected by the exemption will not be prejudiced in consequence of it.

Extension outside Great Britain

15.—(1) Subject to paragraph (2), these Regulations shall apply to and in relation to any activity outside Great Britain to which sections 1 to 59 and 80 to 82 of the 1974 Act apply by virtue of article 4, 6 or 8 of the Health and Safety at Work etc. Act 1974 (Application outside Great Britain) Order 1995 (SI 1995 No. 263) as those provisions apply within Great Britain.

(2) These Regulations shall not extend to Northern Ireland except insofar as they relate to imports of substances and articles referred to in regulation 4(2) into the United Kingdom.

Defence in proceedings for contravention of these Regulations

16. In any proceedings for an offence consisting of a contravention of these Regulations it shall be a defence for any person to prove that he took all reasonable precautions and exercised all due diligence to avoid the commission of that offence.

17. [omitted]

18. [omitted]

Extension of meaning of 'work'

19. For the purposes of Part I of the 1974 Act the meaning of 'work' shall be extended to include any activity involving the consignment, storage or use of any of the biological agents listed in Part V of Schedule 3 and the meaning of 'at work' shall be extended accordingly, and in that connection the references to employer in paragraphs 12 and 13 of that Schedule include references to any person carrying on such an activity.

Modification of section 3(2) of the 1974 Act

20. Section 3(2) of the 1974 Act shall be modified in relation to an activity involving the consignment, storage or use of any of the biological agents referred to in regulation 19 so as to have effect as if the reference therein to a self-employed person is a reference to any person who is not an employer or an employee and the reference therein to his undertaking includes a reference to such an activity.

THE PUBLIC INTEREST DISCLOSURE (COMPENSATION) REGULATIONS 1999
(SI 1999, No. 1548)

3 Compensation

Sections 117 to 127A of the 1996 Act shall apply to compensation awarded, or a compensatory award made, to a person in a case where he is regarded as unfairly dismissed by virtue of section 103A or 105(6A) of the 1996 Act, with the following modifications—

(a) as if, after section 124(1), there was inserted the following subsection—

'(1A) Subsection (1) shall not apply to compensation awarded, or a compensatory award made, to a person in a case where he is regarded as unfairly dismissed by virtue of section 103A or 105(6A)'; and

(b) as if, in section 117(6)—

(i) after paragraph (b), the word 'and' was omitted; and

(ii) after paragraph (c), there was inserted

'and

(d) a dismissal where the reason (or, if more than one, the principal reason)—

(i) in a redundancy case, for selecting the employee for dismissal, or

(ii) otherwise, for the dismissal,

is that specified in section 103A'.

NON-STATUTORY MATERIALS

ACAS CODE OF PRACTICE 1
DISCIPLINARY PRACTICE AND PROCEDURES IN EMPLOYMENT
(Revised 1997)

Formulating policy

5 Management is responsible for maintaining discipline within the organisation and for ensuring that there are adequate disciplinary rules and procedures. The initiative for establishing these will normally lie with management. However, if they are to be fully effective the rules and procedures need to be accepted as reasonable both by those who are to be covered by them and by those who operate them. Management should therefore aim to secure the involvement of employees and all levels of management when formulating new or revising existing rules and procedures. In the light of particular circumstances in different companies and industries trade union officials may or may not wish to participate in the formulation of the rules but they should participate fully with management in agreeing the procedural arrangements which will apply to their members and in seeing that these arrangements are used consistently and fairly.

Rules

6 It is unlikely that any set of disciplinary rules can cover all circumstances that may arise: moreover the rules required will vary according to particular circumstances such as the type of work, working conditions and size of establishment. When drawing up rules the aim should be to specify clearly and concisely those necessary for the efficient and safe performance of work and for the maintenance of satisfactory relations within the workforce and between employees and management. Rules should not be so general as to be meaningless.

7 Rules should be readily available and management should make every effort to ensure that employees know and understand them. This may be best achieved by giving every employee a copy of the rules and by explaining them orally. In the case of new employees this should form part of an induction programme.

8 Employees should be made aware of the likely consequences of breaking rules and in particular they should be given a clear indication of the type of conduct which may warrant summary dismissal.

Essential features of disciplinary procedures

9 Disciplinary procedures should not be viewed primarily as a means of imposing sanctions. They should also be designed to emphasise and encourage improvements in individual conduct.

10 Disciplinary procedures should:

(a) Be in writing.

(b) Specify to whom they apply.

(c) Provide for matters to be dealt with quickly.
(d) Indicate the disciplinary actions which may be taken.
(e) Specify the levels of management which have the authority to take the various forms of disciplinary action, ensuring that immediate superiors do not normally have the power to dismiss without reference to senior management.
(f) Provide for individuals to be informed of the complaints against them and to be given an opportunity to state their case before decisions are reached.
(g) Give individuals the right to be accompanied by a trade union representative or by a fellow employee of their choice.
(h) Ensure that, except for gross misconduct, no employees are dismissed for a first breach of discipline.
(i) Ensure that disciplinary action is not taken until the case has been carefully investigated.
(j) Ensure that individuals are given an explanation for any penalty imposed.
(k) Provide a right of appeal and specify the procedure to be followed.

The procedure in operation

11 When a disciplinary matter arises, the supervisor or manager should first establish the facts promptly before recollections fade, taking into account the statements of any available witnesses. In serious cases consideration should be given to a brief period of suspension while the case is investigated and this suspension should be with pay. Before a decision is made or penalty imposed the individual should be interviewed and given the opportunity to state his or her case and should be advised of any rights under the procedure, including the right to be accompanied.

12 Often supervisors will give informal oral warnings for the purpose of improving conduct when employees commit minor infringements of the established standards of conduct. However, where the facts of a case appear to call for disciplinary action, other than summary dismissal, the following procedure should normally be observed:
(a) In the case of minor offences the individual should be given a formal oral warning or if the issue is more serious, there should be a written warning setting out the nature of the offence and the likely consequences of further offences. In either case the individual should be advised that the warning constitutes the first formal stage of the procedure.
(b) Further misconduct might warrant a final written warning which should contain a statement that any recurrence would lead to suspension or dismissal or some other penalty, as the case may be.
(c) The final step might be disciplinary transfer, or disciplinary suspension without pay (but only if these are allowed for by an express or implied condition of the contract of employment), or dismissal, according to the nature of the misconduct. Special consideration should be given before imposing disciplinary suspension without pay and it should not normally be for a prolonged period.

13 Except in the event of an oral warning, details of any disciplinary action should be given in writing to the employee and if desired, to his or her representative. At the same time the employee should be told of any right of appeal, how to make it and to whom.

14 When determining the disciplinary action to be taken the supervisor or manager should bear in mind the need to satisfy the test of reasonableness in all the circumstances. So far as possible, account should be taken of the employee's record and any other relevant factors.

15 Special consideration should be given to the way in which disciplinary procedures are to operate in exceptional cases. For example:

(a) **Employees to whom the full procedure is not immediately available.** Special provisions may have to be made for the handling of disciplinary matters among nightshift workers, workers in isolated locations or depots or others who may pose particular problems for example because no one is present with the necessary authority to take disciplinary action or no trade union representative is immediately available.

(b) **Trade union officials.** Disciplinary action against a trade union official can lead to a serious dispute if it is seen as an attack on the union's functions. Although normal disciplinary standards should apply to their conduct as employees, no disciplinary action beyond an oral warning should be taken until the circumstances of the case have been discussed with a senior trade union representative or full-time official.

(c) **Criminal offences outside employment.** These should not be treated as automatic reasons for dismissal regardless of whether the offence has any relevance to the duties of the individual as an employee. The main considerations should be whether the offence is one that makes the individual unsuitable for his or her type of work or unacceptable to other employees. Employees should not be dismissed solely because a charge against them is pending or because they are absent through having been remanded in custody.

Appeals

16 Grievance procedures are sometimes used for dealing with disciplinary appeals though it is normally more appropriate to keep the two kinds of procedure separate since the disciplinary issues are in general best resolved within the organisation and need to be dealt with more speedily than others. The external stages of a grievance procedure may however, be the appropriate machinery for dealing with appeals against disciplinary action where a final decision within the organisation is contested or where the matter becomes a collective issue between management and a trade union.

17 Independent arbitration is sometimes an appropriate means of resolving disciplinary issues. Where the parties concerned agree, it may constitute the final stage of procedure.

Records

18 Records should be kept, detailing the nature of any breach of disciplinary rules, the action taken and the reasons for it, whether an appeal was lodged, its outcome and any subsequent developments. These records should be carefully safeguarded and kept confidential.

19 Except in agreed special circumstances breaches of disciplinary rules should be disregarded after a specified period of satisfactory conduct.

Further action

20 Rules and procedures should be reviewed periodically in the light of any developments in employment legislation or industrial relations practice and, if necessary, revised in order to ensure their continuing relevance and effectiveness. Any amendments and additional rules imposing new obligations should be introduced only after reasonable notice has been given to all employees and, where appropriate, their representatives have been informed.

ACAS CODE OF PRACTICE 2
DISCLOSURE OF INFORMATION TO TRADE UNIONS FOR COLLECTIVE BARGAINING PURPOSES
(Revised 1997)

Providing information

9 The absence of relevant information about an employer's undertaking may to a material extent impede trade unions in collective bargaining; particularly if the information would influence the formulation, presentation or pursuance of a claim, or the conclusion of an agreement. The provision of relevant information in such circumstances would be in accordance with good industrial relations practice.

10 To determine what information will be relevant negotiators should take account of the subject-matter of the negotiations and the issues raised during them; the level at which negotiations take place (department, plant, division, or company level); the size of the company; and the type of business the company is engaged in.

11 Collective bargaining within an undertaking can range from negotiations on specific matters arising daily at the work place affecting particular sections of the workforce, to extensive periodic negotiations on terms and conditions of employment affecting the whole workforce in multiplant companies. The relevant information and the depth, detail and form in which it could be presented to negotiators will vary accordingly. Consequently, it is not possible to compile a list of items that should be disclosed in all circumstances. Some examples of information relating to the undertaking which could be relevant in certain collective bargaining situations are given below:

(i) **Pay and benefits:** principles and structure of payment systems; job evaluation systems and grading criteria; earnings and hours analysed according to work-group, grade, plant, sex, out-workers and homeworkers, department or division, giving, where appropriate, distributions and make-up of pay showing any additions to basic rate or salary; total pay bill; details of fringe benefits and non-wage labour costs.

(ii) **Conditions of service:** policies on recruitment, redeployment, redundancy, training, equal opportunity, and promotion; appraisal systems; health, welfare and safety matters.

(iii) **Manpower:** numbers employed analysed according to grade, department, location, age and sex; labour turnover; absenteeism; overtime and short-time; manning standards; planned changes in work methods, materials, equipment or organisation; available manpower plans; investment plans.

(iv) **Performance:** productivity and efficiency data; savings from increased productivity and output; return on capital invested; sales and state of order book.

(v) **Financial:** cost structures; gross and net profits; sources of earnings; assets; liabilities; allocation of profits; details of government financial assistance; transfer prices; loans to parent or subsidiary companies and interest charged.

12 These examples are not intended to represent a check list of information that should be provided for all negotiations. Nor are they meant to be an exhaustive list of types of information as other items may be relevant in particular negotiations.

Restrictions on the duty to disclose

13 Trade unions and employers should be aware of the restrictions on the general duty to disclose information for collective bargaining.

14 Some examples of information which if disclosed in particular circumstances might cause substantial injury are: cost information on individual products; detailed analysis of proposed investment, marketing or pricing policies; and price quotas or the make-up of tender prices. Information which has to be made available publicly, for example under the Companies Acts, would not fall into this category.

15 Substantial injury may occur if, for example, certain customers would be lost to competitors, or suppliers would refuse to supply necessary materials, or the ability to raise funds to finance the company would be seriously impaired as a result of disclosing certain information. The burden of establishing a claim that disclosure of certain information would cause substantial injury lies with the employer.

Trade union responsibilities
16 Trade unions should identify and request the information they require for collective bargaining in advance of negotiations whenever practicable. Misunderstandings can be avoided, costs reduced, and time saved, if requests state as precisely as possible all the information required, and the reasons why the information is considered relevant. Requests should conform to an agreed procedure. A reasonable period of time should be allowed for employers to consider a request and to reply.

17 Trade unions should keep employers informed of the names of the representatives authorised to carry on collective bargaining on their behalf.

18 Where two or more trade unions are recognised by an employer for collective bargaining purposes they should co-ordinate their requests for information whenever possible.

19 Trade unions should review existing training programmes or establish new ones to ensure negotiators are equipped to understand and use information effectively.

Employers' responsibilities
20 Employers should aim to be as open and helpful as possible in meeting trade union requests for information. Where a request is refused, the reasons for the refusal should be explained as far as possible to the trade union representatives concerned and be capable of being substantiated should the matter be taken to the Central Arbitration Committee.

21 Information agreed as relevant to collective bargaining should be made avaialble as soon as possible once a request for the information has been made by an authorised trade union representative. Employers should present information in a form and style which recipients can reasonably be expected to understand.

Joint arrangements for disclosure of information
22 Employers and trade unions should endeavour to arrive at a joint understanidng on how the provisions on the disclosure of information can be implemented most effectively. They should consider what information is likely to be required, what is available, and what could reasonably be made available. Consideration should also be given to the form in which the information will be presented, when it should be presented and to whom. In particular, the parties should endeavour to reach an understanding on what information could most appropriately be provided on a regular basis.

23 Procedures for resolving possible disputes concerning any issues associated with the disclosure of information should be agreed. Where possible such procedures should normally be related to any existing arrangements within the undertaking or industry and the complaint, conciliation and arbitration procedure described in the Act.

ACAS CODE OF PRACTICE 3
TIME OFF FOR TRADE UNION DUTIES AND ACTIVITIES
(Revised 1997)

SECTION 1 TIME OFF FOR TRADE UNION DUTIES
ENTITLEMENT

8 Employees who are officials of an independent trade union recognised by their employer are to be permitted reasonable time off during working hours to carry out certain trade union duties.

9 An official is an employee who has been elected or appointed in accordance with the rules of the union to be a representative of all or some of the union's members in the particular company or workplace.

10 Officials are entitled to time off where the duties are concerned with:

★ negotiations with the employer about matters which fall within section 178(2) of the Trade Union and Labour Relations (Consolidation) Act 1992 (TULR(C)A) and for which the union is recognised for the purposes of collective bargaining by the employer; or

★ any other functions on behalf of employees of the employer which are related to matters falling within section 178(2) TULR(C)A and which the employer has agreed the union may perform.

Matters falling within section 178(2) TULR(C)A are listed in the sub-headings of paragraph 12 below.

11 An independent trade union is recognised by an employer when it is recognised to any extent for the purposes of collective bargaining. Where a trade union is not so recognised by an employer, employees have no statutory right to time off to undertake any duties.

Examples of trade union duties

12 Subject to the recognition or other agreement, trade union officials should be allowed to take reasonable time off for duties concerned with negotiations or, where their employer has agreed, for duties concerned with other functions related to or connected with:

(a) terms and conditions of employment, or the physical conditions in which workers are required to work. Examples could include:

★ pay
★ hours of work
★ holidays and holiday pay
★ sick pay arrangements
★ pensions
★ vocational training
★ equal opportunities
★ notice periods
★ the working environment
★ utilisation of machinery and other equipment;

(b) engagement or non-engagement, or termination or suspension of employment or the duties of employment, of one or more workers. Examples could include:

★ recruitment and selection policies
★ human resource planning
★ redundancy and dismissal arrangements;

(c) allocation of work or the duties of employment as between workers or groups of workers. Examples could include:

★ job grading
★ job evaluation
★ job descriptions
★ flexible working practices;

(d) matters of discipline. Examples could include:

★ disciplinary procedures
★ arrangements for representing trade union members at internal interviews
★ arrangements for appearing on behalf of trade union members, or as witnesses, before agreed outside appeal bodies or employment tribunals;

(e) trade union membership or non-membership. Examples could include:

- ★ representational arrangements
- ★ any union involvement in the induction of new workers;

(f) facilities for officials of trade unions. Examples could include any agreed arrangements for the provision of:

- ★ accommodation
- ★ equipment
- ★ names of new workers to the union;

(g) machinery for negotiation or consultation and other procedures. Examples could include arrangements for:

- ★ collective bargaining
- ★ grievance procedures
- ★ joint consultation
- ★ communicating with members
- ★ communicating with other union officials also concerned with collective bargaining with the employer.

13 The duties of an official of a recognised trade union must be connected with or related to negotiations or the performance of functions both in time and subject matter. Reasonable time off may be sought, for example, to:

- ★ prepare for negotiations
- ★ inform members of progress
- ★ explain outcomes to members
- ★ prepare for meetings with the employer about matters for which the trade union has only representational rights.

PAYMENT FOR TIME OFF FOR TRADE UNION DUTIES

14 An employer who permits officials time off for trade union duties must pay them for the time off taken. The employer must pay either the amount that the officials would have earned had they worked during the time off taken or, where earnings vary with the work done, an amount calculated by reference to the average hourly earnings for the work they are employed to do. There is no statutory requirement to pay for time off where the duty is carried out at a time when the official would not otherwise have been at work.

SECTION 2: TRAINING OF OFFICIALS IN ASPECTS OF INDUSTRIAL RELATIONS

ENTITLEMENT

15 Employees who are officials of an independent trade union recognised by their employer are to be permitted reasonable time off during working hours to undergo training relevant to the carrying out of their trade union duties. These duties must be concerned with:

- ★ negotiations with the employer about matters which fall within section 178(2) TULR(C)A and for which the union is recognised to any extent for the purposes of collective bargaining by the employer; or
- ★ any other functions on behalf of employees of the employer which are related to matters falling within section 178(2) TULR(C)A and which the employer has agreed the union may perform.

Matters falling within section 178(2) TULR(C)A are set out in paragraph 12 above.

What is relevant industrial relations training?

16 Training should be in aspects of industrial relations relevant to the duties of an official. There is no one recommended syllabus for training as an official's duties will vary according to:

- ★ the collective bargaining arrangements at the place of work, particularly the scope of the recognition or other agreement
- ★ the structure of the union
- ★ the role of the official.

17 The training must also be approved by the Trades Union Congress or by the independent trade union of which the employee is an official.

18 Trade union officials are more likely to carry out their duties effectively if they possess skills and knowledge relevant to their duties. In particular, employers should be prepared to consider releasing trade union officials for initial training in basic representational skills as soon as possible after their election or appointment, bearing in mind that suitable courses may be infrequent. Reasonable time off could also be considered, for example:

- ★ for further training particularly where the official has special responsibilities
- ★ where there are proposals to change the structure and topics of negotiation about matters for which the union is recognised; or where significant changes in the organisation of work are being contemplated
- ★ where legislative change may affect the conduct of industrial relations at the place of work and may require the reconsideration of existing agreements.

PAYMENT FOR TIME OFF FOR TRAINING

19 An employer who permits time off for officials to attend training relevant to their duties at the workplace must pay them for the time off taken. The employer must pay either the amount that the officials would have earned had they worked during the time off taken or, where earnings vary with the work done, an amount calculated by reference to the average hourly earnings for the work that they are employed to do. There is no statutory requirement to pay for time off where training is undertaken at a time when the official would not otherwise have been at work.

SECTION 3: TIME OFF FOR TRADE UNION ACTIVITIES

ENTITLEMENT

20 To operate effectively and democratically, trade unions need the active participation of members. It can also be very much in employers' interests that such participation is assured. An employee who is a member of an independent trade union recognised by the employer in respect of that description of employee is to be permitted reasonable time off during working hours to take part in any trade union activity.

What are examples of trade union activities?

21 The activities of a trade union member can be, for example:

- ★ attending workplace meetings to discuss and vote on the outcome of negotiations with the employer
- ★ meeting full-time officials to discuss issues relevant to the workplace
- ★ voting in union elections.

22 Where the member is acting as a representative of a recognised union activities can be, for example, taking part in:

- ★ branch, area or regional meetings of the union where the business of the union is under discussion
- ★ meetings of official policy making bodies such as the executive committee or annual conference
- ★ meetings with full-time officials to discuss issues relevant to the workplace.

23 There is no right to time off for trade union activities which themselves consist of industrial action.

PAYMENT FOR TIME OFF FOR TRADE UNION ACTIVITIES

24 There is no requirement that union members or representatives be paid for time off taken on trade union activities. Nevertheless employers may want to consider payment in certain circumstances, for example to ensure that workplace meetings are fully representative.

SECTION 4: THE RESPONSIBILITIES OF EMPLOYERS AND TRADE UNIONS

GENERAL CONSIDERATIONS

25 The amount and frequency of time off should be reasonable in all the circumstances. Although the statutory provisions apply to all employers without exception as to size and type of business or service, trade unions should be aware of the wide variety of difficulties and operational requirements to be taken into account when seeking or agreeing arrangements for time off, for example:

★ the size of the organisation and the number of workers
★ the production process
★ the need to maintain a service to the public
★ the need for safety and security at all times.

26 Employers in turn should have in mind the difficulties for trade union officials and members in ensuring effective representation and communications with, for example:

★ shift workers
★ part-time workers
★ those employed at dispersed locations
★ workers with particular domestic commitments.

27 For time off arrangements to work satisfactorily trade unions should:

★ ensure that officials are aware of their role, responsibilities and functions
★ inform management, in writing, as soon as possible of appointments or resignations of officials
★ ensure that officials receive any appropriate written credentials promptly.

28 Employers should consider making available to officials the facilities necessary for them to perform their duties efficiently and communicate effectively with their members, fellow lay officials and full-time officers. Where resources permit the facilities could include:

★ accommodation for meetintgs
★ access to a telephone and other office equipment
★ the use of notice boards
★ where the volume of the official's work justifies it, the use of dedicated office space.

REQUESTING TIME OFF

29 Trade union officials and members requesting time off to pursue their industrial relations duties or activities should provide management with as much notice as possible and give details of:

★ the purpose of such time off
★ the intended location
★ the timing and duration of time off required.

30 In addition, officials who request paid time off to undergo relevant training should:

★ give at least a few weeks' notice to management of nominations for training courses

★ if asked to do so, provide a copy of the syllabus or prospectus indicating the contents of the training course.

31 When deciding whether requests for paid time off should be granted, consideration would need to be given as to their reasonableness, for example to ensure adequate cover for safety or to safeguard the production process or the provision of service. Similarly managers and unions should seek to agree a mutually convenient time which minimises the effect on production or services. Where workplace meetings are requested consideration should be given to holding them, for example:

★ towards the end of a shift or the working week

★ before or after a meal break.

32 Employers need to consider each application for time off on its merits; they might also need to consider the reasonableness of the request in relation to agreed time off already taken or in prospect.

SECTION 5: AGREEMENTS ON TIME OFF

33 To take account of the wide variety of circumstances and problems which can arise, there can be positive advantages for employers and trade unions in establishing agreements on time off in ways which reflect their own situations. A formal agreement can help to:

★ provide clear guidelines against which applications for time off can be determined

★ avoid misunderstanding

★ facilitate better planning

★ ensure fair and reasonable treatment.

34 Agreements could specify:

★ the amount of time off permitted

★ the occasions on which time off can be taken

★ in what circumstances time off will be paid

★ to whom time off will be paid

★ the procedure for requesting time off.

35 In addition, it would be sensible for agreements to make clear:

★ arrangements for the appropriate payment to be made when time off relates in part to union duties and in part to union activities

★ whether payment (to which there would be no statutory entitlement) might be made to shift and part-time employees undertaking trade union duties outside their normal working hours.

36 Agreements for time off and other facilities for union representation should be consistent with wider agreements which deal with such matters as constituencies, number of representatives and the election of officials.

37 In smaller organisations, it might be thought more appropriate for employers and unions to reach understandings about how requests for time off are to be made; and more broadly to agree flexible arrangements which can accommodate their particular circumstances.

38 The absence of a formal agreement on time off, however, does not in itself deny an individual any statutory entitlement. Nor does any agreement supersede statutory entitlement to time off.

SECTION 6: INDUSTRIAL ACTION

39 Employers and unions have a responsibility to use agreed procedures to settle problems and avoid industrial action. Time off may therefore be permitted for this purpose particularly where there is a dispute. There is no right to time off for trade union activities which themselves consist of industrial action. However, where an official is not taking part in industrial action but represents members involved, normal arrangements for time off with pay for the official should apply.

SECTION 7: MAKING A COMPLAINT

40 Every effort should be made to resolve any dispute or grievance in relation to time off work for union duties or activities. There is advantage in agreeing ways in which such disputes can be settled and any appropriate procedures to resolve disputes should be followed. Where the grievance remains unresolved, trade union officials or members have a right to complain to an employment tribunal that their employer has failed to allow reasonable time off or, in the case of an official, has failed to pay for all or part of the time off taken. Such complaints may be resolved by conciliation by ACAS and, if this is successful, no tribunal hearing will be necessary. ACAS assistance may also be sought without the need for a formal complaint to a tribunal.

DEPARTMENT OF EMPLOYMENT CODE OF PRACTICE ON PICKETING (REVISED)

Section D
ROLE OF THE POLICE

45 It is not the function of the police to take a view of the merits of a particular trade dispute. They have a general duty to uphold the law and keep the peace, whether on the picket line or elsewhere. The law gives the police discretion to take whatever measures may reasonably be considered necessary to ensure that picketing remains peaceful and orderly.

46 The police have no responsibility for enforcing the civil law. An employer cannot require the police to help in identifying the pickets against whom he wishes to seek an order from the civil court. Nor is it the job of the police to enforce the terms of an order. Enforcement of an order on the application of a plaintiff is a matter for the court and its officer. The police may, however, decide to assist the officer of the court if they think there may be a breach of the peace.

47 As regards the criminal law the police have considerable discretionary powers to limit the number of pickets at any one place where they have reasonable cause to fear disorder. The law does not impose a specific limit on the number of people who may picket at any one place; nor does this Code affect in any way the discretion of the police to limit the number of people on a particular picket line. It is for the police to decide, taking into account all the circumstances, whether the number of pickets at any particular place provides reasonable grounds for the belief that a breach of the peace is likely to occur. If a picket does not leave the picket line when asked to do so by the police, he is liable to be arrested for obstruction either of the highway or of a police officer in the execution of his duty if the obstruction is such as to cause, or be likely to cause, a breach of the peace.

Section E
LIMITING NUMBERS OF PICKETS

48 Violence and disorder on the picket line is more likely to occur if there are excessive numbers of pickets. Wherever large numbers of people with strong feelings are involved there is danger that the situation will get out of control, and that those concerned will run the risk of committing an offence, with consequent arrest and prosecution, or of committing a civil wrong which exposes them, or anyone organising them, to civil proceedings.

49 This is particularly so whenever people seek by sheer weight of numbers to stop others going into work or delivering or collecting goods. In such cases, what is intended is not peaceful persuasion, but obstruction or harassment—if not intimidation. Such a situation is often described as 'mass picketing'. In fact, it is not picketing in its lawful sense of an attempt at peaceful persuasion, and may well result in a breach of the peace or other criminal offences.

50 Moreover, anyone seeking to demonstrate support for those in dispute should keep well away from any picket line so as not to create a risk of a breach of the peace or other criminal offence being committed on that picket line. Just as with a picket itself, the numbers involved in any such demonstration should not be excessive, and the demonstration should be conducted lawfully. Section 14 of the Public Order Act 1986 provides the police with the power to impose conditions (for example, as to numbers, location and duration) on public assemblies of 20 or more people where the assembly is likely to result in serious public disorder; or serious damage to property; or serious disruption to the life of the community; or if its purpose is to coerce.

51 Large numbers on a picket line are also likely to give rise to fear and resentment amongst those seeking to cross that picket line, even where no criminal offence is committed. They exacerbate disputes and sour relations not only between management and employees but between the pickets and their fellow employees. Accordingly pickets and their organisers should ensure that in general the number of pickets does not exceed six at any entrance to, or exit from, a workplace; frequently a smaller number will be appropriate.

Section F
ORGANISATION OF PICKETING

52 Sections B and C of this Code outline aspects of the civil law and the criminal law, as they may apply to pickets, and to anyone, including a trade union, who organises a picket. While it is possible that a picket may be entirely 'spontaneous', it is much more likely that it will be organised by an identifiable individual or group.

53 Paragraphs 36-38 in Section B of this Code describe how to identify whether a trade union is, in fact, responsible in terms of civil law liability, for certain acts. As explained in these paragraphs, the law means, for example, that if such an act takes place in the course of picketing, and if a trade union official has done, authorised or endorsed the act, then the official's union will be responsible in law unless the act is 'effectively repudiated' by the union's national leadership.

Functions of the picket organiser

54 Wherever picketing is 'official' (i.e., organised by a trade union), an experienced person, preferably a trade union official who represents those picketing, should always be in charge of the picket line. He should have a letter of authority from his union which he can show to the police officers or to people who want to cross the picket line. Even when he is not on the picket line himself he should be available to give the pickets advice if a problem arises.

55 A picket should not be designated as an 'official' picket unless it is actually organised by a trade union. Nor should pickets claim the authority and support of a union unless the union is prepared to accept the consequent responsibility. In particular, union authority and support should not be claimed by the pickets if the union

has, in fact, repudiated calls to take industrial action made, or being made, in the course of the picketing.

56 Whether a picket is 'official' or 'unofficial', an organiser of pickets should maintain close contact with the police. Advance consultation with the police is always in the best interests of all concerned. In particular the organiser and the pickets should seek directions from the police on the number of people who should be present on the picket line at any one time and on where they should stand in order to avoid obstructing the highway.

57 The other main functions of the picket organiser should include ensuring that:

- ★ the pickets understand the law and are aware of the provisions of this Code, and that the picketing is conducted peacefully and lawfully;
- ★ badges or armbands, which authorised pickets should wear so that they are clearly identified, are distributed to such pickets and are worn while they are picketing;
- ★ workers from other places of work do not join the picket line, and that any offers of support on the picket line from outsiders are refused;
- ★ the number of pickets at any entrance to, or exit from, a place of work is not so great as to give rise to fear and resentment amongst those seeking to cross that picket line (see paragraph 51 in Section E of this Code);
- ★ close contact with his own union office (if any), and with the offices of other unions if they are involved in the picketing, is established and maintained;
- ★ such special arrangements as may be necessary for essential supplies, services or operations (see paragraphs 62-64 in Section G of this Code) are understood and observed by the pickets.

Consultation with other trade unions

58 Where several unions are involved in a dispute, they should consult each other about the organisation of any picketing. It is important that they should agree how the picketing is to be carried out, how many pickets there should be from each union, and who should have overall responsibility for organising them.

Right to cross picket lines

59 Everyone has the right to decide for himself whether he will cross a picket line. Disciplinary action should not be taken or threatened by a union against a member on the grounds that he has crossed a picket line.

60 If a union disciplines any member for crossing a picket line, the member will have been 'unjustifiably disciplined'. In such a case, the individual can make a complaint to an employment tribunal. If the tribunal finds the complaint well-founded, it will make a declaration to that effect.

61 If the union has not lifted the penalty imposed on the member, or if it has not taken all necessary steps to reverse anything done in giving effect to the penalty, an application for compensation should be made to the Employment Appeal Tribunal (EAT). In any other case, the individual can apply to an employment tribunal for compensation. The EAT or tribunal will award whatever compensation it considers just and equitable in all the circumstances, subject to a specified maximum amount. Where the application is made to the EAT, there will normally be a specified minimum award.

Section G
ESSENTIAL SUPPLIES, SERVICES AND OPERATIONS

62 Pickets, and anyone organising a picket should take very great care to ensure that their activities do not cause distress, hardship or inconvenience to members of the public who are not involved in the dispute. Particular care should be taken to ensure that the movement of essential goods and supplies, the carrying out of essential maintenance of plant and equipment, and the provision of services essential to the life of the community are not impeded, still less prevented.

63 The following list of essential supplies and services is provided as an illustration of the kind of activity which requires special protection to comply with the recommendations in paragraph 62 above. However, the list is not intended to be comprehensive. The supplies and services which may need to be protected in accordance with these recommendations could cover different activities in different circumstances. Subject to this *caveat*, 'essential supplies, services and operations' include:

★ the production, packaging, marketing and/or distribution of medical and pharmaceutical products;

★ the provision of supplies and services essential to health and welfare institutions, e.g., hospitals, old peoples' homes;

★ the provision of heating fuel for schools, residential institutions, medical institutions and private residential accommodation;

★ the production and provision of other supplies for which there is a crucial need during a crisis in the interests of public health and safety (e.g., chlorine, lime and other agents for water purification; industrial and medical gases; sand and salt for road gritting purposes);

★ activities necessary to the maintenance of plant and machinery;

★ the proper care of livestock;

★ necessary safety procedures (including such procedures as are necessary to maintain plant and machinery);

★ the production, packaging, marketing and/or distribution of food and animal feeding stuffs;

★ the operation of essential services, such as police, fire, ambulance, medical and nursing services, air safety, coastguard and air sea rescue services, and services provided by voluntary bodies (e.g., Red Cross and St John's ambulance, meals on wheels, hospital car service), and mortuaries, burial and cremation services.

64 Arrangements to ensure these safeguards for essential supplies, services and operations should be agreed in advance between the pickets, or anyone organising the picket, and the employer, or employers, concerned.

EQUAL OPPORTUNITIES COMMISSION CODE OF PRACTICE FOR THE ELIMINATION OF DISCRIMINATION ON THE GROUNDS OF SEX AND MARRIAGE AND THE PROMOTION OF EQUAL OPPORTUNITY IN EMPLOYMENT

PART 1

RECRUITMENT

12. It is unlawful: unless the job is covered by an exception: to discriminate directly or indirectly on the grounds of sex or marriage
— in the arrangements made for deciding who should be offered a job
— in any terms of employment
— by refusing or omitting to offer a person employment

13. It is therefore recommended that:

(a) each individual should be assessed according to his or her personal capability to carry out a given job. It should not be assumed that men only or women only will be able to perform certain kinds of work;

(b) any qualifications or requirements applied to a job which effectively inhibit applications from one sex or from married people should be retained only if they are justifiable in terms of the job to be done;

(c) any age limits should be retained only if they are necessary for the job. An unjustifiable age limit could constitute unlawful indirect discrimination, for example, against women who have taken time out of employment for child-rearing;

(d) where trade unions uphold such qualifications or requirements as union policy, they should amend that policy in the light of any potentially unlawful effect.

GENUINE OCCUPATIONAL QUALIFICATIONS (GOQs)

14. It is unlawful: except for certain jobs when a person's sex is a genuine occupational qualification (GOQ) for that job to select candidates on the ground of sex.

15. There are very few instances in which a job will qualify for a GOQ on the ground of sex. However, exceptions may arise, for example, where considerations of privacy and decency or authenticity are involved. The SDA expressly states that the need of the job for strength and stamina does not justify restricting it to men. When a GOQ exists for a job, it applies also to promotion, transfer, or training for that job, but cannot be used to justify a dismissal.

16. In some instances, the GOQ will apply to some of the duties only. A GOQ will not be valid, however, where members of the appropriate sex are already employed in sufficient numbers to meet the employer's likely requirements without undue inconvenience. For example, in a job where sales assistants may be required to undertake changing room duties, it might not be lawful to claim a GOQ in respect of *all* the assistants on the grounds that any of them might be required to undertake changing room duties from time to time.

17. It is therefore recommended that:

—A job for which a GOQ was used in the past should be re-examined if the post falls vacant to see whether the GOQ still applies. Circumstances may well have changed, rendering the GOQ inapplicable.

SOURCES OF RECRUITMENT

18. It is unlawful: unless the job is covered by an exception:

—to discriminate on grounds of sex or marriage in the arrangements made for determining who should be offered employment whether recruiting by advertisements, through employment agencies, jobcentres, or career offices.

—to imply that applications from one sex or from married people will not be considered.

—to instruct or put pressure on others to omit to refer for employment people of one sex or married people unless the job is covered by an exception.

It is also unlawful when advertising job vacancies,

—to publish or cause to be published an advertisement which indicates or might reasonably be understood as indicating an intention to discriminate unlawfully on grounds of sex or marriage.

19. It is therefore recommended that:

Advertising

(a) job advertising should be carried out in such a way as to encourage applications from suitable candidates of both sexes. This can be achieved both by wording of the advertisements and, for example, by placing advertisements in publications likely to reach both sexes. All advertising material and accompanying literature relating to employment or training issues should be reviewed to ensure that it avoids presenting men and women in stereotyped roles. Such sterotyping tends to perpetuate sex segregation in jobs and can also lead people of the opposite sex to believe that they would be unsuccessful in applying for particular jobs;

(b) where vacancies are filled by promotion or transfer, they should be published to all eligible employees in such a way that they do not restrict applications from either sex;

(c) recruitment solely or primarily by word of mouth may unnecessarily restrict the choice of applicants available. The method should be avoided in a workforce predominantly of one sex, if in practice it prevents members of the opposite sex from applying;

(d) where applicants are supplied through trade unions and members of one sex only come forward, this should be discussed with the unions and an alternative approach adopted.

Careers Service/Schools

20. When notifying vacancies to the Careers Service, employers should specify that these are open to both boys and girls. This is especially important when a job has traditionally been done exclusively or mainly by one sex. If dealing with single sex schools, they should ensure, where possible, that both boys' and girls' schools are approached; it is also a good idea to remind mixed schools that jobs are open to boys and girls.

SELECTION METHODS

Tests

21.(a) If selection tests are used, they should be specifically related to job and/or career requirements and should measure an individual's actual or inherent ability to do or train for the work or career.

(b) Tests should be reviewed regularly to ensure that they remain relevant and free from any unjustifiable basis, either in contents or in scoring mechanism.

Applications and Interviewing

22. It is unlawful: unless the job is covered by an exception:
To discriminate on grounds of sex or marriage by refusing or deliberately omitting to offer employment.

23. It is therefore recommended that:

(a) employers should ensure that personnel staff, line managers and all other employees who may come into contact with job applicants, should be trained in the provisions of the SDA, including the fact that it is unlawful to instruct or put pressure on others to discriminate;

(b) applications from men and women should be processed in exactly the same way. For example, there should not be separate lists of male and female or married and single applicants. All those handling applications and conducting interviews should be trained in the avoidance of unlawful discrimination and records of interviews kept, where practicable, showing why applicants were or were not appointed;

(c) questions should relate to the requirements of the job. Where it is necessary to assess whether personal circumstances will affect performance of the job (for example, where it involves unsocial hours or extensive travel) this should be discussed objectively without detailed questions based on assumptions about marital status, children and domestic obligations. Questions about marriage plans or family intentions should not be asked, as they could be construed as showing bias against women. Information necessary for personnel records can be collected after a job offer has been made.

PROMOTION, TRANSFER AND TRAINING

24. It is unlawful: unless the job is covered by an exception, for employers to discriminate directly or indirectly on the grounds of sex or marriage in the way they afford access to opportunities for promotion, transfer or training.

25. It is therefore recommended that:

(a) where an appraisal system is in operation, the assessment criteria should be examined to ensure that they are not unlawfully discriminatory and the scheme monitored to assess how it is working in practice;

(b) when a group of workers predominantly of one sex is excluded from an appraisal scheme, access to promotion, transfer and training and to other benefits should be reviewed, to ensure that there is no unlawful indirect discrimination;

(c) promotion and career development patterns are reviewed to ensure that the traditional qualifications are justifiable requirements for the job to be done. In some circumstances, for example, promotion on the basis of length of service could amount to unlawful indirect discrimination, as it may unjustifiably affect more women than men;

(d) when general ability and personal qualities are the main requirements for promotion to a post, care should be taken to consider favourably candidates of both sexes with differing career patterns and general experience;

(e) rules which restrict or preclude transfer between certain jobs should be questioned and changed if they are found to be unlawfuly discriminatory. Employees of one sex may be concentrated in sections from which transfers are traditionally restricted without real justification;

(f) policies and practices regarding selection for training, day release and personal development should be examined for unlawful direct and indirect discrimination. Where there is found to be an imbalance in training as between sexes, the cause should be identified to ensure that it is not discriminatory;

(g) age limits for access to training and promotion should be questioned.

HEALTH AND SAFETY LEGISLATION

26. Equal treatment of men and women may be limited by statutory provisions which require men and women to be treated differently. For example, the Factories Act 1961 places restrictions on the hours of work of female manual employees, although the Health and Safety Executive can exempt employers from these restrictions, subject to certain conditions. The Mines and Quarries Act 1954 imposes limitations on women's work and there are restrictions where there is special concern for the unborn child (e.g., lead and ionising radiation). However the broad duties placed on employers by the Health and Safety at Work, etc., Act, 1974 makes no distinctions between men and women. Section 2(1) requires employers to ensure, so far as is reasonably practicable, the health and safety and welfare at work of *all* employees.

Specific health and safety requirements under earlier legislation are unaffected by the Act.

It is therefore recommended that

— company policy should be reviewed and serious consideration given to any significant differences in treatment between men and women, and there should be well-founded reasons if such differences are maintained or introduced.

TERMS OF EMPLOYMENT, BENEFITS, FACILITIES AND SERVICES

27. It is unlawful: unless the job is covered by an exception: to discriminate on the grounds of sex or marriage, directly or indirectly, in the terms on which employment is offered or in affording access to any benefits, facilities or services.

28. It is therefore recommended that:

(a) all terms of employment, benefits, facilities and services are reviewed to ensure that there is no unlawful discrimination on grounds of sex or marriage. For example, part-time work, domestic leave, company cars and benefits for dependants should be available to both male and female employees in the same or not materially different circumstances.

29. In an establishment where part-timers are solely or mainly women, unlawful indirect discrimination may arise if, as a group, they are treated less favourably than other employees without justification.
It is therefore recommended that:

(b) where part-time workers do not enjoy pro-rata pay or benefits with full-time workers, the arrangements should be reviewed to ensure that they are justified without regard to sex.

GRIEVANCES, DISCIPLINARY PROCEDURES AND VICTIMISATION

30. It is unlawful: to victimise an individual for a complaint made in good faith about sex or marriage discrimination or for giving evidence about such a complaint.

31. It is therefore recommended that:

(a) particular care is taken to ensure that an employee who has in good faith taken action under the Sex Discrimination Act or the Equal Pay Act does not receive less favourable treatment than other employees, for example by being disciplined or dismissed;

(b) employees should be advised to use the internal procedures, where appropriate, but this is without prejudice to the individual's right to apply to an employment tribunal within the statutory time limit, i.e., before the end of the period of three months beginning when the act complained of was done. (There is no time limit if the victimisation is continuing.);

(c) particular care is taken to deal effectively with all complaints of discrimination, victimisation or harassment. It should not be assumed that they are made by those who are over-sensitive.

DISMISSALS, REDUNDANCIES AND OTHER UNFAVOURABLE TREATMENT OF EMPLOYEES

32. It is unlawful: to discriminate directly or indirectly on grounds of sex or marriage in dismissals or by treating an employee unfavourably in any other way.
It is therefore recommended that:

(a) care is taken that members of one sex are not disciplined or dismissed for performance or behaviour which would be overlooked or condoned in the other sex;

(b) redundancy procedures affecting a group of employees predominantly of one sex should be reviewed, so as to remove any effects which could be disproportionate and unjustifiable;

(c) conditions of access to voluntary redundancy benefit should be made available on equal terms to male and female employees in the same or not materially different circumstances;

(d) where there is down-grading or short-time working (for example, owing to a change in the nature or volume of an employer's business) the arrangements should not unlawfully discriminate on the ground of sex;

(e) all reasonably practical steps should be taken to ensure that a standard of conduct or behaviour is observed which prevents members of either sex from being intimidated, harassed or otherwise subjected to unfavourable treatment on the ground of their sex.

PART 2

THE ROLE OF GOOD EMPLOYMENT PRACTICES IN PROMOTING EQUALITY OF OPPORTUNITY

33. This section of the Code describes those employment practices which help to promote equality of opportunity. It gives information about the formulation and implementation of equal opportunities policies. While such policies are not required by law, their value has been recognised by a number of employers who have voluntarily adopted them. Others may wish to follow this example.

FORMULATING AN EQUAL OPPORTUNITIES POLICY

34. An equal opportunities policy will ensure the effective use of human resources in the best interests of both the organisation and its employees. It is a commitment by an employer to the development and use of employment procedures and practices which do not discriminate on grounds of sex or marriage and which provide genuine equality of opportunity for all employees. The detail of the policy will vary according to size of the organisation.

IMPLEMENTING THE POLICY

35. An equal opportunities policy must be seen to have the active support of management at the highest level. To ensure that the policy is fully effective, the following procedure is recommended:

(a) the policy should be clearly stated and, where appropriate, included in a collective agreement;

(b) overall responsibility for implementing the policy should rest with senior management;

(c) the policy should be made known to all employees and, where reasonably practicable, to all job applicants.

36. Trade unions have a very important part to play in implementing genuine equality of opportunity and they will obviously be involved in the review of established procedures to ensure that these are consistent with the law.

MONITORING

37. It is recommended that the policy is monitored regularly to ensure that it is working in practice. Consideration could be given to setting up a joint Management/Trade Union Review Committee.

38. In a small firm with a simple structure it may be quite adequate to assess the distribution and payment of employees from personal knowledge.

39. In a large and complex organisation a more formal analysis will be necessary, for example, by sex, grade and payment in each unit. This may need to be introduced by stages as resources permit. Any formal analysis should be regularly updated and available to Management and Trade Unions to enable any necessary action to be taken.

40. Sensible monitoring will show, for example, whether members of one sex:

(a) do not apply for employment or promotion, or that fewer apply than might be expected;

(b) are not recruited, promoted or selected for training and development or are appointed/selected in a significantly lower proportion than their rate of application;

(c) are concentrated in certain jobs, sections or departments.

POSITIVE ACTION

Recruitment, Training and Promotion

41. Selection for recruitment or promotion must be on merit, irrespective of sex. However, the Sex Discrimination Act does allow certain steps to redress the effects of previous unequal opportunities. Where there have been few or no members of one sex in particular work in their employment for the previous 12 months, the Act allows employers to give special encouragement to, and provide specific training for, the minority sex. Such measures are usually described as Positive Action.

42. Employers may wish to consider positive measures such as:

(a) training their own employees (male or female) for work which is traditionally the preserve of the other sex, for example, training women for skilled manual or technical work;

(b) positive encouragement to women to apply for management posts — special courses may be needed;

(c) advertisements which encourage applications from the minority sex, but make it clear that selection will be on merit without reference to sex;

(d) notifying job agencies, as part of a Positive Action Programme that they wish to encourage members of one sex to apply for vacancies, where few or no members of that sex are doing the work in question. In these circumstances, job agencies should tell both men and women about the posts and, in addition, let the under-represented sex know that applications from them are particularly welcome. Withholding information from one sex in an attempt to encourage applications from the opposite sex would be unlawful.

Other working arrangements

43. There are other forms of action which could assist both employer and employee by helping to provide continuity of employment to working parents, many of whom will have valuable experience or skills.

Employers may wish to consider with their employees whether:

(a) certain jobs can be carried out on a part-time or flexi-time basis;

(b) personal leave arrangements are adequate and available to both sexes. It should not be assumed that men may not need to undertake domestic responsibilities on occasion, especially at the time of childbirth;

(c) child-care facilities are available locally or whether it would be feasible to establish nursery facilities on the premises or combine with other employers to provide them;

(d) residential training could be facilitated for employees with young children. For example, where this type of training is necessary, by informing staff who are selected well in advance to enable them to make child-care and other personal arrangements; employers with their own residential training centres could also consider whether childcare facilities might be provided;

(e) the statutory maternity leave provisions could be enhanced, for example, by reducing the qualifying service period, extending the leave period, or giving access to part-time arrangements on return.

These arrangements, and others, are helpful to both sexes but are of particular benefit to women in helping them to remain in gainful employment during the years of child-rearing.

EQUAL OPPORTUNITIES COMMISSION CODE OF PRACTICE ON EQUAL PAY

SEX DISCRIMINATION IN PAY SYSTEMS

21. Sex discrimination in pay now occurs primarily because women and men tend to do different jobs or to have different work patterns. As a result it is easy to undervalue the demands of work performed by one sex compared with the demands associated with jobs typically done by the other. Such differences can be reinforced by discriminatory recruitment, selection and promotion procedures which may restrict the range of work each sex performs; for example, by allocating the full-time, higher paid, bonus-earning jobs mainly to men.

Different Jobs

22.(a) There is some degree of job segregation in most employing organisations. Frequently the jobs done mainly by men have a higher status and are more highly rewarded than those done by women. Commonly men and women do different jobs within an organisation. It is also common for men to be in the majority at managerial level and women to occupy lower graded jobs. In certain occupations there is further segregation to the extent that there is an even greater concentration of ethnic minority women in lower status, lower paid jobs.

(b) Gender segregation in employment is often historical. Consequently it may be difficult to recognise the discriminatory effects of past pay and grading decisions based on traditional decisions based on traditional values ascribed to 'male' and 'female' work. In addition, the pay and conditions of 'male' and 'female' jobs within a firm might have been bargained separately by different unions. It is not sufficient to explain how the difference in pay came about. Arguments based on 'tradition' or separate bargaining would not justify paying women less than men when their work is of equal value.

(c) The fact that certain jobs are associated with one sex can affect the level of wages for those jobs which in turn can result in discrimination.

(d) Past discriminatory assumptions about the value of what has been regarded as men's or women's work may be reflected in current grading schemes. For example, men and women may be doing the same or very similar work but have different job titles and consequently be in separate grades, with the women's jobs being graded lower. They may on the other hand be doing quite different jobs which are actually of equal value though the women are in lower grades. In both examples the grading scheme could result in discrimination and fail to value the actual work done.

Different Work Patterns

23.(a) Many women take time out of work for pregnancy and maternity. Women also tend to carry the main responsibility for family care. As a result women in general have shorter periods of service than men and more women than men work part-time. This difference in work patterns has contributed to the gender segregation of jobs.

(b) There has been a tendency for payment systems to be designed to reward work patterns traditionally associated with men's employment and fail to recognise the different pattern of 'female' work. For example, a performance pay scheme which relies on an annual appraisal could mean that a woman who begins maternity leave before the appraisal but has performed well for part of the year will be denied a performance pay increase altogether. Another example is where pay benefits, such as occupational pensions or sick pay, are available only to full-time employees. This rule may mean that a group of female employees i.e. those who work part-time, are denied access to important benefits.

24. Most of the discrimination in pay systems takes the form of indirect or hidden discrimination. This occurs where pay rules and agreements appear to be gender neutral but the effect of their application is to disadvantage substantially more of one sex than the other. Whatever the cause of the discrimination and regardless of whether it was intentional or not, once an applicant has established that someone of the opposite sex is paid more for equal work, the employer will be required to show that the difference is not based on sex, using the criteria set out ... under 'Material Factor Defence'and 'Objective Justification'.

REVIEW OF PAY SYSTEMS FOR SEX BIAS

25.(a) Pay arrangements are frequently complicated and the features which can give rise to sex discrimination are not always obvious. Although pay systems reviews are not required by law, they are recommended as the most appropriate method of ensuring that a pay system delivers equal pay free from sex bias.

(b) A pay systems review also provides an opportunity to investigate the amount of information employees receive about their pay. Pay systems should be clear and easy to understand. Where they are not and where pay differentials exist, these may be inferred to be due to sex discrimination ... It is therefore in an employer's interest to have transparent pay systems to prevent unnecessary equal pay claims.

(c) The Equal Opportunities Commission recommends that a pay review should involve the following stages:

Stage One

☐ Undertake a thorough analysis of the pay system to produce a breakdown of all employees, which covers for example, sex, job, title, grade, whether part-time or full-time, with basic pay, performance ratings and all other elements of remuneration.

Stage Two

☐ Examine each element of the pay system against the data obtained in stage one. (See paragraph 27)

Stage Three

☐ Identify any elements of the pay system which the review indicates may be the source of any discrimination.

Stage Four

☐ Change any rules or practices including those in collective agreements which stages 1 to 3 have identified as likely to give rise to discrimination in pay. It is recommended that this should be done in consultation with employees trade unions or staff representations where appropriate. Stages 1 to 3 may reveal that practices and procedures in relation to recruitment, selection and access to training have contributed to discrimination in pay; in that event these matters should also be addressed.

Stage Five

☐ Analyse the likely effects of any proposed changes in practice to the pay system before implementation, to identify and rectify any discrimination which could be caused.

Stage Six

☐ Give equal pay to current employees. Where the review shows that some employees are not receiving equal pay for equal work and the reasons cannot be justified, then a plan must be developed for dealing with this.

Stage Seven

☐ Set up a system of regular monitoring to allow checks to be made to pay practices.

Stage Eight

☐ Draw up and publish an equal pay policy with provision for assessing the new pay system or modification to a system in terms of sex discrimination. Also in the interests of transparency provide pay information as described . . . where this is not already usual practice.

THE PAY REVIEW PROCESS

The following section provides guidance on carrying out stages 1 to 3 of the review process.

Initial Analysis

26. Undertake a thorough analysis of pay systems. This will require a breakdown of all employees to include for example, sex, job title, and grade, whether part-time or full-time, with performance ratings and the distribution of basic pay and all other elements of the remuneration package, to identify potential vulnerability to claims of pay discrimination. This will reveal whether there are any vulnerabilities and what their extent is and enable a plan to be developed to correct any problems.

Identification of Discriminatory Elements

27.(a) Pay systems vary in complexity. Some have more elements than others. In the process of a review, each element will require examination against the statistical data generated at the initial analysis stage. Investigation may show discrimination in written rules and agreements, for example, limiting profit related pay to employees who work above a minimm number of hours; or in the way processes are interpreted and applied, for example, failure to obtain adequate job descriptions during a job evaluation exercise.

(b) Some of the more common pay elements are set out below with examples of facts which could indicate problems of discrimination in pay and suggestions of further questions to be asked to reveal the cause of the pay difference and whether it can be shown to be free of sex bias in the terms explained under 'Material Factor Defence' and 'Objective Justification'....

Basic Pay

28.(a) *Problem:*
Women are consistently appointed at lower points on the pay scale than men.

Recommended Action:
Check the criteria which determine promotion or recruitment starting pay. Are these spelt out clearly?

Examine recruitment and promotion records for evidence of criteria which appear to be disadvantaging women. Can these criteria e.g., qualification requirements, be justified objectively in terms of the demands of the job?

Check the records for evidence of sex bias in the application of managerial discretion.

(b) *Problem:*
Women are paid less per hour than men for doing virtually the same job, but with different job and grade titles.

Recommended Action:
Check whether there are any reasons other than custom and practice for the difference; if so are these reasons justified objectively?

(c) *Problem:*
Women progress more slowly through incremental salary scales and seldom reach higher points.

Recommended Action:
Investigate the criteria applied for progression through the scale. Are these clearly understood? Does any particular criterion e.g., length of service, work to the detriment of women more than men? If so can the use of that criterion or the extent to which it is relied on be justified objectively?

Review the length of the incremental scale. Is the scale longer than it need be? Are there good practical reasons for a scale of that length?

(d) *Problem:*
Women progress more slowly through non-incremental salary ranges and seldom reach higher points.

Recommended Action:
Check the criteria that applied when the structure was introduced and the current criteria for new recruits/promotees to each salary.

Check whether there is a clear, well understood mechanism for progressing through the salary range.

Investigate the criteria for progression through the salary range and whether there are performance, qualification or other bars to upward movement. Can these be justified?

Review the length of the salary range. Can this be justified by real need?

Bonus/Premium Rates/Plus Elements

29.(a) *Problem:*
Female and male manual workers receive the same basic pay but only jobs mainly done by men have access to bonus earnings and those mainly done by women do not.

Recommended Action:
Check the reason why. Does this reflect real differences, for example, in the value of the work or in productivity? Can it be justified objectively on grounds unrelated to sex?

(b) *Problem:*
Where shift and overtime work is available and paid at a premium rate, further full time women employees have access to this higher rated work.

Recommended Action:
Check that women and men employees have equal access to this work and, if not, that the reason can be justified objectively.

(c) *Problem:*
A smaller percentage of women employees have access to enhanced rates for overtime/weekend/shift working.

Recommended Action:
Check the eligibility requirements for this work. Do any of these, for example requiring that employees must be working full-time, work to the disadvantage of women? Can these requirements be justified objectively?

(d) *Problem:*
Average female earnings under a variable payment system are lower than average male earnings (even where some women may have higher earnings than most men).

Recommended Action:
Review the design and operation of the variable payment system. Do these genuinely reflect the demands of the jobs and the productivity needs of the organisation?

In particular, check how factors such as down-time and personal needs breaks are dealt with in a variable payment system covering men and women.

Performance Pay

30.(a) *Problem:*
The performance pay system is applied largely to employees of one sex only and results in a pay discrepancy to the advantage of that group.

Recommended Action:
Investigate the reasons why employees of the other sex are largely excluded from performance pay awards. Are these justified objectively for reasons unrelated to sex?

(b) *Problem:*
Women receive lower performance ratings on average than men.

Recommended Action:
Investigate the performance rating system. Is it really likely that women would on average perform less well than men? What are the possible reasons for this?

Review the criteria for performance rating. Do employees and managers know what these are? Do any of these disadvantage women? Do any of these disadvantage ethnic minority women in particular? If so, are these criteria justified objectively?

Monitor the ratings of individual managers. Do the results of the monitoring suggest a stereotypical interpretation of criteria? Are there appropriate controls on managerial discretion?

(c) *Problem:*
Although women and men receive similar ratings, men achieve higher performance pay awards.

Recommended Action:
Investigate the reasons for this. Is it linked to managerial discretion? Are potentially discriminatory criteria being applied in the linking of ratings to pay? Can these be justified objectively?

Pay Based on Additional Skills or Training

31. *Problem:*
In practice only or mainly male employees receive this supplement.

Recommended Action:
Investigate the reasons for this. Are 'female' skills not recognised? Do women have the same access to any skills or training modules offered?

Review the training/skills/qualification criteria. Do they genuinely reflect enhanced ability to carry out the job duties?

Review the procedures for implementing the supplement. Are managers and employees aware of the procedure? Are they operated fairly as between men and women?

Pay Based on an Assessment of Individual Competencies

32. *Problem:*
There is a pay gap between the male and female employees who are assessed in this way.

Recommended Action:
Review the competencies assessed. Are women and men assessed for the same set of competencies? Are the competencies being interpreted in a consistent way?

Are potentially discriminatory criteria being applied? If so are these justified objectively?

Monitor the assessment of individual managers.

Pay Benefits

33.(a) *Problem:*
A smaller percentage of women employees than men are covered by the organisation's sick pay, pensions, low interest loans, share option schemes.

Recommended Action:
Check eligibility requirements. Are there restrictions which impact negatively on women? For example, are any of these limited to employees working over a minimum number of hours?

Can these requirements be justified objectively?

(b) *Problem:*
Proportionately fewer women are in receipt of contractual benefits, for example, cars, telephone rentals and bills, rent and rates on tied accommodation, reimbursement of council tax in residential occupations.

Recommended Action:
Review the criteria for such benefits and any differences in treatment between male and female dominated groups. Can these differences be justified in terms of the needs of the work?

Review policies for the payment of such benefits between departments within the organisation. Are they consistent and can any differences be justified?

Grading

34. (a) *Problem:*
Jobs predominantly occupied by women are graded lower than jobs predominantly occupied by men.

Recommended Action:
Review the method of grading. Was it devised for the current jobs? Is it adapted from a scheme used in a different organisation? What was the method used to determine job size? Some methods e.g., felt-fair or whole job comparison, are potentially more discriminatory than others e.g., analytical job evaluation. Are separate grading schemes used for jobs predominantly done by women and those predominantly done by men? If so, why, and is this difference objectively justified.

(b) *Problem:*
Some jobs held mainly by men are in higher grades because of 'recruitment and retention' problems.

Recommended Action
Check that there is genuine evidence of a current recruitment and retention problem.

Check that the whole of the difference in pay is attributable to market pressure. If not, investigate the reasons for the rest of the difference.

Consider amending the grading/pay structure so that the 'labour market' element of pay is 'transparent'.

(c) *Problem:*
Red circling, for example, where salary is protected when a job has been downgraded, is mainly applied to male employees.

Recommended Action:
Check the criteria for red circling. Why do they favour male jobs? Can this be justified objectively?

Investigate whether other criteria which are more equitable could be used.

Ensure the difference in pay is phased out as soon as possible so that unequal pay is not unnecessarily perpetuated.

Job Evaluation Method of Grading

35. (a) *Problem:*
An analytical job evaluation scheme has resulted in jobs predominantly done by women being graded lower than those predominantly done by men.

Recommended Action:
Check that all features of the scheme's design and implementation took full account of the need to avoid sex bias. Was the job information collected consistently and accurately? Do the factors and weighting favour characteristics typical of jobs dominated by one sex? If so is this justified objectively? Was training in the avoidance of sex bias given to those responsible for implementing the scheme?

(b) *Problem:*
Jobs which have been evaluated as the same have widely differing salaries, to the detriment of jobs largely held by women.

Recommended Action:
Investigate the possible causes, for example, how were the jobs assimilated to the evaluated structure?

Are different pay scales in use?

Could elements like additional skills payments or performance pay awards be responsible? What part do market rate or productivity considerations play? Can the cause of the difference be justified objectively?

Monitoring

36. Once the current pay systems have been reviewed it is important that periodic checks are made to ensure that discrimination does not creep in. This is best done by incorporating statistics on pay broken down by sex into the existing management information package, so that the necessary information can be checked regularly.

A POLICY ON EQUAL PAY

37. Good equal opportunities practice in employment not only helps to avoid unlawful or unfair discrimination but is also good for business and the right and fair thing to do. Many employers have adopted Equal Opportunities Policies in order to signal to employees and clients or customers that the organisation takes equality issues seriously. Equal pay is an important part of equality at work because pay is the most direct way an organisation values the contribution made by employees and should be covered in any Equal Opportunities Policy.

38. An Equal Pay Policy is an important way of showing commitment to achieving equal pay free of sex bias. The Policy should set out clear objectives which enable priorities for action to be identified and an effective programme to achieve them to be implemented. The internal pay review described [above] would allow the identification of priorities.

39. It is good employment practice for employees to understand how their rate of pay is determined. Information about priorities and proposed action could be communicated to employees as part of the process of informing them about how the pay systems affects them individually. This will serve to assure employees that any sex bias in the payment system is being addressed.

40. Experience shows that the effectiveness of any Equal Pay Policy depends on the following:

A commitment to the policy by senior management.

A recognition by all staff involved in decisions about pay that they share responsibility for the proper implementation of the policy.

Effective training in identifying sex discrimination in pay for all staff who take decisions about the pay and grading of other employees.

Moving beyond a statement of intent to include a provision for a review of the payment system and periodic monitoring to ensure continuing effectiveness.

Information given to employees about the review and any plan of action drawn up as a result.

A suggested Equal Pay Policy is to be found at Annex A.

ANNEX A

SUGGESTED EQUAL PAY POLICY

Equal Pay Statement

This organisation supports the principle of equal opportunities in employment and believes as part of that principle that male and female staff should receive equal pay for the same or broadly similar work, for work rated as equivalent and for work of equal value.

We understand that a right to equal pay between men and women free of sex bias is a fundamental principle of European Community law and is conferred by United Kingdom legislation.

We believe it is in our company's interest and good business practice that pay is awarded fairly and equitably.

We recognise that in order to achieve equal pay for employees doing equal work we should operate a pay system which is transparent, based on objective criteria and free from sex bias.

Action to Implement Policy

In order to put our commitment to equal pay into practice we will:

★ examine our existing and future pay practices for all our employees including those in non-standard employment and those who are absent on pregnancy and maternity leave.
★ carry out regular monitoring of the impact of our practices.
★ inform employees of how these practices work and how their own pay is arrived at.
★ provide training and guidance for managers and supervisory staff involved in decisions about pay and benefits.
★ discuss and agree the equal pay policy with trade unions or staff representatives where appropriate.

We intend through the above action to avoid unfair discrimination, to reward fairly the skills, experience and potential of all staff and thereby to increase efficiency, productivity and competitiveness and enhance the organisation's reputation and image.

COMMISSION FOR RACIAL EQUALITY CODE OF PRACTICE FOR THE ELIMINATION OF RACIAL DISCRIMINATION AND THE PROMOTION OF EQUALITY OF OPPORTUNITY IN EMPLOYMENT

PART 1 The Responsibilities of Employers

1.1 Responsibility for providing equal opportunity for all job applicants and employees rests primarily with employers. To this end it is recommended that they should adopt, implement and monitor an equal opportunity policy to ensure that there is no unlawful discrimination and that equal opportunity is genuinely available.

1.2 This policy should be clearly communicated to all employees — e.g., through notice boards, circulars, contracts of employment or written notifications to individual employees.

Equal Opportunity Policies

1.3 An equal opportunity policy aims to ensure:

(a) that no job applicant or employee receives less favourable treatment than another on racial grounds;

(b) that no applicant or employee is placed at a disadvantage by requirements or conditions which have a disproportionately adverse effect on his or her racial group and which cannot be shown to be justifiable on other than racial grounds;

(c) that, where appropriate and where permissible under the Race Relations Act, employees of under-represented racial groups are given training and encouragement to achieve equal opportunity within the organisation.

1.4 In order to ensure that an equal opportunity policy is fully effective, the following action by employers is recommended:

(a) allocating overall responsibility for the policy to a member of senior management;

(b) discussing and, where appropriate, agreeing with trade union or employee representatives the policy's contents and implementation;

(c) ensuring that the policy is known to all employees and if possible, to all job applicants;

(d) providing training and guidance for supervisory staff and other relevant decision makers, (such as personnel and line managers, foremen, gatekeepers and receptionists) to ensure that they understand their position in law and under company policy;

(e) examining and regularly reviewing existing procedures and criteria and changing them where they find that they are actually or potentially unlawfully discriminatory;

(f) making an initial analysis of the workforce and regularly monitoring the application of the policy with the aid of analyses of the ethnic origins of the workforce and of job applicants in accordance with the guidance in paragraphs 1.34-1.35.

Recruitment, promotion, transfer, training & dismissal

Sources of Recruitment

Advertisements

1.5 When advertising job vacancies it is unlawful for employers: to publish an advertisement which indicates, or could reasonably be understood as indicating, an intention to discriminate against applicants from a particular racial group. (For exceptions see the Race Relations Act). [s 29]

1.6 It is therefore recommended that:

(a) employers should not confine advertisements unjustifiably to those areas or publications which would exclude or disproportionately reduce the numbers of applicants of a particular racial group;

(b) employers should avoid prescribing requirements such as length of residence or experience in the UK and where a particular qualification is required it should be made clear that a fully comparable qualification obtained overseas is as acceptable as a UK qualification.

1.7 In order to demonstrate their commitment to equality of opportunity it is recommended that where employers send literature to applicants, this should include a statement that they are equal opportunity employers.

Employment Agencies

1.8 When recruiting through employment agencies, job centres, careers offices and schools, it is unlawful for employers:

(a) to give instructions to discriminate, for example by indicating that certain groups will or will not be preferred. (For exceptions see the Race Relations Act) [s 30];

(b) to bring pressure on them to discriminate against members of a particular racial group. (For exceptions, as above) [s 31]

1.9 In order to avoid indirect discrimination it is recommended that employers should not confine recruitment unjustifiably to those agencies, job centres, careers offices and schools which, because of their particular source of applicants, provide only or mainly applicants of a particular racial group.

Other Sources

1.10 It is unlawful to use recruitment methods which exclude or disproportionately reduce the numbers of applicants of a particular racial group and which cannot be shown to be justifiable. It is therefore recommended that employers should not recruit through the following methods:

(a) recruitment, solely or in the first instance, through the recommendations of existing employees where the workforce concerned is wholly or predominantly white or black and the labour market is multi-racial;

(b) procedures by which applicants are mainly or wholly supplied through trade unions where this means that only members of a particular racial group, or a disproportionately high number of them, come forward.

Sources for Promotion and Training

1.11 *It is unlawful for employers to restrict access to opportunities for promotion or training in a way which is discriminatory.* It is therefore recommended that [s 4 and s 28]:

—job and training vacancies and the application procedure should be made known to all eligible employees, and not in such a way as to exclude or disproportionately reduce the numbers of applicants from a particular racial group.

Selection for recruitment, promotion, transfer, training & dismissal

1.12 *It is unlawful to discriminate, not only in recruitment, promotion, transfer and training, but also in the arrangements made for recruitment and in the ways of affording access to opportunities for promotion, transfer or training.*

Selection Criteria and Tests

1.13 In order to avoid direct or indirect discrimination it is recommended that selection criteria and tests are examined to ensure that they are related to job requirements and are not unlawfully discriminatory. [s 4 and s 28]. For example:

(a) a standard of English higher than that needed for the safe and effective performance of the job or clearly demonstrable career pattern should not be required, or a higher level of educational qualification than is needed;

(b) in particular, employers should not disqualify applicants because they are unable to complete an application form unassisted unless personal completion of the form is a valid test of the standard of English required for safe and effective performance of the job;

(c) overseas degrees, diplomas and other qualifications which are comparable with UK qualifications should be accepted as equivalents, and not simply be assumed to be of an inferior quality;

(d) selection tests which contain irrelevant questions or exercises on matters which may be unfamiliar to or racial minority applicants should not be used (for example, general knowledge questions on matters more likely to be familiar to indigenous applicants);

(e) selection tests should be checked to ensure that they are related to the job's requirements, i.e., an individual's test markings should measure ability to do or train for the job in question.

Treatment of Applicants, Shortlisting, Interviewing and Selection

1.14 In order to avoid direct or indirect discrimination it is recommended that:

(a) gate, reception and personnel staff should be instructed not to treat casual or formal applicants from particular racial groups less favourably than others. These instructions should be confirmed in writing;

(b) in addition, staff responsible for shortlisting, interviewing and selecting candidates should be:

—clearly informed of selection criteria and of the need for their consistent application;

—given guidance or training on the effects which generalised assumptions and prejudices about race can have on selection decisions;

—made aware of the possible misunderstandings that can occur in interviews between persons of different cultural background;

(c) wherever possible, shortlisting and interviewing should not be done by one person alone but should at least be checked at a more senior level.

Genuine Occupational Qualification

1.15 *Selection on racial grounds is allowed in certain jobs where being of a particular racial group is a genuine occupational qualification for that job.* [s 5, s 5(2)(d)] An example is where the holder of a particular job provides persons of a racial group with personal services promoting their welfare, and those services can most effectively be provided by a person of that group.

Transfers and Training

1.16 In order to avoid direct or indirect discrimination it is recommended that [s 4(2)(b)]:

(a) staff responsible for selecting employees for transfer to other jobs should be instructed to apply selection criteria without unlawful discrimination;

(b) industry or company agreements and arrangements of custom and practice on job transfers should be examined and amended if they are found to contain requirements or conditions which appear to be indirectly discriminatory. For example, if employees of a particular racial group are concentrated in particular sections, the transfer arrangements should be examined to see if they are unjustifiably and unlawfuly restrictive and amended if necessary;

(c) staff responsible for selecting employees for training, whether induction, promotion or skill training should be instructed not to discriminate on racial grounds;

(d) selection criteria for training opportunities should be examined to ensure that they are not indirectly discriminatory.

Dismissal (including redundancy) and Other Detriment

1.17 *It is unlawful to discriminate on racial grounds in dismissal, or other detriment to an employee.* [s 4(2)(c)]

It is therefore recommended that:

(a) staff responsible for selecting employees for dismissal, including redundancy, should be instructed not to discriminate on racial grounds;

(b) selection criteria for redundancies should be examined to ensure that they are not indirectly discriminatory.

Performance Appraisals

1.18 *It is unlawful to discriminate on racial grounds in appraisals of employee performance.* [s 4(2)]

1.19 It is recommended that:

(a) staff responsible for performance appraisals should be instructed not to discriminate on racial grounds;

(b) assessment criteria should be examined to ensure that they are not unlawfully discriminatory.

Terms of Employment, Benefits, Facilities and Services s 4(2)

1.20 *It is unlawful to discriminate on racial grounds in affording terms of employment and providing benefits, facilities and services for employees.* It is therefore recommended that:

(a) all staff concerned with these aspects of employment should be instructed accordingly;

(b) the criteria governing eligibility should be examined to ensure that they are not unlawfully discriminatory.

1.21 In addition, employees may request extended leave from time to time in order to visit relations in their countries of origin or who have emigrated to other countries. Many employers have policies which allow annual leave entitlement to be accumulated, or extra unpaid leave to be taken to meet these circumstances. Employers should take care to apply such policies consistently and without unlawful discrimination.

Grievance, Disputes and Disciplinary Procedures s 4(2) & s 2

1.22 *It is unlawful to discriminate in the operation of grievance, disputes and disciplinary procedures,* for example by victimising an individual through disciplinary measures because he or she has complained about racial discrimination, or given evidence about such a complaint. Employers should not ignore or treat lightly grievances from members of particular racial groups on the assumption that they are over-sensitive about discrimination.

1.23 It is recommended that:
in applying disciplinary procedures consideration should be given to the possible effect on an employee's behaviour of the following:
—racial abuse or other racial provocation;
—communication and comprehension difficulties;
—differences in cultural background or behaviour.

Cultural and Religious Needs
1.24 Where employees have particular cultural and religious needs which conflict with existing work requirements, it is recommended that employers should consider whether it is reasonably practicable to vary or adapt these requirements to enable such needs to be met. For example, it is recommended that they should not refuse employment to a turbanned Sikh because he could not comply with unjustifiable uniform requirements. Other examples of such needs are:
(a) observance of prayer times and religions holidays;
(b) wearing of dress such as sarees and the trousers worn by Asian women.

1.25 *Although the Act does not specifically cover religious discrimination, work requirements would generally be unlawful if they have a disproportionately adverse effect on particular racial groups and cannot be shown to be justifiable.* [s 4(2) and s 28]

Communications and Language Training for Employees
1.26 Although there is no legal requirement to provide language training, difficulties in communication can endanger equal opportunity in the workforce. In addition, good communications can improve efficiency, promotion prospects and safety and health and create a better understanding between employers, employees and unions. Where the workforce includes current employees whose English is limited it is recommended that steps are taken to ensure that communications are as effective as possible.

1.27 These should include, where reasonably practicable:
(a) provision of interpretation and translation facilities, for example, in the communication of grievance and other procedures, and of terms of employment;
(b) training in English language and in communication skills;
(c) training for managers and supervisors in the background and culture of racial minority groups;
(d) the use of alternative or additional methods of communication, where employees find it difficult to understand health and safety requirements, for example:
—safety signs; translations of safety notices;
—instructions through interpreters;
—instruction combined with industrial language training.

Instructions and Pressure to Discriminate
1.28 *It is unlawful to instruct or put pressure on others to discriminate on racial grounds.*
(a) An example of an unlawful instruction is:
—an instruction from a personnel or line manager to junior staff to restrict the numbers of employees from a particular racial group in any particular work [s 30];
(b) An example of pressure to discriminate is:
—an attempt by a shop steward or group of workers to induce an employer not to recruit members of particular racial groups, for example by threatening industrial action. [s 31]

1.29 *It is also unlawful to discriminate in response to such instructions or pressure.*

1.30 The following recommendations are made to avoid unlawful instructions and pressure to discriminate:
(a) guidance should be given to all employees, and particularly those in positions of authority or influence on the relevant provisions of the law;

(b) decision-makers should be instructed not to give way to pressure to discriminate;

(c) giving instructions or bringing pressure to discriminate should be treated as a disciplinary offence.

Victimisation

1.31 *It is unlawful to victimise individuals who have made allegations or complaints of racial discrimination or provided information about such discrimination, for example, by disciplining them or dismissing them.* [s 2]

1.32 It is recommended that:
— guidance on this aspect of the law should be given to all employees and particularly to those in positions of influence or authority.

Monitoring Equal Opportunity

1.33 It is recommended that employers should regularly monitor the effects of selection decisions and personnel practices and procedures in order to assess whether equal opportunity is being achieved.

1.34 The information needed for effective monitoring may be obtained in a number of ways. It will best be provided by records showing the ethnic origins of existing employees and job applicants. It is recognised that the need for detailed information and the methods of collecting it will vary according to the circumstances of individual establishments. For example, in small firms or in firms in areas with little or no racial minority settlement it will often be adequate to assess the distribution of employees from personal knowledge and visual identification.

1.35 It is open to employers to adopt the method of monitoring which is best suited to their needs and circumstances, but whichever method is adopted, they should be able to show that it is effective. In order to achieve the full commitment of all concerned the chosen method should be discussed and agreed, where appropriate, with trade union or employee representatives.

1.36 Employers should ensure that information on individuals' ethnic origins is collected for the purpose of monitoring equal opportunity alone and is protected from misuse.

1.37 The following is the comprehensive method recommended by the CRE.
Analyses should be carried out of:

(a) the ethnic composition of the workforce of each plant, department, section, shift and job category, and changes in distribution over periods of time;

(b) selection decisions for recruitment, promotion, transfer and training, according to the racial group of candidates, and reasons for these decisions.

1.38 Except in cases where there are large numbers of applicants and the burden on resources would be excessive, reasons for selection and rejection should be recorded at each stage of the selection process, e.g., initial shortlisting and final decisions. Simple categories of reasons for rejection should be adequate for the early sifting stages.

1.39 Selection criteria and personnel procedures should be reviewed to ensure that they do not include requirements or conditions which constitute or may lead to unlawful indirect discrimination.

1.40 This information should be carefully and regularly analysed and, in order to identify areas which may need particular attention, a number of key questions should be asked.

1.41 Is there evidence that individuals from any particular racial group:

(a) do not apply for employment or promotion, or that fewer apply than might be expected?

(b) are not recruited or promoted at all, or are appointed in a significantly lower proportion than their rate of application?

(c) are under-represented in training or in jobs carrying higher pay, status or authority?

(d) are concentrated in certain shifts, sections or departments?

1.42 If the answer to any of these questions is yes, the reasons for this should be investigated. If direct or indirect discrimination is found action must be taken to end it immediately. [s 4 and s 28]

1.43 It is recommended that deliberate acts of unlawful discrimination by employees are treated as disciplinary offences.

Positive Action s 38

1.44 *Although they are not legally required, positive measures are allowed by the law to encourage employees and potential employees and provide training for employees who are members of particular racial groups which have been under-represented in particular work.* Discrimination at the point of selection for work, however, is not permissible in these circumstances.

1.45 Such measures are important for the development of equal opportunity. It is therefore recommended that, where there is under-representation of particular racial groups in particular work, the following measures should be taken wherever appropriate and reasonably practicable:

(a) job advertisements designed to reach members of these groups and to encourage their applications: for example, through the use of the ethnic minority press, as well as other newspapers;

(b) use of the employment agencies and careers offices in areas which these groups are concentrated;

(c) recruitment and training schemes for school leavers designed to reach members of these groups;

(d) encouragement to employees from these groups to apply for promotion or transfer opportunities;

(e) training for promotion or skill training for employees of these groups who lack particular expertise but show potential: supervisory training may include language training.

CODE OF PRACTICE FOR THE ELIMINATION OF DISCRIMINATION IN THE FIELD OF EMPLOYMENT AGAINST DISABLED PERSONS OR PERSONS WHO HAVE HAD A DISABILITY

4 The main employment provisions of the Act

DISCRIMINATION

What does the Act say about discrimination?

4.1 The Act makes it unlawful for an employer to discriminate against a disabled person in the field of employment (s. 4). The Act says 'discrimination' occurs in two ways.

4.2 One way in which discrimination occurs is when:

★ for a reason which relates to a disabled person's disability, the employer treats that disabled person less favourably than the employer treats or would treat others to whom the reason does not or would not apply; and

★ the employer cannot show that this treatment is justified (s. 5(1)).

A woman with a disability which requires use of a wheelchair applies for a job. She can do the job but the employer thinks the wheelchair will get in the way in the office. He gives the job to a person who is no more suitable for the job but who does not use a wheelchair. The employer has therefore treated the woman less favourably than the other person because he did not give her the job. The treatment was for a reason related to the disability - the fact that she used a wheelchair. And the reason for treating her less favourably did not apply to the other person because that person did not use a wheelchair.

If the employer could not justify his treatment of the disabled woman then he would have unlawfully discriminated against her.

An employer decides to close down a factory and makes all the employees redundant, including a disabled person who works there. This is not discrimination as the disabled employee is not being dismissed for a reason which relates to the disability.

4.3 A disabled person may not be able to point to other people who were actually treated more favourably. However, it is still 'less favourable treatment' if the employer would give better treatment to someone else to whom the reason for the treatment of the disabled person did not apply. This comparison can also be made with other disabled people, not just non-disabled people. For example, an employer might be discriminating by treating a person with a mental illness less favourably than he treats or would treat a physically disabled person.

4.4 The other way the Act says that discrimination occurs is when:

★ an employer fails to comply with a duty of reasonable adjustment imposed on him by section 6 in relation to the disabled person; and

★ he cannot show that this failure is justified (s. 5(2)).

4.5 [omitted]

What will, and what will not, be justified treatment?

4.6 *The Act says* that less favourable treatment of a disabled person will be justified only if the reason for it is both material to the circumstances of the particular case and substantial (s. 5(3)). This means that the reason has to relate to the individual circumstances in question and not just be trivial or minor.

Someone who is blind is not shortlisted for a job involving computers because the employer thinks blind people cannot use them. The employer makes no effort to look at the individual circumstances. A general assumption that blind people cannot use computers would not in itself be a material reason - it is not related to the particular circumstances.

A factory worker with a mental illness is sometimes away from work due to his disability. Because of that he is dismissed. However, the amount of time off is very little more than the employer accepts as sick leave for other employees and so is very unlikely to be a substantial reason.

A clerical worker with a learning disability cannot sort papers quite as quickly as some of his colleagues. There is very little difference in productivity but he is dismissed. That is very unlikely to be a substantial reason.

An employer seeking a clerical worker turns down an applicant with a severe facial disfigurement solely on the ground that other employees would be uncomfortable working alongside him. This will be unlawful because such a reaction by other employees will not in itself justify less favourable treatment of this sort - it is not substantial. The same would apply if it were thought that a customer would feel uncomfortable.

An employer moves someone with a mental illness to a different workplace solely because he mutters to himself while he works. If the employer accepts similar levels of noise from other people, the treatment of the disabled person would probably be unjustified — that level of noise is unlikely to be a substantial reason.

Someone who has psoriasis (a skin condition) is rejected for a job involving modelling cosmetics on a part of the body which in his case is severely disfigured by the condition. That would be lawful if his appearance would be incompatible with the purpose of the work. This is a substantial reason which is clearly related — material — to the individual circumstance.

4.7 *The Act says* that less favourable treatment cannot be justified where the employer is under a duty to make a reasonable adjustment but fails (without justification) to do so, unless the treatment would have been justified even after that adjustment (s. 5(5)).

An employee who uses a wheelchair is not promoted, solely because the work station for the higher post is inaccessible to wheelchairs - though it could readily be made so by rearrangement of the furniture. If the furniture had been rearranged, the reason for refusing promotion would not have applied. The refusal of promotion would therefore not be justified.

An applicant for a typing job is not the best person on the face of it, but only because her typing speed is too slow due to arthritis in her hands. If a reasonable adjustment - perhaps an adapted keyboard - would overcome this, her typing speed would not in itself be a substantial reason for not employing her. Therefore the employer would be unlawfully discriminating if on account of her typing speed he did not employ her and provide the adjustment.

An employer refuses a training course for an employee with an illness which is very likely to be terminal within a year because, even with a reasonable adjustment to help in the job after the course, the benefits of the course could not be adequately realised. This is very likely to be a substantial reason. It is clearly material to the circumstances. The refusal of training would therefore very likely be justified.

Someone who is blind applies for a job which requires a significant amount of driving. If it is not reasonable for the employer to adjust the job so that the driving duties are given to someone else, the employer's need for a driver might well be a substantial reason for not employing the blind person. It is clearly material to the particular circumstances. The non-appointment could therefore be justified.

4.8-4.11 [omitted]

REASONABLE ADJUSTMENT

What does the Act say about the duty of 'reasonable adjustment'?

4.12 *The Act says* that the duty applies where any physical feature of premises occupied by the employer, or any arrangements made by or on behalf of the employer, cause a substantial disadvantage to a disabled person compared with non-disabled people. An employer has to take such steps as it is reasonable for him to have to take in all the circumstances to prevent that disadvantage — in other words the employer has to make a 'reasonable adjustment' (s. 6(1)).

A man who is disabled by dyslexia applies for a job which involves writing letters within fairly long deadlines. The employer gives all applicants a test of their letter-writing ability. The man can generally write letters very well but finds it difficult to do so in stressful situations. The employer's arrangements would mean he had to begin his test immediately on arrival and to do it in a short time. He would be substantially disadvantaged compared to non-disabled people who would not find such arrangements stressful or, if they did, would not be so affected by them. The employer therefore gives him a little time to settle in and longer to write the letter. These new arrangements do not inconvenience the employer very much and only briefly delay the decision on an appointment. These are steps that it is reasonable for the employer to have to take in the circumstances to prevent the disadvantage — a 'reasonable adjustment'.

4.13-4.16 [omitted]

What 'disadvantages' give rise to the duty?
4.17 *The Act says* that only substantial disadvantages give rise to the duty (s. 6(1)). Substantial disadvantages are those which are not minor or trivial.

An employer is unlikely to be required to widen a particular doorway to enable passage by an employee using a wheelchair if there is an easy alternative route to the same destination.

4.18 An employer cannot be required to prevent a disadvantage caused by premises or by non-pay arrangements by increasing the disabled person's pay.

4.19 [omitted]

What adjustments might an employer have to make?
4.20 The Act gives a number of examples of 'steps' which employers may have to take, if it is reasonable for them to have to do so in all the circumstances of the case (s. 6(3)). Steps other than those listed here, or a combination of steps, will sometimes have to be taken. The steps in the Act are:

★ *making adjustments to premises*
An employer might have to make structural or other physical changes such as: widening a doorway, providing a ramp or moving furniture for a wheelchair user; relocating light switches, door handles or shelves for someone who has difficulty in reaching; providing appropriate contrast in décor to help the safe mobility of a visually impaired person.

★ *allocating some of the disabled person's duties to another person*
Minor or subsidiary duties might be reallocated to another employee if the disabled person has difficulty in doing them because of the disability. For example, if a job occasionally involves going onto the open roof of a building an employer might have to transfer this work away from an employee whose disability involves severe vertigo.

★ *transferring the person to fill an existing vacancy*
If an employee becomes disabled, or has a disability which worsens so she cannot work in the same place or under the same arrangements and there is no reasonable adjustment which would enable the employee to continue doing the current job, then she might have to be considered for any suitable alternative posts which are available. (Such a case might also involve reasonable retraining.)

★ *altering the person's working hours*
This could include allowing the disabled person to work flexible hours to enable additional breaks to overcome fatigue arising from the disability, or changing the disabled person's hours to fit with the availability of a carer.

★ *assigning the person to a different place of work*
This could mean transferring a wheelchair user's work station from an inaccessible third floor office to an accessible one on the ground floor. It could mean moving the person to other premises of the same employer if the first building is inaccessible.

★ *allowing the person to be absent during working hours for rehabilitation, assessment or treatment*
For example, if a person were to become disabled, the employer might have to allow the person more time off during work, than would be allowed to non-disabled employees, to receive physiotherapy or psychoanalysis or undertake employment rehabilitation. A similar adjustment might be appropriate if a disability worsens or if a disabled person needs occasional treatment anyway.

★ *giving the person, or arranging for him to be given, training*
This could be training in the use of particular pieces of equipment unique to the disabled person, or training appropriate for all employees but which needs altering for the disabled person because of the disability. For example, all employees might need to be trained in the use of a particular machine but an employer might have to provide slightly different or longer training for an employee with restricted hand or arm movements, or training in additional software for a visual impaired person so that he can use a computer with speech output.

★ *acquiring or modifying equipment*
An employer might have to provide special equipment (such as an adapted keyboard for a visually impaired person or someone with arthritis), or an adapted telephone for someone with a hearing impairment or modified equipment (such as longer handles on a machine). There is no requirement to provide or modify equipment for personal purposes unconnected with work, such as providing a wheelchair if a person needs one in any event but does not have one: the disadvantage in such a case does not flow from the employer's arrangements or premises.

★ *modifying instructions or reference manuals*
The way instruction is normally given to employees might need to be revised when telling a disabled person how to do a task. The format of instructions or manuals may need to be modified (e.g., produced in braille or on audio tape) and instructions for people with learning disabilities may need to be conveyed orally with individual demonstration.

★ *modifying procedures for testing or assessment*
This could involve ensuring that particular tests do not adversely affect people with particular types of disability. For example, a person with restricted manual dexterity might be disadvantaged by a written test, so an employer might have to give that person an oral test.

★ *providing a reader or interpreter*
This could involve a colleague reading mail to a person with a visual impairment at particular times during the working day or, in appropriate circumstances, the hiring of a reader or sign language interpreter.

★ *providing supervision*
This could involve the provision of a support worker, or help from a colleague, in appropriate circumstances, for someone whose disability leads to uncertainty or lack of confidence.

When is it 'reasonable' for an employer to have to make an adjustment?

4.21 Effective and practicable adjustments for disabled people often involve little or no cost or disruption and are therefore very likely to be reasonable for an employer to have to make. The Act lists a number of factors which may, in particular, have a bearing on whether it will be reasonable for the employer to have to make a particular adjustment (s. 6(4)). These factors make a useful checklist, particularly when considering more substantial adjustments. The effectiveness and practicability of a particular adjustment might be considered first. If it is practicable and effective, the financial aspects might be looked at as a whole — cost of the adjustment and resources available to fund it. Other factors might also have a bearing. The factors in the Act are listed below.

The effectiveness of the step in preventing the disadvantage

4.22 It is unlikely to be reasonable for an employer to have to make an adjustment involving little benefit to the disabled employee.

> A disabled person is significantly less productive than his colleagues and so is paid less. A particular adjustment would improve his output and thus his pay. It is more likely to be reasonable for the employer to have to make that adjustment if it would significantly improve his pay, than if the adjustment would make only a relatively small improvement.

The practicability of the step

4.23 It is more likely to be reasonable for an employer to have to take a step which is easy to take than one which is difficult.

> It might be impracticable for an employer who needs to appoint an employee urgently to have to wait for an adjustment to be made to an entrance. How long it might be reasonable for the employer to have to wait would depend on the circumstances. However, it might be possible to make a temporary adjustment in the meantime, such as using another, less convenient entrance.

The financial and other costs of the adjustment and the extent of any disruption caused

4.24 If an adjustment costs little or nothing and is not disruptive, it would be reasonable unless some other factor (such as practicability or effectiveness) made it unreasonable. The costs to be taken into account include staff and other resources costs. The significance of the cost of a step may depend in part on what the employer might otherwise spend in the circumstances.

> It would be reasonable for an employer to have to spend at least as much on an adjustment to enable the retention of a disabled person — including any retraining — as might be spent on recruiting and training a replacement.

4.25 The significance of the cost of a step may also depend in part on the value of the employee's experience and expertise to the employer.

> Examples of the factors that might be considered as relating to the value of an employee would include:
> — the amount of resources (such as training) invested in the individual by the employer;
> — the employee's length of service;
> — the employee's level of skill and knowledge;
> — the employee's quality of relationships with clients;
> — the level of the employee's pay.

4.26 It is more likely to be reasonable for an employer to have to make an adjustment with significant costs for an employee who is likely to be in the job for some time than for a temporary employee.

4.27 An employer is more likely to have to make an adjustment which might cause only minor inconvenience to other employees or the employer than one which might unavoidably prevent other employees from doing their job, or cause other significant disruption.

The extent of the employer's financial or other resources

4.28 It is more likely to be reasonable for an employer with substantial financial resources to have to make an adjustment with a significant cost, than for an employer with fewer resources. The resources in practice available to the employer as a whole should be taken into account as well as other calls on those resources. The reasonableness of an adjustment will depend, however, not only on the resources in practice available for the adjustment but also on all other relevant factors (such as effectiveness and practicability).

4.29 Where the resources of the employer are spread across more than one 'business unit' or 'profit centre' the calls on them should also be taken into account in assessing reasonableness.

> A large retailer probably could not show that the limited resources for which an individual shop manager is responsible meant it was not reasonable for the retailer to have to make an adjustment at the ship. Such an employer may, however, have a number — perhaps a large number — of other disabled employees in other shops. The employer's expenditure on other adjustments, or his potential expenditure on similar adjustments for other existing disabled employees, might then be taken into account in assessing the reasonableness of having to make a new adjustment for the disabled employee in question.

4.30 It is more likely to be reasonable for an employer with a substantial number of staff to have to make certain adjustments, than for a smaller employer.

> It would generally be reasonable for an employer with many staff to have to make significant efforts to reallocate duties, identify a suitable alternative post or provide supervision from existing staff. It could also be reasonable for a small company covered by the Act to have to make any of these adjustments but not if it involved disproportionate effort.

The availability to the employer of financial or other assistance to help make an adjustment

4.31 The availability of outside help may well be a relevant factor.

> An employer, in recruiting a disabled person, finds that the only feasible adjustment is too costly for him alone. However, if assistance is available e.g., from a Government programme or voluntary body, it may well be reasonable for him to have to make the adjustment after all.

A disabled person is not required to contribute to the cost of a reasonable adjustment. However, if a disabled person has a particular piece of special or adapted equipment which he is prepared to use for work, this might make it reasonable for the employer to have to take some other step (as well as allowing use of the equipment).

> An employer requires his employees to use company cars for all business travel. One employee's disability means she would have to use an adapted car or an alternative form of transport. If she has an adapted car of her own which she is willing to use on business, it might well be reasonable for the employer to have to allow this and pay her an allowance to cover the cost of doing so, even if it would not have been reasonable for him to have to provide an adapted company car, or to pay an allowance to cover alternative travel arrangements in the absence of an adapted car.

Other factors

4.32 Although the Act does not mention any further factors, others might be relevant depending on the circumstances. For example:

★ *effect on other employees*
Employees' adverse reaction to an adjustment being made for the disabled employee which involves something they too would like (such as a special working arrangement) is unlikely to be significant.

★ *adjustments made for other disabled employees*
An employer may choose to give a particular disabled employee, or group of disabled employees, an adjustment which goes beyond the duty — that is, which is more than it is reasonable for him to have to do. This would not mean he necessarily had to provide a similar adjustment for other employees with a similar disability.

★ *the extent to which the disabled person is willing to cooperate*
An employee with a mobility impairment works in a team located on an upper floor, to which there is no access by lift. Getting there is very tiring for the employee, and the employer could easily make a more accessible location available for him (though the whole team could not be relocated). If that was the only adjustment which it would be reasonable for the employer to have to make but the employee refused to work there then the employer would not have to make any adjustment at all.

Could an employer have to make more than one adjustment?
4.33 Yes, if it is reasonable for the employer to have to make more than one.

A woman who is deafblind is given a new job with her employer in an unfamiliar part of the building. The employer (i) arranges facilities for her guide dog in the new area, (ii) arranges for her new instructions to be in Braille and (iii) suggests to visitors ways in which they can communicate with her.

Does an employer have to justify not making an adjustment?
4.34 *The Act says* that it is discrimination if an employer fails to take a step which it is reasonable for him to have to take, and he cannot justify that failure (s. 5(2)). However, if it is unreasonable (under s. 6) for an employer to have to make any, or a particular, adjustment, he would not then also have to justify (under s. 5) not doing so. Failure to comply with the duty of reasonable adjustment can only be justified if the reason for the failure is material to the circumstances of the particular case and substantial (s. 5(4)).

An employer might not make an adjustment which it was reasonable for him to have to make because of ignorance or wrong information about appropriate adjustments or about the availability of help with making an adjustment. He would then need to justify failing in his duty. It is unlikely that he could do so unless he had made a reasonable effort to obtain good information from a reputable source such as contacting the local Placing Assessment and Counselling Team or an appropriate disability organisation.

If either of two possible adjustments would remove a disadvantage, but the employer has cost or operational reasons for preferring one rather than the other, it is unlikely to be reasonable for him to have to make the one that is not preferred. If, however, the employee refuses to cooperate with the proposed adjustment the employer is likely to be justified in not providing it.

A disabled employee refuses to follow specific occupational medical advice provided on behalf of an employer about methods of working or managing his condition at work. If he has no good reason for this and his condition deteriorates as a result, the refusal may justify the employer's subsequent failure to make an adjustment for the worsened condition.

4.35-6.18 [omitted]

Retention of disabled employees

6.19 An employer must not discriminate against an employee who becomes disabled, or has a disability which worsens (s. 4(2)). The issue of retention might also arise when an employee has a stable impairment but the nature of his employment changes.

6.20 If as a result of the disability an employer's arrangements or a physical feature of the employer's premises place the employee at a substantial disadvantage in doing his existing job, the employer must first consider any reasonable adjustment that would resolve the difficulty. The employer may also need to consult the disabled person at appropriate stages about what his needs are and what effect the disability might have on future employment, for example, where the employee has a progressive condition. The nature of the reasonable adjustments which an employer may have to consider will depend on the circumstances of the case.

It may be possible to modify a job to accommodate an employee's changed needs. This might be by rearranging working methods or giving another employee certain minor tasks the newly disabled person can no longer do, providing practical aids or adaptations to premises or equipment, or allowing the disabled person to work at different times or places from those with equivalent jobs (for instance, it may be that a change to part-time work might be appropriate for someone who needed to spend some time each week having medical treatment).

A newly disabled employee is likely to need time to readjust. For example, an employer might allow: a trial period to assess whether the employee is able to cope with the current job, or a new one; the employee initially to work from home; a gradual build-up to full time hours; or additional training for a person with learning disabilities who moves to another workplace.

It may be a reasonable adjustment for an employer to move a newly disabled person to a different post within the organisation if a suitable vacancy exists or is expected shortly.

Additional job coaching may be necessary to enable a disabled person to take on a new job.

In many cases where no reasonable adjustment would overcome a particular disability so as to enable the disabled person to continue with similar terms or conditions, it might be reasonable for the employer to have to offer a disabled employee a lower-paying job, applying the rate of pay that would apply to such a position under his usual pay practices.

If new technology (for instance a telephone or information technology system) puts a disabled person at a substantial disadvantage compared with non-disabled people, then the employer would be under a duty to make a reasonable adjustment. For example, some telephone systems may interfere with hearing aids for people with hearing impairments and the quality of the inductive coupler may need to be improved.

Termination of employment

6.21 Dismissal — including compulsory early retirement — of a disabled person for a reason relating to the disability would need to be justified and the reason for it would have to be one which could not be removed by any reasonable adjustment.

It would be justifiable to terminate the employment of an employee whose disability makes it impossible for him any longer to perform the main functions of his job, if an adjustment such as a move to a vacant post elsewhere in the business is not practicable or otherwise not reasonable for the employer to have to make.

It would be justifiable to terminate the employment of an employee with a worsening progressive condition if the increasing degree of adjustment necessary to accommodate the effects of the condition (shorter hours of work or falling productivity, say) became unreasonable for the employer to have to make.

An employer who needs to reduce the workforce would have to ensure that any scheme which was introduced for choosing candidates for redundancy did not discriminate against disabled people. Therefore, if a criterion for redundancy would apply to a disabled person for a reason relating to the disability, that criterion would have to be 'material' and 'substantial' and the employer would have to consider whether a reasonable adjustment would prevent the criterion applying to the disabled person after all.

HARASSMENT

What does the Act say about harassment?
6.22 The Act does not refer to harassment as a separate issue. However, harassing a disabled person on account of a disability will almost always amount to a 'detriment' under the Act. (Victimisation is covered in paragraphs 4.53-4.54).

Are employers liable for harassment by the employees?
6.23 An employer is responsible for acts of harassment by employees in the course of their employment unless the employer took such steps as were reasonably practicable to prevent it. As a minimum first step harassment because of disability should be made a disciplinary matter and staff should be made aware that it will be taken seriously.

7.1-8.3 and annexes [omitted]

EUROPEAN COMMUNITY MATERIALS

TREATY OF ROME

Note: the following Articles are as amended and re-numbered by the Treaty of Amsterdam.

Article 12 (ex Article 6)

Within the scope of application of this Treaty, and without prejudice to any special provisions contained therein, any discrimination on grounds of nationality shall be prohibited.

The Council, acting in accordance with the procedure referred to in Article 251, may adopt rules designed to prohibit such discrimination.

Article 39 (ex Article 48)

1. Freedom of movement for workers shall be secured within the Community.

2. Such freedom of movement shall entail the abolition of any discrimination based on nationality between workers of the Member States as regards employment, remuneration and other conditions of work and employment.

3. It shall entail the right, subject to limitations justified on grounds of public policy, public security or public health:

(a) to accept offers of employment actually made;

(b) to move freely within the territory of Member States for this purpose;

(c) to stay in a Member State for the purpose of employment in accordance with the provisions governing the employment of nationals of that State laid down by law, regulation or administrative action;

(d) to remain in the territory of a Member State after having been employed in that State, subject to conditions which shall be embodied in implementing regulations to be drawn up by the Commission.

4. The provisions of this Article shall not apply to employment in the public service.

Article 40 (ex Article 49)

The Council shall, acting in accordance with the procedure referred to in Article 251 and after consulting the Economic and Social Committee, issue directives or make regulations setting out the measures required to bring about freedom of movement for workers, as defined in Article 39, in particular:

(a) by ensuring close co-operation between national employment services;

(b) by abolishing those administrative procedures and practices and those qualifying periods in respect of eligibility for available employment, whether resulting from national legislation or from agreements previously concluded between Member States, the maintenance of which would form an obstacle to liberalisation of the movement of workers;

(c) by abolishing all such qualifying periods and other restrictions provided for either under national legislation or under agreements previously concluded between

Member States as impose on workers of other Member States conditions regarding the free choice of employment other than those imposed on workers of the State concerned;

(d) by setting up appropriate machinery to bring offers of employment into touch with applications for employment and to facilitate the achievement of a balance between supply and demand in the employment market in such a way as to avoid serious threats to the standard of living and level of employment in the various regions and industries.

Article 136 (ex Article 117)

The Community and the Member States, having in mind fundamental social rights such as those set out in the European Social Charter signed at Turin on 18 October 1961 and in the 1989 Community Charter of the Fundamental Social Rights of Workers, shall have as their objectives the promotion of employment, improved living and working conditions, so as to make possible their harmonisation while the improvement is being maintained, proper social protection, dialogue between management and labour, the development of human resources with a view to lasting high employment and the combating of exclusion.

To this end the Community and the Member States shall implement measures which take account of the diverse forms of national practices, in particular in the field of contractual relations, and the need to maintain the competitiveness of the Community economy.

They believe that such a development will ensue not only from the functioning of the common market, which will favour the harmonisation of social systems, but also from the procedures provided for in this Treaty and from the approximation of provisions laid down by law, regulation or administrative action.

Article 137 (ex Article 118)

1. With a view to achieving the objectives of Article 136, the Community shall support and complement the activities of the Member States in the following fields:

—improvement in particular of the working environment to protect workers' health and safety;

—working conditions;

—the information and consultation of workers;

—the integration of persons excluded from the labour market, with prejudice to Article 150;

—equality between men and women with regard to labout market opportunities and treatment at work.

2. To this end, the Council may adopt, by means of directives, minimum requirements for gradual implementation, having regard to the conditions and technical rules obtaining in each of the Member States. Such directives shall avoid imposing administrative, financial and legal constraints in a way which would hold back the creation and development of small and medium-sized undertakings.

The Council shall act in accordance with the procedure referred to in Article 251 after consulting the Economic and Social Committee and the Committee of the Regions.

The Council, acting in accordance with the same procedure, may adopt measures designed to encourage cooperation between Member States through initiatives aimed at improving knowledge, developing exchanges of information and best practices, promoting innovative approaches and evaluating experiences in order to combat social exclusion.

(3) However, the Council shall act unanimously on a proposal from the Commission, after consulting the European Parliament, the Economic and Social Committee and the Committee of the Regions in the following areas:

—social security and social protection of workers;

—protection of workers where their employment contract is terminated;

—representation and collective defence of the interests of workers and employers, including co-determination, subject to paragraph 6;
—conditions of employment for third-country nationals legally residing in Community territory;
—financial contributions for promotion of employment and job-creation, without prejudice to the provisions relating to the Social Fund.

4. A Member State may entrust management and labour, at their joint request, with the implementation of directives adopted pursuant to paragraphs 2 and 3.

In this case, it shall ensure that, no later than the date on which a directive must be transposed in accordance with Article 249, management and labour have introduced the necessary measures by agreement, the Member State concerned being required to take any necessary measure enabling it at any time to be in a position to guarantee the results imposed by that directive.

5. The provisions adopted pursuant to this Article shall not prevent any Member State from maintaining or introducing more stringent protective measures compatible with this Treaty.

6. The provisions of this Article shall not apply to pay, the right of association, the right to strike or the right to impose lock-outs.

Article 138 (ex Article 118a)

1. The Commission shall have the task of promoting the consultation of management and labour at Community level and shall take any relevant measure to facilitate their dialogue by ensuring balanced support for the parties.

2. To this end, before submitting proposals in the social policy field, the Commission shall consult management and labour on the possible direction of Community action.

3. If, after such consultation, the Commission considers Community action advisable, it shall consult management and labour on the content of the envisaged proposal. Management and labour shall forward to the Commission an opinion or, where appropriate, a recommendation.

4. On the occasion of such consultation, management and labour may inform the Commission of their wish to initiate the process provided for in Article 139. The duration of the procedure shall not exceed nine months, unless the management and labour concerned and the Commission decide jointly to extend it.

Article 139 (ex Article 118b)

1. Should management and labour so desire, the dialogue between them at Community level may lead to contractual relations, including agreements.

2. Agreements concluded at Community level shall be implemented either in accordance with the procedures and practices specific to management and labour and the Member States or, in matters covered by Article 137, at the joint request of the signatory parties, by a Council decision on a proposal from the Commission.

The Council shall act by qualified majority, except where the agreement in question contains one or more provisions relating to one of the areas referred to in Article 137(3), in which case it shall act unanimously.

Article 140 (ex Article 118c)

With a view to achieving the objectives of Article 136 and without prejudice to the other provisions of this Treaty, the Commission shall encourage cooperation between the Member States and facilitate the coordination of their action in all social policy fields under this chapter, particularly in matters relating to

—employment;
—labour law and working conditions;
—basic and advanced vocational training;

—social security;
—prevention of occupational accidents and diseases;
—occupational hygiene;
—the right of association and collective bargaining between employers and workers.

To this end, the Commission shall act in close contact with Member States by making studies, delivering opinions and arranging consultations both on problems arising at national level and on those of concern to international organisations.

Before delivering the opinions provided for in this Article, the Commission shall consult the Economic and Social Committee.

Article 141 (ex Article 119)

1. Each Member State shall ensure that the principle of equal pay for male and female workers for equal work or work of equal value is applied.

2. For the purpose of this Article 'pay' means the ordinary basic or minimum wage or salary and any other consideration, whether in cash or in kind, which the worker receives directly or indirectly, in respect of his empoyment, from his employer.

Equal pay without discrimination based on sex means:

(a) that pay for the same work at piece rates shall be calculated on the basis of the same unit of measurement;

(b) that pay for work at time rates shall be the same for the same job.

3. The Council, acting in accordance with the procedure referred to in Article 251, and after consulting the Economic and Social Committee, shall adopt measures to ensure the application of the principle of equal opportunities and equal treatment of men and women in matters of employment and occupation, including the principle of equal pay for equal work or work of equal value.

4. With a view to ensuring full equality in practice between men and women in working life, the principle of equal treatment shall not prevent any Member State from maintaining or adopting measures providing for specific advantages in order to make it easier for the under-represented sex to pursue a vocational activity or to prevent or compensate for disadvantages in professional careers.

Article 142 (ex Article 119a)

Member States shall endeavour to maintain the existing equivalence between paid holiday schemes.

TREATY ON EUROPEAN UNION (THE MAASTRICHT TREATY) (O.J. 1992, C/224)

on social policy concluded between the Member States of the European Community

Article 1

The Community and the Member States shall have as their objectives the promotion of employment, improved living and working conditions, proper social protection, dialogue between management and labour, the development of human resources with a view to lasting high employment and the combatting of exclusion. To this end the Community and the Member States shall implement measures which take account of the diverse forms of national practices, in particular in the field of contractual relations, and the need to maintain the competitiveness of the Community economy.

Article 2

1. With a view to achieving the objectives of Article 1, the Community shall support and complement the activities of the Member States in the following fields:

—improvement in particular of the working environment to protect workers' health and safety;

—working conditions;
—the information and consultation of workers;
—equality between men and women with regard to labour market opportunities and treatment at work;
—the integration of persons excluded from the labour market, without prejudice to Article 127 of the Treaty establishing the European Community (hereinafter referred to as 'the Treaty').

2. To this end, the Council may adopt, by means of directives, minimum requirements for gradual implementation, having regard to the conditions and technical rules obtaining in each of the Member States. Such directives shall avoid imposing administrative, financial and legal constraints in a way which would hold back the creation and development of small and medium-sized undertakings.

The Council shall act in accordance with the procedure referred to in Article 189c of the Treaty after consulting the Economic and Social Committee.

3. However, the Council shall act unanimously on a proposal from the Commission, after consulting the European Parliament and the Economic and Social Committee, in the following areas:
—social security and social protection of workers;
—protection of workers where their employment contract is terminated;
—representation and collective defence of the interests of workers and employers, including co-determination, subject to paragraph 6;
—conditions of employment for third-country nationals legally residing in Community territory;
—financial contributions for promotion of employment and job-creation, without prejudice to the provisions relating to the Social Fund.

4. A Member State may entrust management and labour, at their joint request, with the implementation of directives adopted pursuant to paragraphs 2 and 3.

In this case, it shall ensure that, no later than the date on which a directive must be transposed in accordance with Article 189, management and labour have introduced the necessary measures by agreement, the Member State concerned being required to take any necessary measure enabling it at any time to be in a position to guarantee the results imposed by that directive.

5. The provisions adopted pursuant to this Article shall not prevent any Member State from maintaining or introducing more stringent protective measures compatible with the Treaty.

6. The provisions of this Article shall not apply to pay, the right of association, the right to strike or the right to impose lock-outs.

Article 3

1. The Commission shall have the task of promoting the consultation of management and labour at Community level and shall take any relevant measure to facilitate their dialogue by ensuring balanced support for the parties.

2. To this end, before submitting proposals in the social policy field, the Commission shall consult management and labour on the possible direction of Community action.

3. If, after such consultation, the Commission considers Community action advisable, it shall consult management and labour on the content of the envisaged proposal. Management and labour shall forward to the Commission an opinion or, where appropriate, a recommendation.

4. On the occasion of such consultation, management and labour may inform the Commission of their wish to initiate the process provided for in Article 4. The duration of the procedure shall not exceed nine months, unless the management and labour concerned and the Commission decide jointly to extend it.

Article 4

1. Should management and labour so desire, the dialogue between them at Community level may lead to contractual relations, including agreements.

2. Agreements concluded at Community level shall be implemented either in accordance with the procedures and practices specific to management and labour and the Member States or, in matters covered by Article 2, at the joint request of the signatory parties, by a Council decision on a proposal from the Commission.

The Council shall act by qualified majority, except where the agreement in question contains one or more provisions relating to one of the areas referred to in Article 2(3), in which case it shall act unanimously.

Article 5

With a view to achieving the objectives of Article 1 and without prejudice to the other provisions of the Treaty, the Commission shall encourage cooperation between the Member States and facilitate the coordination of their action in all social policy fields under this Agreement.

Article 6

1. Each Member State shall ensure that the principle of equal pay for male and female workers for equal work is applied.

2. For the purpose of this Article, 'pay' means the ordinary basic or minimum wage or salary and any other consideration, whether in cash or in kind, which the worker receives directly or indirectly, in respect of his employment, from his employer.

Equal pay without discrimination based on sex means:

(a) that pay for the same work at piece rates shall be calculated on the basis of the same unit of measurement;

(b) that pay for work at time rates shall be the same for the same job.

3. This Article shall not prevent any Member State from maintaining or adopting measures providing for specific advantages in order to make it easier for women to pursue a vocational activity or to prevent or compensate for disadvantages in their professional careers.

Article 7

The Commission shall draw up a report each year on progress in achieving the objectives of Article 1, including the demographic situation in the Community. It shall forward the report to the European Parliament, the Council and the Economic and Social Committee.

The European Parliament may invite the Commission to draw up reports on particular problems concerning the social situation.

Declarations

1. Declaration on Article 2(2)

The eleven High Contracting Parties note that in the discussions on Article 2(2) of the Agreement it was agreed that the Community does not intend, in laying down minimum requirements for the protection of the safety and health of employees, to discriminate in a manner unjustified by the circumstances against employees in small and medium-sized undertakings.

2. Declaration on Article 4(2)

The eleven High Contracting Parties declare that the first of the arrangements for application of the agreements between management and labour at Community level — referred to in Article 4(2) — will consist in developing, by collective bargaining according to the rules of each Member State, the content of the agreements, and that consequently this arrangement implies no obligation on the Member States to apply the agreements directly or to work out rules for their transposition, nor any obligation to amend national legislation in force to facilitate their implementation.

COUNCIL REGULATION No. 1612/68 (O.J. 1968/475)

on Freedom of Movement for Workers within the Community

Part I—Employment and Workers' Families
Title I—Eligibility for Employment

Article 1

1. Any national of a Member State, shall irrespective of his place of residence, have the right to take up an activity as an employed person, and to pursue such activity, within the territory of another Member State in accordance with the provisions laid down by law, regulation or administrative action governing the employment of nationals of that State.

2. He shall, in particular, have the right to take up available employment in the territory of another Member State with the same priority as nationals of that State.

Article 2

Any national of a Member State and any employer pursuing an activity in the territory of a Member State may exchange their applications for and offers of employment, and may conclude and perform contracts of employment in accordance with the provisions in force laid down by law, regulation or administrative action, without any discrimination resulting therefrom.

Article 3

1. Under this Regulation, provisions laid down by law, regulation or administrative action or administrative practices of a Member State shall not apply:

- where they limit application for and offers of employment, or the right of foreign nationals to take up and pursue employment or subject these to conditions not applicable in respect of their own nationals; or
- where, though applicable irrespective of nationality, their exclusive or principal aim or effect is to keep nationals of other Member States away from the employment offered.

This provision shall not apply to conditions relating to linguistic knowledge required by reason of the nature of the post to be filled.

2. There shall be included in particular among the provisions or practices of a Member State referred to in the first subparagraph of paragraph 1 those which:

(a) prescribe a special recruitment procedure for foreign nationals;

(b) limit or restrict the advertising of vacancies in the press or through any other medium or subject it to conditions other than those applicable in respect of employers pursuing their activities in the territory of that Member State;

(c) subject eligibility for employment to conditions of registration with employment offices or impede recruitment of individual workers, where persons who do not reside in the territory of that State are concerned.

Article 4

1. Provisions laid down by law, regulation or administrative action of the Member States which restrict by number or percentage the employment of foreign nationals in any undertaking, branch of activity or region, or at a national level, shall not apply to nationals of the other Member States.

2. When in a Member State the granting of any benefit to undertakings is subject to a minimum percentage of national workers being employed, nationals of the other Member States shall be counted as national workers, subject to the provisions of the Council Directive of October 15, 1963 (J.O. 1963, 2661).

Article 5

A national of a Member State who seeks employment in the territory of another Member State shall receive the same assistance there as that afforded by the employment offices in that State to their own nationals seeking employment.

Article 6

1. The engagement and recruitment of a national of one Member State for a post in another Member State shall not depend on medical, vocational or other criteria which are discriminatory on grounds of nationality by comparison with those applied to nationals of the other Member State who wish to pursue the same activity.

2. Nevertheless, a national who holds an offer in his name from an employer in a Member State other than that of which he is a national may have to undergo a vocational test, if the employer expressly requests this when making his offer of employment.

Title II—Employment and Equality of Treatment

Article 7

1. A worker who is a national of a Member State may not, in the territory of another Member State, be treated differently from national workers by reason of his nationality in respect of any conditions of employment and work, in particular as regards remuneration, dismissal, and should he become unemployed, reinstatement or re-employment.

2. He shall enjoy the same social and tax advantages as national workers.

3. He shall also, by virtue of the same right and under the same conditions as national workers, have access to training in vocational schools and retraining centres.

4. Any clause of a collective or individual agreement or of any other collective regulation concerning eligibility for employment, remuneration and other conditions of work or dismissal shall be null and void in so far as it lays down or authorises discriminatory conditions in respect of workers who are nationals of the other Member States.

Article 8

1. A worker who is a national of a Member State and who is employed in the territory of another Member State shall enjoy equality of treatment as regards membership of trade unions and the exercise of rights attaching thereto, including the right to vote and to be eligible for the administrative or management posts of a trade union; he may be excluded from taking part in the management of bodies governed by public law and from holding an office governed by public law. Furthermore, he shall have the right of eligibility for workers' representative bodies in the undertaking. The provisions of this Article shall not affect laws or regulations in certain Member States which grant more extensive rights to workers coming from the other Member States.

Article 9

1. A worker who is a national of a Member State and who is employed in the territory of another Member State shall enjoy all the rights and benefits accorded to national workers in matters of housing, including ownership of the housing he needs.

2. Such worker may, with the same right as nationals, put his name down on the housing lists in the region in which he is employed, where such lists exist; he shall enjoy the resultant benefits and priorities.

If his family has remained in the country whence he came, they shall be considered for this purpose as residing in the said region, where national workers benefit from a similar presumption.

Title III—Workers' Families

Article 10

1. The following shall, irrespective of their nationality, have the right to install themselves with a worker who is a national of one Member State and who is employed in the territory of another Member State:

(a) his spouse and their descendants who are under the age of 21 years or are dependants;

(b) dependent relatives in the ascending line of the worker and his spouse.

2. Member States shall facilitate the admission of any member of the family not coming within the provisions of paragraph 1 if dependent on the worker referred to above or living under his roof in the country whence he comes.

3. For the purposes of paragraphs 1 and 2, the worker must have available for his family housing considered as normal for national workers in the region where he is employed; this provision, however, must not give rise to discrimination between national workers and workers from the other Member States.

Article 11

Where a national of a Member State is pursuing an activity as an employed or self-employed person in the territory of another Member State, his spouse and those of the children who are under the age of 21 years or dependent on him shall have the right to take up any activity as an employed person throughout the territory of that same State, even if they are not nationals of any Member State.

Article 12

The children of a national of a Member State who is or has been employed in the territory of another Member State shall be admitted to that State's general educational, apprenticeship and vocational training course under the same conditions as the nationals of that State, if such children are residing in its territory.

Member States shall encourage all efforts to enable such children to attend these courses under the best possible conditions.

COUNCIL DIRECTIVE No. 75/117 (O.J. 1975, L 45/19)

on the approximation of the laws of the Member States relating to the application of the principle of equal pay for men and women

Article 1

The principle of equal pay for men and women outlined in Article 119 of the Treaty, hereinafter called 'principle of equal pay', means, for the same work or for work to which equal value is attributed, the elimination of all discrimination on grounds of sex with regard to all aspects and conditions of remuneration.

In particular, where a job classification system is used for determining pay, it must be based on the same criteria for both men and women and so drawn up as to exclude any discrimination on grounds of sex.

Article 2

Member States shall introduce into their national legal system such measures as are necessary to enable all employees who consider themselves wronged by failure to apply the principle of equal pay to pursue their claims by judicial process after possible recourse to other competent authorities.

Article 3
Member States shall abolish all discrimination between men and women arising from laws, regulations or administrative provisions which is contrary to the principle of equal pay.

Article 4
Member States shall take the necessary measures to ensure that provisions appearing in collective agreements, wage scales, wage agreements or individual contracts of employment which are contrary to the principle of equal pay shall be, or may be declared, null and void or may be amended.

Article 5
Member States shall take the necessary measures to protect employees against dismissal by the employer as a reaction to a complaint within the undertaking or to any legal proceedings aimed at enforcing compliance with the principle of equal pay.

Article 6
Member States shall, in accordance with their national circumstances and legal systems, take the measures necessary to ensure that the principle of equal pay is applied. They shall see that effective means are available to take care that this principle is observed.

COUNCIL DIRECTIVE No. 75/129 (O.J. 1975, L48/29)

on the approximation of the laws of the Member States relating to collective redundancies, as amended by Directive 92/56.

SECTION 1
DEFINITIONS AND SCOPE

Article 1
1. For the purposes of this Directive:

(a) 'collective redundancies' means dismissals effected by an employer for one or more reasons not related to the individual workers concerned where, according to the choice of the member states, the number of redundancies is:
either, over a period of 30 days:

(1) at least 10 in establishments normally employing more than 20 and less than 100 workers;

(2) at least 10% of the number of workers in establishments normally employing at least 100 but less than 300 workers;

(3) at least 30 in establishments normally employing 300 workers or more;
or, over a period of 90 days, at least 20, whatever the number of workers normally employed in the establishments in question;

(b) 'workers' representatives' means the workers' representatives provided for by the laws or practices of the member states.
For the purpose of calculating the number of redundancies provided for in the first subparagraph of point (a), terminations of an employment contract which occur to the individual workers concerned shall be assimilated to redundancies, provided that there are at least five redundancies.

2. This Directive shall not apply to:

(a) collective redundancies affected under contracts of employment concluded for limited periods of time or for specific tasks except where such redundancies take place prior to the date of expiry or the completion of such contracts;

(b) workers employed by public administrative bodies or by establishments governed by public law (or, in member states where this concept is unknown, by equivalent bodies);

(c) the crews of sea-going vessels.

SECTION II
INFORMATION AND CONSULTATION

Article 2

1. Where an employer is contemplating collective redundancies, he shall begin consultations with the workers' representatives in good time with a view to reaching an agreement.

2. These consultations shall, at least, cover ways and means of avoiding collective redundancies or reducing the number of workers affected, and of mitigating the consequences by recourse to accompanying social measures aimed, inter alia, at aid for redeploying or retraining workers made redundant.

Member states may provide that the workers' representatives may call upon the services of experts in accordance with national legislation and/or practice.

3. To enable workers' representatives to make constructive proposals, the employers shall in good time during the course of the consultations:

(a) supply them with all relevant information and

(b) in any event notify them in writing of:

(i) the reasons for the projected redundancies;

(ii) the number of categories of workers to be made redundant;

(iii) the number and categories of workers normally employed;

(iv) the period over which the projected redundancies are to be effected;

(v) the criteria proposed for the selection of the workers to be made redundant in so far as national legislation and/or practice confers the power therefor upon the employer;

(vi) the method for calculating any redundancy payments other than those arising out of national legislation and/or practice.

The employer shall forward to the competent public authority a copy of, at least, the elements of the written communication which are provided for in the first subparagraph, point (b), subpoints (i) to (v).

4. The obligations laid down in paragraphs 1, 2 and 3 shall apply irrespective of whether the decision regarding collective redundancies is being taken by the employer or by an undertaking controlling the employer. In considering alleged breaches of the information, consultation and notification requirements laid down by this Directive, account shall not be taken of any defence on the part of the employer on the ground that the necessary information has not been provided to the employer by the undertaking which took the decision leading to collective redundancies.

SECTION III
PROCEDURE FOR COLLECTIVE REDUNDANCIES

Article 3

1. Employers shall notify the competent public authority in writing of any projected collective redundancies.

This notification shall contain all relevant information concerning the projected collective redundancies and the consultations with workers' representatives provided for in Article 2, and particularly the reasons for the redundancies, the number of workers to be made redundant, the number of workers normally employed and the period over which the redundancies are to be effected.

However, member states may provide that in the case of planned collective redundancies arising from termination of the establishment's activities as the result of a judicial decision, the employer shall be obliged to notify the competent public authority in writing only if the latter so requests.

2. Employers shall forward to the workers' representatives a copy of the notification provided for in paragraph 1.

The workers' representatives may send any comments they may have to the competent public authority.

Article 4

1. Projected collective redundancies notified to the competent public authority shall take effect not earlier than 30 days after the notification referred to in Article 3(1) without prejudice to any provisions governing individual rights with regard to notice of dismissal.

Member states may grant the competent public authority the power to reduce the period provided for in the preceding subparagraph.

2. The period provided for in paragraph 1 shall be used by the competent public authority to seek solutions in the problems raised by the projected collective redundancies.

3. Where the initial period provided for in paragraph 1 is shorter than 60 days, member states may grant the competent public authority the power to extend the initial period to 60 days following notification where the problems raised by the projected collective redundancies are not likely to be solved within the initial period.

Member states may grant the competent public authority wider powers of extension.

The employer must be informed of the extension and the grounds for it before expiry of the initial period provided for in paragraph 1.

4. Member states need not apply this Article to collective redundancies arising from termination of the establishment's activities where this is the result of a judicial decision.

SECTION IV
FINAL PROVISIONS

Article 5

This Directive shall not affect the right of member states to apply or to introduce laws, regulations or administrative provisions which are more favourable to workers or to promote or to allow the application of collective agreements more favourable to workers.

Article 5a

Member states shall ensure that judicial and/or administrative procedures for the enforcement of obligations under this directive are available to the workers' representatives and/or workers.

COUNCIL DIRECTIVE No. 76/207 (O.J. 1976, L 39/40)

on the implementation of the principle of equal treatment for men and women as regards access to employment, vocational training and promotion, and working conditions

Article 1

1. The purpose of this Directive is to put into effect in the Member States the principle of equal treatment for men and women as regards access to employment, including promotion, and to vocational training and as regards working conditions and, on the conditions referred to in paragraph 2, social security. This principle is hereinafter referred to as 'the principle of equal treatment'.

2. With a view to ensuring the progressive implementation of the principle of equal treatment in matters of social security, the Council, acting on a proposal from the Commission, will adopt provisions defining its substance, its scope and the arrangements for its application.

Article 2

1. For the purposes of the following provisions, the principle of equal treatment shall mean that there shall be no discrimination whatsoever on grounds of sex either directly or indirectly by reference in particular to marital or family status.

2. This Directive shall be without prejudice to the right of Member States to exclude from its field of application those occupational activities and, where appropriate, the training leading thereto, for which, by reason of their nature or the context in which they are carried out, the sex of the worker constitutes a determining factor.

3. This Directive shall be without prejudice to provisions concerning the protection of women, particularly as regards pregnancy and maternity.

4. This Directive shall be without prejudice to measures to promote equal opportunity for men and women, in particular by removing existing inequalities which affect women's opportunities in the areas referred to in Article 1(1).

Article 3

1. Application of the principle of equal treatment means that there shall be no discrimination whatsoever on grounds of sex in the conditions, including selection criteria, for access to all jobs or posts, whatever the sector or branch of activity, and to all levels of the occupational hierarchy.

2. To this end, Member States shall take the measures necessary to ensure that:

(a) any laws, regulations and administrative provisions contrary to the principle of equal treatment shall be abolished;

(b) any provisions contrary to the principle of equal treatment which are included in collective agreements, individual contracts of employment, internal rules of undertakings or in rules governing the independent occupations and professions shall be, or may be declared, null and void or may be amended;

(c) those laws, regulations and administrative provisions contrary to the principle of equal treatment when the concern for protection which originally inspired them is no longer well founded shall be revised; and that where similar provisions are included in collective agreements labour and management shall be requested to undertake the desired revision.

Article 4

Application of the principle of equal treatment with regard to access to all types and to all levels, of vocational guidance, vocational training, advanced vocational training and retraining, means that Member States shall take all necessary measures to ensure that:

(a) any laws, regulations and administrative provisions contrary to the principle of equal treatment shall be abolished;

(b) any provisions contrary to the principle of equal treatment which are included in collective agreements, individual contracts of employment, internal rules of undertakings or in rules governing the independent occupations and professions shall be, or may be declared, null and void or may be amended;

(c) without prejudice to the freedom granted in certain Member States to certain private training establishments, vocational guidance, vocational training, advanced vocational training and retraining shall be accessible on the basis of the same criteria and at the same levels without any discrimination on grounds of sex.

Article 5

1. Application of the principle of equal treatment with regard to working conditions, including the conditions governing dismissal, means that men and women shall be guaranteed the same conditions without discrimination on grounds of sex.

2. To this end, Member States shall take the measures necessary to ensure that:

(a) any laws, regulations and administrative provisions contrary to the principle of equal treatment shall be abolished;

(b) any provisions contrary to the principle of equal treatment which are included in collective agreements, individual contracts of employment, internal rules of undertakings or in rules governing the independent occupations and professions shall be, or may be declared, null and void or may be amended;

(c) those laws, regulations and administrative provisions contrary to the principle of equal treatment when the concern for protection which originally inspired them is no longer well founded shall be revised; and that where similar provisions are included in collective agreements labour and management shall be requested to undertake the desired revision.

Article 6
Member States shall introduce into their national legal systems such measures as are necessary to enable all persons who consider themselves wronged by failure to apply to them the principle of equal treatment within the meaning of Articles 3, 4 and 5 to pursue their claims by judicial process after possible recourse to other competent authorities.

Article 7
Member States shall take the necessary measures to protect employees against dismissal by the employer as a reaction to a complaint within the undertaking or to any legal proceedings aimed at enforcing compliance with the principle of equal treatment.

COUNCIL DIRECTIVE No. 77/187
(as amended by Directive No. 98/50, O.J. 1998, L201/88)

on the approximation of the laws of the Member States relating to the safeguarding of employees' rights in the event of transfers of undertakings, businesses or parts of undertakings or businesses

Article 1
1.(a) This Directive shall apply to the transfer of an undertaking, business or part of an undertaking or business to another employer as a result of a legal transfer or merger.

(b) Subject to subparagraph (a) and the following provisions of this Article, there is a transfer within the meaning of this Directive where there is a transfer of an economic entity which retains its identity, meaning an organised grouping of resources which has the objective of pursuing an economic activity, whether or not that activity is central or ancillary.

(c) This Directive shall apply to public and private undertakings engaged in economic activities whether or not they are operating for gain. An administrative reorganisation of public administrative authorities, or the transfer of administrative functions between public administrative authorities is not a transfer within the meaning of this Directive.

2. This Directive shall apply where and in so far as the undertaking, business or part of the undertaking or business to be transferred is situated within the territorial scope of the Treaty.

3. This Directive shall not apply to sea-going vessels.

Article 2
1. For the purposes of this Directive:

(a) 'transferor' means any natural or legal person who, by reason of a transfer within the meaning of Article 1(1), ceases to be the employer in respect of the undertaking, business or part of the undertaking or business;

(b) 'transferee' means any natural or legal person who, by reason of a transfer within the meaning of Article 1(1), becomes the employer in respect of the undertaking, business or part of the undertaking or business;

(c) 'representatives of employees' and related expressions shall mean the representatives of the employees provided for by the laws or practices of the Member States;

(d) 'employee' shall mean any person who, in the Member State concerned, is protected as an employee under national employment law.

2. This Directive shall be without prejudice to national law as regards the definition of contract of employment or employment relationship.

However, Member States shall not exclude from the scope of this Directive contracts of employment or employment relationships solely because:

(a) of the number of working hours performed or to be performed,

(b) they are employment relationships governed by a fixed-duration contract of employment within the meaning of Article 1(1) of Council Directive 91/383/EEC of 25 June 1991 supplementing the measures to encourage improvements in the safety and health at work of workers with a fixed–duration employment relationship or a temporary employment relationship, or

(c) they are temporary employment relationships within the meaning of Article 1(2) of Directive 91/383/EEC, and the undertaking, business or part of the undertaking or business transferred is, or is part of, the temporary employment business which is the employer.

Article 3

1. The transferor's rights and obligations arising from a contract of employment or from an employment relationship existing on the date of a transfer shall, by reason of such transfer, be transferred to the transferee.

Member States may provide that, after the date of transfer the transferor and the transferee shall be jointly and severally liable in respect of obligations which arose before the date of transfer from a contract of employment or an employment relationship existing on the date of the transfer.

2. Member States may adopt appropriate measures to ensure that the transferor notifies the transferee of all the rights and obligations which will be transferred to the transferee under this Article, so far as those rights and obligations are or ought to have been known to the transferor at the time of the transfer. A failure by the transferor to notify the transferee of any such right or obligation shall not affect the transfer of that right or obligation and the rights of any employees against the transferee and/or transferor in respect of that right or obligation.

3. Following the transfer, the transferee shall continue to observe the terms and conditions agreed in any collective agreement on the same terms applicable to the transferor under that agreement, until the date of termination or expiry of the collective agreement or the entry into force or application of another collective agreement.

Member States may limit the period for observing such terms and conditions, with the proviso that it shall not be less than one year.

4.(a) Unless Member States provide otherwise, paragraphs 1 and 3 shall not apply in relation to employees' rights to old-age, invalidity or survivors' benefits under supplementary company or inter-company pension schemes outside the statutory social security schemes in Member States.

(b) Even where they do not provide in accordance with subparagraph (a) that paragraphs 1 and 3 apply in relation to such rights, Member States shall adopt the measures necessary to protect the interests of employees and of persons no longer employed in the transferor's business at the time of the transfer in respect of rights conferring on them immediate or prospective entitlement to old age benefits, including survivors' benefits, under supplementary schemes referred to in subparagraph (a).

Article 4

1. The transfer of an undertaking, business or part of the undertaking or business shall not in itself constitute grounds for dismissal by the transferor or the transferee.

This provision shall not stand in the way of dismissals that may take place for economic, technical or organisational reasons entailing changes in the workforce.

Member States may provide that the first subparagraph shall not apply to certain specific categories of employees who are not covered by the laws or practice of the Member States in respect of protection against dismissal.

2. If the contract of employment or the employment relationship is terminated because the transfer involves a substantial change in working conditions to the detriment of the employee, the employer shall be regarded as having been responsible for termination of the contract of employment or of the employment relationship.

Article 4a

1. Unless Member States provide otherwise, Articles 3 and 4 shall not apply to any transfer of an undertaking, business or part of an undertaking or business where the transferor is the subject of bankruptcy proceedings or any analogous insolvency proceedings which have been instituted with a view to the liquidation of the assets of the transferor and are under the supervision of a competent public authority (which may be an insolvency practitioner authorised by a competent public authority).

2. Where Articles 3 and 4 apply to a transfer during insolvency proceedings which have been opened in relation to a transferor (whether or not those proceedings have been instituted with a view to the liquidation of the assets of the transferor) and provided that such proceedings are under the supervision of a competent public authority (which may be an insolvency practitioner determined by national law) a Member State may provide that:

(a) notwithstanding Article 3(1), the transferor's debts arising from any contracts of employment or employment relationships and payable before the transfer or before the opening of the insolvency proceedings shall not be transferred to the transferee, provided that such proceedings give rise, under the law of the Member State, to protection at least equivalent to that provided for in situations covered by Council Directive 80/987/EEC of 20 October 1980 on the approximation of the laws of the Member States relating to the protection of employees in the event of the insolvency of their employer;

and, or alternatively, that

(b) the transferee, transferor, or person or persons exercising the transferor's functions, on the one hand, and the representatives of the employees on the other hand may agree alterations, insofar as current law or practice permits, to the employees' terms and conditions of employment designed to safeguard employment opportunities by ensuring the survival of the undertaking, business or part of the undertaking or business.

3. A Member state may apply paragraph 2(b) to any transfers where the transferor is in a situation of serious economic crisis, as defined by national law, provided that the situation is declared by a competent public authority and open to judicial supervision, on condition that such provisions already exist in national law by 17 July 1998.

The Commission shall present a report on the effects of this provision before 17 July 2003 and shall submit any appropriate proposals to the Council.

4. Member States shall take appropriate measures with a view to preventing misuse of insolvency proceedings in such a way as to deprive employees of the rights provided for in this Directive.

Article 5

1. If the undertaking, business or part of an undertaking or business preserves its autonomy, the status and function of the representatives or of the representation of the employees affected by the transfer shall be preserved on the same terms and subject to the same conditions as existed before the date of the transfer by virtue of law, regulation, administrative provision or agreement, provided that the conditions necessary for the constitution of the employees' representation are fulfilled.

The first subparagraph shall not apply if, under the laws, regulations, administrative provisions or practice in the Member States, or by agreement with the representatives of the employees, the conditions necessary for the reappointment of the representatives of the employees or for the reconstitution of the representation of the employees are fulfilled.

Where the transferor is the subject of bankruptcy proceedings or any analogous insolvency proceedings which have been instituted with a view to the liquidation of the assets of the transferor and are under the supervision of a competent public authority (which may be an insolvency practitioner authorised by a competent public authority), Member States may take the necessary measures to ensure that the transferred employees are properly represented until the new election or designation or representatives of the employees.

If the undertaking, business or part of an undertaking or business does not preserve its autonomy, the Member States shall take the necessary measures to ensure that the employees transferred who were represented before the transfer continue to be properly represented during the period necessary for the reconstitution or reappointment of the representation of employees in accordance with national law or practice.

Article 6

1. The transferor and the transferee shall be required to inform the representatives of their respective employees affected by a transfer of the following:
— the date or proposed date of the transfer,
— the reasons for the transfer,
— the legal, economic and social implications of the transfer for the employees,
— any measures envisaged in relation to the employees.

The transferor must give such information to the representatives of his employees in good time before the transfer is carried out.

The transferee must give such information to the representatives of his employees in good time, and in any event before his employees are directly affected by the transfer as regards their conditions of work and employment.

2. Where the transferor or the transferee envisages measures in relation to his employees, he shall consult the representatives of his employees in good time on such measures with a view to seeking agreement.

3. Member States whose laws, regulations or administrative provisions provide that representatives of the employees may have recourse to an arbitration board to obtain a decision on the measures to be taken in relation to employees may limit the obligations laid down in paragraphs 1 and 2 to cases where the transfer carried out gives rise to a change in the business likely to entail serious disadvantages for a considerable number of the employees.

The information and consultations shall cover at least the measures envisaged in relation to the employees.

The information must be provided and consultations take place in good time before the change in the business as referred to in the first subparagraph is effected.

4. The obligations laid down in this Article shall apply irrespective of whether the decision resulting in the transfer is taken by the employer or an undertaking controlling the employer.

In considering alleged breaches of the information and consultation requirements laid down by this Directive, the argument that such a breach occurred because the information was not provided by an undertaking controlling the employer shall not be accepted as an excuse.

5. Member States may limit the obligations laid down in paragraphs 1, 2 and 3 to undertakings or businesses which, in terms of the number of employees, meet the conditions for the election or nomination of a collegiate body representing the employees.

6. Member States shall provide that, where there are no representatives of the employees in an undertaking or business through no fault of their own, the employees concerned must be informed in advance of:

— the date or proposed date of the transfer,
— the reason for the transfer,
— the legal, economic and social implications of the transfer for the employees,
— any measures envisaged in relation to the employees.

COUNCIL DIRECTIVE No. 89/391 (O.J. 1989, L/183/1)

on the introduction of measures to encourage improvements in the safety and health of workers at work

SECTION II
EMPLOYERS' OBLIGATIONS

Article 5 General provision

1. The employer shall have a duty to ensure the safety and health of workers in every aspect related to the work.

2. Where, pursuant to Article 7(3), an employer enlists competent external services or persons, this shall not discharge him from his responsibilities in this area.

3. The workers' obligations in the field of safety and health at work shall not affect the principle of the responsibility of the employer.

4. This Directive shall not restrict the option of Member States to provide for the exclusion or the limitation of employers' responsibility where occurrences are due to unusual and unforeseeable circumstances, beyond the employers' control, or to exceptional events, the consequences of which could not have been avoided despite the exercise of all due care.

Member States need not exercise the option referred to in the first subparagraph.

Article 6 General obligations on employers

1. Within the context of his responsibilities, the employer shall take the measures necessary for the safety and health protection of workers, including prevention of occupational risks and provision of information and training, as well as provision of the necessary organization and means.

The employer shall be alert to the need to adjust these measures to take account of changing circumstances and aim to improve existing situations.

2. The employer shall implement the measures referred to in the first subparagraph of paragraph 1 on the basis of the following general principles of prevention:

(a) avoiding risks;
(b) evaluating the risks which cannot be avoided;
(c) combating the risks at source;
(d) adapting the work to the individual, especially as regards the design of work places, the choice of work equipment and the choice of working and production methods, with a view, in particular, to alleviating monotonous work and work at a predetermined work-rate and to reduce their effect on health.
(e) adapting to technical progress;
(f) replacing the dangerous by the non-dangerous or the less dangerous;
(g) developing a coherent overall prevention policy which covers technology, organization of work, working conditions, social relationships and the influence of factors related to the working environment;
(h) giving collective protective measures priority over individual protective measures;
(i) giving appropriate instructions to the workers.

3. Without prejudice to the other provisions of this Directive, the employer shall, taking into account the nature of the activities of the enterprise and/or establishment:

(a) evaluate the risks to the safety and health of workers, *inter alia* in the choice of work equipment, the chemical substances or preparations used, and the fitting-out of work places.

Subsequent to this evaluation and as necessary, the preventive measures and the working and production methods implemented by the employer must:

—assure an improvement in the level of protection afforded to workers with regard to safety and health,

—be integrated into all the activities of the undertaking and/or establishment and at all hierarchical levels;

(b) where he entrusts tasks to a worker, take into consideration the worker's capabilities as regards health and safety;

(c) ensure that the planning and introduction of new technologies are the subject of consultation with the workers and/or their representatives, as regards the consequences of the choice of equipment, the working conditions and the working environment for the safety and health of workers;

(d) take appropriate steps to ensure that only workers who have received adequate instructions may have access to areas where there is serious and specific danger.

4. Without prejudice to the other provisions of this Directive, where several undertakings share a work place, the employers shall cooperate in implementing the safety, health and occupational hygiene provisions and, taking into account the nature of the activities, shall coordinate their actions in matters of the protection and prevention of occupational risks, and shall inform one another and their respective workers and/or workers' representatives of these risks.

5. Measures related to safety, hygiene and health at work may in no circumstances involve the workers in financial cost.

Article 7 Protective and preventive services

1. Without prejudice to the obligations referred to in Articles 5 and 6, the employer shall designate one or more workers to carry out activities related to the protection and prevention of occupational risks for the undertaking and/or establishment.

2. Designated workers may not be placed at any disadvantage because of their activities related to the protection and prevention of occupational risks.

Designated workers shall be allowed adequate time to enable them to fulfil their obligations arising from this Directive.

3. If such protective and preventive measures cannot be organized for lack of competent personnel in the undertaking and/or establishment, the employer shall enlist competent external services or persons.

4. Where the employer enlists such services or persons, he shall inform them of the factors known to affect, or suspected of affecting, the safety and health of the workers and they must have access to the information referred to in Article 10(2).

5. In all cases:

—the workers designated must have the necessary capabilities and the necessary means,

—the external services or persons consulted must have the necessary aptitudes and the necessary personal and professional means, and

—the workers designated and the external services or persons consulted must be sufficient in number

to deal with the organization of protective and preventive measures, taking into account the size of the undertaking and/or establishment and/or the hazards to which the workers are exposed and their distribution throughout the entire undertaking and/or establishment.

6. The protection from, and prevention of, the health and safety risks which form the subject of this Article shall be the responsibility of one or more workers, of one service or of separate services whether from inside or outside the undertaking and/or establishment.

The worker(s) and/or agency(ies) must work together whenever necessary.

7. Member States may define, in the light of the nature of the activities and size of the undertakings, the categories of undertakings in which the employer, provided he is competent, may himself take responsibility for the measures referred to in paragraph 1.

8. Member States shall define the necessary capabilities and aptitudes referred to in paragraph 5.

They may determine the sufficient number referred to in paragraph 5.

Article 8 First aid, fire-fighting and evacuation of workers, serious and imminent danger

1. The employer shall:

—take the necessary measures for first aid, fire-fighting and evacuation of workers, adapted to the nature of the activities and the size of the undertaking and/or establishment and taking into account other persons present,

—arrange any necessary contacts with external services, particularly as regards first aid, emergency medical care, rescue work and fire-fighting.

2. Pursuant to paragraph 1, the employer shall, *inter alia,* for first aid, fire-fighting and the evacuation of workers, designate the workers required to implement such measures.

The number of such workers, their training and the equipment available to them shall be adequate, taking account of the size and/or specific hazards of the undertaking and/or establishment.

3. The employer shall:

(a) as soon as possible, inform all workers who are, or may be, exposed to serious and imminent danger of the risk involved and of the steps taken or to be taken as regards protection;

(b) take action and give instructions to enable workers in the event of serious, imminent and unavoidable danger to stop work and/or immediately to leave the work place and proceed to a place of safety;

(c) save in exceptional cases for reasons duly substantiated, refrain from asking workers to resume work in a working situation where there is still a serious and imminent danger.

4. Workers who, in the event of serious, imminent and unavoidable danger, leave their workstation and/or a dangerous area may not be placed at any disadvantage because of their action and must be protected against any harmful and unjustified consequences, in accordance with national laws and/or practices.

5. The employer shall ensure that all workers are able, in the event of serious and imminent danger to their own safety and/or that of other persons, and where the immediate superior responsible cannot be contacted, to take the appropriate steps in the light of their knowledge and the technical means at their disposal, to avoid the consequences of such danger.

Their actions shall not place them at any disadvantage, unless they acted carelessly or there was negligence on their part.

Article 9 Various obligations on employers

1. The employer shall:

(a) be in possession of an assessment of the risks to safety and health at work, including those facing groups of workers exposed to particular risks;

(b) decide on the protective measures to be taken and, if necessary, the protective equipment to be used;

(c) keep a list of occupational accidents resulting in a worker being unfit for work for more than three working days;

(d) draw up, for the responsible authorities and in accordance with national laws and/or practices, reports on occupational accidents suffered by his workers.

2. Member States shall define, in the light of the nature of the activities and size of the undertakings, the obligations to be met by the different categories of undertakings in respect of the drawing-up of the documents provided for in paragraph 1(a) and (b) and when preparing the documents provided for in paragraph 1(c) and (d).

Article 10 Worker information

1. The employer shall take appropriate measures so that workers and/or their representatives in the undertaking and/or establishment receive, in accordance with national laws and/or practices which may take account, *inter alia*, of the size of the undertaking and/or establishment, all the necessary information concerning:

(a) the safety and health risks and protective and preventive measures and activities in respect of both the undertaking and/or establishment in general and each type of workstation and/or job;

(b) the measures taken pursuant to Article 8(2).

2. The employer shall take appropriate measures so that employers of workers from any outside undertakings and/or establishments engaged in work in his undertaking and/or establishment receive, in accordance with national laws and/or practices, adequate information concerning the points referred to in paragraph 1(a) and (b) which is to be provided to the workers in question.

3. The employer shall take appropriate measures so that workers with specific functions in protecting the safety and health of workers, or workers' representatives with specific responsibility for the safety and health of workers shall have access, to carry out their functions and in accordance with national laws and/or practices, to:

(a) the risk assessment and protective measures referred to in Article 9(1)(a) and (b);

(b) the list and reports referred to in Article 9(1)(c) and (d);

(c) the information yielded by protective and preventive measures, inspection agencies and bodies responsible for safety and health.

Article 11 Consultation and participation of workers

1. Employers shall consult workers and/or their representatives and allow them to take part in discussions on all questions relating to safety and health at work.

This presupposes:

—the consultation of workers,

—the right of workers and/or their representatives to make proposals,

—balanced participation in accordance with national laws and/or practices.

2. Workers or workers' representatives with specific responsibility for the safety and health of workers shall take part in a balanced way, in accordance with national laws and/or practices, or shall be consulted in advance and in good time by the employer with regard to:

(a) any measure which may substantially affect safety and health;

(b) the designation of workers referred to in articles 7(1) and 8(2) and the activities referred to in Article 7(1);

(c) the information referred to in Articles 9(1) and 10;

(d) the enlistment, where appropriate, of the competent services or persons outside the undertaking and/or establishment, as referred to in Article 7(3);

(e) the planning and organization of the training referred to in Article 12.

3. Workers' representatives with specific responsibility for the safety and health of workers shall have the right to ask the employer to take appropriate measures and to

submit proposals to him to that end to mitigate hazards for workers and/or to remove sources of danger.

4. The workers referred to in paragraph 2 and the workers' representatives referred to in paragraphs 2 and 3 may not be placed at a disadvantage because of their respective activities referred to in paragraphs 2 and 3.

5. Employers must allow workers' representatives with specific responsibility for the safety and health of workers adequate time off work, without loss of pay, and provide them with the necessary means to enable such representatives to exercise their rights and functions deriving from this Directive.

6. Workers and/or their representatives are entitled to appeal, in accordance with national law and/or practice, to the authority responsible for safety and health protection at work if they consider that the measures taken and the means employed by the employer are inadequate for the purposes of ensuring safety and health at work.

Workers' representatives must be given the opportunity to submit their observations during inspection visits by the competent authority.

Article 12 Training of workers

1. The employer shall ensure that each worker receives adequate safety and health training, in particular in the form of information and instructions specific to his workstation or job:

—on recruitment,

—in the event of a transfer or a change of job,

—in the event of the introduction of new work equipment or a change in equipment,

—in the event of the introduction of any new technology.

The training shall be:

—adapted to take account of new or changed risks, and

—repeated periodically if necessary.

2. The employer shall ensure that workers from outside undertakings and/or establishments engaged in work in his undertaking and/or establishment have in fact received appropriate instructions regarding health and safety risks during their activities in his undertaking and/or establishment.

3. Workers' representatives with a specific role in protecting the safety and health of workers shall be entitled to appropriate training.

4. The training referred to in paragraphs 1 and 3 may not be at the workers' expense or at that of the workers' representatives.

The training referred to in paragraph 1 must take place during working hours.

The training referred to in paragraph 3 must take place during working hours or in accordance with national practice either within or outside the undertaking and/or the establishment.

SECTION III
WORKERS' OBLIGATIONS

Article 13

1. It shall be the responsibility of each worker to take care as far as possible of his own safety and health and that of other persons affected by his acts or Commissions at work in accordance with his training and the instructions given by his employer.

2. To this end, workers must in particular, in accordance with their training and the instructions given by their employer:

(a) make correct use of machinery, apparatus, tools, dangerous substances, transport equipment and other means of production;

(b) make correct use of the personal protective equipment supplied to them and, after use, return it to its proper place;

(c) refrain from disconnecting, changing or removing arbitrarily safety devices fitted, e.g., to machinery, apparatus, tools, plant and buildings, and use such safety devices correctly;

(d) immediately inform the employer and/or the workers with specific responsibility for the safety and health of workers of any work situation they have reasonable grounds for considering represents a serious and immediate danger to safety and health and of any shortcomings in the protection arrangements;

(e) cooperate, in accordance with national practice, with the employer and/or workers with specific responsibility for the safety and health of workers, for as long as may be necessary to enable any tasks or requirements imposed by the competent authority to protect the safety and health of workers at work to be carried out;

(f) cooperate, in accordance with national practice, with the employer and/or workers with specific responsibility for the safety and health of workers, for as long as may be necessary to enable the employer to ensure that the working environment and working conditions are safe and pose no risk to safety and health within their field of activity.

SECTION IV
MISCELLANEOUS PROVISIONS

Article 14 Health surveillance

1. To ensure that workers receive health surveillance appropriate to the health and safety risks they incur at work, measures shall be introduced in accordance with national law and/or practices.

2. The measures referred to in paragraph 1 shall be such that each worker, if he so wishes, may receive health surveillance at regular intervals.

3. Health surveillance may be provided as part of a national health system.

Article 15 Risk groups

Particularly sensitive risk groups must be protected against the dangers which specifically affect them.

COUNCIL DIRECTIVE No. 93/104 (O.J. 1993, L307/18)

concerning certain aspects of the organisation of working time

SECTION I
SCOPE AND DEFINITIONS

Article 1 Purpose and scope

1. This Directive lays down minimum safety and health requirements for the organisation of working time.

2. This Directive applies to:

(a) minimum periods of daily rest, weekly rest and annual leave, to breaks and maximum weekly working time; and

(b) certain aspects of night work, shift work and patterns of work.

3. This Directive shall apply to all sectors of activity, both public and private, within the meaning of Article 2 of Directive 89/391/EEC, without prejudice to Article 17 of this Directive, with the exception of air, rail, road, sea, inland waterway and lake transport, sea fishing, other work at sea and the activities of doctors in training;

4. The provisions of Directive 89/391/EEC are fully applicable to the matters referred to in paragraph 2, without prejudice to more stringent and/or specific provisions contained in this Directive.

Article 2 Definitions

For the purposes of this Directive, the following definitions shall apply:

1. *working time* shall mean any period during which the worker is working, at the employer's disposal and carrying out his activity or duties, in accordance with national laws and/or practice;

2. *rest period* shall mean any period which is not working time;

3. *night time* shall mean any period of not less than seven hours, as defined by national law, and which must include in any case the period between midnight and 5 a.m.;

4. *night worker* shall mean:

(a) on the one hand, any worker, who, during night time, works at least three hours of his daily working time as a normal course; and

(b) on the other hand, any worker who is likely during night time to work a certain proportion of his annual working time, as defined at the choice of the Member State concerned:

(i) by national legislation, following consultation with the two sides of industry; or

(ii) by collective agreements or agreements concluded between the two sides of industry at national or regional level;

5. *shift work* shall mean any method of organising work in shifts whereby workers succeed each other at the same work stations according to a certain pattern, including a rotating pattern, and which may be continuous or discontinuous, entailing the need for workers to work at different times over a given period of days or weeks;

6. *shift worker* shall mean any worker whose work schedule is part of shift work.

SECTION II

MINIMUM REST PERIODS — OTHER ASPECTS OF THE ORGANISATION OF WORKING TIME

Article 3 Daily rest

Member States shall take the measures necessary to ensure that every worker is entitled to a minimum daily rest period of 11 consecutive hours per 24-hour period.

Article 4 Breaks

Member States shall take the measures necessary to ensure that, where the working day is longer than six hours, every worker is entitled to a rest break, the details of which, including duration and the terms on which it is granted, shall be laid down in collective agreements or agreements between the two sides of industry or, failing that, by national legislation.

Article 5 Weekly rest period

Member States shall take the measures necessary to ensure that, per each seven-day period, every worker is entitled to a minimum uninterrupted rest period of 24 hours plus the 11 hours' daily rest referred to in Article 3.

The minimum rest period referred to in the first subparagraph shall in principle include Sunday.

If objective, technical or work organisations conditions so justify, a minimum rest period of 24 hours may be applied.

Article 6 Maximum weekly working time

Member States shall take the measures necessary to ensure that, in keeping with the need to protect the safety and health of workers:

1. the period of weekly working time is limited by means of laws, regulations or administrative provisions or by collective agreements or agreement between the two sides of industry;

2. the average working time for each seven-day period, including overtime, does not exceed 48 hours.

Article 7 Annual leave

1. Member States shall take the measures necessary to ensure that every worker is entitled to paid annual leave of at least four weeks in accordance with the conditions for entitlement to, and granting of, such leave laid down by national legislation and/or practice.

2. The minimum period of paid annual leave may not be replaced by an allowance in lieu, except where the employment relationship is terminated.

SECTION III
NIGHT WORK — SHIFT WORK — PATTERNS OF WORK

Article 8 Length of night work

Member States shall take the measures necessary to ensure that:

1. normal hours of work for night workers do not exceed an average of eight hours in any 24-hour period;

2. night workers whose work involves special hazards or heavy physical or mental strain do not work more than eight hours in any period of 24 hours during which they perform night work.

For the purposes of the aforementioned, work involving special hazards or heavy physical or mental strain shall be defined by national legislation and/or practice or by collective agreements or agreements concluded between the two sides of industry, taking account of the specific effects and hazards of night work.

Article 9 Health assessment and transfer of night workers to day work

1. Member States shall take the measures necessary to ensure that:

(a) night workers are entitled to a free health assessment before their assignment and thereafter at regular intervals;

(b) night workers suffering from health problems recognised as being connected with the fact that they perform night work are transferred whenever possible to day work to which they are suited.

2. The free health assessment referred to in paragraph 1(a) must comply with medical confidentiality.

3. The free health assessment referred to in paragraph 1(a) may be conducted within the national health system.

Article 10 Guarantees for night-time working

Member States may make the work of certain categories of night workers subject to certain guarantees, under conditions laid down by national legislation and/or practice, in the case of workers who incur risks to their safety or health linked to night-time working.

Article 11 Notification of regular use of night workers

Member States shall take the measures necessary to ensure that an employer who regularly uses night workers brings this information to the attention of the competent authorities if they so request.

Article 12 Safety and health protection

Member States shall take the measures necessary to ensure that:

1. night workers and shift workers have safety and health protection appropriate to the nature of their work;

2. appropriate protection and prevention services or facilities with regard to the safety and health of night workers and shift workers are equivalent to those applicable to other workers and are available at all times.

Article 13 Pattern of work

Member States shall take the measures necessary to ensure that an employer who intends to organise work according to a certain pattern takes account of the general principle of adapting work to the worker, with a view, in particular, to alleviating monotonous work and work at a predetermined work-rate, depending on the type of activity, and of safety and health requirements, especially as regards breaks during working time.

SECTION IV
MISCELLANEOUS PROVISIONS

Article 14 More specific Community provisions

The provisions of this Directive shall not apply where other Community instruments contain more specific requirements concerning certain occupations or occupational activities.

Article 15 More favourable provisions

This Directive shall not affect Member States' right to apply or introduce laws, regulations or administrative provisions more favourable to the protection of the safety and health of workers or to facilitate or permit the application of collective agreements or agreements concluded between the two sides of industry which are more favourable to the protection of the safety and health of workers.

Article 16 Reference periods

Member States may lay down:

1. for the application of Article 5 (weekly rest period), a reference period not exceeding 14 days;

2. for the application of Article 6 (maximum weekly working time), a reference period not exceeding four months.

The periods of paid annual leave, granted in accordance with Article 7, and the periods of sick leave shall not be included or shall be neutral in the calculation of the average;

3. for the application of Article 8 (length of night work), a reference period defined after consultation of the two sides of industry or by collective agreements or agreements concluded between the two sides of industry at national or regional level.

If the minimum weekly rest period of 24 hours required by Article 5 falls within that reference period, it shall not be included in the calculation of the average.

Article 17 Derogations

1. With due regard for the general principles of the protection of the safety and health of workers, Member States may derogate from Article 3, 4, 5, 6, 8 or 16 when, on account of the specific characteristics of the activity concerned, the duration of the working time is not measured and/or predetermined or can be determined by the workers themselves, and particularly in the case of:

(a) managing executives or other persons with autonomous decision-taking powers;

(b) family workers; or

(c) workers officiating at religious ceremonies in churches and religious communities.

2. Derogations may be adopted by means of laws, regulations or administrative provisions or by means of collective agreements or agreements between the two sides of industry provided that the workers concerned are afforded equivalent period of compensatory rest or that, in exceptional cases in which it is not possible, for objective reasons, to grant such equivalent periods of compensatory rest, the workers concerned are afforded appropriate protection:

2.1. from Articles 3, 4, 5, 8 and 16:

(a) in the case of activities where the worker's place of work and his place of residence are distant from one another or where the worker's different places of work are distant from one another;

(b) in the case of security and surveillance activities requiring a permanent presence in order to protect property and persons, particularly security guards and caretakers or security firms;

(c) in the case of activities involving the need for continuity of service or production, particularly:

(i) services relating to the reception, treatment and/or care provided by hospitals or similar establishments, residential institutions and prisons;

(ii) dock or airport workers;

(iii) press, radio, television, cinematographic production, postal and telecommunications services, ambulance, fire and civil protection services;

(iv) gas, water and electricity production, transmission and distribution, household refuse collection and incineration plants;

(v) industries in which work cannot be interrupted on technical grounds;

(vi) research and development activities;

(vii) agriculture;

(d) where there is a foreseeable surge of activity, particularly in:

(i) agriculture;

(ii) tourism;

(iii) postal services;

2.2 from Articles 3, 4, 5, 8 and 16:

(a) in the circumstances described in Article 5(4) of Directive 89/391/EEC;

(b) in cases of accident or imminent risk of accident;

2.3. from Articles 3 and 5:

(a) in the case of shift work activities, each time the worker changes shift and cannot take daily and/or weekly rest periods between the end of one shift and the start of the next one;

(b) in the case of activities involving periods of work split up over the day, particularly those of cleaning staff.

3. Derogations may be made from Articles 3, 4, 5, 8 and 16 by means of collective agreements or agreements concluded between the two sides of industry at national or regional level or, in conformity with the rules laid down by them, by means of collective agreements or agreements concluded between the two sides of industry at a lower level.

Member States in which there is no statutory system ensuring the conclusion of collective agreements or agreements concluded between the two sides of industry at national or regional level, on the matters covered by this Directive, or those Member States in which there is a specific legislative framework for this purpose and within the limits thereof, may, in accordance with national legislation and/or practice, allow derogations from Articles 3, 4, 5, 8 and 16 by way of collective agreements or agreements concluded between the two sides of industry at the appropriate collective level.

The derogations provided for in the first and second subparagraphs shall be allowed on condition that equivalent compensating rest periods are granted to the workers concerned or, in exceptional cases where it is not possible for objective reasons to grant such periods, the workers concerned are afforded appropriate protection.

Member States may lay down rules:

— for the application of this paragraph by the two sides of industry, and

—for the extension of the provisions of collective agreements or agreements concluded in conformity with this paragraph to other workers in accordance with national legislation and/or practice.

4. The option to derogate from point 2 of Article 16, provided in paragraph 2, points 2.1. and 2.2. and in paragraph 3 of this Article, may not result in the establishment of a reference period exceeding six months.

However, Member States shall have the option, subject to compliance with the general principles relating to the protection of the safety and health of workers, of allowing, for objective or technical reasons or reasons concerning the organisation of work, collective agreements or agreements concluded between the two sides of industry to set reference periods in no event exceeding 12 months.

Before the expiry of a period of seven years from the date referred to in Article 18(1)(a), the Council shall, on the basis of a Commission proposal accompanied by an appraisal report, re-examine the provisions of this paragraph and decide what action to take.

Article 18 Final provisions

1. (a) Member States shall adopt the laws, regulations and administrative provisions necessary to comply with this Directive by 23 November 1996, or shall ensure by that date that the two sides of industry establish the necessary measures by agreement, with Member States being obliged to take any necessary steps to enable them to guarantee at all times that the provisions laid down by this Directive are fulfilled.

(b) (i) However, a Member State shall have the option not to apply Article 6, while respecting the general principles of the protection of the safety and health of workers, and provided it takes the necessary measures to ensure that:

—no employer requires a worker to work more than 48 hours over a seven-day period, calculated as an average for the reference period referred to in point 2 of Article 16, unless he has first obtained the worker's agreement to perform such work,

—no worker is subjected to any detriment by his employer because he is not willing to give his agreement to perform such work,

—the employer keeps up-to-date records of all workers who carry out such work,

—the records are placed at the disposal of the competent authorities, which may, for reasons connected with the safety and/or health of workers, prohibit or restrict the possibility of exceeding the maximum weekly working hours,

—the employer provides the competent authorities at their request with information on cases in which agreement has been given by workers to perform work exceeding 48 hours over a period of seven days, calculated as an average for the reference period referred to in point 2 of Article 16.

Before the expiry of a period of seven years from the date referred to in (a), the Council shall, on the basis of a Commission proposal accompanied by an appraisal report, re-examine the provisions of this point (i) and decide on what action to take.

(ii) Similarly, Member States shall have the option, as regards the application of Article 7, of making use of a transitional period of not more than three years from the date referred to in (a), provided that during that transitional period:

—every worker receives three weeks' paid annual leave in accordance with the conditions for the entitlement to, and granting of, such leave laid down by national legislation and/or practice, and

—the three-week period of paid annual leave may not be replaced by an allowance in lieu, except where the employment relationship is terminated.

(c) Member states shall forthwith inform the Commission thereof.

COUNCIL DIRECTIVE No. 94/45 (O.J. 1994, L254/64)

on the establishment of a European Works Council or a procedure in Community-scale undertakings and Community-scale groups of undertakings for the purposes of informing and consulting employees

SECTION I
GENERAL

Article 1 Objective

1. The purpose of this Directive is to improve the right to information and to consultation of employees in Community-scale undertaking and Community-scale groups of undertakings.

2. To that end, a European Works Council or a procedure for informing and consulting employees shall be established in every Community-scale undertaking and every Community-scale group of undertakings, where requested in the manner laid down in Article 5(1), with the purpose of informing and consulting employees under the terms, in the manner and with the effects laid down in this Directive.

3. Notwithstanding paragraph 2, where a Community-scale group of undertakings within the meaning of Article 2(1)(c) comprises one or more undertakings or groups of undertakings which are Community-scale undertakings or Community-scale groups of undertakings within the meaning of Article 2(1)(a) or (c), a European Works Council shall be established at the level of the group unless the agreements referred to in Article 6 provide otherwise.

4. Unless a wider scope is provided for in the agreements referred to in Article 6, the powers and competence of European Works Councils and the scope of information and consultation procedures established to achieve the purpose specified in paragraph 1 shall, in the case of a Community-scale undertaking, cover all the establishments located within the Member States and, in the case of a Community-scale group of undertakings, all group undertakings located within the Member States.

5. Member States may provide that this Directive shall not apply to merchant navy crews.

Article 2 Definitions

1. For the purposes of this Directive:

(a) 'Community-scale undertaking' means any undertaking with at least 1,000 employees within the Member States and at least 150 employees in each of at least two Member States;

(b) 'group of undertakings' means a controlling undertaking and its controlled undertakings;

(c) 'Community-scale group of undertakings' means a group of undertakings with the following characteristics:

— at least 1,000 employees within the Member States,

— at least two group undertakings in different Member States, and

— at least one group undertaking with at least 150 employees in one Member State and at least one other group undertaking with at least 150 employees in another Member State;

(d) 'employees' representatives' means the employees' representatives provided for by national law and/or practice;

(e) 'central management' means the central management of the Community-scale undertaking or, in the case of a Community-scale group of undertakings, of the controlling undertaking;

(f) 'consultation' means the exchange of views and establishment of dialogue between employees' representatives and central management or any more appropriate level of management;

(g) 'European Works Council' means the council established in accordance with Article 1(2) or the provisions of the Annex, with the purpose of informing and consulting employees;

(h) 'special negotiating body' means the body established in accordance with Article 5(2) to negotiate with the central management regarding the establishment of a European Works Council or a procedure for informing and consulting employees in accordance with Article 1(2).

2. For the purposes of this Directive, the prescribed thresholds for the size of the workforce shall be based on the average number of employees, including part-time employees, employed during the previous two years calculated according to national legislation and/or practice.

Article 3 Definition of 'controlling undertaking'

1. For the purposes of this Directive, 'controlling undertaking' means an undertaking which can exercise a dominant influence over another undertaking ('the controlled undertaking') by virtue, for example, of ownership, financial participation or the rules which govern it.

2. The ability to exercise a dominant influence shall be presumed, without prejudice to proof to the contrary, when, in relation to another undertaking directly or indirectly:

(a) holds a majority of that undertaking's subscribed capital; or

(b) controls a majority of the votes attached to that undertaking's issued share capital; or

(c) can appoint more than half of the members of that undertaking's administrative, management or supervisory body.

3. For the purposes of paragraph 2, a controlling undertaking's rights as regards voting and appointment shall include the rights of any other controlled undertaking and those of any person or body acting in his or its own name but on behalf of the controlling undertaking or of any other controlled undertaking.

4. Notwithstanding paragraphs 1 and 2, an undertaking shall not be deemed to be a 'controlling undertaking' with respect to another undertaking in which it has holdings whre the former undertaking is a company referred to in Article 3(5)(a) or (c) of Council Regulation (EEC) No 4064/89 of 21 December 1989 on the control of concentrations between undertakings.

5. A dominant influence shall not be presumed to be exercised solely by virtue of the fact that an office holder is exercising his functions, according to the law of a Member State relating to liquidation, winding up, insolvency, cessation of payments, compositions or analogous proceedings.

6. The law applicable in order to determine whether an undertaking is a 'controlling undertaking' shall be the law of the Member State which governs that undertaking.

Where the law governing that undertaking is not that of a Member State, the law applicable shall be the law of the Member State within whose territory the representative of the undertaking or, in the absence of such a representative, the central management of the group undertaking which employs the greatest number of employees is situated.

7. Where, in the case of a conflict of laws in the application of paragraph 2, two or more undertakings from a group satisfy one or more of the criteria laid down in that paragraph, the undertaking which satisfies the criterion laid down in point (c) thereof shall be regarded as the controlling undertaking, without prejudice to proof that another undertaking is able to exercise a dominant influence.

SECTION II
ESTABLISHMENT OF A EUROPEAN WORKS COUNCIL OR AN EMPLOYEE INFORMATION AND CONSULTATION PROCEDURE

Article 4 Responsibility for the establishment of a European Works Council or an employee information and consultation procedure

1. The central management shall be responsible for creating the conditions and means necessary for the setting up of a European Works Council or an information and consultation procedure, as provided for in Article 1(2), in a Community-scale undertaking and a Community-scale group of undertakings.

2. Where the central management is not situated in a Member State, the central management's representative agent in a Member State, to be designated if necessary, shall take on the responsibility referred to in paragraph 1.

In the absence of such a representative, the management of the establishment or group undertaking employing the greatest number of employees in any one Member State shall take on the responsibility referred to in paragraph 1.

3. For the purposes of this Directive, the representative or representatives or, in the absence of any such representatives, the management referred to in the second subparagraph of paragraph 2, shall be regarded as the central management.

Article 5 Special negotiating body

1. In order to achieve the objective in Article 1(1), the central management shall initiate negotiations for the establishment of a European Works Council or an information and consultation procedure on its own initiative or at the written request of at least 100 employees or their representatives in at least two undertakings or establishments in at least two different Member States.

2. For this purpose, a special negotiating body shall be established in accordance with the following guidelines:

(a) The Member States shall determine the method to be used for the election or appointment of the members of the special negotiating body who are to be elected or appointed in their territories.

Member States shall provide that employees in undertakings and/or establishments in which there are no employees' representatives through no fault of their own, have the right to elect or appoint members of the special negotiating body.

The second subparagraph shall be without prejudice to national legislation and/or practice laying down thresholds for the establishment of employee representation bodies.

(b) The special negotiating body shall have a minimum of three and a maximum of 17 members.

(c) In these elections or appointments, it must be ensured:

—firstly, that each Member State in which the Community-scale undertaking has one or more establishments or in which the Community-scale group of undertakings has the controlling undertaking or one or more controlled undertakings is represented by one member,

—secondly, that there are supplementary members in proportion to the number of employees working in the establishments, the controlling undertaking or the controlled undertakings as laid down by the legislation of the Member State within the territory of which the central management is situated.

(d) The central management and local management shall be informed of the composition of the special negotiating body.

3. The special negotiating body shall have the task of determining, with the central management, by written agreement, the scope, composition, functions, and term of office of the European Works Council(s) or the arrangements for implementing a procedure for the information and consultation of employees.

4. With a view to the conclusion of an agreement in accordance with Article 6, the central management shall convene a meeting with the special negotiating body. It shall inform the local managements accordingly.

For the purpose of the negotiations, the special negotiating body may be assisted by experts of its choice.

5. The special negotiating body may decide, by at least two-thirds of the votes, not to open negotiations in accordance with paragraph 4, or to terminate the negotiations already opened.

Such a decision shall stop the procedure to conclude the agreement referred to in Article 6. Where such a decision has been taken, the provisions in the Annex shall not apply.

A new request to convene the special negotiating body may be made at the earliest two years after the abovementioned decision unless the parties concerned lay down a shorter period.

6. Any expenses relating to the negotiations referred to in paragraphs 3 and 4 shall be borne by the central management so as to enable the special negotiating body to carry out its task in an appropriate manner.

In compliance with this principle, Member States may lay down budgetary rules regarding the operation of the special negotiating body. They may in particular limit the funding to cover one expert only.

Article 6 Content of the agreement

1. The central management and the special negotiating body must negotiate in a spirit of cooperation with a view to reaching an agreement on the detailed arrangements for implementing the information and consultation of employees provided for in Article 1(1).

2. Without prejudice to the autonomy of the parties, the agreement referred to in paragraph 1 between the central management and the special negotiating body shall determine:

(a) the undertakings of the Community-scale group of undertakings or the establishments of the Community-scale undertaking which are covered by the agreement;

(b) the composition of the European Works Council, the number of members, the allocation of seats and the term of office;

(c) the functions and the procedure for information and consultation of the European Works Council;

(d) the venue, frequency and duration of meetings of the European Works Council;

(e) the financial and material resources to be allocated to the European Works Council;

(f) the duration of the agreement and the procedure for its renegotiation.

3. The central management and the special negotiating body may decide, in writing, to establish one or more information and consultation procedures instead of a European Works Council.

The agreement must stipulate by what method the employees' representatives shall have the right to meet to discuss the information conveyed to them.

This information shall relate in particular to transnational questions which significantly affect workers' interests.

4. The agreements referred to in paragraphs 2 and 3 shall not, unless provision is made otherwise therein, be subject to the subsidiary requirements of the Annex.

5. For the purposes of concluding the agreements referred to the paragraphs 2 and 3, the special negotiating body shall act by a majority of its members.

Article 7 Subsidiary requirements

1. In order to achieve the objective in Article 1(1), the subsidiary requirements laid down by the legislation of the Member State in which the central management is situated shall apply:

—where the central management and the special negotiating body so decide, or

—where the central management refuses to commence negotiations within six months of the request referred to in Article 5(1), or

—where, after three years from the date of this request, they are unable to conclude an agreement as laid down in Article 6 and the special negotiating body has not taken the decision provided for in Article 5(5).

2. The subsidiary requirements referred to in paragraph 1 as adopted in the legislation of the Member States must satisfy the provisions set out in the Annex.

SECTION III
MISCELLANEOUS PROVISIONS

Article 8 Confidential information

1. Member States shall provide that members of special negotiating bodies or of European Works Councils and any experts who assist them are not authorised to reveal any information which has expressly been provided to them in confidence.

The same shall apply to employees' representatives in the framework of an information and consultation procedure.

This obligation shall continue to apply, wherever the persons referred to in the first and second subparagraphs are, even after the expiry of their terms of office.

2. Each Member State shall provide, in specific cases and under the conditions and limits laid down by national legislation, that the central management situated in its territory is not obliged to transmit information when its nature is such that, according to objective criteria, it would seriously harm the functioning of the undertakings concerned or would be prejudicial to them.

A Member State may make such dispensation subject to prior administrative or judicial authorisation.

3. Each Member State may lay down particular provisions for the central management of undertakings in its territory which pursue directly and essentially the aim of ideological guidance with respect to information and the expression of opinions, on condition that, at the date of adoption of this Directive such particular provisions already exist in the national legislation.

Article 9 Operation of European Works Council and information and consultation procedure for workers

The central management and the European Works Council shall work in a spirit of cooperation with due regard to their reciprocal rights and obligations.

The same shall apply to cooperation between the central management and employees' representatives in the framework of an information and consultation procedure for workers.

Article 10 Protection of employees' representatives

Members of special negotiating bodies, members of European Works Councils and employees' representatives exercising their functions under the procedure referred to in Article 6(3) shall, in the exercise of their functions, enjoy the same protection and guarantees provided for employees' representatives by the national legislation and/or practice in force in their country of employment.

This shall apply in particular to attendance at meetings of special negotiating bodies or European Works Councils or any other meetings within the framework of the agreement referred to in Article 6(3), and the payment of wages for members who are on the staff of the Community-scale undertaking or the Community-scale group of undertakings for the period of absence necessary for the performance of their duties.

Article 11 Compliance with this Directive

1. Each Member State shall ensure that the management of establishments of a Community-scale undertaking and the management of undertakings which form part of a Community-scale group of undertakings which are situated within its territory and their employees' representatives or, as the case may be, employees abide by the obligations laid down by this Directive, regardless of whether or not the central management is situated within its territory.

2. Member States shall ensure that the information on the number of employees referred to in Article 2(1)(a) and (c) is made available by undertakings at the request of the parties concerned by the application of this Directive.

3. Member States shall provide for appropriate measures in the event of failure to comply with this Directive; in particular, they shall ensure that adequate administrative or judicial procedures are available to enable the obligations deriving from this Directive to be enforced.

4. Where Member States apply Article 8, they shall make provision for administrative or judicial appeal procedures which the employees' representatives may initiate when the central management requires confidentiality or does not give information in accordance with that Article.

Such procedures may include procedures designed to protect the confidentiality of the information in question.

Article 12 Link between this Directive and other provisions

1. This Directive shall apply without prejudice to measures taken pursuant to Council Directive 75/129/EEC of 17 February 1975 on the approximation of the laws of the Member States relating to collective redundancies, and to Council Directive 77/187/EEC of 14 February 1977 on the approximation of the laws of the Member States relating to the safeguarding of employees' rights in the event of transfers of undertakings, businesses or parts of businesses.

2. This Directive shall be without prejudice to employees' existing rights to information and consultation under national law.

Article 13 Agreements in force

1. Without prejudice to paragraph 2, the obligations arising from this Directive shall not apply to Community-scale undertakings or Community-scale groups of undertakings in which, on the date laid down in Article 14(1) for the implementation of this Directive or the date of its transposition in the Member State in question, where this is earlier than the abovementioned date, there is already an agreement, covering the entire workforce, providing for the transnational information and consultation of employees.

2. When the agreements referred to in paragraph 1 expire, the parties to those agreements may decide jointly to renew them.

Where this is not the case, the provisions of this Directive shall apply.

Article 14 Final provisions

1. Member States shall bring into force the laws, regulations and administrative provisions necessary to comply with this Directive no later than 22 September 1996 or shall ensure by that date at the latest that management and labour introduce the required provisions by way of agreement, the Member States being obliged to take all necessary steps enabling them at all times to guarantee the results imposed by this Directive. They shall forthwith inform the Commission thereof.

2. When Member States adopt these measures, they shall contain a reference to this Directive or shall be accompanied by such reference on the occasion of their official publication. The methods of making such reference shall be laid down by Member States.

Article 15 Review by the Commission
Not later than 22 September 1999, the Commission shall, in consultation with the Member States and with management and labour at European level, review its operation and, in particular examine whether the workforce size thresholds are appropriate with a view to proposing suitable amendments to the Council, where necessary.

ANNEX
SUBSIDIARY REQUIREMENTS

referred to in Article 7 of the Directive

1. In order to achieve the objective in Article 1(1) of the Directive and in the cases provided for in Article 7(1) of the Directive, the establishment, composition and competence of a European Works Council shall be governed by the following rules:

(a) The competence of the European Works Council shall be limited to information and consultation on the matters which concern the Community-scale undertaking or Community-scale group of undertakings as a whole or at least two of its establishments or group undertakings situated in different Member States.

In the case of undertakings or groups of undertakings referred to in Article 4(2), the competence of the European Works Council shall be limited to those matters concerning all their establishments or group undertakings situated within the Member States or concerning at least two of their establishments of group undertakings situated in different Member States.

(b) The European Works Council shall be composed of employees of the Community-scale undertaking or Community-scale group of undertakings elected or appointed from their number by the employees' representatives or, in the absence thereof, by the entire body of employees.

The election or appointment of members of the European Works Council shall be carried out in accordance with national legislation and/or practice.

(c) The European Works Council shall have a minimum of three members and a maximum of 30.
Where its size so warrants, it shall elect a select committee from among its members, comprising at most three members.

It shall adopt its own rules of procedure.

(d) In the election or appointment of members of the European Works Council, it must be ensured:

—firstly, that each Member State in which the Community-scale undertaking has one or more establishments or in which the Community-scale group of undertakings has the controlling undertaking or one or more controlled undertakings is represented by one member,

—secondly, that there are supplementary members in proportion to the number of employees working in the establishments, the controlling undertaking or the controlled undertakings as laid down by the legislation of the Member State within the territory of which the central management is situated.

(e) The central management and any other more appropriate level of management shall be informed of the composition of the European Works Council.

(f) Four years after the European Works Council is established it shall examine whether to open negotiations for the conclusion of the agreement referred to in Article 6 of the Directive or to continue to apply the subsidiary requirements adopted in accordance with this Annex.

Articles 6 and 7 of the Directive shall apply, *mutatis mutandis*, if a decision has been taken to negotiate an agreement according to Article 6 of the Directive, in which case 'special negotiating body' shall be replaced by 'European Works Council'.

2. The European Works Council shall have the right to meet with the central management once a year, to be informed and consulted, on the basis of a report drawn up by the central management, on the progress of the business of the Community-scale undertaking or Community-scale group of undertakings and its prospects. The local managements shall be informed accordingly.

The meeting shall relate in particular to the structure, economic and financial situation, the probable development of the business and of production and sales, the situation and probable trend of employment, investments, and substantial changes concerning organisation, introduction of new working methods of production processes, transfers of production, mergers, cut-backs or closures of undertakings, establishments or important parts thereof, and collective redundancies.

3. Where there are exceptional circumstances affecting the employees' interests to a considerable extent, particularly in the event of relocations, the closure of establishments or undertakings or collective redundancies, the select committee or, where no such committee exists, the European Works Council shall have the right to be informed. It shall have the right to meet, at its request, the central management, or any other more appropriate level of management within the Community-scale undertaking or group of undertakings having its own powers of decision, so as to be informed and consulted on measures significantly affecting employees' interests.

Those members of the European Works Council who have been elected or appointed by the establishments and/or undertakings which are directly concerned by the measures in question shall also have the right to participate in the meeting organised with the select committee.

This information and consultation meeting shall take place as soon as possible on the basis of a report drawn up by the central management or any other appropriate level of management of the Community-scale undertaking or group of undertakings, on which an opinion may be delivered at the end of the meeting or within a reasonable time.

This meeting shall not affect the prerogatives of the central management.

4. The Member States may lay down rules on the chairing of information and consultation meetings.

Before any meeting with the central management, the European Works Council or the select committee, where necessary enlarged in accordance with the second paragraph of point 3, shall be entitled to meet without the management concerned being present.

5. Without prejudice to Article 8 of the Directive, the members of the European Works Council shall inform the representatives of the employees of the establishments or of the undertakings of a Community-scale group of undertakings or, in the absence of representatives, the workforce as a whole, of the content and outcome of the information and consultation procedure carried out in accordance with this Annex.

6. The European Works Council or the select committee may be assisted by experts of its choice, in so far as this is necessary for it to carry out its tasks.

7. The operating expenses of the European Works Council shall be borne by the central management.

The central management concerned shall provide the members of the European Works Council with such financial and material resources as enable them to perform their duties in an appropriate manner.

In particular, the cost of organising meetings and arranging for interpretation facilities and the accommodation and travelling expenses of members of the European Works Council and its select committee shall be met by the central management unless otherwise agreed.

In compliance with these principles, the Member States may lay down budgetary rules regarding the operation of the European Works Council. They may in particular limit funding to cover one expert only.

COUNCIL DIRECTIVE No. 97/81 (O.J. 1998, L14/9)

Concerning the Framework Agreement on part-time work concluded by UNICE, CEEP and the ETUC

FRAMEWORK AGREEMENT ON PART-TIME WORK

Clause 1: Purpose

The purpose of this Framework Agreement is:

(a) to provide for the removal of discrimination against part-time workers and to improve the quality of part-time work;

(b) to facilitate the development of part-time work on a voluntary basis and to contribute to the flexible organisation of working time in a manner which takes into account the needs of employers and workers.

Clause 2: Scope

1. This Agreement applies to part-time workers who have an employment contract or employment relationship as defined by the law, collective agreement or practice in force in each Member State.

2. Member States, after consultation with the social partners in accordance with national law, collective agreements or practice, and/or the social partners at the appropriate level in conformity with national industrial relations practice may, for objective reasons, exclude wholly or partly from the terms of this Agreement part-time workers who work on a casual basis. Such exclusions should be reviewed periodically to establish if the objective reasons for making them remain valid.

Clause 3: Definitions

For the purpose of this agreement:

1. The term 'part-time worker' refers to an employee whose normal hours of work, calculated on a weekly basis or on average over a period of employment of up to one year, are less than the normal hours of work of a comparable full-time worker.

2. The term 'comparable full-time worker' means a full-time worker in the same establishment having the same type of employment contract or relationship, who is engaged in the same or a similar work/occupation, due regard being given to other considerations which may include seniority and qualification/skills.

Where there is no comparable full-time worker in the same establishment, the comparison shall be made by reference to the applicable collective agreement or, where there is no applicable collective agreement, in accordance with national law, collective agreements or practice.

Clause 4: Principle of non-discrimination

1. In respect of employment conditions, part-time workers shall not be treated in a less favourable manner than comparable full-time workers solely because they work part time unless different treatment is justified on objective grounds.

2. Where appropriate, the principle of *pro rata temporis* shall apply.

3. The arrangements for the application of this clause shall be defined by the Member States and/or social partners, having regard to European legislation, national law, collective agreements and practice.

4. Where justified by objective reasons, Member States after consultation of the social partners in accordance with national law, collective agreements or practice and/or social partners may, where appropriate, make access to particular conditions of employment subject to a period of service, time worked or earnings qualification. Qualifications relating to access by part-time workers to particular conditions of employment should be reviewed periodically having regard to the principle of non-discrimination as expressed in Clause 4.1.

Clause 5: Opportunities for part-time work

1. In the context of Clause 1 of this Agreement and of the principle of non-discrimination between part-time and full-time workers:

(a) Member States, following consultations with the social partners in accordance with national law or practice, should identify and review obstacles of a legal or administrative nature which may limit the opportunities for part-time work and, where appropriate, eliminate them;

(b) the social partners, acting within their sphere of competence and through the procedures set out in collective agreements, should identify and review obstacles which may limit opportunities for part-time work and, where appropriate, eliminate them.

2. A worker's refusal to transfer from full-time to part-time work or vice-versa should not in itself constitute a valid reason for termination of employment, without prejudice to termination in accordance with national law, collective agreements and practice, for other reasons such as may arise from the operational requirements of the establishment concerned.

3. As far as possible, employers should give consideration to:

(a) requests by workers to transfer from full-time to part-time work that becomes available in the establishment;

(b) requests by workers to transfer from part-time to full-time work or to increase their working time should the opportunity arise;

(c) the provision of timely information on the availability of part-time and full-time positions in the establishment in order to facilitate transfers from full-time to part-time or vice versa;

(d) measures to facilitate access to part-time work at all levels of the enterprise, including skilled and managerial positions, and where appropriate, to facilitate access by part-time workers to vocational training to enhance career opportunities and occupational mobility;

(e) the provision of appropriate information to existing bodies representing workers about part-time working in the enterprise.

INTERNATIONAL OBLIGATIONS

COUNCIL OF EUROPE

EUROPEAN CONVENTION FOR THE PROTECTION OF HUMAN RIGHTS AND FUNDAMENTAL FREEDOMS

Article 9 Freedom of thought, conscience and religion

1. Everyone has the right to freedom of thought, conscience and religion; this right includes freedom to change his religion or belief and freedom, either alone or in community with others and in public or private, to manifest his religion or belief, in worship, teaching, practice and observance.

2. Freedom to manifest one's religion or beliefs shall be subject only to such limitations as are prescribed by law and are necessary in a democratic society in the interests of public safety, for the protection of public order, health or morals, or for the protection of the rights and freedoms of others.

Article 10 Freedom of expression

1. Everyone has the right to freedom of expression. This right shall include freedom to hold opinions and to receive and impart information and ideas without interference by public authority and regardless of frontiers. This Article shall not prevent States from requiring the licensing of broadcasting, television or cinema enterprises.

2. The exercise of these freedoms, since it carries with it duties and responsibilities, may be subject to such formalities, conditions, restrictions or penalties as are prescribed by law and are necessary in a democratic society, in the interests of national security, territorial integrity or public safety, for the prevention of disorder or crime, for the protection of health or morals, for the protection of the reputation or rights of others, for preventing the disclosure of information received in confidence, or for maintaining the authority and impartiality of the judiciary.

Article 11 Freedom of Assembly and Association

1. Everyone has the right to freedom of peaceful assembly and to freedom of association with others, including the right to form and to join trade unions for the protection of his interests.

2. No restrictions shall be placed on the exercise of these rights other than such as are prescribed by law and are necessary in a democratic society in the interests of national security or public safety, for the prevention of disorder or crime, for the protection of health or morals or for the protection of the rights and freedoms of others. This Article shall not prevent the imposition of lawful restrictions on the exercise of these rights by members of the armed forces, of the police or of the administration of the State.

Article 14 Prohibition of Discrimination

The enjoyment of the rights and freedoms set forth in this Convention shall be secured without discrimination on any ground such as sex, race, colour, language, religion, political or other opinion, national or social origin, association with a national minority, property, birth or other status.

COUNCIL OF EUROPE

EUROPEAN SOCIAL CHARTER
(Revised 1996)

[Note: the United Kingdom has not yet ratified the revised version]

Article 1
The right to work
With a view to ensuring the effective exercise of the right to work, the Contracting Parties undertake:

1. to accept as one of their primary aims and responsibilities the achievement and maintenance of as high and stable a level of employment as possible, with a view to the attainment of full employment;
2. to protect effectively the right of the worker to earn his living in an occupation freely entered upon;
3. to establish or maintain free employment services for all workers;
4. to provide or promote appropriate vocational guidance, training and rehabilitation.

Article 2
The right to just conditions of work
With a view to ensuring the effective exercise of the right to just conditions of work, the Parties undertake:

1. to provide for reasonable daily and weekly working hours, the working week to be progressively reduced to the extent that the increase of productivity and other relevant factors permit;
2. to provide for public holidays with pay;
3. to provide for a minimum of four weeks annual holiday with pay;
4. to eliminate risks in inherently dangerous or unhealthy occupations, and where it has not yet been possible to eliminate or reduce sufficiently these risks, to provide for either a reduction of working hours or additional paid holidays for workers engaged in such occupations;
5. to ensure a weekly rest period which shall, as far as possible, coincide with the day recognised by tradition or custom in the country or region concerned as a day of rest.
6. to ensure that workers are informed in written form, as soon as possible, and in any event not later than two months after the date of commencing their employment, of the essential aspects of the contract or employment relationship;
7. to ensure that workers performing night work benefit from measures which take account of the special nature of the work.

Article 3
The right to safe and healthy working conditions
With a view to ensuring the effective exercise of the right to safe and healthy working conditions, the Parties undertake, in consultation with employers' and workers' organisations:

1. to formulate, implement and periodically review a coherent national policy on occupational safety, occupational health and the working environment. The primary aim of this policy shall be to improve occupational safety and health and to prevent accidents and injury to health arising out of, linked with or occurring in the course of

work, particularly by minimising the causes of hazards inherent in the working environment;

2. to issue safety and health regulations;

3. to provide for the enforcement of such regulations by measures of supervision;

4. to promote the progressive development of occupational health services for all workers with essentially preventive and advisory functions.

Article 4
The right to a fair remuneration
With a view to ensuring the effective exercise of the right to a fair remuneration, the Parties undertake:

1. to recognise the right of workers to a remuneration such as will give them and their families a decent standard of living;

2. to recognise the right of workers to an increased rate of remuneration for overtime work, subject to exceptions in particular cases;

3. to recognise the right of men and women workers to equal pay for work of equal value;

4. to recognise the right of all workers to a reasonable period of notice for termination of employment;

5. to permit deductions from wages only under conditions and to the extent prescribed by national laws or regulations or fixed by collective agreements or arbitration awards.

The exercise of these rights shall be achieved by freely concluded collective agreements, by statutory wage-fixing machinery, or by other means appropriate to national conditions.

Article 5
The right to organise
With a view to ensuring or promoting the freedom of workers and employers to form local, national or international organisations for the protection of their economic and social interests and to join those organisations, the Parties undertake that national law shall not be such as to impair, nor shall it be so applied as to impair, this freedom. The extent to which the guarantees provided for in this Article shall apply to the police shall be determined by national laws or regulations. The principle governing the application to the members of the armed forces of these guarantees and the extent to which they shall apply to persons in this category shall equally be determined by national laws or regulations.

Article 6
The right to bargain collectively
With a view to ensuring the effective exercise of the right to bargain collectively, the Parties undertake:

1. to promote joint consultation between workers and employers;

2. to promote, where necessary and appropriate, machinery for voluntary negotiations between employers or employers' organisations and workers' organisations, with a view to the regulation of terms and conditions of employment by means of collective agreements;

3. to promote the establishment and use of appropriate machinery for conciliation and voluntary arbitration for the settlement of labour disputes;

and recognise:

4. the right of workers and employers to collective action in cases of conflicts of interest, including the right to strike, subject to obligations that might arise out of collective agreements previously entered into.

Article 7 The right of children and young persons to protection

With a view to ensuring the effective exercise of the right of children and young persons to protection, the Contracting Parties undertake:

1. to provide that the minimum age of admission to employment shall be 15 years, subject to exceptions for children employed in prescribed light work without harm to their health, morals or education;
2. to provide that a higher minimum age of admission to employment shall be 18 with respect to prescribed occupations regarded as dangerous or unhealthy;
3. to provide that persons who are still subject to compulsory education shall not be employed in such work as would deprive them of the full benefit of their education;
4. to provide that the working hours of persons under 18 years of age shall be limited in accordance with the needs of their development, and particularly with their need for vocational training;
5. to recognise the right of young workers and apprentices to a fair wage or other appropriate allowances;
6. to provide that the time spent by young persons in vocational training during the normal working hours with the consent of the employer shall be treated as forming part of the working day;
7. to provide that employed persons of under 18 years of age shall be entitled to a minimum of four weeks' annual holiday with pay;
8. to provide that persons under 18 years of age shall not be employed in night work with the exception of certain occupations provided for by national laws or regulations;
9. to provide that persons under 18 years of age employed in occupations prescribed by national laws or regulations shall be subject to regular medical control;
10. to ensure special protection against physical and moral dangers to which children and young persons are exposed, and particularly against those resulting directly or indirectly from their work.

Article 8 The right of employed women to protection of maternity

With a view to ensuring the effective exercise of the right of employed women to the protection of maternity, the Contracting Parties undertake:

1. to provide either by paid leave, by adequate social security benefits or by benefits from public funds for women to take leave before and after childbirth up to a total of at least fourteen weeks;
2. to consider it as unlawful for an employer to give a woman notice of dismissal during the period from the time when she notifies her employer that she is pregnant until the end of her maternity leave or to give her notice of dismissal at such a time that the notice would expire during such absence;
3. to provide that mothers who are nursing their infants shall be entitled to sufficient time off for this purpose;
4. to regulate the employment in night work of pregnant women, women who have recently given birth and women nursing their infants;
5. to prohibit the employment of pregnant women, women who have recently given birth or who are nursing their infants in underground mining and all other work which is unsuitable by reason of its dangerous, unhealthy or arduous nature and to take appropriate measures to protect the employment rights of these women.

Article 20 Right to equal opportunities and equal treatment in matters of employment and occupation without discrimination on the grounds of sex

1. With a view to ensuring the effective exercise of the right to equal opportunities and equal treatment in matters of employment and occupation without discrimination on the grounds of sex, the Parties undertake to recognise that right and to take appropriate measures to ensure or promote its application in the following fields:

—access to employment, protection against dismissal and occupational resettlement;
—vocational guidance, training, retraining and rehabilitation;
—terms of employment and working conditions including remuneration;
—career development including promotion.

Article 21 Right to information and consultation

1. With a view to ensuring the effective exercise of the right of workers to be informed and consulted within the undertaking, the Parties undertake to adopt or encourage measures enabling workers or their representatives, in accordance with national legislation and practice:

(a) to be informed regularly or at the appropriate time and in a comprehensible way about the economic and financial situation of the undertaking employing them, on the understanding that the disclosure of certain information which could be prejudicial to the undertaking may be refused or subject to confidentiality; and

(b) to be consulted in good time on proposed decisions which could substantially affect the interests of workers, particularly on those decisions which could have an important impact on the employment situation in the undertaking.

Article 22 The Right to take part in the determination and improvement of the working conditions and working environment

1. With a view to ensuring the effective exercise of the right of workers to take part in the determination and improvement of the working conditions and working environment in the undertaking, the Parties undertake to adopt or encourage measures enabling workers or their representatives, in accordance with national legislation and practice, to contribute:

(a) to the determination and the improvement of the working conditions, work organisation and working environment;

(b) to the protection of health and safety within the undertaking;

(c) to the organisation of social and socio-cultural services and facilities within the undertaking;

(d) to the supervision of the observance of regulations on these matters.

INTERNATIONAL LABOUR ORGANISATION
Convention (No. 87) concerning Freedom of Association and Protection of the Right to Organise

PART I. FREEDOM OF ASSOCIATION

Article 1

Each Member of the International Labour Organisation for which this Convention is in force undertakes to give effect to the following provisions.

Article 2

Workers and employers, without distinction whatsoever, shall have the right to establish and, subject only to the rules of the organisation concerned, to join organisations of their own choosing without previous authorisation.

Article 3

1. Workers' and employers' organisations shall have the right to draw up their constitutions and rules, to elect their representatives in full freedom, to organise their administration and activities and to formulate their programmes.

2. The public authorities shall refrain from any interference which would restrict this right or impede the lawful exercise thereof.

Article 4
Workers' and employers' organisations shall not be liable to be dissolved or suspended by administrative authority.

Article 5
Workers' and employers' organisations shall have the right to establish and join federations and confederations and any such organisation, federation or confederation shall have the right to affiliate with international organisations of workers and employers.

Article 6
The provisions of Articles 2, 3 and 4 hereof apply to federations and confederations of workers' and employers' organisations.

Article 7
The acquisition of legal personality by workers' and employers' organisations, federations and confederations shall not be made subject to conditions of such a character as to restrict the application of the provisions of Articles 2, 3 and 4 hereof.

Article 8
1. In exercising the rights provided for in this Convention workers and employers and their respective organisations, like other persons or organised collectivities, shall respect the law of the land.
2. The law of the land shall not be such as to impair, nor shall it be so applied as to impair, the guarantees provided for in this Convention.

Article 9
1. The extent to which the guarantees provided for in this Convention shall apply to the armed forces and the police shall be determined by national laws or regulations.
2. In accordance with the principle set forth in paragraph 8 of Article 19 of the Constitution of the International Labour Organisation the ratification of this Convention by any Member shall not be deemed to affect any existing law, award, custom or agreement in virtue of which members of the armed forces or the police enjoy any right guaranteed by this Convention.

Article 10
In this Convention the term 'organisation' means any organisation of workers or of employers for furthering and defending the interests of workers or of employers.

PART II. PROTECTION OF THE RIGHT TO ORGANISE

Article 11
Each Member of the International Labour Organisation for which this Convention is in force undertakes to take all necessary and appropriate measures to ensure that workers and employers may exercise freely the right to organise.

INTERNATIONAL LABOUR ORGANISATION
Convention (No. 98) concerning the Application of the Principles of the Right to Organise and to Bargain Collectively

Article 1
1. Workers shall enjoy adequate protection against acts of anti-union discrimination in respect of their employment.
2. Such protection shall apply more particularly in respect of acts calculated to—
(a) make the employment of a worker subject to the condition that he shall not join a union or shall relinquish trade union membership;

(b) cause the dismissal of or otherwise prejudice a worker by reason of union membership or because of participation in union activities outside working hours or, with the consent of the employer, within working hours.

Article 2

1. Workers' and employers' organisations shall enjoy adequate protection against any acts of interference by each other or each other's agents or members in their establishment, functioning or administration.

2. In particular, acts which are designed to promote the establishment of workers' organisations under the domination of employers or employers' organisations, or to support workers' organisations by financial or other means, with the object of placing such organisations under the control of employers or employers' organisations, shall be deemed to constitute acts of interference within the meaning of this Article.

Article 3

Machinery appropriate to national conditions shall be established, where necessary, for the purpose of ensuring respect for the right to organise as defined in the preceding Articles.

Article 4

Measures appropriate to national conditions shall be taken, where necessary, to encourage and promote the full development and utilisation of machinery for voluntary negotiation between employers or employers' organisations and workers' organisations, with a view to the regulation of terms and conditions of employment by means of collective agreements.

Article 5

1. The extent to which the guarantees provided for in this Convention shall apply to the armed forces and the police shall be determined by national laws or regulations.

2. In accordance with the principle set forth in paragraph 8 of Article 19 of the Constitution of the International Labour Organisation the ratification of this Convention by any Member shall not be deemed to affect any existing law, award, custom or agreement in virtue of which members of the armed forces or the police enjoy any right guaranteed by this Convention.

Article 6

This Convention does not deal with the position of public servants engaged in the administration of the State, nor shall it be construed as prejudicing their rights or status in any way.

INDEX

BLACKSTONE'S STATUTES
TITLES IN THE SERIES

Commercial and Consumer Law Statutes
Company Law Statutes
Contract, Tort and Restitution Statutes
Criminal Law Statutes
EC Legislation
Employment Law Statutes
Environmental Law Statutes
Evidence Statutes
Family Law Statutes
International Human Rights Documents
International Law Documents
Intellectual Property Statutes
Landlord and Tenant Statutes
Medical Law Statutes
Planning Law Statutes
Property Law Statutes
Public Law and Human Rights Statutes